Helion & Company Limited
26 Willow Road
Solihull
West Midlands
B91 1UE
Tel. 0121 705 3393
Fax 0121 711 4075
Email: info@helion.co.uk
Website: www.helion.co.uk
Twitter: @helionbooks
Visit our blog http://blog.helion.co.uk/

Published by Helion & Company 2015

Designed and typeset by Bookcraft Limited, Stroud, Gloucestershire
Cover designed by Euan Carter, Leicester (www.euancarter.com)
Printed by Gutenberg Press Limited, Tarxien, Malta

Text © Igor Nebolsin 2014. English edition translated and edited by Stuart Britton, ©
Helion & Company Limited 2014.
Maps © Helion & Company Limited 2014. Maps designed by Paul Hewitt, Battlefield
Design (www.battlefield-design.co.uk)
Photographs used came from the Russian State Archive of Film and Photo Documents
(RGAKFD), the photo album "Odna iz Shesti" ["One of Six"], the site "Voennyi Al'bom"
["Military Album"], the Museum of Combat Glory of the Second Guards "Hero of the
Soviet Union N.M. Teliakov" Red Banner Tank Army, and a number of open sources via
the author.
Originally privately published in 2012 by the author as *Vtoraia Gvardeiskaia Tankovaia
Armiia: Boevoi put' 2-I Gvardeiskoi Krasnoznamennoi Tankovoi Armii; dokumental'naia
monografiia.*

ISBN 978 1 909982 15 4

British Library Cataloguing-in-Publication Data.
A catalogue record for this book is available from the British Library.

For details of other military history titles published by Helion & Company Limited contact
the above address, or visit our website: http://www.helion.co.uk.

We always welcome receiving book proposals from prospective authors.

# Contents

List of Photographs                                                              iv

List of Maps                                                                     xii

List of Tables                                                                   xiii

Preface                                                                          xvi

Foreword                                                                         xvii

Introduction                                                                     xix

1    The Origins of the 2nd Tank Army                                            21

2    In the Battle of Kursk 1943                                                 75

3    The Orel Offensive Operation, 1943                                          137

4    In the Sevsk Operation, 1943                                               173

5    Vinnitsa and Korsun'-Shevchenkovskii, 1944                                  206

6    The Uman' Operation                                                         281

7    The Army's Battles in Moldavia and Romania, 1944                            333

Bibliography                                                                     429

Index                                                                            432

# List of Photographs

P.Kh. Molochkov. xvi

Ia.F. Nebolsin. xvi

Major General Anatolii Shvebig. xvii

Semen Bogdanov, 2nd Guards Tank Army commander. xviii

Veteran of the 2nd Guards Tank Army medal. xviii

Prokofii Romanenko, the first commander of the 2nd Tank Army. 23

Aleksei Rodin, the second commander of the 2nd Tank Army. 23

Petr Latyshev. 25

Aleksei Maslov – 16th Tank Corps. 25

Ivan Lazarev – 11th Tank Corps. 25

Mikhail Goncharov. 25

Nikolai Bubnov – 11th Guards Tank Brigade. 25

Infantry and motorized rifle units go on the offensive, February 1943. 35

Tanks of the 2nd Tank Army move up into forward positions, February-March 1943. 40

A gun crew in the Sevsk area prepares to fire. The Russian caption above the photograph read "Over open sights, Sevsk area". 41

Tanks go on the attack, Central Front 1943. 43

The 11th Guards Tank Brigade receives its tanks from the "Tambov Collective Farmer". 54

Knocked-out armor of the 4th Panzer Division, March 1943, Sevsk area. 55

Disabled and bogged down equipment of the 4th Panzer Division, March 1943, Sevsk area. 56

Knocked-out T-34 tanks in the Sevsk area, March 1943. 59

T-34 tanks of the 16th Tank Corps, which had sunk into the Usozha River in March 1943, but were towed out of the water in the middle of April 1943. 60

The presentation of combat decorations in the 16th Tank Corps' 164th Tank Brigade, April 1943. In the center is Major Mansvetov. 70

Technician-Lieutenant Ivan Lubov. 71

V.G Pirozhenko. 71

A.N. Chesnokov. 71

Battalion commander of the 1st Tank Battalion, Ivan Korol'kov. 71

V.I. Nesvetailov. 71

Guards Senior Lieutenant Kazachenko's tank crew. 71

Guards Lieutenant Aleksandr Lugansky. 71

M.G. Mikhailov. 71

Senior Lieutenant Aleksei Petrukhin's T-34 tank crew: Left to right Lapin, Kotenov, Petrukhin and Patepko. 72

Platoon commander of the 1st Tank Battalion of the 11th Guards Tank Brigade Junior Lieutenant Aleksandr Shilov's tank crew, summer of 1943. 72

Another shot of Petrukhin's tank crew. From left to right Lapin, Kotenov, Petrukhin and Patepko.                                                                                      72

Guards Lieutenant Ivan Kvasha.                                                          73

Guards Sergeant Major Lev Everskov.                                                     73

Guards Lieutenant V. Dashinsky.                                                         73

Nikolai Bubnov, commander of the 11th Guards Tank Brigade.                              73

Guards Junior Lieutenant Aleksandr Shilov.                                             73

Grigorii Kalustov, deputy political commander of the 11th Guards Tank Brigade.          73

Aleksei Rodin.                                                                          76

Maksim Sinenko – 3rd Tank Corps.                                                        76

Georgii Kokurin – 51st Tank Brigade.                                                    76

Petr Latyshev.                                                                          76

Vasilii Grigor'ev – 16th Tank Corps.                                                    76

Georgii Maksimov – 103rd Tank Brigade.                                                  76

Grigorii Preisman.                                                                      76

Nikolai Bubnov – 11th Guards Tank Brigade.                                              76

Fedor Konovalov – 50th Tank Brigade.                                                    76

Nikolai Teliakov – 107th Tank Brigade.                                                  77

Mikail Tsikalo – Commander of Artillery.                                                77

Ashraf Galimov, Chief of Intelligence Department.                                      77

Nikolai Kopylov – 164th Tank Brigade.                                                   77

Vladimir Chizh – Chief of Operations.                                                   77

Isak Levin – Commander of Engineer Troops.                                              77

Petr Akimochkin – 15th Motorized Rifle Brigade.                                         77

Iosif Smoly – Chief of Signals Department.                                              77

Mikhail Goncharov – Deputy Commander for Rear Services.                                 77

Tankers of the 11th Guards Tank Brigade. Fourth from the left is Aleksandr Lugansky; fifth from left is A. Shagin; sixth from left is Shkvornikov; and seventh from left, Nesvetailov (summer of 1943).                                                               78

The crew of tank company commander Senior Lieutenant Konstantin Blinov, 103rd Tank Brigade, 3rd Tank Corps, on the eve of combat in the Kursk bulge. The Russian caption read: "Hero of the Soviet Union Guards Senior Lieutenant K.M. Blinov talks with his crew."                                                                           78

The command of the 16th Tank Corps poses with a group of top-rated tank drivers in the village of Sotnikovo, Central Front, 24 May 1943.                                       82

The caption reads, "Presentation of the 107th Tank Brigade's Combat Red Banner. Deputy Commander of the 16th Tank Corps Colonel A.A. Vitruk presents – Brigade commander Colonel N.M. Teliakov receives."                                                 82

A series of photos showing knocked-out tanks of the 16th Tank Corps in the Butyrki area, 6 July 1943.                                                                         99

Knocked out German tanks and assault guns in the area of Ponyri, July 1943.            115

Another knocked-out German tank in the area of Ponyri, July 1943                        116

Units of the 2nd Tank Army on the battlefield, July 1943.                              116

Units of the 2nd Tank Army on the battlefield, July 1943.                              117

Units of the 2nd Tank Army on the battlefield, July 1943.                              118

The post-action inspection of knocked-out German tanks                                        119

The SU-152 of the commander of the 1541st Self-propelled Artillery Regiment Major
   Aleksei Sankovsky, July 1943.                                                               120

The commander of the 1541st Self-propelled Artillery Regiment Guards Major Aleksei
   Sankovsky, July 1943, Kursk bulge. Guards Major Sankovsky demonstrated courage
   and resolve as a commander. In combat in the Step' – Podsoborovka area, skillfully
   directing the batteries of the 1541st Self-propelled Artillery Regiment under enemy
   air and artillery attack, he brought his regiment to the indicated area without losses.
   Under his direct leadership, the regiment destroyed more than 30 enemy tanks and
   assault guns, including 5 Tigers.                                                           120

Junior Lieutenant Andrei Stoliarov [upper left], Junior Lieutenant Konstantin Blinov
   [upper right], Senior Lieutenant Fedor Donkov [lower left] and Guards Lieutenant
   Ivan Kvasha [lower right].                                                                  121

Corporal Krivsun's squad of sappers, 9th Separate Combat Engineer Battalion, 16th
   Tank Corps, July 1943.                                                                      124

The commander of the 3rd Tank Corps' 24th Reconnaissance Battalion, Captain
   Surzhikov, gives an order to Captain Zakrevsky's group, July 1943.                         126

The commander of the 24th Separate Reconnaissance Battalion Captain Surzhikov (3rd
   Tank Corps] in the forward detachment, July 1943.                                          126

Captain D. Zakrevsky's scouts prepare to tow a captured German tank, 10 July 1943.
   Below: Another German tank left abandoned on the battlefield.                              127

A scout of Captain Zakresvsky's group proudly poses in front of the captured German
   tank.                                                                                      127

"A line has been taken. It is necessary to dig in."                                           132

Major General Latyshev presents the Order of the Red Banner and the Order of the
   Patriotic War to Captains Zakrevsky and Bystritsky, for their participation in a
   reconnaissance mission into the enemy rear.                                                132

Forces of the 2nd Tank Army on the march, July 1943.                                          144

Tanks of the 2nd Tank Army, July 1943.                                                        144

At the command post prior to the offensive, August 1943. On the left is Army
   commander Lieutenant General S.I. Bogdanov. Next to him is Military Council
   member Major General P.M. Latyshev.                                                        156

Tank combat on the Orel axis, July-August 1943: A burning T-34 is in the foreground.          156

Battalion commander Major Zaerniuk gives a combat assignment, August 1943.                    157

The Soviet photo caption read 'The crew of a combat machine: (from left to right) A.
   Lugansky, A. Vysotsky, V. Ivanov, I. Chudin.'                                              157

From left to right: G.Sh. Kalustov, N.M. Koshaev, P.L. Bormotov, N.M. Bubnov and
   V.V. Iablokov.                                                                             163

Aleksandr Lugansky of the 11th Guards Tank Brigade.                                           172

Brigade commander Maksimov – 103rd Tank Brigade.                                              172

Georgii Semenov of the 103rd Tank Brigade.                                                    172

Semen Bogdanov.                                                                               174

Fedor Artamonov – 25th Guards Mechanized Brigade.                                             174

Ivan Korchagin – 7th Guards Mechanized Corps.                                                 174

Aleksandr Khalaev – 103rd Tank Brigade.                                                       174

Soldiers of the Red Army on a Sevsk road.                                                     190

Senior Sergeant Migunov's machine gunners, city of Sevsk. 190

Soldiers of the Red Army in the Sevsk area. 191

Sergeant Kotylev's anti-aircraft gun crew. 191

In liberated Sevsk, on Lenin Street. 192

Semen Bogdanov. 207

Ivan Dubovoi. 207

Petr Akimochkin. 207

Petr Latyshev. 207

Nikolai Koshaev. 207

Nikolai Kopylov. 207

Aleksandr Shamshin. 207

Semen Mirvoda. 207

Tikhon Abramov. 207

Commander of the 50th Tank Brigade R.A. Liberman (left) and the brigade's chief of staff A.M. Kovalevsky. A 1944 photo. 208

The commander of the 2nd Tank Army S. Bogdanov (right) with the commander of the 11th Guards Tank Brigade Hero of the Soviet Union N. Koshaev. 208

Tanks of the 3rd Tank Corps before an attack in the area of Lipovets Station, January 1944 – the Russian caption read, "In ambush – the 3rd Tank Corps." 217

A T-34 tank crew, January 1944 (a photo of an exposition by the Museum of the Korsun'-Shevchenkovskii Battle). 217

Motorized infantry of the 16th Tank Corps moving into positions, January 1944. 217

Tanks of the 2nd Tank Army on the march, January 1944 (a photo from an exposition by the Museum of the Korsun'-Shevchenkovskii Battle). 218

A T-34 rolls across a short bridge. "January 1944: The march in the Vinnitsa area." 221

Tanks of the 2nd Tank Army, February 1944 (from the archive of Guards Colonel Vitruk). 233

Officers of the 2nd Tank Army, with tanks of the 3rd Tank Corps in the background, winter 1944. 234

Moments later, these same officers have stopped to confer. 234

Tanks of the 2nd Tank Army moving out toward their jumping-off positions. 255

Abandoned German vehicles and equipment in the Korsun'-Shevchenkovskii area, February 1944. 255

A T-34 with tank riders aboard passes a burning Tiger tank. 264

A German Panther, knocked out by Lieutenant Kravtsev's SU-85. The photograph was taken from the driver-mechanic's hatch. 264

Prokofii Kalashnikov – 11th Guards Tank Brigade. 274

Ivan Ostroverkhov – 16th Tank Corps (battalion commander). 274

Vladimir Nesvetailov – 11th Guards Tank Brigade. 274

I.I. Gorbunov – 50th Tank Brigade. 274

Alexei Pustovalov – 11th Guards Tank Brigade. 274

Sergei Matsapura – 107th Tank Brigade. 274

I.O. Pozdeev – 107th Tank Brigade. 275

Alexandr Rybin – 15th Motorized Rifle Brigade. 275

I.A. Kozhevnikov – 11th Guards Tank Brigade. 275

V. Voloznev – 107th Tank Brigade. 275

Nikandr Panfilov – 51st Tank Brigade. 275

I.V. Chupakhin – 11th Guards Tank Brigade. 275

K.A. Ishchenko – 109th Tank Brigade. 275

M.F. Vdovchenko – 11th Guards Tank Brigade. 275

Petr Krupinov – 11th Guards Tank Brigade. 275

V.M. Ochkin – 11th Guards Tank Brigade. 276

M.I. Konev – 3rd Tank Corps. 276

I.B. Ostrous –86th Guards Mortar Regiment. 276

M.P. Gedzhadze – 11th Guards Tank Brigade. 276

V.P. Oskov – 3rd Tank Corps. 276

O.G. Antiasov – 107th Tank Brigade. 276

M.N. Zhuchkov – 11th Guards Tank Brigade. 276

P.A. Annikov – 86th Guards Mortar Regiment, 16th Tank Corps. 276

M.O. Elkin – 107th Tank Brigade. 276

Commander of the 50th Tank Brigade, Roman Liberman. 278

Commander of the 11th Guards Tank Brigade Nikolai Koshaev (on left) and the brigade's deputy political commander Karp Zhuravlev. 279

An aerial view of the city of Uman', March 1944, showing a devastated German column of armor and trucks. 288

Disabled German armor in the Potash area, March 1944. 291

Knocked-out and abandoned Tigers of the 503rd Heavy Panzer Battalion, Potash area, March 1944. 291

Knocked-out and abandoned Panthers and Tigers of Heavy Panzer Regiment *Bäke*, March 1944. 292

Booty of the 2nd Tank Army: Abandoned German tanks in the area of Man'kovka, March 1944 (from Guards Colonel S.M. Terekhov's personal collection of photographs). 293

Units of the 16th Tank Corps crossing a flooded stream, March 1944. 294

Uman' after the battle. An abandoned German Nebelwerfer is in the foreground. Note also the camouflage pattern on the abandoned German car. 294

A devastated German motorized column in the area of Man'kovka, March 1944. A handwritten Cyrillic caption read, "Abandoned enemy equipment". 294

Abandoned German trucks and self-propelled guns in Uman', 1944. 295

Disabled and abandoned German Pz. IV tanks, March 1944. Both tanks might have been used as salvage by the Germans; note that both are missing their drive wheels, and the tank in the foreground is missing several bogey wheels. 295

Another shot of abandoned German vehicles on an Uman' city street, 1944. 295

Vehicles of the 2nd Tank Army, passing between knocked-out and captured German armor, March 1944. 296

A knocked-out German Pz. IV in the area of Uman', March 1944. 296

An abandoned German StuG in the same area. 296

German tanks and halftracks destroyed by forces of the 2nd Tank Army in the area of Uman', March 1944. A Cyrillic caption read, "After accurate strikes". 297

The command staff of the 51st Tank Brigade. In the center is Colonel Mirvoda, and on the right is Lieutenant Colonel Pisunkov (from S.M. Terekhov's personal collection of photographs).   297

The award ceremony on 1.10.1944 in the village of Tur, Volynsk Oblast, bestowing the Order of the Red Banner for the liberation of Uman'. On the right is General Latyshev, member of the 2nd Tank Army's Military Council.   297

Tanks of the 11th Guards Tank Brigade crossing the Southern Bug River, March 1944.   301

T-34 tanks of the 11th Guards Tank Brigade being ferried across the Southern Bug, March 1944.   302

Hero of the Soviet Union Vladimir Kosarev and his tank crew of the 16th Tank Corps' 51st Separate Motorcycle Regiment enjoy a smoke.   302

A Cyrillic caption read, "As it happened". Red Army soldiers in this blurry photo are standing next to their truck, which has become stuck in the deep mud on the road.   303

Tanks of the 2nd Tank Army in the area of Uman, March 1944.   308

Red Army troops happily inspect a knocked-out German Panther tank.   309

A T-34 waits in ambush – 2nd Tank Army, March 1944. The Cyrillic caption read "In ambush".   313

Attacking motorized infantry of the 2nd Tank Army dismount from a halted tank, March 1944.   314

"Where has their arrogance gone?".   314

"What sort of 'technological wonder' is this?"   314

A bridge over the Dnestr River, spring 1944.   315

German prisoners, taken in the Uman' area, March 1944.   315

Hero of the Soviet Union Captain Fedor Donkov and his tank crew inspect a destroyed German Panther, March 1944. Several days later, the tankers of Donkov's tank company (107th Tank Brigade) would conduct their final exploit in the Pirlița Sat area.   316

Units of the 2nd Tank Army crossing the Dnestr River, March 1944. The Cyrillic captions read, "The crossing of the 34th Guards Motorized Rifle Brigade over the Dnestr River. Motorized rifle brigade commander Colonel P.N. Akimochkin directs the crossing."   316

Donkov and his crew inspecting the same knocked-out Panther. The Cyrillic text read, "But what is it like close-up?"   317

A tank of the 2nd Tank Army enters a Moldavian village, April 1944.   318

Evgeni Tyshchik – 50th Tank Brigade.   329

Mikhail Sanachev – 51st Tank Brigade.   329

Boris Makeev – 107th Tank Brigade.   329

Fedor Mekhnin – 50th Tank Brigade.   329

Alexandr Rybin – 15th Motorized Rifle Brigade.   329

Melnikov – 8th Guards Heavy Tank Regiment.   329

Fedor Donkov – 107th Tank Brigade.   329

Nikolai Savin – 8th Guards Heavy Tank Regiment.   329

Iakov Telechenko – 11th Guards Tank Brigade.   329

Tankers of the 2nd Tank Army after being decorated.   331

Semen Bogdanov.   333

Nikolai Matiushin.   334

Grigorii Plaskov.                                                                        334

Boris Eremeev.                                                                          334

Aleksei Radzievsky.                                                                    334

Vasilii Mishulin.                                                                        334

Iosif Cheriapkin.                                                                        334

Il'ia Bazanov.                                                                            334

Ivan Dubovoi.                                                                           334

Pavel Shamardin.                                                                       334

Tanks of the 2nd Tank Army being greeted by locals, 1944.                             337

Motorized infantry of the 2nd Tank Army rest before the offensive, April 1944.        339

Tanks of the 11th Guards Tank Brigade on the march, April 1944.                        340

Major General Latyshev at the 11th Guards Tank Brigade's award ceremony. On the right
is brigade commander Guards Colonel Boris Eremeev.                                     340

The commander of the 2nd Tank Army Lieutenant General Semen Bogdanov, on the
right, bestows an Order to the 11th Guards Tank Brigade. On his right is brigade
commander Guards Colonel Boris Eremeev.                                                340

Boris Eremeev, commander of the 11th Guards Tank Brigade.                              341

Captain Petr Zlenko, battalion commander with the 11th Guards Tank Brigade.            341

Army commander S.I. Bogdanov taking a look at something off-camera.                    341

Lieutenant Spesivyi's tank crew, which distinguished itself in the fighting in Moldavia
and Romania, 1944.                                                                     341

Soviet tankers examine their "work".                                                   342

The 2nd Tank Army's intelligence chief Colonel Galimov, second from right, and on his
right, his deputy Lieutenant Colonel Kostromin, 1944.                                  342

Tankers of the 50th Tank Brigade of the 2nd Tank Army's 3rd Tank Corps examining a
German howitzer that they've knocked out.                                              342

A Cyrillic caption read, "May 1944. Romania. An elderly Romanian presents his last
remaining sheep to the soldier-liberators of the brigade, who were the first to fight their
way into the village."                                                                 343

Tankers of the 11th Guards Tank Brigade. On the right is Guards Lieutenant Vladimir
Tolstikov.                                                                             343

Army commander General Bogdanov and Military Council member General Latyshev
converse with the commander of the 5th Guards Tank Army General Rotmistrov and
staff officers.                                                                        343

Tankers of the 11th Guards Tank Brigade, April 1944; on the left is Guards Lieutenant
Vladimir Tolstikov.                                                                    344

"Fuel for tanks".                                                                      348

At the command post of the 2nd Tank Army. Seated at the table on the right is the army
commander, General Bogdanov.                                                           355

Romania, April-May, 1944.                                                              357

Tanks of the 2nd Tank Army ford the Prut River – April 1944.                          357

Two views of an SU-85 seized by the enemy in the Pirliţa Sat area, Romania, April 1944.  371

Joseph Stalin tanks of the 6th Guards Heavy Tank Regiment knocked-out in the area of
Târgu Frumos, May 1944.                                                                379

| 5.7 | Data on the availability of tanks in the 2nd Tank Army's formations as of 9.00 on 11.2.1944 | 237 |
|---|---|---|
| 5.8 | Data on the condition of the 2nd Tank Army's tank pool as of 7.00 on 29.2.1944 | 248 |
| 5.9 | Irrecoverable losses in armor of the 3rd Tank Corps from 25.1 to 23.2.1944 | 256 |
| 5.10 | Data on losses in personnel of the 3rd Tank Corps' units from 25.01 to 25.02.1944 | 257 |
| 5.11 | Data on the losses in personnel of the 16th Tank Corps over the period of combat actions between 27.01 and 25.02.1944 | 258 |
| 5.12 | Condition of non-serviceable tanks and assault guns | 261 |
| 5.13 | Number of tanks and assault guns repaired by the army-level repair services and the repair shops of the army's units and formations | 261 |
| 6.1 | The condition of the 2nd Tank Army's tank pool on the eve of the Uman' operation at midnight on 3.3.1944 | 283 |
| 6.2 | The operational status of the 2nd Tank Army's tanks as of midnight on 5.3.1944 | 285 |
| 6.3 | Status of the 2nd Tank Army's armor pool on 5 March 1944 | 286 |
| 6.4 | Data on the 2nd Tank Army's available tanks and assault guns as of 20 March 1944 | 311 |
| 6.5 | Data on the losses suffered by the 2nd Tank Army over the period between 5 March and 19 March 1944 | 311 |
| 7.1 | Data on the materiél of the 2nd Tank Army at 6.00 on 18.4.1944 | 363 |
| 7.2 | Data on the materiél of the 2nd Tank Army at 6.00 on 23.4.44 | 364 |
| 7.3 | Data on the material and supply levels of the forces of the 2nd Tank Army at 15.00 on 28 April 1944 | 365 |
| 7.4 | The amount of artillery in the 2nd Tank Army in firing positions on 28.4.44 | 368 |
| 7.5 | Data on the status of the tanks and self-propelled guns of the 2nd Tank Army on 14 May 1944 | 403 |
| 7.6 | Composition of the serviceable armor in the 2nd Tank Army at 6.00 on 2 June 1944 | 405 |
| 7.7 | Data on the personnel and materiél of the units and formations of the 2nd Tank Army as of 30 May 1944 | 415 |

# Preface

This book is devoted to the combat path of the 2nd Guards Tank Army. It attacked along the most important strategic axis. Its rank and file, non-commissioned officers and staff officers covered themselves with unfading glory and displayed combat skill, courage, heroism and resolve. The army's actions were marked by particular impetuousness. For example, over 15 days its troops advanced with fighting more than 700 kilometers from the Vistula to the Oder. During the war years more than 103,000 troops of the 2nd Guards Tank Army were decorated with medals and Orders for feats of combat heroism, and 221 of them earned the title Hero of the Soviet Union.

The book has been written on the basis of documents of the Russian Federation Ministry of Defense's Central Archives (TsAMO) and the recollections of war veterans. For the first time, complete information on the army's combat roster and its losses in each combat operation, strictly drawn from archival documents, are given in print. The sections on the army's combat lessons, with analysis of tactical situations at the company and battalion level, and the recommendations of 2nd Guards Tank Army commander Marshal of Armored Forces Semen Bogdanov on the modernization of the organizational structure of tank armies and the design and construction of main battle tanks might be of particular interest to specialists and readers.

I dedicate this book to my grandfathers, Captain Petr Kharitonovich Molochkov of the 133rd Tank Brigade (subsequently the 11th Guards Separate Tank Brigade), and Guards Major Iakov Filippovich Nebolsin, who commanded an assault battalion of the 178th Guards Rifle Regiment, 34th Guards Rifle Corps, 5th Guards Army. Guards Major General Anatolii Petrovich Shvebig, and Natalia Konstantinovna Zelenova, the director of the "Hero of the Soviet Union N.M Teliakov Museum of the 2nd Guards Tank Army's Combat Glory" in Moscow School No. 324 gave me invaluable help while working on this book.

P.Kh. Molochkov.

Ia.F. Nebolsin.

# Foreword

Major General Anatolii Shvebig.

Many articles, memoirs and other literature have been written about the combat operations of tank brigades, tank corps and tank armies. However, still many documents about the heroic actions of our 2nd Guards Tank Army and its troops have yet to be published. Much still remains in the archives and in the collective memory of its veterans. Since, it wasn't possible to write about everything back in Soviet times and because a lot of archival material was still classified, there are a lot of inaccuracies in the books that have been published.

The combat path of the 2nd Guards Tank Army is well-known to me. From April 1943 to February 1948, I was at different times the deputy technical commander of the 2nd Guards Tank Army's 12th and 16th Guards Tank Corps. The army had to fight primarily against select panzer and motorized divisions of Nazi Germany, and the victory over them was achieved in heavy and bloody combats. Thousands of tankers of the 2nd Guards Tank Army gave their lives for the freedom of their Motherland. Their selfless service to the Motherland, their loyalty to their military duties, and their courage are an example as well for today's young generation. The author has dedicated a lot of research work, gathered documentary archival materials, and broadly used the recollections of the army's veterans, resulting in an honest book about the glorious combat operations of the Guards tank army. Time passes inexorably. Veterans of the war – eyewitnesses of the fighting – are passing away, and together with them their priceless combat experience. In the book, the reader will read about such legendary personalities of the 2nd Guards Tank Army as Aleksandr Lugansky, Fedor Donkov, Boris Makeev, Mikhail Sanachev, Oleg Matveev, Sergei Matsapur, Ashot Amatun' and many others.

In my life I have read hundreds of books on the history of World War II that have been published in the Soviet Union and Russia both for public and internal use. However, the combat history of the 2nd Guards Tank Army written by Igor Nebolsin represents a completely new type of study. In my opinion, it is most likely the best book on this subject I have seen. And finally, Marshal of the Armor troops, Commander-in-Chief of the 2nd Guards Tank Army S.I. Bogdanov in one of our talks, told me about his conversation with the Supreme Commander which took place shortly after the war. In this conversation, Stalin stated that until the Berlin operation of 1945 he considered the 1st Guards Tank Army the best army, but after combats in Berlin and upon his overall assessment of the war, the number 1 position in the Soviet tank forces was taken by the 2nd Guards Tank Army.

Major General Anatolii Shvebig, deputy technical commander of the
12th Guards Tank Corps, 2nd Guards Tank Army

Semen Bogdanov, 2nd Guards Tank Army
commander.

Veteran of the 2nd Guards Tank Army
medal.

# Introduction

Over the years of the Second World War, the 2nd Guards Tank Army traveled a combat path of 6,000 kilometers. In the course of the fighting, the tankers, together with other troops of the Red Army, swept the enemy from a territory covering 27,000 square kilometers and liberated 3,730 towns and villages, including 49 major cities. The army was involved in some of the largest battles of the Great Patriotic War. The 2nd Guards Tank Army primarily faced elite enemy panzer formations on the battlefield along almost the entire extent of its combat path. At various times, they included the *Wehrmacht*'s *Grossdeutschland* and 4th Panzer Divisions; the *Luftwaffe*'s *Herman Goering* Division, SS panzer divisions such as *Leibstandarte Adolf Hitler*, *Totenkopf*, and *Wiking*; the 505th and 506th Heavy Panzer Battalions of Tiger tanks; and the Heavy Panzer Regiment *Bäke*. The army's troops passed these tests with honor and in the course of the engagements and battles inflicted blows upon a powerful, technically equipped foe.

In the assessment of Marshal Konev, the commander of the 1st Ukrainian Front, as part of which the 2nd Tank Army took part in the Uman operation and in the battles in Romania: "It was a well-forged army, superbly trained and organized in a combat respect, and in operations it was distinguished by its audacity and high activity." Marshal Rokossovsky, the commander of the Central Front and later the 1st Belorussian Front, as part of which the 2nd Guards Tank Army took part in the Battle of Kursk and in the Orel, Sevsk and Lublin operations, assessed the army's performance in the following manner: "The operations of the 2nd Tank Army to smash the enemy's Liubomil – Liublin, Pulawy – Dęblin and Prague groupings is a model of the classic use of tank and mechanized formations of the Red Army." General Radzievsky, who commanded the army during the Liublin – Prague Operation of 1944, wrote: "Nurtured in the spirit of impetuous forward advances, the 2nd Tank Army always fought in a Guards fashion without actually yet being a Guards formation. Serving with selfless dedication to its Motherland and acting boldly in battles, the ARMY gained a number of glittering victories over the foe and with its BLOOD earned the right to the GUARDS title."

The army, with fighting, traveled a glorious combat path from Sevsk to the city of Iaşi [Iassy, Jassy], then from Kovel to Warsaw, and ended its combat path in the city of Berlin. The army participated in 12 *front*- and army-level operations. Over the period of combat operations, the army's Guardsmen disabled or destroyed approximately 3,000 German tanks, up to 700 assault guns, and approximately 7,000 guns and mortars. For its successful combat operations, 145 Combat Orders decorated the banners of the army's units, many of which earned honorific titles: "Sevsk", "Uman", "Vapniarka" and "Berlin". Combat traditions developed and were faithfully upheld. The officers, sergeants and the rank and file gained experience and became forged in combat. Through its combat operations, the army earned the high assessment of the Supreme Commander-in-Chief Marshal Stalin, who 24 times publicly thanked the army's entire officers' staff and men. The 2nd Guards Tank Army achieved major triumphs in the fighting at Orel, Korsun-Shevchenkovskii, Uman, Vapnairka and in Poland, and on 21 April 1945 was the first to reach the northern outskirts of Berlin. For their exemplary fulfillment of combat orders at the front, 221 privates, sergeants and officers of the army were awarded the title Hero of the Soviet Union, while 103,352 troops were decorated with combat Orders and medals. The Guardsmen warriors demonstrated stubbornness and resolve on the defensive, and decisiveness and boldness on the offensive. By its glorious traditions, they added to the combat traditions of the Russian armed forces.

# 1

# The Origins of the 2nd Tank Army

The combat path of the 2nd Guards Tank Army begins with the People's Commissar of Defense Directive No. 787391 from 1 September 1942 on the forming of the 3rd Reserve Army, with Kalinin designated as the location of the army's headquarters. According to the army's journal of combat operations, the operations group of the army's headquarters arrived in Kalinin already on 5 September 1942 and set to work on forming the army and organizing the training and combat preparations in the units of the army's subordinate formations. One of the first to arrive was deputy army commander Major General Bondarev and the chief of the operations department Lieutenant Colonel Chizh. Initially, the army received the 15th, 20th, 23rd and 33rd Separate Rifle Brigades, the 43rd Guards Latvian Rifle Division, the 183rd and 374th Rifle Divisions, the 9th Separate Signals Regiment and a number of other units. The divisions and separate units that arrived in the army started work on combat preparations on 1 October 1942. At the same time, the army's field command began to prepare for combat operations, and it was fully hammered together by 1 December 1942. At 18.00 on 10 January 1943, the directive on forming the 2nd Tank Army on the basis of Briansk Front's 3rd Reserve Army was signed:

> Directive of the *Stavka* of the Supreme High Command No. 46002 to the Commander of the Briansk Front about Forming the 2nd Tank Army:

> The *Stavka* of the Supreme High Command orders: By 1 February 1943 form the 2nd Tank Army as part of the forces of Briansk Front in the area Efremov, Rossoshnia Station, Elets. Designate Lieutenant General Romanenko as commander of the 2nd Tank Army. Under the command of the 2nd Tank Army, include: the command of the 3rd Reserve Army with its support units, service facilities and army rear services, having changed the name of the 3rd Reserve Army's command to that of the 2nd Tank Army. Location – Ploskoe (20 kilometers north of Elets); the 11th Tank Corps and the 11th Separate Guards Tank Brigade – include tank brigades equipped with domestically-produced tanks; the 16th Tank Corps on the unit roster of a tank corps; the 29th and 30th Separate Guards Heavy Tank Regiments; two armored transport battalions and one motorcycle battalion under the control of the commander of the armored and mechanized troops; the 60th, 112th and 194th Rifle Divisions and three ski brigades; two destroyer anti-tank artillery regiments; one Guards mortar regiment; two engineering battalions; and three motorized supply battalions.

> [Signed] *Stavka* of the Supreme Commander-in-Chief I. Stalin

General Nikolai Biriukov, deputy commander of the armored-tank forces, made the following entry into his service diary on this subject:

8 January 1943: <u>Comrade Stalin's Order:</u> Choose a member of the Military Council for the 2nd Tank Army who would understand armored warfare. Begin forming the 2nd Tank Army in the area of Efremov. Present a draft directive on this. The army is to have two tank corps and three rifle divisions. Take the tank brigades from Briansk Front. The self-propelled artillery regiment is to have 16 76mm and 8 120mm self-propelled guns. The tank army is to have two tanks corps (the 11th and 16th), one tank brigade (the 11th Guards), three rifle divisions (the 60th, 112th and 194th), two motorized supply battalions with 200 vehicles, and one self-propelled artillery regiment. The mortar regiment is to have 36 mortars. Issue an order about appointing Romanenko as commander of the 2nd Tank Army for signing. Present for the People's Commissar's approval: c) the organization of the 2nd Tank Army's units; d) the directive for forming the 2nd Tank Army; e) the order regarding the appointment of the commander, the Military Council member, the chief of staff, and the deputy commander.

On 13 January 1943, an order was received to shift location and to transport the units of the 3rd Reserve Army by rail to a new assembly area. On 14 January 1943, the army's headquarters loaded onto a train at Kalinin Station and at 18.00 headed out along the route Kalinin – Moscow – Elets – Lozovaia Station. On 19 January 1943, the first train arrived at Lozovaia Station; work proceeded to unload it until 22.00.

The "birthday" of the 2nd Guards Tank Army is considered to be 15 January 1943 – the day of receiving the 3rd Reserve Army's field command pursuant to the *Stavka* directive about converting the 3rd Reserve Army into the 2nd Tank Army. Those were the victorious days of the Red Army's grand winter offensive along the enormous extent of the Soviet-German front. With the Red Army's going over to a decisive offensive, the role of the mobile tank and mechanized formations grew immeasurably. In accordance with the *Stavka* directive, trains arrived every day in the area of the army's assembly, loaded with troops, combat equipment, fuel, ammunition and rations. At night, the rumble of motors never ceased along the roads in the frontal zone: units that had been transferred to the army's command were coming up; artillery and engineering troops were being brought up; and combat supply and service units were arriving. According to the journal of combat operations, on 21 January 1943, the commander of the 2nd Tank Army Lieutenant General Prokofii Romanenko arrived. Departments of the army headquarters were wrapping up their work to set up office space and were preparing to receive the formations and separate units that were arriving in the army. On this same day, Major General of Tank Forces Ivan Lazarev's 11th Tank Corps arrived; assigned to the 2nd Tank Army, it consisted of the 53rd, 59th and 160th Tank Brigades, and the 12th Motorized Rifle Brigade.

On 20 January 1943, the 11th Guards Separate Tank Brigade under the command of the experienced Guards Colonel Nikolai Bubnov joined the 2nd Tank Army. The 16th Lithuanian Rifle Division arrived in the army on 23 January 1943 and on this same day took part together with the 11th Tank Corps in training exercises on the theme "March in anticipation of a meeting battle, and the meeting battle". In the period between 25 January and 1 February 1943, the 563rd and 567th Destroyer Anti-tank Artillery Regiments, the 37th Guards Motorcycle Regiment, and the 29th Separate Guards Breakthrough Heavy Tank Regiment joined the army. Around this same time, Major General of Tank Forces Aleksei Maslov's 16th Tank Corps arrived, which prior to this had been part of the Don Front. This corps had been formed in June 1942 and had taken part in the Battle of Stalingrad. It included the 107th, 109th and 164th Tank Brigades, and the 15th Motorized Rifle Brigade. Other units and elements were arriving in the army's assembly area. Together with the formations, which had combat experience, fresh young replacements were also coming in. Thus from the first days of the 2nd Tank Army's mustering, important significance was given to education work. Commanders, political staff and veterans of the units held talks regarding the situation at the front, and passed along the combat traditions of the units and elements in which the young replacements were to serve. The fresh replacements studied the KV, T-34 and T-70 tanks, as well as the other combat equipment and weapons that had arrived to equip the tank army. Tireless work was conducted to knit together the crews of the tanks, as well as the tank, artillery and rifle elements. The great amount of focused work and combat training in all of the tank army's units helped prepare the tankers both in a combat and political sense for the looming offensive on the Orel – Briansk axis under wintertime conditions.

Soon after the destruction of the enemy's Stalingrad grouping and the successful offensive by the Voronezh Front's forces, the question arose about smashing the enemy's major grouping in the Kromy – Orel area. The 2nd Tank Army (consisting of the 11th and 16th Tank Corps, the 11th Guards Tank Brigade, the 29th Guards Tank Regiment, the 37th Guards Mortar Regiment, the 9th Separate Signals Regiment, the 60th and 112th Rifle Divisions, the 563rd and 567th Destroyer Anti-tank Artillery Regiments and the 115th Separate Rifle Brigade) transferred from the control of Briansk Front to Central Front and was given the assignment to launch an enveloping attack against the enemy's Kromy – Orel grouping. By 1 February 1943, the 2nd Tank Army with its main forces had assembled in the Liubovsha – Verkhov'e – Solov'evka – Prostor – Srevo-Petrovskoe area (all points lying 30-50 kilometers north and northeast of Livny. Once there, it conducted Red vs Blue combat maneuvers, and prepared to carry out its first combat assignment.

On 12 February 1943, a new commander arrived to take command of the 2nd Tank Army: Hero of the Soviet Union Guards Lieutenant General of Tank Forces Aleksei Rodin. Lieutenant General Prokofii Romanenko had departed to be placed at the disposal of the *Stavka*. On 12 February the 2nd Tank Army was transferred to the Central Front and on the night of 12-13 February, started out on a 200-kilometer march.

Prokofii Romanenko, the first commander of the 2nd Tank Army.

Aleksei Rodin, the second commander of the 2nd Tank Army.

## THE 1943 DMITRIEV – SEVSK OPERATION

On the eve of the 2nd Tank Army's first offensive, its command staff consisted of the following:

**Command Staff of the 2nd Tank Army**
Commander – Lieutenant General Aleksei Rodin
Chief of Staff – Major General Dmitrii Onuprienko
1st Member of the Military Council – Major General Petr Latyshev
2nd Member of the Military Council – Major General Vladimir Sosnovikov
Deputy Commander for Rear Services – Major General Mikhail Goncharov
Deputy Chief of Staff – Colonel Belkov
Commander of Artillery – Colonel Mikhail Tsikalo
Commander of Engineering troops – Colonel Isak Levin
Chief of Operations Department – Colonel Vladimir Chizh
Chief of Signals Department – Lieutenant Colonel Iosif Smoly

**11th Tank Corps** – Major General of Tank Forces Ivan Lazarev
Chief of Staff – Colonel Petr Kalinichenko
53rd Tank Brigade – Lieutenant Colonel Il'ia Latypov
59th Tank Brigade – Lieutenant Colonel Sergei Kozikov
160th Tank Brigade – Lieutenant Colonel Nikita Davydenko
12th Motorized Rifle Brigade – Lieutenant Colonel Georgii Vinokurov

**16th Tank Corps** – Major General Aleksei Maslov
Chief of Staff – Colonel Leonid Pupko
107th Tank Brigade – Lieutenant Colonel Nikolai Teliakov
109th Tank Brigade – Colonel Vasilii Arkhipov
164th Tank Brigade – Colonel Andrei Kuznetsov
15th Motorized Rifle Brigade – Major Illarion Lomako

**112th Rifle Division** – Major General Porfirii Furt
**194th Rifle Division** – Guards Colonel Pavel Opiakin
**60th Rifle Division** – Colonel Ignatii Kliaro
**115th Separate Rifle Brigade** – Colonel Sankovsky
**11th Separate Guards Tank Brigade** – Guards Colonel Nikolai Bubnov
**9th Separate Signals Regiment** – Major Andrei Savchenko

**Units directly subordinate to Army headquarters:**
27th Separate Guards Breakthrough Heavy Tank Regiment
29th Separate Guards Breakthrough Heavy Tank Regiment
37th Guards Mortar Regiment
143rd Mortar Regiment (120mm) – arrived at the end of the operation
563rd Destroyer Anti-tank Artillery Regiment
567th Destroyer Anti-tank Artillery Regiment
1118th Destroyer Anti-tank Artillery Regiment – arrived at the end of the operation
51st Motorcycle Battalion

**Command Staff of the 2nd Tank Army – February 1943:**

Petr Latyshev.

Mikhail Goncharov.

Aleksei Maslov – 16th Tank Corps.

Nikolai Bubnov – 11th Guards Tank Brigade.

Ivan Lazarev – 11th Tank Corps.

## The 2nd Tank Army's Supply Situation

As of 1 February 1943, the 2nd Tank Army's supply situation in its staging area was fully satisfactory. The relatively short distance from the army's bases and supply dumps (ammunition, food and fodder were at Stanovaia Station, 70 kilometers from the army's formations; fuel and lubricants were in Babarykino Station, 100 kilometers away) enabled the full delivery of supplies to the troops.

## The Numerical Strength of the 2nd Tank Army as of 1 February 1943

**11th Tank Corps** – 6,447 men, 192 tanks, 80 guns and mortars, 116 anti-tank rifles
**16th Tank Corps** – 6,491 men, 161 tanks, 99 guns and mortars, 105 anti-tank rifles
**11th Guards Tank Brigade** – 1,086 men, 55 tanks, 10 guns and mortars, 6 anti-tank rifles.
**60th Rifle Division** – 8,111 men, 247 guns and mortars, 162 anti-tank rifles
**563rd and 567th Destroyer Anti-tank Artillery Regiments** – each had 20 anti-tank guns
**37th Guards Mortar Regiment** – 24 *Katiusha* rocket launchers, 1 anti-tank gun, 1 anti-tank rifle

Table 1.1: Armaments as of 2 February 1943

|  | Rifles | HMGs | A-A MGs | LMGs | SMGs | Mortars | Guns | A-T Guns | Trucks and Cars | Tanks |
|---|---|---|---|---|---|---|---|---|---|---|
| 11th Tank Corps | 3,119 | 18 | 18 | 79 | 859 | 52 | 13 | 15 | 577 | 192 |
| 16th Tank Corps | 3,716 | 36 | 16 | 179 | 1,575 | 52 | 24 | 23 | 401 | 161 |
| 11th Guards Tank Brigade | 497 | 4 | – | 20 | 171 | 6 | – | 4 | 94 | 55 |
| 60th Rifle Division | 6,030 | 89 | 9 | 177 | 708 | 178 | 36 | 33 | 74 | – |
| 567th Anti-tank Regiment | 167 | – | – | 5 | 37 | – | – | 20 | 35 | – |
| 563rd Anti-tank Regiment | – | – | – | – | – | – | – | 20 | 35 | – |
| 37th Guards Mortar Regiment | 450 | – | 2 | 10 | 3 | 24 launchers | – | 1 | 80 | – |
| 51st Motorcycle Brigade | 10 | – | – | 12 | 193 | 5 | – | – | 15 |  |

Table 1.2: Fuel and lubricant supplies as of 5 February 1943

| Formation | Refills | | | |
|---|---|---|---|---|
|  | Diesel fuel | KB-70 (high-octane) | Benzene 2s | Lubricants |
| 11th Tank Corps | 3.1 | 3.5 | 1.5 | 3.5 |
| 16th Tank Corps | 1.8 | 2.2 | 1.8 | 0.34 |
| 11th Guards Tank Brigade | 2.1 | 2.8 | 2.2 | 2.6 |
| 60th Rifle Division | – | – | – | – |

**Table 1.3: Ammunition supplies as of 5 February 1943**

| Formation | Combat Loads of Ammunition | | | |
|---|---|---|---|---|
| | 122mm shells | 76mm shells | 45mm shells | 120mm and 50mm mortar rounds |
| 11th Tank Corps | – | 1.9 | 3.2 | 2 |
| 16th Tank Corps | – | 1.9 | 2.3 | 0.6 |
| 11th Guards Tank Brigade | – | 3.1 | 1.3 | – |
| 60th Rifle Division | One combat load each | | | |

**Table 1.4: Condition of the Army's motorized transport on 10 February 1943**

| | Total number of available vehicles | | Vehicles under repair | | Vehicles yet to arrive | |
|---|---|---|---|---|---|---|
| | ZIS-5 | GAZ-AA | ZIS-5 | GAZ-AA | ZIS-4 | GAZ-AA |
| 816th Separate Motorized Transport Battalion | – | 144 | – | 56 | – | 89 |
| 850th Separate Motorized Transport Battalion | 37 | 108 | 7 | 37 | 30 | 71 |
| 193rd Horse-Drawn Transport Company | 104 wagons | | 35 wagons | | 69 wagons | |

Note: Each wagon of the horse-drawn transport company was pulled by a two-horse team.

The 2nd Tank Army's main supply base was at Elets. Several trains were moved to Krasnaia Zaria Station. Such a force disposition and supply basing for the army presumed its use in the role of follow-on echelon to develop a breakthrough in the western direction. As a result of the successful offensive by the Briansk Front's left flank, a favorable situation for introducing the 2nd Tank Army on this axis had arisen.

## The March of the Army's Formations

The 2nd Tank Army received an assignment to begin shifting to the Svoboda – Melekhino Station – Verkhnee Ol'khovatoe – Novaia Svoboda area (all points 15-30 kilometers south and southeast of Zolotukhino) from the morning of 13 February 1943. While en route, the army's assembly area was changed; its formations were instead to arrive in the Fatezh – Dubrovka – Telegino – Annenkovo area by 15 and 16 February 1943. Because of the lack of communications and due to the impass-ability of the roads, the army's headquarters was unable to transmit the change in destination in time, and several formations such as the 60th Rifle Division marched to the originally-designated assembly area, which led to great confusion and the scattering of units. The conditions for the army's march to the new area of assembly were very unfavorable: strong snowstorms made the roads virtu-ally impassable for wheeled vehicles. The army had no means of its own for clearing the roads, while the Front offered no assistance. Consequently, all of the army's formations were supposed to make a march of 200 kilometers in conditions of no trafficable roads. The supply bases and the dumps of fuel and rations had been left behind at the army's former location, while restaging them involved enormous difficulties and required a lot of time. Not only the 2nd Tank Army, but the entire Front, was moving day and night (or more often, not moving) over a single road, which enabled the enemy to detect the introduction of the new 2nd Tank Army and precluded any possibility of surprise.

The army's primary formations – the tank corps – only reached the designated assembly area on 24 February (instead of 15 and 16 February). After completing the march, their condition was such that they were unable to conduct combat operations because of the lack of fuel and lubricants, and due to the fact that they had lost half their tanks en route due to breakdowns or becoming bogged in snow drifts. The 60th Rifle Division didn't reach the assembly area by 19 February 1943. With the start of the march, the army's lines of communication became stretched, the available supplies among the troops were being expended, while the one motorway assigned to serve the Army was nearly impassable for the trucks, as a result of which the 2nd Tank Army's forces arrived in their jumping-off area without fuel, ammunition and rations.

The deep snow cover, the frequent snowfalls and snowstorms in the situation of a shortage of repair and recovery means and the absence of rear units told negatively on the status of the armor pool, while the insufficient supply of spare parts and repair tools worsened the condition of the armored vehicles.

**Table 1.5: Availability of tanks upon arrival in the new assembly area**

|  | Number of tanks in previous staging area | Number of tanks present in new assembly area | Tanks remaining in old assembly area | Tanks lagging behind en route |
|---|---|---|---|---|
| 16th Tank Corps | 161 | 38 | 44 | 79 |
| 11th Tank Corps | 192 | 104 | 39 | 49 |
| 11th Guards Tank Brigade | 55 | 40 | 13 | 2 |
| Total: | 408 (100%) | 182 (45%) | 96 (23.5%) | 130 (31.5%) |

**Table 1.6: Availability of fuel and lubricants, and ammunition by 21 February 1943**

|  | Fuel and Lubricants (refills) | Ammunition (combat loads) |
|---|---|---|
| 16th Tank Corps | 0.1 | 1.5 |
| 11th Tank Corps | 0.25 | 2.0 |
| 11th Guards Tank Brigade | 0.1 | 2.5 |

The march of a tank army along a single road, which was also being used by troops of the entire Front and the 2nd Guards Cavalry Corps, and along which ammunition was being brought up and the wounded and property were being evacuated, created excessively difficult conditions for the movement of the army's formations. The wheeled transport that was bringing up fuel and ammunition spent a long time en route, and the inadequate number of vehicles in the motorized transport battalions made the army's situation even worse. The absence of fuel, spare parts and repair tools in the army's formations led to the fact that of the army's 408 tanks, only 182 arrived in the jumping-off position for the offensive, and most of those needed short-term repairs. As a result of all this, the tank corps, virtually without fuel, had little combat capability prior to 1 March 1943. Here's how this march was described in the combat journal of the 11th Tank Corps:

At this time, the 11th Tank Corps, which had become part of the 2nd Tank Army, received an order from the army commander General Rodin: via night marches, reach the area Vasilevskoe, Kasimovo, Konevo. The corps commander Major General Ivan Lazarev decided to conduct the march in a single column by echelon, and by 3.00 14 February, the corps was to assemble in the area Iamskaia Svoboda, Barkovo. The headquarters staff under the leadership of the chief of staff Colonel P.I. Kalinichenko worked out a detailed plan for the march. Staff officers were sent out to the units in order to render assistance in organizing the night march. So that the corps' units weren't delayed on the march, reinforced detachments for supporting the movement were created, consisting of the 32nd Mine-Engineering Company and two motorized rifle companies of the 12th Motorized Rifle Brigade; in addition, each brigade had tanks with attached snowplows at the head of the column in order to clear the snow-covered roads. An unprecedented blizzard began on the morning of 13 February. It was possible to move only with the greatest difficulty. At 17.00 the units of the corps set out on the march. The blizzard wasn't subsiding. The depth of the snow cover was more than a meter. It seemed as if nature had erected an obstacle in front of the troops, and was striving to check their forward movement. No sooner had the snowplow-equipped tank managed to advance 100-200 meters, along with two or three vehicles in its immediate wake, when the road would again be blanketed with snow. Because of this, the wheeled vehicles were unable to make headway through the deep drifts of snow; the corps' fuel and lubricants transport company as well as the rear services of the brigades lagged behind their units and formations. This threatened to disrupt the timely supply of the units with fuel.

The movement of the 2nd Tank Army to its new area of assembly was not organized by either the army's headquarters or the Front's headquarters. The army's headquarters didn't have the time or the means for this, while the Front obviously didn't trouble itself with these questions at all: the roads were not plowed, and no reserves of fuel, lubricants and rations had been stockpiled in proximity to the army's new area of assembly. No measures whatsoever were taken to secure a concealed march. As a result, the army's formations that managed to reach the new assembly area were not combat-capable. The isolation from supply bases and dumps, the poor condition of the roads, and the lack of motorized transport – all this taken together placed the army's forces in difficult circumstances prior to the start of carrying out its combat assignment. The army's operation was not supported materially. The lengthy march in the conditions where the road was nearly impassable and the weather was so bad exhausted the tank formations, and rendered the tank forces almost combat-ineffective.

## Description of the terrain in the sector of the 2nd Tank Army's operations

The 2nd Tank Army's operations unfolded in the Svapa River (with its tributaries) – Osmanka – Sev River – Osozha area. The Svapa and Sev Rivers cut through the terrain in the 2nd Tank Army's sector from north to south, and presented obstacles to tank movement along their entire courses. The Svapa River and its tributaries lie in a broad valley with a commanding western bank, which offered good defensive positions and fine observation over the approaches to the Svapa River. The terrain along the line running from Dmitriev to Sevsk and further along the Sev River is sharply divided into two parts: the northern area is densely cut by balkas and ravines, forested, and has large populated places, making the area unfavorable for tank operations; the southern portion is more open, with fewer populated places and forested patches, making itself more favorable for the broad use of tank forces with the aim of bypassing strongpoints in the enemy's defense. The cities of Dmitriev and Sevsk, situated on the right bank of the rivers presented natural defensive strongpoints that commanded the surrounding terrain. The Usozha River, which flowed through the sector of the army's operations from east to west, represented an advantageously located switch position, which threatened any successful offensive operations to the west of the line of the Usozha – Sevsk highway. There were no other trafficable roads in the sector of the 2nd Tank Army's offensive. The roads Dmitriev – Sevsk and Dmitriev – Lokot' had been mined and demolished. Major populated places Dmitriev, Deriugino, Krasnyi Klin and Evdokimovo, as well as others had been timely prepared for a lengthy defense (embrasures for heavy machine guns and infantry guns had been cut through walls, and the approaches to them had been mined). Thus, the terrain in the northern portion of the 2nd Tank Army's sector of advance was unfavorable for tank forces.

## Meteorological conditions during the operation

The army's combat operations began in the latter half of February and continued until the end of March. The February and March snowstorms and frequent snowfalls made the available roads largely impassable, as a result of which it was necessary to take urgent steps to clear the roads, to mobilize the local population and to assign command staff and troops for maintaining the roads. However, despite all the adopted measures, the prolonged snowstorms and snow drifts made the roads impassable, and the possibility for movement along the roads would be curtailed for 2-3 days at a time. The weather conditions were plainly unsatisfactory for developing the combat operations of the 2nd Tank Army's formations.

## Preparation for combat operations

Pursuant to a Central Front Headquarters' Combat Order No. 022/OP from 19 February 1943, the army's troops moved into their jumping-off position for the offensive, with the task to crush enemy resistance on the line Mikhailovka – Ratmanovo – Staryi Gorod – Sukhoi Rovets, and then to attack in the general direction of Dmitriev and Sevsk.

**Table 1.7: Correlation of forces at the start of the tank corps' motorized infantry combat operations**

|  | On the entire front | | | Per kilometer of front | |
| --- | --- | --- | --- | --- | --- |
|  | Our force | Enemy force | Correlation | Our force | Enemy force |
| Battalions | 22 | 12 | 2:1 | 1.2 | 0.7 |
| Heavy machine guns | 106 | 104 | 1:1 | 5.6 | 5.5 |
| Light machine guns | 506 | 400 | 1.2:1 | 27 | 22 |
| Anti-tank rifles | 364 | 108 | 3:1 | 20.2 | 6 |
| Mortars |  |  |  |  |  |
| 50mm | 90 | 108 | 0.9:1 | 5 | 6 |
| 82mm | 159 | 72 | 2.2:1 | 8.8 | 4 |
| 120mm | 36 | – | – | – | – |
| Guns | 80 | 119 | 0.8:1 | 4.5 | 6.5 |

Note: The correlation of forces was calculated without regard for the limited supply of ammunition for the attacking formations and the impossibility of rapidly delivering ammunition to the firing positions.

The advantageous position of the defenders and the adaptation of the western bank of the Svapa River and populated places for defense, as well as the enemy's saturation with weapons and ammunition made things difficult for the attackers to carry out their assignment. The lack of reinforcing artillery, the lagging behind of their own artillery and the insignificant stockpiles of shells created additional problems. The impunity with which the enemy employed his bombers told most heavily on the operations of the attacking formations.

## The 2nd Tank Army's Combat Baptism

At 9.30 on 20 February 1943, the 2nd Tank Army's headquarters received Central Front Headquarters' No. 022/OP that had been issued the evening before at 18.30 on 19 February 1943, according to which the troops of the 2nd Tank Army were to move into a jumping-off position on the line Mikhailovka – Ratmanovo – Staryi Gorod – Sukhoi Rovets for an offensive in the general direction of Dmitriev-L'govskii, Sevsk and Trubchevsk:

## Central Front's Combat Order No.022/OP to the 2nd Tank Army, 19 February 1943

I.   Clarification of tasks: On 23.2.1943, as part of the Central Front the 2nd Tank Army (with the rifle and motorized rifle formations) in collaboration with the 65th Army and Kriukov's Cavalry Group breaks through the enemy's defenses in the sector Mikhailovka, Morshneva, Dmitriev, L'govskii, Arbuzovo and destroys the opposing units of the 707th Infantry Division and the 5th Regiment of Kaminsky's Brigade. With the introduction of the tank corps, develop the success into the operational depth in the general direction of Trubchevsk, Unecha. The army's immediate task is to cut the Briansk – Konotop railroad, its ultimate objective – reach the northwestern bank of the Desna River and seize Trubchevsk. Subsequently the army must be ready for operations in the Pochep and Unecha directions. The army, under the Front's direction, carries out one of the primary tasks, and is a powerful battering ram, which will split the northern and southern enemy groupings facing the Briansk and Central Fronts. When carrying out the immediate assignment, it is necessary with two rifle divisions and the motorized infantry of the first echelon in conjunction with partisan brigades to destroy the enemy troops in his tactical zone of defense and to secure the operation of the tank corps from the southwest direction in the course of 48 hours. When carrying out subsequent assignments, the army secures its main grouping from possible enemy counterattacks from the directions of Briansk, Pochep, Pogar or Gremiach. The overall depth of the operation – 120 kilometers. The initial objective – reaching the northwestern bank of the Desna River – 35 kilometers. The pace of advance for the tank formations and motorized infantry on the third day – 40-45 kilometers, for the infantry – 25-30 kilometers after destroying the enemy in the tactical zone.

II.  Decision: a) Operation's aim: The army with the force of two rifle divisions and the motorized infantry of the tank corps, and part of the strength of 132nd Rifle Division in cooperation with the 65th Army and Kriukov's Cavalry Group breaks through the enemy's defense, wipes out his personnel in the tactical zone, and will introduce its tank corps into the operational depth with the aim of dividing the enemy's Briansk and southern grouping and seizing the railroad in the Kokorevka – Suzemka sector. The army's immediate task – to reach the front Kokorevka, Suzemka; subsequent task – reach the northwestern bank of the Desna River and seize Trubchevsk.
b) The army's deployment: Conduct the army's regrouping and the combat deployment in the days before the breakthrough. Complete the bringing up of the army's forces only at night time. Arrange the combat formation in the jumping-off position in three echelons. In the first echelon – two rifle divisions, the motorized infantry, two regiments of the 132nd Rifle Division, and all the artillery of the rifle divisions and the motorized rifle brigades. Second echelon – two tank corps, one tank regiment. Third echelon – one tank brigade, one rifle brigade.

III. The operation's stages: Conduct the operation in three stages: The preparatory stage – 48 hours. All of the work of the preparatory stage concludes in the assembly area. The jumping-off area is the only place for supplementary reconnaissance, intelligence gathering, and topping up the vehicles with fuel for the first echelon. The first stage – 3-4 days for the tank formations, 5-6 days for the infantry. The second stage – presumably in the Pochep and Unecha directions, 2-3 days for the tank formations, 3-4 days for the infantry. Tasks for the stages of the operation for the formations and units – in correspondence with combat instructions and orders.

IV.   Ensuring the operation
Intelligence: In the preparatory stage – establish the enemy's system of fire in the frontal zone. Pinpoint the enemy's artillery in the frontal zone and in the depth. Detect the areas of assembly of the closest reserves, especially in the areas of Konotop and Bakhmach. In the first stage – pinpoint the arrangement of defensive weapons in the zone of the tactical defense. Pay particular attention to establishing the location of anti-tank weapons and areas. Establish the possibility of regrouping the Hungarian VIII Army Corps and the approach of operational reserves from the areas of Konotop and Bakhmach, as well as the enemy's grouping and path of retreat. Ascertain the system of defensive fortifications along the Desna River.

V.   Material support for the operation – For the operation, the army should have: 3 combat loads of ammunition; 5-6 refills for the combat vehicles; 8 refills for the transport vehicles; and 10 days of provisions. The rifle divisions should have two combat loads. For the successful carrying out of the operation, it is necessary to reinforce the army: with two destroyer anti-tank regiments – 76mm; two light artillery regiments; two howitzer artillery regiments; and with two aviation divisions (composite).

[Signed] RODIN, LATYSHEV, ONUPRIENKO

Given the text of the order, it was plainly too ambitious given the wintry conditions and the severe problems they were causing during the 2nd Tank Army's movement into the jumping-off positions. The army was to be ready to attack on the morning of 23 February 1943. In order to carry out this order, the formations would have to conduct a 70-kilometer march and make ready to attack. Refer back to Table 5 for the condition of the tank corps at this time.

All of the artillery and the mortars of the corps' motorized infantry were lagging behind en route. The 60th and 112th Rifle Divisions and the 115th Separate Rifle Brigade were still on the march and hadn't yet arrived in the area of the 2nd Tank Army's assembly. Thus it is obvious that Combat Order No. 022/OP was issued without regard for time and distance, or the real condition of the army's formations, and with no consideration of its feasibility. All of this was reported by code to Chief of the General Staff Marshal Vasilevsky and Colonel Gromov of the General Staff, who was responsible for coordinating the Central Front's actions. After discussions, the 2nd Tank Army commander and the Central Front commander reached a compromise solution – to attack with the motorized infantry alone, without tanks and artillery, since the latter were still en route. The general task of the 2nd Tank Army was formulated as follows: "The 2nd Tank Army with the forces of the motorized brigades and motorized rifle battalions of the 11th and 16th Tank Corps and the 11th Guards Tank Brigade on 23.2 will go on the offensive with the task to crush resistance in the sector Pervo-Maiskii, Morshneva, Dmitriev, Chernaia Griaz' and will seize the line Kruglinskii, Deriugino, Bugry, Merkulovka, Ul'ianovka."

The infantry of the 11th Tank Corps on 22 February 1943 under the leadership of the commander of the 12th Motorized Rifle Brigade Lieutenant Colonel G. Vinokurov moved out on foot and aboard trucks toward the area of its jumping-off position, and by the end of the day was assembling in readiness to attack toward Fateevka. The corps' tank brigades had stopped in place, waiting for fuel to come up.

The agitation of the 2nd Tank Army command over the dire supply situation and the attenuation of his tank force en route to the new assembly area is evident in Order No. 0057/OP from 23 February 1943 to all of the army's subordinate commanders:

> Due to the unfavorable meteorological conditions, as well as the tardy organization and execution by the commanders of the formations, units and army rear, the impermissible straggling not only of the rear services, but also of the combat units has come about. As a result, the Army's troops failed to carry out a combat order regarding the movement to a new assembly area. More than 50 percent of the combat vehicles have been left behind on the road due to the lack of fuel and to mechanical breakdowns. If this disorganization and tardiness isn't immediately rectified, the Army will be confronted with the threat of failing to carry out a combat assignment. THE ARMY'S MILITARY COUNCIL DEMANDS:
>
> 1. The commanders of the formations and units are quickly to take under their own personal leadership the organization of clearing the roads in their sectors [leading] from the areas of assembly.
> 2. In order to secure the uninterrupted movement of supply vehicles to the areas of assembly and of food from the areas of assembly to their sectors, keep constant teams of the local population on the roads, led by representatives of the units, not only to keep the roads clear, but also to push wheeled transport through difficult to pass sectors.
> 3. Take all measures for the total mobilization of the local population to clear the roads and for keeping them in constant trafficable condition.
> 4. Seek out containers based upon the calculation of transporting fuel – two refills, not including one refill for the vehicles. Consider the restoration of the roads and the bringing up of fuel and ammunition as the execution of a combat order. Recommend those commanders of the units and elements, who carry out the order on time and without interruptions, for decorations; remove those officers who fail to carry out the order or who are slow in carrying out the order from their posts and turn them over to the Court of Military Tribunal. Responsibility for maintaining the army's line of communications Livy – Zolotukhino rests upon the Chief of the Motor Road Department. Zolotukhino – Fatezh and Fatezh – Dmitriev-L'govskii – upon my Deputy of the Engineering Troops.
> 5. In the course of 23.2 and 24.2.43, bring up three refills of fuel and 2 combat loads of ammunition to the assembly areas. Take ¾ of a combat load of ammunition and one refill for the tanks. Supply the crews with five days of dry rations and 3-4 normal meals. Deliver two refills, two combat loads of ammunition, and 5-7 days' worth of provisions to the rifle formations. Take all measures to procure foodstuffs at the expense of local means. The main line of communications for more movement of supplies and wheel and tracked transport: Fatezh – Dmitriev-L'govskii.
> 6. The Military Council forewarns that no meteorological conditions or road difficulties whatsoever should be an obstacle to the timely delivery of fuel and ammunition and to the uninterrupted supply of the units when carrying out combat tasks.

At 19.00 on 23 February 1943, the 2nd Tank Army's chief of operations Lieutenant Colonel Chizh produced a report showing the availability of combat-ready tanks in the army's subordinate armor units:

**Table 1.8: Available combat-ready tanks in the 2nd Tank Army's tank formations as of 19.00 on 23 February 1943**

| Unit | Tank Type | | | | | | Total | Headquarters |
|---|---|---|---|---|---|---|---|---|
| | KV | T-34 | T-70 | T-60 | Matilda | Valentine | | |
| **11th Tank Corps** | | | | | | | | |
| 53rd TBr. | 10 | 16 | – | – | – | – | 26 | Dovgoletovo |
| 59th TBr. | – | – | – | 9 | 3 | 18 | 30 | Kochetki |
| 160th TBr. | – | – | – | 10 | 28 | – | 38 | Shmarnoe |
| Total: | 10 | 16 | – | 19 | 31 | 18 | 94 | Dubrovka |
| **16th Tank Corps** | | | | | | | | |
| 107th TBr. | – | 12 | 1 | – | – | – | 13 | Soleevka |
| 109th TBr. | – | 11 | 11 | – | – | – | 22 | Koshurovka |
| 164th TBr. | – | 7 | – | – | – | – | 7 | Tikhonovka |
| Total: | – | 30 | 12 | – | – | – | 42 | Milenino |
| **11th GTBr.** | – | 23 | – | 16 | – | – | 39 | Sorokovye Dvory |
| **29th GTRgt.** | 12 | – | – | – | – | – | 12 | Konevo |
| Total for the Army | 22 | 69 | 12 | 35 | 31 | 18 | 187 | Sergeevskoe |

## Course of the operation between 22.00 23 February and 11.00 24 February 1943

At 22.00 on 23 February 1943, the 16th Tank Corps' 15th Motorized Rifle Brigade with a limited number of guns and mortars, as well as the motorized rifle battalions of the 107th and 164th Tank Brigades went on the offensive from the line of the Svapa River out of jumping-off positions in the woods north of Voropaevo in the direction of Pal'tsevo, Glotovka. Having in the course of the night cleared the enemy from the eastern bank of the Osmanka River, by 11.00 on 24 February the Red Army infantry was locked in combat with the enemy on the line: eastern outskirts of Pal'tsevo, Glotovka. The motorized infantry, encountering the enemy's stubborn resistance in positions that had been previously prepared for defense and taking enemy artillery fire from the vicinities of Hill 233.3 (2 kilometers northwest of Morshneva) and Hill 225.2 (2 kilometers southwest of Kil'kino), was unable to carry out its assignment and by the end of the day began to dig in on the line it had reached.

The lead 934th Rifle Regiment of the 194th Rifle Division on the morning of 24 February went on the attack out of the area of Ratmanovo and the heights north of Ratmanovo in the direction of Polozovka together with motorized infantry of the 16th Tank Corps, and by 11.00 was engaged in street fighting in the eastern outskirts of Polozovka, having cracked the enemy's first line of defense. The 194th Rifle Division's 616th and 470th Rifle Regiments, having deployed out of the area of Pervomaiskii and outflanking Polozovka from the north, went on the offensive in the area of Rogozino, Zelenyi Gai, Novaia Pershina and throughout 24 February attacked in the direction of Petrovskoe and Bykhovka.

As a result of the first day of fighting, the eastern bank of the Osmanka River and the Svapa River were swept clean of the enemy, and the forward edge of the enemy's defense in the Polozovka – Pal'tsevo area was ruptured. The tank corps, the 60th Rifle Division and the 115th Separate Rifle Brigade were all continuing to assemble in the jumping-off areas for the offensive. The motorized infantry of the 16th Tank Corps lost 410 men in the course of the day. The 194th Rifle Division lost 156 men. Over this same period of combat, the enemy left more than 300 soldiers and officers dead on the battlefield. Trophies: 2 serviceable guns and 2 prisoners. Three populated places were liberated on this day.

Infantry and motorized rifle units go on the offensive, February 1943.

Plainly, the attack with motorized infantry alone, without tanks, artillery or mortars, was unjustified and yielded meagre results. Undertaken with the aim of destroying the enemy as quickly as possible, without waiting for the all-arms formations to come up and for the restoration of the tanks' combat readiness, the attack failed to reach its objective. The forces were committed piecemeal, which enabled the Germans to detect the new formations and to take corresponding countermeasures in response. The specialized infantry, which had been trained to attack together with tanks, suffered significant, pointless losses.

On the morning of 24 February 1943, as the fruitlessness of the attacks became evident, the Central Front's deputy chief of operations Colonel Kramar issued a situation report that labeled the attacks by the infantry of the 2nd Tank Army as a "reconnaissances-in-force":

The 2nd Tank Army – with motorized rifle units on foot by the end of 23.2.1943 reached the jumping-off line of the Svapa River, and from the morning of 24.2.1943 is conducting a reconnaissance-in-force. The 194th Rifle Division – on the line Pervomaiskii, Polozovka (15 kilometers northeast of Dmitriev-L'govskii) from the morning of 23.2 has been conducting a reconnaissance-in-force. The 60th Rifle Division – began assembling in the area Romanovka, Belyi Kolodez', Dmitrievskaia Koloniia (12 kilometers southeast of Dmitriev-L'govskii). The artillery of these units is still on the march. The tank formations are located in the areas: 16th Tank Corps – Bugry, Milenino, Soleevka; the 11th Tank Corps – Shmarnoe, Kasilovo, Kochetki; the 11th Guards Tank Brigade – Bychek, Trubitsyn (Sorokovye Dvory); the 29th Guards Tank Regiment – Konevo; the fuel and the materiél that has lagged behind are being brought up. The tank formations will move into their jumping-off positions at the end of 26.2.1943 and will begin operations on the morning of 27.2. **Condition:** 11th Tank Corps – serviceable 11 KV, 1 T-34, 41 T-60 and T-70, 49 Mk II and Mk III [Matildas and Valentine tanks], altogether 102 tanks; the 16th

Tank Corps – serviceable 33 T-34, 14 T-60 and T-70, altogether 47 tanks; 11th Guards Tank Brigade – serviceable 25 T-34 and 15 T-70, altogether 40 tanks; the 29th Guards Separate Tank Regiment – 15 KV tanks operational. By the start of stepping off on the offensive, 33 [additional] tanks of the 11th Tank Corps and 23 [additional] tanks of the 16th Tank Corps will either come up or be made serviceable.

In order to replenish the tank formations, 85 tanks for the army are coming by railroad, which are beginning to arrive at Livy Station on 24.2.43. The large loss of equipment in the 16th Tank Corps is explained by poor management on the part of the corps commander Major General Maslov and his chief of staff – Colonel Pupko. [Author's note: On 24 February 1943 General Maslov was removed from command of the 16th Tank Corps; on 8 March 1943, Colonel V.E. Grigor'ev assumed command of the corps.] There was enough fuel at the end of 23.2 for one refueling, in addition, canisters with fuel, which have been sent to the army by the rear command are still on their way. The army has one transport container, enough for a single refill, and this complicates bringing up the fuel. There isn't enough oil. There are captured lubricants in Kursk, which are now being tested for possible use. The assets – the 1188th Destroyer Anti-tank Regiment and the 143rd Mortar Regiment – on the march from the Elets area – have passed through Livny. The 567th and 563rd Destroyer Anti-tank Artillery Regiments are on the march from Livny. As much as 50 percent of their towing vehicles (Willys jeeps) have broken down. The 10th Anti-aircraft Division is finishing assembly in the area east of Fatezh. The Guards Mortar units: the 37th Guards Mortar Regiment – moving as part of the 2nd Tank Army, passed through Zolotukhino on the morning of 24.2; the 86th Guards Mortar Regiment – also. The 1188th Destroyer Anti-tank Artillery Regiment and the 143rd Mortar Regiment – after unloading are on their way to join the 2nd Tank Army; their location on the march is being ascertained; the 10th Anti-aircraft Division has joined the Tank Army and is finishing its assembly in the Ol'khovatka area.

[Signed] Deputy chief of operations of the Central Front Colonel Kramar

On 24-25 February 1943, the 194th, 112th and 60th Rifle Divisions, and the 29th Guards Tank Regiment were transferred to the 2nd Tank Army. The tanks received fuel and could begin combat operations.

## Combat operations from 11.00 24 February to 26 February 1943

In the course of 24.2.1943, the 60th Rifle Division was moving into its jumping-off area for the offensive. The motorized infantry of the 16th Tank Corps and the 194th Rifle Division were continuing to attack and by 18.00 on 25.2.1943 the 194th Rifle Division, having overcome the enemy's stubborn resistance, took possession of Polozovka with the forces of the 954th Rifle Regiment. The 616th Rifle Regiment was fighting in the eastern outskirts of Kamenka, having overcome the enemy's defenses on the western bank of the Svapa River; the 470th Rifle Regiment seized the southern outskirts of Pal'tsevo after a hard fight, and for the rest of the day was engaged in street fighting. The motorized infantry of the 16th Tank Corps, lacking artillery and unsupported by tanks, was unable to continue its attack and at the end of 25.2.1943, they were continuing to dig in on the lines they had achieved. The motorized infantry of the 11th Tank Corps, having breached the enemy's defenses on the western bank of the Svapa River on the front Zlobino, Chernaia Griaz', Arbuzovo by the end of the day 25.2.1943 seized Petrovskoe and Etenevka and was continuing to attack to the northwest.

By the end of 25.2.1943, the enemy's line of defense on the flanks of the main defensive strong-point Dmitriev had been breached; the 2nd Tank Army had its greatest success on its left flank. The evident success of the army on its left flank and the losses among the 16th Tank Corps' motorized infantry compelled the command to conduct a partial regrouping with the aim of taking the Briansk Front's combat-ineffective 132nd Rifle Division out of the line and reducing the attacking front of the 16th Tank Corps' motorized infantry through the commitment of the 112th and 60th Rifle Divisions and the 115th Separate Rifle Brigade that were coming up from the rear. The 2nd Tank Army's troops spent 26 and 27 February 1943 conducting the regrouping, improving their positions, and sending out reconnaissance patrols, while the tank formations were finishing their assembly in the jumping-off areas for the offensive.

In order to better handle the forces of the first echelon, the army headquarters shifted to General'shino, and its forward field command post to Ratmanovo. As a result of the combat operations between 24 and 27 February 1943, the enemy's defense along the western bank of the Svapa River was ruptured, which allowed the subsequent possibility of using the tank corps on the western side of the river. In addition, the axis of the army's further efforts to encircle the enemy's Dmitriev grouping was determined. This enemy grouping consisted of the 137th and 707th Infantry Divisions, plus the 9th, 10th and 11th Battalions of Kaminsky's Brigade.

On the morning of 28.2.1943, the augmented 2nd Tank Army stepped off to fulfill this assignment. By Rodin's Combat Order No. 1 from 27.2.1943, the assignments were given to the subordinate forces for the general offensive that would begin on the morning of 28.2.1943. As specified by Combat Order No. 1, the overall task facing the troops was to launch a two-pronged attack against the flanks of the enemy's defending forces in the Dmitriev area. On the right wing of the army, the 16th Tank Corps and the 194th Rifle Division, reinforced by the 29th Guards Tank Regiment attacked in the general direction toward Deriugino Station, Krasnyi Klin, and Pogodino. On the left, the 11th Tank Corps attacked in the direction of Dobrovod'e and Sevsk; the 60th Rifle Division, reinforced by the 53rd Separate Tank Brigade attacked toward Kuznetsovka, Popovkino and Belyi Kolodez'. The 112th Rifle Division attacked in the center, toward Dmitriev itself, having replaced units of the 194th and 60th Rifle Divisions. The 11th Guards Tank Brigade, which was concentrated in the area of Shcherbachevo, was located in the 2nd Tank Army's reserve.

Units of the enemy's 137th Infantry Division were defending in front of the 2nd Tank Army on the line Polozovka – Dmitriev. On the front Dmitriev – Zlydino, units of the 707th Infantry Division, which had been strongly battered in the previous fighting, were defending. In Dmitriev itself, there was up to battalion of Brigade Commander Kaminsky's police brigade. The enemy's defenses primarily rested upon foxholes and trenches dug into the snow. There were only a handful of earth-and-timber weapon emplacements. Thus the enemy's main resistance was expected on the 2nd Tank Army's right flank. The line Dmitriev – Beliteno was being held by units that had suffered heavy losses and which were to a known extent already demoralized.

The overall sector of the 2nd Tank Army's attack was 36 kilometers in width. The main attack was launched by the 11th Tank Corps on a front of 5 kilometers in the direction of Dobrovod'e and Sevsk, to a depth of 30 kilometers. Secondary attacks were launched by the 194th Rifle Division in the direction of Boguslovka, Pervoavgustovskii and Deriugino Station, and by the 60th Rifle Division in the direction of Melovoe and 1st Oktiabr'skii, with the ultimate objective of encircling the enemy's Dmitriev grouping. The army's combat formation was arranged in a single echelon. The 112th Rifle Division was supposed to operate in a second echelon behind the 11th Tank Corps, but at the moment of the offensive's start, it was still on the march.

Table 1.9: The correlation of forces (on a front of 36 kilometers)

| | On the entire front | | | Per kilometer of the front | |
| --- | --- | --- | --- | --- | --- |
| | Our forces | Enemy forces | Correlation | Our forces | Enemy forces |
| Battalions | 24 | 12 | 2:1 | 0.6 | |
| Heavy MGs | 223 | 104 | 2.1:1 | 6.2 | |
| Light MGs | 606 | 400 | 1.5:1 | 16.9 | |
| Anti-tank rifles | 535 | 108 | 5:1 | 15.0 | |
| **Mortars:** | | | | | |
| 50mm | 262 | 108 | 2:1 | 7.2 | |
| 82mm | 145 | 72 | 2:1 | 4.0 | |
| 120mm | 48 | – | – | 1.3 | |
| **Guns:** | | | | | |
| Heavy | 18 | 12 | 1.5:1 | 0.5 | |
| Anti-tank | 143 | 59 | 2.4:1 | 4.0 | |
| Light | 115 | 48 | 2.2:1 | 3.2 | |
| **Tanks:** | | | | | |
| Heavy | 21 | – | – | 0.58 | |
| Medium | 109 | – | – | 3 | |
| Light | 68 | – | – | 1.9 | |

The direction of the main attack was correct. The deployment of the combat forces, and the distribution and correlation of forces ensured the carrying out of the army's tasks. The army head-quarters didn't conduct any detailed planning of the operation, as the Front's combat order didn't assign the army tasks that were strictly determined according to phase lines and a time schedule; indeed, the 2nd Tank Army's final roster of units wasn't determined until after the start of the operation: the 112th Rifle Division and the 115th Separate Rifle Brigade didn't arrive until much later. Other than with their own motorized infantry, the tanks didn't cooperate with other types of forces. The 2nd Tank Army had no artillery of the Supreme Command Reserve, nor any avia-tion. The artillery of the motorized rifle brigades and of the tank brigades was attached to the rifle divisions, which is explained by the absence of roads and the impossibility for the artillery to follow the tanks. Cooperation between the infantry and the artillery was properly organized. **The offensive operation was not supported materially.** The army had no railroad. Its main supply base was back in Livny. The roads between Livny and Dmitriev, because of the snowstorms, were impassable to motorized vehicles. All this forced the army's formations to begin the offensive with just one refill and with less than one standard combat load of shells for the divisional artillery.

## Combat operations from 28 February 1943

At 12.15 on 28.2.1943, the 2nd Tank Army's forces went on the offensive along its entire front, but having run into stubborn enemy resistance, on the right flank they were unable to carry out their orders.

Table 1.10: Serviceable tanks of the 2nd Tank Army in the operation from 21 February to 28 February 1943

| | | Serviceable tanks over the course of the operation (excluding tanks under repair) | | | | | | |
|---|---|---|---|---|---|---|---|---|
| | | 21.02 | 23.02 | 24.02 | 25.02 (5.00) | 25.02 (18.00) | 27.02 | 28.02 |
| **11th Tank Corps** | | | | | | | | |
| 53rd TBr | KV | 9 | 10 | 10 | 10 | 10 | 7 | 9 |
| | T-60 | 16 | 16 | 16 | 16 | 16 | 14 | – |
| 59th TBr | T-60 | 5 | 9 | 9 | 9 | 10 | 6 | 12 |
| | Mk-2 | – | 3 | 3 | 2 | – | 2 | 3 |
| | Mk-3 | 18 | 18 | 18 | 21 | 30 | 23 | 22 |
| 160th TBr | T-60 | 13 | 10 | 10 | 10 | 9 | 10 | – |
| | Mk-2 | 29 | 28 | 28 | 30 | 2 | 30 | 21 |
| | Mk-3 | – | – | – | – | 21 | – | – |
| Total: | | 90 | 94 | 94 | 98 | 98 | 92 | 67 |
| **16th Tank Corps** | | | | | | | | |
| 107th TBr | T-34 | 6 | 12 | 12 | 13 | 13 | 10 | 11 |
| | T-70 | 3 | 1 | 1 | 1 | 6 | – | – |
| 109th TBr | T-34 | 8 | 11 | 11 | 12 | 12 | 9 | 9 |
| | T-70 | 11 | 11 | 11 | 11 | 13 | 12 | 12 |
| 164th TBr | T-34 | 8 | 7 | 7 | 13 | 13 | 8 | 8 |
| | T-70 | – | – | – | – | – | – | – |
| **Total:** | | 36 | 42 | 42 | 50 | 50 | 39 | 40 |
| 11th GTBr | T-34 | 22 | 23 | 23 | 26 | 27 | 26 | 26 |
| | T-70 | 16 | 16 | 16 | 16 | 16 | 16 | 18 |
| 29th GTR | KV | 19 | 12 | 14 | 14 | 14 | 11 | 7 |
| 27th GTR | KV | | | | | 14 | | |
| **Overall Total:** | | 183 | 187 | 189 | 204 | 226 | 184 | 158 |

The 194th Rifle Division, having reached a brook southwest of the Deriuginskii State Farm with its right flank and the eastern outskirts of Polozovka and Pal'tsevo with its left flank, dug-in on the line it had achieved. The attached battalion of the 29th Guards Tank Regiment reached Boguslavka, but there it came under heavy enemy artillery fire and lost 3 tanks. The motorized infantry of the 16th Tank Corps, attacking in the center of the 194th Rifle Division's combat formation, battled their way across the Svapa River and became tied up in fighting on the western bank. Tanks of the 16th Tank Corps were held up at the crossing over the Svapa River in the Polozovka area and were unable to support the infantry's attack. The 15th Motorized Rifle Brigade, operating in the direction of Glotovka and Morshneva, was continuing to fight on the eastern outskirts of these villages, but was unable to seize them without the support of artillery and mortars. On the right flank, in the course of the day and night, fierce combat went on with the stubbornly defending enemy units.

On the army's left flank, the 60th Rifle Division, which had been thrown into the fighting, took full possession of Kuznetsovka by the end of 28.2.1943, having killed more than 100 German soldiers in the process, and reached a machine-tractor station 2 kilometers southeast of Dmitriev and the road fork 2 kilometers southwest of Staryi Gorod, Lugavoi and Kuznetsovka, where it ran into heavy fire from the line Staryi Gorod – Lipki – Tomilinskii. The 2nd Tank Army obtained its greatest success on its left wing as a result of the timely introduction of tanks of the 11th Tank Corps. By the end of 28.2.1943, the army's left wing, with the forward detachment of tanks mounting tank riders, seized Probozh'e Pole and cleared the enemy out of 15 settlements, and over the course of the day penetrated 16 kilometers into the depth of the enemy's defenses. In the course of the day 28.2, the army's left wing breached the tactical zone of the enemy's defense and with the tanks of the 11th Tank Corps broke into the operational depth, which disrupted the orderliness of the enemy's defense of Dmitriev.

Tanks of the 2nd Tank Army move up into forward positions, February-March 1943.

In the course of the night 28 February/1 March 1943, the 2nd Tank Army conducted a partial regrouping for the subsequent attack and a replenishment of matériel. The 60th Rifle Division with night actions seized Ivanovskii, while the 12th Motorized Rifle Brigade captured Popovkino and Mikhailovka.

## Combat operations on 1 March 1943

On the morning of 1 March 1943, the 2nd Tank Army continued its offensive across its entire front. The right wing, consisting of the 194th Rifle Division together with the 29th Guards Tank Regiment and a composite tank brigade of the 16th Tank Corps inflicted a major defeat to the right flank of the 137th Infantry Division, and by the end of the day was fighting for Boguslavka and the eastern outskirts of Kamsu, having liberated Borenkov, Kamenka, Kil'kino, Rozhenskii, Pal'tsevo, Glotovka, and Morshneva. The 16th Tank Corps' 15th Motorized Rifle Brigade, attacking in the center of the 194th Rifle Division's combat formation, having seized Kil'kino, became tied up in savage fighting for possession of settlements on the approaches to Deriugino. In the course of the day, the first line of the enemy's defenses, which ran along the western bank of the Svapa River opposite the army's right flank, was fully ruptured. The enemy, having lost up to 500 men killed, fell back to the second defensive line west of Deriugino. The western bank of the Svapa River was now free of the enemy, which permitted the introduction of tanks of the 16th Tank Corps across the river for further cooperation with the attacking infantry of the right wing.

In the center of the army's combat deployment, the 112th Rifle Division moved into position and prepared to attack toward Dmitriev. On the army's left wing, the 60th Rifle Division engaged in heavy combat with the enemy in the Lipki area; twice, the division's training battalion attacked toward Lipki, but was thrown back each time. Up to two enemy companies, which were defending in the area of Lipki, inflicted major casualties upon the attackers with heavy fire from automatic weapons, and only after an outflanking maneuver by the left wing of the 1283rd Rifle Regiment was the enemy compelled to pull out of Lipki in a northerly direction. By the end of the day, the center of the division advanced into Lipki as the left flank reached the southern bank of the Kharasev River, having seized Iuzhnaia Merkulovka. The 11th Tank Corps, having broken into operational space in the enemy's rear, was continuing its offensive on the morning of 1.3.1943 – with motorized infantry from the line of Mikhailovka toward Dobrovod'e, and with the tank brigades, from the line of Lazlivy toward Sevsk. In the course of the day, the 11th Tank Corps smashed the enemy's defense on the western bank of the Sev River by 17.00, rolled into Sevsk, and cut the roads leading out of Sevsk in the north, south and west. The corps' motorized infantry, having taken control of Dobrovod'e, used part of its force to help destroy the enemy garrison that was defending Sevsk.

As a result of the fighting on 1 March 1943, the 2nd Tank Army fully broke through the enemy's first line of defense on both the right and left flanks, emerged into operational depth, and seized the line of the Sev River and the city of Sevsk, having thereby cut the main roads that connected the enemy's Orel and Southern groupings. Over the course of this day, the army's forces liberated 19 populated places from the enemy, including the city of Sevsk, and eliminated more than 600 of the enemy's soldiers and officers.

In the street fighting for Sevsk, a tank crew under the command of Lieutenant Loginov (his driver mechanic was Sergeant Major Chapenko) of the 160th Tank Brigade distinguished itself. Lieutenant Colonel Kozikov's 59th Tank Brigade and Lieutenant Colonel Davydenko's 160th Tank Brigade turned in superb performances. In accordance with the Front commander's Combat Order No. 12/Op, the 27th Guards Tank Regiment was transferred to the 70th Army. By day's end, however, there was an acute shortage of fuel and shells in all the formations. It was difficult to bring up more supplies over the long distances and abysmal road conditions.

A gun crew in the Sevsk area prepares to fire. The Russian caption above the photograph read "Over open sights, Sevsk area".

Table 1.11: Combat strength of the 2nd Tank Army on 1 March 1943 (asterisks denote information gathered on 25 February 1943)

| Unit | Total men | Of which, of service and supply units | Total horses | Total rifles | Machine guns Heavy | Machine guns Anti-aircraft | Machine guns Light | PPD and PPSh | Mortars, all types | Field Guns | Field Guns 76 mm | 122 mm | 152 mm | 203 mm | Anti-tank guns | Anti-tank rifles | Motor vehicles | Tanks of all types | Anti-aircraft guns | Armored cars |
|---|---|---|---|---|---|---|---|---|---|---|---|---|---|---|---|---|---|---|---|---|
| 60th RD | 7,550 | 1,318 | 1,074 | 6,030 | 89 | 9 | 177 | 703 | 178 | 36 | 27 | 9 | — | — | 33 | 162 | 78 | — | — | — |
| 194th RD | 5,945 | — | 1,212 | 5,365 | 48 | 3 | 228 | 720 | 172 | 37 | 28 | 9 | — | — | 30 | 137 | 102 | — | 15 | — |
| 112th RD | 9,297 | — | 941 | 6,217 | 108 | — | 478 | 1,001 | 160 | 44 | 32 | 12 | — | — | 48 | 198 | 76 | — | — | — |
| 10th Anti-Air Bn.* | 1,276 | — | — | 596 | — | 80 | 1 | 4 | — | — | — | — | — | — | — | — | 164 | — | 48 | — |
| 115th Special RB* | 5,943 | — | 476 | 3,927 | 75 | — | 145 | 1,214 | 96 | 19 | — | — | — | — | 20 | 156 | 49 | — | — | — |
| **11th TC:** | | | | | | | | | | | | | | | | | | | | |
| Command and corps units* | 768 | — | — | 326 | — | — | 6 | 111 | — | — | — | — | — | — | — | 20 | 131 | 3 | — | 17 |
| 53rd TBr* | 1,054 | — | — | 428 | 3 | 3 | 16 | 168 | 6 | 3 | 3 | — | — | — | 1 | 15 | 91 | 25/32 | 4 | — |
| 59th TBr* | 1,121 | — | — | 521 | 4 | 1 | 13 | 171 | 6 | 3 | 3 | — | — | — | 1 | 2 | 99 | 23/47 | — | — |
| 60th TBr* | 1,134 | — | — | 426 | 3 | — | 16 | 107 | 6 | 2 | 2 | — | — | — | — | 6 | 92 | 51/19 | — | — |
| 12th MRB* | 3,043 | — | — | 1,446 | 8 | — | 24 | 513 | 37 | 5 | 5 | — | — | — | 8 | 69 | 157 | 1/3 | — | 4 |
| Total: | 7,120 | — | — | 3,147 | 18 | 4 | 75 | 1,070 | 55 | 13 | 13 | — | — | — | 10 | 119 | 570 | 103/101 | 4 | 21 |
| **16th TC:** | | | | | | | | | | | | | | | | | | | | |
| Command and corps units | 439 | — | — | 179 | — | — | 1 | 47 | — | — | — | — | — | — | — | — | 114 | 0/2 | — | — |
| 107th TBr | 953 | — | — | 637 | 4 | 2 | 20 | 116 | 6 | 4 | 4 | — | — | — | — | 6 | 91 | 37/16 | 2 | — |
| 109th TBr | 1,003 | — | — | 455 | 2 | 2 | 25 | 121 | 6 | 4 | 4 | — | — | — | — | 7 | 77 | 39/14 | 2 | — |
| 164th TBr | 1,075 | — | — | 482 | 4 | 2 | 24 | 170 | 6 | 4 | 4 | — | — | — | — | 11 | 106 | 18/35 | 2 | — |
| 15th MRB | 2,416 | — | — | 1,167 | 26 | 12 | 114 | 1,122 | 36 | 12 | 12 | — | — | — | 12 | 70 | 117 | — | 5 | — |
| Total: | 5,889 | — | — | 2,920 | 36 | 18 | 184 | 1,576 | 54 | 24 | 24 | — | — | — | 12 | 94 | 505 | 94/67 | 11 | — |
| 11th Gds TBr | 1,087 | 240 | — | 497 | 2 | 2 | 20 | 171 | 6 | — | — | — | — | — | — | 6 | 95 | 45/11 | — | — |
| 51st MC Btn. | 265 | 48 | — | 16 | — | — | 12 | 195 | 6 | — | — | — | — | — | — | 2 | 17 | — | — | — |
| 29th GTR | 244 | 82 | — | 53 | — | — | — | 25 | — | — | — | — | — | — | — | — | 41 | 8/9 | — | — |
| 27th GTR | 221 | — | — | 53 | — | — | — | 57 | — | — | — | — | — | — | — | — | 35 | 21 | — | — |
| 37th | 700 | — | — | 455 | — | 2 | 10 | 37 | 24 | — | — | — | — | — | — | 24 | 85 | — | — | — |
| 86th | 735 | — | — | 397 | — | — | — | 27 | 24 | — | — | — | — | — | — | 24 | 90 | — | 7 | — |
| 563rd ATR | 254 | — | — | 175 | — | — | — | 37 | — | — | — | — | — | — | 20 | — | 35 | — | — | — |

Tanks go on the attack, Central Front 1943.

## Combat operations on 2 March 1943

From the morning of 2 March, the 2nd Tank Army's troops continued to attack with the aim of further smashing the enemy's defending 137th and 707th Infantry Divisions. The 194th Rifle Division, acting together with the 16th Tank Corps, on the morning of 2 March launched an attack from the line Boguslavka – Pt. 307.2 – Pt. 228.4 in the direction of Mel. Gora, Pervoavgustovskii with its right flank, and with its left flank toward the 1st of May State Farm. The 29th Guards Tank Regiment was left idle in Boguslavskii without fuel. The enemy was putting up stiff resistance, striving at whatever the cost to hold onto the line Deriugino – 1st of May State Farm – Deriugino Station, in order to keep the Soviets from cutting the Dmitriev – Lokot' highway and railroad. In the course of 2 March 1943, there was bitter combat on the 2nd Tank Army's right flank, which at times reached the point of hand-to-hand fighting. The composite tank brigade of the 16th Tank Corps together with motorized infantry fought for possession of the 1st of May State Farm, where they wiped out up to a battalion of enemy infantry, cut the main road linking Dmitriev and Komarichi, and burst into Deriugino Station. The motorized infantry, following behind the tanks, was stopped by fire in the area of 1st of May State Farm and became pinned down. The tanks, without infantry support, were unable to consolidate their grip on the railroad station.

The 112th Rifle Division, which was attacking in the center of the 2nd Tank Army's formation, conducted a strong reconnaissance probe in the direction of Dmitriev. By 8.00 that morning, with bold actions a battalion of submachine gunners took Doktorovo and Kuznetsovka, while another battalion on the left entered Staryi Gorod. The division command immediately took advantage of the successful reconnaissance probe, and committing its main forces into the fighting, by 13.00 on

2 March 1943 the division took possession of Dmitriev, having in the process seized 115 prisoners, 1 mortar, 5 light machine guns, 33 wagons containing combat materiél and 4 food warehouses, while losing only 2 men in return.

On the 2nd Tank Army's left wing, the 60th Rifle Division, having regrouped its main force to its left flank with the aim of attacking in the direction of Popovkino, Osotskoe and Belyi Kolodez' for further joint actions with the 16th Tank Corps and the 194th Rifle Division, seized the villages of Blagodatnyi and Khinetskoe. The 11th Tank Corps, retaining possession of Sevsk, finished mopping up the enemy's garrison in the city and sent out a combat reconnaissance in the direction of Suzemka and Seredina-Buda. The mobile group from the 11th Tank Corps seized Suzemka and cleared the enemy out of 10 other populated places, including the town of Suzemka and the Suzemka railroad station. Over 2 March 1943, the enemy left behind on the battlefield 5 anti-tank guns, 3 horses, 1 mortar, and 6 wagons carrying rations; 51 soldiers were taken prisoner in the Dobrovod'e area, of which 36 were Hungarian and 15 were Russian. But the main achievement of the day was the seizure of Dmitriev together with its railroad station.

## Combat operations on 3 and 4 March 1943

Over 3 and 4 March, the 2nd Tank Army's forces continued attacking with the aim of sealing the pocket around the enemy's Dmitriev grouping and reaching the line of the Usezha – Sevsk road. On the right flank, the 194th Rifle Division, having broken stubborn enemy resistance in the Pervoavgustovskii – Bychki area, continued attack with its right flank in the direction of Lobanovskii and with its left flank in the direction of Oktiab'rskii, while simultaneously mopping up nests of enemy defenders in the area of Mel. Gora. In the course of the day, the 194th Rifle Division came under repeated enemy air attacks. The 29th Guards Tank Regiment, consisting of 8 KV tanks, was in the area of Boguslavskii, but without fuel or lubricants. The 16th Tank Corps, as a result of the fighting on 3 and 4 March 1943, having broken the enemy resistance in the area of Pervomaiskii and Deriugino Station, by 3.00 seized Deriugino and by 8.00 4 March took possession of Krasnyi Klin. As a result of the fighting, the enemy left behind more than 500 dead in the area of Deriugino Station and Krasnyi Klin. They also abandoned 16 guns, 5 vehicles, 30 wagons with combat materiél, and a battery in its firing positions. As a result of the seizure of the Deriugino Station by the 16th Tank Corps' composite tank brigade, the enemy's strongpoints of Deriugino, Bychki and Pervoavgustovskii fell, and the possibility of a further advance of the right wing in the direction of Nikolaevka and Evdokimovo appeared, with the aim of blocking the enemy's path of retreat to the northwest. In the center, the 112th Rifle Division consolidated in the Dmitriev area, but conducted a reconnaissance foray with one regiment in the direction of Pervomaiskii and Voronki, having seized the latter village and Vol'nye Dvory by the end of 4 March 1943.

On the left flank, the 60th Rifle Division, overcoming enemy resistance seized Melovoe, Bugry, Volchek, and Bel. Kolodez', and went in pursuit of two enemy battalions that were retreating to the north. Three KV tanks of the 53rd Tank Brigade that were supporting the 60th Rifle Division, burst into the retreating enemy columns and forced the enemy to abandon the road and to continue to retreat in small groups through the wilderness. The 60th Rifle Division's 1283rd Rifle Regiment besieged Evdokimovo. The 11th Guards Tank Brigade, which had been committed into the fighting, had come under intensive enemy bombing while crossing the Svapa River at Chernaia Griaz', but in the further course of the day cooperated with the 60th Rifle Division to destroy the enemy groups that were retreating to the north. The tank brigade continued to pursue retreating enemy columns to the north of Evdokimovo and inflicted heavy losses upon them. The enemy, abandoning his heavy equipment, fled in small groups across the Usozha River. The 11th Tank Corps continued to remain in the Sevsk – Suzemka area and topped up with fuel and ammunition, then sent out a combat reconnaissance and seized Seredina-Buda at 21.00 3 March, while taking more than 500 enemy soldiers and officers prisoner. Having seized Suzemka and Seredina-Buda, the 11th Tank Corps made contact with the "For the power of the Soviets" and "In the name of Molotov" partisan detachments.

Over the period of combat on 3 and 4 March 1943, the enemy's Dmitriev grouping was conclusively smashed; only remnants of it were retreating beyond the Usozha River in small groups. The 2nd Tank Army in return between 28 February and 5 March 1943 lost 2 T-34 and 3 T-70 tanks burned out; 2 T-70 tanks that were blown up; and 13 T-34 and 10 T-70 tanks that were disabled. The 2nd Tank Army also lost 248 killed, 469 wounded, and 9 missing in action.

## Conclusions Regarding the Offensive between 28 February and 4 March 1943

As a result of the conducted offensive, only the 11th Tank Corps fulfilled its mission, having seized Sevsk and Suzemka. Meanwhile, the remaining formations of the 2nd Tank Army in essence were making little progress and were unable to encircle the enemy's Dmitriev grouping. The main reasons for the offensive's failure were as follows:

1.  The 2nd Tank Army's unit roster wasn't set before the offensive began, which didn't give a possibility to the army command to get to know the rifle formations and in the future assign them appropriate tasks commensurate with their strength and abilities. For example, the army command had the opportunity to keep on its roster either the 112th Rifle Division or the more fully-equipped 115th Separate Rifle Brigade, and selected the latter. This brigade, however, proved to be completely unready for combat operations, and after the long marches and its first combat actions, it had lost almost all of its personnel and weapons. In the future it would be necessary to determine the army's composition at least 5 to 10 days before the start of combat operations, and not in the midst of them.

2.  The 2nd Tank Army's right flank, which was to complete the encirclement of the enemy's Dmitriev grouping when it reached Deriugino Station, proved to be relatively weak. The 194th Rifle Division, which was operating on a broad front and was reinforced only by a composite brigade of the 16th Tank Corps numbering 28 tanks that didn't take part in the fighting on the first day, faced the entire German 137th Infantry Division and was unable to carry out its assignments. It was necessary to strengthen the right flank by weakening the forces on the central axis opposite Dmitriev.

3.  There was not enough ammunition, which didn't allow the artillery to provide the necessary support to the infantry and tank attacks. In the future for the same reasons, the rifle divisions, seeing the enemy's retreat, were unable to hinder it and unable to begin a pursuit (for example, the 60th Rifle Division on 2 March 1943). Thus, although the army had three times the amount of artillery than the enemy, the Germans had seemingly a limitless number of shells, which the army didn't have. In reality, fire superiority was on the adversary's side. This led to heavy losses in our rifle formations. The calculation of the correlation of force based on the number of artillery tubes doesn't give a correct picture. It is necessary to include the amount of shells available to the artillery in the calculation, and reckon that the enemy had three combat loads per artillery tube (albeit no precise data are available), while our artillery had whatever was at hand.

4.  The uninterrupted enemy airstrikes against our combat formations and immediate rear greatly hampered ground operations. The absence of air support for the attacks and cover of our forces by our fighters reduced the pace of the offensive and led to our losses.

## Combat operations from 5 March to 7 March 1943

At 19.45 on 4 March 1943, the Central Front's Combat Order No. 970 was received. It directed the 11th Tank Corps to attack on the morning of 5 March with all its forces in the direction of Usozha, Komarichi and Radogoshch. In order to carry out this assignment, the 11th Tank Corps would have to conduct with part of its forces a march of 60 kilometers, but it didn't have enough fuel for this. In the little time available between receipt of the order and the start of the attack, it was also necessary to conduct reconnaissance, issue orders and organize cooperation. All this was impossible to complete in the given amount of time, while the lack of fuel simply precluded the execution of the order. Thus, once again the Central Front headquarters issued an order with no consideration of time or the condition of the tank corps. The 2nd Tank Army's forces in the course of 5, 6 and 7 March 1943 were continuing to pursue the retreating enemy in a northward direction, and reached the southern bank of the Usozha River with its forward units. However, because of their condition, the 11th and 16th Tank Corps were unable to go on the offensive. The 29th Guards Tank Regiment was stuck in the area of Polozovka with no fuel or lubricants. The 194th Rife Division was covering the army's regrouping, defending on the line Lobanovskii, Zazheleznodorozhnyi, Litii.

The army's forces, by an order from Front headquarters, were given a new mission to launch an attack to the northeast with the Karachev area as the objective. Major General Kriukov's Mounted-Rifle Group, which was continuing to operate on the left, was given the combat sector in the Seredina-Buda area in view of the 2nd Tank Army's pivot to the northeast. On the right, continuing its offensive operations was General Batov's 65th Army. By a combat order of the 2nd Tank Army's Military Council, the troops on the morning of 8 March 1943 were given the task to go on the offensive from the line of the Usozha River in the direction of Komarichi, Lokot' and Radogoshch. On the 2nd Tank Army's left flank, the partisan detachments "For the power of the Soviets" and "In the name of Molotov" were ordered to resume operations.

## Combat operations from 8 March to 12 March 1943

The enemy's defenses along the northern bank of the Usozha River had been timely prepared, and prior to the arrival of the 2nd Tank Army's troops, the enemy had converted all of the villages situated on the river's northern bank into defensive strongpoints, while simultaneously bringing up reserves to the line of the Usozha River. In the period between 8 March and 12 March 1943, the fresh 45th and 72nd Infantry Divisions were fully committed by the enemy into the fighting. On the morning of 8 March, the 2nd Tank Army's infantry, overcoming heavy enemy fire, pushed across to the northern bank of the river, but having encountered enemy strongpoints in the vicinities of Dobruchik, Ugrevichi and Mostechnia, was unable to advance any further. In the course of the entire period, the infantry in the bridgehead across the river had to repel strong enemy attacks and were ceaselessly subjected to enemy airstrikes.

On its right flank, the 2nd Tank Army with the forces of the 194th Rifle Division seized Litizh, but was stopped there by enemy resistance. The 29th Guards Tank Regiment was in the area of Kil'kino, again waiting for fuel to come up. The 11th Guards Tank Brigade was assembled in the area of Evdokimovo as the army's reserve.

As a result of the fighting from 8 to 12 March, the 2nd Tank Army's infantry continued to hold their present lines and were unable to make headway against the heavy enemy fire. The tank formations spent the days between 8 and 12 March replenishing fuel and ammunition, and were assembling in their jumping-off areas for the offensive. By this time, the 11th Tank Corps had just 36 tanks, the 16th Tank Corps had only 14 tanks and the 11th Guards Tank Brigade had 36 tanks. Enemy aircraft in the course of the entire period subjected the army's combat dispositions on both sides of the Usozha River to constant bombing.

On 9 March 1943, the tank corps received a combat order from the command of the Central Front, giving the 2nd Tank Army the assignment to attack to the north. The immediate task was to reach the Nizhnee Gorodishche – Brasovo line. Subsequently, the tank corps were to advance to cut the Orel – Briansk road in the Karachev area. The offensive was set to begin at 9.00 on 13 March 1943. However, because of the great distance from their supply bases and the poor road conditions, fuel and lubricants and ammunition weren't brought up in time, which forced the army commander Lieutenant General Rodin on 12 March 1943 to hold a talk with Major General Boikov over a direct line, and to request a delay of 1-2 days in order to prepare the forces. As a result of these talks, the start of the offensive was pushed back to 17 March 1943.

## Combat Report of the Commander of the 2nd Tank Army to the Commander of the Central Front on the Course of the Offensive

12 March 1943

The Army, having initiated a semi-prepared operation on 23.2.1943, in the course of 15 days has been involved in constant fighting up to the present day. Over this period the Army has broken through the enemy's defensive belt on the Osmanka, Svapa and Kharaseia Rivers. It has smashed the [enemy's] 707th Infantry Division, one regiment of the 108th Infantry Division (of Hungarians), and thoroughly mauled the 137th Infantry Division. It has wiped out up to 6,000 soldiers and officers, taken prisoner up to 1,500 soldiers and officers, liberated 220 populated places, including the district centers Dmitriev, Sevsk, Seredina-Buda and Suzemka. Considering that the operation began almost from the march, given a limited amount of ammunition and fuel, as well as the total dissolution of the roads, the offensive in the course of four days was conducted by the rifle divisions and motorized infantry with a limited amount of artillery and without any tanks, which led to excessive losses in infantry and motorized infantry. As a result of the elongation of the supply lines up to 200 kilometers, the absence of roads, and the extremely limited amount of fuel and motorized transport, especially in the rifle divisions, less than 50 percent of the combat vehicles and the same amount of artillery have joined the fighting. To the present day, the fuel situation has not improved, nor has the situation with respect to ammunition; the infantry and a portion of the tanks are continuing to fight, while entire units and formations are standing idle in the rear without fuel – the 1st Anti-aircraft Artillery Division, the 1188th Destroyer Anti-tank Artillery Regiment, the 37th Guards Mortar Regiment, and up to 50 percent of the artillery and tanks. The Army's arrival with its left wing at the line Suzemka, Seredina-Buda and the pivot of the main forces in the directions of Komarichi and Lokot' have created a plain threat of dismemberment to the enemy's Orel – Briansk grouping. The Army's successful advance in the western and northern directions have compelled the enemy urgently to shift up to three infantry divisions (72nd, 45th and an SS division) and up to 100 aircraft to the Komarichi, Igritskoe, Lokot' area and to take up a defense along the line of the Usozha River with the forces of the 72nd and 45th Infantry Divisions, as well as a secondary defensive belt along the Nerussa River with the SS division. As a result, the Army's forces have met strong enemy resistance on the Usozha River, which is daily supported by bomber aircraft with up to 75-100 individual sorties a day in groups of 3 to 15 aircraft, while on 11.3.1943, up to 50 aircraft bombed the Litizh area. The enemy is daily counterattacking in the Litizh, Ugrevichi directions in company to battalion strength, with the support of 7-10 tanks. The ceaseless counterattacks and daily bombing of the combat formations have had their effect on the attacking troops. As a result of the suffered losses and the lagging behind of the materiél in the rear because of the lack of fuel, the operational position of the Army and the correlation of forces at the present day are as follows:

The enemy: With the aims of blocking a further advance of our forces to the north and the encirclement of the enemy's Orel – Kromy grouping, the enemy is offering stubborn resistance on the line they are defending with the remnants of the 137th and 707th Infantry Divisions that are falling back to the line of the Usozha River, having brought up fresh infantry and tank units, and with fire and frequent counterattacks of infantry and tanks with air support. The most fortified points of the enemy's defense on the forward edge are Mal'tsevskii, Kozinka, Dobreichik, Ugrevichi and Mostechnia, and in the depth of the defense – Komarichi, Lokot', Brasovo and Krasnyi Kolodez'. The enemy has in the first line of defense the remnants of the 707th Infantry Division (the 727th and 747th Regiments) and the 45th Infantry Division's 133rd Infantry Regiment; the 124th and 105th Infantry Regiments of the 72nd Infantry Division and the 313th Security Battalion – altogether up to five infantry regiments are defending in the first line, reinforced with artillery and tanks, and one security battalion – a total of 16 battalions. The enemy has two infantry regiments of the 45th Infantry Division and one regiment of the 72nd Infantry Division in the role of divisional reserves. The enemy's operational reserves – an SS cavalry division in the area of Nerusskie Dvoriki, the 102nd Infantry Division (Hungarian) in the area of Lokot', and the 7th Panzer Division, which is situated in the Komarichi, Nerusskie Dvorki area.

The enemy's artillery: Anti-tank – 167 guns; regimental – 46 guns; divisional – 120 guns; heavy – 35 guns; mortars – 306.

Tanks: one tank division with 70-80 tanks (4th Panzer Division)

Aviation: up to 100 aircraft.

Our forces: The 2nd Tank Army, operating on the outflanking wing of the Central Front in cooperation with the 65th Army and partisans, destroying opposing enemy units, is reaching the Briansk – Orel rail and main roads, completing the operational encirclement of the enemy's Orel – Kromy grouping. The Army is carrying out the primary task as part of the Central Front.

By the end of 11.3.1943, the Army has:

Infantry – the 194th and 60th Rifle Divisions, the 115th Rifle Brigade, the 12th and 15th Motorized Rifle Brigades, and the motorized rifle battalions of the tank brigades – altogether 35 battalions (which have suffered losses of up to 40 percent as a result of 15 days of offensive combat operations).

Artillery: Anti-tank – 135 guns, with 58 additional guns coming up; regimental – 19 guns, with 4 more guns on the way; divisional – 42 guns, with 53 more guns coming up; no heavy artillery; 379 mortars; rocket artillery – 14 rocket launchers, with 29 more launchers on the way. (The artillery still on the approach march is on average 90 kilometers away from the area of combat operations).

Tanks: The 16th and 11th Tank Corps and the 11th Guards Tank Brigade – altogether 100 operational tanks, with 21 on the march to their jumping-off areas for the offensive; located without fuel in their previous assembly areas – 41.

Supplies: ammunition – 16th Tank Corps, 11th Tank Corps and 11th Guards Tank Brigade have one standard combat load each, the 194th Infantry Division – 0.1 combat load; the 60th Rifle Division – 0.5 combat load; the 115th Rifle Brigade – 0.1 combat load; fuel: the 11th Guards Tank Brigade has 0.3 of a refill, the 16th Tank Corps – 0.1 of a refill, and the 11th Tank Corps – 0.5 of a refill.

The lengthy supply lines, the poor condition of the roads, the inadequate availability of army-level transport and the lack of fuel and lubricants at the front- and army-level bases, as well as of ammunition at the Front's base Fatezh, prevents a possibility of bringing up the necessary materiél for supporting the operation. For normal movement of carrying out a combat assignment, it is necessary to have 3 refills of fuel for the combat vehicles, 5-6 refills for the transport vehicles and no less than two standard combat loads of ammunition for all the army's formations.

Conclusion: The enemy's Second Panzer Army, reinforced at the expense of the Western Front with the 72nd and 137th Infantry Divisions, and with 75-100 aircraft, is stubbornly holding a defensive line along the Usozha River on the left wing and a number of populated points north of the Usozha River on the right wing, launching frequent counterattacks, supported by tanks and aircraft. The enemy has as his aim to throw back our units on the right wing to the southern bank of the Usozha River, and in the future in cooperation with the Dmitriev – Orel grouping – to launch a general offensive to the southeast. The Army, having suffered heavy losses in infantry and motorized infantry, and also as a consequence of the lack of fuel and ammunition and the tethering of the artillery and tanks in the deep rear, having encountered fresh enemy divisions in the second defensive line, with its present forces and combat materiél will not be in a condition to carry out the designated task prior to bringing up all the serviceable tanks and artillery and the replenishing of the motorized rifle and rifle formations with personnel. The fulfillment of the given order given the absence of the army's reserves will place the Army in an extremely difficult situation. The absence of the Army's artillery regiments does not give the possibility to suppress the main foci of resistance and the enemy's artillery. Following from all the above, the Army's Military Council requests: a) Not to start the operation before providing the Army with fuel and ammunition; b) To replenish the motorized rifle and rifle formations with personnel; c) To strengthen the Army with one rifle division in the role of a reserve; d) To provide air cover of the Army's main grouping in the preparatory phase and to support the Army's offensive with bomber and fighter aircraft; e) To strengthen the Army with artillery from the Supreme Command Reserve. The main task of the Army in the period of preparing the operation will be the holding of the occupied lines, primarily the northern bank of the Usozha River.

[Signed] RODIN, LATYSHEV

The tank and combined-arms formations after the long marches and battles between 23 February and 4 March 1943 had suffered significant losses in personnel and equipment. Their condition can be described by the following figures:

Operational in the 11th Tank Corps on 16 March 1943: the 53rd Tank Brigade – 5 KV and 6 T-60; the 59th Tank Brigade – 2 Matilda Mk. II, 31 Valentine Mk. III and 6 T-60; 160th Tank Brigade – 26 Matilda Mk. II and 8 T-60 (left in reserve of the army commander).

Operational in the 16th Tank Corps: 7 T-34 and 22 T-70. The 11th Guards Tank Brigade had been dropped from the army's roster and placed at the disposal of the commander of the 2nd Guards Cavalry Corps, having 26 T-34 and 15 T-70.

The 60th Rifle Division had 385 "active bayonets" plus 90 submachine gunners and 200 men of untrained replacements lacking uniforms;

The 115th Separate Rifle Brigade in reality had no more than one full-strength battalion on its roster.

**Thus, the 2nd Tank Army by 17 March 1943 had in actual fact been reduced to the equivalent of one rifle division and two tank brigades.**

The enemy by this time had on the northern bank of the Usozha River one regiment of the 137th Infantry Division, two regiments of the 45th Infantry Division, and the 72nd Infantry Division with the authorized amount of artillery and an ample quantity of shells. The enemy ground troops were being supported by powerful bomber aviation. Even a simple comparison of the relative strength of the two sides shows that the 2nd Tank Army, without air support, no heavy artillery of the Supreme Command Reserve, and only a limited amount of ammunition supplies, could not fulfill the tasks given to it by the Front command. True, in his talks with the army commander, Major General Boikov no longer set Karachev as the army's objective, but insisted only that it take Komarichi; however, the army was not even capable of fulfilling this assignment. The offensive was continuing through inertia, with no regard for the enemy's real strength and his possibilities.

### Combat operations from 12 March to 17 March 1943

The 2nd Tank Army continued to hold its occupied positions on its entire front, repelling strong counterattacks by enemy infantry and tanks, while also conducting reconnaissance probes and taking in ammunition and fuel. The situation facing the army was developing not at all to its favor. General Kriukov's 2nd Guards Cavalry Corps operating on its left was subjected to a powerful counterattack by superior enemy forces and with heavy fighting had to fall back in the direction of Sevsk, daily losing the territory it had gained.

The enemy, having brought up the 4th Panzer Division, began to shove the units of the 2nd Guards Cavalry Corps back from the Desna River to the east, and on 15 March 1943, the Germans regained control of Seredina-Buda. At an order from the Central Front commander, the 11th Guards Tank Brigade was withdrawn from the 2nd Tank Army roster and sent to the area of Sevsk to reinforce the cavalry corps. Here, on 16 March 1943 in the vicinity of Sevsk, there occurred the first recorded collision between forces of the 2nd Tank Army and a German panzer formation. Units of Colonel Bubnov's 11th Separate Guards Tank Brigade (temporarily subordinated to the 2nd Guards Cavalry Corps) joined battle with General Schneider's 4th Panzer Division. As is confirmed by documents, the Germans had a numerical superiority in tanks in these clashes, and the *Luftwaffe* reigned supreme in the skies. The 11th Guards Tank Brigade went into the battle having 46 operational tanks (29 T-34 and 17 T-70) against 82 tanks and assault guns of the German 4th Panzer Division. The following documents give an insight into the details of these tank clashes:

### Conclusions drawn by the headquarters of the Central Front's 2nd Tank Army from an analysis of the 11th Tank Brigades combat actions when defending Sevsk

22 May 1943

On the offensive, the enemy as before employs tanks en mass, supporting their actions with self-propelled artillery. The combat experience demonstrated that when under an attack by superior enemy tank forces, our tanks can struggle against them successfully, firing from fixed ambush positions and using maneuvers on the battlefield with the aim of inflicting a surprise blow against the enemy tank elements from the flank or from the rear. Such a modus operandi of our tank formation yields the possibility to inflict significant losses in equipment and personnel on the enemy, to seize possession of the initiative, and leads to the complete destruction of the enemy's attacking tanks and infantry formations.

Example: The enemy, having brought up the 4th Panzer Division, began to drive units of the 2nd Guards Cavalry Corps back from the Desna River to the east, and on 15.3.1943 seized Seredina-Buda.

The 11th Guards Tank Brigade, at the order of the 2nd Tank Army commander, had assembled on the southern outskirts of Sevsk by the morning of 16.3.1943 and came under the temporary command of the commander of the 2nd Guards Cavalry Corps, having 29 T-34 and 17 T-70, a total of 46 tanks, a motorized rifle battalion, and an anti-tank battery of three 76mm guns.

At 9.00 on 17.3, the brigade together with the 3rd Guards Cavalry Division took up a defense of the line Borisovo, Bukovishche, Moritskii and Streletskaia, with the task to prevent a breakthrough by enemy tanks and infantry toward Sevsk. On the basis of the brigade commander's decision, the tank elements and motorized infantry were deployed: the 1st Tank Battalion with a company of submachine gunners, comprising the reserve of the brigade commander, on the southern outskirts of Sevsk; the 2nd Tank Battalion with two companies of motorized riflemen were arranged in separate groups of T-70 and T-34 tanks in ambush positions in the areas: 6 T-70 tanks on the southwestern outskirts of Borisovo, 3 T-70 tanks – on the southwestern outskirts of Lemeshok, 6 T-70 tanks on the northwestern outskirts of Bukovishche, 3 T-34 tanks – on the western outskirts of Moritskii, the anti-tank battery – at the observation post in the vicinity of the fork in the roads 1 kilometer south of Sevsk with the assignment to prevent a breakthrough by enemy tanks from the directions of Sosnitsy and Lipitsy. The motorized infantry was dug-in behind the separate tank elements and separate tanks with the goal to prevent enemy infantry from approaching our tanks, especially at nighttime. At 14.00 on 17.3.1943, the enemy went on the attack out of Berestok with 12 tanks and up to a battalion of infantry toward Borisovo. The 6 T-70 tanks in Borisovo and the 3 T-70 tanks in Lemeshki opened sudden fire from their ambush positions; 3 T-34 tanks launched a counterattack out of Moritsy through Bukovishche into the flank of the enemy's group of tanks, which had gone on the attack toward Borisovo out of Korostovka. After stubborn fighting, which lasted until the onset of darkness, the enemy was thrown back to their jumping-off positions, suffering losses: 7 tanks were left burning and 10 tanks were knocked out; 2 self-propelled guns were destroyed and up to a 100 soldiers and officers were killed. At 12.00 on 18.3.1943, the enemy went on the offensive, launching the main attack in the direction of Korostovka, Bukovishche and Sevsk. Up to 30 tanks and up to a battalion of infantry – out of Mikhailovskii, Berestovka toward Borisovo; more than 40 tanks and up to a regiment of infantry – out of Korostovka along the highway to Sevsk; up to 30 tanks out of Kalinovskii toward Kudiiar. Altogether, the brigade faced more than 100 heavy and medium tanks and up to two regiments of infantry. In order to repel the enemy's tank and infantry attack, the brigade's command sent 3 T-34 tanks out of its reserve to Kniaginino, from which point together with three more T-34 tanks that were positioned there, they launched a counterattack through Borisovo toward Korostovka. Three T-70 tanks in ambush positions in Borisovo were supporting the counterattack. The enemy tank attack out of Korostovka was repulsed, after which our tanks moved to repel the enemy tank and infantry attack in the direction of Mikhailovskii. In order to repel the attack of the 30 enemy tanks out of Kalinovskii toward Kudiiar, six more T-34 tanks were committed into the fighting out of the brigade commander's reserve and directed to Kudiiar. These tanks with heavy fire from fixed positions and flanking fire from the three T-34 tanks in Moritskii stopped the enemy tank and infantry attack toward Kalinovskii. As a result of this battle, the enemy suffered heavy losses: 33 tanks were left burned-out and 22 more tanks were knocked out; 4 guns, 3 machine guns, and 9 vehicles were destroyed, and more than 650 of the enemy's soldiers and officers were killed. While involved in the hard combat with superior numbers of enemy tanks until 27.3.1943, the 11th Guards Tank Brigade inflicted heavy losses upon the enemy in men and equipment. The enemy was forced to call off any further attacks and to go over to the defense. In these battles between 17 and 27 March 1943, the 11th Guards Tank Brigade inflicted the following losses upon the enemy: 75 tanks burned out and 47 tanks knocked out; 23 self-propelled guns, 42 machine guns, 21 vehicles, 1 armored car, 3 mortars and 3 anti-tank rifles were destroyed; and 2,355 soldiers and officers were killed. Over this same period of time, the brigade lost: 33 tanks burned out or abandoned on the battlefield, and 53 dead and 102 wounded.

Conclusions:

1. The main type of combat of our tank formations when defending against superior forces of enemy tanks was the method of ambushes, which were necessary to set up on the probable axes of the enemy tanks' appearance. In addition, it was necessary to have a mobile tank reserve for reinforcing the ambushes or for setting up ambushes on new directions of the enemy's advance, as well as for launching a counterattack against the enemy tank elements from the flank or rear.

2. It was necessary to have at least a minimal cover of our tanks by our infantry against enemy infantry, especially at night. In this case, given the absence of infantry of other units, it was necessary to have the infantry of the tank brigade's motorized rifle battalion dig in behind the tank elements or even isolated tanks.

3. Command and control over the brigade's elements in the battle was implemented by radio. All the radios were working on the same wavelength. In this fashion, rapidity of information and knowledge of the situation was obtained by all the commanders of radio-equipped tanks, all the battalion headquarters, and the brigade's headquarters on all the sectors of the brigade's actions.

4. During the combat, not only the battalion commanders, but also the platoon commanders quickly learned of the brigade commander's decisions.

[Signed] The deputy chief of staff of the 2nd Tank Army Lieutenant Colonel Chizh; Senior assistant of the chief of the 2nd Tank Army's operations department for the study of the war's experience Major Borisenko

The German side confirms that the lead elements of Major General Erich Schneider's 4th Panzer Division arrived from the march in the area of Novgorod-Severskii on 8 March 1943. The 4th Panzer Division's official history reports that the division from 8 March to 27 March 1943 was involved in fighting in the Novgorod-Severskii – Sevsk area.

On 5 March 1943, the 4th Panzer Division (I/Pz.Rgt. 35, Pz.Jg.Abt. 49) together with attached units (StuG.Gesch.Abt. 904) had **82 tanks and assault guns:** 21 Pz. IV (75mm L/43), 3 Pz. IV (75mm L/24), 7 Pz. III (50mm L/42), 5 Pz. II, 26 Marder II, and 20 StuG III L/43. The 4th Panzer Division had been located on the Eastern Front without interruption since 1941. Of its personnel, 73 had been considered worthy of the Knight's Cross, 10 had achieved the Knight's Cross with Oak Leaves, and one – the Knight's Cross with Oak Leaves and Swords. On 31 March 1943, the 4th Panzer Division had 60 tanks and assault guns fit for combat: 16 Pz. IV (75mm L/43), 1 Pz. IV (75mm L/24), 6 Pz. III (50mm L/42), 5 Pz. II, 19 Marder II and 13 StuG III L/43. The official history of the 4th Panzer Division maintains that 3 Pz. IV L/43 and 4 assault guns (2 StuG III and 2 Marder) could not be repaired and were written off as irrecoverable losses. According to the information from the German side, 2 Pz. IV tanks were destroyed by Russian tank fire on the day of 18 March 1943 in the area of Kudiiar, and one more Pz. IV tank was destroyed by Russian tankers on the evening of 19 March 1943 on the northern outskirts of Sevsk. The two Marder II self-propelled guns were irrecoverably lost on the morning of 21 March 1943 during a counterattack by Russian tanks and infantry on the northern outskirts of Sevsk. The two StuG III assault guns were lost in the same area. In addition to this, 16 tanks and self-propelled guns (2 Pz. IV (75mm L/43), 2 Pz. IV (75mm L/24), 1 Pz. III (50mm L/42), 6 Marder and 5 StuG III L/43) among the number of tanks that had been knocked out or damaged were evacuated and put under repair. In addition to the armor losses, the 4th Panzer Division in the fighting near Sevsk in March 1943 lost 227 soldiers and officers killed, 876 wounded, and 23 men missing in action.

Colonel Kazakov recalls:

> This was the first combat that the Guardsmen of the 11th Guards Tank Brigade took on in their T-34s, which had been gifted to the brigade on the eve of the operation by the Tambov collective farm workers. Here are excerpts from the brigade's journal of combat operations, which were submitted daily to higher headquarters:
>
> "At 9.20 16 March 1943, the brigade together with units of the 2nd Guards Cavalry Corps arrived in the line of defense and received the task to block the enemy's advance along the Severnye Budy [sic] – Sevsk road. At 16.00 the enemy went on the attack out of the Grudskaia area toward Svetovo with 8 tanks, and seized it. The 2nd Company of the 1st Battalion launched a counterattack and drove back the enemy."
>
> "At 14.00 on 17 March 22 enemy tanks and up to a battalion of infantry attacked out of the area of Berestok toward Borisovo. Heavy fighting continued until darkness. Seven German tanks were left burned out and 10 more were knocked out, 2 self-propelled guns were destroyed, and up to 100 soldiers and officers were killed. The losses of the brigade: 3 tanks left burned out, 2 were knocked out, and 5 men were killed …"
>
> "At 12.00 18 March, the enemy attacked again, launching the main blow toward Korostovka, Bukovishe [sic] and Sevsk. Up to 30 tanks and two battalions of infantry out of Mikhailovskii and Berestok toward Borisovo, and more than 40 tanks and up to a regiment of infantry attacked toward Sevsk. Altogether, the brigade faces more than 100 tanks and up to two regiments of infantry. Enemy losses: 33 tanks burned out, 22 knocked out, 4 guns destroyed, and up to 650 soldiers and officers. Our losses: 12 tanks burned out, 2 knocked out, and 16 men killed, including Hero of the Soviet Union Savel'ev."

These are the dry lines of combat reports. But if it is recalled that the brigade, having 46 tanks, knocked out approximately 30 hostile machines over the first three days of fighting, then this gives the right to recognize the combat skill and courage of our Guardsmen, and the iron will and superb command qualities of Colonel Bubnov and the other commanders, who were able with fewer forces and artful maneuver to repel the enemy's onslaught, disrupt his plans, and inflict heavy losses upon him.

The intense combat actions of the 2nd Tank Army's infantry, the difficult conditions for the tank formations' operations, the lack of spare parts and repair tools, the impossibility of bringing up supplies because of the poor road conditions, as well as the inadequate amount of fuel significantly reduced the 2nd Tank Army's attacking power and prevented the tanks from cooperating with the infantry, as a result of which the infantry suffered extremely heavy losses. **By the end of 17.3.1943, the 2nd Tank Army was on the verge of exhausting its attacking capabilities.**

The 11th Guards Tank Brigade receives its tanks from the "Tambov Collective Farmer".

Knocked-out armor of the 4th Panzer Division, March 1943, Sevsk area.

Disabled and bogged down equipment of the 4th Panzer Division, March 1943, Sevsk area.

## Combat operations from 17 March to 19 March 1943

At 8.00 on 17 March 1943, after a 15-minute artillery preparation, forces of the 2nd Tank Army went on the offensive in two groups with the aim of seizing Komarichi and reaching the line of the Nerussa River. The Army's right-hand group, consisting of the 16th Tank Corps (which had just 28 tanks remaining) and the 194th Rifle Division, having attacked in the direction of Mal'tsevskii and Oktiabr'skii, was met by the enemy's heavy small arms and anti-tank fire, and as a result of flanking fire from the southern outskirts of Mal'tsevskii, the infantry, advancing behind the tanks, was cut off from them and then pinned down by enemy bombers. The tanks continued on to Oktiabr'skii without the infantry, where they ran into heavy anti-tank fire and were unable to advance any further. The 16th Tank Corps fell back to the start line on the night of 17/18 March, having suffered large losses (10 T-34 and 9 T-70). During the attack, the 37th Guards Mortar Regiment with 15 rocket launchers had been supporting the 194th Rifle Division and the 16th Tank Corps.

In the center the 60th Rifle Division ran into stubborn enemy resistance in the area of Dobruchik and Ugrevichi. Repelling strong counterattacks by German tanks and infantry while being subjected to constant attacks from the air, it failed to make any headway.

On the left, the 11th Tank Corps (minus its 160th Tank Brigade) attacked together with the 115th Separate Rifle Brigade. Reaching the left bank of the Usozha River, the tank corps encircled Apazha with tanks, while the infantry of the 115th Separate Rifle Brigade attacked Mostechnia and Preobrazhenskii. After a day of combat, the 2nd Tank Army's left-hand group was unable to take these settlements. The 11th Tank Corps, while on the approach to Apazha, was attacked five times by the enemy's specialized anti-tank aircraft in groups of 18, 8, 11, 7 and 6 aircraft. One of the German aircraft was shot down in the area of Izbichni and its crew was taken prisoner. The 11th Tank Corps' losses from anti-tank artillery fire and aerial attacks were as follows: the 53rd Tank Brigade – 2 KV and 10 T-60; the 59th Tank Brigade – 15 Valentine Mk. III and 2 T-60.

On 18 March 1943 the offensive was supposed to continue, but the infantry was unable to budge from their jumping-off positions. The growing resistance of the enemy defenders, the lack of progress made by the neighbor on the right, the heavy defensive fighting of General Kriukov's Mounted-Rifle Group and the weakened composition of the 2nd Tank Army prevented the possibility of further offensive operations. By an order of the Central Front commander, the 2nd Tank Army on the night of 18/19 March went over to a defensive posture with its main forces in the sector Khlebtovo, Iasnyi Luch, Ivichni, Lepeshino, Hill 207, Hill 221.7, having direct contact with the 65th Army in the Khlebtovo area and General Kriukov's Mounted-Rifle Group in the Shvednikovsk area. The 11th Tank Corps' 160th Tank Brigade, which was located in the 2nd Tank Army's reserve, was as we've seen transferred by an order of the Front commander to reinforce the 2nd Guards Cavalry Corps.

Conclusions: The combat order of the Central Front, which demanded a resumption of the offensive on 5 March, its postponement to 9 March and then to 17 March, and finally the order to go on the defensive on 18 March fully shows that the army's tasks had been set without regard for time, distances or the real correlation of forces. The offensive was organized not as the result of an assessment of the real situation, but only out of inertia. All this led to the result that the 2nd Tank Army, without achieving any successes, suffered needless losses. The army command exerted every effort to carry out the task that had been set for it by the Front command, and justly raised the question about the impossibility of attacking within the time period indicated by the Front. However, on the eve of 17 March, it did not raise the issue of the difficulty of fulfilling the orders with the army's available capabilities, given the present correlation of forces and the stabilization of the enemy's defense.

The combat history of the 11th Tank Corps states bluntly:

> The failure of the 11th Tank Corps' combat operations in the direction of Komarichi is explained by the fact that because of the lack of fuel and ammunition, the corps went on the attack with a delay of six days, which allowed the enemy to shift the 72nd Infantry Division from Rzhev to the Lokot', Komarichi area. This division converted every settlement on the direction of the corps' attack into defensive strongpoints, interlaced by an overall system of fire. Mobile groups of tanks and self-propelled guns had been organized in the depth of the defense.

## The losses of the two sides over the period of the 2nd Tank Army's offensive

Over the period of the Army's combat operations from 23 February to 23 March 1943 inclusively, the enemy suffered the following losses: Destroyed -- 6,041 soldiers and officers, 146 guns of various calibers, 16 trucks, 14 prime movers, 4 field kitchens, 5 supply dumps, **5 self-propelled guns**, 3 armored turrets, 292 supply wagons with materiél, a battalion headquarters, a regiment headquarters, 1 motorcycle, and 5 guns mounted on all-terrain vehicles. Seized -- 1,650 soldiers and officers taken prisoner, 73 guns of various calibers, **3 tanks**, 27 mortars, 189 machine guns, 510 rifles, 10 submachine guns, 8 radio sets, 25 trucks, 11 supply dumps, 1 armored car, 38 serviceable and unserviceable tractors, 528 horses, 5 field kitchens, 100 kilometers of telephone cable, 230 boxes of shells, 15,000 cartridges plus an additional 260 boxes of cartridges, 830 hand grenades, 1 all-terrain vehicle, and 33.5 tons of food and fodder. The number of wounded enemy soldiers and officers isn't given.

In return, from 22 February to 20 March 1943 the 2nd Tank Army lost 3,520 killed, 7,599 wounded, 882 missing in action and 1,694 due to illness or other causes, for a total of 13,695 men. The **11th Tank Corps** irreparably lost 1 T-34, 6 T-60, 18 Mk. II, and 31 Mk. III, for a total of **56 tanks**. The **16th Tank Corps** irreparably lost 26 T-34 and 20 T-70, and another 22 T-34 and 14 T-70 disabled, of which 3 T-34 and 5 T-70 were not evacuated and left abandoned on the battlefield. Thus corps had to write off 30 T-34 and 21 T-70, and its **total losses were 82 tanks.** The fully-intact **11th Guards Tank Brigade** was placed at the disposal of the 2nd Guards Cavalry Corps commander.

These figures demonstrate that the 2nd Tank Army suffered significant losses. These losses would have been considerably fewer, had the army possessed a normal amount of ammunition and if the tank attacks had received air support.

## Combat operations from 19 March to 21 March 1943

From the morning of 19 March 1943, the 2nd Tank Army's forces were occupying a defensive belt, busily engaged with digging in, camouflaging the positions, preparing fire support and anti-infantry defenses, and conducting reconnaissance and observation of the enemy. The tank formations were pulled out of combat in order to refit

## Combat operations from 21 March to 24 March 1943

The 2nd Tank Army continued to hold its occupied lines. At 14.30 on 21 March 1943, it came under an intensive bombing from enemy aircraft, followed by a probe by enemy infantry and tanks out of the area of Lepeshino toward Izvichni. On the night of 21/22 March 1943, the enemy infiltrated the boundary with its neighbor on the left and seized Shvedchikovii with a sudden attack, while on the morning of 22 March, the Germans launched a powerful attack out of the

Knocked-out T-34 tanks in the Sevsk area, March 1943.

T-34 tanks of the 16th Tank Corps, which had sunk into the Usozha River in March 1943, but were towed out of the water in the middle of April 1943.

Lepeshino area in strength of two infantry regiments with tanks toward Izvichni, and up to a regiment of infantry out of the Usozha direction toward Shirokaia Roshcha and Mal. Prudki. After a lengthy combat and suffering heavy losses, the enemy managed to seize Izvichni, Svetlyi Put' and Pavlovskii and to cut a sector of the Komarichi – Sevsk road. By 23 March, a serious situation had arisen with the threat of a possible breakthrough of the defenses in the direction of Berezovets and Prichim. All combat-ready tanks and motorized infantry were thrown back into combat with the aim of restoring the situation and recapturing Shirokaia Roshcha and Mal. Prudki

As a result of the counterattack by tanks, supported by infantry of the 194th Rifle Division, Shirokaia Roshcha was regained. The enemy's growing offensive activity compelled a withdrawal of units of the 60th Rifle Division and 115th Separate Rifle Brigade, which had been weakened by combat, to the Lukinki line, where with the arrival of the fresh 181st Rifle Division the 2nd Tank Army's left wing consolidated. By an order Central Front commander, the 2nd Tank Army was withdrawn into the Front reserve in the Fatezh area, after passing control of the 194th Rifle Division, the 60th Rifle Division and the 115th Separate Rifle Brigade to the 65th Army command. The army's headquarters and the remaining materiél of the 11th and 16th Tank Corps by 24.00 24 March 1943 began to move out to the new assembly area. The 11th Guards Tank Brigade remained subordinate to the 2nd Guards Cavalry Corps. It became involved in heavy fighting in the Sevsk area, and only between 12 April and 15 April 1943 did it pass back to the control of the 2nd Tank Army and reassemble in the Dubrovka area after handing over its remaining serviceable tanks to the 65th Army's 19th Tank Corps. In the period of the 2nd Tank Army's entire offensive operations, 217 populated places were liberated, including the cities of Dmitriev, Sevsk, Suzemka and Seredina-Buda. Territory was also liberated in the area of the Svapa and Sev Rivers.

Table 1.12: Serviceable tanks of the 2nd Tank Army over selected dates in the operation from 25 February to 30 March 1943

| 2nd Tank Army | Serviceable tanks over the course of the operation (excluding tanks under repair) | | | | | | | | |
|---|---|---|---|---|---|---|---|---|---|
| | 25.02 | 27.02 | 1.03 | 4.03 | 10.03 | 15.03 | 20.03 | 28.03 | 30.03 |
| **11th Tank Corps** | | | | | | | | | |
| 53rd TBr | 26 | 21 | 25 | 17 | 26 | 24 | 12 | 11 | 11 |
| 59th TBr | 40 | 31 | 23 | 36 | 36 | 38 | 10 | 4 | 4 |
| 160th TBr | 32 | 40 | 51 | 34 | 44 | 34 | 24 | 22 | 22 |
| Corps units | – | – | 4 | 4 | 3 | 3 | – | 1 | 1 |
| Total: | **98** | **92** | **103** | **91** | 109 | 99 | 46 | 38 | 38 |
| **16th Tank Corps** | | | | | | | | | |
| 107th TBr | 19 | 10 | 37 | 13 | 20 | 11 | 12 | 27 | 27 |
| 109th TBr | 25 | 21 | 30 | 7 | 13 | 6 | 1 | 0 | 0 |
| 164th TBr | 13 | 8 | 18 | 9 | 20 | 9 | 0 | 8 | 8 |
| Corps units | – | – | – | – | 2 | 2 | – | – | |
| **Total:** | **57** | **39** | **94** | **29** | **55** | **28** | **13** | **35** | **35** |
| 11th GTBr | 43 | 42 | 45 | 39 | 33 | 33 | | 24 | |
| 29th GTR | 14 | 11 | 8 | 8 | 10 | | | | |
| 27th GTR | 14 | | 21 | | | | | | 10 |
| Overall total: | 226 | 184 | 271 | 167 | 207 | 160 | 59 | 97 | 83 |

## The operational significance of the 2nd Tank Army's operations

In its initial stage, the 2nd Tank Army's offensive, which started from the line of the Svapa River, inflicted a serious defeat upon the enemy's defending 137th and 707th Infantry Divisions and units of the Kaminsky Brigade. The threat of the emergence of the army's main forces in the rear of the enemy's Orel – Kromy grouping compelled the *Wehrmacht* command to shift hastily the 72nd Infantry Division from in front of the Kalinin Front and the 45th Infantry Division from in front of the Briansk Front, and also to bring up reserves from the depth. At the same time, however, the 2nd Tank Army was unable to carry out fully its operational orders due to lack of supplies and support while conducting the operation.

## Assessment of the operation by the command of the 2nd Tank Army – Generals Rodin, Latyshev and Onuprienko

THE MAIN SHORTCOMINGS IN CONDUCTING THE ARMY'S OPERATION:
1.  The lengthy march in abysmal road conditions, which extended for 250-300 kilometers from the assembly area to the area of the Army's proposed operational use, as well as the poor training of the tank crews led to the fact that only 182 of [its] 408 tanks arrived in the area of operational deployment.
2.  The Army entered the operation from the march and introduced its main force – the tanks and artillery – in a piecemeal fashion, which is to say as they arrived at the front.
3.  The operation began with an extremely limited quantity of ammunition that was available to the troops, especially in the rifle divisions, which, not having a sufficient amount of motorized transport or the authorized number of horses were unable to bring up combat supplies given the terrible road conditions, while the tank formations, having expended their available fuel on the march and having no fuel at their supply bases at this moment, being now 250 kilometers from their rear support services, could not be committed into the fighting.
4.  The deep snow cover hindered the maneuver of medium and heavy tanks and almost fully precluded the operations of the light T-60, T-70 and Mk. III tanks
5.  The rifle formations, which were arriving in the Army from the march, were untrained, while the 115th Separate Rifle Brigade was absolutely unprepared for combat and in the course of 3-4 days of combat operations lost all of its personnel and combat materiél.
6.  The 143rd Mortar Regiment (120mm) and the 1118th Destroyer Anti-Tank Artillery Regiment (76mm) arrived in the battlefield zone only at the end of the operation.
7.  While conducting the operation, the 29th and 27th Guards Tank Regiments, the 112th Rifle Division, the 1188th Destroyer Anti-Tank Artillery Regiment, two engineer battalions, the 11th Guards Tank Brigade and the 11th Tank Corps' 160th Tank Brigade were all taken from the Army, which prevented it from having under its control at least a small reserve, in order to parry attacks and to restore the situation in individual sectors.
8.  The lack of evacuation means led to the fact that the Army could not either tow away unserviceable materiél or evacuate [disabled] tanks from the battlefield. Evacuation companies arrived in the Army only on 28 March 1943, and they required not less than 10-15 days of repair. The lack of a refueling battalion in the Army raised and still raises the threat of a disruption in fuel supplies.
9.  In the process of the operation, the Army never at all received replenishments of either rank and file personnel or junior command staff. The engineering and sapper battalions had no sort of mechanized machinery; road work was done only through manual labor, which slowed the pace of work. The absence of a road-building battalion extremely complicated and frequently delayed the timely entry of tanks into combat, since the sapper companies of the corps have few men, while

the engineering battalions, having no equipment for carrying out road and bridging work, were unable to manage with these tasks.

**Conclusion:** For the most effective use of the tank army it is ESSENTIAL to give at least 7-10 days of time to prepare for an operation; and to bring up to the jumping-off areas by the start of the operation all of the attached means of reinforcement and to furnish them with an adequate amount of combat supplies. All of the rifle formations and units of reinforcement should be assigned to the Army prior to the start of the operation with the aim of training them and the determination of where the rifle formation should be placed in the Army's combat formation. Strengthen the operation of the tank army with motorized infantry formations, artillery of the Supreme Command Reserve, and aviation. Have reserves of motorized infantry and tanks in the depth behind the tank army for exploiting a success, for augmenting a blow from the depth. The basis for the success of the operation of a tank army is its adequate supply with matériél. Do not allow the army to become too separated from the Front's rear echelon, making good roads available for the axis of the tank army's operation.

## General conclusions regarding the Army's operation

The General Staff's senior officer with the headquarters of the 2nd Tank Army, General Strogy, offered the following assessment of the recently concluded offensive:

With all obviousness it has been confirmed on the experience of the march and [subsequent] operations of the 2nd Tank Army that the violation of provisions in regulations leads to negative consequences. In addition, a number of new questions arose that require your resolution. Of the old and new questions, the following merit attention:

- The 270-300 kilometer-march of the tank formations in the conditions of almost a total absence of roads led to 180 tanks that dropped out of the column, which amounted to 32 percent of the total complement of tanks of the two corps. This once again proves that our armored vehicles, especially when being handled by inexperienced drivers, are poorly adapted to lengthy movements by their own march. Such lengthy marches should be employed only in exceptional cases, with the personal approval of the Front's Commander of Armored and Mechanized Forces. In the given case, there was no need for a march of 270 kilometers.

- The planning of the Army's operation in the period from the middle of February to the middle of March, that is to say, in a period of the largest number of snowstorms and the deepest snow cover, led to the fact that the T-60 and T-70 tanks were usually unable to operate off-road, and sometimes became stuck even on the roads. There cannot even be any talk about the deployment of the corps. Tank operations occurred primarily in small groups along roads. For such operations, separate regiments and tank brigades, working in close cooperation with the infantry, were more suitable and would have achieved no less result. Considering that such unwieldy formations as a corps couldn't be kept supplied with a sufficient amount of fuel because of the impassability of the roads, it must be stated frankly that the use of corps-level formations didn't justify itself.

- In the initial phase of the operation from 23 February to 4 March 1943, an offensive sector was allocated to the Army. The allotment of a sector for the Army's tanks, in my opinion, places responsibility for the entire sector upon the command and deprives, to a certain extent, freedom of maneuver, compelling it to operate like a typical all-arms army. I consider it more expedient not to give the tank armies a separate offensive sector. The Tank Army should begin to operate in someone else's sector, and then exploit success along well-defined axes of advance, placing the consolidation of this success upon the ordinary armies following in its wake.

- As indicated above, the Army's tasks were set by the Front with no regard for time, distances, or the real condition of the units. The period of time allotted between receiving the order and beginning the operation was extremely limited. Thus, for example, the Central Front's Combat Order No.0022/OP was received by the Army's headquarters at 18.30 on 20 February 1943. According to it, it was necessary to begin the offensive on the morning of 22 February, having first completed a 70-kilometer march. Combat Order No. 970, received at 19.45 on 4 March 1943, demanded the offensive begin on the morning of 5 March 1943. As a result, the combat orders were issued hastily by the army headquarters and corps headquarters, while the commanders of the brigades and elements usually had no time at all to prepare for battle, and in crude violation of the requirements of all regulations.

- Over the time of the Army's operations, the formations never received any air support or cover. All the while, the mandates of NKO [People's Commissariat of Defense] Order No. 325 were being crudely violated: "Our air force with its actions strikes the enemy's anti-tank defense, blocks the approach of his tanks to the battlefield, covers the armor combat formations against enemy air attacks, and constantly and incessantly supports the combat operations of the tank units with aerial reconnaissance." None of this was observed and the Army, lacking a single artillery regiment from the Supreme Command Reserve, operated without any artillery or air support. In contrast the enemy's air force continuously and actively operated against our combat formations, which severely impeded the offensive, and inflicted significant losses and disrupted the movement of supplies. It is necessary to ban operations by the tank armies without air support, and to demand from the command of all levels to carry out the mandates of Order No. 325 precisely.

- The Army's operations were implemented without any logistical support: the supply bases were 200-300 kilometers away; often they did not have the necessary types of fuel; and the roads for the motorized transport were impassable. As a result the tank corps were very often left without fuel and were not combat-ready. When planning the Army's operations, the directive of Part 1 of the Combat Regulations of the Red Army's Armored and Mechanized Forces were completely forgotten: "Tanks not timely provided with fuel, ammunition and means of repair lose all the properties of a menacing combat weapon and turn into a helpless and even burdensome heap of metal." All of this happened during the operations of the 2nd Tank Army. In the future, it is forbidden in any event to commit Tank Armies without preparing for their operations in a material-technical respect.

## Ultimate conclusions regarding the operation

The gradual, piecemeal introduction of the army's units into combat to a significant degree affected the course of the operation and its results as a whole. The enemy, which had previously had weak forces in the sector of the 2nd Tank Army's offensive managed to create a powerful shock group and forced the army's forces to assume a defensive posture. The enemy resistance was accompanied by the intensive activity of *Luftwaffe* bombers. In the first stage of the offensive, the 2nd Tank Army inflicted a serious defeat upon the enemy's Dmitriev – L'gov grouping. The threat of the emergence of the army's main forces in the rear of the enemy's Orel – Kromy grouping forced him hastily to transfer forces from the sectors of the Kalinin and Briansk Front to the area of the breakthrough. Over the period of combat operations, the army advanced 150 kilometers with fighting, in the process liberating 217 villages and towns. Based on the experience of the conducted approach march, the Army received a great lesson on the staging of the materiél and equipment for conducting all the measures connected with the approach march. The army's troops received the combat experience of conducting offensive and defensive fighting in harsh winter conditions. The army's troops learned how to operate simultaneously in several areas that were not connected with the overall line of the front. The experience of the fighting demonstrated that the pace of advance cannot be equal on separate directions, and that a bold and decisive maneuver (the 11th Tank Corps) secures a rapid tempo of the development of combat operations. This operation served as an object lesson for organizing command and control and for supporting the combat with everything necessary on the part of the command and leadership. Here the army acquired the experience for an independent breakthrough of an enemy's defensive belt and the organization of a defense in the operational depth. In the period of the 2nd Tank Army's first offensive, the army's soldiers received their combat baptism. Already in the first combats, the tankers and motorized infantry showed themselves to be fearless warriors, capable of striking and smashing the enemy. The offensive battles showed that the 2nd Tank Army with its powerful and menacing equipment was capable of resolving major operational tasks.

**Thus was born the glory and combat traditions of the 2nd Guards Tank Army.**

## An exerpt from the Act of Acceptance and Transfer of the 2nd Tank Army's 194th and 60th Rifle Divisions and its 115th Special Rifle Brigade to the 65th Army – 23 March 1943

1.  The acceptance and transfer was conducted in a situation of active enemy operations and the withdrawal of the indicated formations to a line according to the attached map. The enemy's advance wasn't stopped.

2.  The 194th Rifle Division – Division commander – Guards Colonel Opiakin. The division has up to 4,500 men. It is occupying a defensive sector of 12 kilometers. The division is fully combat-capable, and is distinguished by the tight teamwork and precision of the headquarters. All enemy counterattacks are being repelled.

3.  The 60th Rifle Division – Division commander – Colonel Kliaro. The division on 23 March 1943 is not sufficiently combat-fit. There is no clear cut command at the company-battalion-regiment levels. By the end of 23 March 1943, there remained 80-90 active bayonets reporting for duty in each rifle regiment.

4.  The 115th Special Rifle Brigade – Brigade commander – Colonel Sankovsky. By the end of 22 March 1943, in the brigade there were 30-35 men in each battalion. The brigade is totally unfit for combat. Combat leadership is lacking. The brigade's headquarters is not well-knit. Of the battalion commanders, only one is still on active duty. The 2nd Battalion commander was shot on 22 March 1943 for showing cowardice.

## Guards Colonel Kazakov recalls:

On 25 February 1943, the offensive of the Central Front's forces began. However, the situation on this sector of the front was developing adversely for our troops. The 2nd Guards Cavalry Corps, which was operating here, was subjected to a counterattack by superior enemy forces, and began to fall back to the Sevsk area with heavy fighting. At an order of the Central Front commander, our 11th Guards Separate Tank Brigade was urgently shifted to the Sevsk area. I was at the headquarters vehicle, when a cavalry commander in the broadest black cloak came galloping up on a foaming horse:

"Where is Bubnov?" he asked.

I pointed to the vehicle. The rider hastily dismounted and tossed his cloak onto the snow. At that moment, the door of the cab opened and Nikolai Matveevich emerged from it.

"Are you Bubnov?" the cavalryman asked.

Nikolai Matveevich calmly looked down at the agitated commander and said, "Yes, I am Bubnov. And who are you?"

The cavalryman gave his surname and hastily added in a pleading voice: "Come bail us out, Comrade Bubnov. The fascists are on a roll, and they have tanks … And what can you do against them on this?" he said, as he pointed at his horse.

"This is the first time I've seen a cavalryman, who refers to his war horse so disgracefully," the Colonel noted with venom, before angrily asking, "And where are your fighters? They, perhaps, also gave a wave at their horses? Perhaps help is pointless over there, if the commander himself has lost his head?"

The brigade commander disliked commanders who lost control of themselves as a situation grew complicated. The cavalryman was apparently one of them. However, Bubnov didn't waste time with an interrogation: "Come over here, show me on the map," he said; "Where is he, the German?" Then he added, "Kazakov, come here."

From the cavalryman's story, a bad scene emerged. Under enemy attack, a breach had been created in the corps' defense, through which the hostile troops had rushed. Every hour mattered, and Bubnov had immediately given an order to a tank battalion to block the path of the German units that were moving toward Sevsk. At this time the radio operator Senin, who was maintaining contact with the commander of the tank battalion, reported that the battalion commander was concerned about ammunition, which was already running low, while the fascists were continuing to press. Bubnov immediately ordered a truck loaded with shells to be sent there. They reported that Guards Major Iurii Telly had set off in the truck. Several minutes later, Senin received a report from the battalion commander that he could see a truck with ammunition approaching on the road and that the Germans were firing at it. An alarmed silence descended over the headquarters vehicle. It continued, probably, for around five minutes. Bubnov began to get agitated. "Report on Telly," he demanded.

"The vehicle is making its way through the snow under a storm of mortar shells and artillery fire," the radio operator reported. Then again there was silence.

"The vehicle has stopped. A shell exploded beside it. It isn't clear what has happened with it through the smoke and swirling snow," Senin passed along. The tense minutes stretched on. However, then there was an even more alarming report: "A shell hit the vehicle. It is burning. Telly and his driver are hauling the boxes out and dragging them to one side. The barrage is intensifying."

Bubnov stood up, lit a cigarette, but then immediately tossed it aside with anger. It was perceptible that his nerves had given out for a moment. However, he immediately regained his self-control. On the outside he was again calm, but plainly he was seething inside, suffering over the fate of the major and the driver, worried for the tankers, who almost had no shells left and were incapable of helping Telly and the driver. Meanwhile over the radio they were reporting that the major and driver were at a crawl under the artillery barrage, dragging more boxes of shells from the burning truck.

"Fine men! Heroes!" exclaimed Bubnov. Neglecting the danger, Telly and the driver delivered two boxes of shells to the tankers, returned to the truck, and again, under mortar fire, fighting for every meter across the snow-covered landscape, started dragging boxes. Then suddenly a new report: "Guards Major Telly has been killed …" This ordinary toiler of the war had suddenly become a hero, the self-sacrificial act of whom was later long praised by our Guardsmen.

March 1943 was also difficult for our tankers. The winter in this year was snowy. There had been a lot of snow as well around Sevsk, where Aleksandr Lugansky, who was now the commander of a tank platoon, was able to demonstrate his ability to strike the fascists. We'll recall an entry in the journal of combat reports about a clash that flared up on 17 March at the village of Borisovo. Back then, Lugansky's platoon had been ordered to drive back the enemy that was advancing on the village. Across the deep snow, which hindered maneuver, the commander led his platoon to a point that blocked the path to the Nazis and took up a favorable position. The hostile vehicles approached. "Seven … ten … 12," Lugansky was counting. The correlation of four to one was not in favor of our tankers. Stout nerves and iron belief in one's capabilities were necessary in order not to flinch. Lugansky calmly asked his crew, "Do you see how many there are?"

"We see."

"Will we hold out?"

"We'll hold out! We won't let them pass!"

"Right. Fire only at my command."

Lugansky glanced at the clock dial. It was 1400, when he gave the first command. Then immediately the field ahead, where wisps of windblown snow were dancing, erupted with shell explosions. Lugansky watched as first one enemy tank brewed up, and then another. This instantly cooled the ardor of the attacking fascists. The enemy vehicles reduced speed and some of them stopped. Lugansky's crews increased their fire and knocked out yet another tank. Now almost all the foe's tanks had stopped, while others began to retire.

"Aha, they've turned yellow, the bastards!" Lugansky swore, seeing the enemy's confusion.

Senior Lieutenant Korol'kov was observing the course of the battle. "Counterattack!" he transmitted to the platoon leader. The tanks, upon which the words *Tambovskii kolkhoznik* [Tambov collective farmer] starkly stood out, and raising clouds of snow, began to rush at the enemy. Unable to withstand the onslaught, he began to turn around and retreat.

A new day dawned, and fresh enemy attacks began. Now Lugansky's platoon was shifted to the village of Kudiiar, where the enemy was exerting especial pressure. On this day as well, the tank duel ended with a counterattack by our tankers, in the course of which the commander personally left one hostile tank blazing. Another vehicle was seized as a trophy. When the enemy was thrown back, the driver-mechanic Vysotsky asked the platoon commander, "Perhaps we can check it out?"

"Let's go," the commander eagerly agreed.

Having climbed out of the T-34, they approached the German tank. The hatches were open, and there was no one inside. Vysotsky took a seat in the driver's position and pressed the starter button. The engine coughed, but wouldn't start. Vysotsky clambered into the combat compartment, scrutinized it, climbed out and reported: "Everything is fully operational and there are shells. They skedaddled!"

"This isn't '41," the platoon commander replied.

The fighting didn't subside until the end of March. Every single day, Aleksandr Lugansky was in the thickest of the fighting. On 26 March he was wounded while repelling an enemy attack, but he managed to destroy one more German tank. In the fighting for Sevsk, many other of the brigade's Guardsmen had similar feats.

### From the memoirs of Guards Senior Lieutenant Razukanny, *Tanki evakuirovanny [The tanks have been evacuated]*:

In the month of February 1943, our tank battalion, which belonged to a tank brigade of the 16th Tank Corps, began an offensive on the Central Front. Our tanks covered not an insignificant number of kilometers on the heels of the retreating enemy. In the area of the village of Litezh, having encountered fierce enemy resistance, we took up a defense. The enemy had a lot of infantry and artillery in the narrow sector of our battalion. Moreover, the enemy forces were surrounding the battalion on three sides. Taking advantage of such a great superiority, the enemy hurled his infantry into an attack against our forces. Our tanks fought courageously and didn't take a step back in retreat. While repelling the counterattack, our battalion left six tanks that were knocked out by the Germans on the battlefield. They had to be evacuated. Despite the heavy enemy fire, the deputy commander for maintenance and technical support summoned the battalion's repair element and the deputy commanders of the technical support companies. He gave a specific task to each one regarding the evacuation of the tanks. As soon as it began to get dark, the repair personnel Polikarpov, Matiushchenko and Gusak under the leadership of Senior Lieutenant Proskurin set to work. With the support of our artillery, they had to approach each tank in bounds of 20-30 meters, so that the enemy couldn't detect the location of the evacuation. Despite the difficult work conditions, the repairmen carried out the combat assignment that had been placed up on them with honor, and all the tanks were evacuated. Four of them were repaired that same night and by morning they were already in defensive positions. The command recommended a government decoration for all the participants in the evacuation effort.

## From the memoirs of Guards Major General Anatolii Shvebig:

In Kursk, having arrived at the headquarters of the Central Front, I quickly searched out the commander of the armored forces. General Orel literally on the fly familiarized me with the situation and sent me to the headquarters of the 2nd Tank Army, where I was presented to its commander Lieutenant General Rodin. He looked unhappy. Right off the bat, he began to dress me down: "Why have they sent you? What is Moscow thinking about?" Stunned by such a reception, I stood quietly before the angered commander. But he continued: "Why aren't you answering? We don't need any taciturn people around here." Finally, when he fell silent, I rather curtly asked if he had an order for me. At that point I was ready to head back to Moscow once again in order to receive an appointment to any post in a different army. The commander looked at me with surprise and now said affably, "Enough chit-chat, engineer! Go to the 16th Tank Corps and put things in order there with their equipment." Having snappily turned around according to regulations, I stepped out of the headquarters hut, lost in thought, wondering what had prompted such wrath from General Rodin toward me. Soon the situation became clear. It turned out that General Rodin had his own candidate for the post of deputy corps commander, but Moscow hadn't agreed with him.

"This in fact had upset the army commander," the deputy commander for vehicle maintenance and technical support Engineer-Colonel Krupenin told me with a chuckle, when I had reported to him after the conversation with the General. "But don't pay any attention to his cold reception," he added; "Our commander values good workers."

Soon upon my arrival, I met with the commander of the 16th Tank Corps and the chief of staff Colonel Kocherin. After reporting, the corps commander amicably said to me, "We'll fight side-by-side." Then after stepping over to a staff map that had been spread out on a table he continued:

"The corps is in the second echelon of the Central Front's defense. A very difficult situation has come about with the equipment. For the first time, the condition of the combat vehicles is unsatisfactory. Of the available 152 tanks, only 57 are fit for combat. While completing the winter march by our units along the 200-kilometer-long march routes, we left behind 35 tanks that had broken down with a variety of technical problems. It still isn't known where they are now and in what condition. The rest of the vehicles are in the area of combat operations and require repair. The tanks must be found and repaired by 1 June 1943. That will be the first task for you and your subordinates. Then organize the reception of 20 combat vehicles from the 11th Tank Corps. Quickly familiarize yourself with the staff of the technical department and get to work."

As it turned out, the officers of the corps' technical department consisted of more qualified specialists, having tremendous experience with working in frontline conditions. The repair and evacuation of vehicles was headed by Major Ivan Gur'ev. His assistant for supplies and inventory was Engineer Major Ekeleovsky, about whom it was said that he had memorized all the catalog numbers of the tank parts.

Together with these officers and Senior Lieutenant Kucherov, on the first day of my arrival in the corps we discussed in detail how best to carry out the given assignment. The weather complicated matters. Spring was claiming its own rights with more insistence. The muddy season had turned all the roads into quagmires. One couldn't even think about traveling over them to search for the abandoned tanks. Colonel Kocherin came to our aid, having placed at my personal disposal a PO-2 airplane from an aviation flight attached to the corps. Guards Captain Aleksandr But, a splendid pilot, was assigned to fly it. He knew how to land on any dry clump of land and how to take off from it. For three days, officers of the technical department flew patrols over the former march routes used by the tank columns, searching for the abandoned machines. Often it was necessary to find the crews in the villages where they had been posted. It was also necessary to determine the places and sectors of artillery barrages. They forced the crews to dig tank emplacements and moved the [disabled] tanks into the positions with prime movers. At any time they could be used as firing positions while work was underway to repair them. The mechanical problems were various, but they all, as a rule, required a lot of time to fix. Over the three days of flying over the area of the tank columns' movement routes, officers of the maintenance and technical support department found all of the abandoned machines. Then the repair teams got to work.

### From the letter of commendation for the commander of the 11th Tank Corps General Ivan Lazarev:

Major General Lazarev is a willful, energetic, well-prepared corps commander. Units of the corps under his command in the period from 13 to 27 February 1943 conducted a 320-kilometer march in the most difficult meteorological conditions. Thanks to good organization, they arrived in formation at the jumping-off position for the offensive. Subsequent combat operations of the units were decisive, bold and rapid. In the period from 28 February to 10 March 1943, the corps took the cities of Sevsk, Seredina-Buda and Suzemka and liberated several dozen populated points from the Germans. Over this time, the corps destroyed 2,172 enemy soldiers and officers, 30 heavy and light machine guns, and 2 guns. Captured were 1,757 enemy soldiers and officers, 36 trucks, 18 mortars, 33 heavy machine guns and 18 guns. He has been awarded the Order of the Red Banner.

### Soldiers of the 2nd Tank Army who distinguished themselves in the Dmitriev – Sevsk operation:

Senior Lieutenant Vladimir **Konstantinov**, company commander with the 352nd Tank Battalion, 11th Tank Corps. In the battle for Sevsk, he demonstrated guts and resolve, and he skillfully directed the combat. His tank was the first to break into the city and to receive enemy fire. As a result of the combat, his tank knocked out a 75mm gun and wiped out up to 40 enemy soldiers and officers. In the fight for the settlement of Vladimirskii and the village of Mostechnia, being

The presentation of combat decorations in the 16th Tank Corps' 164th Tank Brigade, April 1943. In the center is Major Mansvetov.

wounded, he continued to direct the combat. He destroyed two anti-tank guns, a Pz. III tank, and up to a company of enemy personnel. He came off the field of battle only after an order from the battalion commander. Awarded the Order of the Red Banner.

Senior Lieutenant Nikolai **Kudriavtsev**, company commander in the 352nd Tank Battalion, 160th Tank Brigade, 11th Tank Corps. In the battle for Seredina-Buda, he led an operation to block the enemy's path of retreat to Novgorod-Severskii. Two settlements were seized by two T-34 tanks under the leadership of Kudriavtsev (Romashkovo and Nezamozhnik), as were a wagon with ammunition, 4 guns, 5 machine guns and a headquarters. Taken prisoner were 34 enemy soldiers and officers, and up to 40 Hitlerites were wiped out. Awarded the Order of the Red Banner.

Major Tikhon **Kartashev**, deputy commander of the 107th Tank Brigade. Temporarily assumed command of the 107th Tank Brigade. Having composite tank battalions of tank brigades under his command in the period of offensive fighting from 23 February to 8 March 1943, he knew how to forge the combat collective of his brigade. Being up front in the line of battle, by his personal example he inspired the personnel to carry out their assigned task. Under his leadership, the brigade seized 13 settlements, including Deriugino, Litizh and others. More than 2,000 enemy soldiers and officers, 59 guns of various calibers, and more than 150 machine guns were destroyed. Awarded the Order of the Red Banner.

Captain Anatolii **Khombakh**, commander of the 310th Tank Battalion of the 109th Tank Brigade. While breaking through the enemy defenses in the area of the village and station of Deriugino and the 1st of May State Farm on 3 March 1943, and during the subsequent pursuit of the enemy up to 12 March 1943, he was always located in the battalion's combat formations, inspiring the battalion's personnel to carry out their combat tasks. He organized command and control over the battle in exemplary fashion. Up to 900 German soldiers and officers, 3 self-propelled guns, approximately 40 guns of various calibers, and up to 100 machine guns were destroyed by his battalion. Awarded the Order of the Red Banner.

## Tankers of the 11th Guards Tank Brigade – 1943

Technician-Lieutenant Ivan Lubov.

Battalion commander of the 1st Tank Battalion, Ivan Korol'kov.

Guards Lieutenant Aleksandr Lugansky.

V.G Pirozhenko.

V.I. Nesvetailov.

M.G. Mikhailov.

A.N. Chesnokov.

Guards Senior Lieutenant Kazachenko's tank crew.

Senior Lieutenant Aleksei Petrukhin's T-34 tank crew: Left to right Lapin, Kotenov, Petrukhin and Patepko.

Another shot of Petrukhin's tank crew. From left to right Lapin, Kotenov, Petrukhin and Patepko.

Platoon commander of the 1st Tank Battalion of the 11th Guards Tank Brigade Junior Lieutenant Aleksandr Shilov's tank crew, summer of 1943.

Guards Lieutenant
Ivan Kvasha.

Guards Lieutenant V.
Dashinsky.

Guards Junior Lieutenant
Aleksandr Shilov.

Guards Sergeant Major
Lev Everskov.

Nikolai Bubnov, commander
of the 11th Guards Tank
Brigade.

Grigorii Kalustov, deputy
political commander of the
11th Guards Tank Brigade.

Guards Senior Lieutenant Aleksandr **Lugansky**, platoon commander in the 1st Tank Battalion, 11th Guards Tank Brigade. On 18.3.1943, commanding a platoon of 3 T-34 tanks at Kudiiar, while repelling an attack of 20 German tanks, he brewed up enemy tanks and knocked out another, and captured one that was completely serviceable, full of fuel and ammunition. On 26.3.1943, at 19.30, the enemy hurled 12 tanks with the support of artillery and aviation at the line of defense of Lugansky's platoon. Having joined battle with the German tanks, Lugansky with his very first shot set fire to one enemy tank, while his platoon knocked out 6 more tanks. Awarded the Order of Aleksandr Nevsky.

Junior Lieutenant Grigorii **Kazachenko**, T-34 tank commander, 2nd Tank Battalion, 11th Guards Tank Brigade. Over the period of combat from 17.3 to 19.3.1943 in the area of the village of Bukovishche, Hill 216.6 and the city of Sevsk, he demonstrated exceptional resolve, courage and bravery. He personally brewed up 6 tanks, knocked out 4 tanks, and destroyed up to 80 Hitlerites. Awarded the Order of the Red Banner.

Guards Lieutenant Iakov **Karachker**, platoon commander, 1st Tank Battalion, 11th Guards Tank Brigade. In the combat at the village of Borisovo on 18.3.1943, he demonstrated exemplary courage, bravery and military skill. With his bold and decisive actions, at the head of 3 T-34 tanks he swept the settlement of Borisovo clean of 8 German tanks, of which two were left burned out and two were knocked out, and destroyed up to 100 enemy soldiers and officers. He stopped the attack of German tanks against the 15th and 16th Cavalry Regiments, thereby securing the withdrawal of these units and the evacuation of their equipment, for which he received the gratitude of the cavalry corps commander. In action he is bold and decisive. Awarded the Order of the Red Banner.

Sergeant Major Ivan **Nestruga**, T-34 driver-mechanic, 107th Tank Brigade. In the fighting for Litizh in March 1943, the enemy launched a counteroffensive; the tanks of the brigade in view of the snowdrifts arrived late at the place of combat. The tank of "Guardsman" driver-mechanic Nestruga had to repel four enemy counterattacks. He destroyed 16 pillboxes, 4 anti-tank guns, 6 machine guns and up to 100 Hitlerites. His tank was attacked by enemy aircraft and Nestruga was badly wounded. Awarded the Order of the Red Banner.

Guards Junior Lieutenant Sergei **Savenko**, platoon commander of medium tanks, 2nd Tank Battalion, 11th Guards Tank Brigade. Over the period of combat between 4.3 and 19.3.1943 in the area of the villages of Evdokimovo and Borisovo, his platoon brewed up 6 tanks, knocked out 5 tanks, and destroyed 2 anti-tank guns and more than 40 soldiers and officers. Awarded the Order of the Red Banner.

Guards Senior Lieutenant Pavel **Tolstikov**, T-34 tank company commander, 2nd Tank Battalion, 11th Guards Tank Brigade. Commanding the company, in the area of the village of Bukovishche and Hill 216.6 over the period from 16.3 to 19.3.1943, he proved himself to be a bold and decisive commander. His company repulsed fierce enemy attacks. Tolstikov himself knocked out 2 tanks and killed up to 18 Hitlerites. Awarded the Order of the Red Banner.

Guards Sergeant Major Aleksei **Shchetinin**, driver-mechanic of a T-34 tank, 2nd Tank Battalion, 11th Guards Tank Brigade. On 17 March 1943 in the village of Bukovishche, repelling enemy attacks, his tank was set ablaze. Under enemy fire he evacuated the crew from the burning tank. The neighboring machine was also burning. Shchetinin put out the fire, rescued the injured crew, took a seat in the driver's position, and drove it to cover. Awarded the Order of the Red Banner.

Captain Mikhail **Ivanov**, commander of a motorized rifle battalion, 109th Tank Brigade. In combat from 23.2 to 6.3.1943, he was a model of bravery, courage and resolve, leading all the personnel. The battalion was serving as tank riders. At top speeds, the soldiers leaped off the tanks and with their fire killed enemy personnel. On 3.3.1943 it [the battalion] seized Deriugino Station with an outflanking maneuver, which thereby secured an assembly point for tanks. More than 600 enemy soldiers and officers were destroyed by the battalion, 120 supply wagons were destroyed, and prisoners and valuable documents were seized. He personally killed up to 20 Hitlerites. Awarded the Order of the Red Banner.

Major Aleksandr **Zhernokleev**, mortar battalion commander, 15th Motorized Rifle Brigade. In combat for Deriugino Station, up to 100 enemy infantrymen were destroyed by the battalion, and 4 heavy machine guns and 7 light machine guns and 2 anti-tank guns were knocked out by the fire of the mortar battalion. By his personal example he led the battalion's soldiers in carrying out their combat assignments. Awarded the Order of the Red Banner.

# 2

# In the Battle of Kursk 1943

**Command Staff of the 2nd Tank Army**
Commander – Guards Lieutenant General Aleksei Rodin
1st Member of the Military Council – Major General Petr Latyshev
2nd Member of the Military Council – Major General Vladimir Sosnovikov
Chief of Staff – Major General Grigorii Preisman
Deputy Commander for Rear Services – Major General Mikhail Goncharov
Deputy Commander for Vehicle Maintenance and Technical Support – Colonel Samuil Krupenin
Commander of Artillery – Colonel Mikhail Tsikalo
Chief of Intelligence Department – Lieutenant Colonel Ashraf Galimov
Chief of Engineering Troops – Colonel Isak Levin
Chief of Operations Department – Colonel Vladimir Chizh
Chief of Signals Department – Lieutenant Colonel Iosif Smoly

**3rd Tank Corps** – Major General Maksim Sinenko
50th Tank Brigade – Colonel Fedor Konovalov
51st Tank Brigade – Lieutenant Colonel Georgii Kokurin
103rd Tank Brigade – Colonel Georgii Maksimov
57th Motorized Rifle Brigade – Lieutenant Colonel Anton Arzhba
121st Anti-aircraft Artillery Regiment – Major Ia. Tutov
Also the 234th Mortar Regiment, the 881st Destroyer Anti-tank Artillery Regiment, the 74th Motorcycle Brigade and the 728th Destroyer Anti-tank Artillery Battalion

**16th Tank Corps** – Major General Vasilii Grigor'ev
107th Tank Brigade – Lieutenant Colonel Nikolai Teliakov
109th Tank Brigade – Lieutenant Colonel Petr Babkovsky
164th Tank Brigade – Lieutenant Colonel Nikolai Kopylov
15th Motorized Rifle Brigade – Colonel Petr Akimochkin
Also the 226th Mortar Regiment, the 614th Destroyer Anti-tank Artillery Regiment, the 51st Motorcycle Battalion, and the 729th Destroyer Anti-tank Artillery Battalion

11th Guards Tank Brigade – Guards Colonel Nikolai Bubnov
9th Separate Signals Regiment – Lieutenant Colonel Petr Pavlov

**Command Staff of the 2nd Tank Army – July 1943**

Aleksei Rodin.

Petr Latyshev.

Grigorii Preisman.

Maksim Sinenko – 3rd Tank Corps.

Vasilii Grigor'ev – 16th Tank Corps.

Nikolai Bubnov – 11th Guards Tank Brigade.

Georgii Kokurin – 51st Tank Brigade.

Georgii Maksimov – 103rd Tank Brigade.

Fedor Konovalov – 50th Tank Brigade.

Nikolai Teliakov – 107th Tank Brigade.

Nikolai Kopylov – 164th Tank Brigade.

Petr Akimochkin – 15th Motorized Rifle Brigade.

Mikail Tsikalo – Commander of Artillery.

Vladimir Chizh – Chief of Operations.

Iosif Smoly – Chief of Signals Department.

Ashraf Galimov, Chief of Intelligence Department.

Isak Levin – Commander of Engineer Troops.

Mikhail Goncharov – Deputy Commander for Rear Services.

### On the Eve of the Battle of Kursk, Summer of 1943

Tankers of the 11th Guards Tank Brigade. Fourth from the left is Aleksandr Lugansky; fifth from left is A. Shagin; sixth from left is Shkvornikov; and seventh from left, Nesvetailov (summer of 1943).

The crew of tank company commander Senior Lieutenant Konstantin Blinov, 103rd Tank Brigade, 3rd Tank Corps, on the eve of combat in the Kursk bulge. The Russian caption read: "Hero of the Soviet Union Guards Senior Lieutenant K.M. Blinov talks with his crew."

As a result of the winter offensive by the Central and Voronezh Fronts, which had pushed ahead of the neighboring *fronts*, but had then been pushed back by German counterattacks at Khar'kov and Sevsk, a bulge had been created on the Eastern Front along the line Bolkhov, Sevsk, Ryl'sk, Belgorod, with Kursk at its center. The frontline had stabilized on this line and was maintained between March and July 1943. The forces positioned within the interior of the bulge were continually under the threat of fighting in encirclement, since it was advantageous to the enemy to break through the front of our defending forces at the base of the bulge with a concentrated attack, and force the defenders to fight on two fronts. Two most likely variants of the enemy's plan of attack were assumed. According to the first variant, the enemy would attack from Orel toward Livny and from Belgorod toward Kastornoe with the aim of cutting our main lines of communication that supplied our *fronts*, and by this place the troops of both *fronts* in a difficult situation. According to the second alternative, the enemy would launch an attack from the north from Orel toward Kursk, and from the south from Belgorod through Oboyan' also toward Kursk with the immediate aim of erasing the Kursk salient, and the further aim of creating favorable conditions for a subsequent offensive toward Moscow.

The enemy created major force groupings on either side of the base of the bulge: one in the Orel – Kromy area consisting of seven panzer, two motorized and eleven infantry divisions, for a total of 20 divisions; and the second in the Belgorod area, consisting of ten panzer, one motorized and seven infantry divisions, for a total of 18 divisions. With these forces the enemy planned to break through our defenses with a concentric attack in the general direction of Kursk, and to encircle and destroy our defending troops positioned within the bulge. In accordance with the situation that had developed and the possible alternatives of the enemy's planned offensive, a plan was developed by our command to counter the enemy's possible intentions, and major tank and artillery formations were brought up to the Kursk bulge. The 2nd Tank Army was assembled in the areas north and south of Kursk, occupying an advantageous position for maneuvers to the north, west or south with the aim of counterattacking the enemy's mobile groups in the event of a breakthrough into the depth of our defenses, before going over to a decisive offensive. Deployed in the area of the populated points of Kondrinka, Brekhovo and Kochetki, the 2nd Tank Army was subsequently designated for operations against the enemy main grouping located south of Orel.

The troops of the 2nd Tank Army spent the months of April to July 1943 preparing for a defensive battle. Particular attention was paid to preparing the elements, units and formations for their employment on the defense in accordance with the defensive plan. The personnel went through intensive combat training. One important aspect of that training, especially for the inexperienced soldiers, was presentations by soldiers who had distinguished themselves in combat and who had skillfully mastered their equipment and weapon. According to General Radzievsky's testimony, the experienced tanker Hero of the Soviet Union Konstantin Blinov, a commander of one of the tank companies, often gave talks to the personnel of the 2nd Tank Army's 103rd Tank Brigade. He had earned the title Hero of the Soviet Union after he and his crew had destroyed an enemy vehicle column that contained the headquarters of an infantry division, a signals battalion, an anti-tank battalion and a motorcycle company. That was, naturally, why he was selected to instruct the inexperienced troops. Great attention was given to preparing the troops for night actions. Not less than one-third of all the training exercises were conducted under nighttime conditions. The tankers practiced firing from both fixed positions and while on the move, learned to alter positions quickly and stealthily, and in suitable circumstances, to emerge boldly from their cover and to counterattack vigorously.

On 1 June 1943, the 3rd Tank Corps under the command of Major General of Tank Forces Maksim Sinenko arrived from the Supreme Command Reserve to replace the departed 11th Tank Corps. It included the 50th, 51st and 103rd Tank and the 57th Motorized Rifle Brigades. The 3rd Tank Corps also had available Major Ia. Tutov's 121st Anti-Aircraft Artillery Regiment, Major A. Ponomarev's 74th Separate Motorcycle Battalion, the 64th Chemical Defense Company, the 8th Separate Aviation Signals Flight, the 234th Mortar and 881st Destroyer Anti-tank Artillery Regiments, the 728th Destroyer Anti-Tank Artillery Battalion, the 90th Separate Sapper Battalion and the 411th Separate Signals Battalion. Prior to this, the 3rd Tank Corps had taken an active part in battles, and its personnel had extensive combat experience. Before the Battle of Kursk, the corps was fully brought up to table strength with personnel, equipment and weapons. It had 2.1 combat loads of ammunition for the tanks, 2.5 for the anti-tank artillery, 2.8 for the anti-aircraft artillery, and 2 for small arms; 3.3 refills of diesel fuel for the tanks, 3.5 refills for the remaining vehicles; and 6 days of rations.

## Equipping of the Army with combat matériel

According to a report by the 2nd Tank Army's Deputy Commander for Vehicle Maintenance and Technical Support Guards Engineer-Colonel Samuil Krupenin:

> At the moment of the 2nd Tank Army's introduction into the fighting [i.e., on 5 July 1943], it was in top fighting condition, and consisted of the 3rd and 16th Tank Corps and the 11th Guards Tank Brigade. The personnel of the Army's formations were fully equipped, armed,

well-trained and ready to carry out any combat assignment of the command. The strength and condition of the Army's armor as of 5 July 1953 was as follows:

**In tanks:** 317 T-34 tanks, 126 T-70 tanks and 17 T-60 tanks. **Total: 460 tanks**. Of the total number of tanks, **457** were serviceable (314 T-34, 126 T-70 and 17 T-60), which amounted to 99.3 percent of all the tanks in its inventory. Three T-34 tanks were undergoing repair work to replace engines or parts that had exceeded their service lifetimes between overhauls, which amounted to 0.7 percent of the tank park. In addition, three more tanks (2 T-34 and 1 T-60) had been transferred to the 227th Reserve Training Regiment in the month of May so that the contingent of reserve tankers under training could have practical experience with the tanks.

Separately for the corps and the types of vehicles, the amount of operating hours on the tank engines as of 5 July 1943 and the number of operating hours still remaining before needed replacement are shown in Table 2.1:

**Table 2.1: Operating hours remaining on the 2nd Tank Army's tank engines at the start of the Battle of Kursk**

|  | Type | Hours on the tank engines from the start of their use | Hours remaining before scheduled overhaul | Total tanks on 5 July 1943 |
|---|---|---|---|---|
| 3rd Tank Corps | T-34 | 42 | 159 | 195 (of which 1 was under repair) |
|  | T-70 | 36 | 164 |  |
| 16th Tank Corps | T-34 | 46 | 154 | 206 (of which 4 were under repair) |
|  | T-70 | 40 | 160 |  |
|  | T-60 | 20 | 180 |  |
| 11th Guards Tank Brigade | T-34 | 40 | 160 | 54 (all serviceable) |
|  | T-70 | 41 | 159 |  |

The technical maintenance done on the tanks was completely up to date. The tanks were fully fueled and lubricated, and they were carrying full ammo loads. The tank drivers were assessed according to their ability, and as of 5 July 1943, the 2nd Tank Army had 34 highly skilled tank mechanic-drivers, 41 mechanic-drivers of the 1st Class, 61 mechanic-drivers of the 2nd Class, and 149 mechanic-drivers of the 3rd Class.

## Endowment with recovery vehicles

The 2nd Tank Army's formations had not been provided with an adequate number of recovery vehicles. For example, the 3rd Tank Corps, which by TO&E should have had 17 ChTZ-65 tractors had only 2. The 16th Tank Corps had only 5 ChTZ-65 tractors, of which 3 were under long-term repair, while the other 2 required the replacement of worn-out parts. Instead of 5 tractors, as foreseen by the TO&E, the 11th Guards Tank Brigade didn't have a single one. Thus, all the work to evacuate disabled tanks from the battlefield was done primarily by two recovery companies that were directly subordinate to the Command of Armored Supplies and Repair and the 2nd Tank Army headquarters, which were also badly under-equipped according to table strength. At the moment that combat operations began, the evacuation companies had 17 ChTZ-65 tractors instead of the authorized 30. The tractors for the 77th and 78th Evacuation Companies, which had arrived in the Command of Armored Supplies and Repair from Briansk Front, required immediate repairs. After a great deal of training on the recovery of disabled or bogged vehicles, the tractors were overhauled and prepared for the July 1943 battles. The personnel of the evacuation companies and of the brigade's evacuation platoons had practical experience, and for the most part had been chosen from brave men, who were dedicated to the Motherland, which had enormous significance in the forthcoming combat operations.

## Supply of fuel and lubricants

By the start of combat operations, the Army's formations had a sufficient reserve of fuel and lubricants in containers and crates that had been assembled at the formations' supply bases. The quantity of refills (in tons) by type of fuel or lubricant on 5 July 1943 is shown in Table 2.2:

**Table 2.2: Amount of fuel and lubricants available to the 2nd Tank Army on 5 July 1943**

| Fuel or lubricant | Quantity in metric tons | Quantity in refills |
|---|---|---|
| KB-70 high-octane fuel[1] | 270.81 | 5.70 |
| Diesel fuel | 681.11 | 3.34 |
| Petrol[2] | 788.60 | 5.92 |
| Track grease | 85.65 | 4.26 |
| Motor oil | 47.50 | 4.96 |

Notes:

1 This high-octane fuel was used by Soviet aircraft, but also by Soviet T-60 and T-70 tanks that were present at Kursk.

2 This was a lower octane fuel used by GAZ-5, GAZ-AA and other Soviet trucks.

Fuel and lubricants were transported in jerricans, containers and in metal drums, which were mounted aboard special-purpose vehicles designed to carry them.

## Supply of ammunition for the combat vehicles

Ammunition for the combat formations arrived in timely fashion and was delivered to the units and distributed among the tanks, with the simultaneous creation of a significant reserve of ammunition at temporarily organized dumps. As of 5 July 1943, the following types and amounts of ammunition had been brought up to the fighting units: a) 76mm shells – 3.5 standard combat loads; b) 45mm shells – 3 standard combat loads; 20mm shells – 3.8 standard combat loads. The transport of ammunition in the period of the Army's defensive and offensive operations was performed primarily by vehicles that had been set aside for these purposes.

## Supply of the Army with spare parts and components

As of 5 July 1943, the 2nd Tank Army had in supply 6 V-2 engines and up to 70 metric tons of various parts; after 5 July, it received 5 more V-2 engines from Front supply dumps, 2 transmission gear boxes, 2 T-34 steering clutches, 1 T-34 engine clutch, 1 T-34 drive wheel and up to 10 more metric tons of spare parts. Between 5 July 1943 and 15 July 1943, the following parts and components were distributed to the units: 10 V-2 engines, 2 transmission gear boxes and up to 20 metric tons of spare parts. Between 5 July 1943 and 15 July 1943, the following parts and components were forwarded to the Front depots for the repair and rehabilitation of tanks: 9 V-2 engines, 3 T-34 transmission gear boxes, 3 T-70 transmission gear boxes, and up to 15 metric tons of various components.

In addition to its regular roster of tank formations, on 5 July 1943 the **19th Tank Corps** was made operationally subordinate to the 2nd Tank Army. It had 8,156 officers and men, as well as the following amount of serviceable armor: 107 T-34, 25 T-70, 36 T-60, 19 Mk II and Mk III (Maltildas and Valentines), 39 armored cars and armored troop carriers, 30 76mm guns and 12 45mm guns, 2 37mm anti-aircraft guns, 271 machine guns and 64 mortars.

The caption reads, "Presentation of the 107th Tank Brigade's Combat Red Banner. Deputy Commander of the 16th Tank Corps Colonel A.A. Vitruk presents – Brigade commander Colonel N.M. Teliakov receives."

The command of the 16th Tank Corps poses with a group of top-rated tank drivers in the village of Sotnikovo, Central Front, 24 May 1943.

Table 2.3: Data on the effective combat strength of the 2nd Tank Army on 5 July 1943

| Unit | Men | | | | Rifles | Machine guns | | | | Mortars | | | Artillery | | | | Anti-tank rifles | Motor vehicles | Tanks | Armored cars | Anti-aircraft guns |
|---|---|---|---|---|---|---|---|---|---|---|---|---|---|---|---|---|---|---|---|---|---|
| | Command staff | Junior command staff | Enlisted men | Total | Total | PPD, PPSh | Light | Heavy | Anti-aircraft | 120mm | 82mm | 50mm | 107mm-203mm | 76mm ZiS-3 divisional | 76mm regimental | 45mm | | | | | |
| **3rd Tank Corps:** | | | | | | | | | | | | | | | | | | | | | |
| Command and corps units | 303 | 580 | 965 | 1,848 | 798 | 480 | 24 | | | | 4 | | | | | | | 228 | 32/1 | 52 | |
| 50th Tank Brigade | 212 | 455 | 456 | 1,123 | 409 | 267 | 20 | 4 | 10 | | 6 | | | 4 | | | 24 | 111 | 55 | 3 | |
| 51st Tank Brigade | 215 | 455 | 436 | 1,106 | 388 | 292 | 20 | 4 | 10 | | 6 | | | 4 | | | 24 | 111 | 53 | 3 | |
| 103rd Tank Brigade | 213 | 455 | 460 | 1,128 | 489 | 229 | 20 | 4 | 10 | | 6 | | | 4 | | | 24 | 115 | 53 | 3 | |
| 57th Motorized Rifle Brigade | 295 | 1,002 | 1,910 | 3,207 | 1,206 | 1,374 | 111 | 45 | 9 | 6 | 30 | | | 12 | | | 86 | 276 | | 19 | |
| 234th Mortar Regiment | 80 | 170 | 428 | 678 | 434 | 154 | 6 | | | 36 | | | | | | | | 112 | | | |
| 881st Anti-tank Regiment | 32 | 87 | 134 | 253 | 169 | 56 | | | | | | | 12 | | | 20 | 36 | 43 | | | |
| 728th Anti-tank Battalion | 26 | 70 | 130 | 226 | 69 | 132 | | | | | | | | | | 12 | 12 | 33 | | | |
| 121st Anti-aircraft Regiment | 39 | 103 | 250 | 392 | 258 | 112 | | | 16 | | | | | | | | | 48 | | | 0/16 |
| Total in the corps: | 1,415 | 3,377 | 5,169 | 9,961 | 4,220 | 3,096 | 201 | 57 | 56 | 42 | 52 | | 12 | 24 | | 32 | 206 | 1,077 | 193/1 | 80 | 0/16 |
| **16th Tank Corps:** | | | | | | | | | | | | | | | | | | | | | |
| Command and corps units | 299 | 646 | 902 | 1,847 | 872 | 316 | 50 | | | | 4 | | | | | | 20 | 193 | 40/3 | 27 | |
| 107th Tank Brigade | 213 | 425 | 451 | 1,089 | 482 | 343 | 20 | 4 | | | 6 | | | 4 | | | 24 | 87 | 55/1 | 2 | |
| 109th Tank Brigade | 195 | 424 | 458 | 1,077 | 403 | 350 | 18 | 4 | | | 6 | | | 4 | | | 24 | 80 | 53 | | |
| 164th Tank Brigade | 210 | 438 | 446 | 1,094 | 446 | 315 | 23 | 4 | | | 6 | | | 4 | | | 24 | 93 | 54 | | |
| 15th Motorized Rifle Brigade | 288 | 874 | 1,910 | 3,070 | 1,301 | 1,371 | 110 | 45 | 9 | 6 | 30 | | | 12 | | | 83 | 113 | | | |
| 226th Mortar Regiment | 79 | 155 | 364 | 598 | 434 | 144 | | | | 36 | | | | | | | | 28 | | | |
| 614th Anti-tank Regiment | 36 | 87 | 129 | 252 | 170 | 37 | | | | | | | 12 | | | 20 | 36 | 39 | | | |
| 729th Anti-tank Battalion | 28 | 70 | 126 | 224 | 69 | 132 | | | | | | | | | | 12 | 12 | 33 | | | |
| 1085th Anti-aircraft Regiment | 30 | 54 | 124 | 208 | 135 | 15 | 15 | | 9 | | | | | | | | | 15 | | | 0/11 |
| Total in the corps: | 1,378 | 3,173 | 4,910 | 9,461 | 4,312 | 3,023 | 221 | 57 | 18 | 42 | 52 | | 12 | 24 | | 32 | 223 | 681 | 202/4 | 29 | 0/11 |
| 11th Guards Tank Brigade | 198 | 505 | 401 | 1,104 | 389 | 281 | 20 | 4 | | | 6 | | | 4 | | | 24 | 86 | 54 | | |
| 51st Separate Motorcycle Battalion | 30 | 75 | 172 | 277 | 16 | 230 | 15 | | | | 4 | | | | | | 2 | 16 | | | |
| 24th Separate Reconnaissance Battalion | 35 | 104 | 63 | 202 | 56 | 86 | | | | | | | | | | | | 13 | | | |
| Grand Total | 3,036 | 7,234 | 10,715 | 21,005 | 8,993 | 6,716 | 457 | 118 | 74 | 84 | 114 | | 24 | 52 | | 64 | 455 | 1,873 | 449/5 | 109 | 0/27 |

## Preparatory measures for the operation

The task of the 2nd Tank Army was set on 27 May 1943 on the basis of the personal instructions of the Central Front's chief of staff Lieutenant General Malinin as given to the 2nd Tank Army's chief of staff Major General of Tank Forces Preisman, and on this day the army headquarters set to work on a plan for the defensive operation. There was sufficient time available to work out the operation's plan thoroughly and in detail. The plan eventually elaborated by the headquarters of the 2nd Tank Army consisted of three versions. Each version anticipated the 2nd Tank Army's action on one of three probable directions of enemy actions:

The First Option: The enemy would launch the main attack against the Nizh. Sergeevka, Panskaia sector in the direction of Fedorovka and Livny
The Second Option: The enemy would launch the main attack along the railroad to the south in the general direction of Ponyri and Zolotukhino
The Third Option: The enemy would launch the main attack out of the Kromy – Trosna area in the direction of Fatezh

According to the first option, that is, given a German offensive in the direction of Alekseevka, Droskovo and Livny, the 3rd and 16th Tank Corps were to shift to the Verkh. Sosna, Ivan', Andreevka area, and on the second or third day of the operation launch an attack in conjunction with the 17th Guards Rifle Corps in the general direction of Panskaia, i.e, at the base of the enemy penetration. If the enemy chose the second option and launched the main attack in the direction of Ponyri, Zolotukhino and Kursk, the 2nd Tank Army overnight before the second day of the operation was to move to the Berezovets, Ol'khovatka area and take up suitable jumping-off areas for launching counterattacks, with the 3rd Tank Corps positioned east of the Orel – Kursk railroad, and the 16th Tank Corps west of it. In dependence on the axis of the enemy offensive, one of the tank corps would receive the German attack, while the other tank corps would position itself on the flank of the enemy's main grouping and launch a flank attack against it. The execution of this plan was hindered by the Snova River, which was impassable to tanks, so additional bridges were constructed across it, while existing bridges were strengthened. According to the third plan option, if the enemy launched the main attack in the direction of Fatezh and Kurk, the 3rd and 16th Tank Corps would move to the Samodurovka area with the assignment to launch a counterattack toward Trosna.

In all three options, the jumping-off areas for deploying the tank corps were located 25-40 kilometers away from the army's area of concentration. The plan gave each corps two routes for its movement to its jumping-off area, and the movement was to be conducted at night with the calculation that the tank corps would be in their jumping-off positions by 10:00 on the following morning after the start of the enemy offensive. If the unfolding situation forced the tank corps to take up their jumping-off positions in daylight hours, then the tank corps would conduct the march in short columns (company, battalion), using byroads to conceal the movement. In that case, according to the preliminary calculations of the army headquarters, the assembly of the tank corps in their jumping-off areas would require 6-7 hours of time.

With the aim of keeping this plan of employment for the tank army secret, copies of it were not made, and only the original hand-written document of the plan was kept with the army's chief of staff. According to the plan, there would be no correspondence regarding it; all amendments and directions were given verbally, by means of travel to the units, as well as by the means of summoning the officers who were to implement the plan to army headquarters.

Since Germans adopted the Option No. 2, we shall take a closer look at the Central Front's plan to counter it. Given the enemy's main attack toward Ponyri, the rifle divisions of the 13th Army, which were deployed in the first line of defense, were to delay the attacking enemy, inflicting losses to attackers with the fire of the entire defensive system and with counterattacks by their second echelons. They were to hold their occupied sectors stubbornly and exhaust the enemy's strength. It was thought that no matter how strong the enemy attack might be, the troops of the 13th Army's first line of defense, relying upon the extensive and elaborate system of defensive fortifications, the support of their second echelons and the powerful artillery fire of the artillery corps, would be able to check the enemy advance for at least one day and not allow the Germans to reach the second line of defenses. The second defensive belt ran along the line: Maloarkhangel'sk, Fedorovka, Hill 257.1, 1st of May, northern outskirts of the Ponyri railroad station, Hill 248.5, Hill 244.2, Hill 223.0, Hill 231.1, northern outskirts of Podsoborovka and further along the line of the Svapa River. On average, the second defensive line lay 9-10 kilometers behind the first defensive line. While the Germans battered their way through the first line of defense and the intermediary lines in front of the second line of defense, which according to the Central Front's thinking would require anywhere from 24 hours to 2-3 days, the 17th and 18th Guards Rifle Corps situated in the 13th Army's reserve were to move up and occupy the line Mamoshino, Progress, Prilepy, Hill 256.9, Karpun'evka, Bitiug, Kashara. Independently of the hour of the start of the German attack, the 2nd Tank Army was to move out and be in position to counterattack by 10:00 on the following morning. The start line would run along Hill 264.2, Hill 256.9, Hill 248.6, 2nd Ponyri, Kutyrki, Leninskii; thus, the minimal time for the 2nd Tank Army to reach this line was calculated to be ten hours. With the German troops now out in the open, and with the German artillery compelled to change firing positions, and especially with the enemy strength worn down by the combat for the first line of defense and enmeshed within the defensive system, the troops of the 13th Army, introducing into the battle its fresh 17th and 18th Guards Rifle Corps, were to launch a general counteroffensive together with the forces of the 2nd Tank Army, to hurl the enemy back to his old positions, and on his heels break through his front line and develop the offensive in the general direction of Buzuluk, Krivye Verkhi, Baranovskii, Lazovets. Simultaneously, the 48th and 70th Armies were to go on the offensive. The 19th Tank Corps would be activated only in the event the Germans chose the third plan variant, in which case it was to occupy a defense along the Svapa River in the Molotychi – Iasenok sector. The 9th Tank Corps was in Central Front reserve.

## Preparation for the operation

Among the list of measures taken in the preliminary period were the following: the study of the enemy by means of using intelligence from *front* and army headquarters; the reconnoitering of the roads by the commanders of formations, units and elements and the study of the terrain in the sector of the pending operations; staff exercises directly on the ground of each of the possible variants of combat actions with officers of the corps; training with the troops to work out issues of cooperation between the tanks and the infantry and artillery; the analysis of the defensive fortifications in the second belt of our defenses, and of jumping-off and firing positions, ambush positions, observation posts and command posts, and mine fields; the preparation of the movement routes (repairing roads, building and repairing bridges, laying down portable road matting, arranging detours and improving fords); and the compilation of plans for logistic support.

On 2 June 1943, 2nd Tank Army headquarters sent Directive No.00381/OP to the subordinate corps headquarters and the headquarters of the 11th Guards Tank Brigade, which informed their commanders of the following: a) movement routes and alternate routes; b) jumping-off areas; c) lines of deployment; d) likely directions of attack; e) with whom to cooperate and with what; f) the locations for the headquarters of the army, the corps and 11th Guards Tank Brigade; g) and the general orders given to the commanders of the 3rd and 16th Tank Corps and of the 11th Guards Tank Brigade.

They were to study the routes of movement with the command staff down to the level of the company commanders inclusively, and the directions of attack down to the level of the platoon commanders inclusively. In addition, on the directions of attack, they were to determine: the jumping-off areas; the locations of the command post, an alternate command post, the observation post and an alternate observation post; the lines of deployment; the lanes of fire for actions out of ambushes and assembly areas; and simultaneously they were to establish the amount of needed work on bridges, down-grades, up-grades and so forth.

In order to fulfill the above given directive of the army headquarters, the subordinate headquarters and troops had to do a lot of work. The schedule of moving out, the time necessary for the marches, the loads for the wheeled transport, and the schedule for the movement of the loads and equipment, the artillery, ammunition, etc. were worked out in detail. By a special instruction of the army headquarters, the army's units performed a rehearse loading of the matériel onto the trucks. Officers of the Operations Department were assigned to the units to offer assistance with the haulage calculations and to check the correctness of the loading. As a result of this, the transport was fully relieved of unnecessary loads and was used maximally to transport ammunition supplies, gear, artillery and motorized infantry. The entire command staff down to the company commanders drove out to reconnoiter the routes, the jumping-off areas and the lines of deployment. Places were also identified for observations posts, operation posts and command posts, ambush positions and concealed lateral movements, and so forth. Areas for mine fields, located on the probable sectors of their actions, were studied and reported down to platoon commanders. An enormous amount of work was done to prepare the movement routes. Many bridges, roads, down-grades and bypasses were repaired and strengthened through the efforts of the army. For example, 69 bridges were built, 10 bridges were repaired, 29 bridges were reinforced, and 10 fords were arranged. Considering the presence of water obstacles in the area of the 2nd Tank Army's future operations, a sophisticated transportable wooden bridge on trestle supports was designed by the army's chief of engineering Colonel Levin. Before the start of the operation, a company of sappers was able to assemble this 20-meter-long transportable wooden bridge in just 90 minutes. During the army's combat operations, transportable plank bridges were used in the area of Ol'khovatka; under enemy fire, four such bridges were constructed, over which more than 250 tanks passed. The bridges were able to withstand the loading and showed great durability and solidity.

By way of personal visits and the exchange of documents regarding signals and plans, all matters of mutual cooperation were dovetailed by the army command and the command of the corps, and together with the units and headquarters of the 13th Army, 16th Air Army, 19th Tank Corps and with other units. Plans for the material, technical and artillery support for the operation were worked out in the headquarters of the army, the corps and the brigades.

On the basis of the personal reconnoitering by the commander of the 2nd Tank Army, Hero of the Soviet Union Guards Lieutenant General of Tank Forces Aleksei Rodin, the commanders of the formations were given instructions on where and how to operate (where to set up ambushes, where to dig in the tanks, where to place mobile reserves, where to position the artillery and so forth. At the same time, the question about occupying Hills 274.5 and 272.9 (5 kilometers east of Khmelevoe) was resolved. These two hills were outside the army's formal area of operation, but were key terrain for the Germans in order to reach operational space. This was subsequently confirmed by events: the enemy made strenuous efforts to take them, in order to break through along the highway leading to Fatezh and along the roads leading to Zolotukhino.

In the plan, documents regarding command and control over the troops were fully developed: radio signal tables and call signs of the command staff were compiled; maps were encoded; and documents regarding communications were produced. Plans for providing anti-aircraft cover while on the march and in the jumping-off areas were devised, as were decisions regarding the combat formations for the attacks and counterattacks.

With the aim of maintaining secrecy of the finished plan, the corps headquarters and the army headquarters were authorized to have only one hand-written copy of the document each. Correspondence regarding the plan was kept to a minimum. All directions, amendments and corrections were made verbally, by means of traveling out to the units or by summoning key individuals to the army headquarters. In order to keep the 2nd Tank Army's location concealed the use of radios while conducting the planning and preparatory work was banned. Several times in the month of June, massive sweeps were conducted in the areas of the army's dispositions to clean them of suspicious elements. The sweeps identified deserters, people who had previously collaborated with the Germans, and several clear spies.

As the planning was underway, group exercises were conducted with the command staff of the corps and brigades with visits to the actual ground along the planned approach routes, of the jumping-off positions and along the probable directions of attack. The exercises included command staff down to the battalion commanders inclusively. Systematic and intense exercises were conducted with the troops with an emphasis on gunnery and marches. The maneuvers as a rule were always "Red versus Blue".

The plan was ultimately finished by the middle of June, and adjusted in all its details by 25 June 1943. All the measures to prepare for the implementation of the plan were completed in the second half of June. The remaining time before the start of the offensive was used for troop drills, analysis of the situation and repair of the road network. The resolutely conducted preparatory measures to a significant degree facilitated the successful fulfillment by the troops of the 2nd Tank Army of the combat assignments they'd been given. By the start of the operation, the army had increased its stockpiles of artillery shells (3 combat loads), mortar shells (5 combat loads), fuel and lubricants (3 refills), and rations (7 days).

## The terrain

The combat operations of the 2nd Tank Army unfolded in a sector bounded on the right by the Snova River and on the left by a provisional line that passed through Verkh. Tagino, Teploe and Khmelevoe. The ground in the area of combat operations was cut by deep ravines and streams with steep, boggy and peaty banks, which complicated the movement of armor and artillery. The few patches of woods and brush, as well as the fact that the villages were only in the valleys of the streams and rivers greatly hindered the camouflaging of tanks and didn't allow maneuvers to be kept concealed from enemy eyes; this prompted the need for nighttime movements that were difficult to organize, time-consuming, and increased the overall fatigue of the personnel.

On the left flank of the 2nd Tank Army and in the area of Hills 274.5 and 272.9, the ground was less rough; the hills dominated the surrounding terrain and allowed observation of the battlefield, with views that extended out to a distance of 2 to 6 kilometers. In general, though, the terrain in army's sector of operations was open, but with a great number of streams and ravines, which complicated the army's operations. The area of operations was split from north to south by the Snova River, which as mentioned above was impassable for tanks and to a significant extent cramped the maneuver of the tank forces. Maneuver of tanks along the front was also complicated by the ravines and the large number of streams in the sector, which flowed into the Snova River from the east. To the west of the Snova River lay an elevated sector of ground, which served as the divide between the Snova and Usozha watersheds with their numerous tributaries. This ground was more suitable for tank operations, though as you proceed from north to south, the streams and ravines in places created corridors with a width of only 3-4 kilometers, which also constricted the maneuver of armor.

In general, the terrain in the sector of the 2nd Tank Army's operations facilitated the organization and conducting of defensive fighting; at the same time, the presence of the Snova River and the ravines and streams that cramped the freedom of maneuver of large armor formations on our side also cramped the enemy's movement. The nature of the terrain required thorough study and its preparation in an engineering sense for the success of the army's operations. While working out the second plan option, the terrain features were learned through numerous reconnaissance forays and exercises on the ground that included the command staff down to the platoon commanders inclusively. The roads and bridges were repaired, and corduroy roads, temporary crossings, up-grades, down-grades and fords were constructed.

## The overall situation and the Army's task

By the start of the July defensive operations, the Germans had assembled eight infantry, six panzer and two motorized divisions with a large quantity of reinforcing artillery units and separate panzer battalions in front of and on the flanks of the 13th Army, in the sector of which the 2nd Tank Army was operating. Of the 1,450 German tanks and assault guns opposite the Central Front, more than 1,000 had been concentrated by the Germans in front of the 13th Army and opposite the right flank of the 70th Army. Here, the following enemy panzer divisions had been identified by Soviet intelligence: the 2nd, 4th, 9th and 18th Panzer (of the XXXXI Panzer Corps); the 20th Panzer (of the XXXXVI Panzer Corps); and the 12the Panzer (of the XXXXVII Panzer Corps). In addition, the forces on this axis had been reinforced with the 505th Heavy Panzer Battalion (with 45 Tiger tanks), the 216th Battalion of 150mm Sturmpanzers (45 Brummbär), and one regiment of heavy tank destroyers (90 Ferdinands).

The bulk of the Central Front's tank forces were concentrated on the axis of the expected main enemy attack, which is to say, in the sector of the 13th Army and on the 70th Army's right flank. Here, in addition to the 129th Tank Brigade and eight tank regiments that were attached to the armies, were the Front's reserves, namely: the 2nd Tank Army consisting of the 3rd and 16th Tank Corps and the 11th Guards Tank Brigade in the Kondrinio – Khmelevoe – Banino – Koneva area; the 19th Tank Corps (the 79th, 101st and 202nd Tank Brigades) in the Verkh. Liubazh – Buzets Station area; and the 9th Tank Corps (the 23rd, 95th and 108th Tank Brigades and the 8th Motorized Rifle Brigade) in the Tsvetovo area.

The total number of Red Army tanks in the sector of the Germans' forthcoming offensive was 1,150. Thus, in the sector of the 13th Army and on the right flank of the 70th Army, our forces had a slight numerical superiority in tanks and self-propelled guns. However, the enemy had more heavy tanks, and in addition, the Germans had created a denser grouping of armor on the axis of the main attack, where they had managed to concentrate up to 45 tanks per kilometer of front. The 2nd Tank Army, reinforced with the 130th and 563rd Destroyer Anti-tank Artillery Regiments, the 226th and 234th Mortar Regiments, and the 121st Anti-aircraft Artillery Regiment, in dependence on the axis of the enemy's offensive was to conduct combat operations according to one of the variants, foreseen by the Central Front's plan.

## The adversary and the organization of reconnaissance

### The enemy grouping

On the northern shoulder of the Kursk bulge, the enemy had more than 1,000 tanks and assault guns facing the opposing forces of the Central and Briansk Fronts. As of 5 July 1943, the panzer formations consisted of the following:

2nd Panzer Division – 118 tanks (60 Pz. IV, 40 Pz. III, 12 Pz. II and 6 Pz. Bef)
4th Panzer Division – 101 tanks (80 Pz. IV, 15 Pz. III, 6 Pz. Bef)
9th Panzer Division – 98 tanks (38 Pz. IV, 53 Pz. III, 1 Pz. II and 6 Pz. Bef)

18th Panzer Division – 72 tanks (34 Pz. IV, 30 Pz. III, 5 Pz. II and 3 Pz. Bef)
505th Heavy Panzer Battalion – 45 Tigers
656th Heavy Panzerjäger Regiment, consisting of:
    653rd Heavy Panzerjäger Battalion: 45 Ferdinands
    654th Heavy Panzerjäger Battalion: 45 Ferdinands
    216th Sturmpanzer Battalion: 45 "Brummbär"
12th Panzer Division – 83 tanks (37 Pz. IV, 36 Pz. III, 6 Pz. II and 4 Pz. Bef)
20th Panzer Division – 82 tanks (49 Pz. IV, 17 Pz. III, 9 Pz38(t), 7 Pz. Bef)
78th Sturm Division equipped with Marder II and Marder III tank destroyers
10th Panzer Grenadier Division – (7th Panzer Battalion, 110th Panzer Reconnaissance Battalion, and a battalion of Marder II and Marder III)
177th Assault Gun Battalion – 31 StuG
185th Assault Gun Battalion – 32 StuG
189th Assault Gun Battalion – 31 StuG
244th Assault Gun Battalion – 31 StuG
245th Assault Gun Battalion – 31 StuG
904th Assault Gun Battalion – 31 StuG
909th Assault Gun Battalion – 31 StuG

The group's flanks were secured by:
5th Panzer Division – 102 tanks (76 Pz. IV, 17 Pz. III and 9 Pz. Bef)
8th Panzer Division – 100 tanks (22 Pz. IV, 55 Pz. III, 14 Pz. II, 3 Pz. 38(t) and 6 Bef)

## Intelligence regarding the enemy

Prior to the start of the operation, the 2nd Tank Army's Intelligence Department obtained intelligence about the enemy by means of organizing a broad network of observation posts in the sectors of the rifle divisions, which were run by the intelligence departments of the corps and the army; additional intelligence on the enemy from the headquarters of the rifle divisions operating on the Nikol'skii axis; aerial reconnaissance; and intelligence from the 13th Army's Intelligence Department and the Central Front's Intelligence Department. Based on the information regarding the enemy from these sources, the 2nd Tank Army's Intelligence Department was constantly updated about the size of the enemy's grouping, its disposition, the appearance of reserves, and his maneuvers. All of this information was promptly passed up to the army's Military Council and reported to subordinate forces. By the start of the enemy offensive on the Orel – Kursk axis, the 2nd Tank Army was fully aware of the enemy's attack grouping. In the assessment of the enemy's operational-tactical situation, given on 1 July 1943, it was ultimately determined that the enemy had created a shock grouping in the Zmievka – Kromy area, in readiness to go on the offensive in the Panskoe – Voronezh sector in a general direction toward Kursk.

By 5 July 1943, the enemy's 216th, 36th, 86th, 6th, 7th and 258th Infantry Divisions, 78th Sturm Division, and the 18th, 9th, 20th and 12th Panzer Divisions had assembled in the Panskoe – Arkhangel'skoe Voronezh – Glazunovka – Gremiachevo area and were ready to attack. The enemy was also bringing up the 2nd and 4th Panzer Divisions, the 292nd and 31st Infantry Divisions, and the 10th Panzer Grenadier Division out of the Karachev and Orel areas. Reinforcing assets included two heavy artillery regiments from the *Führer* Reserve, the 216th, 654th and 656th Assault Gun Battalions, the 53rd Mortar Regiment, and the 653rd Heavy Panzerjäger Battalion. In sum, eight infantry and five panzer divisions of the enemy had been identified in front of and on the flanks of the 13th Army, and in the immediate German rear.

According to prisoners from the 20th Panzer Division, the Germans were making intense preparations to go on the offensive. A captured German pilot of I/KG 53 indicated that his squadron was preparing to support a German ground offensive, and that the aim of the offensive was to encircle the Russian Kursk grouping. On 3 July 1943, information arrived that the enemy, having created a shock grouping in the Zmievka – Kromy area, was supposed to launch an offensive in the general direction of Kursk in the period between 3 July and 6 July 1943. On 4 July 1943, a German combat engineer from an army-level sapper battalion, who was taken prisoner in the area of Verkh. Tagino, gave the precise hour when the offensive would begin – at 03.00 on 5 July 1943. Thus, the enemy offensive on the Orel – Kursk axis was not a surprise to the army headquarters and didn't catch the army's troops unaware. By the moment of the German offensive, his grouping, its time of going on the offensive, and his likely directions of attack had been revealed. It remained to determine the boundaries of the offensive's front, which was revealed already in the process of the first day of fighting.

### The start of the operation

On the morning of 5 July 1943, the enemy went on the offensive in the Panskoe – Morozikha sector on a front of 45 kilometers, launching the main attack with the forces of the 9th, 18th, 20th and 12th Panzer Divisions, the 78th Sturm Division and the 86th, 6th, 7th and 258th Infantry Divisions. In reserve to exploit a success were the 2nd and 4th Panzer Divisions, the 31st and 292nd Infantry Divisions, and the 10th Panzer Grenadier Division. After a powerful artillery preparation and airstrikes, the enemy forces moved out and at the cost of enormous losses managed to make a 4-6 kilometer advance into the depth of our rifle divisions' defenses. Having no success in the course of 5-6 July 1943 in breaching our defenses and exploiting it with his mobile units into operational space, the enemy on 7 and 8 July 1943 committed the reserve 2nd and 4th Panzer Divisions and the 31st and 292nd Infantry Divisions into the battle, and shifted the 18th Panzer Division laterally from the area of Protasovo to the area of Ponyri.

With the introduction of the 2nd Tank Army into the fighting, thanks to the broad network of mobile observation posts, the active operations of reconnaissance groups, captured enemy documents and prisoners, the appearance of the fresh enemy units – the 4th and 9th Panzer Divisions, the 292nd Infantry Division and the 10th Panzer Grenadier Division – was timely revealed. The commitment of the 4th Panzer Division into the fighting on 8 July 1943 was detected by the seizure of a prisoner by our scouts. From an intercepted combat order to the 18th Panzer Division's 52nd Panzer Grenadier Regiment, the objectives of the 18th and 9th Panzer Divisions and the 252nd Infantry Division were learned. The timely exposure of the enemy's grouping and intentions allowed the army to take necessary countermeasures.

In the course of 8-11 July 1943, the enemy continued stubborn attacks in the Ponyri – Teploe sector, directing his main efforts against the center and left wing of the 2nd Tank Army, striving to break through to the south and southwest. By 11 July 1943, at the cost of heavy losses – up to 50 percent of tanks and more than 50 percent of men – the enemy managed to create a breach at the boundary between the 13th and 70th Armies and make a 6- to 15-kilometer advance into the depth of the defenses, and to reach the line Protasovo – Sidorovka – Ponyri Station – Berezovyi Log – Kashara – Teploe – Samodurovka.

By 12 July 1943, as a result of heavy losses, the enemy's shock grouping had run out of steam and went over to a defense on the aforementioned line. The enemy began a force regrouping, replacing the panzer divisions with infantry, and urgently shifted the 2nd, 9th, 12th, 18th and 20th Panzer Divisions northward to counter the breakthroughs made by the Briansk and Western Fronts. The enemy's shift to a defensive posture and the transfer of the panzer divisions indicated above to the north was timely revealed by the active operations of our reconnaissance groups and other types of intelligence.

In the period of the offensive, the enemy used the following attacking methods: a) powerful armored strike forces, reinforced with Ferdinand tank destroyers, were created with the task to breach our defenses, so that mobile units could be introduced into this breach; b) tanks were employed en masse, in groups of 30-200 in narrow sectors of the front, behind which infantry advanced, which consolidated points that were seized by the panzers; c) to foster the successful panzer operations, the tanks were supported by a large amount of artillery and aircraft. On the main axis of attack, the density of artillery amounted to 52 guns per kilometer. Air support for the panzers was expressed by the simultaneous appearance of up to 200 enemy aircraft above the combat formations of our forces on the front line. In the first days of the fighting, the enemy daily made up to 1,000 individual aircraft sorties against the 2nd Tank Army; d) the German panzers adopted a "bell" formation on the attack, with the heavy Pz. VI tanks and Ferdinands in the lead and on the flanks; e) on the defense, the enemy employed tanks as immobile firing positions, dug into the ground, intended for struggle with our tanks, or used them as a mobile reserve for counterattacks against our infantry; f) a new tactic employed by the enemy's panzer formations was to to avoid close-range combat with our tanks and to engage our tanks and anti-tank artillery with fire from a range no closer than 1,000 to 1,500 meters.

The enemy failed to break that line being held by the 2nd Tank Army and could not penetrate into the depth of our combat dispositions. The enemy's primary principles and tactic was confirmed in the offensive – to break through our defenses with panzer formations with the simultaneous introduction of mobile forces into the breach.

## Actions of the 2nd Tank Army in the defensive operation

The 13th Army and the 2nd Tank Army that opposed the enemy's eight infantry and five panzer divisions consisted of 11 rifle divisions and three tank corps. The yields the following correlation of forces on a front of 32 kilometers in the period between 5 and 8 July 1943 (see Table 2.4):

## Situation at the Kursk bulge by 5 July 1943

### Combat Operations of the 2nd Tank Army

Excerpts from the journal of daily entries of the Operations Department of the 2nd Tank Army's headquarters trace the response to the launching of the German offensive:

1. A conversation over the high frequency radio between Front Commander Colonel General Rokossovsky with Guards Lieutenant General Rodin, which took place at 9.30 on 5.7.43: "Operate according to Option 2. Move out immediately. Operate in small groups."
2. A conversation over Soviet teletype between Guards Lieutenant General Rodin and Major General Grigor'ev, which took place at 10.30 on 5.7.43: "Comrade Grigor'ev! Move out according to Option 2. Concealed movement in company-battalion elements. Fighter aircraft will cover you from the air. Immediately make contact with the infantry, artillery and tanks operating in front of you. Take up firing lines in the jumping-off area as defined by Option 2 and meet the enemy with fire from fixed positions. Further operations according to my orders. Step off immediately. Report on implementation." Further instructions followed: "Complete assembling by 20.00. Get situational reports from the units located in front of you. Report every two hours. Pay attention so that all personnel clearly know [the location of] our mine fields while operating."

**Table 2.4: Correlation of forces on the front of the 2nd Tank Army and 13th Army in the period from 5 July to 13 July 1943**

| | Tanks | | | Guns | | | | Mortars | Total guns and mortars | Anti-tank rifles | Machine guns | Aircraft |
|---|---|---|---|---|---|---|---|---|---|---|---|---|
| | Heavy | Medium | Total | Heavy | Light | Medium | Total | | | | | |
| Germans: 2nd Panzer Army: 216, 78, 86, 6, 7, 36, 292 and 31 ID; 18, 20, 2, 9, and 4 PzD; 653 Tiger Bn. and artillery reinforcements | 224 | 650 | 874 | 248 | 767 | 669 | 1,684 | 1,533 | 3,217 | 1,038 | 7,200 | 700 |
| Red Army: 2nd Tank Army: 3, 16 and 19 TC, 11 GTBr; | – | 607 | 607 | – | 110 | 72 | 182 | 258 | 440 | 645 | 912 | |
| 13th Army: 8, 148, 81 and 15 RD, 129 TBr and 5 separate tank regiments; | – | 260 | 260 | 152 | 930 | 441 | 1,523 | 616 | 2,139 | 848 | 2,416 | |
| 9, 18 and 17 RC and 13 RD of 70th Army; | – | 208 | 208 | – | 640 | 386 | 1,026 | 1,258 | 2,284 | 2,125 | 4,851 | |
| 16th Air Army | – | – | – | – | – | – | – | – | – | – | – | 500 |
| Total: | – | 1,075 | 1,075 | 152 | 1,680 | 899 | 2,731 | 2,132 | 4,863 | 3,617 | 8,179 | 500 |
| *Average operational density per kilometer of front* | | | | | | | | | | | | |
| Germans | 7 | 20 | 27 | 8 | 24 | 21 | 53 | 48 | 101 | 32 | 225 | 22 |
| Red Army | – | 34 | 34 | 5 | 52 | 28 | 85 | 66 | 151 | 113 | 225 | 16 |
| *Correlation of Forces:* | | | | | | | | | | | | |
| Germans | | | 1 | | | | 1 | 1 | 1 | 1 | 1 | 1.4 |
| Red Army | | | 1.3 | | | | 1.6 | 1.4 | 1.5 | 3.5 | 1 | 1 |

3.   Conversation between Lieutenant General Rodin and Major General Sinenko over teletype, which took place at 10.37 on 5.7.43: "Immediately move out according to Option 2. Move in small groups of a company and not more than a battalion. Assembly on the lines in the new area by 20.00. Take up firing positions in the new area and meet the enemy with fire from place; employ ambushes. Further actions from the new area by a following order. Aviation covers you from 12.00. Direct the personnel's attention to awareness of [our] mine fields to avoid a detonation. Immediately send out reconnaissance and a screening detachment, and establish contact with the units that are operating in front of you. Grigor'ev is operating on your left. In front of you are our units in [their] former composition. Report on the initiation of moving out and subsequently every two hours. Position the command post according to the previously foreseen plan." Sinenko: "Everything is clear. I'm moving out."

4.   Combat Order No. 042/OP from the commander of the 2nd Tank Army, at 12.00 5.7.43: "From 5.30 5.7.43, up to three infantry divisions and up to three tank divisions of the enemy went on the attack across the entire front of the 13th Army. By 10.40 [the enemy] seized Protasovo, the northern outskirts of Buzuluk, Ochki, Sokol'niki, Hill 243.9, Ozerki and Novaia Poliana. The 2nd Tank Army's formations are to take up a jumping-off position by 19.00 5.7.43: 3rd Tank Corps – the villages Gorianovo, Ponyri Heights, northern outskirts of Berezovets, northern outskirts of Gorodishche. Corps headquarters – grove west of Hill 258.5. 16th Tank Corps – 2nd Ponyri, Kutyrki. Corps headquarters – woods 1 kilometer south of Hill 251.4. 11th Guards Tank Brigade – initiate movement at 22.00 5.7.43." By Combat Order No. 043/OP, the Guards Brigade began moving out at 19.00 5.7.43. "The Army's formations are to be ready to launch a counterattack at dawn on 6.7.43 in the general direction of Arkhangel'sk. Upon reaching the jumping-off areas take up firing lines and meet the enemy with fire from place. Further operations at my direction. Link operations with the units of the 13th Army located in front. The entire command staff of the acting units is to know the mine fields in the areas of their operations. Pay particular attention to securing the flanks, to the organization of reconnaissance, and to the maintenance of communications with the cooperating units according to Variant No. 2. Report: on the time of the attack at 14.00, and subsequently every two hours and on the time of the assembly at 19.00."

5.   Telegram from the 3rd Tank Corps over the signature of Major General Sinenko, received at 22.00 5.7.43: "The 3rd Tank Corps at 19.30 5.7.43 according to Option 2 has assembled in full."

6.   Radiogram from the 11th Guards Tank Brigade over the signature of Captain Nosenko, received at 21.00 5.7.43: "The 11th Guards Tank Brigade at 20.00 has assembled in full according to Variant No. 2."

7.   Report from Colonel Kocherin to Colonel Preisman over the telephone at 21.00 5.7.43: The 16th Tank Corps at 20.00 5.7.43 has assembled: 107th Tank Brigade – on the line Point 246.9, Kutyrki; the 109th Tank Brigade – in the woods west of Osinovyi; 164th Tank Brigade – Gnedovishche, Point 240.0; the 614th Destroyer Anti-tank Artillery Regiment – has occupied firing positions on the line: northwestern outskirts of Bitiug, 1.5 kilometers northwest of Point 246.9; the 15th Motorized Rifle Brigade – with one battalion west of Ol'khovatka, two battalions – northern outskirts of Stanovoe. The Corps' complement and supplies, with the exception of fuel and lubricants, are without change."

The enemy began its artillery preparation at 3.30 on 5 July 1943, and after a 40-minute barrage and with the accompaniment of several hundred aircraft, the infantry and tanks went on the attack in the sector Panskaia – Maloarkhangel'sk Station, which is to say against the right flank of the 13th Army. The 216th and 86th Infantry Divisions, the 78th Storm Division, several *Jaeger* battalions and the 18th Panzer Division were committed to the opening attack. However, this was only an auxiliary attack, which was quickly repelled by the forces of the 13th Army. The enemy's main attack was launched in a sector only 10-12 kilometers wide that stretched between Arkhangel'skoe and Verkh. Tagino with the forces of two panzer divisions (the 20th and 2nd Panzer) and two infantry divisions (the 6th and 7th Infantry). This attack struck the 81st and 15th Rifle Divisions. Under the effects of powerful artillery fire and airstrikes, and with their lines disrupted by enemy tanks that were breaking through, the divisions in places began to retreat, while in other locations isolated units of these divisions continued to fight in encirclement. The enemy, accompanied by the fire of artillery and mortars as well as airstrikes, began to advance into the depth of our defenses. The enemy artillery and mortars concentrated their fire on all the heights, gullies and locations of expected troop concentrations, or on aggregations of reserves and of artillery batteries. The *Luftwaffe* in groups of 60-80 aircraft were constantly in the air above the battlefield and were working over each 100 square meters of terrain, laying down a path for the tanks and infantry.

The combat formation adopted by the German forces had the heavy Ferdinand self-propelled guns attacking in the front, followed by Tigers and medium tanks. The Tigers and Ferdinands attacked along the elevated crests in single file. If it was necessary to change direction, the tank or self-propelled gun would stop, back up into cover, change direction, and then continue to carry out its assigned combat task in the new direction. Fire was usually conducted from a range of 1.5 to 2 kilometers. Behind the heavy tanks and self-propelled guns, maneuvering, were the medium and light tanks. Infantry followed behind the tanks. Artillery by its fire would secure the advance of this entire combat formation.

Characteristically, the enemy artillery and air force were only working over the first belt of our defenses. The second defensive belt was untouched by enemy air or artillery attack, while the railroad, train stations where supplies and troops were unloaded, and ground routes of communication were not subjected to enemy air raids. The enemy unleashed all of its powerful airstrikes only against the forward edge of the defenses.

The panzers attacked in two groups. On the secondary axis, 100 armored vehicles were attacking simultaneously on a front of 10-12 kilometers, while up to 200 armored vehicles attacked within a 6- to 8-kilometer front on the main axis of attack.

In connection with the withdrawal of the 13th Army's combat formations, already at 9.30 on 5 July 1943, the Front commander issued a combat order over high-frequency radio to the commander of the 2nd Tank Army: "Immediately go into action according to Option 2. Move to the jumping-off area in small groups: company or battalion." At 10.30 on 5.7.1943, the commander of the 2nd Tank Army personally gave a combat order to the commanders of 3rd and 16th Tank Corps over teletype: "Operate according to the second variant. Move out immediately, and complete assembly by 19.00 5.7.1943." Located in Army reserve, the 11th Guards Tank Brigade was given its order via a signals officer.

Each corps and the 11th Guards Tank Brigade marched along its own routes. Each corps was given two main routes, in addition to alternate routes. Forward detachments (the composition and assignment of which were determined while working out the plan variant) were sent ahead to secure the assembly areas of the tank corps. In addition, the individual tank brigades sent forward reconnaissance and combat security detachments along their routes. The 2nd Tank Army's march was covered by fighters of the 16th Air Army, beginning at 13.00 on 5.7.1943.

The 2nd Tank Army didn't have its own sector (front) of defense, but was situated within the combat dispositions of the 13th Army, which created difficulties in command and control over the battle. The advancing combat formations of the 2nd Tank Army ran into retreating units of the 13th Army that were jamming the roads, which were also being used by the 17th and 18th Rifle Corps to move up to the front. One after another of the combat formations of the infantry and artillery units merged and became intermingled, which created confusion and chaos in command. When it came time for the tank corps to counterattack the enemy together with the infantry, the commanders of the tank brigades, having difficulty locating the commanders of the rifle divisions, were unable to organize cooperation with them, while because of the intermingling of the rifle units, command and control by the commanders of the rifle divisions over their own subordinate troops was temporarily disrupted totally. If the commanders of the 2nd Tank Army hadn't had a firm grasp of their destinations and assignments, then the disorder created by the simultaneously withdrawing and approaching units might have seriously and adversely affected the 2nd Tank Army's successful combat.

At 12.00 on 5.7.1943, the tank corps were already on the move and advancing in short columns along their routes toward the areas that had been designated for them, outpacing the units of the 17th Rifle Corps, which were also being brought up to the breakthrough area. The 2nd Tank Army commander had instructed the tank corps to move into firing positions and deploy into ambush positions upon reaching the new areas. However, as the tanks corps of the 2nd Tank Army were moving up, the situation on the front of the 13th Army deteriorated, and the left wing of that army, albeit slowly, was retreating to the south. At 12.00, the Central Front commander Rokossovsky issued a supplementary order to the commander of the 2nd Tank Army – with the forces of the 16th Tank Corps and the 11th Guards Tank Brigade, to counterattack the enemy tanks that had supposedly broken through to the Ol'khovatka, Kashara area.

However, this counterattack on 5 July 1943 never took place, because actually there were no enemy tanks in this area; inaccurate information on the lines reached by the adversary was arriving at the Front and army headquarters. At this time, the enemy was still fighting on the line Ochki – Okop. Besides this, the tank corps were still on the approach to their jumping-off areas and were stretched out along the entire march routes in small groups. They could only have been thrown into the attack piecemeal, which didn't correspond to the situation.

While the 3rd and 16th Tank Corps were on the move toward their assigned areas, unaffected by enemy aircraft, which were occupied with the task of securing their own tanks' advance, the 19th Tank Corps, which according to the initial plan had been designated for actions as part of the 70th Army, by an order of the Front commander at 12.20 passed instead to the 2nd Tank Army, with the mission to reach the line Molotychi, Petroselki, Novoselki, Sergeevka, Iasenok. There it was to meet the enemy with fire from place and to be ready to launch a counterattack along previously indicated directions. The start time for the counterattack was supposed to be given by a following message. By 19.00 on 5 July, the 19th Tank Corps reached the area that had been designated for it and received an order from the chief of staff of the Central Front's Armored and Mechanized Forces to move out to the Krasavka – Nikol'skoe – Samodurovka area and to counterattack the enemy immediately in the direction of Podolian'.

The enemy by this time had taken Saborovka with tanks and had broken through to Samodurovka. However, the counterattack of the 19th Tank Corps also didn't take place on this day, because the corps didn't have its own artillery, and for the counterattack it was supposed to receive cooperation and support from the artillery of the rifle divisions that were operating on this axis. While the corps was trying to arrange this and to get a grasp of the operational situation, darkness fell and the counterattack was postponed to the next day.

By the end of 5 July 1943, the 2nd Tank Army had reached its assigned jumping-off area, and was situated as follows: 3rd Tank Corps – woods northwest of Brusovoe, Point 250.0, southern outskirts of Berezovets, northern outskirts of Brusovoe; 16th Tank Corps – between 2nd Ponyri, Ol'khovatka and Osinovyi; the 19th Tank Corps in the course of the night was moving up into its assigned jumping-off area for the counterattack and only by 6.00 6.7.1943 had it assembled in the area Nikol'skoe – Krasnoplavskii and the northeastern outskirts of Teploe – Molotychi; the 11th Guards Tank Brigade had assembled by 20.30 in some woods 2 kilometers northeast of Gornyi. From the first day until the final day of the operation, the commander of the 2nd Tank Army Lieutenant General Rodin was at the command post of the 16th Tank Corps commander in some woods west of Osinovyi. The army headquarters remained in the area of Skorodnoe-1 and served to link Rodin with Front headquarters and the headquarters of neighboring formations.

The tank corps, having reached the areas designated for them by order of the army commander, began to dig in and to camouflage their positions thoroughly; in their own orders, the corps commanders had stressed that the main method of battling with the enemy should be "with actions out of ambush positions; from fixed positions shoot up the enemy's tanks that have broken through and wipe out the infantry" (from Combat Order No. 1 of the 16th Tank Corps issued at 15.15 on 5.7.1943). The enemy by the end of the day had made on average a 6- to 8-kilometer advance and had been stopped by troops of the 13th Army and the arriving 17th Guards Rifle Corps on the line: northern outskirts of Trosna, southern outskirts of Soglasnyi, Kleniniskii, north of Rzhavets, Druzhovetskii, Bobrik, and by the neighboring 132nd Rifle Division of the 70th Army on the line Gnilets, Probuzhdenie, Izmailovo. Thus, the enemy on the first day of the offensive had been unable to breach completely the 13th Army's first belt of defenses. According to a Soviet estimate, the enemy on the first day of the battle had lost 138 tanks in mine fields alone. In order to resume the offensive on the next day, the enemy introduced fresh forces and shifted its main efforts to the boundary between the 13th Army and the 70th Army, having as its aim to reach the Orel – Fatezh highway.

Thus, on 5 July the tank corps of the 2nd Tank Army and the 19th Tank Corps did not enter the fighting. The entire day was spent moving to the jumping-off areas that had been set for them. By the end of 5 July, the direction of the enemy's main attack, which ran somewhat to the west of the Orel – Kursk railroad had been conclusively identified. In these operational conditions, the forces, deployed according to Option 2, which anticipated an enemy offensive along the railroad, didn't fully respond to the existing situation, and thus the Front commander made corresponding adjustments to the plan. At 22.00 5 July 1943, an order from the Central Front commander arrived in the headquarters of the 2nd Tank Army, in which the army was given a new task:

> The 3rd Tank Corps is to go over to a defense on the line Gorianovo, Gorodishche; the 16th Tank Corps in cooperation with units of the 17th Guards Rifle Corps is to go on the attack at dawn on 6 July in the general direction toward Step' and Butyrki, with the mission to restore the situation on the 13th Army's left flank; the 19th Tank Corps will launch an attack toward Saborovka and Podolian'. The commanders of the 13th and 70th Armies, making use of the tank corps' attacks, are to regain the previous position on the front of their armies and are to dig in firmly.

The night of 5/6 July was used to prepare for the counterattack in correspondence with the Front commander's order. The 16th Tank Corps took up jumping off positions in the vicinity of 2nd Ponyri and Kutyrki; the 19th Tank Corps, having received the assignment to attack in a direction that was new for it, lost a lot of time reconnoitering the terrain and preparing passages through the combat formations of friendly infantry. In particular a lot of time was spent on creating passages through the minefields and other anti-tank obstacles, which had been set up by our troops in the depth of the defense, since no one could accurately indicate where they had been placed. As a result, the 19th Tank Corps was not only unready to attack by morning, but even by noon on the following day, and thus took no part in the counterattack that was launched by units of the 16th Tank Corps and the 17th Guards Rifle Corps.

## The 2nd Tank Army's counteroffensive on 6 July 1943

By the morning of 6 July, the 13th Army had been reinforced by the 15th and 17th Guards Rifle Corps from the Front reserve, which were occupying the second defensive line in front of the 2nd Tank Army, thereby covering the tank corps. At 5.00 6 July 1943, the 16th Tank Corps launched a disorganized counterattack with two brigades in a general direction toward Ol'khovatka, Step' and Butyrki. The attack was supported by the 4th Breakthrough Artillery Corps and two self-propelled artillery regiments. The 107th Tank Brigade led off the attack, moving out from the line Snova – Podsoborovka in the direction of Hill 231.1, Step', and Okop.

With the start of the counterattack, German artillery and self-propelled guns opened fire at the combat formations of the 107th Tank Brigade. The infantry following behind the tanks, taking casualties, began to lag somewhat behind. With a further advance, the enemy allowed the tanks into the depth of their positions, and there met them with the fire of 16 Tiger tanks and up to 70 medium and light tanks. Ferdinand tank destroyers also contributed to the maelstrom of enemy anti-tank fire. The 107th Tank Brigade, having lost 29 T-34 and 17 T-70 knocked-out or left burning in a short period in this action, with its remaining four tanks fell back behind its infantry and re-assembled in some woods west of Osinovyi.

An hour after the unsuccessful attack by the 107th Tank Brigade, the 164th Tank Brigade went on the attack from the line Kashara, Samodurovka in the Podsoborovka, Step' direction. The brigade encountered up to 150 enemy tanks, and in the unequal contest with the enemy's superior tank forces lost 17 T-34 and 6 T-70, before being compelled to fall back to its jumping-off position.

So instead of a synchronized, powerful counterattack by the 16th and 19th Tank Corps, units of the 107th and 164th Tank Brigades were thrown piecemeal into the attack and suffered large losses (89 tanks). Having repelled the uncoordinated counterattack by the tank brigades of the 16th Tank Corps, the enemy infantry and tanks resumed their advance in the direction of Ol'khovatka with intensive air support. Units of the 17th Guards Rifle Corps, left without armor, went over to a defense on the line they had reached, hurling back fierce attacks by the German panzers and infantry. Although the counterattack by the 16th Tank Corps was indeed a failure, nevertheless it had pre-empted and disrupted the planned staging of a powerful assault by the enemy, which had assembled up to 300 tanks in the area of Butyrki for this purpose. This to a significant extent eased the task of the defending 17th Guards Rifle Corps.

The commander of the 19th Tank Corps, having received word of the results of the counterattack by the 107th and 164th Tank Brigades, refrained from making an immediate attack and appealed to the commanders of the 132nd and 15th Rifle Divisions for artillery support. The 19th Tank Corps spent almost the entire day organizing cooperation and preparing for the counterattack by clearing mines to create passages through the minefields, and thus it went on the offensive only at 18.30. By 20.00, the corps' brigades were fighting with enemy tanks on the line: 79th Tank Brigade – Samodurovka, Krasavka; the 101st Tank Brigade – western outskirts of Saborovka; and the 202nd Tank Brigade – western outskirts of Bobrik. The enemy met the attacking tanks with artillery fire from concealed positions and the fire of heavy tanks. The enemy also struck the combat formations of the tank brigades from the air with up to 100 aircraft. The motorized rifle battalions of the tank brigades became separated from the tanks by the enemy artillery fire. In view of this, and as well the losses already suffered, the attack was cancelled and the corps received the order of the 2nd Tank Army commander to take up a defense in the Teploe, Krasavka area, with two brigades in reserve.

At the same time as the meeting engagements with enemy tanks were occurring on the 2nd Tank Army's left flank, on the right flank of the 13th Army the enemy in strength of two infantry and one panzer division was attacking the defensive positions of the 81st Rifle Division, and forced it to retreat. The 74th and 307th Rifle Divisions of the 15th Rifle Corps and the 103rd Tank Brigade of the 3rd Tank Corps were brought up to this point of danger. At 10.00 30 enemy tanks advanced out of the Ponyri area, and passing through the combat positions of the infantry of the 13th Army, they attacked units of the 3rd Tank Corps. With the fire of the 3rd Tank Corps' 881st Destroyer Anti-tank Artillery Regiment and with counterattacks by its 103rd Tank Brigade, the enemy tanks were driven back. At 11.30, the enemy made another attack with up to 40 tanks with artillery and air support. This attack was again repelled with heavy losses for the enemy. The

881st Destroyer Anti-tank Artillery Regiment and the 103rd Tank Brigade in this battle destroyed a total of 40 enemy tanks. Having repelled the attacks of up to 100 enemy tanks, by the end of the day they had stopped the enemy and had dug in, with the 74th Rifle Division on the line Sidorovka, Dobrovka and the 307th Rifle Division on the line 2nd Nikol'skoe, 1st of May State Farm, northern outskirts of Ponyri. Backing them up was the 3rd Tank Corps on the defensive lines it had occupied the evening before.

The enemy's main attack on this day, however, had been concentrated west of the railroad. Having repelled the disorganized counterattacks by the 16th Tank Corps' tank brigades in the morning, the enemy went on the offensive with the 2nd and 20th Panzer Divisions of the XXXXI Panzer Corps and the 6th and 7th Infantry Divisions, supported by massed airstrikes, and pressed back the units of the 15th and 132nd Rifle Divisions, which were positioned in front of the 2nd Tank Army's left flank. With the commitment of the 17th Rifle Corps into the fighting, the enemy advance was stopped. In order to secure the boundary between the 70th Rifle Division and the 19th Tank Corps, at 15.40 on 6 July Lieutenant General Rodin deployed his reserve, the 11th Guards Tank Brigade, on the line Hill 274.5, Molotychi, and ordered the brigade to organize an anti-tank region.

The enemy, having detected the relocation of the 11th Guards Tank Brigade and the work that it was conducting, struck the brigade's position at 18.00 with 48 Stuka dive bombers. As a result of the bombing, 2 tanks caught fire, but the crews were able to suppress the flames and kept the tanks serviceable. There were no losses in men.

By Combat Order No. 045/OP, the commander of the 2nd Tank Army instructed all the corps to dig-in their tanks on the lines they occupied and to screen the infantry, and with an organized system of fire not to allow a single enemy tank to pass through their combat positions. On 6 July 1943 the 2nd Tank Army also received an order from the commander of the Central Front about shifting the 3rd Tank Corps to a defensive posture. Having moved out to the second defensive belt, the 3rd Tank Corps went on the defense on the line Berezovets, Gorodishche. At the decision of the corps commander General M.S. Sinenko, the 57th Motorized Rifle and the 51st and 103rd Tank Brigades were deployed in the first echelon of the defense, while the 50th Tank Brigade was in reserve.

The 57th Motorized Rifle Brigade assumed a defense on a line running between Berezovskie Vyselki and a hut on the railroad (2 kilometers south of Ponyri), having created three anti-tank regions on a front of 9 kilometers. The 728th Destroyer Anti-tank Battalion and the 881st Destroyer Anti-tank Regiment were occupying firing positions behind the first echelon of the motorized rifle brigade. The tank brigades received the assignment to hold the areas they occupied stubbornly, and to be ready to launch counterattacks. Tank ambushes were deployed in order to cover the flanks and to secure the boundaries.

As a result of the second day of combat, the enemy at the cost of heavy losses managed to advance another 1 to 2 kilometers and to close upon the forward edge of the 13th Army's second defensive belt, which was directly in front of the area of the 2nd Tank Army's deployment. The enemy attacks, which continued for the entire day of 6 July, had been fruitless; not a single enemy tank broke through the combat formations of the 2nd Tank Army.

### From the Operational Summary of Central Front headquarters No. 00283/op to the Chief of the General Staff on the Course of the Defensive Operation

6 July 1943, 22.00

The troops of the Central Front on the Orel – Kursk axis continued defensive fighting with attacking enemy infantry and tanks during the day of 6.7. On the rest of the front, our troops were defending and holding their existing lines, and conducting reconnaissance of the enemy. With part of its force, the 2nd Tank Army in cooperation with units of the 13th Army fought to repel enemy attacks. The 16th Tank Corps – the 107th Tank Brigade together with infantry of the 13th Army launched a counterattack in the direction of Step', but having run into an ambush by **18 enemy Pz. VI Tiger tanks** [Author's emphasis] and organized artillery fire, the brigade lost as a result of the combat 29 T-34 tanks, 17 T-70 tanks, with 2 T-70 tanks missing in action. The 164th Tank Brigade – after combat in the Druzhevitskii area was withdrawn to the line: woods north of Kashara, Ponyri. The 109th Tank Brigade, 15th Motorized Rifle Brigade and 226th Mortar Regiment are on the line 2nd Ponyri, Ol'khovatka. The 3rd Tank Corps is in its previous area. At 11.30, forces of the 103rd Tank Brigade and 881st Destroyer Anti-tank Artillery Regiment fought against 40 enemy tanks in the area south of 1st Ponyri. As a result of the action, 8 [enemy] tanks were destroyed, and the remaining enemy tanks were scattered. The 11th Guards Tank Brigade at 16.30 was deployed on the line Hill 274, Molotychi.

Malinin, KRAMAR

## Results of the second day of fighting

The enemy, having assembled 100-200 tanks on a front of 2 to 3 kilometers, attempted to break through the defense of the rifle units. In order to support the ground troops, the enemy on the front of the 2nd Tank Army and 13th Army conducted 2,293 individual aircraft sorties. As a result of the fighting the enemy, having lost several dozen tanks in mine fields, in combats with tanks and from artillery fire, advanced by 2-3 kilometers and closed upon the forward edge of

A series of photos showing knocked-out tanks of the 16th Tank Corps in the Butyrki area,
6 July 1943.

A series of photos
showing knocked-out
tanks of the 16th Tank
Corps in the Butyrki
area, 6 July 1943.

the 13th Army's second defensive belt. The 2nd Tank Army with a portion of its tanks in cooperation with the 17th Guards Rifle Corps and rifle divisions of the 13th Army counterattacked the enemy and repelled major enemy tank attacks. Over the day of combat, the Army lost 69 tanks. The losses in tanks might have been smaller, if the actions of the 16th and 19th Tank Corps been better coordinated. However, the efforts of the 16th Tank Corps were not in vain. The enemy in the course of the day tried repeatedly to develop the offensive, but the appearance of our tanks, the presence of a well-organized anti-tank system of fire and the well-designed fortified belt affected the enemy's actions. The enemy attacked quite cautiously and slowly. The enemy's XXXXI Panzer Corps (the 2nd and 20th Panzer Divisions) deployed on a front of 8-10 kilometers and prepare to continue the offensive. However, this attack, with the appearance of the 107th and 164th Tank Brigades, broke up into several nodes of combat, and this eased the struggle with the attacking enemy tanks for the artillery of the 17th Guards Rifle Corps, which was fully deployed into firing positions.

General Bogdanov later summarized the day:

> On 6 July 1943, with no consideration of the situation, two tank brigades of the 2nd Tank Army were hurled into a counterattack with the task of liquidating a breakthrough by the enemy's tank groups. The 107th Tank Brigade was operating in front, and echeloned behind it was the 164th Tank Brigade. Over two hours of combat, the brigades forced the enemy to fall back a short distance, but subsequently on the 107th Tank Brigade was met by the fire of 16 Tiger tanks and of medium tanks. Having lost 46 tanks, the 107th Tank Brigade pulled back to its jumping-off position. After the withdrawal of the 107th Tank Brigade, the 164th Tank Brigade continued to attack, and having run into 150 tanks, engaged them in battle. As a result of the unequal combat, the brigade lost 23 tanks and fell back to its jumping-off position. This example speaks to the fact that with no consideration of the enemy's strength, the tank brigades, launching the counteroffensive, suffered significant losses, without achieving any success.

## Actions of the 2nd Tank Army on 7 July 1943

On the third day of the operation, the army continued to repel strong enemy attacks from the Ponyri – Saborovka – Bobrik direction. The enemy in the course of the day brought down heavy artillery and mortar fire on the combat formations of the Soviet forces and conducted frequent massed bombing raids. Over the course of the day, they flew more than 800 individual combat sorties against the forces of the 2nd Tank Army. The enemy's efforts were concentrated on three directions: along the railroad in the 3rd Tank Corps' sector of defense; between Bitiug and Kashara in the 16th Tank Corps' sector of defense; and at Samodurovka, Teploe at the boundary between the 16th and 19th Tank Corps. The enemy, having replenished the battered divisions of the XXXXI Panzer Corps with reserve tanks, also committed the fresh 9th Panzer Division into the fighting and made another attempt to breach the front of the defending 13th Army and 2nd Tank Army.

After a powerful mortar and artillery preparation, with the accompaniment of 100-150 combat aircraft the 18th Panzer Division attacked the 307th Rifle Division and pushed it back. By 12.30 the Soviet division had abandoned the 1st of May State Farm and Ponyri. German tanks and infantry managed to break into Ponyri and to seize this key railroad hub on the Orel – Kursk road. However, a counterattack by Colonel G.M. Maksimov's 103rd Tank Brigade (3rd Tank Corps), supported by the 1023rd Rifle and 881st Destroyer Anti-tank Regiments drove the Germans back out of Ponyri. The Nazis left 30 burned-out tanks on the battlefield. The 103rd Tank Brigade lost 7 tanks. At 15.00 the enemy attempted again to attack on this same axis, but had no success.

In the sector of defense of the 16th Tank Corps' 109th Tank Brigade, the enemy introduced the 9th Panzer Division. Having deployed up to 150 tanks and assault guns on a front of 9-10 kilometers between Hill 243.8 and Snova, the Germans broke through the defenses of the 6th Rifle Division, shoved back its left flank, and seized Bitiug. Met on this line by the fire of dug-in tanks of the 109th Tank Brigade and tanks of the 48th and 58th Tank Regiments, as well as by the fire of the 614th Destroyer Anti-tank Artillery Regiment, the Germans were stopped and were unable to make any further advance.

At 15.30, up to two enemy infantry divisions with the support of up to 150 tanks of the 2nd Panzer Division, among which were Tiger tanks, and with artillery and air support, attempted to break through the defenses of the 75th Guards Rifle Division and the 140th Rifle Division in the sector of Hill 257.0 in the direction of Kashara. Thanks to the organized fire of the rifle divisions and the dug-in tanks of the 16th Tank Corps, the enemy was compelled to fall back, having left more than 40 knocked-out tanks on the battlefield.

The 19th Tank Corps by dawn on 7 July 1943 had only just taken up a defense in the sector of operations designated for it and was in the process of digging in its tanks. The disposition and tasks of the 19th Tank Corps' subordinate brigades were as follows: the 79th Tank Brigade – Point 240.0 – Teploe, with the task in conjunction with the 140th Rifle Division to prevent an enemy breakthrough in the Samodurovka, Teploe direction; the 26th Motorized Rifle Brigade – eastern outskirts of Krasavka – Hill 252.2, with the task to secure the boundary between the 175th and 132nd Rifle Divisions and to prevent an enemy breakthrough toward Nikol'skoe. In reserve were the 101st Tank Brigade (eastern outskirts of Molotychi) and the 202nd Tank Brigade (eastern outskirts of Nikol'skoe).

Over the day, the enemy undertook several attacks in the 19th Tank Corps' sector of defense. The first attack by infantry and tanks was launched at 13.00 in two directions: from Podsoborovka toward Samodurovka in the sector of the 140th Rifle Division; and from Gnilets toward Nikol'skoe at the boundary between the 175th and 132nd Rifle Divisions. With the support of tanks of the 79th Tank Brigade, the German attack was repulsed. Toward the end of the day, the enemy undertook a second attack with the support of 60 tanks in the vicinity of Samodurovka, but fell back to Podsoborovka when met by a counterattack of the 101st Tank Brigade.

## Enemy situation at the end of 7 July 1943

Despite the desperate attempts of the enemy to penetrate the defenses of the 2nd Tank Army and break through it, the 2nd Tank Army in cooperation with the 13th Army foiled every enemy attack and stubbornly clung to its positions. Thus, in the course of 7 July, the enemy managed to achieve only a slight success in the Bitiug area. Thanks to the presence of a large number of tanks, the infantry's defenses, which had been breached in several places, were quickly restored. Only in one sector of the front did enemy tanks break through to the defensive positions of the 109th Tank Brigade, but having encountered an organized rebuff, they were compelled to retreat. In other sectors of the front, tanks of the 3rd, 16th and 19th Tank Corps that had moved out into counterattacks sealed gaps in the infantry's positions. Over the day of fighting, the enemy lost 149 tanks from artillery and tank fire, and in minefields; of this total number, 70 were claimed by the 2nd Tank Army. Over the day of fighting, the 2nd Tank Army lost 84 tanks (52 T-34, 17 T-70, 8 T-60, 3 Mk III and 4 Mk IV). All of the army's corps and units worked around the clock to make improvements in their defensive fortifications. The 16th Air Army over the day of fighting conducted 837 individual combat sorties, while the enemy made 800 individual combat sorties against the forces of the 2nd Tank Army. Thus, the correlation in the air was relatively equal. The air units of both sides that appeared above the battlefield concentrated their attacks on formations of ground troops.

The commander of the 2nd Tank Army, summing up the results of the day of fighting, issued Combat Order No. 047/OP at 23.00 on 7 July for the following day of the operation, which stated:

> Located in presently occupied areas, cooperating with the rifle units to prevent a breakthrough by enemy tanks in the sectors: a) 3rd Tank Corp, bounded on its right by the line Bazhenova, Nikol'skoe, Zabolot'e and on its left by the line – 1st Ponyri, Karpun'evka, Leninskii; b) the 16th Tank Corps, bounded on its right by the 3rd Tank Corps and extending along the line Saborovka – Samodurovka – Khmelevoe; c) the 19th Tank Corps, bounded on its right by the 16th Tank Corps and on the left by the line Gnilets – Nikol'skoe – Vetrenka. The reserve 11th Guards Tank Brigade is presently occupying an area to secure the boundary between the 16th and 19th Tank Corps with fire from place and with counterattacks in the directions: a) Hill 234.0, Kashara; b) Hill 238.1, Samodurovka.

From the cited excerpt it is possible to establish that in contrast with the combat operations of the preceding days, for 8 July the army commander assigned only one tank brigade for counterattacks, while the commanders of all the corps were given responsibility for defending defined sectors.

Placing responsibility on the commanders of the tank corps for the defense of the sectors assigned to them, the headquarters of the 2nd Tank Army failed to indicate how the tank corps were to cooperate with the rifle divisions that were operating on this sector of the front. However, in the course of the battle, the cooperation of the tank corps with the other types of forces was implemented at the initiative of the commanders of the tank and rifle units and formations. The question of who was subordinate to whom – the tank corps to the rifle divisions or the rifle divisions operationally subordinated to the tank corps – wasn't defined. The commanders of the rifle corps that were operating on their directions also set tasks only for their rifle divisions, making only general mention of cooperation with tanks in their orders. The senior officer who was located directly on the battlefield and who was directing the combat operations in the sector between the Snova River and the 70th Army was the commander of the 2nd Tank Army. It seemed to Rodin that all the forces positioned in this sector should be subordinated to him. In reality, there were two army commanders in this sector, the commander of the 2nd Tank Army and the commander of the 13th Army, neither of which was subordinate to the other, and only the mutual understanding of the overall task and the identical assessment of the situation that had arisen was creating unity of command.

On the night of 7/8 July, by order of the commander of the Central Front, the 19th Tank Corps was removed from the operational control of the 2nd Tank Army and was made subordinate to the commander of the 70th Army. However, this corps kept its place on the left flank of the 2nd Tank Army until the end of the defensive battle.

General Bogdanov comments, "On 7 July facing the attacking enemy tank forces were the dug-in tanks of the 103rd and 51st Tank Brigades, which with fire from place, suffering single-digit losses, blunted the attack of the enemy tanks."

## Actions of the 2nd Tank Army on 8 July 1943

From the morning of 8 July 1943, the 3rd Tank Corps with two brigades was supporting a counterattack by the 307th Rifle Division toward the 1st of May village in order to regain the positions that had been lost the preceding day. The 51st and 103rd Tank Brigades went on the attack at 6.00, and by 9.00, having driven the enemy out of 1st of May and the northern outskirts of Ponyri, took up a position with the 51st Tank Brigade on the northern outskirts of 1st of May and the 103rd Tank Brigade on the northern outskirts of Ponyri. The enemy had no intention to yield 1st of May and Ponyri, so decided to re-take them. In the afternoon, after an artillery preparation and with air support, the enemy deployed 35 tanks behind Hill 257.1, some of which were Tigers, and launched an attack toward 1st of May. Having lost on this axis 6 Tigers and 12 medium tanks that had been knocked-out at point-blank range, the enemy retreated. The enemy also hurled up to 40 tanks, 15 of them heavy, into an attack toward Ponyri Station. With the sudden massed fire of large-caliber artillery, anti-tank fire over open sights, and fire from dug-in tanks, 10 Tigers and 12 medium tanks were knocked out. The surviving tanks, firing as they moved, threw their tanks into reverse gear and fell back behind cover. The Germans made no further attempts to attack, and the front on this sector became stabilized.

Ferocious fighting on this day developed for possession of Hill 257. In the course of the day the Germans attacked this hill three times in groups of 60-100 tanks simultaneously from the northeast and north. The 17th Guards Rifle Corps that was defending this hill received great assistance from the 107th and 109th Tank Brigades, which with fire from fixed positions repelled the enemy attacks. Only by 17.00 did the enemy manage to seize this hill at the cost of heavy losses. An attempt by the Germans to make a further advance broke up against the tenacious anti-tank defenses of the 17th Guards Rifle Corps and 16th Tank Corps.

The enemy's main efforts on this day were aimed at the boundary between the 70th and 13th Armies in the general direction toward Teploe and Hill 274.5, striving to reach the Kromy – Fatezh highway at a point 12 kilometers west of Khmelevoe over terrain that was most suitable for tank operations. Having deployed the 4th and 20th Panzer Divisions between the woods east of Podsoborovka and the upper reaches of the Svapa River, the enemy launched a number of attacks upon Kashara and Samodurovka in the direction of Hill 274.5 and Teploe, striving to take the commanding heights held by the 16th Tank Corps, the 11th Guards Tank Brigade and the 19th Tank Corps.

Having broken through the defenses of the 140th Rifle Division, the enemy took possession of Kashara and began to exploit this success in the sector of the 16th Tank Corps toward Hill 274.5 and Teploe. The 109th Tank Brigade, with fire from fixed positions, repulsed enemy tank attacks from the direction of Point 257.0. The 11th Guards Tank Brigade, which was defending on Hill 274.5, exchanged fire with enemy tanks that had broken through from the area of Teploe and Hill 240.0, knocking out several tanks and brewing up one Tiger. The 15th Motorized Rifle Brigade threw the enemy back north of Kutyrki. The 107th Tank Brigade, with fire from its dug-in tanks, repelled enemy tanks and infantry attacks in the course of the day.

Until the end of the day, the enemy was unable to breach the defensive line held by the 16th Tank Corps. The 11th Guards Tank Brigade throughout the day was subjected to repeated enemy airstrikes in groups of 9-16 aircraft, as a result of which it lost one tank.

In the second half of the day, more than 200 enemy tanks attacking out of the Samodurovka area broke through the combat positions of the 140th Rifle Division and reached the eastern outskirts of Teploe by 16.00. Bypassing it from the west, the Germans twice attacked the position of the 11th Guards Tank Brigade. Twelve panzers took part in the first attack, and 16 in the second. Both attacks were repulsed by the brigade with fire from fixed positions. The enemy lost 6 Tigers and 3 medium tanks, and halted its attacks against Hill 274. Our infantry, despite the penetration made by the German tanks, continued to fight along the line 2nd Ponyri, northern outskirts of Kutyrki, Hill 238.1, Samodurovka, creating thereby a pocket, in which the enemy thrashed around, outflanked by the 16th and 19th Tank Corps, which continued to hold their occupied positions.

Toward the evening of 8 July, the 2nd Tank Army's intelligence system detected large aggregations of enemy tanks and infantry in front of the army's forward edge of defense. The army's chief of staff made an appeal to the commander of the 16th Air Army to bomb these tempting targets at dawn on 9 July, while the army's forces were given orders to be ready to repel enemy attacks. As a result of the combat on 8 July 1943, the 3rd and 16th Tank Corps lost 48 tanks either knocked out or burned out, of which the greater number of losses (44) was at the expense of the 3rd Tank Corps. However, an entry in the Army's war diary reveals that the Army received 35 T-34 and 23 T-70 replacement tanks from the Front reserve on this day.

## Actions of the 2nd Tank Army on 9 and 10 July 1943

At sunrise on 9.7.43, the 16th Air Army conducted a heavy airstrike against an aggregation of enemy infantry and tanks. Simultaneously, strong artillery fire was directed on the same location.

Around that time, a German motorcyclist was killed by scouts of the 3rd Tank Corps, and on his body an attack order for the 18th Panzer Division's 52nd Panzer Grenadier Regiment was found, from which it was established that the start of the attack on 9 July 1943 was supposed to begin at 16.15. The Germans launched the attack, on all sectors, at 11.00. The attack had almost been disrupted by the air raids and powerful artillery fire. Captured prisoners indicated that the enemy's losses over the last two days of combat had been enormous. For example, the 6th Infantry Division was down to around 25 men each in its companies.

In the course of 9 and 10 July, units of the 3rd Tank Corps cooperated with the 307th Rifle Division in contesting for possession of the villages of 1st of May and Ponyri, which repeatedly changed hands until the rifle units of the 13th Army, with the active participation of the 3rd Tank Corps, took final control of them. The 16th Tank Corps was continuing to defend the line it occupied, repelling enemy attacks from the direction of Hill 257.0. The enemy attacks everywhere were driven back with heavy losses for the attackers.

Already by 9 July 1943, rolls of barbed wire began to appear along the enemy's forward edge, the first sign of the enemy's recognition of their failures on this axis. West of the railroad, the enemy continued attacks at the boundary between the 13th and 70th Armies; in the course of the fighting, the Germans managed to shove back the 19th Tank Corps and rifle units of the 70th Army and to seize Teploe, but the enemy was unable to make any further advance beyond this point. The commanding heights located between Kutyrki and Molotychi remained behind the 2nd Tank Army, and the enemy was unable to seize them. The enemy was not in the condition to break the resistance of the dug-in tank brigades.

The foe continued fierce attacks against Ponyri on 9 July. The Germans were striving to crush the 3rd Tank Corps, to attack the flank of the 16th Tank Corps and to emerge in the rear of the 2nd Tank Army. However, on 9 July as well, the 3rd Tank Corps held out. The enemy at first placed the 103rd Tank Brigade's right flank under pressure, and then began to threaten a breakthrough in the center of the brigade's positions. In order to counter the Nazis, the corps commander General Maksim Sinenko moved up the 728th Destroyer Anti-tank Artillery Battalion to the point of the threatened breakthrough. Simultaneously, he concentrated fire from the 234th Mortar Regiment upon the enemy's tanks and infantry. The corps commander ordered the commander of the 103rd Tank Brigade to commit his reserves, to stop and throw back the enemy, and then to seize Ponyri in cooperation with the 51st Tank Brigade. Sinenko demanded from the commander of the 51st Brigade Lieutenant Colonel G.A. Kokurin to increase pressure on the foe – to help its neighbor with fire and with a counterattack into the flank of the attacking Nazis. The commander of the 103rd Tank Brigade Colonel Georgii Maksimov introduced a destroyer anti-tank battery into the fighting, as well as his reserve – Hero of the Soviet Union Senior Lieutenant Blinov's company.

The attack of this tank company was bold and impetuous. Several tanks dueled with penetrating German tanks, while the company commander, sharply altering the left-flank platoon's axis of attack, led it around the German flank, intending to break into the enemy's rear. The hostile tanks spotted this maneuver, and fearing to wind up cut-off from their supporting infantry, they began to retreat, but came under the devastating fire of the company's tankers. In an hour of intense combat, the Soviets destroyed 15 German tanks. Among the number of burned-out tanks were 4 tanks that had been shot up at point-blank range by Blinov's crew; however, the company commander's tank took a direct hit from an armor-piercing shell. Senior Lieutenant Blinov was mortally wounded.

The brigades of the 3rd Tank Corps stopped the enemy. Then the 103rd and 51st Tank Brigades, supported by reserves, in cooperation with troops of the 307th Rifle Division drove the Germans out of Ponyri. The Germans had been unable to break the anti-tank defenses of the 13th Army, reinforced by the dug-in tanks of the 2nd Tank Army and the 19th Tank Corps. In essence, with this victory at Ponyri, the defensive operation of the forces of the 13th Army and 2nd Tank Army came to an end.

## The actions of the 2nd Tank Army between 11 and 14 July 1943

On 11 and 12 July 1943, the enemy continued fruitless attacks on a number of directions. The Germans also brought down heavy artillery fire on the 2nd Tank Army's dispositions and conducted frequent airstrikes. Units of the 2nd Tank Army in cooperation with the 13th Army, repelling enemy attacks with fire and counterattacks, inflicted heavy damage upon the enemy in personnel and equipment, and firmly held the area they were defending. On 13 July along the entire front, the Germans went over to the defensive and began to pull back their battered panzer divisions to the immediate rear for their subsequent transfer to the Mtsensk – Bolkhov area to counter the successfully developing offensive by Briansk Front. On 13 and 14 July, the exhausted and weakened enemy conducted no active operations, limiting themselves to conducting artillery and mortar fire and making reconnaissance probes. The units of the 2nd Tank Army used the lull to conduct a partial regrouping and to repair and replenish materiél, while simultaneously improving their positions in preparation for a counteroffensive.

## Results of the 2nd Tank Army's Conducted Operation

The main and basic point in the given operation consists in the fact that the large panzer offensive undertaken by the Germans failed to breach the defensive lines of the 13th Army and 2nd Tank Army. The heavy Ferdinand self-propelled guns and Tiger tanks failed to fulfill the mission that had been entrusted to them. The appearance of these armored monsters on the battlefield was not a surprise for our troops, and our units were well-prepared to meet this new equipment. The German air force was operating over the battlefield in large numbers at a very shallow tactical depth, trying to prepare the way forward for the ground troops. Through the efforts of the 13th and 2nd Tank Armies, the enemy was stopped and suffered heavy losses. Over 10 days of fighting, in addition to a lot of other war materiél, the forces of the 2nd Tank Army destroyed 340 guns of various calibers; 344 various tanks and assault guns, including 34 Ferdinands; shot down 35 German aircraft; and killed 9,296 enemy soldiers and officers.

The Germans, having initiated a battle that was unfavorable for them, suffered a defeat. The Germans had been bled white, and their actions had failed to gain elbow room for the panzer operations. Once the offensive stalled, the initiative again passed into the hands of the Red Army. In addition to all this, a staging area had been preserved for the Red Army's subsequent counteroffensive.

The 2nd Tank Army entered the battle on 5 July 1943 with a total of 460 operational tanks (317 T-34, 126 T-70 and 17 T-60). In addition, during the battle the army received another 96 tanks from the Central Front reserve (71 T-34, 25 T-70). Thus, the 2nd Tank Army had 556 tanks available to it.

Between 5 and 14 July 1943, the 2nd Tank Army lost 845 soldiers and officers killed, 1,452 wounded, and 122 missing in action, for a total of 2,429 men or about 11 percent of the army's total number.

According to a report from the deputy commander of the 2nd Tank Army for vehicle maintenance and technical support Guards Engineer-Colonel Krupenin:

Over the period of defensive combat between 6 and 15 July 1943 inclusively, the Army had the following losses in tanks: a) out of action as the result of combat damage: 154 T-34 tanks, 70 T-70 tanks, and 5 T-60 tanks, for a total of 229 tanks; b) disabled as a result of combat operations due to mechanical problems: 5 T-34, 3 T-70, for a total of 8 tanks. Thus, the total tank losses of the 2nd Tank Army were 237. Of this total number, irrecoverable losses amount to 90 T-34 tanks and 49 T-70, for a total of 139 tanks. The main cause of the combat losses was enemy tank and artillery fire; this was the case in 204 of the tanks, or 88.7 percent of the Army's total combat losses in tanks. The greatest number of losses came in the first three days of the Army's defensive actions; on 6, 7 and 8 July 1943, the Army lost 172 machines. The subsequent days of the battle up until 15 July inclusively were characterized by weakening pressure from the German forces, which is reflected in the insignificant combat losses relative to the first days of fighting; 65 machines over the period 9.7 to 15.7.1943. The losses of tanks due to enemy aviation amounted to 19 machines, and 6 machines were knocked out by mines. In addition to the irrecoverable losses numbering 139 tanks, 198 tanks required urgent repair, with the exception of those tanks requiring capital repair. The repair pool is distributed across the tank types and type of repair: a) minor repair: 79 T-34, 35 T-70 and 8 T-60, for a total of 122 tanks; b) light overhaul: 47 T-34, 10 T-70, for a total of 57 tanks; c) major overhaul: 12 T-34, 6 T-70 and 1 T-60, for a total of 19 tanks.

Recognizing that the success of the Army's defensive fighting depends upon the availability of operational combat machines, the repair personnel of the 2nd Tank Army, frequently under ceaseless enemy fire and in exceptionally difficult meteorological conditions worked to repair the combat vehicles. The crews of the knocked-out tanks not only contributed with their personal labor to get the tanks running again as quickly as possible, but often didn't take their machines requiring a difficult repair back to the repair stations, but with the help of field mechanics, who had set to work on the tanks, they took measures to make it operational again directly on the battlefield, under heavy artillery and mortar fire and enemy air attack. Incidents of the death of mechanics while carrying out their military duty were not isolated. For example, the electrician of the 3rd Tank Corps' 50th Tank Brigade Malenkov, while fixing a problem in a tank, died courageously, but got the machine running.

Over this period from 5.7 to 15.7.1943, combat damage was repaired by the 2nd Tank Army's mechanics: a) 16 T-34, 6 T-70 and 4 T-60, for a total of 26 tanks with minor repair; b) 25 T-34 and 7 T-70, for a total of 32 tanks with a light overhaul. Over this same period, worn out components were replaced and combat damage that didn't disable the tank was fixed: a) 55 T-34, 25 T-70, 4 T-60 with minor repair, for a total of 84 tanks; b) 14 T-34, 2 T-70 with a light overhaul:, for a total of 16 tanks. Altogether for the Army, 158 tanks were repaired. Of them, a) 71 T-34, 31 T-70 and 8 T-60, for a total of 110 tanks requiring minor repairs; and b) 39 T-34 and 9 T-70, for a total of 48 tanks requiring light overhauls.

The Army's Military Council highly valued the self-sacrificial work of the mechanics and technicians, recommending those who had most distinguished themselves for government awards. In addition, the Army's Military Council, considering the level of stress in the work, and the accompanying expenditure of strength and energy, issued a decree on supplying the repair workers with 1st Category rations and on distributing the supplementary special food packets for the officer's staff, as established by the government, to the entire contingent of repair personnel. Such an important decision by the Army's Military Council increased the enthusiasm in work among the mechanics and technicians.

In the defensive fighting, the timely evacuation of combat machines from the battlefield and no-man's land has great significance. It is not at all coincidental that the paying of monetary bonuses for the evacuation of tanks was foreseen by order of the USSR's People's Commissariat of Defense. On the basis of the data on the work that was done, which was constantly associated with a great risk to life, the Army's Military Council gave an excellent evaluation to the work of the recovery companies and recovery teams in the period of the 2nd Tank Army's defensive fighting. Given that they didn't have the authorized number of recovery vehicles or personnel, it was only thanks to the persistence and initiative of the personnel that 49 T-34, 25 T-70 and 1 T-60 were recovered from the battlefield and no-man's land and delivered to the SPAMs [disabled vehicle collection stations] of the tank corps and the 11th Guards Tank Brigade, for a total of 75 tanks. Of the indicated number, 15 (8 T-34, 6 T-70 and 1 T-60) were evacuated to Zolotukhino Station and sent via railroad to industrial factories for major overhauls on 15 July 1943.

The insignificant losses of tanks due to mines is explained by the fact that the command staff of the 2nd Tank Army when preparing for the operation studied and knew the minefield locations, and the minefields were always cleared or passages were made through them. The army lifted an enormous number of mines, because this sector had a lot of minefields.

The losses of the 2nd Tank Army (including those of the 19th Tank Corps) in materiél amounted to approximately 46.4 percent of the army's tank park, and 49 percent of all the losses were irrecoverable. The table above does not include data for the 19th Tank Corps, since this tank corps only participated in the fighting under the 2nd Tank Army's operational control for three days. On the first day, that is to say on 6 July 1943, it had no losses; on 7 July, the corps lost 41 tanks, and on 8 July – it again had no losses.

**Table 2.5: Characteristics of the combat losses of tanks of the 2nd Tank Army in the period from 5 to 15 July 1943 (the defensive operation)**

| Tank type | Knocked out by artillery fire | | Burned out by artillery fire | | Burned out by enemy air attack | | Blown up on mines | | Sunk | | Total | | Of which, irrevocably lost | |
|---|---|---|---|---|---|---|---|---|---|---|---|---|---|---|
| | No. | % | No. | % | No. | % | No. | % | No. | % | No. | % of starting No. | No. | % |
| T-34 | 12 | 14.5 | 64 | 77.0 | 6 | 7.2 | – | – | 1 | 1.2 | 83 | 21.4 | 64 | 77.0 |
| T-70 | 9 | 18.5 | 36 | 73.0 | 3 | 6.5 | 1 | 2.0 | – | – | 49 | 32.5 | 36 | 73.0 |
| Total | 21 | 15.5 | 100 | 76.0 | 9 | 7.0 | 1 | 1.5 | 1 | 0.75 | 132 | 23.7 | 100 | 76.0 |

Note: In the original document, the percentages of T-34 and T-70 tanks left burned out by artillery fire, the percentages of the starting number of T-34 and T-70 tanks lost in combat, and the percentages of T-34 and T-70 tanks irrevocably lost were all circled by hand.

## Conclusions regarding the conducted operation

Occupying a defense, the 2nd Tank Army as a rule had the destroyer anti-tank artillery regiments and the motorized rifle battalions of the motorized rifle and tank brigades in the first line; the tanks were positioned a certain distance behind them. Each brigade and corps commander had his own mobile reserve. This arrangement allowed the opportunity to influence the course of the fighting in a timely manner, to hold the defense on any sector stubbornly, and to inflict large losses upon the enemy. In those places where the tanks were immediately involved in repelling enemy attacks, the tanks were dug in. Thanks to superb camouflaging and the presence of emplacements for the tanks, the 11th Guards Tank Brigade had insignificant losses, although it was almost constantly under enemy artillery fire. The struggle to hold a defensive line by employing the tactic of dug-in tanks and the launching of frequent counterattacks contributed to the staying power of the major tank formations in the course of the defensive operation. The data on the losses of tanks, for example, in the 2nd Tank Army's 3rd and 16th Tank Corps, and in the 11th Guards Tank Brigade, speak to this. The table below gives the number of irrecoverable tank losses across the days of the operation:

**Table 2.6: Data on the irrecoverable tank losses of the 2nd Tank Army over the period from 6 to 15 July 1943**

| | | 6.7 | 7.7 | 8.7 | 9.7 | 10.7 | 11.7 | 12.7 | 15.7 | Total |
|---|---|---|---|---|---|---|---|---|---|---|
| **3rd Tank Corps** | | | | | | | | | | |
| 50th Tank Brigade | T-34 | – | – | – | – | 2 | – | – | 2 | 4 |
| | T-70 | – | – | – | – | – | – | – | 1 | 1 |
| 51st Tank Brigade | T-34 | – | – | 15 | – | 1 | – | – | – | 16 |
| | T-70 | – | – | 15 | – | – | – | – | 2 | 17 |
| 103rd Tank Brigade | T-34 | – | 13 | – | 4 | – | – | – | – | 17 |
| | T-70 | – | 7 | – | 1 | – | – | – | – | 8 |
| Total: | | | | | | | | | | 63 |
| **16th Tank Corps** | | | | | | | | | | |
| 107th Tank Brigade | T-34 | 29 | – | – | – | – | – | – | – | 29 |
| | T-70 | 16 | – | – | – | – | – | – | – | 16 |
| 109th Tank Brigade | T-34 | – | – | – | – | – | – | – | – | – |
| | T-70 | – | – | – | – | – | – | – | – | – |
| 164th Tank Brigade | T-34 | 15 | 7 | – | – | – | – | 1 | – | 23 |
| | T-70 | 2 | 5 | – | – | – | – | – | – | 7 |
| Total: | | | | | | | | | | 75 |
| **11th Guards Tank Brigade** | T-34 | – | – | – | – | – | 1 | – | – | 1 |
| | T-70 | – | – | – | – | – | – | – | – | – |
| Total: | | 1 | | | | | | | | |
| Total for the Army | T-34 | 44 | 20 | 15 | 4 | 3 | 1 | 1 | 2 | 90 |
| | T-70 | 18 | 12 | 15 | 1 | 0 | 0 | 0 | 3 | 49 |
| **Grand Total:** | | 62 | 32 | 30 | 5 | 3 | 1 | 1 | 5 | 139 |

The cited figures give the following description of the irrecoverable tank losses. Of the total number of 139 tanks that were irrecoverably lost, 101 were destroyed by fire as a result of shell hits; 21 were destroyed by artillery fire; 9 were knocked out of action by enemy air strikes; 1 blew up in a minefield, and 7 tanks were lost for other reasons.

Consequently, artillery (including anti-tank artillery) and tanks remained the main foe of the tanks. The increase in the caliber of anti-tank artillery, the increased in the initial muzzle velocity of shells, and the use of special shells yielded the quite large percentage of irrecoverable tanks losses relative to the total number of knocked-out tanks. Of the 214 knocked-out tanks, 139 were irrecoverably lost, which amounts to almost 65 percent. The high percentage of irrecoverable losses was also the result of a change in the tactics of struggling with tanks. The German anti-tank artillery, tanks and self-propelled guns didn't cease firing at a tank, if it had stopped as a result of a shell hit, but continued to fire at the immobile target until it caught fire. Such a tactic against attacking tanks leads to large irrecoverable losses in their formations. In contrast, the effectiveness of air strikes against tanks, hunkered down in a positional defense, is quite insignificant.

In the process of the operation, the 2nd Tank Army received 96 tanks from the Front reserve, and between 6 and 13 July it repaired 64 tanks in its repair shops, which means on average it returned 10-12 tanks to action each day. As a result of the steady arrival of tanks, the army's combat strength was maintained throughout the operation at almost the same level. The 107th Tank Brigade, which suffered the most damage in the operation, was put back into action on 8 July, just two days after the disastrous 6 July counterattack. The number of combat-ready tanks in the 2nd Tank Army across the days of the operation is shown in the table below:

**Table 2.7: Serviceable tanks in the 3rd and 16th Tank Corps and the 11th Guards Tank Brigade, by day of operation**

|  | 5.07 | 6.07 | 7.07 | 8.07 | 9.07 | 10.07 | 11.07 | 12.07 | 13.07 | 14.07 |
|---|---|---|---|---|---|---|---|---|---|---|
| 3rd Tank Corps | 195 | 192 | 179 | 130 | 100 | 121 | 111 | 123 | 130 | 132 |
| 16th Tank Corps | 206 | 117 | 83 | 144 | 157 | 161 | 161 | 162 | 165 | 174 |
| 11th Guards Tank Brigade | 54 | 54 | 54 | 54 | 54 | 54 | 54 | 52 | 52 | 52 |
| Total: | 455 | 362 | 316 | 328 | 311 | 336 | 326 | 337 | 347 | 358 |

The table shows that the army's tank strength was lowest on the fifth day of the operation, on 9 July. By this day, the number of operational tanks had fallen by 30 percent since the start of the operation. On the following days, the army's number of serviceable tanks began to rise steadily, and the army launched its counteroffensive with a number of tanks that was 20 percent less than it had on 5 July 1943.

## Observations on the operation conducted by the 2nd Tank Army

The defensive operation was based on the principle of organizing a rugged defense, with a field army located in the first echelon of the defense, and a tank army in the second echelon. The task of both armies was to stop the enemy in the defense's tactical zone, to bleed white his forces and to strip them of the capability of developing a tactical success into an operational success. With the efforts of the 13th Army and 2nd Tank Army, this task was fully implemented. The offensive undertaken by the Germans continued for 6-7 days, before they were compelled to go over to a defense on the lines they had reached, and then to fall back to their start line. It is necessary to note the very high density of fortifications that featured in the construction of them. The attacking side was superior to the defenders only in number of aircraft. With respect to ground forces, the defending Red Army had the upper hand. A distinguishing feature of this operation was that major Front reserves took part in the fighting on the very first day. This deprived the Germans of tactical superiority, which they had at the start of their offensive in certain sectors of the front. The enemy began to lose the tactical advantage already from the second day of the operation, which is shown in the table below on the rate and breadth of the enemy's advance over the days of the operation.

Table 2.8: The frontage of the German attacks and the width and depth of the German advance, by date of operation

|  | 5.7 | 6.7 | 7.7 | 8.7 | 9.7 | 10.7 | 11.7 |
|---|---|---|---|---|---|---|---|
| Frontage of the German attacks by day of operation, in kilometers | 50 | 50 | 35 | 25 | 20 | 10 | 0 |
| Width of the enemy's advance, in kilometers | 45 | 40 | 15 | 2 | 2 | 0 | 0 |
| Depth of the enemy's advance, in kilometers | 4-6 | 3-5 | 1-2 | 0.5-1 | 0.5-1 | 0 | 0 |

From the table it is obvious that already from 6 July the width of the sector of the offensive began to dwindle from day to day, while the depth of the advance decreased, which is particularly noticeable after 7 July. The closer the enemy approached the line held by the 2nd Tank Army, the more his progress slowed, before stopping completely. The short distance between the disposition of the Front's reserves and the breakthrough sector allowed them to be present on the threatened axis already by the end of the first day. The commitment of the 2nd Tank Army already on the first day created the front's needed resilience. The 2nd Tank Army by plan was to take part in the defensive operation from the second day and was to reach the designated jumping-off areas overnight before the second day. The situation required it to complete the march in daylight hours, since a need for the tank corps already began to ripen on the afternoon of the first day.

The broadly done engineered-defensive work played a large role in the operation. The elaborate engineering work eased the conducting of the defense for the troops of the 13th Army and 2nd Tank Army. The timely-prepared and analyzed movement routes for the 2nd Tank Army enabled the army's tank corps to reach the areas that had been designated for them without excessive delays, in 6-7 hours.

The leaders of the operation to repulse the German offensive on the axis of the main attack were the commanders of the 2nd Tank Army and the 13th Army. However, in fact the 2nd Tank Army commander controlled all of the rifle formations that were positioned in the 2nd Tank Army's defensive belt. Thus, even though the 2nd Tank Army was defending a defined sector, in this sector there were troops of two different armies, each subordinate to their own commander. For example, in the 2nd Tank Army's area of operations there was the 17th Guards Rifle Corps, which was receiving combat orders from the commander of the 13th Army. If the tasks set for the 17th Guards Rifle Corps hadn't been thoroughly coordinated between the two headquarters, then a lack of cohesion in the operations between the 2nd Tank Army and the 17th Guards Rifle Corps wouldn't have been excluded. In order to avoid this and to simplify command and control, it was necessary to subordinate the 17th Guards Rifle Corps to the commander of the 2nd Tank Army.

The size of the 2nd Tank Army, consisting of two tank corps and one tank brigade, was too small. On the most intense days of struggle, between 6 July and 8 July 1943, the 2nd Tank Army was controlling three tank corps (the 3rd, 16th and 19th Tank Corps). In addition, the 17th Guards Rifle Corps and the 15th Rifle Corps were operating in tight tactical cooperation with the tank corps. Thus, there was two rifle corps for three tank corps. Given the positional struggle, it was necessary to have more firepower, and maneuverability was less important. Thus the Tank Army, placed on the defensive against a major enemy tank grouping, could successfully execute its mission with a roster of 3-5 corps given a correlation of 2-3 tank corps to 1-2 rifle corps. The Tank Army justified its role in a positional defense only given the need to counter an offensive by major enemy tank groupings. The capability of the tank army to maneuver quickly and to dig-in quickly allowed it to be kept in the reserve of the main command until the situation became clear, and then to be shifted rapidly to the needed axis, in essence making it a "mobile" fortified district.

Dug-in tanks and artillery were the basis of the tank army's defense. Up to 50 man-hours of work is required in order to prepare a tank to serve as a fixed firing point, which means to excavate an emplacement, to clear a field of fire, etc. The tank's crew, given a short time period to prepare a defense and to do all the ground work, is not in the condition to carry out this work in one day and needs assistance. Thus, the period of time it took each tank corps, and subsequently the tank army itself, to be ready for a defense depended entirely on the number of people that could be recruited to help the crews construct the defenses. In order to carry out special engineering tasks in the army's sector and in order to deploy minefields, the tank army's unit roster must include an engineering brigade.

The tank army also had to have self-propelled artillery regiments, equipped with guns of a caliber between 85mm and 122mm. It was senseless to have self-propelled artillery regiments armed with a caliber of guns smaller than 85mm, because the tanks were armed with 76mm guns. The self-propelled artillery should be superior to the tanks in firepower and have the necessary means of observation and control, in order to resolve their tasks flexibly. One self-propelled artillery regiment, operating out of ambush positions, could counter a group of attacking enemy tanks two or three times in size, which is to say that 20 self-propelled guns could successfully struggle against 40-60 enemy tanks or defend a sector 1 or 2 kilometers wide. A Tank Army was able to receive its own sector of operations for a self-sufficient defense. The width of the sector depended primarily on the army's complement of formations and on the importance of the particular axis.

The 2nd Tank Army was defending a sector equivalent to 25 kilometers. The 2nd Tank Army, including the 19th Tank Corps and the 17th Guards Rifle Corps, had 607 tanks, 1,400 guns and mortars, 1,500 anti-tank rifles, and 2,800 machine guns, which yields an average density of 26 tanks, 55 guns and mortars, 6 anti-tank rifles and 110 machine guns per kilometer of front. Given the disposition of the tank army on the defense, it was necessary to determine the forward edge of the defenses not by the line of the machine-gun positions, as is the usual practice when defending against an enemy that has no tanks or has them in a limited number, but along the line of the anti-tank guns and dug-in tanks. The infantry in this case was located in the intervals between the guns and tanks. The combat dispositions of the 3rd and 16th Tank Corps can serve as an example. In the first two days of the operation, the 3rd and 16th Tank Corps placed tank brigades on the defense, and kept the motorized rifle brigades in reserve behind the tank brigades. The tank corps in the operation cooperated closely with the infantry that was deployed in front of them, but there was not a single instance, when one corps gave assistance to a neighboring corps. The 3rd Tank Corps on 6 July 1943 during the counterattack launched by the 16th Tank Corps was totally preoccupied with carrying out its own tasks. The 16th Tank Corps, when launching its counterattack, was counting upon the assistance of the 19th Tank Corps, but was unable even to organize the simultaneous attack of its own two brigades (the 107th and 164th Tank Brigades). The 19th Tank Corps, following the order of the 2nd Tank Army's commander, launched a counterattack only late in the day on 6 July. On 7 and 8 July 1943, when the struggle for Ponyri became particularly fierce, the 3rd Tank Corps was repelling all the enemy attacks independently, without the participation of the 16th Tank Corps. The Snova River, after the destruction of the bridges across it by the enemy, became an impenetrable barrier between the two tank corps and prevented the organization of mutual assistance. Only in the final stage of the Front's defensive operation, once the 2nd Tank Army went on the counteroffensive to regain the lost ground, did the tank corps receive freedom of maneuver.

The combat operations of the 2nd Tank Army were so intertwined with the combat operations of the 13th Army that it is impossible to examine them separately. Both armies halted the enemy offensive, and 2-3 days after the enemy was stopped, launched a successful counteroffensive. This once again emphasizes that the density of the defenses on this sector of defense of the Central

Front was excessively high, and that the task could have been resolved given a different correlation of force. Tanks and artillery played the decisive role in turning back the enemy offensive, with the active assistance of other types of forces. For the tank commanders, a positional defense and its aspect of combat actions had been inadequately studied, so this somewhat justifies the dense saturation of the defensive zone with tanks and artillery. The correlation of forces with the enemy was such that for the defending side it proved excessive, but once going on the offensive, it proved inadequate before the enemy became heavily worn down.

The battle on the Orel – Kursk axis was decided as a result of the attempts by the Germans to break through our defenses with a frontal assault. The German groupings' axis of attack was identified on 5 July, and thus it was possible that a more correct solution would have been to shift the 2nd Tank Army to a jumping-off area east of the line Maloarkhangel'sk, Kursk, so as to resolve the task with an offensive solution by launching a flank attack at the base of the German penetration. In order to answer the given question, it is necessary to consider that evidence of the enemy's concentration of major forces in the Orel, Kromy area had arrived long before, but the direction of the Germans' attacks became clear only on 3 July 1943, just a couple of days before the start of the offensive. Judging by the fact that the boundary between the 13th and 48th Armies was especially well covered by field works, and that the 13th Army's headquarters was on the Shchigry axis, it is possible to assume that for a long time it had been thought that the enemy would more likely launch the attack to the southeast, and thus the initial positioning of the 2nd Tank Army was more suitable.

In addition, it is necessary to consider another circumstance. The diameter of the Kursk salient through Kursk was equal to 180 kilometers. Accordingly, the enemy's northern and southern groupings would each have to cover 90 kilometers in order to link up. However, the distance from Ryl'sk, at the tip of the salient, to Kursk is 100 kilometers. Accordingly, a retreat by the defending units positioned west of Kursk to the east would have placed them in a difficult position. As became known later, the Germans planned to conduct the operation to take Kursk in three days, that is to say, at a rate of advance of 30 kilometers per day. Possibly, if the tank armies had not been positioned on the path of attack of the German shock groupings, then the Germans might have been able to create a serious situation for the Soviet forces defending along the perimeter of the bulge west of Kursk. It is even more probable by the fact that the terrain was unsatisfactory for launching a counterattack from east to west, and had a lot of suitable lines for a defense from the west to the east. Thus the positioning of the tank armies to the north and south of Kursk better conformed to the situation. A defensive operation for a tank army is not its primary mission, but it is necessary to know how to organize and conduct one, and to apply it according to the situation.

## The Result of the Defensive Fighting 5-15 July 1943

Going on the offensive on a front of 45 kilometers from the morning of 5 July and launching the main attack with four panzer and five infantry divisions, with two panzer divisions, two infantry divisions and one motorized division in close reserve, the enemy after a powerful artillery preparation, at the cost of enormous losses, on the first day of the offensive made a 4-6 kilometer penetration into the defenses of the Soviet forces. The German attack was so strong, that the Central Front command was compelled to adjust its plan of operations somewhat by committing on the very first day of the battle the 18th and 17th Guards Rifle Corps and the 2nd Tank Army, which had been designated for a counteroffensive. Having achieved no success on 5 or 6 July 1943 in breaching the defense of the Soviet forces, the enemy in the course of 7 and 8 July introduced reserve units into the fighting, and in the course of 8-11 July continued stubborn attacks in the Ponyri – Teploe sector, directing the main efforts to break through the center and left wing of the 2nd Tank Army. By 11 July 1943, at the cost of enormous losses (up to 50 percent), the enemy managed to make a penetration of 6-15 kilometers into the depth of the defenses at the boundary between the 13th and 70th Armies, and to reach the line Protasovo, Ponyri Station, Berezovyi Log, Bitiug, Koshara, Teploe, Samodurovka. By 12 July the main enemy grouping, as a result of the heavy fighting, had lost its striking power and went over to a defense on the lines it had achieved. At the same time, the enemy began to regroup his forces and replaced the panzer divisions with infantry divisions.

In this defensive operation, the 2nd Tank Army acquired rich experience in combatting the enemy's major tank forces. The initially applied method of a counterattack against major enemy tank forces, given the latter's superiority, did not justify itself, and in the future when facing enemy tank attacks, our tanks were dug-in, and firing over open sights, inflicted heavy damage upon the enemy, eliminated their superiority in tank numbers, and then went over to a counteroffensive. The success of the defensive fighting is explained by the fact that the personnel of the 2nd Tank Army, when preparing for the operation, had studied and become familiar with the forthcoming theater of operations.

**The minimal total losses of Army Group Center**, which opposed the forces of the Central Front on the northern side of the Kursk bulge **over the period from 5 to 12 July 1943 amounted to 89 tanks and assault guns**. This figure includes 35 Pz. IV tanks, 4 Tigers, 19 Ferdinands, 17 StuG III, 10 Sturmpanzer IV, and 5 Pz. III. In addition, a large number of tanks and assault guns were knocked out or disabled by mines, but were evacuated and put under repair. Since during the subsequent retreat, a significant number of the machines under repair were lost irrecoverably, the real total losses of the German grouping on the northern shoulder of the Kursk bulge significantly exceeded the official statistic of 89 machines. As an example, one can cite the losses of the 656th Heavy Tank Destroyer Battalion, which officially lost 19 Ferdinands, but another 20 Ferdinands that were under repair in fact never did get repaired and had to be written off as irreplaceable losses in August 1943. The 505th Heavy Panzer Battalion, on 7 July alone in addition to the Tigers written off as destroyed, evacuated 23 Tigers damaged by enemy fire or disabled by mines, 4 of which had damage to the bogie wheels and tracks from enemy fire, 16 of which had been disabled by mines, and 3 of which had transmission damage. Over one day of combat alone, the 505th Heavy Panzer Battalion lost 25 of the 31 Tigers (more than 80 percent) with which it had started on 5 July. From 5 to 11 July 1943, the German Ninth Army lost 22,273 in killed. Casualties in the combat units approached 26.1 percent of the officers and men. According to the data given by Newton, from 4 July to 9 July 1943 alone, the combat numbers of the XXXXVI Panzer Corps decreased by 35 percent (from 14,947 to 9,723 men), the combat numbers of the LVII Panzer Corps dropped by 25 percent (from 15,165 to 11,340 men), and the XXIII Army Corps by 26 percent (from 75,713 to 55,941 men). For the eleven divisions that took part in the battle in the period from 5 to 9 July, the average human losses were sizeable – 45 percent for the combat soldiers who took part in combat actions.

Throughout the entire 2nd Tank Army resounds the fame of the fearless hero-tanker of the 16th Tank Corps' 107th Tank Brigade, Junior Lieutenant **Andrei Stoliarov**, who on 6 July 1943 rammed a German tank with his burning T-34 and destroyed it together with its crew.

**Junior Lieutenant Konstantin Blinov** – Commander of a T-34 tank company in the 3rd Tank Corps' 103rd Tank Brigade. A Hero of the Soviet Union who fell heroically in battle.

**Guards Lieutenant Ivan Kvasha** – A tank company commander in the 11th Guards Tank Brigade. In combat for Teploe Station on 8 July, he brewed up two enemy medium tanks. His tank emerged undamaged.

Knocked out German tanks and assault guns in the area of Ponyri, July 1943.

Another knocked-out German tank in the area of Ponyri, July 1943

Units of the 2nd Tank Army on the battlefield, July 1943.

Units of the 2nd Tank Army on the battlefield, July 1943.

Units of the 2nd Tank Army on the battlefield, July 1943.

The post-action inspection of knocked-out German tanks

The SU-152 of the commander of the 1541st Self-propelled Artillery Regiment Major Aleksei Sankovsky, July 1943.

The commander of the 1541st Self-propelled Artillery Regiment Guards Major Aleksei Sankovsky, July 1943, Kursk bulge. Guards Major Sankovsky demonstrated courage and resolve as a commander. In combat in the Step' – Podsoborovka area, skillfully directing the batteries of the 1541st Self-propelled Artillery Regiment under enemy air and artillery attack, he brought his regiment to the indicated area without losses. Under his direct leadership, the regiment destroyed more than 30 enemy tanks and assault guns, including 5 Tigers.

Junior Lieutenant Andrei Stoliarov [upper left], Junior Lieutenant Konstantin Blinov [upper right], Senior Lieutenant Fedor Donkov [lower left] and Guards Lieutenant Ivan Kvasha [lower right].

**Senior Lieutenant Fedor Donkov** – A tank company commander in the 16th Tank Corps' 107th Tank Brigade. In combats for the settlements of Butyrki and Aleksandrovka, he demonstrated tenacity and courage. His company destroyed 6 tanks, 5 anti-tank guns and up to 150 enemy soldiers and officers. When Donkov's T-34 tank was knocked out by an enemy shell, he switched to a different tank and continued to direct the company in battle.

**Lieutenant Shmal' (T-70) and Lieutenant Anepriev (T-70)** showed themselves to be brave tankers in combats. They boldly went into fierce attacks against German medium and even heavy tanks in their T-70s. Despite the fact that the main gun of the "70s" was significantly weaker in their firepower than the main guns of the German tanks, the heroic crews of Lieutenant Shmal' and Lieutenant Anepriev, thanks to high combat skills, destroyed 4 German medium tanks, 2 by Shmal's crew and 2 by Anepriev's crew.

**Sergeant Krainov** – A driver-mechanic of a T-70 (103rd Tank Brigade). Seventeen times he drove his tank right up to the combat formations of German tanks and with aimed fire he brewed up three enemy tanks.

**Lieutenant Filonenko** (T-34) and his driver-mechanic **Zhirnov**. Their tank with a replaced engine ran for 1,000 hours. Through excellent care for the machine, the skillful employment of it in any conditions, artful maneuver on the battlefield, and their ability to adapt to the terrain –the crew won the glory of the unconquerable; 59 times the crew went on the attack against the foe and they came out not only with their vehicle intact, but also themselves, inflicting no small damage to the enemy in personnel and equipment.

**Sergeant Major Metel'nikov**, driver-mechanic **Ishkov**. The crew shows excellent teamwork. With a nearly unspoken understanding of each other, the tankers skillfully make use of the terrain; using the reverse slopes of hills and bringing their machine out from under enemy fire, they inflicted serious damage upon the enemy. They brewed up or knocked out 8 German tanks, and destroyed 14 cannons, 20 mortars and more than 40 enemy soldiers and officers. Sergeant Major Metel'nikov and driver-mechanic Ishkov were awarded with government decorations.

**Driver-mechanic Sergeant Major Lesiuk** – was badly wounded in the arm. Bleeding heavily, steering the tank with one hand, he brought his machine out from under enemy shellfire and inflicted major damage to the foe. He personally destroyed 6 enemy tanks, one artillery battery, several cannons and approximately 100 enemy soldiers and officers.

**Sergeant Petr Panov** – The commander of an anti-tank gun in the 729th Separate Destroyer Anti-tank Battalion (**16th Tank Corps**), Sergeant Panov in combat near the village of Ol'khovatka on 6 July 1943 over several hours destroyed or knocked out 11 enemy tanks. Awarded the title Hero of the Soviet Union on 7 August 1943.

**Sergeant Sergei Fadeev** – A gun layer of the 729th Separate Destroyer Anti-tank Battalion (**16th Tank Corps**). Fadeev distinguished himself in the fighting at the village of Ol'khovatka. On 6 July 1943 while repelling enemy tanks, together with the gun's crew he knocked out or brewed up 11 enemy tanks. He was wounded, but didn't leave the battlefield – Hero of the Soviet Union.

**Senior Sergeant Amantai Daulitbekov** – The commander of a gun of the 1180th Destroyer Anti-tank Artillery Regiment (13th Destroyer Anti-tank Brigade, 2nd Tank Army). Daulitbekov in the battle on 9 July 1943, covering the main road in the area of Ponyri Station, was surrounded by enemy tanks and infantry. When his gun was disabled, together with the other surviving artillerymen he lunged into hand to hand combat. He was killed in this melee. Hero of the Soviet Union.

**Lieutenant Grigorii Koshkarov** – Commander of a gun platoon in a battery of anti-tank guns of the 15th Motorized Rifle Brigade (**16th Tank Corps**), Lieutenant Koshkarov on 7 July 1943 together with the gun crews repulsed enemy tank attacks west of the village of Ponyri. He replaced the battery commander and skillfully organized the defense. On 8-10 July the battery repeatedly repelled up to 5-6 attacks a day. The artillerymen held the positions they occupied. Killed in action on 11 July 1943. Hero of the Soviet Union.

**Junior Lieutenant Vasilii Uvarov** – Commander of a platoon of the 1180th Destroyer Anti-tank Artillery Regiment (13th Separate Destroyer Anti-tank Brigade, 2nd Tank Army), Junior Lieutenant Uvarov distinguished himself in the fighting for Ponyri Station. On 9 July 1943 he repelled 8 enemy attacks, in the process destroying 8 tanks and up to 2 companies of infantry. When his gun was smashed, he rallied his fighters into a counterattack. He was killed in this action. Hero of the Soviet Union.

**Captain Dmitrii Zakrevsky** – The deputy commander of a reconnaissance battalion, leader of a reconnaissance group. The group conducted a successful raid into the enemy rear. It destroyed up to a platoon of submachine gunners and seized an enemy tank.

## From the Recollections of Guards Major General Anatolii Shvebig:

On the night of 4/5 July 1943, the commander of the 16th Tank Corps and his deputies were at the headquarters. No one was sleeping. No one was sitting in the stuffy dugout either. Chatting quietly, the officers were out smoking in the fresh air. I had a thought that it had never been so quiet at the front. It was hard to believe that war was lurking quite nearby. Then suddenly the calm that was reigning over the nearby frontline was shattered by the roar of thousands of guns and the deep rumble of bombers that instantly appeared from behind the forests.

"It has started!" exclaimed Colonel Kocherin.

Turning, he rushed into the dugout to the telephones. Before moving to follow him, I automatically took a glance at the illuminated dial on the watch. The hands were showing 0230.

By midday it had become known that despite the stubborn resistance, the enemy with a powerful tank wedge had managed to breach the first line of defenses in the sector of the 13th Army and to advance in the direction of Ol'khovatka. It was here that that the Hitlerites launched their main attack north of Kursk. Our 16th Tank Corps was moved out together with other formations to meet the foe. Instantly, the seemingly empty ravines and groves came alive. Tank columns began to move out on their routes of advance. The dust hadn't managed to settle behind them on the roads, when maintenance support companies following behind them appeared. Overtaking the slowly moving columns of the maintenance personnel, our spritely Willys jeep moved to catch up with the tank brigades. My driver Sergeant Makar Gapochka and I found the tank brigades in the assembly area, where they were waiting for an order. During a meeting with me, the deputy brigade commanders, who well understood that they couldn't avoid losses in the upcoming fighting, in one voice expressed their concerns about the plainly inadequate number of recovery vehicles that they had. Instead of the authorized number of 17 tractors, we had only 5. Moreover these were slow moving machines that had little horsepower, which had been used previously in agriculture. The speed of the evacuation didn't exceed 2-3 kilometers an hour, while the insufficient horsepower of their engines led to the point where one tank required two or three tractors to tow it. It was necessary to violate the commander's order and to give an order in case of urgent need to use combat tanks to evacuate damaged machines.

By 2000 on 5 July 1943, the corps' brigades had moved into their jumping-off positions. For the rest of the night, the crews readied their combat machines for battle, and at 0600 the 107th Tank Brigade under the command of Lieutenant Colonel Nikolai Teliakov, in support of the 75th Guards Rifle Division, attacked the Nazis in the Butyrki – Step' area, but met by organized artillery fire and a counterattack by 50 tanks, lost 47 tanks knocked-out.

From the very first minutes of the battle, I was at the main observation and communications point together with Karakozov. Then the corps commander Colonel Grigor'ev summoned me. I no longer recall the details of the brief conversation between us. Something else stuck in my memory. We were talking about whether Brigade Commander Teliakov should be punished, since he failed to carry out his orders. It is difficult to impart in words what I was feeling at the time. Anything happens in war, but to accuse a brigade commander of cowardice, who had been up in the combat formations and who had lost his own tank in battle – such a thing had never happened before in my experience. It was hellishly hot, but I shivered with the thought that now a torrent of slander and abuse would be unleashed upon

Teliakov. He personally directed the combat and had lost almost his entire brigade. Now he would have to report to the corps commander that the brigade no longer existed. It is a good thing that I had spare tanks. Quickly the brigade was refitted.

However, a representative from the Front ordered the brigade commander's arrest and that he be tried for cowardice. I reported to the corps commander: "Comrade General, I was there myself. I watched how it all happened together with the brigade's deputy for technical service Major Karakozov. They knocked out his tank, and the brigade commander was barely able to clamber out of it." The corps commander ordered me to say more. I then told him, "What, you don't believe me? The deputy corps commander saw it all. They knocked out his tank, it caught fire, what more needs to be said?" My arguments were convincing. The charged situation dissipated, and the brigade commander headed off to rally his brigade.

### From the recollections of the commander of a combat engineer squad, Guards Corporal Krivsun:

In the fighting at the Orel – Kursk bulge, I had to carry out a lot of tasks to mine the forward edge of our defense at Ponyri Station. On the night of 6/7 1943, my squad was ordered to mine the ground of our forward edge that was favorable for tank movement, in order to prevent the possibility that the German tanks would break through the defenses of our units in that location. Having gathered 6 anti-tank mines each, in single file we stealthily began to make our way to the place for mining, having determined its location earlier that day. The enemy now and then swept the ground with a machine gun. Having strictly allocated the duties of each while emplacing the mines, we started work. Quickly, without casualties, we emplaced 42 mines. One German blew up the next day in the minefield, and the Germans opted not to try to break through the defenses or to hurl their tanks forward in this sector. For carrying out this combat assignment, I was decorated with the medal "For Combat Services".

Corporal Krivsun's squad of sappers, 9th Separate Combat Engineer Battalion,
16th Tank Corps, July 1943.

## From the recollections of Guards Captain Egorov:

In the area of the village of Ponyri, Kursk Oblast, on 5.7.1943 the battalion was given an order: to move out to meet the attacking enemy and to stand on the defense with the aim of restraining and destroying the attacking enemy tanks, and to deprive them of the possibility to cut the main road leading from Ponyri Station to Ol'shanka. In order to fulfill this mission, at the decision of battalion commander Major Khombakh, the 1st Tank Company under the command of Senior Lieutenant Karasev was given an order. The company, numbering 10 T-34/76 tanks, occupied defensive positions on the fringe of a grove at Osinovaia, with its front facing Ponyri Station. The company commander Senior Lieutenant Karasev, wasting no precious time, ordered emplacements to be dug for the tanks and personnel, while he himself decided to study the map and to walk the ground lying out in front, and to organize fire support between the platoons and to set up reference points. On the morning of 6.7.43 at 6.00 groups of enemy aircraft began to bomb the Osinovaia grove and continued to do so for the next four hours. On the morning of 7.7, enemy aircraft repeated their strikes on the grove, but in smaller groups of 10-15 aircraft. Simultaneously under air cover, the enemy went on the attack against the Osinovaia grove with infantry and groups of tanks. The tankers were ready, waiting for the right moment to open fire. The weather had turned hot, and the ground was scorched from the incessant bombing and the explosion of shells. The dust raised by the shell explosions restricted line of sight and observation by the crews. The tank commanders had to stand in the open hatch in order to observe the enemy. The tanks were coming closer and closer. Junior Lieutenant Chikomasov spotted the lead tank at a range of 700 meters and reported this immediately to the company commander. The company commander ordered everyone to hold their fire and to allow the tanks to approach to within a range of 300 meters. Having allowed the German tanks to close, Senior Lieutenant Karasev's company opened targeted fire from all the tanks. German tanks were brewing up one after another; they couldn't withstand the proffered resistance and turned back. The German attack had been repulsed. The enemy left 11 burned-out tanks and 6 knocked-out tanks on the battlefield. The company had no tank losses.

## Ilia Bystritsky's recollections of a night patrol:

We were 11 men. We were moving north of the district center of Ponyri. At that time, once darkness fell, there were people in no-man's land: there were a significant number of damaged enemy vehicles here, and repair-recovery teams were to get the evacuation of tanks and guns up and running. Soldiers of our tank and artillery repair shops were also at work. The weather that day had turned gray. That evening the skies became clouded, and by nightfall a fine, cold drizzle was falling. The group of our soldiers, armed with light machine guns, submachine guns, grenades and knives, was moving across no-man's land. Yet here a surprise was waiting for them. For some reason the fascists ceased all work in no-man's land, and began increasingly to illuminate the sky with flares. The group commander **Captain Dmitrii Zakrevsky** then made a decision: to move deeper into the enemy rear.

Now the neutral zone was behind us. The group was moving under the rainfall in absolute silence, passing 1 kilometer … 2 kilometers. Somewhere around 5-6 kilometers in the enemy rear, the scouts noticed a mound by some sort of building. At first they thought it was simply a pile of dirt. When they approached more closely, someone gave the opinion that it was a bunker. Suddenly one of the scouts reported to the commander, "I see a light."

This wasn't a dirt pile or a bunker, but a fascist headquarters tank camouflaged by canvas. A light was burning in the machine, but there was no one around. The guys cautiously approached the tank's armor, and through the open hatch we could see that

The commander of the 3rd Tank Corps' 24th Reconnaissance Battalion, Captain Surzhikov, gives an order to Captain Zakrevsky's group, July 1943.

The commander of the 24th Separate Reconnaissance Battalion Captain Surzhikov (3rd Tank Corps] in the forward detachment, July 1943.

Captain D. Zakrevsky's scouts prepare to tow a captured German tank, 10 July 1943.
Below: Another German tank left abandoned on the battlefield.

A scout of Captain Zakresvsky's group proudly poses in front of the captured German tank.

there was no one inside the machine either. So imagine our surprise, when we lowered ourselves through the hatch, we found a small, portable table with field maps of the fascist command spread out upon it, along with various secret papers and documents. A functioning radio set was working here. Then a daring thought struck us: to bring the tank back under its own power to our side of the lines. The railroad leading back to Ponyri was chosen as the direction of movement. The engine started up and the machine lurched forward, toward our positions.

As soon as the tank started moving, we could hear shouts, swearing and random gunfire behind us. Several minutes later the Germans came to their senses and opened fire from mortars. Hearing the gunshots and explosions in their own rear, the Nazi sentries in the front-line woke up. At full speed, we burst into the German main line of resistance. The scouts, who remained on the tank's armor, were firing from machine guns and hurling grenade bundles. At last, the German pursuit fell behind. Now there was the enemy's first line of trenches. The machine hurtled across it and continued onward. The Nazis thought this signaled the start of an attack, and their infantry rose up and "went into battle" behind us. Immediately machine guns fired at them from the tank. The fascists were taken aback and dropped to the ground, but the tank continued on at full speed toward our positions. As the machine was moving across no-man's land, I got a swastika flag, and having folded the banner so that only the red fabric showed, I began to wave it at our frontline. Even though the sentries of the division were suspicious, they nevertheless didn't open fire at the tank. The fascist tank crossed the frontline under its own power, and all of the military booty of this night raid was promptly delivered to headquarters. When the Hitlerites realized what had happened, they sent an artillery spotter plane out over our positions. Soon, a massive artillery barrage fell upon the grove where the German tank was parked. However, by this time all of the documents had already been transferred, as they say in the army, "up the ladder".

## Recollections of Vasilii Torgaev:

I didn't join the Great Patriotic War right away. After I was conscripted, they sent me not to the front, but to the Gor'kii Automobile Factory. I worked there for a while as a machinist together with Volodia Shchetinin. We found defects in the vehicles that were coming off the line and worked to repair them. Over a shift, we would each go over 20 vehicles. I submitted a request to be sent to the front, and they honored it. I wound up in the 2nd Tank Army. It was April 1943. Our army was located in the area of Alekseevka Station and in the village of Ilovoi. Then they loaded us aboard trains and we traveled as far as Livny Station. Meanwhile, the T-34 tanks were moving to the front under their own power as far as Krasnoarmeisk, where they were made ready for combat. A ZIS-5 fuel truck was assigned to me. I was supposed to handle refueling and to deliver diesel fuel oil, heating oil and lubricant for the tanks. It was clear that they were preparing for a large battle.

This battle began on 5 July 1943. My supply platoon joined the roster of the 119th Tank Battalion of the 3rd Tank Corps' 103rd Tank Brigade. The tanks were refueled only at night-time, without illumination. In those days we were fighting for 1st Ponyri. Indeed, it kept changing hands up until 14 July. Then at last we eliminated the last pockets of resistance and took Ponyri-1, Ponyri-2 and Ponyri-3. General Bogdanov was now commanding our tank army. A strapping, stately man of more than 6'6 in height, as soon as he barked out orders, it felt like ants were running up and down your spine. On the attack he was always in a tank and he feared nothing, not even the Devil himself. He only took exception to the tanks. They were too small for him. Even the "KV" wasn't very suitable. The soldiers talked that Stalin himself had ordered a special tank to be made for him. It is likely just a joke.

On 25 August Bogdanov visited our brigade; we assembled in formation, and he told us loudly and briefly: "Men, beat the fascists, and don't spare the cartridges or shells. Beat the stuffing out of them, so that their trousers fall down, and then so that their trousers can't stand it and run away!" We roared with laughter. It was a good quip about the trousers.

On 27 August, there was an artillery preparation before moving out to capture Sevsk. Even though there were a lot of Germans there, our 103rd Tank Brigade took it without particularly high losses and we acquired the honorific title "Sevsk". But over the entire two months of fighting, the casualties were heavy. My commander Hero of the Soviet Union Senior Lieutenant Kostia Blinov was killed. He was a Muscovite by birth. After the war, they re-named one street in Kursk "In the name of Hero Blinov". Our 103rd "Sevsk" Brigade was sent to the vicinity of L'gov in Kursk Oblast for rest and refitting.

## From the recollections of Guards Captain Kavkin:

The enemy increased the pressure on Ponyri Station, but had no success. On 7 July 1943 he introduced fresh forces, which had to be identified; in order to establish the enemy's strength and the composition of his fresh units, it was necessary to "grab a tongue" [Editor's note: A prisoner to interrogate]. For this purpose, at the order of the corps' intelligence department, a recon group consisting of 10 men was sent out with the task to capture a "tongue" in the area of Ol'khovatka. At 11.00 7 July 1943, a 10-man group under the command of Lieutenant Ivanin set off toward a hill 8 kilometers to the north of Ol'khovatka. The group was equipped with 10 submachine guns, 2 light machine guns, and each man was carrying 3 hand grenades. Everyone was dressed in a summer uniform. Since there was little time to prepare for the mission, the entire recon team, with no documents or insignia of rank, was brought up to the jumping-off line, where the men began observing the enemy. They also diligently studied the terrain, across which they would have to move. The surveillance established that an enemy group of up to a platoon of submachine gunners had infiltrated along a communications trench, which had been abandoned by our troops in front of their own tanks, and had stopped there for the night. The recon team commander split his men into three groups: one group that would conduct the snatch operation, and two that would cover it. The first cover group had the task to isolate the right-hand part of the communications trench and to deprive the enemy of the possibility of coming to the aid of their comrades. The second cover group was to secure the operation of the snatch group in the event of an enemy counterattack. As the snatch group withdrew with its prize, the cover groups would take turns covering its withdrawal. Each member of the team received detailed information regarding their roles. When night fell, the recon team slipped out and crept to within 50-60 meters of the communications trench, where it opened fire from machine guns at the right-hand sector. The snatch group moved in and captured one German officer, gathered documents from the dead, and guarded by the two covering groups, made its way back to the start line. Having scattered the platoon of submachine gunners, the scouts suffered no casualties and successfully carried out their mission.

As a result of thorough observation of the enemy and the attentive study of the terrain and communication trenches, as well as the proper use of the machine guns on the flank, the recon team carried out its mission and captured a "tongue". The prisoner provided valuable information.

Captain Kavkin continues:
In the period from 7 to 8 July 1943, the enemy conducted powerful tank attacks supported with infantry, artillery and aircraft in the direction of Ponyri Station and somewhat shoved

back our units. It was assumed that the enemy had as its task to reach the Zolotukhino railroad station, thereby cutting all the dirt roads and railroads over which our troops positioned in the northern portion of the Kursk bulge received supplies, in order to leave our units without supplies of ammunition and rations and then to destroy them.

The situation and the enemy's intentions on the line Teploe – Khmelevoi – Stanovets were unclear. The corps' intelligence department gave a task to a reconnaissance detachment to clarify the enemy's situation on the line Teploe – Khmelevoi – Stanovets and to find out his intentions in the given sector. In order to carry out the given assignment, one ORD [Separate Reconnaissance Patrol] was organized consisting of one platoon of light armored vehicles and one platoon of armored cars. Three observation posts were set up among the combat positions of our infantry units in the Teploe – Khmelevoi – Stanovets sector, and from 12.00 7 July 1943, surveillance of the combat formations of the enemy's units and their activities was maintained. The results of the surveillance were reported to the chief of the ORD, who at 19.00 7 July 1943 conducted a personal reconnaissance of the given area and confirmed the intelligence received from the observation posts. At the same time, exercises were conducted with the personnel to rehearse the ORD's actions in the enemy's main line of resistance, ammunition was replenished, and the vehicles and guns were checked. When everything was ready, the troops were given a two-hour rest. Personal documents and insignia were collected and turned over to headquarters. All of the unit identification numbers on the vehicles were removed. The ORD was ready for action.

By 20.00, the ORD had moved into its jumping-off line in the area of Ol'khovatka, where it was given its task for the reconnaissance. The ORD operated in a single column. One armored personnel carrier and one armored car moved out as a forward detachment. The column's rear guard consisted of the same. The rest of the patrol was moving together in a single group. In the event of an enemy encounter, the ORD would deploy into battle line and destroy the enemy, but given superior enemy forces, the ORD, covered by the fire of the forward detachment, was either to bypass the enemy or to return to the jumping-off line at the order of the ORD commander. The vehicles of the main group were to keep within a viewing range of 100-150 meters of each other.

The ORD, exploiting features of the terrain and the dark night, bypassing separate groups of enemy tanks, infiltrated to a forest lying 8 kilometers away from the village of Teploe, and conducted a reconnaissance in the enemy rear from that point by sending out pairs or individual vehicles, as well as groups on foot. By the operation of the ORD it was established that the enemy was in the process of shifting more than 100 tanks from his left flank to his right flank. At dawn, up to two regiments of panzer grenadiers were moved to the same place. Artillery was being brought up. Having gained this intelligence, the ORD reported it over the radio to the corps' observation posts and began to withdraw over the same route, under the covering fire of two armored personnel carriers and two armored cars. The losses of the ORD were 1 armored personnel carrier and 5 submachine gunners. Now it was clear that the enemy was planning to launch his main attack in the Fatezh – Kursk direction. In fact, on 8 July 1943 the enemy indeed began an offensive on this axis. However, thanks to the fact that additional forces of our troops had been transferred there, the enemy lost up to 50 tanks and withdrew to his previous positions.

In order to identify fresh enemy forces that had been moved to the area of Ol'khovatka (the area of Ponyri Station), a second reconnaissance team was dispatched under the command of Senior Sergeant Khomenko. The team consisted of 5 men, armed with submachine guns and 3 hand grenades for each man. Early on the morning of 8 July 1943, the team arrived in the combat positions of the 15th Motorized Rifle Brigade, from which point it kept watch over the enemy for the rest of the day. In the area of Ol'khovatka, there was a knocked-out enemy tank, which the Germans were preparing to evacuate. Senior Sergeant Khomenko decided to set up an ambush at this tank, and on the night of 8 July the team, making use of the darkness, moved into ambush positions. They didn't have to wait long. A group of 6 Germans approached the tank and began final preparations to evacuate it. The sound of hammering and German conversation was audible. There was no need to wait any longer. At a signal, the ambush team opened fire from submachine guns, and having hurled their grenades, rushed the tank. Five of the Germans were killed and one was wounded. Having seized the wounded tanker, the papers on the bodies of the dead Germans, maps, and the tank's radio, the team returned with no losses. Since heavy rifle and machine-gun fire was opened at the team, the scouts had to crawl on their bellies for 1.5 kilometers together with the wounded German. The seized documents and maps from the tank yielded valuable intelligence about the enemy.

Thanks to excellent observation and an excellent assessment of the situation, as well as the bold and daring operation by the scouts, the task was fulfilled.

## THE CENTRAL FRONT'S KURSK COUNTEROFFENSIVE

On 13 July 1943, the commander of the 2nd Tank Army issued an order for the army, together with the field armies, to go over to a general counteroffensive, with the aim of destroying the enemy in the Krivtsovo – Kunach' – Mal. Bobriki – Nizh. Tagino – Probuzhdenie – Teploe – Bitiug – Ponyri – Protasovo area. The army was to launch its main attack in the direction of Snova, Sen'kovo and Gremiachevo. The army's offensive would begin after the 13th Army reached the Soglasnyi, Buzuluk, Shirokoe Boloto, Druzhovetskii, Saborovka line; from this point it was to pass through the lines of the 17th and 18th Guards Rifle Corps and by the end of 17 July 1943, it was to reach the Ol'gino, Ozerna, Gnilusha, Shusherovo area with its main forces, with a subsequent development of the attack toward Nikol'skoe and Nesterovo. In order to reinforce the 2nd Tank Army, the 9th Tank Corps was added to it out of the Front reserve. In accordance with the given order, the 2nd Tank Army commander on the night of 14/15 July 1943 determined the sectors of attack for the tank corps and the dates by which they were to reach the indicated objectives. In accordance with Lieutenant General Rodin's Combat Dispatch No.0147/OP to the commander of the Central Front Colonel General Rokossovsky that was sent at 20.00 on 16 July 1943, the forces of the 2nd Tank Army were in their jumping-off positions in readiness for forthcoming operations before noon on 16 July.

The composition, location and strength of the 2nd Tank Army's formations for the counteroffensive were as follows:

**3rd Tank Corps:** 50th Tank Brigade with the 1441st Self-propelled Artillery Regiment, 881st Destroyer Anti-tank Artillery Regiment, 1323rd Destroyer Anti-tank Artillery Regiment, and the 1068th Anti-aircraft Artillery Regiment was in its jumping-off positions in the area of the northwestern slopes of Point 253.5 and the village of 1st of May; the 51st Tank Brigade with the 449th Destroyer Anti-tank Artillery Regiment, the 728th Destroyer Anti-tank Artillery Battalion, and the 121st Anti-aircraft Artillery Regiment was in the 1st Nikol'skoe, Prilepy area; the 103rd Tank Brigade with the 1180th Destroyer Anti-tank Artillery Regiment held the sector between Prilepy and Goreloe area; the sector of the 57th Motorized Rifle Brigade with the 234th Mortar Regiment extended from the southwestern outskirts of Goreloe to Ponyri and Hill 239.8; and the 74th Separate Motorcycle Battalion and the 1329th and 567th Destroyer Anti-tank Artillery Regiments were in corps' reserve. The **3rd Tank Corps at 20.00 on 16.7.43** had 99 T-34 tanks and 37 T-70 tanks that were combat-fit and 25 T-34 tanks and 5 T-70 that were under repair. Thus, altogether the 3rd Tank Corps had 136

"A line has been taken. It is necessary to dig in."

Major General Latyshev presents the Order of the Red Banner and the Order of the Patriotic War to Captains Zakrevsky and Bystritsky, for their participation in a reconnaissance mission into the enemy rear.

operational tanks and 30 tanks under repair. It had 2 combat loads of ammunition, 3 refills with fuel and lubricants, and 6 days' of rations.

**16th Tank Corps** had the 164th Tank Brigade in the area of woods southwest of Ponyri-2 with the attached 729th Separate Destroyer Anti-tank Artillery Battalion, three batteries of the 1085th Anti-aircraft Regiment, and one company of the 205th Sapper Battalion; the sector of the 109th Tank Brigade with the 1541st Self-propelled Artillery Regiment, one battery of the 1085th Anti-aircraft Regiment and one company of the 205th Sapper Battalion extended from the western fringe of the woods northeast of Hill 264.9 to the woods 1 kilometer west of Hill 264.9; the 15th Motorized Rifle Brigade was in the Step' area together with the 226th Mortar Regiment and the 1042nd Anti-aircraft Regiment; and the 107th Tank Brigade and the 614th Destroyer Anti-tank Artillery Regiment were in corps reserve in the Hill 261.4, Hill 243.1 area. The **16th Tank Corps at 20.00 16.7.1943** had 100 T-34, 37 T-70 and 15 T-60 tanks that were combat-ready, for a total of 152 tanks. It had 2 combat loads of ammunition and 2.2 refills of fuel and lubricants.

The **11th Guards Tank Brigade** was holding its previous defensive lines and had 43 T-34 tanks and 10 T-70 tanks for a total of 53 tanks.

Thus as of 16 July 1943, the situation with the tanks in the 2nd Tank Army was as follows:

**Table 2.9: Status of the 2nd Tank Army's tanks as of 16 July 1943**

| | Authorized | Serviceable | Under repair | | | Irrevocable losses, not yet written off |
|---|---|---|---|---|---|---|
| | | | Minor repair | Medium repair | Major overhaul | |
| T-34 | 205 | 167 | 8 | 8 | 12 | 10 |
| T-70 | 84 | 67 | 4 | – | 6 | 7 |
| T-60 | 17 | 16 | – | – | 1 | – |
| Total: | 306 | 250 | 12 | 8 | 19 | 17 |

Of those operational tanks, including the recent batch of replenishments, most still had a considerable number of hours remaining on their engines before the next scheduled overhaul:

**Table 2.10: Status of the tank engines in the 2nd Tank Army's tanks**

| Tank type | Number of tanks | Of which, operational | Hours remaining on the tank engines of those operational tanks before scheduled overhaul | | | |
|---|---|---|---|---|---|---|
| | | | Less than 50 hours | From 50 to 100 hours | From 100 to 200 hours | 200 hours and above |
| T-34 | 276 | 238 | – | 167 | 71 | – |
| T-70 | 109 | 92 | – | 67 | 25 | – |
| T-60 | 17 | 16 | – | 16 | – | – |
| Total: | 402 | 346 | – | 250 | 96 | – |

## The 2nd Tank Army's counteroffensive in the Ponyri – Ol'khovatka sector of the front from 15 to 17 July 1943

Having suffered a defeat in the offensive stage of their operation, the Germans from 12 July began to go over to the defense, digging in on the line that had been reached, while simultaneously conducting a regrouping and transferring the 2nd, 9th, 12th, 18th and 20th Panzer Divisions to the area north and east of the city of Orel. As of 15 July 1943, in the sector facing the 2nd Tank Army, the enemy had the 78th, 86th, 292nd and 6th Infantry Divisions; the 4th and 9th Panzer Divisions; the 10th Panzer Grenadier Division; and the 304th Panzer Grenadier Regiment of the 2nd Panzer Division. The quick transition of the Soviet forces from defense to a large-scale offensive didn't allow the German troops to conduct a re-organization and to complete the processes of repair and restoration. According to dispatches from the attacking units of the 13th Army, all of the captured German mobile repair shops were still jammed with damaged vehicles and equipment.

At 19.30 on 15 July 1943, the 2nd Tank Army went on the offensive with the right-flank forces of the 3rd Tank Corps, while the army's left flank remained on its jumping-off line, because the rifle units, which had carried the heavy burden of the defensive fighting, weren't ready to attack. At the start of its offensive, the 2nd Tank Army had on its roster 240 T-34 tanks, 93 T-70 tanks and 15 T-60 tanks, for a grand total of 348 tanks.

The enemy resisted stubbornly. Wishing to disrupt the counteroffensive, the enemy in the course of 15 July launched counterattacks on all the sectors in groups of company to battalion size with the support of 10-15 tanks. The enemy also had a large quantity of anti-tank guns and self-propelled artillery positioned in strongpoints.

As a result of the day's action, the 3rd Tank Corps together with units of the 13th Army by 20.00 15 July reached a line 1 kilometer south of Buzuluk with two brigades. Meanwhile, its 103rd Tank Brigade was repelling enemy attacks toward Ponyri-1, covering the rest of the 3rd Tank Corps from the west. By the end of the day, the 3rd Tank Corps was given the task over the course of the night to withdraw units of the corps to the 1st of May – Prilepy – Goreloe area. The losses of the 3rd Tank Corps for 15 July 1943 were 64 killed and 71 wounded, with 1 T-34 tank burned-out, and 14 T-34 and 3 T-70 knocked out, which were recovered and made serviceable again.

## Combat Operations on 16 July 1943

Prior to 17.00, the 2nd Tank Army was located in its jumping-off areas in readiness for the offensive. The army had a total of 334 operational tanks: 228 T-34, 91 T-70 and 15 T-60.

At 17.00, the 16th Tank Corps went on the attack in the direction of Rzhavets and Druzhovetskii. That morning, the enemy had begun to pull back a portion of his forces to a new defensive line, covered by specially designated rear guard detachments from each of the regiments. The covering detachments were composed of 6-12 tanks, self-propelled guns, and a group of submachine gunners with a large number of artillery and mortars in support. As a result of the fighting, by 19.20 the 16th Tank Corps had reached the line Hill 244.2 – southern outskirts of Rzhavets. On the night of 16/17 July, an order was issued for the entire 2nd Tank Army to go on the attack at 4.00 17 July 1943 together with troops of the 13th Army, with the objective to reach the Mal. Bobrik – Kamenka – Plotavets – Sen'kovo area by the end of the day. Losses of the 2nd Tank Army for 16 July were 43 T-34, 1 T-70 and 1 T-60 knocked-out. Enemy losses were 12 anti-tank guns destroyed, and up to 18 tanks either burned-out or knocked-out.

## Combat Operations on 17 July 1943

With a total of 346 tanks (245 T-34, 86 T-70 and 15 T-60), the 2nd Tank Army resumed its offensive on the morning of 17 July. The enemy offered stubborn resistance with fire and counter-attacks, while simultaneously withdrawing a portion of his forces to the line they had held before launching the Kursk offensive. Groups of up to 50 enemy aircraft bombed the combat formations of our units. The 3rd Tank Corps, continuing to develop the offensive on the Ochki axis, as a result of tenacious fighting reached the line Buzuluk Station, Maloarkhangel'sk Station, Shirokoe Boloto, Ponyri-1, Rzhavets, Aleksandrovka, Druzhovetskii farmstead, Podsoborovka, Saborovka and Bobrik. Lieutenant Colonel Borisov's 51st Tank Brigade and Colonel Konovalov's 50th Tank Brigade, reinforced with artillery, were advancing in the first echelon of General Sinenko's 3rd Tank Corps. Lieutenant Colonel Arzhba's 57th Motorized Rifle Brigade was following in the wake of the first echelon tank brigades. The 103rd Tank Brigade was in corps' reserve. The 51st and 50th Tank Brigades attacked the enemy after a brief artillery barrage. A hard battle with hostile artillery and tanks developed. The tankers of the 3rd Tank Corps demonstrated resolve and bravery in this fighting.

The soldiers of Major I. Meerovsky's 255th Tank Battalion of the 51st Tank Brigade fought with particular bravery. They destroyed two enemy battalions and brewed up several tanks, of which two were destroyed by the battalion commander himself together with his crew. Pursuing the foe, the battalion destroyed three anti-tank guns and up to a company of infantry.

The tank commanders served as an example of self-sacrificial courage when carrying out combat assignments. For example, Captain Vasilii Filin's 94th Tank Battalion (51st Tank Brigade) in the area north of the village of Ochki destroyed 19 enemy self-propelled and field guns, three Pz. III and Pz. IV tanks, and up to a battalion of infantry. Captain Filin himself destroyed two anti-tank guns, a tank, and killed up to 50 Germans. For this he was awarded the Order of the Red Banner. Lieutenant Nikolai Zotov, a tank company commander of the 51st Tank Brigade's 255th Tank Battalion skillfully directed the combat in the area of Ochki and Lomovets, and in two separate actions destroyed five tanks (including one Tiger), 13 anti-tank guns and 24 machine-gun nests. He was decorated with the Order of the Red Banner.

Fearing a breakthrough of his defenses, the enemy on 17 July 1943 introduced the 10th Panzer Grenadier Division and the 292nd Infantry Division, which had previously been withdrawn into the reserve in the Sen'kovo area, into the fighting in the sector of the 2nd Tank Army. Having thrown the Germans back to the lines that they had occupied prior to the launching of Operation Citadel, the 2nd Tank Army received an order at 22.00 on 17 July: "In the course of the night of 17/18 July and the day of 18 July, assemble in the areas: Molotychi, Khmelevoe, Brekhovo, Iasenok, and Verkh. and Nizh. Liubazh. The 11th Guards Tank Brigade numbering 43 T-34 and 10 T-70 will be in the army commander's reserve."

Thus, over three days of fighting, the 2nd Tank Army together with the 13th Army had driven the enemy back to his start lines, thereby liquidating all of his offensive gains resulting from Operation Citadel. However, the 2nd Tank Army was unable to exploit the operation on this axis due to the receipt of a new assignment – an introduction into a breakthrough in the sector of the neighboring 70th Army.

The first three days of the 2nd Tank Army's counteroffensive, 15-17 July, are also characteristic with respect to combat losses in tanks. As a result of combat damage, 112 of its tanks had been knocked out.

The losses of the 3rd Tank Corps for 17 July 1943: 39 killed, 72 wounded and 11 men missing in action. Eleven T-34 tanks and one T-70 were left burned-out. Eleven more T-34 tanks and 1 T-70 were knocked-out, but all were evacuated. The losses inflicted on the enemy: 1,136 soldiers and officers, 9 medium tanks, 25 self-propelled guns, 3 vehicles and 31 guns of various calibers.

The 3rd Tank Corps was left with 128 serviceable tanks (91 T-34 and 37 T-70). Seventeen more tanks were under repair: 11 T-34 and 6 T-60.

The losses of the 16th Tank Corps over 16 and 17 July 1943: 307 men killed and wounded, 12 45mm anti-tank guns destroyed or damaged, and 13 T-34 and 4 T-70 left burned-out. Another 26 T-34 and 2 T-70 were knocked-out. The losses inflicted upon the enemy: 22 tanks and 3 self-propelled guns knocked-out and 2 artillery batteries destroyed. At the end of this period, the 16th Tank Corps had 95 serviceable tanks: 55 T-34, 28 T-70 and 12 T-60. Another 57 tanks were under repair: 42 T-34 and 15 T-70.

In the offensive battles of 16 and 17 July 1943, Captain Khombakh's 310th Tank Battalion and Captain Gvozdikov's 309th Tank Battalion (both of the 109th Tank Brigade), Captain Chigarko's 307th Tank Battalion (107th Tank Brigade) and Captain Eremenko's 360th Tank Battalion (164th Tank Brigade) all stood out. For example, Lieutenant Ivan Parshin's platoon of the 310th Tank Battalion was one of the first to break into Aleksandrovka Station, and with the fire from their tanks, contributed to the infantry's advance and the mopping up of the village. The commander of a T-34 tank Lieutenant Il'ia Chikomasov in his tank was the first to enter the village, and for a long time exchanged fire with the Germans. Senior Lieutenant Nikolai Rybak, the commander of a T-34 tank company in the 360th Tank Battalion, destroyed two enemy tanks and killed up to 20 enemy soldiers and officers in an offensive battle in the Aleksandrovka area. Rybak himself was badly wounded. The commander of a T-34 tank Lieutenant Zhigunov broke through to Hill 257.0 and fired from his tank at enemy artillery batteries, but with two direct hits against his turret, his tank erupted in flames and he was killed.

The commander of a tank company in the 309th Tank Battalion, Lieutenant Petr Sibriaev skillfully handled his company in the fight for Aleksandrovka village. Five enemy anti-tank guns, two machine-gun nests and up to 50 Nazis were wiped out by his company. Lieutenant Sibriaev himself was severely wounded, but refused to yield command of the company until an order from the battalion commander. Lieutenant Nikolai Talalov took command of the tank company in his place. In this same battle, his crew destroyed another heavy enemy gun. Talalov's tank caught fire after a hit from a German anti-tank shell, but even though he was also severely wounded, he continued to conduct fire from the tank until he was killed when his tank blew up. In these combats, the T-34 tank commanders Lieutenants Mikhail Piatin, Il'ia Chikimasov, Nikolai Zhigunov and Il'ia Parshin were all killed in combat. They were all posthumously awarded the Order of the Patriotic War.

## The 2nd Tank Army's march from 18 July to 21 July 1943

At midnight on 17 July, units of the 2nd Tank Army were on the move out of the Ponyri-1, Druzhovetskii, Ol'khovatka area, and by 14.00 on 18 July 1943, it had re-assembled with its main forces in the Molotychi, Vetrenka, Redogoshch', Nizh. Liubazh, Zherdovo, Brekhovo area, where the units were brought back into order. The army's headquarters was in Novoselki from 12.00 on 18 July. That evening, the army conducted a regrouping and by 18.30 18 July, it had moved into its area of jumping-off positions for the new offensive. The 3rd Tank Corps was in the Shepelovo, Nov. Tur'i, Raznovil'e area. The 16th Tank Corps' sector extended from the ravine southwest of Shepelovo to Proletarskii. The 11th Guards Tank Brigade moved into the area of Malakhova Sloboda at 20.30. The 2nd Tank Army received its new orders: "With the arrival of the infantry on the line Gorchakov, Monastyrshchina, Lomovets and in cooperation with the 19th Tank Corps, it is to seize the Kromy area, and in the future to operate in the direction of Orel or Naryshkino."

# 3

# The Orel Offensive Operation, 1943

**Command Staff of the 2nd Tank Army:**
Commander Lieutenant General Aleksei Rodin; after 2 August 1943 – Semen Bogdanov
Member of the Military Council – Major General Petr Latyshev
Chief of Staff – Major General Grigorii Preisman

**3rd Tank Corps** – Major General Maksim Sinenko
50th Tank Brigade – Colonel Fedor Konovalov; Lieutenant Colonel Vasilii Bzyrin
51st Tank Brigade – Lieutenant Colonel Pavel Borisov
103rd Tank Brigade – Lieutenant Colonel Aleksandr Khalaev
57th Motorized Rifle Brigade – Lieutenant Colonel Anton Arzhba
234th Mortar Brigade, 881st Destroyer Anti-tank Artillery Regiment, 74th Motorcycle Battalion,
728th Destroyer Anti-tank Battalion, 1441st Self-propelled Artillery Regiment

**16th Tank Corps** – Major General Vasilii Grigor'ev
107th Tank Brigade – Lieutenant Colonel Nikolai Teliakov
109th Tank Brigade – Lieutenant Colonel Petr Babkovsky
164th Tank Brigade – Lieutenant Colonel Nikolai Kopylov
15th Motorized Rifle Brigade – Colonel Petr Akimochkin
226th Mortar Regiment, 614th Destroyer Anti-tank Artillery Regiment, 51st Motorcycle Battalion,
729th Destroyer Anti-tank Battalion, 1541st Self-propelled Artillery Regiment

**11th Guards Tank Brigade** – Guards Colonel Nikolai Bubnov
**9th Separate Communications Regiment** – Lieutenant Colonel Petr Pavlov

On 20 July 1943, the 2nd Tank Army was in its jumping-off areas, awaiting commitment into a breakthrough. However, the attack by the units of the 70th Army had no success, and on the night of 20/21 July 1943, the 2nd Tank Army was shifted even further westward at an order from the Central Front to woods in the Ladyrevskii Heights, Ozerki, Novyi Svet area.

The army was prepared for an offensive in the general direction: Pokrovskoe, Verkh. Slobodka, Hill 268.2, Parnyi, Chern', Novo-Ryzhkovskii, Bel'diazhki, Kromy. The army's troops spent the day observing the enemy, cleaning and lubricating their equipment, and making minor repairs to the tanks, artillery and small arms.

Table 3.1: Data on the manpower and materiél of the 2nd Tank Army on 20 July 1943

| Unit | Men | | | | Rifles | | Machine guns | | | Mortars | | | Artillery | | | | Anti-tank rifles | Motor vehicles | Tanks | Armored cars | Anti-aircraft guns |
| --- | --- | --- | --- | --- | --- | --- | --- | --- | --- | --- | --- | --- | --- | --- | --- | --- | --- | --- | --- | --- | --- |
| | Command staff | Junior command staff | Enlisted men | Total | Total | PPD, PPSh | Light | Heavy | Anti-aircraft | 120mm | 82mm | 50mm | 85mm | 76mm howitzers | 76mm field | 45mm | | | | | |
| **3rd Tank Corps:** | | | | | | | | | | | | | | | | | | | | | |
| Command and corps units | 285 | 463 | 954 | 1702 | 834 | 480 | 24 | | 9 | 4 | 4 | | | | | | 2 | 226 | 2 | 52 | |
| 50th Tank Brigade | 199 | 408 | 412 | 1019 | 450 | 242 | 21 | 4 | 10 | | 6 | | | 4 | | | 24 | 112 | 46/3 | 3 | |
| 51st Tank Brigade | 204 | 390 | 372 | 966 | 397 | 293 | 20 | 4 | 9 | | 6 | | | 4 | | | 24 | 111 | 30/12 | 3 | |
| 103rd Tank Brigade | 206 | 371 | 356 | 933 | 362 | 294 | 20 | 4 | 9 | | 6 | | | 4 | | | 24 | 115 | 46/9 | 3 | |
| 57th Motorized Rifle Brigade | 275 | 798 | 1,502 | 2,575 | 1,186 | 1,375 | 109 | 43 | 9 | | 30 | | | 12 | | 11 | 85 | 276 | | 4 | |
| 234th Mortar Regiment | 81 | 168 | 386 | 635 | 434 | 154 | | | | 35 | | | | | | | | 120 | | | |
| 881st Anti-tank Regiment | 32 | 65 | 133 | 230 | 170 | 57 | | | | | | | | | | 20 | 36 | 43 | | | |
| 728th Anti-tank Battalion | 25 | 64 | 116 | 205 | 69 | 132 | | | | | | | | | | | 12 | 33 | | | |
| 121st Anti-aircraft Regiment | 38 | 94 | 233 | 370 | 257 | 112 | | | 16 | | | | 12 | | | | | 48 | | | 0/15 |
| Total in the corps: | 1,345 | 2,826 | 4,464 | 8,635 | 4,159 | 3,169 | 194 | 55 | 52 | 39 | 52 | | 12 | 24 | | 31 | 207 | 1,034 | 124/24 | 80 | 0/15 |
| **16th Tank Corps:** | | | | | | | | | | | | | | | | | | | | | |
| Command and corps units | 244 | 485 | 897 | 1,626 | 845 | 313 | 46 | | 9 | 6 | 4 | | | | | | 18 | 189 | 10 | ? | |
| 107th Tank Brigade | 224 | 435 | 350 | 1,009 | 443 | 303 | 17 | 4 | 9 | | 6 | | | 2 | | | 21 | 87 | 34/4 | ? | |
| 109th Tank Brigade | 184 | 403 | 329 | 916 | 403 | 329 | 20 | 4 | | | 6 | | | 4 | | | 24 | 75 | 34/11 | ? | |
| 164th Tank Brigade | 213 | 398 | 335 | 946 | 391 | 236 | 20 | 4 | | | 6 | | | 4 | | | 19 | 86 | 44/6 | ? | |
| 15th Motorized Rifle Brigade | 271 | 640 | 1,588 | 2,494 | 1,285 | 1,331 | 110 | 45 | | | 30 | | | 12 | | 12 | 82 | 112 | | ? | |
| 226th Mortar Regiment | 81 | 151 | 366 | 598 | 434 | 144 | | | | 36 | | | | | | | | 26 | | ? | |
| 614th Anti-tank Regiment | 31 | 57 | 71 | 159 | 147 | 33 | | | | | | | | | | | 36 | 31 | | ? | |
| 729th Anti-tank Battalion | 22 | 55 | 100 | 177 | 61 | 110 | | | | | | | | | | 7 | 10 | 24 | | ? | |
| 1085th Anti-aircraft Regiment | 31 | 54 | 121 | 206 | 135 | 15 | | | | | | | 7 | | | | | 14 | | ? | 0/11 |
| Total in the corps: | 1,301 | 2,678 | 4,157 | 8,136 | 4,144 | 2,814 | 213 | 56 | 18 | 42 | 52 | | 7 | 22 | | 19 | 210 | 644 | 122/21 | ? | 0/11 |
| 11th Guards Tank Brigade | 205 | 505 | 392 | 1,102 | 329 | 311 | 20 | 4 | | | 6 | | | 4 | | | 24 | 86 | 54 | | |
| 51st Separate Motorcycle Battalion | 30 | 76 | 170 | 276 | 16 | 230 | | | | | 4 | | | | | | 2 | 16 | | | |
| 24th Separate Reconnaissance Battalion | 34 | 103 | 61 | 198 | 54 | 86 | 15 | | | | | | | | | | | 13 | | | |
| **Grand Totals:** | 2,915 | 6,188 | 9,244 | 18,347 | 8,704 | 6,610 | 442 | 115 | 70 | 81 | 114 | | 19 | 50 | | 50 | 443 | 1,840 | 299/45 | ? | 0/26 |

On the eve of the attack on 20 July 1943, the 3rd Tank Corps had 122 operational tanks, including 82 T-34 and 40 T-70. Its subordinate 50th Tank Brigade had 29 T-34 and 19 T-70; the 51st Tank Brigade had 23 T-34 and 7 T-70; and the 103rd Tank Brigade had 30 T-34 and 17 T-70. It had available 2 combat loads of ammunition and 3 refills of fuel and lubricants. The 16th Tank Corps had 115 operational tanks, including 67 T-34, 24 T-70 and 14 T-60. Its subordinate 107th Tank Brigade had 17 T-34 and 20 T-70; the 109th Tank Brigade had 14 T-34, 2 T-70 and 12 T-60; and the 164th Tank Brigade had 30 T-34, 1 T-70 and 1 T-60. In corps' reserve were 6 T-34, 1 T-70 and 1 T-60. It had available 2.2 combat loads of ammunition, 2.9 refills of fuel and lubricants, and 7 days of rations.

On 21 July 1943 at 22.00, the Central Front commander issued Combat Order No.00442/op to the commander of the 2nd Tank Army regarding the offensive in the direction of Kromy. Here is the relevant excerpt:

> The 2nd Tank Army with all its forces simultaneously together with the infantry of the 70th Army is to launch an offensive from the line Khitrovka, Novo-Tsvetushchii, and developing the attack in the general direction of Novo-Ryzhkovskii, Krasnikov, Bel'diazhki, it is to reach the Kromy area by the end of 22.7.1943. While carrying out the task, keep in mind that Rybalko's forces went on the offensive at 15.00 on 21.7.1943 out of the Zolotorevo area (20 kilometers east of Orel) in the general direction of Kromy. Confirm receipt. Malinin.

## The 2nd Tank Army's opening attack in the Zhukovka – Pokhnisevo sector, 22 July 1943

At 10.00 on the morning of 22 July 1943, in conjunction with the 70th Army, the 2nd Tank Army went on the offensive with its main forces. The enemy with the units of Manteuffel's group – the 9th, 10th and 11th *Jäger* Battalions and the 102nd Infantry Division – had been defending the line Trosna, Lavrovo, Krasnoe Znamia, Zolotoe Dno for the previous four months, and had fortified it. The defenses were based on a collection of strongpoints and nests of resistance. There were well-built trenches along the entire forward edge, densely saturated with machine guns and mortars. In places there were barbed wire obstacles; the enemy had 2-3 earth and timber bunkers and up to 8 machine-gun nests per each kilometer of the frontline. The most strongly fortified points in the frontline sector were Trosna, Lomovets, Pokhvisnevo and Krasnaia Zaria. There were minefields at Trosna, Hill 195.1, southwestern outskirts of Lavrovo, Hill 237.5 and Hill 238.6. The enemy had up to 12-13 guns per kilometer of front. Trosna, Krasnikovo and Pokhvisnevo had been converted into anti-tank regions. On the morning of 22 July, the Germans reinforced his grouping, having transferred the 7th Infantry Division and the 4th Panzer Division to this sector from the Voronets – Sen'kovo area.

In the course of the day 22 July, the 2nd Tank Army, battling its way through minefields and across anti-tank ditches while subjected to enemy air strikes and heavy anti-tank fire and counterattacks by enemy tanks and infantry, pushed forward and at 19.00 seized Koz'mino, Iur'evskii, Zhukovka, Lomovets, Verkh. Slobodka, and Pokhvisnevo. The toll was heavy: 53 T-34 tanks and 27 T-70 tanks knocked-out; 10 T-34, 5 T-70 and 1 T-60 destroyed; and 13 T-34 that became disabled by mines. Thus altogether for the day of 22 July 1943, the 2nd Tank Army lost 111 tanks. In addition, 91 men were killed, 291 men wounded and 24 men went missing-in-action. At the same time, the enemy suffered the following damage: up to 2,456 officers and soldiers were wiped out; 40 tanks, 13 self-propelled guns, 18 mortars, 74 machine guns, 40 guns of various sorts and 4 vehicles were destroyed. In addition, one ammo dump was blown up and the headquarters of an infantry battalion was overrun and destroyed. Three German artillery batteries were silenced.

The tank battalions of Captain Khombakh and Gvozdikov stood out in the fighting. On 22 July 1943, the commander of the 310th Tank Battalion (109th Tank Brigade) Captain Anatolii Khombakh during an attack against Hill 264.0 (east of Krasnikovo) skillfully directed the fighting.

From his own tank, he personally knocked out four medium German tanks. The commander of the 309th Tank Battalion (109th Tank Brigade) Captain Ivan Gvozdikov, attacking the eastern outskirts of Krasnikovo and pursuing the retreating enemy, personally crushed three anti-tank guns with his tank. Deafened by the fighting, he refused to leave the battlefield and continued to command the battalion. In the fighting for possession of Hill 231.1, T-34 tank company commander Senior Lieutenant Vasilii Pavlov skillfully conducted the attack. In the fighting on 22 July 1943 in the area of Verkhniaia Slobodka and Novo-Ryzhkovskii, the commander of a T-34 tank company Senior Lieutenant Pavel Grudev (119th Tank Battalion, 50th Tank Brigade) distinguished himself. From his own tank he destroyed three cannons, 8 bunkers and up to 50 enemy officers and soldiers. In the combat in the area of Gnezdilovo and Krasnikovo, T-34 tank commander Aleksandr Chichikov (420th Tank Battalion, 103rd Tank Brigade) displayed exceptional tenacity on the attack. With fire from his own tank, he destroyed a self-propelled gun, three anti-tank guns, two earth and timber bunkers and up to 50 enemy soldiers and officers. He was decorated with the Order of the Patriotic War.

According to Combat Dispatch No.0154/OP from 23 July 1943, the army's combat losses for 22 July amounted to the following:

> 3rd Tank Corps – 54 killed, 130 wounded, 24 missing-in-action; 29 T-34 and 21 T-70 knocked-out, 9 T-34 burned-out and 2 T-34 blown up on mines.

> 16th Tank Corps – 37 killed and 161 wounded; 26 T-34 and 6 T-70 knocked-out, 1 T-34 burned-out and 11 T-34, 5 T-70 and 1 T-60 disabled or destroyed by mines. In addition, 1 T-34 and 1 T-70 were being sought.

In the assessment of the commander of the 2nd Tank Army Lieutenant General Aleksei Rodin and his assistant for vehicle maintenance and technical support Engineer-Colonel Samuil Krupenin, the greatest number of combat losses of tanks – 147 – for the entire operation occurred on 22 July 1943, when the formations of the 2nd Tank Army were operating on the left flank of the 70th Army in the areas of Chern' and Pokhvisnevo. The enemy, having brought up major reserves of anti-tank artillery and having assembled a large quantity of aircraft, attempted to blunt the advance of the 2nd Tank Army on 22 July 1943; however, regardless of the strong anti-tank artillery fire and strikes from the air, the army's units operating in the indicated area, having broken the German resistance, continued to push ahead.

The causes for the loss of combat vehicles on 22 July 1943 were:

a)  From anti-tank artillery fire: 44 T-34, 24 T-70, 4 T-60 for a total of 72 tanks;
b)  From mines: 15 T-34, 7 T-70, 2 T-60 for a total of 24 tanks;
c)  From airstrikes: 22 T-34, 5 T-70 for a total of 27 tanks;
d)  Caught fire and burned out: 3 T-34 and 1 T-70 for a total of 4 tanks;
e)  Due to mechanical problems: 12 T-34, 6 T-70 and 2 T-60 for a total of 20 tanks

This yields a grand total of 147 tanks lost on 22 July 1943. Having withdrawn the tanks by 2 to 3 kilometers on the night of 22/23 July 1943, the 2nd Tank Army on 23 July, remaining in a defensive posture, repelled enemy counterattacks by tanks and infantry.

## Combat operations on 24 July 1943

The Germans spent the day fortifying the line they held and shelling the 2nd Tank Army's combat formations, while bringing up tanks and infantry to the frontline. The 2nd Tank Army was occupying its current area, limiting itself to conducting reconnaissance probes, minefield clearing, and organizing cooperation with the 70th Army. Artillery and mortars fired at aggregations of enemy infantry and machines. Simultaneously, the 2nd Tank Army transferred the remaining equipment and personnel of the 51st Tank Brigade to the 50th Tank Brigade. The 51st Tank Brigade was withdrawn for refitting.

Combat Order No.020/OP from the Headquarters of the 3rd Tank Corps at 14.00 on 24 July 1943 specified:

> The commander of the 50th Tank Brigade Colonel Konovalov is to take the combat matériel from the 51st Tank Brigade, numbering 19 operational T-34 and 6 operational T-70, along with their crews and is to add them to the roster of the 50th Tank Brigade. The commander of the 51st Tank Brigade Lieutenant Colonel Borisov is to hand over the aforementioned matériel to Colonel Konovalov. Complete the transfer and acceptance of the matériel by 18.00 on 24.7.1943 and report upon the completion. The commander of the 51st Tank Brigade is to withdraw the remaining equipment and personnel to the wooded area 1 kilometer south of Khitrovka, where he is to put everything in order, be brought back up to table strength in personnel through the Personnel Department of the Corps Headquarters, camouflage thoroughly, and to organize combat training.
>
> [Signed] Commander of the 3rd Tank Corps Major General Comrade Sinenko and Chief of Staff – Colonel Deviatov

## Combat operations on 25 July 1943

Throughout the day, the enemy repeatedly launched counterattacks in groups of a company or battalion of infantry and up to 20 tanks. All the counterattacks were driven back with heavy losses to the enemy. All of the enemy's efforts were focused on strengthening his grouping in the Lomovets – Zhiriatino sector with the aim of protecting the southern flank of the retreating Orel grouping of his forces. Efforts by units of the 70th Army to breach the enemy's front in this sector had no success. The 2nd Tank Army spent the day of 25 July in its current area, readying its personnel and equipment for forthcoming operations. According to Lieutenant General Rodin's Combat Dispatch No.0156 from 25 July to the commander of the Central Front General Rokossovsky, at 20.00 the 2nd Tank Army had in its inventory: 3rd Tank Corps – 68 T-34 tanks and 29 T-70 tanks serviceable, and 13 T-34 and 1 T-70 under repair; 16th Tank Corps – 67 T-34, 24 T-70 and 7 T-60 operational, and 18 T-34, 10 T-70 and 9 T-60 under repair; 11th Guards Tank Brigade – 41 T-34 and 10 T-70, all combat-ready. On the night of 25/26 July 1943, by order of the Central Front, the 2nd Tank Army was shifted to a wooded area at Ladyrevskii Heights and south of Svetlyi Dunai. There, the 2nd Tank Army put its ordnance into combat readiness. The formations' headquarters reconnoitered the routes they would take to reach their jumping-off positions.

At 00.30 on 26 July 1943, the commander of the 2nd Tank Army received Order No.00465/op from the Central Front Commander regarding the introduction of the army into a planned breakthrough:

> 2nd TA – with the arrival of the infantry and tanks of the 70th Army on the line Grankino, Iablonovets, Maslovskii will enter the breach in the Zhiriatino, Kammenyi Kolodez' sector with the task to reach the Krasnaia Roshcha, Gnezdilovo, Chuvardino area by the end of day 27.7.1943; in the future have in mind operations toward Staroe Gnezdilovo and Verkhniaia Boevka. The 2nd TA's introduction into the breakthrough will be supported by a) all the artillery of the 55th Rifle Division, 29th Rifle Corps and a large portion of the 4th Artillery

Corps; and b) by a large portion of the 16th Air Army's forces. The commander of the 2nd TA is to use the day of 26.7.1943 for thorough preparation of the 2nd TA's offensive and for the organization of cooperation with troops of the 70th Army (especially with the 4th Artillery Corps) and with the 16th Air Army. Confirm receipt.

[Signed] Rokossovsky

On the night of 26/27 July 1943, by Combat Order No.061/OP, the 2nd Tank Army was shifted to the Khitrovka – Komarnik – Kucheriaevka area with the task to be ready to enter the planned breakthrough in the Zhiriatino – Kammenyi Kolodez' sector once the 29th Rifle Corps reached the line: Grankino, Iablonovets, Maslovskii. Unfortunately, the 29th Rifle Corps' attacks on 27 and 28 July 1943 made no headway, and thus the units of the 2nd Tank Army on 27 July remained idle on this axis.

## Combat operations on 28 July 1943

At 16.00 on 28 July, an order was given to the 3rd Tank Corps to go on the attack in the sector: Hill 260.1, Topkovo, Grankino. The 16th Tank Corps and the 11th Guards Tank Brigade were to stand by in readiness to move out behind the 3rd Tank Corps and to exploit its success. The enemy, with fire and counterattacks by infantry and tanks repulsed our units' attack. By 19.30, the 3rd Tank Corps with one brigade (the 50th Tank Brigade) had fought its way to an area 1 kilometer southeast of Topkovo, and with its main forces was approaching Nezhivka. Before setting out, the 3rd Tank Corps had 72 T-34 and 29 T-70 that were combat-ready. The 16th Tank Corps moved out at 19.30 in the wake of the 3rd Tank Corps. Before setting out for the march, the 16th Tank Corps had 73 T-34 tanks, 21 T-70 tanks and 6 T-60 tanks in formation. In the 227th Reserve Rifle Regiment, there were 2 T-34, 1 T-70 and 1 T-60. The 11th Guards Tank Brigade was still in its former area, having 42 T-34 and 10 T-70 operational. The 9th Separate Communications Regiment had 5 combat-fit T-34.

## Combat operations on 29 July 1943

The 2nd Tank Army throughout the day remained in the positions that it held at the end of the previous day, with part of its forces engaged in combat from 13.00 on the line Hill 260.1 – Hill 243.5. The enemy in the course of the day was putting up fierce resistance with fire and counter-attacks. At 15.30, after a 10-minute artillery preparation, the Germans counterattacked out of the areas of Hill 256.1, northern outskirts of Novaia Ialta and Martynovskii in strength of up to an infantry regiment with 40 tanks. The enemy attack was repulsed with heavy losses for him. However, the units of the 70th Army and the 2nd Tank Army were unable to achieve significant results either, since the enemy grouping, reinforced with the 7th Infantry Division and 4th Panzer Division was tenaciously holding a heavily fortified sector of the German defenses and preventing any breakthrough in this sector of the front. The losses of the 3rd Tank Corps for 29 July 1943 amounted to 31 killed, 98 wounded, and 5 T-34 tanks and 2 T-70 tanks that were knocked-out. After this, the 3rd Tank Corps had 63 T-34 tanks and 20 T-70 tanks still serviceable, with 19 T-34 and 8 T-70 under repair. The 16th Tank Corps had 64 T-34 tanks and 23 T-70 tanks operational. The 11th Guards Tank Brigade was still in its previous assembly area. At 20.00 on 29 July 1943, the units of the 2nd Tank Army were withdrawn by Combat Order No.029/OP to the wooded area at Ladyrevskii Heights and south of Svetlyi Dunai.

## Combat operations on 30-31 July 1943

By 16.00, the 2nd Tank Army had assembled in the above-mentioned wooded area. The units were busy with the repair and rehabilitation of materiél and weapons. Routes for the passage of tanks were reconnoitered and improved, and temporary bridges were constructed. The tank corps' headquarters spent the day discussing cooperation with the 70th Army's formations. On 31 July 1943, the units and headquarters of the 2nd Tank Army prepared to resume the offensive according to Order No.009/OP from 30 July 1943 for the army.

As a result of the fighting between 15 and 31 July 1943, the 2nd Tank Army had the following casualties: 856 men killed, 1,790 men wounded, and 46 men missing-in-action, for a total of 2,692 men. Tank losses were 57 T-34 and 22 T-70 destroyed; 82 T-34 and 29 T-70 knocked-out; and 10 T-34 and 7 T-70 that were disabled by mines, for a grand total of 207 tanks. The German side also suffered heavy losses. According to Soviet reports, 12,936 soldiers and officers were killed; and 164 tanks, 68 self-propelled guns, 213 guns of various caliber, 87 mortars, 288 machine guns, 108 vehicles and 6 aircraft were destroyed.

The commander of the 2nd Tank Army Lieutenant General Aleksei Rodin and his assistant for vehicle maintenance and technical support Engineer-Colonel Krupenin reported that as a result of the combat operations of the army between 16 July and 31 July 1943 inclusively, the following number of tanks were knocked-out: a) due to combat damage – 235 T-34, 70 T-70, and 10 T-60, for a total of 315 tanks; b) due to mechanical breakdowns: 71 T-34, 20 T-70 and 9 T-60, for a total of 100 tanks. Thus, a grand total of 415 tanks of the 2nd Tank Army were knocked-out or disabled. Of this indicated number, 78 tanks (61 T-34 and 17 T-70) were irrecoverably lost in the period from 16 July to 31 July 1943.

Altogether over this same period, the 2nd Tank Army repaired 307 tanks. The repair work on the combat machines was done in a compressed period of time. The fact that the formations were provided with necessary spare parts and components played a great role in the successful operations of the repair teams. Having temporarily halted the offensive in order to repair and rehabilitate the tanks, technical maintenance was done on 30 and 31 July on the tanks, including replacing the oil, cleaning of filters, tuning up the engines and charging the batteries.

## The penetration by the 2nd Tank Army of the enemy's strongly-fortified defenses in the Zhukovka – Shepelovo sector and the subsequent exploitation of the breakthrough, from 1 to 11 August 1943

By 1 August 1943, the enemy, striving to prevent the encirclement and destruction of his Orel grouping, had withdrawn his forces from the Orel area. In order to strengthen the southern flank, the enemy reinforced his grouping on the sector Lomovets – Krasnikovo – Novaia Zhizn' with the 7th Infantry Division, 4th Panzer Division, 63rd and 43rd Artillery Regiments, the 18th Mortar Battalion, the 620th and 851st Artillery Battalions, and a battalion of assault guns. In the Lomovets – Krasnikovo – Novaia Zhizn' sector, the enemy had positioned up to four infantry regiments of the 7th and 102nd Infantry Divisions, reinforced by two artillery battalions of the 43rd Artillery Regiment, the 851st Assault Gun Battalion and units of the 4th Panzer Division (70-90 tanks). His divisional reserves were located in the Krasnyi Pakhar' – Maiskii Tsvetok area. The defensive line in this sector had been improved by the enemy over the four previous months. The strongpoints were densely packed with machine guns and anti-tank guns. By 1 August 1943, the density of the fortified works consisted of 3-4 earth and timber bunkers and 8-11 machine-gun nests, and up to 20-23 guns (including mortars) per kilometer of front. In addition, there were up to 60 tanks and 20 Ferdinand heavy tank destroyers in this sector.

In the days of intensive work to prepare for the offensive, heavy rain fell on 28, 29 and 30 July. The area of the 2nd Tank Army's operations had no hard-surfaced roads at all, and the dirt roads in the black earth soil between the villages turned into quagmires, and became impassable for wheeled vehicles. Tracked vehicles could advance only with difficulty. The offensive was set to begin on 2 August 1943, but having received information that the enemy had started to withdraw some of his units, an order was given to begin the offensive on 1 August. As a result of this, the majority of the firing targets, previously designated and agreed upon with the artillery battalions, became superfluous in view of the entry of our units into these areas. The guns of the artillery battalions fired at unplanned targets or conducted area fire, which placed a familiar burden on the tanks of the 2nd Tank Army in carrying out their assignments.

Forces of the 2nd Tank Army on the march, July 1943.

Tanks of the 2nd Tank Army, July 1943.

On 1 August 1943, the 2nd Tank Army had 222 operational tanks, including 166 T-34, 50 T-70 and 6 T-60. These were distributed among the subordinate formations as follows:

The **3rd Tank Corps** had 54 T-34 and 20 T-70 operational, and another 30 T-34 and 12 T-70 under repair. The 1441st Self-propelled Artillery Regiment had 3 operational assault guns and 2 assault guns and 1 T-34 tank under repair. The 1442nd Self-propelled Artillery Regiment had 12 operational assault guns, plus 1 assault gun and 1 T-34 tank under repair. The corps had available 2 combat loads of ammunition, 3 refills of fuel and lubricants, and 5 days of rations.

The **16th Tank Corps** had 73 T-34, 20 T-70 and 6 T-60 operational, plus another 12 T-34, 9 T-70 and 9 T-60 under repair. In the 227th Reserve Rifle Regiment there were four operational tanks, 2 T-34, 1 T-70 and 1 T-60. The 1541st Heavy Self-propelled Artillery Regiment had 7 heavy self-propelled guns operational and 1 KV-1S. The corps had available 2.1 combat loads of ammunition, 2.7 refills of fuel and lubricants, and 6 day of rations.

The **11th Guards Tank Brigade** had 52 serviceable tanks (42 T-34 and 10 T-70). Another T-34 was under repair. It had available 2.2 combat loads of ammunition, 3.1 refills of fuel and lubricants, and 9 days of rations. The 9th Separate Communications Regiment had 5 T-34, all operational.

A report by the 2nd Tank Army's deputy commander for vehicle maintenance and technical support Guards Engineer-Colonel Krupenin stated that the 2nd Tank Army had the following number of tanks by the third stage of the operation, i.e. by 1 August 1943 (See Table 3.2):

**Table 3.2: Status of the 2nd Tank Army's tanks as of 1 August 1943**

|  | Authorized | Serviceable | Under repair | | | Irrevocable losses, not yet written off |
|  |  |  | Minor repair | Medium repair | Major overhaul |  |
|---|---|---|---|---|---|---|
| T-34 | 226 | 147 | 5 | 14 | 16 | 44 |
| T-70 | 85 | 44 | 1 | 4 | 15 | 21 |
| T-60 | 16 | 7 | – | – | 9 | – |
| Total: | 327 | 198 | 6 | 18 | 40 | 65 |

**Table 3.3: Status of the tank engines in the tanks of the 2nd Tank Army as of 1 August 1943**

| Tank type | Number of tanks | Of which, operational | Hours remaining on the tank engines of those operational tanks before scheduled overhaul | | | |
|  |  |  | Less than 50 hours | From 50 to 100 hours | From 100 to 200 hours | 200 hours and above |
|---|---|---|---|---|---|---|
| T-34 | 226 | 147 | – | 147 | – | – |
| T-70 | 85 | 44 | – | 44 | – | – |
| T-60 | 16 | 7 | – | 7 | – | – |
| Total: | 327 | 198 | – | 198 | – | – |

At 11.00 on 1 August 1943, the forces of the 2nd Tank Army in cooperation with the 70th Army's 29th Rifle Corps went on the attack in the general direction of Hill 260.1, Hill 256.9, Hill 262.7, and Rzhava. At 15.30, the forward units of the 2nd Tank Army caught up with the infantry on the line Hill 269.0, Krasnikovo and west of the slopes of Hill 260.1. The enemy was putting up fierce resistance, launching counterattacks and conducting frequent massed airstrikes on the combat formations of the 2nd Tank Army's units.

The 2nd Tank Army, overcoming the Germans' network of anti-tank fire and anti-tank obstacles, by 21.00 on 1 August 1943 reached the line running from a grove south of Hill 263.0 to Hill 260.1. Because of the presence of minefields, heavy artillery fire and enemy tank fire from fixed positions, the army's units were unable to make any further gains on 1 August. The infantry of the 70th Army were lagging behind. The 2nd Tank Army in the course of the day lost 16 T-34 and 5 T-70 burned-out, and 19 T-34 and 8 T-70 knocked-out, for a total of 48 tanks.

In the fighting on 1 August 1943 for the village of Krasnyi Kommunar, the commander of a tank company in the 103rd Tank Brigade's 119th Tank Battalion Lieutenant Aleksandr Petrukhin stood out for his performance. He operated together with his subordinate company decisively and daringly. He destroyed 2 enemy trucks filled with troops, 2 guns and more than 50 enemy soldiers and officers. In this same action, Lieutenant Boris Garbuzov of the 119th Tank Battalion also showed himself to be a courageous and seasoned commander. His tank crew destroyed 4 anti-tank guns, 9 bunkers and 50 enemy soldiers and officers. Tank platoon commander Lieutenant Vasilii Bratersky (50th Tank Battalion) destroyed 4 cannons, 3 mortars and 25 hostile soldiers and officers. When his company commander's tank was knocked out of action, he skillfully directed the company's combat. All three were killed in action. Lieutenants Petrukhin, Bratersky and Garbuzov were all posthumously awarded the Order of the Patriotic War.

## Combat operations on 2 August 1943

At 5.30, the army's forces resumed the offensive in the general direction of Rzhava and Sharykino. Overcoming tenacious enemy resistance and receiving heavy flanking fire from a grove to the east of Rossokhovets and Krasnyi Kommunar, the army in the course of the day was involved in heavy fighting on the northwestern slopes of Hill 262.7 and in the Progress – Novaia Zaria area, repelling enemy tank and infantry counterattacks. The infantry of the 70th Army on the 2nd Tank Army's left flank was making very slow progress in the Krasnikovo – Topkovo sector, and at times made no advance at all, which allowed the enemy to concentrate all of his artillery fire on the 2nd Tank Army, and gave him the opportunity to launch counterattacks from the west into the army's exposed flank. The army's units suffered heavy losses – over the day of combat, 22 tanks were irrevocably lost. Also, on 2 August 1943, the deputy chief of staff of the 2nd Tank Army Colonel Belkov, the 3rd Tank Corps' chief of staff Colonel Deviatov, and the commander of the 11th Guards Tank Brigade Colonel Bubnov were all killed in action. In heavy fighting in the area of Hill 263.0, the deputy commander of the 50th Tank Brigade Colonel Ushakov and its commander Colonel Konovalov were both killed. The lack of progress and the recent heavy losses led to the dismissal of Lieutenant General Aleksei Rodin as the commander of the 2nd Tank Army. Lieutenant General Semen Bogdanov assumed command of it.

On the morning of 2 August 1943, when the 2nd Tank Army had reached Hill 263.0 with the 3rd Tank Corps, Hill 262.7 with the 11th Guards Tank Brigade and Hill 269.0 with the 16th Tank Corps, by an order from the deputy commander of the Central Front Lieutenant General Zakharkin, the army received the mission to force a crossing of the Tishinka River in the Sharykino, Progress and Guniavka areas and to emerge in the rear of the enemy group that was defending in the Krasnikovo, Grankino, Krupyshino area. All of the army's attempts to breakthrough to the west in the designated places had no success, because the approaches to the settlements were mined and were being blanketed with heavy artillery fire from the northwestern bank of the Tishinka River. There were no fords on the river, and all the bridges across it had been demolished. Having no success, the 2nd Tank Army by the end of the day was compelled to continue to attack in the general direction of Rzhava and Sharykino. As a result of the day's action, units of the 2nd Tank Army by 20.00 on 2 August 1943 had battled its way forward to a line that stretched from a point north of Hill 258.1 to a point 1 kilometers south of Rzhava with intense fighting, including being subjected to strikes from the air by groups of 20 to 50 German aircraft.

## Combat operations on 3 August 1943

In the course of the day, the enemy's left flank continued to hold its positions, while the right-flank forces, offering stubborn resistance, made a fighting withdrawal to the northwest. The *Luftwaffe* repeatedly bombed the 2nd Tank Army's combat formations in groups of up to 40 aircraft. Major General of Tank Forces Maksim Sinenko, the commander of the 3rd Tank Corps, was up among the combat formations of the main forces. Skillfully handling the formations and units on the spot, he was able to make the proper decisions at the most critical moments. Analyzing the course of the fighting, the corps commander came to the conclusion that the enemy still hadn't deciphered the Soviet command's plan or the axis of the main attack. General Sinenko ordered the 50th and 51st Tank Brigades to increase their pressure on the enemy. He strengthened his 103rd Tank Brigade, which was attacking with an open flank, with his reserve 881st Destroyer Anti-tank Regiment.

The 16th Tank Corps, developing the offensive, seized Zelenaia Roshcha at 10.00 on 3 August 1943. The corps' human losses amounted to 63 killed, 173 wounded and 3 men missing-in-action. With respect to tanks, the 16th Tank Corps lost 18 T-34 and 2 T-70 knocked-out; and 9 T-34 that were destroyed. Another 4 T-34 and 1 T-70 were damaged by mines. In return, according to Soviet reports the Germans lost one Me-109 shot down, one tank knocked-out and 7 mortar batteries, 4 artillery batteries, 13 machine-gun nests and 3 earth and timber bunkers that were destroyed. In addition, up to 500 enemy soldiers and officers were killed.

## Combat operations on 4 August 1943

The enemy remained in his current grouping, making a fighting withdrawal to the north and northwest with stubborn resistance; the *Luftwaffe* continued to strike the combat formations of our units in groups of 15 to 20 aircraft. The 2nd Tank Army's attack on 4 August began in the morning, having 68 T-34 and 19 T-70 in formation (although two T-70 tanks lacked crews). The 9th Tank Corps, consisting of the 23rd Tank Brigade, the 108th Tank Brigade, and the 95th Tank Brigade, as well as the 8th Motorized Rifle Brigade, became operationally subordinate to the 2nd Tank Army on this day. It was operating on the Kolko – Glinki, Kutafino – Leshnia axis, with 33 T-34 and 27 T-70 still serviceable, and 5 T-34 and 3 T-60 under repair. By this time the 3rd Tank Corps was down to 32 operational tanks (23 T-34 and 9 T-70), though 6 of the T-34 tanks and 2 of the T-70 tanks lacked crews. It also had 28 T-34 and 1 T-70 that were in the repair shop. The 16th Tank Corps had been reduced to just 31 operational tanks, 16 T-34 and 5 T-70. The 11th Guards Tank Brigade counted 29 T-34 and 5 T-70 that were still operational. By the morning of 5.8.1943, it had put two more T-34 back into service.

The 2nd Tank Army in the course of 4 August 1943 continued to attack and seized Kutafino and Rozhkovskii. It was fighting for possession of the road west of Hill 245.2, and with a portion of its forces forced a crossing of the Kroma River in the sector south of Glinki and Kutafino, while its 11th Guards Tank Brigade crossed the Nezhivka River southwest of Rozhkovskii. The enemy, falling back behind the Nezhivka River, had destroyed all the bridges.

## Combat operations on 5 August 1943

The enemy on 5 August stubbornly defended the southwestern bank of the Nezhivka River with fire and counterattacks. Enemy aircraft in groups of up to 100 bombed the 2nd Tank Army's combat formations and especially concentrated their efforts on destroying the pontoon bridges across the Nezhivka River.

The 2nd Tank Army on the morning of 5 August 1943 had 88 operational tanks: 66 T-34 and 22 T-70. The 9th Tank Corps was withdrawn into the reserve of the Central Front and was located in woods east of Raikino and Shirokaia Poliana, where it performed maintenance and service on its tanks and weapons and worked to make itself combat-ready. Overcoming enemy resistance, by 16.00 the 2nd Tank Army with its main forces had completed the crossing of the Nezhivka River, but only with great difficulty, since the swampy flood plain of the Nezhivka River was 300 to 400 meters wide and consisted of boggy muck. It was often impossible to recover mired machines and guns even with tractors because of the swampy ground. Moreover, the crossing was conducted under German artillery fire and strong enemy air activity. Once again, the 70th Army had made no progress, lagged behind, and gave the enemy the opportunity to unleash most of his artillery fire and air strikes against units of the 2nd Tank Army, especially at the places where the river was being crossed.

Having completed the river crossing by 16.00, primarily with tanks and motorized infantry, the 2nd Tank Army expanded its bridgehead against enemy resistance, and by 17.30 it had seized Krasnaia Iagoda and was fighting for the southeastern outskirts of Krasnaia Roshcha. In the combat in the area of the Nezhivka River, T-34 tank commander Lieutenant Tkachenko of the 103rd Tank Brigade's 119th Tank Battalion stood out. With fire from his main gun and machine gun, he knocked out an enemy tank and a self-propelled gun, and killed more than 80 enemy soldiers and officers. In the combat in the area of Volobuevo on 5 August, another T-34 tank commander with the 119th Tank Battalion, Junior Lieutenant Vladimir Riabovol, who had an assignment to scout out a crossing for the tanks, pushed far in front of the rest of the battalion. In the process, he destroyed two guns and five machine guns, and killed 70 Nazis. Riabovol's tank was set ablaze by a direct hit from a heavy German shell. He clambered out of the burning tank with difficulty, tossing grenades, and killed up to 10 enemy soldiers and officers before being killed himself.

The new commander of the 2nd Tank Army Lieutenant General Semen Bogdanov, soon after taking command of the army, issued Combat Order No.069/OP at 23.30 on 5 August. It was in effect a dressing down of his subordinate commanders and a harsh criticism of their performance:

> To the commanders of the 3rd, 9th and 16th Tank Corps and the 11th Guards Tank Brigade:
>
> The army's combat assignment has not been carried out. A further pattern of failing to carry out a combat order by the commanders of the tanks corps and of the 11th Guards Tank Brigade is intolerable. The army's Military Council believes that the causes for the failures are the fact that the corps commanders are not directing the tank combat formations and especially not the artillery. There is no artillery in the combat formations to place direct fire. The tanks attacks are not being prepared by directed, massed artillery fire. The artillery commanders of the corps are being idle and are not directing the artillery. Command and control by the corps commanders has been organized in an unsatisfactory manner. For example, the commanders of the 16th Tank Corps and the 11th Guards Tank Brigade had no communications link with me for one and a half days and failed to show any concern. Reconnaissance and surveillance of the battlefield hasn't been organized by the headquarters, while the chiefs of staff give no significance to this matter. The artillery headquarters are not

scouting the enemy's system of fire at all. Cooperation both within the corps and between the corps and the 11th Guards Tank Brigade, and with the attached assets is entirely absent. The corps commanders and the commander of the 11th Guards Tank Brigade are failing to show the requisite initiative with respect to cooperation.

I AM ORDERING:

The commanders of the corps and of the 11th Guards Tank Brigade are to put reconnaissance and command and control into that order and system that have been personally directed by me. The work is to be carried out by 16.00 on 6.8.1943. I demand that you direct the artillery and the artillery headquarters. By 22.00 on 6.8.1943, replenish the units' combat formations at the expense of the rear services by removing 35 percent of the personnel from the rear areas. I am placing personal responsibility for these measures on the deputy political commanders of the corps. Pay especial attention to the timely repair and timely return of the tanks to the combat formations. Don't busy yourselves with paperwork.

According to the testimony of the assistant commanders for technical services, there are the following number of tanks that are combat-ready: in the 3rd Tank Corps – at 20.00 on 5.8.43, on paper there were 23 operational tanks, but in reality there are 12 tanks; in the 16th Tank Corps at 22.00 on 4.8.43, there were 53 serviceable tanks on paper, but in fact there were only 18.

The army's Military Council demands the elimination of the shortcomings mentioned in this combat order. I am warning the commander of the 11th Guards Tank Brigade Guards Colonel Bormotov about his heedless attitude to service and to my orders. I am pointing Guards Engineer-Colonel Krupenin's attention to his formal attitude toward important work and [directing him] not to be busy henceforth with departmentalism, but to be genuinely engaged with the problems of putting tanks back into service in the combat formations.

[Signed] Commander of the 2nd Tank Army Guards Lieutenant General Comrade Bogdanov, Member of the Military Council Major General Comrade Latyshev and Deputy Chief of Staff Colonel Chizh

The official document *Boevoi put' 2-oi Gv. TA* [*Combat path of the 2nd Guards Tank Army*] comments upon General Bogdanov's initial steps once he took command, as well as the 2nd Tank Army's initial operations under Bogdanov's direction:

Having arrived at the headquarters of the 2nd Tank Army, the [new] commander attentively studied the situation facing the army and its neighbors. The shape of the frontlines was such that our forces were looming over a hostile grouping that deeply extended to the east. With a successful development of the 2nd Tank Army's offensive, the army would emerge in the rear of the German grouping, thereby creating the threat of its encirclement. This would compel the German command to increase its forces and put up fierce resistance against the 2nd Tank Army, in order prevent a breakthrough.

Indeed, General Bogdanov took advantage of this situation. He decided to conduct a regrouping of the army in the span of one night and to launch a focused attack on a narrow sector of the front. Subsequently, given a successful development of the offensive, the commander proposed using the maneuverability of the tank corps in order to alter the direction of the attack in the course of the offensive, if this would be prompted by the situation. General Bogdanov disagreed with the suggestion of the chief of staff General Preisman, who was recommending that the tank army's efforts be shifted to the sector of the 70th Army, where the enemy had weakened his forces. "In the opposite case, we risk a head-on attack, instead of maneuver," declared the chief of staff at the end of his report.

To this point, the tank army had been commonly used to exploit a success in the sectors of the combined-arms armies. However, the situation that had developed was demanding immediate actions, in order to prevent the enemy from organizing a solid defense. Bogdanov said, "In the given situation, independent operations by the tank army are sensible, even though we don't have such experience." Addressing the chief of staff, he continued, "You are saying it is a risk that we'll attack head-on, but to know how to take sensible chances is a necessary quality of a commander. In battle, the commander's will manifests itself in a risk. But in order not to be a speculative adventure, the risk should be grounded in reality. That is why we are attacking head-on."

The 3rd Tank Corps after a series of regroupings at the order of the commander launched a focused attack in a narrow sector of the front, seized Rzhava and Bel'diazhki, and cut the Kromy – Dmitriev – Sevsk highway. Lieutenant Colonel Arzhba'a 57th Motorized Rifle Brigade and the 51st Tank Brigade attacked toward Kromy. However, here the corps met stubborn enemy resistance. The German command began hastily to bring up its reserves and anti-tank means to this area. The pace of the tank corps' advance perceptibly slowed. General Bogdanov watched as the right-flank 57th Motorized Rifle Brigade was stopped by an enemy counterattack, and several elements of it were pushed back. This was creating the threat of an enemy attack into the right flank of the 3rd Tank Corps. Bogdanov traveled to the observation post of the corps commander General Sinenko, who reported to him that he had been compelled to advance the 51st Tank Brigade out of his reserve to the right flank. The army commander agreed with this decision, but ordered that the 51st Tank Brigade must attack, to create the impression in the enemy that the army was striving for the Kromy area. At the order of the army commander, the army's main forces halted their attack toward Kromy and abruptly pivoted to the west. This maneuver protected the 51st Tank Brigade and 57th Motorized Rifle Brigade, which were continuing to attack on the Kromy axis. At the same time, he threw the enemy into confusion regarding the real direction of the attack.

The main forces of the 3rd Tank Corps and of the 2nd Tank Army at the decision of the Front commander were pivoted to launch a powerful attack to the west toward Kolki and Tolmachevo, into the flank of the enemy's Orel grouping. The tank corps from the march forced the Nezhivka River. This maneuver by the tank army came as a surprise for the enemy. Although the wide, swampy river basin indeed hindered the movement of tanks, and though the bridges had been blown, the tanks rapidly overcame a line that the German command hadn't had time to set up for a defense. It hadn't expected that our tanks would so swiftly change the direction of attack and go on the offensive in this relatively impassable terrain. Continuing to advance doggedly, the tank corps took possession of Tolmachevo and Gnezdilovo. Thereby the threat of encirclement from the south of the enemy grouping that was operating in the Orel area was created.

## Combat operations on 6 August 1943

The enemy was continuing to check the offensive by the 2nd Tank Army's units with stubborn defense, while pulling back his main forces to the west; the *Luftwaffe* was bombing the army's combat formations and the pontoon bridges on the Nezhivka River in groups of up to 20 aircraft. The 2nd Tank Army on 6 August 1943 had a total of 73 tanks operational, including 50 T-34 and 23 T-70, and was continuing to attack in the Krasnaia Roshcha – Krasnaia Step' – Novo-Gnezdilovo direction. By 18.00 it reached a line running from 1 kilometer southwest of Krasnaia Roshcha to 2 kilometers northwest of Krasnaia Iagoda. The subordinate formations of the 2nd Tank Army were now down to 16 serviceable tanks in the 3rd Tank Corps (9 T-34 and 7 T-70), 20 serviceable tanks in the 16th Tank Corps (17 T-34 and 3 T-70) and 27 serviceable tanks in the

11th Guards Tank Brigade (25 T-34 and 2 T-70). Over the period from 24 July to 6 August 1943, the army had made a 115-kilometer advance with fighting and had liberated 22 populated places.

At 23.50 on 6 August 1943, the commander of the Central Front issued Order No.00525/op to the commanders of the 3rd Guards and 2nd Tank Armies and the 16th Air Army:

> The enemy is retreating to the west, and clinging to opportune, unprepared lines, is striving to delay the offensive of our forces and by this secure the orderly withdrawal of the Orel grouping. The 3rd Guards Tank Army and the 2nd Tank Army, despite a situation that has developed favorably for us and in spite of my order, has been spinning their wheels for three days and have not carried out their tasks. This is a consequence of the fact that the commanders of the tank formations and units are showing indecisiveness, do not know how to force their subordinates to carry out assignments, and are handling the combat of their units, formations and armies exceptionally poorly. I am ordering the 3rd Guards Tank Army and 2nd Tank Army with all their forces to break through the front of the enemy's units on the morning of 7.8.1943, and exploiting the attack in the general direction of Shablykino, to cut-off the path of retreat of his Orel grouping to the west and southwest from the line Naryshkino, Ostanino, Korov'e Boloto, Nizhniaia Fedotovka. The 2nd Tank Army is to breach the defensive front of the enemy's covering units in the sector Krasnaia Roshcha, Volobuevo, and developing the attack toward Gnezdilovo, is to seize the Efimovka, Goncharovka, Gnezdilovo, Gorodishche area by the end of 7.9.1943; in the future attack in the general direction of Zhikharevo, Lobki, Kolosok and seize the Gavrilovo, Turishchevo, Kolosok area. The commanders of the 3rd Guards Tank Army and 2nd Tank Army are to demand the precise and unconditional fulfillment of orders from the entire officer staff. In no case allow an attack with scattered groups; demand an attack by the entire mass of tanks and motorized infantry of the corps and armies. Bring the commanders of the units and formations who fail to carry out their assignments to strict accounting, right up to trial in front of a military tribunal. Confirm receipt.
>
> [Signed] Rokossovsky

## Combat operations on 7 August 1943

The enemy, covered by fire and counterattacks, continued to withdraw his main forces. The *Luftwaffe* in groups of up to 10 aircraft continued to strike the combat formations of our units. The 2nd Tank Army continued to attack with a total of 60 tanks (47 T-34, 13 T-70). At this time, up to 50 repaired tanks of various marks, which had been dispatched from the disabled vehicle collection points, were on the move toward the battlefield or were positioned at river crossings. The 11th Guards Tank Brigade at 6.00 seized Krasnaia Roshcha, and subsequently at 14.00 with an impetuous attack took possession of Gnezdilovo after a clash with enemy tanks. The 3rd Tank Corps at 9.00 was approaching Goncharovka and at 11.00 seized Tolmachevo. The enemy, fearing envelopment by units of the 2nd Tank Army, withdrew his units on the left flank, thereby giving units of the 70th Army the possibility to advance.

The commander of the 2nd Tank Army Lieutenant General Bogdanov issued Combat Order No.071/op at 20.00 on 7 August 1943, in which he demanded from the army's formations:

> Continue to scout out the condition of crossings and bypasses. Go around all obstacles met on the path, do no get tied up in combats for populated points, and make constant forward progress. Do not permit an offensive in scattered groups, but attack en masse with the tanks, motorized infantry and artillery. Keep firm, continuous contact among the corps and the 11th Guards Tank Brigade; cooperate without interruptions on the battlefield. I categorically

demand from the entire officer staff the punctual and unconditional carrying out of assignments. On the night of 7/8 August 1943, organize reconnaissance and send out forward detachments with the assignment not to allow the enemy to dig in and to pursue him actively in the directions of the army's operations. Report every two hours.

## Combat operations on 8 August 1943

The units of the 2nd Tank Army ran into heavy enemy artillery and mortar fire, as well as enemy tank fire, in front of Hills 247.7 and 266.0. The 2nd Tank Army by 8 August 1943 had only 36 operational tanks (which took part in the fighting): 26 T-34 and 10 T-70. Primarily the offensive was being sustained by the motorized rifle brigades, the motorized infantry – machine-gun battalions of the tank brigades, and the corps' artillery. Having lost so many tanks in the preceding fighting, the army had expended its main shock power to a significant degree and no longer had the capability to break through enemy defenses. The personnel, especially the tank crews, were extremely worn out, and thus the army could not breach the enemy front on this sector. The terrain, which was strongly cut by water obstacles that were difficult to cross, was another cause that hindered the army from carrying out of its tasks. Attempts to outflank the enemy positions from the south had no success, and by day's end the 2nd Tank Army was fighting on a line east of Lebiazh'e – Goncharovka and on the southwestern slopes of Hill 251.0.

## Combat operations on 9 August 1943

By Directive No.00531/op, the 3rd Tank Corps, the 15th Motorized Rifle Brigade, the 13th Destroyer Anti-tank Brigade and the 1541st Heavy Self-propelled Artillery Regiment became operationally subordinate to the 70th Army. Having handed their remaining tanks to the 3rd Tank Corps, on the morning of 9 August the 16th Tank Corps and the 11th Guards Tank Brigade prepared for a march, and at 13.00 they set out to a new assembly area. By the Central Front's directive, the 2nd Tank Army was pulled out of combat and re-assembled in the Pavlovskii – Trofimovka – Vysokoe area. The 3rd Tank Corps remained under the operational control of the 70th Army, and on 9 and 10 August continued to be involved in combat.

The 2nd Tank Army commander issued the following combat order (No.073/OP) at 4.40 on 9 August 1943:

**To the commanders of the 3rd and 16th Tank Corps and of the 11th Guards Tank Brigade:**

On the basis of Directive No.00531/OP of 9.8.43 from the Central Front's Military Council, I AM ORDERING: the 3rd Tank Corps from 9.8.43 is to become operationally subordinate to the 70th Army. Prior to 11.00 9.8.43, all the tanks and self-propelled guns of the 16th Tank Corps and of the 11th Guards Tank Brigade together with their crews will be handed over to the 3rd Tank Corps. The 16th Tank Corps' 15th Motorized Rifle Brigade and the 1442nd and 1541st Self-propelled Artillery Regiments from 9.00 9.8.43 will be subordinate to the 3rd Tank Corps commander. Material support for the 3rd Tank Corps will remain the 2nd Tank Army's responsibility. Report on the execution [of this order] at 11.00 9.8.43.

[Signed] Commander of the 2nd Tank Army Guards Lieutenant General Bogdanov, Military Council member Major General Comrade Latyshev, and deputy chief of staff Colonel Chizh

This order was followed by one from the headquarters of the 3rd Tank Corps to its subordinate units. Combat Order No.031/OP from 9.8.43 stated:

**To the commanders of the 103rd and 50th Tank Brigades, and the Artillery Commander and the Chief of Rear Services of the 3rd Tank Corps:**

On the basis of Combat Order No.072/OP of 9.8.43 from the headquarters of the 2nd Tank Army, the 3rd Tank Corps will pass to the operational control of the 70th Army, having received all the tanks from the 16th Tank Corps and 11th Guards Tank Brigade together with their crews. I AM ORDERING: the commander of the 103rd Tank Brigade will accept all of the serviceable tanks of the 16th Tank Corps and of the 11th Guards Tank Brigade, together with their crews by 10.30, leaving them in their combat sectors until the end of the day. By 15.00 9.8.43, the commander of the 50th Tank Brigade is to take all of the tanks requiring repair from the 16th Tank Corps and the 11th Guards Tank Brigade, together with their crews, and is immediately to organize their repair. Control over the acceptance of the matériel is placed on my assistant for technical services Engineer-Lieutenant Colonel Khokhlov. By 10.30 9.8.43, the commander of the corps' artillery is to accept the self-propelled guns of the 16th Tank Corps and 11th Guards Tank Brigade and is to subordinate them to the 1442nd and 1541st Self-propelled Artillery Regiments. Supply of the 3rd Tank Corps remains the responsibility of the 2nd Tank Army. Report on the execution at 10.30 9.8.43. Present a map of the dispositions and data on the combat strength and total strength.

[Signed] Commander of the 3rd Tank Corps Major General Comrade Sinenko; chief of staff of the 3rd Tank Corps Colonel Safronov

## Combat operations on 9 August 1943

Having completed a night march, the 2nd Tank Army arrived in its new assembly area without the 3rd Tank Corps. Lieutenant General Bogdanov gave directions on the withdrawal of his 2nd Tank Army (minus the 3rd Tank Corps and 15th Motorized Rifle Brigade) into the Front reserve from 9 August 1943:

The 11th Guards Tank Brigade (without tanks), having turned over its combat sector to the 3rd Tank Corps at 21.00 on 9.8.43 is to set out on the route: Hill 257.0, Lubianki, Koshelovo, Rzhavchik, Uspenskii, Pavlovskii, and by 5.00 10.8.43 is to assemble in the Gurovka area. The 16th Tank Corps (without its tanks and its 15th Motorized Rifle Brigade) is to set out on two routes and is to assemble in the Proletarskii, Novo-Alekseevskii, Petrovskii area by 5.00 10.8.43. Assemble in the new area in complete concealment. Pay special attention to concealment when withdrawing the units from their combat positions, and to concealing the movement of tanks, especially at river and stream crossings. Quickly begin reconnoitering the routes and crossings that will require repair. Send out security detachments and traffic officers. Dig in all the vehicles once in the assembly area over the course of 10.8 and 11.8. Build dugouts or put up tents for the personnel, and dig slit trenches. Allow all the men to bathe, and put all the uniforms and matériel back into order. Begin regular combat training exercises from 12.8.43.

The deputy commander of the 2nd Tank Army for vehicle maintenance and technical support Engineer-Colonel Krupenin reported that as a result of the army's combat operations, over the period from 1 to 11 August 43 inclusively the army had the following combat losses:

a)   Due to combat damage: 337 T-34, 98 T-70, 8 T-60, for a total of 443 tanks.

b)   Due to mechanical problems: 4 T-34 tanks.

In addition, 34 T-34, 14 T-70 and 5 T-60 tanks either suffered combat damage that didn't render the tanks unserviceable, or required the replacement of worn-out parts, for a total of 53 tanks. Of the total number of tanks that suffered combat damage, irrecoverable losses amounted to 71 T-34 and 16 T-70, for a total 87 tanks.

The entire period of the offensive that began on 15 July 1943 was characterized by the use of a tank army to provide direct support to the infantry with its tanks; in the process the 2nd Tank Army, having expended its breakthrough capabilities, achieved no success. The experience of the fighting demonstrated that it was senseless to use a tank army in order to break through the tactical zone of the enemy's defense, since by the time a breach was created, the tank army, worn out by the intense combat to create it, could no longer be used for actions in the operational depth.

In the course of the offensive campaign, the army repeatedly maneuvered from one axis of attack to another. The tankers persistently attacked the foe, but each time they were met by organized enemy resistance. This was because the maneuver was insufficiently rapid. It is known that the use of maneuver can lead to great success, but only when it comes as a surprise to the enemy. However, the 2nd Tank Army failed to achieve the element of surprise. Each time, the army conducted its regrouping of forces to a new axis in direct proximity of the front line, which made it easy for enemy intelligence to detect. In addition, the rifle corps didn't have their own tanks, so as soon as Soviet armor appeared on one or another sector of the front, the enemy command immediately suspected the appearance of the 2nd Tank Army's tank corps, and would bring up its anti-tank reserves to that sector. The organization of the offensive was conducted hastily, without taking adequate measures to support the tank attacks with artillery fire and airstrikes. As a result, the enemy's anti-tank means were not suppressed, and the tanks had to struggle against them on their own.

General Radzievsky's assessment of the operation stressed its teaching points:

In the Orel operation of 1943, on average the 2nd Tank Army lost 160 men per day, but on specific dates its human losses amounted to 282 (17 July) and 452 (22 July) men. In the first case the army was repelling a counterattack by the enemy's 10th Panzer Grenadier Division and 292nd Infantry Division, on a day when the *Luftwaffe* reigned supreme in the skies. In the latter case, its formations were trying to break through a deeply-echeloned defense of the German fascist forces, without any support. The army expended a significant amount of its shock force not in actions in the operational depth, as was proper for a tank formation, but while helping the rifle divisions, which were still exhausted from the preceding battles, break through the enemy's defense. From the date of 15 July 1943, when the 2nd Tank Army was committed into the battle in order to break through a deeply-echeloned defense with heavy fighting with the enemy, in the course of which it had to gnaw its way through one position after another, the army lost 393 tanks, and had only 36 serviceable machines by the end of the operation. This led to the fact that having expended its shock power in the fighting leading up to the penetration, the army only slowly emerged in the operational depth of the enemy's defense, could not sustain the pace of the offensive, and was unable fully to carry out its direct assignment as a means to exploit the success. The experience of the Orel operation indicated that without certain damage to the enemy's system of fire, such a use of the tank armies would lead to heavy losses, in connection with which the Front's forces would be deprived of a powerful means of exploiting a success. This experience was considered in subsequent operations.

General Radzievsky deserves respect for the fact that the data he gives on the losses in the Orel operation, which he cited in his 1978 book *Tankovyi udar* [*Tank attack*], were fully in line with the archival data found in the Ministry of Defense's Central Archives.

General Bogdanov was less forthcoming: "It isn't possible to establish any sort of pattern in the irrecoverable tank losses over a day of combat. One can only cite isolated figures. On 17 July 1943, the 2nd Tank Army irrecoverably lost 10 percent of its serviceable tanks. On 1 and 2 August 1943, the army lost 7 percent and 11 percent, respectively. The average irrecoverable losses per day of fighting in the operation amounted to 1.6 percent. Fifty-three tanks, or 11.6 percent according to the results of the operation, were sent back to factories for major overhauls."

## Army Group Center's Tank Losses

In the assessment of the British historian Stephen Newton, the German Ninth Army and Second Panzer Army lost approximately 56 percent of its combat strength in personnel, not including rear and supply personnel, over one month of combat (July 1943). The minimal irrecoverable losses in tanks of Army Group Center for July 1943 amounted to 304 of the 746 serviceable tanks which it possessed on 30 June 1943 (37 percent of the total number at the start of Operation Citadel), including 6 Tigers of the 505th Heavy Panzer Battalion. In August 1943, the 505th Heavy Panzer Battalion irrecoverably lost another 12 Tigers. Of the 90 Ferdinand heavy tank destroyers that were available at the start of Operation Citadel, 39 were irrecoverably lost. In addition to the tanks that had to be written off, a significant number of tanks and assault guns were damaged, but had been evacuated and were under repair. These machines weren't included in the German statistic of combat losses and were counted instead as "available tanks presently in short-term or long-term repair." In Newton's opinion, there is an enormous difference between "available tanks" and "combat-ready" tanks.

The opinion of Adolf Hitler himself on this question, which he expressed on 19 November 1943 at a daily conference with the Chief of the General Staff General Zeitler, is interesting: "They tell me about the rapid rehabilitation and repair of temporarily knocked-out tanks; however, they never return to service. Yet whenever I ask when these very same tanks will again be combat-ready, I always hear the answer: 'Very soon'."

## Operations of the 11th Guards Tank Brigade in the period of fighting between 1 and 9 August 1943

On 1 August 1943 at the verbal order of 2nd Tank Army's commander, units of the brigade went on the march from a wooded area 1 kilometer south of 1st of May, and by 16.00 it had re-assembled in the area of Hill 264.5 with 44 serviceable tanks (34 T-34 and 10 T-70). At 18.00 the brigade arrived in the area of Hill 262.7, from where it attacked the enemy. By 20.00, units of the 11th Guards Tank Brigade reached the northern slopes of Hill 269.0. The enemy was putting up strong fire resistance to the advance of our units, supporting their defense with bomber aircraft. In the course of the day, 4 officers were wounded, as were 6 sergeants and privates.

At 5.00 on 2 August 1943, the brigade's units resumed their attacks, having 42 operational T-34 and 10 operational T-70. The enemy, in small groups of infantry with heavy artillery, tank and air support, put up stiff localized resistance. The enemy was pulling back his main forces to the northwest. At 7.00 on 2 August 1943, brigade commander Guards Colonel Bubnov and the assistant chief of staff for intelligence Guards Major Evdokimov were killed at an observation post.

At the command post prior to the offensive, August 1943. On the left is Army commander
Lieutenant General S.I. Bogdanov. Next to him is Military Council member
Major General P.M. Latyshev.

Tank combat on the Orel axis, July-August 1943: A burning T-34 is in the foreground.

Battalion commander Major Zaerniuk gives a combat assignment, August 1943.

The Soviet photo caption read 'The crew of a combat machine: (from left to right) A. Lugansky, A. Vysotsky, V. Ivanov, I. Chudin.'

Table 3.4: Data on the personnel losses in the combat units of the 2nd Tank Army from 5 July to 10 August 1943

| Dates | KIA or died during medical evacuation | | | Evacuated to hospitals with wounds, concussions, burns, etc. | | | Evacuated to hospitals with illness | | | Missing in action | | | Taken prisoner | | | Other causes | | | Total losses | | | Grand total |
|---|---|---|---|---|---|---|---|---|---|---|---|---|---|---|---|---|---|---|---|---|---|---|
| | Command staff | Jr. command staff | Enlisted men | Command staff | Jr. command staff | Enlisted men | Command staff | Jr. command staff | Enlisted men | Command staff | Jr. command staff | Enlisted men | Command staff | Jr. command staff | Enlisted men | Command staff | Jr. command staff | Enlisted men | Command staff | Jr. command staff | Enlisted men | |
| From 5.7 to 10.7.43 | 74 | 225 | 230 | 86 | 249 | 501 | 1 | 5 | 7 | 6 | 30 | 64 | | | | | 1 | 3 | 167 | 510 | 805 | 1482 |
| From 11.7 to 14.7.43 | 23 | 94 | 111 | 56 | 172 | 262 | | | 18 | 1 | 3 | 6 | | | | | 3 | 2 | 80 | 272 | 399 | 751 |
| Total from 5.7 to 14.7.43 | 97 | 319 | 341 | 142 | 421 | 763 | 1 | 5 | 25 | 7 | 33 | 70 | | | | | 4 | 5 | 247 | 782 | 1,204 | 2.233 |
| For 15 July | | 2 | 7 | 5 | 7 | 15 | | | 2 | | | | | | | | | | 5 | 9 | 24 | 38 |
| For 16 July | 3 | 23 | 30 | 11 | 44 | 69 | | 1 | 1 | | 4 | 5 | | | | | | | 14 | 72 | 105 | 191 |
| For 17 July | 8 | 25 | 32 | 10 | 48 | 108 | | 3 | 1 | 2 | 8 | 17 | | 4 | 16 | | | | 20 | 88 | 174 | 282 |
| Total from 15.7 to 17.7.43 | 11 | 50 | 69 | 26 | 99 | 192 | | 4 | 4 | 2 | 12 | 22 | | 4 | 16 | | | | 39 | 169 | 303 | 511 |
| For 18 July | 15 | 37 | 39 | 16 | 51 | 134 | | | | 2 | 3 | 18 | | | | | | | 33 | 91 | 191 | 315 |
| For 19 July | 6 | 20 | 13 | 8 | 29 | 70 | | | | 1 | 4 | 7 | | | | | | | 15 | 53 | 90 | 158 |
| For 20 July | | 2 | 1 | 5 | 17 | 28 | | | | | | 1 | | | | | | | 5 | 19 | 30 | 54 |
| For 21 July | 2 | 8 | 4 | 2 | 4 | 10 | | | | 1 | | 5 | | | | | | | 5 | 12 | 19 | 36 |
| Total from 18.7 to 21.7.43 | 23 | 67 | 57 | 31 | 101 | 242 | | | | 4 | 7 | 31 | | | | | | | 58 | 175 | 330 | 563 |
| For 22 July | 20 | 50 | 41 | 50 | 113 | 177 | | | | | | 1 | | | | | | | 70 | 163 | 219 | 452 |
| For 23 July | 12 | 20 | 29 | 19 | 75 | 51 | | | | 2 | 18 | 35 | | | | | | | 33 | 113 | 115 | 261 |
| For 24 July | | | 1 | 1 | 10 | 9 | | | 1 | | | | | | | | | | 1 | 10 | 11 | 22 |
| For 25 July | 2 | 6 | 17 | 10 | 24 | 81 | 1 | | 1 | | | | | | | | | | 13 | 30 | 99 | 142 |
| For 26 July | 2 | 6 | 5 | 1 | 4 | 6 | | | | | | | | | | | | 1 | 3 | 10 | 12 | 25 |
| Total from 22.7 to 26.7.43 | 36 | 82 | 93 | 81 | 226 | 324 | 1 | | 2 | 2 | 18 | 36 | | | | | | 1 | 120 | 326 | 456 | 902 |
| For 27 July | 1 | 7 | 9 | 4 | 25 | 30 | 1 | | | | | | | | | | | | 6 | 32 | 39 | 77 |
| For 28 July | | 4 | 10 | 4 | 20 | 22 | 1 | | | | | | | | | | | | 5 | 24 | 32 | 61 |
| For 29 July | 7 | 11 | 19 | 10 | 28 | 63 | | | 2 | | | 1 | | | | | | | 17 | 39 | 85 | 141 |
| For 30 July | 4 | 1 | 5 | 1 | 20 | 28 | | 1 | 2 | 1 | 1 | 12 | | | | | | | 6 | 23 | 47 | 76 |
| For 31 July | 3 | 12 | 22 | 7 | 65 | 45 | | | | | | | | | | | | | 10 | 77 | 67 | 154 |
| Total from 27.7 to 31.7.43 | 15 | 35 | 65 | 26 | 158 | 188 | 2 | 1 | 4 | 1 | 1 | 13 | | | | | | | 44 | 195 | 270 | 509 |

Table 3.4 (continued)

| Dates | KIA or died during medical evacuation | | | Evacuated to hospitals with wounds, concussions, burns, etc. | | | Evacuated to hospitals with illness | | | Missing in action | | | Taken prisoner | | | Other causes | | | Total losses | | | Grand total |
|---|---|---|---|---|---|---|---|---|---|---|---|---|---|---|---|---|---|---|---|---|---|---|
| | Command staff | Jr. command staff | Enlisted men | Command staff | Jr. command staff | Enlisted men | Command staff | Jr. command staff | Enlisted men | Command staff | Jr. command staff | Enlisted men | Command staff | Jr. command staff | Enlisted men | Command staff | Jr. command staff | Enlisted men | Command staff | Jr. command staff | Enlisted men | |
| For 1 August | 4 | – | 11 | 12 | 12 | 80 | | | | 2 | 3 | 5 | | | | | | | 18 | 15 | 96 | 129 |
| For 2 August | 19 | 49 | 94 | 49 | 102 | 281 | 1 | 1 | 10 | 1 | 2 | | | | | | | | 70 | 154 | 385 | 609 |
| For 3 August | 12 | 26 | 63 | 28 | 105 | 154 | | | | | | | | | | | | | 40 | 131 | 217 | 388 |
| For 4 August | 7 | 17 | 20 | 21 | 44 | 66 | 1 | 1 | | | | | | | | | | | 29 | 62 | 86 | 177 |
| For 5 August | 24 | 88 | 194 | 22 | 314 | 536 | | | | | | | | | | | | | 46 | 403 | 730 | 1179 |
| For 6 August | 10 | 22 | 45 | 21 | 184 | 153 | | | | | | | | | | | | | 31 | 206 | 198 | 435 |
| For 7 August | 5 | 4 | 16 | 9 | 28 | 51 | 3 | | | | | | | | | | | | 17 | 32 | 67 | 116 |
| For 8 August | 6 | 11 | 24 | 19 | 43 | 79 | | | | | | | | | | | | | 25 | 54 | 103 | 182 |
| For 9 August | – | 2 | 1 | 2 | 11 | 13 | | | | | | | | | | | | | 2 | 13 | 14 | 29 |
| **Total from 1.8 to 9.8.43** | **87** | **219** | **468** | **183** | **843** | **1413** | **5** | **2** | **10** | **3** | **5** | **5** | | | | | | | **278** | **1,070** | **1,896** | **3,244** |
| **For entire period from 5.7 to 9.8.43** (according to updated data) | **332** | **827** | **1,078** | **559** | **2,013** | **3,289** | **6** | **3** | **23** | **16** | **50** | **137** | | **4** | **16** | **9** | **30** | **67** | **922** | **2,937** | **4,608** | **8,467** |

Note: The totals for each period do not always add up to the total for the entire period from 5 July to 9 August 1943. The latter figure was based upon revised data, which generally increased the casualty figures.

Table 3.5: Manpower and matériel of the 2nd Tank Army on 10 August 1943

*Column groups: Men (Command staff, Junior command staff, Enlisted men, Total); Rifles; Machine guns (Light, Heavy, Anti-aircraft); Mortars (120mm, 82mm, 50mm); Artillery (85mm, 76mm howitzers, 76mm field, 45mm).*

| Unit | Command staff | Junior command staff | Enlisted men | Total | Rifles | PPD, PPSh | Light | Heavy | Anti-aircraft | 120mm | 82mm | 50mm | 85mm | 76mm howitzers | 76mm field | 45mm | Anti-tank rifles | Motor vehicles | Tanks | Armored cars | Anti-aircraft guns |
|---|---|---|---|---|---|---|---|---|---|---|---|---|---|---|---|---|---|---|---|---|---|
| **3rd Tank Corps:** | | | | | | | | | | | | | | | | | | | | | |
| Command and corps units | 271 | 368 | 877 | 1,516 | 827 | 475 | 24 | 4 | 9 | | 4 | | | 4 | | | 2 | 223 | 2 | 25/2 | |
| 50th Tank Brigade | 138 | 218 | 232 | 588 | 406 | 272 | 20 | 4 | 9 | | 6 | | | 4 | | | 19 | 111 | | 3 | |
| 51st Tank Brigade | 155 | 245 | 376 | 776 | 381 | 217 | 19 | 4 | 9 | | 6 | | | 2 | | | 21 | 97/14 | | 2/1 | |
| 103rd Tank Brigade | 174 | 372 | 424 | 970 | 306 | 152 | 20 | 4 | 11 | | 6 | | | | | | 24 | 105 | | 3 | |
| 57th Motorized Rifle Brigade | 150 | 340 | 788 | 1,278 | 664 | 852 | 28 | 15 | | 3 | 20 | | | 7 | | 6 | 28 | 243 | | 4 | 17 |
| 234th Mortar Regiment | 76 | 168 | 330 | 544 | 454 | 154 | | | | 30 | | | | | | | 35 | 108 | | | |
| 881st Anti-tank Regiment | 26 | 51 | 113 | 190 | 154 | 55 | | | | | | | | | | | | 32 | | | |
| 728th Anti-tank Battalion | 17 | 57 | 90 | 164 | 61 | 105 | | | | | | | | | | | 10 | 21 | | | |
| 121st Anti-aircraft Regiment | 32 | 81 | 182 | 295 | 257 | 111 | 13 | | | | | | 6 | | | | | 21 | | | 13 |
| Total in the corps | 1,039 | 1,900 | 3,412 | 6,351 | 3,510 | 2,403 | 124 | 27 | 38 | 33 | 42 | | 6 | 17 | | 6 | 139 | 961/14 | 2 | 37/3 | 30 |
| **16th Tank Corps:** | | | | | | | | | | | | | | | | | | | | | |
| Command and corps units | 258 | 447 | 819 | 1,524 | 821 | 313 | 42 | 4 | 9 | | 4 | | | 4 | | | 17 | 176 | | 26 | |
| 107th Tank Brigade | 184 | 345 | 376 | 905 | 446 | 300 | 18 | 4 | 9 | | 6 | | | 4 | | | 17 | 87 | | 1 | |
| 109th Tank Brigade | 172 | 238 | 305 | 715 | 326 | 298 | 12 | 4 | | | 6 | | | 4 | | | 17 | 75 | | 3 | |
| 164th Tank Brigade | 179 | 330 | 325 | 834 | 322 | 200 | 20 | 3 | | | 6 | | | | | | 22 | 85 | | 3 | |
| 15th Motorized Rifle Brigade | 247 | 509 | 1,109 | 1,865 | 1,229 | 1,280 | 110 | 45 | 9 | 6 | 30 | | | 12 | | | 81 | 109/11 | | | |
| 226th Mortar Regiment | 79 | 130 | 325 | 534 | 424 | 142 | | | | 36 | | | | | | | 28 | 44 | | | |
| 614th Anti-tank Regiment | 31 | 49 | 96 | 176 | 152 | 33 | | | | | | | | | | 7 | | 32 | | | |
| 729th Anti-tank Battalion | 27 | 58 | 92 | 177 | 61 | 113 | | | | | | | | | | | 10 | 27 | | | |
| 1085th Anti-aircraft Regiment | 31 | 59 | 104 | 194 | 117 | 14 | | | | | | | 6/0 | | | | | 13 | | | 0/9 |
| Total in the corps | 1,208 | 2,165 | 3,551 | 6,924 | 3,898 | 2,693 | 202 | 56 | 18 | 42 | 52 | | 6/0 | 24 | | 7 | 192 | 643/11 | | 33 | 0/9 |
| 11th Guards Tank Brigade | 165 | 355 | 315 | 835 | 305 | 250 | 11 | 4 | | | 5 | | | 4 | | | 11 | 83 | | 33 | |
| 51st Separate Motorcycle Battalion | 28 | 72 | 147 | 247 | 16 | 230 | 14 | | | | 3 | | | | | | | 15 | | | |
| 24th Separate Reconnaissance Battalion | 32 | 99 | 54 | 185 | 56 | 86 | | | | | | | | | | | | 5/8 | | | |
| **Grand Totals:** | 2,472 | 4,591 | 7,479 | 14,542 | 7,785 | 5,662 | 351 | 87 | 56 | 75 | 76 | | 12 | 45 | | 13 | 342 | 1,712/33 | 2 | ? | 30/9 |

**Table 3.6: Expenditure of fuel by the tanks of the 2nd Tank Army over the period of fighting from 5 July to 11 August 1943**

| Tank type | Fuel type | Dates | Average delivery per day | Expenditure of fuel | | | | Average running hours on tank motors | |
|---|---|---|---|---|---|---|---|---|---|
| | | | | Over the entire period | | Average expenditure per day | | On average over the entire period for the army | Average running time in hours per day for the army |
| | | | | In tons | In refills | In tons | In refills | | |
| Defense, 5 July to 15 July 1943 | | | | | | | | | |
| T-34 | Diesel | 5-15.7.43 | 248 | 124.34 | 1.253 | 11.3 | 0.113 | 819.3 | 1.72 |
| T-70 | KB-70 | 11 days | 110 | 58.66 | 1.380 | 5.33 | 0.13 | 821.1 | 1.9 |
| Offensive, 16 July to 31 July 1943 | | | | | | | | | |
| T-34 | Diesel | 16-31.7.43 | 195 | 231.97 | 2.974 | 14.5 | 0.187 | 29.6 | 1.80 |
| T-70 | KB-70 | 16 days | 77 | 112.07 | 3.82 | 10.19 | 0.24 | 31.0 | 2.0 |
| Offensive, 1 August to 11 August 1943 | | | | | | | | | |
| T-34 | Diesel | 1-11.8.43 | 80 | 185.2 | 5.8 | 16.8 | 0.53 | 63.7 | 5.8 |
| T-70 | KB-70 | 11 days | 29 | 62.25 | 5.65 | 5.67 | 0.51 | 65.2 | 5.9 |

Note: To the right side of this table there were handwritten comments for each category of the 2nd Tank Army's basic posture and dates. Next to the first category, "Defense, 5 July to 15 July 1943", was the comment "The average daily expenditure of fuel when on the defensive amounted to 0.2 refills; for separate formations – up to 0.3, 0.4 refills." Next to the second category, "Offensive, 16 July to 31 July 1943", was the comment "The average daily expenditure of fuel during the offensive fighting with a slow tempo of advance – up to 0.3 refills, and for separate formations – up to 0.5 refills. Next to the final category, "Offensive, 1 August to 11 August 1943", was the observation "The average daily expenditure of fuel during the offensive fighting with a large advance into the depth of the enemy's defenses – up to 0.75 refills, and for separate formations up to 1 refill."

**Table 3.7: Irrecoverable tank losses of the 2nd Tank Army in the 1943 Orel operation**

| Report on the irrecoverable tank losses of the 2nd Tank Army between 16 and 29 July 1943 | | 16.07 | 17.07 | 21.07 | 22.07 | 25.07 | 28.07 | 29.07 | Total |
|---|---|---|---|---|---|---|---|---|---|
| **3rd Tank Corps** | | | | | | | | | |
| 50th Tank Brigade | T-34 | – | 5 | 1 | 9 | – | 1 | – | 16 |
| | T-70 | – | – | – | 6 | – | 2 | 1 | 9 |
| 51st Tank Brigade | T-34 | – | 7 | – | 8 | – | – | – | 15 |
| | T-70 | – | – | – | – | – | – | – | – |
| 103rd Tank Brigade | T-34 | – | 2 | – | 1 | – | – | 2 | 5 |
| | T-70 | – | – | – | – | – | – | – | – |
| Total: | | | | | | | | | 45 |
| **16th Tank Corps** | | | | | | | | | |
| 107th Tank Brigade | T-34 | – | 10 | – | – | – | – | – | 10 |
| | T-70 | – | 4 | – | 1 | 1 | – | – | 6 |
| 109th Tank Brigade | T-34 | – | 8 | – | 3 | – | – | – | 11 |
| | T-70 | – | – | – | 1 | – | – | – | 1 |
| 164th Tank Brigade | T-34 | – | 1 | – | 3 | – | – | – | 4 |
| | T-70 | 1 | – | – | – | – | – | – | 1 |
| Total: | | | | | | | | | 33 |
| 11th Guards | T-34 | – | – | – | – | – | – | – | – |
| Tank Brigade | T-70 | – | – | – | – | – | – | – | – |
| Total for the army: | T-34 | 1 | 33 | 1 | 24 | – | 1 | 2 | 61 |
| | T-70 | – | 4 | – | 8 | 1 | 2 | 1 | 17 |
| Grand Total: | | **1** | **37** | **1** | **32** | **1** | **3** | **3** | **78** |

Table 3.8: Irrecoverable tank losses of the 2nd Tank Army in the 1943 Orel operation

| Report on the irrecoverable tank losses of the 2nd Tank Army between 1 and 11 August 1943 | | | | | | | | | | | |
|---|---|---|---|---|---|---|---|---|---|---|---|
| | | 1.08 | 2.08 | 3.08 | 4.08 | 6.08 | 7.08 | 8.08 | 9.08 | 10.08 | Total |
| **3rd Tank Corps** | | | | | | | | | | | |
| 50th Tank Brigade | T-34 | 3 | 10 | – | – | – | – | – | – | – | 13 |
| | T-70 | 2 | – | – | – | – | – | – | – | – | 2 |
| 51st Tank Brigade | T-34 | – | – | – | – | – | – | – | – | – | – |
| | T-70 | – | – | – | – | – | – | – | – | – | – |
| 103rd Tank Brigade | T-34 | 2 | – | – | 6 | 9 | – | 1 | – | – | 18 |
| | T-70 | 5 | – | – | – | – | – | – | – | – | 5 |
| Total: | | | | | | | | | | | **38** |
| **16th Tank Corps** | | | | | | | | | | | |
| 107th Tank Brigade | T-34 | 1 | 5 | 1 | – | – | – | – | – | – | 7 |
| | T-70 | – | – | 5 | 1 | – | – | – | – | – | 6 |
| 109th Tank Brigade | T-34 | 4 | – | 1 | – | – | – | – | – | – | 5 |
| | T-70 | – | – | – | – | – | – | – | – | – | – |
| 164th Tank Brigade | T-34 | – | – | – | – | 5 | – | 1 | – | 6 | 12 |
| | T-70 | – | 1 | – | – | – | – | – | 1 | – | 2 |
| **Total:** | | | | | | | | | | | **32** |
| 11th Guards Tank Brigade | T-34 | – | 6 | – | – | 5 | 2 | – | – | 3 | 16 |
| | T-70 | – | – | – | – | – | – | 1 | – | – | 1 |
| Total: | | | | | | | | | | | **17** |
| Total for the army: | T-34 | 10 | 21 | 2 | 6 | 19 | 2 | 2 | – | 9 | 71 |
| | T-70 | 7 | 1 | 5 | 1 | – | – | 1 | 1 | – | 16 |
| Grand Total: | | **17** | **22** | **7** | **7** | **19** | **2** | **3** | **1** | **9** | **87** |

Table 3.9: Status of the 2nd Tank Army's tanks on 11 August 1943 (the day of the withdrawal from combat)

| | Tank type | On the list | Serviceable | Requiring repair | | | Irrecoverable losses not yet written off |
|---|---|---|---|---|---|---|---|
| | | | | Light | Light overhaul | Major overhaul | |
| 3rd Tank Corps | T-34 | 111 | 45 | 10 | 17 | 31 | 5 |
| | T-70 | 37 | 20 | 1 | 1 | 11 | – |
| 16th Tank Corps | T-34 | 30 | 4 | 1 | 11 | 14 | – |
| | T-70 | 19 | 2 | – | 3 | 13 | 1 |
| | T-60 | 7 | 1 | – | – | 6 | – |
| 11th Guards Tank Brigade | T-34 | 10 | – | 4 | – | 4 | 2 |
| | T-70 | 3 | – | – | – | 2 | 1 |
| 9th Separate Signals Regiment | T-34 | 5 | 5 | – | – | – | – |
| **Total:** | | **222** | **77** | **16** | **36** | **84** | **9** |

From left to right: G.Sh. Kalustov, N.M. Koshaev, P.L. Bormotov, N.M. Bubnov and V.V. Iablokov.

Colonel Kazakov recalls:

The offensive was developing to the north, toward Kromy. On 2 August, the brigade's tank column, moving at high speeds along a deep balka, reached the line of attack in the area of the village of Rzhava. Submachine gunners of our battalion, and I along with them, were riding on the armor. About another 300 meters, and we were to enter combat. The balka, along which our tanks were moving, made a sharp turn to the left. Part of the vehicles disappeared around the bend. The column stopped. At that moment, a torrent of enemy artillery fire rained down on the bend in the balka. A blast wave of an explosion blew me over the turret to the opposite side. The ravine seethed and boiled with the explosions of heavy shells. The motorized riflemen quickly took cover, some in the tanks and others beneath the machines. The artillery barrage ceased after several minutes, without inflicting any particular damage to us. We sighed with relief, shaking off the dust and dirt. At this moment, Guards Colonel Bubnov came driving past us in a Willys. A minute or two later, and an order was passed down the column: "Battalion commanders, to the head of the column". The brigade commander was gathering them to give them their combat orders.

Soon the tanks began to clamber out of the balka, moving into a combat formation. Bubnov also climbed onto a knoll, in order to watch as the brigade went into action. At that moment, the enemy began another concentrated artillery barrage. Nikolai Matveevich was caught in a whirlwind of erupting shells – he didn't even have time to take cover in a tank. A shell fragment cut down our brigade commander. This tragic death of Bubnov was most unseemly. Just several minutes before he had driven past our tank – spirited, focused, inspired by the success of our offensive. Yet now he was no longer among the living. We knew how he had thirsted for the offensive, how much he had dreamed about that day, when the Guardsmen would develop into all their Bogatyr' might and begin to drive the foe off of native soil. Now this day had arrived. We were pursuing the Nazis, and destroying them pitilessly. But a perfidious death was literally stalking Bubnov, waiting for just that moment to strike him down at the very start of its realization.

Guards Colonel Bormotov took command of the brigade. The brigade's losses were 4 T-34 totally destroyed and 5 T-34 and 2 T-70 knocked-out. Two more T-70 tanks were serviceable, but lacked crews. Seven of the officers' staff and 5 of the sergeants' staff were killed; 8 more officers were wounded, as were 26 sergeants and 16 men.

The enemy was laying down heavy fire from all types of weapons from the area east of Puzeevo and from the northern slopes of Hill 258.0, putting up strong resistance to our attacking units. But by the end of the day, units of the brigade seized Hill 258.0.

On 3.8.43, units of the brigade were given the order to take Rzhava and Bel'diazhki, and to reach the Kromy – Dmitrovsk road, thereby cutting off the enemy's path of retreat to the west toward Chuvardino. This in fact was accomplished by 10.00. Subsequent offensive actions unfolded in the direction of Hill 280.5. Before reaching it, our troops arrived in the area of Hill 245.2. In the course of the day, the neighbors on the right and left of the 11th Guards Tank Brigade hadn't been correctly informed about the position of our units and those of the enemy. For example, they had received information about the taking of Kolki, but in reality, that village wasn't taken in the morning.

Over the day of combat on 3.8.43, the 11th Guards Tank had 1 T-34 burned-out and 1 T-34 knocked-out. At day's end, the brigade's units dug in, conducted an inspection, and topped up their tanks with fuel. At the order of the 2nd Tank Army commander, units of the brigade launched a night attack to the northwest against the enemy, seized two populated points, and with their attack assisted our infantry in forcing a crossing of the Kromy River and to establish a bridgehead on its northern bank.

The enemy was covering their retreat with artillery, self-propelled guns and small rearguard detachments of infantry. By 6.20 on 4.8.43, units of the 11th Guards Tank Brigade reached the eastern bank of the Nezhevka River. With the arrival of our units at the Nezhevka River, the enemy blew up a bridge in the vicinity of the Rozhkovskii State Farm and continued to withdraw to the northwest. There was no success in forcing a crossing of the Nezhevka River, as the approaches to it and the banks of the river were boggy, and there were no bypasses or fords. The further advance of the brigade's units was stopped, while the rifle units failed to take advantage of the success and failed to dig in on the western bank of the Nezhevka River, which gave an opportunity to the enemy to fortify positions in the vicinity of Krasnaia Roshcha and to bring up reserves.

Engineers of the 2nd Tank Army rebuilt the bridge only by 6.00 on 5.8.43, but the enemy smashed the crossing with artillery fire and bombing raids, and only by 18.00 did units of the brigade manage to make it across to the western bank of the Nezhevka River and reach the southeastern slopes of Hill 208.3, in readiness together with units of the 3rd Tank Corps to attack the enemy in the Krasnaia Roshcha area.

All of the attacks on the day of 6.8.43 toward Krasnaia Roshcha were repulsed by the enemy, and the attempt to take the town failed. By the end of day 6.8.43, the brigade had 31 serviceable tanks (25 T-34 and 6 T-70). The decision was make to launch a night-time outflanking attack from the west. With an impetuous attack, the brigade carrying motorized riflemen aboard the tanks broke into the town at 4.20 on 7.8.43, and seized it. Subsequently the units attacked Tolmachevo, but the enemy continued to put up stubborn resistance. From the northern bank of the Kromy River, the enemy was conducting heavy fire from artillery and heavy tanks at the flanks of our tanks. With swift actions the tanks passed Novo-Gnezdilovo and by the end of the day they had reached the southern slopes of Hill 289.3, attacking the enemy in the direction of Lebiazh'e and Goncharovka. However, there they ran into a strong anti-tank front, and further advance was stopped. In this combat, brigade commander Guards Colonel Bormotov and the brigade's deputy political commander Guards Colonel Kalustov were both killed. The brigade's chief of staff Guards Colonel Koshaev assumed command of the 11th Guards Tank Brigade.

On the 30th Anniversary of Victory, we, the veterans of the 2nd Tank Army, gathered in Moscow. We swapped stories about the battles. Here is what Nikolai Koshaev told me about the events of that day. That evening back in August 1943, Bormotov, Kalustov and Koshaev were summoned to a meeting of the 2nd Tank Army's Military Council. There, the army commander General S.I. Bogdanov gave them a sharp tongue-lashing for their failure to ensure the completion of their assigned task. Kalustov was very upset. Over his time in the post of commissar, and then in the post of deputy political commander, he had never heard such reproaches, and now, on the fourth day after Bubnov's death, he was forced to listen to such bitter words. They returned from the Military Council meeting late at night. On the way back they discussed who and what each man would do immediately. Usually the deputy political commander strove to be wherever his presence was most necessary. That morning, before the attack itself, he told Koshaev: "If you will, I will be in the same tank with Bormotov." Koshaev shrugged his shoulders in bewilderment. "Don't you have any advice?" Kalustov asked him with agitation. Koshaev replied, "Yes, Bormotov might interpret this action incorrectly, and will think that you don't trust him, and you will take take his actions under control." Kalustov then told Koshaev, "Bubnov never thought that way, even when I was his commissar. But I must be next to Bormotov. Petr Leont'evich needs the support." Koshaev simply told him, "Perhaps you're right. Decide for yourself."

The brigade command conducted a regrouping of the forces, agreed about increasing the artillery support, and arranged closer cooperation between the battalions and neighbors. At the designated hour, the battalions went on the attack. The resistance of the Nazis in Rzhava was broken, and they were driven out of the hamlet of Bel'diazhki. The tankers impetuously advanced. On the next day, the brigade reached the small Nezhevka River, a tributary of the Kromy River. The fascists had dug in behind it. A fierce exchange of tank fire developed. Bormotov in his tank was compelled to join it. But when the success of our elements was already plainly apparent, an enemy shell struck the commander's tank and it burst into flames. Guards Corporals Grigorii Nestiforov and Ivan Krichun were the first to see this. Under enemy fire they rushed to the tank. Both Bormotov and Kalustov were badly wounded. They dragged the deputy political commander from the tank first. With the help of Krichun, Grigorii hoisted Kalustov on his back and crawled back toward the rear. Ivan helped Petr Leont'evich get out of the burning tank. However, they couldn't find any cover. The Nazis opened up heavy mortar fire. "It's nothing, nothing, Comrade Commissar," Nestiforov said to Kalustov, "We'll make it, absolutely we'll make it." A mortar shell exploded quite nearby. The deputy political commander heavily moaned and then fell silent. "Comrade Commissar, Comrade Guards Colonel," Grigorii prompted him. But Kalustov was already dead.

A post-action account of the 11th Guards Tank Brigade's actions between 1 and 9 August, produced by the brigade's senior command, for the headquarters of the 2nd Tank Army:

In the course of 8.8.43, the enemy repelled our attacks with artillery and tanks, and the attempt to seize Lebiazh'e and Goncharovka from the east failed. At the decision of the brigade commander, our tanks moved around them from the south, before turning to attack the enemy to the north, bypassing Goncharovka and Lebiazh'e to the west of the villages. All attempts to break through into the depth of the enemy's defenses were repulsed by artillery fire. By 13.00 the offensive was halted, while the artillery received an order to suppress the enemy's firing points. However, because the artillery fire was weak and inaccurate, the attacks that resumed at 15.15 were also unsuccessful. By the end of the day the tanks reached the southern slopes of Hill 261.0. By this time the 11th Guards Tank Brigade had just 24 service-able tanks (16 T-34 and 8 T-70). The brigade's casualties amounted to 12 killed (3 officers, 8 sergeants and 1 private) and 20 wounded (2 officers, 6 sergeants and 12 privates). On 9 August 1943, all of the 11th Guards Tank Brigade's tanks were handed over to the 3rd Tank Corps together with their crews at an order from the 2nd Tank Army's headquarters, while the brigade's units were withdrawn into the 2nd Tank Army's reserve. On 10 August 1943, the brigade assembled in the woods 1 kilometer southwest of Gurovka, where an inspection was conducted and repairs were made to the wheeled transport. The personnel were brought back into order.

This same account by the command of the 11th Guards Tank Brigade offered the following conclusions about the lessons learned during the operation:

The enemy when retreating in the period of our offensive puts up strong fire resistance with his rearguard units – small groups of infantry of up to a company or battalion, with the strong support of artillery, self-propelled guns and tanks (primarily heavy tanks), and secures his withdrawal with heavy air cover. The main forces meanwhile strive to avoid coming under attack. [The enemy] often leaves behind little groups of submachine gunners in the rear of [our] tanks, which cut off our infantry. He places artillery and tanks on hills and fires from long ranges.

The infantry, as a rule, lags behind the tanks during attacks, since on foot they can't keep up with the tanks, which complicates the operation of the tank units. It is necessary for the infantry to move up on the tanks as closely as possible, but no closer than 1,500 meters. The artillery poorly scouts the forward edge of the enemy's defense and often fires on our own units. The artillery positions are located far to the rear, and fire is conducted primarily on areas, and not at targets, and thusly it doesn't suppress the firing positions that are hinder-ing the advance of the tanks and infantry. The air force acts en masse and courageously, but despite established signals with the ground troops, often bomb their own front line. The fighter aircraft rarely take on the enemy's bombers. Engineer units aren't conducting enough reconnaissance. Our units often unexpectedly run into anti-tank obstacles: minefields and anti-tank ditches. Bridges destroyed by the enemy are being slowly repaired, thereby holding up the further advance of the tanks and transport.

It is necessary to point out the inadequate work of the headquarters of the brigade's battal-ions: often they are lagging far behind the forward elements and don't help the commander to direct the combat. Information arrives late in brigade headquarters; they don't count their own losses or the damage inflicted on the enemy with adequate accuracy. Radio communica-tions in the brigade performed well. Management of a battle was implemented through radio communications.

This same account from the senior command of the 11th Guards Tank Brigade also offers descriptions of heroic episodes of the men of the brigade in the period between 1 August and 9 August 1943:

On 1 August 1943 during an attack, a company commander was wounded. Fedorchuk, being the commander of a T-34 tank platoon, took command of the company and with his capable actions and decisions he pursued the enemy, while displaying boldness, courage and heroism. He personally destroyed one self-propelled gun, two anti-tank guns, and killed 10 enemy infantry. Two enemy tanks were left burning by his company; it destroyed 2 mortars, 6 guns of various calibers, 5 machine guns, 2 vehicles with loads, and 160 enemy soldiers and officers.

Also on 1 August, while on reconnaissance, the commander of a company of T-70 light tanks Guards Captain Piatizventsev was wounded. Disregarding it, he didn't leave the battlefield, but continued to direct his platoon, and carrying out the order from the command, he inflicted damage to the enemy in personnel and equipment. His company destroyed 2 guns, 2 bunkers, 1 staff vehicle with its officers aboard, one car and 95 enemy infantry.

In an action on 2 August 1943 on Hill 263.7, the platoon commander of a motorized rifle battalion engaged in hand-to-hand combat with a group of Nazis. Guards Corporal Mironenko acted to defend his platoon commander and in a hand-to-hand struggle killed one enemy soldier and one enemy officer.

On 7 August 1943, in offensive fighting for the village of Lebiazh'e, the T-70 tank commander Guards Lieutenant Il'chenko and his driver-mechanic Guards Sergeant Kharitonov, pursuant to an order from higher command, broke through the enemy's defense, and having penetrated into the depth of the defense, destroyed enemy personnel and equipment with fire and the tracks of his tank. [Il'chenko's] tank was hit and began to burn. The Germans surrounded the burning tank and waited for the crew to surrender. However, Guards Lieutenant Il'chenko and Guards Sergeant Kharitonov kept firing at the Germans at point-blank range until their final breath, and perished in the tank as heroes.

From the recollections of Guards Sergeant Major Mistriukov:

At last my desire was granted, and I joined the ranks of a large formation – the 2nd Tank Army, with which I was to travel a lengthy combat path. On 15 July 1943, our units, going on the counteroffensive, took Ponyri Station, which had changed hands several times. This was a fierce battle, where the struggle went on for each meter of ground. Men, biting into the ground, fought mercilessly and set enemy tanks aflame. At this time I was transferred to the radio station that handled combat command and communications, which was headed by Lieutenant Kukarov. Our work as radio operators at that time was very hard, because the telephone network at times was disrupted, either by enemy artillery fire or by treads of tanks.

We were working at the command post. Contact was maintained with the units, which required constant burdensome work, because this communications link was of very great importance. Even in those minutes when enemy aircraft were bombing the grove or ravine in which we were located, we didn't cease work.

True, for the first few days it was somewhat frightening, but after several days we became accustomed to life at the front. On 31 July 1943, I was manning a radio set. Suddenly I was contacted by the radio of a formation commander, which was set up in a Willys jeep and was always located with the formation commander. I was asked to take a very important radio message. I agreed. At this moment, German Messerschmitts began to wing over into a dive directly above our vehicle, which was parked in a ravine. Someone shouted, "Air raid". Whoever was off-duty took cover in slit trenches, but I couldn't leave the radio, because the incoming message was very important, and it was from a formation commander. So I stayed at the radio set and already began to jot down the first groups [of code]. When three bombs exploded, I was momentarily deafened and I missed two words, but I continued to work. Other bombs were exploding further away, before suddenly the transmission was broken in mid-word, though I could hear the sound of distant, exploding bombs. I tried re-establishing contact – nothing was audible; I called once, twice, but there was no answer. About 30 minutes later, a different radio, one located at an observation post, made contact. It was set up in the tank of the formation commander, and with its help I managed to take the rest of the message. They reported that the radio operator and his driver had been killed. That was how I found out why the transmission had been disrupted. The chief of the radio station Sergeant Major Bludov and his driver had been killed; he was working alone at the radio post, because he had no radio operators.

At 4.00 on 1 August 1943, when dew was still covering the grass, we set off to the observation post together with Major Marin. We hadn't even had time to emerge from the ravine, in which we were parked, when we came under artillery fire. Major Marin told the driver, "Well, Kvasov, step on it, or we'll be blown to pieces." The vehicle flew along through hollows and over knolls. Shells fell to the right, to the left and behind our vehicle, and only tiny slivers flew with a whistle into the bodies of the radio vehicles. Despite the hurricane of fire, we had to drive over this little hill. We reached the front line, but we couldn't locate the observation post. We turned around and drove for about 3 kilometers and stopped in a ravine. Major Marin gave me the assignment to find the observation post.

I headed out on foot. I walked where the tanks were moving. The road ran again over a hill, where the enemy would open fire as soon as targets appeared on it. I had just reached this hill, when a barrage began. I dropped into a chest-high entrenchment to wait out the barrage. At this time five tanks were climbing the hill at full speed. Enemy aircraft appeared in the sky and dove on the tank column, which had drawn level with my entrenchment. I dropped flat in the trench and only heard explosions, at first distant, and then two bombs exploded 10 meters away from the far side of the road that ran past my trench. The soil was loose and crumbly, and the trench collapsed atop me. I was suffocating. With my final strength, I managed to dig my way out of the trench.

I headed back, when I came upon a telephone cable, and I followed it to the observation post. At the observation post we worked with the call signs of the formation commander and were able to make contact with any network. We had to work at several frequencies, because only our single radio set was located at the observation post. We maintained contact with the army commander, the network of the formation headquarters, the liaison network, and the network of the units and their headquarters. Despite the intense work, we nevertheless had to maintain contact without interruptions. All of the particularly important radio messages, as well as the orders and signals were transmitted punctually.

The 3rd Tank Corps commander Major General Sinenko would come in and order us to call one or another of his unit commanders. Making contact, we'd quickly summon them and duly facilitate the discussions. Several times during important discussions, enemy aircraft bombed us, but the conversations went on normally. In several places, the body and track assembly bore the holes of shell fragments.

While resting and refitting, the 11th Guards Tank Brigade's commander Guards Colonel Koshaev and his chief of staff Guards Major Rodionov submitted a report to the headquarters of the 2nd Tank Army on the results of the recent fighting:

**Table 3.10: Losses in the period from 1.8 to 9.8.43**

| | | | |
|---|---|---|---|
| T-34 tanks: | Burned out | 15 | |
| | Knocked out | 20 | |
| T-70 tanks: | Burned out | 1 | |
| | Knocked out | 3 | |
| | | | |
| Personnel: | Killed: | Officers' staff | 28 |
| | | Sergeants' staff | 25 |
| | | Enlisted men | 7 |
| | Wounded: | Officers' staff | 31 |
| | | Sergeants' staff | 90 |
| | | Enlisted men | 71 |

| | | |
|---|---|---|
| Losses inflicted upon the enemy from 1.8 to 9.8.43: | | |
| Tanks burned out | 25 | |
| Tanks knocked out | 7 | |
| Destroyed: | Guns of various calibers | 98 |
| | Of which, self-propelled | 9 |
| | Vehicles | 38 |
| | Mortars | 55 |
| | Machine guns | 116 |
| | Anti-tank rifles | 18 |
| | Loaded wagons | 26 |
| | Radio sets | 2 |
| | Dugouts | 2 |
| | Tractors | 9 |
| | Motorcycles | 1 |
| | Earth and timber bunkers | 1 |
| | Ammunition dumps | 1 |
| Taken prisoner: | 27 | |
| Killed soldiers and officers: | Up to 840 | |

The 3rd Tank Corps's commander Major General of Tank Forces Sinenko and his chief of staff Colonel Safronov also submitted a report on the results of the recent fighting:

As a result of defensive and offensive fighting, units of the corps inflicted the following damage to the enemy:

**Table 3.11: As a result of the defensive and offensive battles, the corps' units inflicted the following damage to the enemy:**

**Destroyed:**

| | | | |
|---|---|---|---|
| Tanks | 280 | Self-propelled guns | 131 |
| Guns of various calibers | 285 | Mortars | 101 |
| Machine guns | 253 | Firing points | 175 |
| Anti-tank rifles | 85 | Dugouts | 112 |
| Motorcycles | 16 | Vehicles | 163 |
| Aircraft | 20 | Supply dumps | 4 |
| Soldiers and officers | Up to 22,802 | | |

**Captured:**

| | | | |
|---|---|---|---|
| Tanks | 2 | Guns of various calibers | 5 |
| Self-propelled guns | 6 | Heavy machine guns | 30 |
| Light machine guns | 7 | Mortars | 7 |
| Rifles | 89 | Submachine guns | 78 |
| Tank radios | 9 | Vehicles | 5 |
| Taken prisoner | 84 | | |

**Over this same period, the corps' units lost:**

| | | | |
|---|---|---|---|
| In personnel: | Wounded | 3,238 | |
| | Killed | 1,601 | |
| | Missing-in-action | 68 | |
| | | | |
| In materiél: | T-34 tanks | 92 | (knocked out) |
| | | 107 | (burned out) |
| | | 18 | (blown up by mines) |
| | T-70 tanks | 35 | (knocked out) |
| | | 45 | (burned out) |
| | | 2 | (blown up by mines) |
| | | | |
| | SU-122 | 4 | (knocked out) |
| | | 6 | (burned out) |

| | | | |
|---|---|---|---|
| Mortars | 12 | Vehicles | 55 |
| Submachine guns | 40 | Guns of various calibers | 10 |
| | | Rifles | 56 |
| | | Anti-tank rifles | 9 |

**Warriors of the 2nd Tank Army, who Distinguished Themselves in the 1943 Orel Operation**

Guards Colonel Nikolai **Bubnov**, commander of the 11th Guards Tank Brigade. On 2 August 1943, while organizing the brigade's attack in the direction of Rzhava and Bel'diazhki, he fell bravely in battle. Hero of the Soviet Union.

Guards Colonel Grigorii **Kalustov**, deputy political commander of the 11th Guards Tank Brigade. On 7 August 1943, located together with the brigade commander on the battlefield and directing the offensive combats, he fell bravely in battle. Hero of the Soviet Union.

Captain Anatolii **Khombakh**, tank battalion commander in the 109th Tank Brigade. Before the start of combat operations, he was able to hammer together the brigade's personnel, having taught them to carry out combat assignments. In the period of offensive operations, he capably maneuvered under heavy enemy mortar and artillery fire, and acted decisively and daringly. On 22 July 1943, during an attack on Hill 264.0 east of Krasnikovo, from his tank he personally knocked out 4 medium German tanks. Awarded the Order of Aleksandr Nevsky.

Guards Senior Lieutenant Aleksandr **Lugansky**, company commander of medium tanks of the 11th Guards Tank Brigade's 1st Tank Battalion. In fighting for the villages of Novaia Zaria and Bel'diazhki, he demonstrated courage and audacity. He knows how to inspire the personnel to carry out an assigned task. During the combats between 1.8 and 8.8.43, his company brewed up 9 tanks, knocked out 5 tanks, and destroyed 11 guns, 5 machine guns, 14 mortars, 3 anti-tank guns, 14 vehicles, 10 wagons, 4 tractors, and more than 450 enemy soldiers and officers. Awarded the Order of the Red Banner.

Guards Lieutenant Dmitrii **Barabash**, platoon commander of T-34 of the 11th Guards Tank Brigade's 1st Tank Battalion. On 2.8.1943 in combat at the Novaia Zaria, with his tanks he destroyed two self-propelled guns and 6 vehicles. He brewed up one enemy tank and disabled another. In combat he is exceptionally bold and decisive, which inspires the rest of the crews to carry out their assigned task. Awarded the Order of the Red Banner.

Guards Lieutenant Ivan **Diachenko**, platoon commander of the 11th Guards Tank Brigade's motorized rifle battalion. In an offensive combat he displayed exceptional boldness and courage. During his platoon's attack against Hill 208.3, under heavy artillery fire and automatic weapons' fire, he broke into the enemy trenches, where a hand-to-hand struggle erupted. In this combat, the platoon under Diachenko's command emerged as the victors. He himself in the close combat shot four German officers at point-blank range, while his platoon killed 49 Nazis, and destroyed one mortar and two guns. Awarded the Order of the Red Banner.

Aleksandr Lugansky of the 11th Guards
Tank Brigade.

Georgii Semenov of the 103rd Tank Brigade.

Brigade commander Maksimov – 103rd Tank
Brigade.

# 4

# In the Sevsk Operation, 1943

**Command Staff of the 2nd Tank Army:**
Commander – Lieutenant General Semen Bogdanov
Military Council Member – Major General Petr Latyshev
Chief of Staff – Major General Grigorii Preisman
Chief of Operations Department – Colonel Vladimir Chizh
Commander of Artillery – Guards Colonel Mikhail Tsikalo

**3rd Tank Corps** – Major General Maksim Sinenko
50th Tank Brigade – Lieutenant Colonel Vasilii Bzyrin
51st Tank Brigade – Lieutenant Colonel Pavel Borisov
103rd Tank Brigade – Lieutenant Colonel Aleksandr Khalaev
57th Motorized Rifle Brigade – Lieutenant Colonel Anton Arzhba
234th Mortar Regiment, 881st Destroyer Anti-tank Artillery Regiment, 74th Motorcycle Battalion, 728th Destroyer Anti-Tank Battalion, 1441st Self-propelled Artillery Regiment, 121st Anti-aircraft Artillery Regiment

**7th Guards Mechanized Corps** – Guards Lieutenant General Ivan Korchagin
25th Guards Mechanized Brigade – Guards Lieutenant Colonel Fedor Artamonov
26th Guards Mechanized Brigade – Guards Major General David Barinov
57th Guards Tank Brigade – Guards Lieutenant Colonel Ivan Silov
24th Guards Mechanized Brigade – Guards Colonel Vladimir Maksimov
468th Mortar Regiment, 291st Destroyer Anti-tank Artillery Regiment, 288th Anti-aircraft Artillery Regiment, 57th Destroyer Anti-tank Battalion, 1418th Self-propelled Artillery Regiment, 772nd Separate Signals Battalion, 33rd Coastal Artillery Battery, 9th Separate Signals Regiment

In the opinion of General Bogdanov, of all the operations conducted by the 2nd Tank Army in 1943, the Sevsk Operation presents the greatest interest; it signaled a German general retreat to the west on the Central Front, although all the prisoners were maintaining that they were only pulling back to the Desna River, where the Germans had prepared a tough line of defense.

## The preliminary period

The 2nd Tank Army from 10 August 1943 was located in Central Front's reserve in the area: Gurovka woods, Proletarskii, Hill 239.6, Petrovskii, Vysokoe. Consisting of the 3rd Tank Corps, the 16th Tank Corps, the 7th Guards Mechanized Corps (which became part of the 2nd Tank Army on 14 August 1943) and the 11th Guards Tank Brigade, the 2nd Tank Army was repairing equipment and weapons. On 14 August, Operational Directive No.00553/OP was received from Central Front headquarters. It directed the 2nd Tank Army to cross the Sev River in the Novo-Iamskoe (south) – Sevsk sector once the infantry of the 65th Army reached the line Novo-Iamskoe – Kniaginino – Moritskii – Sosnitsa, to pass through the infantry of the 65th Army on

Semen Bogdanov.

Ivan Korchagin – 7th Guards
Mechanized Corps.

Fedor Artamonov – 25th Guards
Mechanized Brigade.

Aleksandr Khalaev – 103rd Tank Brigade.

the Kniaginino – Moritskii line, and exploiting the success on the Korostovka – Orliia – Seredina-Buda – Chernatskoe axis, to seize subsequently the areas: a) Torlopovo, Strachevo, Filippovo, Orliia on the first day of the army's offensive; b) Chernatskoe, Romashkovo, Seredina-Buda on the second day of the army's offensive. In the future it was to attack in the direction of Pigarevka, Duplikovka and Kolievka, with the task to seize crossings on the Desna River in the Novgorod-Severskii area.

Carrying out the assigned task, the army's forces were given a combat order to conduct a march to the Dedovod'e, Krasnyi Klin, Bugry, Budennyi village, Pervoavgustovskii, Karpeevskii area. The movement of the 2nd Tank Army to the new assembly area was to be made at night time, concealed from the enemy, with the observation of all measures of camouflage and deception. The 2nd Tank Army was to re-assemble fully in the indicated area by 5.00 on 18 August 1943. As a result of an internal reshuffling of personnel and equipment and the creation of new combat units necessitated by the heavy losses during the Orel offensive, the 2nd Tank Army was able to resume combat operations only with the 3rd Tank Corps and 7th Guards Mechanized Corps, which were brought up to strength at the expense of the 16th Tank Corps and the 11th Guards Tank Brigade. The 3rd Tank Corps and 7th Guards Mechanized Corps began the operation with a total of 236 serviceable tanks (168 T-34 and 68 T-70). The 16th Tank Corps and 11th Guards Tank Brigade were now without tanks and other materiél, didn't prepare for the operation, and took no part in the fighting.

## Work of the 2nd Tank Army Staff to Prepare for the Offensive

The plan for the operation, which was worked out by the 2nd Tank Army headquarters, foresaw four stages for the army's operation:

First Preliminary Stage (two days):
This stage anticipated the completion of all the work in a holding area. More precisely, the work entailed the scouting of crossings and the distribution of scouts and observation posts among the infantry's combat formations; the reconnoitering of jumping-off areas and the routes of approach to the river crossings; the preparation of bridging means to cross the Sev River and their concentrations in proximity to the vicinities of the crossings; the coordination of all types of cooperation; the organization of communications in the jumping-off areas; the selection of locations for command posts and observation posts; the formation of reconnaissance detachments and traffic control detachments; the organization of artillery and air cover from the flanks in the jumping-off areas; occupying the jumping-off locations for the offensive; and taking over the passages through the minefields from the 65th Army.

The Second Stage (one day):
This stage would entail the forcing of a crossing of the Sev River and passage through the infantry on the Kniaginino – Moritskii line, with the subsequent arrival in the Torlopovo, Strachevo, Orliia area. Pontoon bridges would be laid down. This stage would see the organization of the cover for the bridges by the 1st Anti-aircraft Division; the organization of artillery cover of the flanks in the areas of the bridges; and night-time management of the traffic at the bridges. The 2nd Tank Army's left flank would be secured along the northern edge of the woods south of Byki and Podlesnye. Scouts and reconnaissance detachments would emerge on the line Shepetlivo – Seredina-Buda – Mikhailovskii farmstead – Podyvot'e.

The Third Stage (one day)
The 2nd Tank Army in this stage was to cut the railroad and to seize the Chernatskoe, Romashkovo, Seredina-Buda area. The left flank of the army would be secured by placing artillery fire on the Mikhailovskii farmstead. With the actions of night bombers targeting the Ulitsa, Pigarevka, Kamenka, and Mikhailovskii farmstead areas, the concentration of enemy reserves in these areas would be prevented. Intelligence organs and reconnaissance detachments were to arrive on the Pervomaiskii – Bol. Berezka – Krasichka – Duplikovka – Belitsa – Setnoe line.

The Fourth Stage (two days):
Operating in the general direction of Duplikovka, Kalievka and Novgorod-Severskii, the forward units were to arrive on the western bank of the Desna River and seize crossings in the Novgorod-Severskii area.

Directed by the operation's plan, on 17 August 1943 a combat order was issued by the 2nd Tank Army's headquarters, on the basis of which the corps commanders, brigade commanders and battalion commanders in the course of 18 and 19 August were to scout the routes to the jumping-off areas, the areas of the jumping-off positions, the locations of observation posts, and the approach routes of the formations from the jumping-off areas to the crossings on the Sev River. On 23 August, army staff checked the combat readiness and the organization of collaboration within the army's forces, as well as the completion of combat documentation and the command staff's knowledge of their tasks down to the platoon commander level inclusively. All documents were collated, and the ability of the commanders of the corps and brigade headquarters to use them correctly was verified. Radio stations were shut down, with the exception of the main stations, which operated only to receive communications.

According to the testimony of the commander of the 2nd Tank Army General Bogdanov, on 20 August 1943 the commander of the Central Front General Rokossovsky and the Central Front's chief of staff listened to his decisions for the operation, which amounted to the following: It was necessary to prepare 9 pontoon bridges on the Sev River for the 2nd Tank Army – 6 operational bridges and 3 reserve bridges. The 65th Army was to build these bridges once its infantry had crossed to the western bank of the Sev River. Units of the 65th Army would seize Sevsk and Streletskoe. At that moment, the 2nd Tank Army would begin crossing. The 16th Air Army would provide air cover for the operation.

On 26 August 1943, the 2nd Tank Army's combat formations were deployed in the following manner for the offensive: The 7th Guards Mechanized Corps was to advance on the right, with its 34th Mechanized Brigade, 33rd Tank Brigade and 43rd Mechanized Brigade arrayed respectively from left to right in the first echelon. The 33rd Tank Brigade in the center had the immediate support of the 734th Separate Destroyer Anti-tank Battalion and the 1418th Self-propelled Artillery Regiment. The 43rd Mechanized Brigade on the right had the 79th Destroyer Anti-tank Artillery Regiment in support. The 18th Mechanized Brigade was in reserve. The artillery supporting the 7th Guards Mechanized Corps' attack is shown in Table 4.1.

The 3rd Tank Corps was on the left, with its 103rd Tank Brigade and 50th Tank Brigade deployed in the first echelon. The latter tied in with the 7th Guards Mechanized Corps' 34th Mechanized Brigade on its right. The two tank brigades had the direct support of the 1442nd Self-propelled Artillery Regiment, as well as the 881st Destroyer Anti-tank Artillery Regiment and the 728th Separate Destroyer Anti-tank Artillery Battalion. The 57th Motorized Rifle Brigade was to advance in the second echelon, together with the 121st Anti-aircraft Artillery Regiment. The artillery supporting the 3rd Tank Corps' attack is shown in Table 4.2.

Table 4.1: The type and amount of artillery available in the 7th Guards Mechanized Corps on 26 August 1943

| Unit | Number of mortars and guns | | | | | | | | | |
| | Mortars | | AT Guns | | | Other | | | | |
| | 82mm | 120mm | 45mm | 76mm | 85mm | 76mm | SU-122 | 37mm | M-13 (RL) | Hvy MG (A-A) |
|---|---|---|---|---|---|---|---|---|---|---|
| 79th Anti-tank Rgt. | – | – | 15 | – | – | – | – | – | – | – |
| 734th Anti-tank Bn. | – | – | – | – | 12 | – | – | – | – | – |
| 468th Mortar Regiment | – | 26 | – | – | – | – | – | – | – | – |
| 1706 Anti-aircraft Artillery Rgt. | – | – | – | – | – | – | – | 16 | – | 16 |
| 1418th Self-propelled Artillery Rgt. | – | – | – | – | – | – | 9 | – | – | – |
| 410th Separate Guards Mortar Bn. | – | – | – | – | – | – | – | – | 7 | – |
| Remaining artillery | 42 | 13 | 20 | 25 | – | 12 | – | – | – | – |
| 14th Destroyer Brigade | 8 | 4 | 12 | 16 | – | – | – | – | – | – |
| Total for the 7th Guards Mechanized Corps | 50 | 53 | 47 | 41 | 12 | 12 | 9 | 16 | 7 | 16 |

Table 4.2: Amount and type of artillery available in the 3rd Tank Corps on 26 August 1943

| Unit | Number of guns | | | | | | | | |
| | Mortars | | Anti-tank | | | 76mm | SU-122 | 37mm | Hvy MG (A-A) |
| | 82mm | 120mm | 45mm | 76mm | 85mm | | | | |
|---|---|---|---|---|---|---|---|---|---|
| 881st Anti-tank Artillery Regiment | – | – | 20 | – | – | – | – | – | – |
| 728th Anti-tank Artillery Battalion | – | – | – | – | 11 | – | – | – | – |
| 234th Mortar Regiment | – | 36 | – | – | – | – | – | – | – |
| 121st Anti-aircraft Artillery Regiment | – | – | – | – | – | – | – | 16 | 14 |
| 1442nd Self-propelled Artillery Regiment | – | – | – | – | – | – | 7 | – | – |
| Remaining artillery | 48 | 6 | 8 | 12 | – | 12 | | | |
| Total for the 3rd Tank Corps | 48 | 42 | 28 | 12 | 11 | 12 | 7 | 16 | 14 |

The 2nd Tank Army was to carry out the Front's assignment according to the following schedule: On the first day, the 7th Guards Mechanized Corps was to take Torlopovo and Starchevo, while the 3rd Tank Corps seized Orliia and Filippovo. On the second day, the 7th Guards Mechanized Corps was to take Seredina-Buda, while the 3rd Tank Corps took Romashkovo. On the third day, forward detachments were to advance to the Desna River. In addition to on-the-spot coordination and documentation in the form of timetables, the cooperation with the infantry, artillery, engineers and aviation was also played out on sand tables. There was full agreement in all the details between the commanders of the 65th Army and 2nd Tank Army, and among the staffs, the corps and brigade commanders, the artillery commanders, etc. Prior to 25 August, all the questions of cooperation with the 65th Army and 16th Air Army were fully worked out and documented in a schedule of cooperation.

General Bogdanov recalled, "I obtained the agreement of the Front commander (General Rokossovsky) that the 2nd Tank Army would be introduced only once the infantry reached the Kniaginino – Moritskii line and had actually breached the enemy's defenses."

At 20.00 on 25 August, the 2nd Tank Army, consisting of the 3rd Tank Corps and the 7th Guards Mechanized Corps, completed the march into the area of its jumping-off positions, and by 4.00 on 26 August, it had assembled in a wooded area east of Uspenskii, south of Pokrovskii, east of Lesovoi, and north and south of Postelinskii and Dobrovod'e, in readiness to carry out its assignment.

## Characteristics of the terrain

The terrain on the axis of the army's operations favored a defender and significantly complicated the army's offensive. The main obstacle confronting the 2nd Tank Army was the Sev River, which in the army's sector had a width of 8 to 16 meters, a depth of 0.3 to 2 meters, and a current speed of 0.2 meters a second. The basin of the Sev River was 1 to 2 kilometers wide, and was wet meadowland with boggy soil above a firm layer; in the summertime it was passable only for trucks and wagons. The eastern bank of the Sev River is gently sloping and open; in the area of Sevsk, the western bank is steep and rises significantly above the eastern bank. Populated places are located on the western bank of the Sev River: Streletskaia and the city of Sevsk with their brick buildings loomed across the entire front on the axis of the main attack. In the depth of the enemy's defenses, the terrain is cut by deep ravines and is open from the air.

## The adversary

By the start of the operation, on 26 August 1943, the enemy had the 251st Infantry Division occupying a front of 12 kilometers in the Rozhdestvenskii – Lipnitsa sector. In reserve the enemy had the 61st Infantry Regiment of the 7th Infantry Division. There was also the Kaminsky Brigade (consisting of traitors of the Motherland) under the command of Filatov, with a total strength of up to 3 battalions in the Korostovka, Borisovo and Byki areas. An unidentified German infantry regiment was in the area of Seredina-Buda, and on the approach to the area west and northwest of Sevsk were units of the 31st Infantry Division and the 8th Panzer Division. The Germans strengthened this sector with the 69th Artillery Regiment and the 604th Artillery Division from the *Führer* Reserve, plus an unidentified battalion of assault guns (20-30 self-propelled guns). Up to 65 tanks and self-propelled guns had been detected in the Iupiter – Lipnitsa area, standing ready to counterattack any penetrations of the frontline defenses. The reinforcement of the enemy's Sevsk grouping was connected with the fact that the enemy managed to detect the 65th Army's preparations for an offensive ahead of time.

Later, General Bogdanov provided his assessment of the enemy's defenses:

The Germans had spent more than 5 months strengthening the defensive line Shirokaia Roshcha, Iupiter, Novo-Iamskoe, Sevsk, Dubki. In the first line was the 251st Infantry Division with the 451st, 459th and 491st Infantry Regiments, all positioned in a single line, with up to 10,000 men. German reserves were located in Kniaginino – 20 tanks and up to a regiment of infantry; in woods west of Lepnitsa – up to an infantry regiment; and up to two regiments of Vlasovites [the Kaminsky Brigade] in Seredina-Buda. In the vicinity of Lokot', the Germans had an area of reforming and refitting, where the 4th, 8th and 12th Panzer Divisions and the 31st, 7th and 6th Infantry Divisions were located. From 10 August to 26 August 1943, the enemy began to conduct a regrouping of forces east of Sevsk. The enemy, from aerial reconnaissance, knew that the gathering of our forces was underway, and prisoners revealed that the Germans were aware of our [pending] offensive. Therefore the enemy began to concentrate forces in and around Sevsk, and by 25 August 1943 had introduced the 86th Infantry Division in the Iupiter – Rozhdestvenskii sector, had fleshed out the combat ranks of the 251st Infantry Division, and had brought up the 7th, 31st and 82nd Infantry Divisions and the 4th and 8th Panzer Divisions to the area west of Sevsk.

The enemy's defenses facing the 65th Army and 2nd Tank Army presented a rather serious obstacle. In addition to minefields and anti-tank ditches, the Sev River itself, 8 to 16 meters in width, was a major obstacle. The city of Sevsk and town of Streletskaia with their brick buildings, and especially Sevsk with its stone fences and churches, were fortified. The western bank commanded the eastern bank, which could be swept by German fire out to 2 to 3 kilometers from the direction of Sevsk. The terrain was exposed from the air.

The official *Boevoi put' 7-go mexanizirovannogo korpusa* [*Combat path of the 7th Mechanized Corps*] states:

General S.I. Bogdanov's 2nd Tank Army was committed into the fighting in the sector of General Batov's 65th Army. The 7th Guards Mechanized Corps, which had received tanks and personnel replacements from Rybalko's 3rd Guards Tank Army, became operationally subordinate to the 2nd Tank Army on 14 August 1943. The enemy had created a firm defense in the Sevsk area. Numerous earth and timber bunkers, armored turrets, trenches with shelters, anti-tank ditches, minefields and barbed wire barriers were clearly visible in the rough terrain. The front line ran along the Sev River. Units of the 137th, 251st and 86th Infantry Divisions were holding the defenses in front of the 7th Guards Mechanized Corps.

General Bogdanov initiated the preparation of the offensive with a conference. It took place in a spacious home on the edge of a forest. "As soon as the enemy begins to retreat," said the commander, we will introduce armored units into the breach. Pursuing the enemy, we must strive to encircle him, while the 65th Army will complete the elimination [of the pocket]. Soon Front commander K.K. Rokossovsky drove up. He quickly went to the table, greeted everyone, and immediately went to work:

"Comrade Commanders. You must understand that a breakthrough is a relative concept, since the enemy's defenses extend far in depth; therefore, don't expect easy conditions in the enemy's rear and don't search for justifications for failures. With the introduction of the 2nd Tank Army into the battle, we will assemble large forces of aviation in the breakthough sector. Do not fear separation from the rifle units. It is their duty to hasten after the tanks, while your task is to advance, as quickly and as far as possible."

According to the plan of the operation, the 7th Guards Mechanized Corps, outflanking Sevsk on its northwestern side, was to attack in the direction of Seredina-Buda Station. The corps commander and headquarters staff went to work on preparations: they got a clearer picture of the contours of the [German] front line, established movement routes and crossing places on the Sev River, and began laying down corduroy roads to the river crossings.

Soon General Bogdanov arrived in the corps. He met with the officer staff and visited the 26th Brigade. The start of the offensive was drawing closer. By this time the 7th Guards Mechanized Corps had assembled in the Pokrovskoe, Uspenskii staging area. On 25 August 1943 the army commander again gathered the commanders and chiefs of staff. At the map, marked all over with red and blue arrows, and at the relief map of the terrain, they reported their decisions regarding the arrangement of the offensive and of joint actions with their neighbors and among types of forces.

To reiterate, the 16th Tank Corps and the 11th Guards Tank Brigade had turned over all their tanks and a portion of their men and artillery to the 3rd Tank Corps, and they took no part in the fighting. The 2nd Tank Army, consisting of the 3rd Tank Corps and 7th Guards Mechanized Corps had 168 T-34 and 68 T-70 tanks, 16 SU-122 self-propelled guns, 207 guns of various calibers, and 193 mortars. Guards Major Potemkin, chief of the 7th Guards Mechanized Corps' Operations Department, generated a report on the availability and condition of the armored vehicles among the corps' units on 21 August 1943 (see Table 4.3):

Table 4.3: Data on the availability and condition of the armored vehicles in the units of the 7th Guards Mechanized Corps on 21 August 1943

| Unit | Type | According to TO&E | On the list | Serviceable | Under repair | |
|---|---|---|---|---|---|---|
| | | | | | Minor | Light overhaul |
| 33rd Tank Brigade | T-34 | 32 | 34 | 31 | 2 | 1 |
| | T-70 | 21 | 21 | 18 | 1 | 2 |
| | BA-64 | | 2 | 1 | – | – |
| 18th Mechanized Brigade | T-34 | 32 | 34 | 21 | 11 | 2 |
| | T-70 | 7 | 8 | 7 | 1 | – |
| | BA-64 | | 4 | 1 | – | 3 |
| 34th Mechanized Brigade | T-34 | 32 | 34 | 28 | 2 | 4 |
| | T-70 | 7 | 7 | 7 | – | – |
| | BA-64 | | 5 | 3 | – | 2 |
| 43rd Mechanized Brigade | T-34 | 32 | 27 | 25 | – | 2 |
| | T-70 | 7 | 7 | 7 | – | – |
| | BA-64 | | 5 | 2 | 1 | 2 |
| 772nd Separate Signals Battalion | T-34 | 3 | 3 | 2 | – | 1 |
| | BA-64 | | 10 | 3 | – | 7 |
| 33rd Separate Coastal Artillery Battery | T-70 | 7 | 6 | 5 | 1 | – |
| | BA-64 | | 15 | 13 | – | 1 |
| 1418 Self-propelled Artillery Regiment | SU-122 | 16 | 12 | 10 | – | 2 |

On 23 August 1943, the 2nd Tank Army's Military Council received a report from the 7th Guards Mechanized Corps at 19.00:

1.   Units of the 7th Guards Mechanized Corps are in their present assembly area.
     The personnel are occupied with combat training: individual training of the soldier in line drills; tactical training -- the attack of rifle and tank platoons against a defending enemy.
2.   Officers of the Corps headquarters from 7.00 to 17.00 on 23.8.43 conducted an inspection of the organization and course of combat training, of the troop dispositions, and of the digging in and camouflaging of the personnel and equipment of brigade and corps units.
3.   A reconnaissance group of the 68th Separate Motorcycle Battalion is keeping the enemy defenses under observation from Hill 197.9.
4.   The reception of personnel replacements and their distribution across the brigades:
     18th Mechanized Brigade – 292 men;
     34th Mechanized Brigade – 288 men;
     43rd Mechanized Brigade – 207 men
     Total: 787 men
5.   Presence of combat vehicles, located in the holding area, ready for combat operations on 23 August 1943:
     a)   33rd Tank Brigade – 32 T-34, 18 T-70, 1 BA-64
     b)   18th Mechanized Brigade – 24 T-34, 7 T-70, 1 BA-64, 7 M3A1
     c)   34th Mechanized Brigade – 28 T-34, 6 T-70, 3 BA-64, 8 M3A1
     d)   43rd Mechanized Brigade – 25 T-34, 7 T-70, 1 BA-64, 7 M3A1
     e)   1418th Self-propelled Artillery Regiment – 1 T-34, 9 SU-122
     f)   772nd Separate Signals Battalion – 2 T-34, 3 BA-64, 1 M3A1
     g)   33rd Separate Coastal Artillery Battery – 6 T-70, 13 BA-64
     h)   68th Separate Motorcycle Battalion – 4 M3A1, 60 motorcycles
     Total for the corps: 112 T-34, 44 T-70, 22 BA-64, 27 M3A1, 9 SU-122
     The corps has 1.7 combat loads of ammunition, 2 refills of diesel fuel and lubricants, 3.5 refills of KV-70, 1.5 refills of low-grade benzene, and 5 days of rations.
6.   Communications with the formations and units of the corps – via staff officers and by telephone.

## I HAVE DECIDED:

1.   To continue combat training, primarily with drills and tactical exercises.
2.   To continue the repair of combat and transport vehicles and to put the personnel and equipment in order.
     [Signed] Commander of the 7th Guards Mechanized Corps Guards Lieutenant General Korchagin; deputy chief of staff of the 7th Guards Mechanized Corps Guards Major Potemkin

The next day, the headquarters of the 3rd Tank Corps submitted an operational summary to the headquarters of the 2nd Tank Army at 21.00. It stated:

1.   The units of the corps in the course of the day didn't alter their positions.
2.   The personnel of the corps' units are occupied with combat training, in accordance with the given plan.

| | |
|---|---|
| 50th Tank Brigade: 29 T-34, 10 T-70; | 2.0 combat loads of ammo |
| | 1.7 refills of fuel and lubricants |
| | 5.0 days of rations |
| 51st Tank Brigade: 0 tanks, refitting | 1.9 combat loads of ammo |
| | 1.6 refills of fuel and lubricants |
| | 6.0 days of rations |
| 103rd Tank Brigade: 24 T-34, 10 T-70; | 2.0 combat loads of ammo |
| | 1.3 refills of fuel and lubricants |
| | 5.0 days of rations |
| 57th Motorized Rifle Brigade: 0 AFV; | 2.0 combat loads of ammo |
| | 1.9 refills of fuel and lubricants |
| | 4.5 days of rations |
| 234th Mortar Regiment: 36 120mm mortars; | 1.0 combat loads of ammo |
| | 1.4 refills of fuel and lubricants |
| | 3.0 days of rations |
| 881st Destroyer AT Regiment: 19 45mm guns; | 1.2 combat loads of ammo |
| | 1.0 refills of fuel and lubricants |
| | 4.0 days of rations |
| 728th Destroyer AT Battalion: 11 85mm guns; | 1.0 combat loads of ammo |
| | 1.0 refills of fuel and lubricants |
| | 7.0 days of rations |
| 1442nd Self-propelled Artillery Regiment: 7 SU-122; | 2.0 combat loads of ammo |
| | 2.0 refills of fuel |
| | 5 days of rations |
| 121st Anti-aircraft Regiment: 16 27mm AA guns; 14 DShK MG; | 2.0 combat loads of ammo |
| | 2.0 refills of fuel and lubricants |
| | 5.0 days of rations |

2. Communications with the corps' units – over the telephone and via signal officers.

3. Command post in its previous location.

[Signed] Temporary chief of staff of the 3rd Tank Corps Colonel Shvetsov

## Course of the operation

At 8.17 on 26 August 1943, the preparatory artillery barrage began, and at 9.00 the infantry of the 65th Army went on the attack. By 11.00, 65th Army headquarters was reporting that the attacking infantry had seized Streletskaia; at 12.00 Novo-Iamskoe; at 12.45 Sevsk; at 14.00 Shvedchikovy, etc. As a result of checks by the 2nd Tank Army headquarters, the corps commanders, and the observation network organized by the 2nd Tank Army, by 15.00 it had become clear that only Streletskaia had been taken. The other objectives were being placed under artillery fire, but the infantry had been pinned down. By this time our air force had conducted up to 370 individual sorties. By the end of the day on 26 August, the 65th Army had failed to carry out its assignment; at the moment of the 2nd Tank Army's "introduction into the breach", the infantry had still not taken Novo-Iamskoe, Kniaginino, Moritskii or Sevsk. The 2nd Tank Army remained in its jumping-off area, having the assignment to begin crossing the Sev River with the onset of darkness. By the morning of 27 August, it was crossing the Sev River to the western bank in order to carry out its task.

Thus, the units of the 65th Army by the end of the day on 26 August in the sector of the 2nd Tank Army's introduction on the axis of the main attack had made an advance of only 3 kilometers, where it had been halted by strong resistance within the enemy's previously prepared lines, which extended 12 to 15 kilometers in depth. Here, given the situation that had developed, the element of surprise had been lost, and the adversary had the opportunity to bring up reserves. With the sunset on 26 August, the 65th Army had only managed to create a 5.5-kilometer wide bridgehead on the western bank of the Sev River, to a depth of 3 to 4 kilometers. To the left, the enemy continued to hold the main defensives stronghold – the city of Sevsk.

At the decision of the Central Front commander, the 2nd Tank Army was thrown into the fighting in order to breach the enemy's defenses. The enemy had destroyed the bridges across the Sev River and was preventing the construction of temporary bridges in the Novo-Iamskoe – Sevsk area with mortar fire and direct artillery fire. The curtain of fire was well-placed. As a result of every effort by the sappers of the 2nd Tank Army, which only had seven sapper battalions, just three of the nine planned bridges were built. This created a traffic jam leading to the available three crossings in the Rozhdestvenskii – northern outskirts of Sevsk sector tying up the 2,000 vehicles of the 2nd Tank Army, artillery, and the supply wagons of the 65th Army. The 2nd Tank Army's crossing was completed with great difficulty by 7.30 on 27 August, and the corps' deployed into their combat formations northwest of the Streletskaia area on the western bank of the Sev River. According to Operational Summary No.327 from 27 August 1943, the 2nd Tank Army at the start of its offensive had 212 operational armored vehicles (142 T-34, 58 T-70 and 12 SU-122).

At 10.00 on 27 August, a 3rd Tank Corps headquarters' staff officer quickly compiled a report on the condition of the corps' subordinate tank brigades (see Table 4.4). In his hurry, he committed a simple mathematical error:

**Table 4.4: Data on the condition of the 3rd Tank Corps' subordinate tank brigades at 10.00 on 27 August 1943**

| | Tanks: | On the list | | Serviceable | | En route | |
|---|---|---|---|---|---|---|---|
| 50th Tank Br. | T-34 | 30 | | T-34 | 25 | T-34 | 5 |
| | T-70 | 10 | | T-70 | 10 | T-70 | – |
| 103rd Tank Br. | T-34 | 34 | | T-34 | 30 | T-34 | 4 |
| | T-70 | 12 | | T-70 | 12 | T-70 | – |
| Total | T-34 | 64 | | T-34 | 45 (sic) | | |
| | T-70 | 22 | | T-70 | 22 | | |
| Command tanks | T-34 | 2 | | T-34 | 2 | | |
| | T-70 | 2 | | T-70 | 2 | | |
| Altogether: | T-34 | 66 | | T-34 | 47 (sic) | | |
| | T-70 | 24 | | T-70 | 24 | | |
| Supplies: | with ammunition – | | | 2 combat loads | | | |
| | with fuel and lubricants – | | | 2.3 refills | | | |
| | with rations – | | | 6 days' worth | | | |

General Bogdanov recalls,

> At 8.30 on 27 August 1943, after a 5-minute opening artillery barrage, the 2nd Tank Army went on the attack; by 10.00 the motorcycle battalion and the 33rd Tank Brigade seized Kniaginino, in the process of which it took prisoners of the 7th Infantry Division and the 23rd Panzer Grenadier Regiment of the 8th Panzer Division (the presence of which was unknown to the 65th Army and the Central Front). Conducting a reconnaissance toward Chemlyzh, by the end of the day the 7th Guards Mechanized Corps had seized Berestochek and the Revolution State Farm, and had taken prisoners from the 31st Infantry Division's 12th Infantry Regiment. By midnight, the 7th Guards Mechanized Corps was taking possession of Zaul'e and Mikhailovskii, and here again the presence of the 31st Infantry Division, the 7th Infantry Division and the 8th Panzer Division was detected.
>
> The 3rd Tank Corps with its 50th and 103rd Tank Brigades began slowly to attack toward a triangular-shaped patch of woods, but was met by heavy artillery fire and airstrikes. It spent the entire day of 27 August grinding its wheels in place and accomplished nothing. The 50th Tank Brigade had been ordered to attack in the wake of the [7th Guards Mechanized Corps'] 34th Mechanized Brigade, but the commander of the 50th Tank Brigade tarried with carrying out the order, wandered into a ravine, and remained there until nightfall. In the area of the triangular patch of woods, men of the 7th Infantry Division were captured. As a result of the attacks, on 27 August 1943 the 2nd Tank Army revealed the presence of the 7th Infantry Division, the 31st Infantry Division, and the 8th Panzer Division, in addition to the 251st Infantry Division, about which the 65th Army and the Central Front already knew.
>
> On the night of 27/28 August, a forward detachment was created and sent out to scout in the direction of the corps' advance. The observation post of the 2nd Tank Army's commanders moved into western Streletskaia. At 5.00 on 28 August 1943, the 2nd Tank Army had operational a total of 147 tanks, 83 T-34 and 64 T-70. Thus, the losses on 27 August amounted to 97 tanks.

The 2nd Tank Army's journal of combat operations observes:

> At 7.50 after a 5-minute artillery preparation, the troops of the army went on the attack in the general direction of Kniaginino, Borisovo and Berestok, and by 10.00 a portion of its forces seized Kniaginino. Because the enemy had concealed his front line, the opening barrage had fallen on his belt of outposts. The enemy, with units of the 7th Infantry Division, the 251st Infantry Division, the 69th Artillery Regiment and the 604th Artillery Battalion in the course of the day offered stubborn resistance to the attack of our units. The enemy air force in groups of 15-30 aircraft bombed the combat formations of our forces, and patrolled over our roads in pairs with accompanying bombing. Altogether over the day, up to 120 individual aircraft sorties were counted. With the efforts of the 7th Guards Mechanized Corps, the army breached the enemy's defenses and seized the Zaul'e – Ivnik line, where it ran into a natural obstacle in the form of the Ul'iana River, which was being covered by heavy enemy fire. Continuing to attack, the army's forces over the day of combat took Kniaginino, Moritskii and Bukovishche, and by day's end the 7th Guards Mechanized Corps was fighting on a line 1 kilometer southwest of Chemlyzh, 2 kilometers northwest of Kniaginino, 2 kilometers east of Mikhailovskii, and Hill 194.7; the 3rd Tank Corps had reached a line running from 1 kilometer south of Hill 194.1 through a ravine 1 kilometer east of Borisovo to a point 700 meters southeast of Lemeshok.
>
> The 3rd Tank Corps, taking advantage of the 7th Guards Mechanized Corps' advance in the direction of Berestok, resumed its offensive, seized the settlement of Korostovka, and

continued to exploit in the Svetova – Mikhailovskii farmstead direction. The enemy units that were defending Sevsk began to retreat to the west. At this time the 103rd Tank Brigade jointly with units of the 69th Rifle Division impetuously attacked the enemy, and after bitter fighting, took full possession of Sevsk by the end of 27 August. After the taking of Sevsk, by order of the Supreme Commander, gratitude was expressed to the personnel of the 3rd Tank Corps, while the 3rd Tank Corps' 103rd Tank Brigade and the 26th Guards Mechanized Brigade (formerly the 43rd Mechanized Brigade) of the 7th Guards Mechanized Corps were awarded the honorific title "Sevsk". At 20.00 on 27 August 1943, the 3rd Tank Corps had 38 T-34 and 16 T-70 still serviceable.

Thus, the 2nd Tank Army broke through the enemy's defenses, but in the process it had expended its strength (having lost 97 tanks alone over the day of combat), and it was unable to exploit the breach. Over the day of fighting on 27 August 1943, the 2nd Tank Army captured Kniaginino, Moritskii, Zaul'e, Mikhailovskii, Ivnik, the Revolution State Farm, and Sevsk.

At 10.30 on 27 August 1943, the commander of the 2nd Tank Army expressed frustration with the slow pace of advance in his Combat Order No.090/OP to the commanders of the 3rd Tank Corps and 7th Guards Mechanized Corps:

Once again you are failing to carry out an order and a combat assignment. Once again you are criminally spinning your wheels in place, suffering casualties to no avail. The Military Council categorically demands a change of the method of leadership and the handling of the battle. I AM ORDERING: Use massed, resolute attacks with tanks. Use massed fire of all types. Quickly organize the combat and carry out the assignment you've been given. Report on the execution. Confirm receipt.

[Signed] Commander of the 2nd Tank Army Lieutenant General Bogdanov and Military Council Member Major General Latyshev

The German Lieutenant General Rudolf Freiherr von Roman, the commander of the defending XX Army Corps, later wrote:

The Russians began the attack on 26 August 1943 with an artillery preparation along the entire front lines of XX Corps; [artillery] fire was concentrated primarily on General Feltzman's 251st Infantry Division and General Weidling's 86th Infantry Division. Soon we determined that the barrage on the 45th and 137th Infantry Divisions was rather weak and represented harassing fire. However, along the front of the 251st and 86th Infantry Divisions, serious fighting was occurring, which went on for several days.

After a lot of fighting the Soviets, often turning to the help of their airplanes and tanks, broke through the defenses of the 251st Infantry Division on both sides of Sevsk. On the northwestern side of the city, enemy forces had broken through on a narrow sector, aimed in the direction of Seredina-Buda, which was located approximately 20 kilometers to the west of Sevsk, and had already traveled almost half the distance to that town.

We had no information whatsoever about the situation south of Sevsk. The murkiest spot was the wooded section on the boundary between XX and XIII Corps. It was totally unknown to us, how far the Soviets had managed to penetrate behind our front. General Weiss ordered Lieutenant General von Rappard's 7th Infantry Division to support our ranks, but it was totally unable to improve the situation. The 7th Infantry Division had been so worn out in the fighting west of Dmitriev, that to release it into the battle was totally inadmissible.

General von Rappard was compelled to send his battalions into the battle as each arrived at the front line. The operation was unsuccessful.

On 27 August 1943 the Russians launched 25 attacks (in strength of a battalion to a division) against the left flank of the 251st Infantry Division northwest of the Sev River and against the right flank of the 86th Infantry Division. We drove back all these attacks, and the Soviets suffered serious losses. This happened largely owing to the unexpected, but timely appearance of General Fichtner's 8th Panzer Division, which didn't allow the Russians to complete a breakthrough in the Novo-Iamskoe area, on the boundary between the 251st and 86th Infantry Divisions.

## Combat operations on 28 August 1943

The enemy in the course of 28 August with units of the 7th, 31st and 251st Infantry Divisions and the 8th and 4th Panzer Divisions, with fire and counterattacks of up to a battalion of infantry with tank support put up stubborn resistance to the advance of our units. Enemy aircraft in groups of 14 to 30 bombed the combat formations of our units. At 11.30 the enemy in strength of up to a company of infantry with the support of tanks counterattacked our units in the direction of Borisovo out of the northern outskirts of Korostovka; the counterattack was repulsed. At 18.00, up to a battalion of enemy infantry with the support of up to 26 tanks counterattacked our units in the direction of Bukovishche out of the area of Hill 244.0 and took Bukovishche, but was thrown back to its jumping-off position by a counterattack of our units. Our aerial reconnaissance established that in the course of the day the enemy was bringing up fresh units to the zone of combat operations. The movement of 120 motor vehicles with 40 towed guns was detected en route from Suzemka toward Negino, and another 320 vehicles, including 25 tanks, was observed in motion from Seredina-Buda toward Orliia. Staff documents captured in the area of Kniaginino confirmed the presence of the 4th and 8th Panzer Divisions.

The 2nd Tank Army (3rd Tank Corps and 7th Guards Mechanized Corps) at 5.00 on 28 August resumed the offensive, and by 12.00, having driven back a counterattack of 30 enemy tanks out of Bezgorodovka and Glinki and having overcome stubborn enemy resistance with combat, seized Berestok, Lemeshok and reached a line 1 kilometer south of Berestok. By the end of the day, overcoming heavy enemy fire out of the areas of Glinki, Bezgorodkova and Korostovka, and repelling counterattacks of enemy infantry and tanks with the forces of the 3rd Tank Corps, the 2nd Tank Army was fighting on the line: northern outskirts of Berestok – northeastern slopes of Hill 217.0 – western outskirts of Borisovo. By Combat Order No.092/OP, the 2nd Tank Army went temporarily over to a defense on the line it had achieved, with the task of destroying the enemy's fresh tank divisions and to prevent a German breakthrough to the east. The army was to be ready for the defense by 21.00 on 28 August 1943. At this time, the 3rd Tank Corps had just 25 serviceable tanks (16 T-34 and 9 T-70). The corps' losses for the day amounted to 9 T-34 and 5 T-70.

General Bogdanov remembers,

By the morning of 28.8.1943, the enemy was organizing strong opposition with fire on the entire front of the 2nd Tank Army's offensive, and was launching counterattacks. He was putting up especially bitter resistance in the area of the triangular patch of woods and Bukovishche. From the morning of 28.8.1943, the 2nd Tank Army was continuing to carry out its assignment. The 7th Guards Mechanized Corps reached the Ul'ianovka River and began to prepare a crossing. The 3rd Tank Corps bypassed the triangular patch of woods, and having driven back four counterattacks out of Bukovishche, seized three prisoners of the 4th Panzer Division. At 12.00 on 28.8.43, the 2nd Tank Army received an order to pivot to the south and to seize Mikhailovskii Station. By this time the neighboring 60th Army was making rapid progress to the west. The 9th Tank Corps, encountering slight enemy resistance, emerged in the depth and rear of the enemy, and subsequently the 9th Tank Corps took Glukhov. Therefore the 2nd Tank Army was pivoted to the south in order to encircle the enemy's southern grouping. With the attacks on 27 and 28 August, the enemy grouping consisting of the 8th Panzer Division (Glinki, Zaul'e), 31st Infantry Division (Zaul'e), 4th Panzer Division, 7th Infantry Division (Berestok, Korostovka) and the 251st Infantry Division was hurled back to the north and south. According to the testimonies of prisoners, the 8th Panzer Division had 120 tanks, while the 4th Panzer Division had up to 105 tanks.

At 11.30 on 28.8.43, the enemy undertook a number of counterattacks from the areas of Korostovka, Bukovishche, Borisov and Lemeshok against the 3rd Tank Corps' 57th Motorized Rifle Brigade and 103rd Tank Brigade, but the envelopment by the 50th, 33rd and 43rd Tank Brigades forced the enemy to fall back to his jumping-off positions ….

Units of the 8th Panzer Division (45 tanks) and up to two infantry regiments were assembled in the area northwest of Zaul'e. The 61st Infantry Regiment of the 7th Infantry Division and the 4th Panzer Division, consisting of seven battalions and 105 tanks, were assembled in the Korostovka area and in the ravines southwest of Berestok with the aim of launching counterattacks in the direction of Lemeshok and the woods to the east of it. Altogether on the breakthrough sector, the enemy had brought together up to 200 tanks and 30 self-propelled guns.

As noted above, the 2nd Tank Army had overcome heavy enemy fire coming from the directions of Bezgorodovka and Glinki, and having repelled four enemy counterattacks, by 20.00 on 28 August it was fighting on the line: northern outskirts of Berestok – northern slopes of Hill 217.0 – western and northern outskirts of Borisovo – woods east of Lemeshok – Hill 217.5. The infantry of the 65th Army, having reached the line Novo-Iamskoe – Kniaginino – Hill 209.6 and the northern section of Sevsk, made no further headway.

The document "Combat path of the 7th Guards Mechanized Corps" notes:

Enemy resistance had grown noticeably. That night Bogdanov decided to pivot the mechanized corps to the south, in order to assist the 3rd Tank Corps, which had been stopped short of Lemeshok, in seizing Sevsk, on the approaches to which heavy fighting was also going on. But there was no one to which to hand over its sector – the rifle units had lagged behind and the offensive on the southern axis was also going slowly. Only on the morning of 28 August 1943 did the 26th and 57th Brigades reach Borisovo, having left behind a portion of their artillery and mortars, as well as their rear elements, in the vicinity of Revolution State Farm. Their approach march took place under constant barrages and bombing attacks. On the approach to Borisovo, enemy tanks had been spotted. The commander of the 26th Brigade's artillery Lieutenant Colonel Zaglodin advanced Captain Gudkov's artillery battalion to meet them. The gun crews quickly prepared for combat and opened fire. In the brief clash, the artillerymen destroyed four tanks and killed up to 70 Nazis. While driving around the firing positions on the running board of his Studebaker, Captain Gudkov was killed.

In the afternoon, the enemy counterattacked again and cut off the 5th Company from the rest of its motorized rifle battalion. Senior Sergeant Ignatov's platoon of submachine gunners was sent to its relief. The soldiers imperceptibly filtered into the German rear and took cover. About two hours later, two battalions repeated the attack. Our submachine gunners opened fire from the rear. The battalion linked up with the company and together with tankers threw back the foe. Maksimov's and Artamonov's brigades reached the village of Berestok.

The sun had dropped below the horizon, when the army commander's Willys appeared on the forest road. Korchagin quickly walked out to meet him. Bogdanov pulled a map out of a satchel and spread it out directly on the hood of the jeep.

"The situation has become complicated in front of your corps", he said. "Fresh units of the 4th and 8th Panzer Divisions and of the 7th and 31st Infantry Divisions have appeared. According to all the evidence, they intend to break through to Sevsk. Halt the offensive. Prepare to repel a counterattack."

Bogdanov drove off. The units were given the order: "Assume a defensive posture. The brigade commanders are to arrive at the corps command post."

The conference began when it was already dark. Korchagin began:

"General Bogdanov drove up and announced that the enemy was preparing a counterattack. We also have in our possession intelligence about the movement of German tanks and infantry. The Germans are laying down a corodoy road across the swamp from the direction of the village of Berestochka. The road between Kniaginino and the Revolution State Farm is being constantly shelled. The main attack is anticipated here. It is necessary to bring back Silov's brigade to this area. The remaining brigades are to hold their positions. Get all the weapons ready. Dig in deeper into the ground."

General Bogdanov recalls, "Thus, the plain threat of a powerful counterattack by major tank groups of the 8th and 4th Panzer Divisions against the base of the salient, which had been created by the breakthrough, was emerging. At the decision of the 2nd Tank Army commander, at 20.00 on 28.8.43 the 7th Guards Mechanized Corps went on the defensive on the line Revolution State Farm – Berestok – Korostovka – southern outskirts of Borisovo, with the mission to annihilate the enemy's tanks and personnel with the fire of artillery and tanks from ambush positions, not giving him the possibility to break through to the east."

According to archival evidence, the grouping of German forces in the Sevsk area which was opposing the 2nd Tank Army had more than 200 tanks and assault guns on its list as of 20 August 1943, including:

**8th Panzer Division – 97 tanks** (37 Pz. IV, 32 Pz. III, 7 Pz. II, 6 Pz. Bef, and 15 Marders)

**4th Panzer Division – 131 tanks** (57 Pz. IV, 9 Pz. III, 14 Pz. Bef, 21 Marders, and 12 Wespe, 6 Hummel and 12 Grille self-propelled artillery vehicles)

Attached assets included Stu.Gesch.Abt. 244, with 24 StuG III and 5 StuH 42 assault guns; Stu. Gesch.Abt 909, with 19 StuG III; s.Pz.Abt 505, with 25 Tigers; and *Kampfgruppe* Kall (elements of sPzJg.Rgt. 656), with 12 Ferdinands and 14 Sturmpz. IV.

German Lieutenant General Rudolf Freiherr von Roman, commander of XX Corps, later wrote:

Unfortunately, the situation in the southwest in the forested zone reached a crisis point, and thus on 28 August 1943, General Weiss withdrew the 8th Panzer Division from the area of Novo-Iamskoe and transferred it to the threatened sector. Thus after a successful counterattack, the forward units of the division abandoned the area, while the main forces followed them on 29 August 1943. The Second Army was planning to replace it at Novo-Iamskoe with General Grossman's 6th Infantry Division, which was being withdrawn into the army group's reserve, but by the moment of the departure of the main forces of tanks, only motorized elements of the 6th Combat Engineer Battalion and other forward units of the 6th Infantry Division had managed to arrive. These weak forces were incapable of holding back the Russian offensive. The enemy managed to seize ground southwest of Novo-Iamskoe just as the motorized column with the main forces of the 6th Infantry Division was arriving on the evening of 29 August. Once again, it was necessary to throw separate regiments and companies into the battle immediately upon their arrival. Despite these difficulties, the 6th and 86th Infantry Divisions through their joint efforts were able to hold our second line of defenses, which ran from the southern boundary of Novo-Iamskoe through Sveshnikovo along the road to Glebovo. By this time, a tense situation had arisen with supplies; the main supply road, over which they were brought up, ran southwest of Lokot', which had been temporarily turned over for the movement of the 4th and 8th Panzer Divisions. Field Marshal Klüge had ordered these two divisions to relocate from the Ninth Army's sector to the Second Army's sector, in order to overcome the crisis southwest of Sevsk.

## Combat operations on 29 August 1943

With the forces of the 8th Panzer Division's 28th Panzer Grenadier Regiment, the rest of the 8th Panzer Division, the 31st Infantry Division's 12th Infantry Regiment, the 7th Infantry Division's 61st Infantry Regiment, the 451st Infantry Division and units of the 4th Panzer Division, the enemy with fire and counterattacks by two infantry regiments supported by 14-40 tanks, was putting up stubborn resistance. The *Luftwaffe* was launching solitary reconnaissance aircraft to scout the combat formations and supply routes of our forces.

At 16.00 the enemy in strength of up to two infantry regiments with the support of 40 tanks counterattacked in the direction of Revolution State Farm in the Berestochek – Zaul'e sector. The counterattack was thrown back. At 17.00, the enemy in strength of two companies of infantry with the support of 15 tanks unsuccessfully counterattacked out of Korostovka toward Bukovishche. In the course of the day, the enemy conducted strong artillery fire out of the areas of Zaul'e, Poliana and Bezgodkovo.

The 2nd Tank Army in the course of the day was defending on the line Kniaginino – Revolution State Farm – Berestok – Borisovo with its right flank. With its left-flank 3rd Tank Corps, the army was attacking in the direction of Korostovka from the Lemeshok line, overcoming stubborn resistance and repelling frequent counterattacks by enemy infantry and tanks. By 21.00, combat was continuing on the Borisovo line. The infantry of the 65th Army remained on its previous line.

Thus, on 29 August 1943, the 7th Guards Mechanized Corps was defending on the line it had attained, while the 3rd Tank Corps was battling its way toward Korostovka. At 20.00 on 29 August, the 3rd Tank Corps was down to 31 combat-fit tanks (8 T-34 and 6 T-70 in the 50th Tank Brigade; 4 T-34 and 6 T-70 in the 103rd Tank Brigade; 3 T-34 in the 51st Tank Brigade; and 2 T-34 and 2 T-70 with the corps' headquarters). The 7th Guards Mechanized Corps had 48 combat-fit tanks (8 T-34 and 4 T-70 in the 33rd Tank Brigade; 7 T-34 and 4 T-70 in the 34th Tank Brigade; 9 T-34 and 3 T-70 in the 43rd Mechanized Brigade; and 7 T-34 and 6 T-70 in the 18th Mechanized Brigade).

General Bodgdanov recalls the day of 28 August 1943:

> At 16.30 the enemy went on the attack with the 8th and 28th Panzer Grenadier Regiments and 40 tanks of the 8th Panzer Division's 10th Panzer Regiment, supported by the 31st Infantry Division's 12th Infantry Regiment in the Berestochek – Zaul'e sector toward Revolution State Farm. The enemy attack was anticipated and thus it was met by artillery fire from the 2nd Tank Army's artillery reserve and by a counterattack by the 33rd Tank Brigade. As a result, the enemy, suffering heavy losses (up to 50 percent of the infantry and 16 tanks left burning on the battlefield), fell back to the jumping-off position.
>
> At the same time, the enemy with units of the 4th Panzer Division (36 tanks, including 6 Tiger tanks) and up to two battalions of infantry attacked out of Bezgotkovo area toward Berestok, and with a group of 15 tanks and two infantry companies out of Korostovka toward Bukovishche. These enemy counterattacks were also driven back.

Soldiers of the Red Army on a Sevsk road.

Senior Sergeant Migunov's machine gunners, city of Sevsk.

Soldiers of the Red Army in the Sevsk area.

Sergeant Kotylev's anti-aircraft
gun crew.

In liberated Sevsk, on Lenin Street.

The document "Combat path of the 7th Guards Mechanized Corps" offers a fuller description of the fighting on 29 August:

> The night passed in uneasy anticipation, but relatively quietly. It was also quiet after sunrise. Then an exchange of gunfire began. German aircraft appeared. Enemy infantry units with the support of 40 tanks went on the attack. As was expected, the main blow fell in the sector between Revolution State Farm and Kniaginino. The German tanks burst into the combat positions of Captain Karpov's battalion through a tall hemp field. From the observation post of the chief of staff Senior Lieutenant Larikov of a mortar battery of the 26th Brigade, it was clearly visible that the motorized riflemen were falling back. Larikov had direct communications with the brigade's command post. He reported to the brigade chief of staff Prokof'ev, "Enemy tanks and infantry have shoved back the 3rd Battalion and are approaching out positions." The reply was "Ascertain the enemy strength. Support the battalion with your fire."
>
> Guns and mortars opened up on the enemy tanks and infantry. Soldiers of the rear elements took up a defense in the trenches. Columns of dirt and smoke from exploding shells approached ever closer. Now shots were audible from every direction. The Germans were striving to envelop us. Observation of the battlefield was hindered by smoke from a burning tank. Acrid smoke of burning oil wafted across the hemp field. Under the pressure of superior enemy forces, our light T-70 tanks and motorized riflemen began to retreat. Tigers with yellow patches of camouflage paint rumbled after them. Under their cover, German submachine gunners were dashing toward our position.
>
> Eighteen of our mortars and two batteries of 76mm anti-tank guns were firing intensively. The hostile submachine gunners were now just 100 meters away, and in order to hold, it was necessary to counterattack. Gainanov, the commander of the mortar men, leapt out of the trench and led his soldiers into the attack. Bayonets, sapper shovels and knives were freely employed in the hand-to-hand combat. Everyone fought desperately. The fascists were thrown

back, but only 50-60 men remained in our ranks. The hot August sun hung over the battle-field. The soldiers, drenched with sweat, were dragging up the final cases of ammunition. Tanks were burning.

Once again, the German rocket launchers began to howl – the signal for the next attack. Mortar battery commander Riazantsev requested authorization to change his position. The brigade commander cut him off: "I forbid a retreat! Help will soon arrive!" A shell exploded on the brigade command post. Communications were interrupted. German submachine gunners began to envelop the command post from two directions. Now even the brigade commander had to retreat. He hadn't had time to take a seat in the armored transporter, when a small-caliber shell struck its rear.

The brigade commander ordered Khaitovich to attack with tanks, and for Churiukin's mortar men to open up with blocking fire. At the most critical moment, when it seemed everything was lost, twenty tanks rushed at the foe, and the mortar men of the batteries opened up with rapid fire. The German attack in this sector faltered. Nevertheless, they had managed at first to take possession of Revolution State Farm and to push back the 26th Brigade. Toward evening, the Nazis were driven back out of the State Farm and thrown back to their jumping-off line.

Enemy attacks ensued as well in the Berestok and Bezgodkovo area, where infantry elements and approximately 20 tanks attempted unsuccessfully to penetrate the defenses of the 57th Brigade. Four German tanks and infantry broke through into the rear of the 24th Brigade. Mortar men, engineers and signalers joined in the fighting. Here and there, the fascists began to push back our fighters. However, the mortar men didn't lose heart; they deployed their heavy mortars and blanketed the enemy with shells.

The corps commander General Korchagin sent staff officers to these sectors, while he himself traveled to the Revolution State Farm. On this day, the enemy lost 1,500 soldiers and officers killed and wounded; 14 tanks; and a lot of other equipment and weapons.

According to a report of the chief of staff of the 7th Guards Mechanized Corps Guards Colonel Petrovsky for the period between 26 and 29 August 1943, the corps inflicted the following damage on the enemy: 1,773 soldiers and officers killed or wounded, 20 tanks, 41 vehicles, 10 cannons, 6 self-propelled guns, 18 anti-tank guns, 26 mortars and 27 machine guns. In addition, 13 soldiers and officers were taken prisoner. Over this same period, the corps' 33rd Tank Brigade had 46 dead and 86 wounded, and lost 11 T-34 and 6 T-70 totally destroyed, plus 13 T-34 and 4 T-70 knocked-out; the 34th Tank Brigade had 45 dead and 302 wounded, and lost 8 T-34 and 4 T-70 totally destroyed and 5 T-34 and 4 T-70 knocked-out; the 43rd Mechanized Brigade had 56 dead and 266 wounded, and lost 3 T-34 and 1 T-70 totally destroyed, and 4 T-34 and 3 T-70 knocked-out; and the 18th Mechanized Brigade had 58 dead and 126 wounded, and lost 10 T-34 and 1 T-70 knocked-out.

## Combat Operations on 30 August 1943

On the morning of 30 August, the 2nd Tank Army had a total of 82 serviceable tanks (48 T-34 and 34 T-70). The enemy in his same grouping was continuing to put of stiff resistance to our units with fire and counterattacks in strength of up to two companies of infantry with the support of 12 tanks and self-propelled guns. The *Luftwaffe* was continuing to conduct solitary reconnaissance patrols above our combat positions and supply routes. Enemy artillery was firing out of the areas: Chemlyzh – with up to two artillery batteries and two mortar batters; Zaul'e – with up to a battalion of artillery and two mortar batteries; and Korostovka – with up to two artillery battalions, two mortar batteries, and six-barreled rocket launchers.

At 8.30 the enemy in strength of up to two infantry companies with the support of a dozen tanks and self-propelled guns counterattacked out of the Bezgodkovo area toward Berestok. Simultaneously, up to two infantry companies and a dozen tanks attacked the southern outskirts of Berestok from the vicinity of Hill 217.0. The counterattacks were repulsed.

As over the day before, the 2nd Tank Army's 7th Guards Mechanized Corps was holding its line and continuing to mop-up the remaining enemy in Berestok; this process was completed at 13.00. The corps also assisted the attack of the 3rd Tank Corps with fire. Against fierce enemy opposition, by the end of the day the 3rd Tank Corps reached the northwestern outskirts of Korostovka. The infantry of the 65th Army remained in its positions in the area of the breakthrough.

Having repelled the enemy counteroffensive, the 7th Guards Mechanized Corps on 30 August 1943 received a new task – to turn over its sector of defense to infantry and to attack to the southwest. The handing over of the sector dragged out due to the lagging of the infantry. The 3rd Tank Corps by this time seized Korostovka and was continuing to attack toward Svetova. In connection with this, the 7th Guards Mechanized Corps had its orders changed. It was now to attack toward Seredina-Buda.

At 20.00 on 30.8.1943, the 3rd Tank had 11 T-34 and 13 T-70 still operational. For 48 hours, heavy fighting hadn't subsided. The defeat of the major German counteroffensive was a large success for the Guardsmen. General Bogdanov formally expressed his gratitude to the personnel of the corps.

## Combat operations on 31 August 1943

On the morning of 31 August, the 2nd Tank Army had a total of 72 operational tanks (40 T-34 and 32 T-70) and 16 self-propelled guns. Due to mechanical problems, 10 of these self-propelled guns were unable to move under their own power. In the course of the night, the 2nd Tank Army with part of its forces had continued to hold its defensive positions while turning over the sector to the 65th Army, while another part of its forces was mopping up Korostovka of the enemy. By 6.20, they took full possession of Korostovka together with units of the 246th Rifle Division.

The enemy in the course of the day was making a fighting withdrawal to the west. The enemy air force was bombing our combat positions with groups of up to 9 aircraft and conducting reconnaissance patrols above our rear areas and the routes being used to move up our forces.

The 2nd Tank Army's forces with its main forces went on the offensive at 7.00, and by 8.30 had taken Svetlaia Poliana. By the end of the day, the army's forces, overcoming stubborn enemy resistance, seized Bezgodkovo, Orliia, and Svetova and was fighting on the line: Hill 222.3 – Slobodka – southern slopes of Hill 232.0. At 21.00 on 31 August, the 3rd Tank Corps had 18 serviceable tanks: 6 T-34 and 3 T-70 in the 50th Tank Brigade; 5 T-34 and 2 T-70 in the 103rd Tank Brigade; 1 T-34 in the 51st Tank Brigade; and 1 T-34 with corps headquarters.

Following orders, the 7th Guards Mechanized Corps seized Bezgodkovo on 31 August, but having run into bitter resistance, it soon received again the combat order to attack to the southwest. By the end of the day on 31 August, the corps took Orliia, while units of the 3rd Tank Corps reached Svetova. The fighting took on a protracted character. The troops of the tank army, repelling counterattacks by major enemy forces of infantry and tanks, were advancing, albeit slowly. The pace of the offensive was slackening, and the tank formations were unable to exploit the successes of the rifle divisions. Enemy counterattacks were coming one after the other. Since the 2nd Tank Army's attack was launched in a relatively narrow sector of the front, the enemy had the possibility to increase his forces on this direction quickly at the expense of weakening other sectors.

Lieutenant General Freiherr von Roman's manuscript notes:

> Only this road had the adequate trafficability for the movement of the two panzer divisions, but a powerful storm, which began on the evening of 29 August 1943, made it impassable in many places. The unfavorable consequences of the XX Corps' lack of supplies were deepened by the fact that our main base of supplies was located 45 kilometers behind the front. Such a distance was too great for the supply columns to bring up supplies regularly. The Russians had broken through our front south of Sevsk and had advanced to a depth of 46 kilometers. The Red Army forces were already beginning to pivot to the north with the obvious intention of cutting off all of the German divisions located east of the Desna River. In connection with this, a retreat became absolutely necessary. The combat strength of the infantry divisions of XX Corps (the 102nd, 137th and 6th Infantry Divisions) was significantly weakened during the fighting around Sevsk and the retreat. Only 45 to 70 men remained in the infantry battalions.

## Combat operations on 1-2 September 1943

By the order of the Central Front commander, the 3rd Tank Corps and 7th Guards Mechanized Corps were to turn over their combat sectors to the 65th Army. The 3rd Tank Corps was then to assemble in a grove east of Lemeshok and in the areas of Hill 216.6 and the ravines south of Hill 209.6. The 7th Guards Mechanized Corps was withdrawn into the reserve of the Central Front and was to assemble in the Berestok – Borisovo – Moritskii area.

In the course of the day, the enemy with artillery and mortar fire and with counterattacks by infantry with tank support tried to drive the units of the 18th Mechanized Brigade out of Svetova. All the counterattacks were repulsed. By the morning of 2 September, the forces of the 2nd Tank Army had turned over their combat sectors to the 65th Army. The 2nd Tank Army had 82 remaining operational tanks, including 46 T-34 and 36 T-70. On 2 September 1943, the 3rd Tank Corps handed over its materiél and motorized infantry to the 7th Guards Mechanized Corps. Altogether, 28 T-34 and 11 T-70 tanks passed to the 7th Guards Mechanized Corps, as well as 1,522 officers, non-commissioned officers and men. The 7th Guards Mechanized Corps, having 94 tanks and more than 12,000 men, was withdrawn from operational subordination to the 2nd Tank Army and came under the operational control of the 60th Army.

Over the period of fighting between 27 August and 2 September 1943, the 2nd Tank Army inflicted the following damage to the enemy: 12,210 soldiers and officers were killed; 141 guns of various calibers, 77 heavy machine guns, 14 light machine guns, 245 vehicles, 5 motorcycles and 229 wagons with loads were destroyed. In addition, 48 prisoners were taken, and 20 vehicles, 1 armored transport, 48 rifles, 23 machine guns, 21 guns of various calibers, 70 submachine guns, 9 motorcycles, 7 mortars, 3 cars, 21 radio sets, 2 all-terrain vehicles, 1 tractor, 1 ammo dump and 1 fuel dump were captured.

The chief of staff of the 3rd Tank Corps Colonel Safronov and the chief of its Operations Department Colonel Shvetsov issued the following report on the losses suffered by the tank corps and the damage inflicted on the enemy in the Sevsk operation:

**Table 4.5: Personnel losses of the 2nd Tank Army over the period from 27 August to 2 September 1943**

|                        | Officers | Sergeants | Enlisted men | Total: |
|------------------------|----------|-----------|--------------|--------|
| Killed                 | 108      | 350       | 365          | 823    |
| Wounded                | 280      | 1,293     | 1,936        | 3,509  |
| Evacuated with illness | 3        | 2         | 4            | 9      |
| Missing-in-action      | 2        | 20        | 49           | 71     |
| Total:                 | 393      | 1,665     | 2,354        | 4,412  |

**Table 4.6: Tank losses of the 2nd Tank Army over the period of combat from 27 August to 2 September 1943**

|                      | T-34 | T-70 | Total: |
|----------------------|------|------|--------|
| Mechanical breakdowns| 16   | 10   | 26     |
| Damaged              | 73   | 10   | 83     |
| Destroyed            | 58   | 22   | 80     |
| Stuck in swamps      | 6    | –    | 6      |
| Total:               | 153  | 42   | 195    |

**Table 4.7: Data on the losses of personnel of the combat units of the 2nd Tank Army from 27 August to 2 September 1943**

| Date | Killed or died during medical evacuation | | | Wounded, concussed, burned, etc. with evacuation to hospital | | | Evacuated to hospital with illness | | | Missing-in-action | | | Total Losses | | | Grand Totals |
|------|---------|----------------|--------------|---------|----------------|--------------|---------|----------------|--------------|---------|----------------|--------------|---------|----------------|--------------|--------------|
|      | Command | Junior command | Enlisted men | Command | Junior command | Enlisted men | Command | Junior command | Enlisted men | Command | Junior command | Enlisted men | Command | Junior command | Enlisted men |              |
| 27.8.43 | 27 | 50 | 62 | 39 | 122 | 146 |   | 1 | 2 |   |   |   | 66 | 173 | 210 | 449 |
| 28.8.43 | 29 | 80 | 102 | 55 | 229 | 248 |   |   |   |   |   |   | 86 | 399 | 350 | 745 |
| 29.8.43 | 14 | 58 | 120 | 54 |    | 897 |   |   |   |   |   |   | 78 |    | 1,075 | 1,153 |
| 30.8.43 | 10 | 34 | 40 | 17 | 160 | 139 |   |   |   |   |   |   | 27 | 194 | 179 | 400 |
| 31.8.43 | 7 | 13 | 11 | 20 | 132 | 54 |   |   |   |   |   |   | 27 | 146 | 65 | 237 |
| Total: | 87 | 235 | 335 | 195 | 643 | 587 |   | 1 | 2 |   |   |   | 284 | 821 | 804 |    |
| Corrected from 27.8 to 31.8.43 | 90 | 389 | 347 | 206 | 1,120 | 1,468 | 4 | 6 | 18 |   | 2 | 6 | 300 | 1,517 | 1,839 | 3,656 |

Note: The categories for "Frostbitten with evacuation to hospital", "Taken prisoner" and "Other causes" had no entries in the original document, and thus were omitted from this table to save space.

**Table 4.8: Data on losses and the damage inflicted on the enemy by units of the 3rd Tank Corps over the period of fighting from 26 August to 1 September 1943**

| Destroyed: | | Suppressed: | |
|---|---|---|---|
| Tiger tanks | 14 | Artillery batteries | 14 |
| Pz IV tanks | 55 | Mortar batteries | 29 |
| Self-propelled guns | 10 | Firing points | 11 |
| Guns of various calibers | 35 | Scattered and partially destroyed soldiers and officers | 1,050 |
| Mortars | 28 | | |
| Artillery batteries | 2 | | |
| Mortar batteries | 6 | | |
| Machine guns of various calibers | 38 | Trophies: | |
| Rifles | 250 | Guns of various calibers | 15 |
| Submachine guns | 170 | Mortars | 4 |
| Anti-tank rifles | 8 | Heavy machine guns | 5 |
| Anti-tank guns | 44 | Submachine guns | 53 |
| Vehicles with loads | 87 | Rifles | 15 |
| Armored personnel carriers | 4 | All-terrain vehicles | 2 |
| Ammunition dumps | 2 | Tractors | 1 |
| Wagons with various loads | 50 | Vehicles | 9 |
| Dugouts | 7 | Motorcycles | 4 |
| Aircraft | 17 | | |
| Soldiers and officers | 4,430 | Taken prisoner | 19 |
| | | | |
| LOSSES: | | | |
| In materiél: | | | |
| T-34s burned out | 27 | 27mm small-caliber anti-aircraft artillery | 2 |
| T-34s knocked out | 7 | 76mm guns | 1 |
| T-70s burned out | 6 | Armored personnel carriers | 2 |
| T-70s knocked out | 3 | ZIS-5 trucks | 2 |
| SU-122s burned out | 2 | GAZ-AA trucks | 8 |
| 120mm mortars | 1 | Willys jeeps | 7 |
| 85mm mortars | 7 | Studebaker trucks | 1 |
| 45mm anti-tank guns | 5 | Radio sets | 1 |
| Armored cars | 1 | | |
| Telephone devices | 14 | | |

| In personnel: | Officers | Sergeants | Enlisted men |
|---|---|---|---|
| Killed: | 35 | 91 | 152 |
| Wounded: | 116 | 490 | 809 |
| | Total losses: | 1,543 men | |
| | There were no deserters | | |

## Losses of the German Panzer Divisions

Of the 96 tanks (Pz. III and Pz. IV) available to the 4th Panzer Division on 1 July 1943, it had only 25 tanks (Pz. III and Pz. IV) on 1 September 1943. Since this panzer division received no replenishments with tanks over the indicated period, this means the irrecoverable losses for July-August 1943 amounted to 71 tanks. In addition to this, 11 of the available tanks were not combat-ready and were under repair. From 1 to 31 August 1943 alone, the 4th Panzer Division lost 241 killed and 952 wounded, 70 missing in action, 17 ill and 14 discharged for other reasons. Over the period of the Sevsk operation between 20 August and 1 September 1943, the 4th Panzer Division irrecoverably lost 6 Pz. IV tanks, 4 self-propelled guns (1 Marder, 1 Wespe and 2 Hummel). In addition, over the period between 20 August and 1 September 1943, it had 28 tanks knocked out of action and requiring repair (3 Pz. III with the 75mm L/24, 23 Pz. IV with the 75mm L/43 and L/48, and 2 Pz.Beob. III), as well as 15 Marder self-propelled guns.

Of the 49 Pz. III and 20 Pz. IV tanks available to the 8th Panzer Division on 1 July 1943, only 21 Pz. III and 38 Pz. IV were still available. Since in July 1943 this division received an additional 42 Pz. IV tanks from the factories, then its irrecoverable losses over July-August 1943 amounted to 52 tanks (28 Pz. III and 24 Pz. IV). In addition to this, 34 of the available tanks were not combat-ready and were under repair. Between 1 and 31 August 1943 inclusively, the 8th Panzer Division lost 219 killed, 926 wounded, 168 missing in action, 241 ill and 60 discharged for other reasons. Over the period of the Sevsk operation between 20 August and 1 September 1943 inclusively, the 8th Panzer Division irrecoverably lost 2 tanks (1 Pz. III with the 50mm L/60 and 1 Pz. IV with the 75mm L/43 or L/48) and 3 Marder self-propelled guns. Over the period from 20 August to 1 September 1943, another 46 tanks (18 Pz. III with the 50mm L/60, 2 Pz. III with the 75mm L/24, 23 Pz. IV with the 75mm L/43 and L/48, and 3 Pz.Bef. III) and 6 Marder self-propelled guns of this panzer division were out of action and under repair.

As a result of the offensive between 26 August and 2 September 1943, the 2nd Tank Army overcame a strongly-fortified belt of enemy defenses, attracted significant German reserves, and inflicted heavy losses on the Germans. With its advance in the southwestern direction and the seizure of Orliia and Svetova, the 2nd Tank Army created the threat of encirclement of the enemy grouping facing the left-flank 60th Army, forced it to retreat, and gave the relatively insignificant forces of the 60th Army together with the 9th Tank Corps the opportunity to exploit the success with an eventual emergence on the banks of the Desna River. Over this period the 2nd Tank Army advanced 30 kilometers with heavy fighting, liberated 19 populated places, and broke through the enemy's tactical belt of defenses, but being bled white by the fighting, it was unable to develop the success.

In the assessment of the commander of the 2nd Tank Army General Bogdanov, the moment when he timely allowed the 7th Guards Mechanized Corps to assume a defensive posture, considering the situation that had developed, was characteristic and worthy of attention and study. This decision allowed the defenders to inflict heavy damage to the counterattacking enemy, which had an advantage in tank numbers, and to even out the contending forces, before resuming a decisive offensive.

## Commander of the 2nd Tank Army General Bogdanov's conclusions regarding the offensive operation of July-August 1943 (made on 15 October 1943)

1.  The enemy, obviously, plainly assumed that the units of the Central Front might create not only a threat of encirclement, but actual encirclement as well; the Central Front had sufficient strength for this operation. Thus the enemy on the northern sector of the Central Front, at first against the 13th Army, and then against the 65th and 70th Armies, created a large grouping of mobile artillery, Pz. IV and Pz. VI tanks, and Ferdinand tank destroyers.

2.  The constant activity of the enemy air force. The enemy air force operated in the following fashion: until 14.00 or 15.00, groups of 10-15 Messerschmitts were working over our formations, which in individual pairs would strike tanks, vehicles and artillery. After 14.00-15.00, dive bombers would appear above the battlefield. At 19.00 to 20.00, bombers would show up and would bomb from an altitude of 4 to 5 kilometers. Taken together with the frequent counterattacks, out units were slowed down and attrited.

3.  The 2nd Tank Army and 3rd Guards Tank Army didn't break through into an operational depth due to the following reasons: a) we were late in understanding that the enemy on that axis, where the armies were operating, had created 3-4 lines of artillery-mortar barriers with a depth of 10-15 kilometers. The artillery laid down indirect and direct fire with the support of massed air strikes; b) the intelligence of all types didn't yield necessary information on the enemy, which led to the encounter with various surprises in the course of the fighting, in the form of fire and tank ambushes and undetected minefields and other obstacles, which affected the course of battle; c) there were no feints or the necessary masking of the attack. Everyone was in a hurry, fearing the enemy would escape; d) there was no depth to the attack of the tank armies, and as a consequence of this the battle wasn't organized in full teamwork; e) not a single time did the infantry of the 13th, 70th and 65th Armies breach the enemy's defenses. As a consequence of this, the tanks suffered needless losses. The tank corps were not conserved for their main task – to break through into an operational depth; f) strong reconnaissance – we have no experience with a reconnaissance-in-force with the forces of a reinforced brigade or rifle division. The motorcycle battalions in these conditions can do nothing.

4.  The marches were conducted only at night, since the enemy air force was always present in the air.

5.  As the offensive unfolded, the infantry units lagged behind the tanks, which gave the enemy the opportunity to concentrate all his firepower on the army's tanks. Such a situation is a consequence of the incomplete joint teamwork.

6.  The officer staff of the 2nd Tank Army is now (15.10.1943) working on all these matters, with the aim of preventing those mistakes, which took place in the 2nd Tank Army, from re-occurring in forthcoming battles.

7.  The concept that the Tank Army is a means of exploiting a success still hasn't been instilled in the all-arms commanders, nor do they grasp that with its proper use, it is able to launch a decisive blow against the enemy with the development of it into the operational depth.

Once again, the premature introduction of the 2nd Tank Army into battle, when the infantry had not yet breached the enemy's defenses, led to the fact that the 2nd Tank Army was unable to break through into an operational depth, but was compelled together with the infantry to create a breach, as a result of which the tanks, suffering losses, failed to carry out their primary task – the exploitation of a success. While grinding through the enemy's defenses, as a result of the unfolding situation, the 2nd Tank Army was compelled temporarily to assume a defensive posture in order to liquidate the enemy's temporary superiority in tanks, and then resume the offensive once again.

By the end of the operation (1 September 1943), the 2nd Tank Army had a total of 82 operational tanks (46 T-34 and 36 T-70). The tank losses over the period of combat between 26 August and 2 September 1943 amounted to 153 T-34 and 42 T-70. Of these, 80 were totally destroyed. The 2nd Tank Army also lost 57 cannons and mortars of various calibers. At the beginning of September 1943, the 2nd Tank Army was withdrawn to the L'gov area, where it underwent rest and replenishment and engaged in combat training from September to December 1943.

The July-August battles of 1943 demonstrated that the 2nd Tank Army had further hardened and had become a menacing and powerful force, capable of inflicting serious blows against the enemy. In the Sevsk Operation, the troops of the 2nd Tank Army gained great experience in conducting an offensive battle that combines attack with defense.

### From the technical report on the staging and conducting of the 2nd Tank Army's combat operations from 16 August to 1 September 1943

...

As a result of the 2nd Tank Army's operations conducted in the course of July-August 1943, the fitting of the army with combat equipment was weakened to a significant degree, and as of 15 August 1943, the amount and condition of its tanks were as follows:

**Table 4.9 The quantity and status of tanks in the 2nd Tank Army as of 15 August 1943**

| Formation | | Type | Including tanks and self-propelled guns | | | |
|---|---|---|---|---|---|---|
| | | | Serviceable | Minor repairs | Light overhaul | Major overhaul |
| 3rd Tank Corps | 50th Tank Brigade | T-34 | 27 | 1 | 1 | 11 |
| | | T-70 | 10 | – | 1 | 9 |
| | 103rd Tank Brigade | T-34 | 32 | – | 10 | 24 |
| | | T-70 | 12 | – | – | 7 |
| Total for the corps | | T-34 | 59 | 1 | 11 | 35 |
| 9th Separate Signals Battalion | | T-34 | 5 | – | – | – |
| Total for the 2nd Tank Army | | T-34 | 64 | 1 | 11 | 35 |
| | | T-70 | 22 | – | 1 | 15 |

Note: This was "Table 3" in the report.

Note: The 16th Tank Corps and 11th Guards Tank Brigade, which had been withdrawn into the reserve, had turned over their tanks to the 3rd Tank Corps. At this time the 7th Guards Mechanized Corps arrived in the 2nd Tank Army with the following combat materiél:

**Table 4.10: The quantity and status of tanks in the 7th Guards Mechanized Corps when joining the 2nd Tank Army**

| Formation | | Type | Including tanks and self-propelled guns | | | |
|---|---|---|---|---|---|---|
| | | | Serviceable | Minor repairs | Light overhaul | Major overhaul |
| 7th Guards Mechanized Corps | 33rd Tank Brigade | T-34 | 29 | 4 | – | – |
| | | T-70 | 19 | – | 2 | – |
| | 18th Mech. Brigade | T-34 | 23 | 3 | 2 | – |
| | | T-70 | 5 | 2 | – | – |
| | 34th Mech. Brigade | T-34 | 24 | 5 | 1 | – |
| | | T-70 | 8 | – | – | – |
| | 43rd Mech. Brigade | T-34 | 25 | – | – | – |
| | | T-70 | 6 | – | – | – |
| | 772nd Signals Battalion | T-34 | 3 | – | – | – |
| | 33rd Coastal Artillery Battalion | T-70 | 6 | – | – | – |
| Total for the corps: | | T-34 | 104 | 12 | 3 | – |
| | | T-70 | 44 | 2 | 2 | – |
| | Total tanks: | | 148 | 14 | 5 | |

Note, this was Table 4 in the report.

**Table 4.11 The condition of the 2nd Tank Army on 17 August 1943**

| Formation | | Type | Including tanks and self-propelled guns | | | |
|---|---|---|---|---|---|---|
| | | | Serviceable | Minor repairs | Light overhaul | Major overhaul |
| 7th Guards Mechanized Corps | 33rd Tank Brigade | T-34 | 29 | 4 | – | – |
| | | T-70 | 19 | – | 2 | – |
| | 18th Mech. Brigade | T-34 | 23 | 3 | 2 | – |
| | | T-70 | 5 | 2 | – | – |
| | 34th Mech. Brigade | T-34 | 24 | 5 | 1 | – |
| | | T-70 | 8 | – | – | – |
| | 43rd Mech. Brigade | T-34 | 25 | – | – | – |
| | | T-70 | 6 | – | – | – |
| | 772nd Signals Battalion | T-34 | 3 | – | – | – |
| | 33rd Coastal Artillery Battalion | T-70 | 6 | – | – | – |
| Total for the corps | | T-34 | 104 | 12 | 3 | – |
| | | T-70 | 44 | 2 | 2 | – |
| | Total: | | 148 | 14 | 5 | – |
| 3rd Tank Corps | 50th Tank Brigade | T-34 | 27 | 1 | 1 | 11 |
| | | T-70 | 10 | – | 1 | 9 |
| | 103rd Tank Brigade | T-34 | 32 | – | 10 | 24 |
| | | T-70 | 12 | – | – | 7 |
| Total for the corps | | T-34 | 59 | 1 | 11 | 35 |
| | | T-70 | 22 | – | 1 | 16 |
| 9th Separate Signals Battalion | | T-34 | 5 | | | |
| Total for the 2nd Army | | T-34 | 168 | 13 | 14 | 35 |
| | | T-70 | 66 | 2 | 3 | 16 |
| | Total number of tanks: | | 234 | 15 | 17 | 51 |

Note: This was Table 5 in the report.

This total number of tanks had an average remaining running time before overhaul of 51 hours on the engines of the T-34 tanks and 45 hours on the T-70 engines. As is apparent from the figures in Tables 3 [Table 4.9] and 4 [Table 4.10] above, 32 tanks required maintenance or light overhauls, including 27 T-34 and 5 T-70. When the 7th Guards Mechanized Corps was conducting its march to the assembly area, as a result of the driver-mechanics' lack of practical experience with handling a tank and the lack of necessary disciplinary control by the officers' staff, 32 tanks had dropped out of the column due to mechanical breakdowns, including 27 T-34 and 5 T-70. But altogether 64 tanks required repair through the efforts and means of the army's mechanics and technicians, including 54 T-34 and 10 T-70. Moreover, in the schedule of preparations for forthcoming combat operations, the entire available materiél was subjected to close mechanical inspection. In the process, another 68 tanks were found to be in need of repair. This entire pool of tanks in need of repair work, consisting of 132 tanks (106 T-34 and 26 T-70), was fully processed through the efforts of the army's mechanics and technicians by 25 August 1943, i.e., by the moment of the 2nd Tank Army's departure to the area of its jumping-off positions. The search for components and parts, including their scrounging from tanks that had been written-off, their timely delivery to the repair teams, and the proper allocation of the repair teams and resources to a significant degree contributed to the most rapid completion of the large amount of repair work.

As a result of these measures, the number of combat-ready machines by the start of combat operations amounted to 266 tanks. The systematic training of the personnel of the 3rd Tank Corps on the equipment had a totally beneficial effect on keeping the tanks in good working order. Over the entire period of combat operations, the 3rd Tank Corps had just 8 cases of tanks disabled by mechanical problems, while over this same period the 7th Guards Mechanized Corps, which hadn't undergone such training, had 48 cases. The most commonly encountered reasons for mechanical breakdowns were: burned-out master clutches; inoperable starters; malfunctioning pressure and temperature gauges; damage to the rolling wheels and the ball bearings of the idler wheels; worn or broken teeth in the gearshift mechanism; breakage of the steering clutch linkage; and pinching of the line to the water pump.

In the period of combat operations from 27.8 to 1.9.1943, the 2nd Tank Army had the following number of combat-ready tanks across the given days:

Table 4.12: The quantity of serviceable tanks of the 2nd Tank Army across the given dates between 27 August and 1 September 1943 inclusively

|  |  | 27.08 | 28.08 | 29.08 | 30.08 | 31.08 | 1.09 |
|---|---|---|---|---|---|---|---|
| 3rd Tank Corps |  |  |  |  |  |  |  |
| 50th Tank Brigade | T-34 | 21 | 21 | 13 | 8 | 8 | 8 |
|  | T-70 | 8 | 9 | 7 | 7 | 7 | 7 |
| 103rd Tank Brigade | T-34 | 19 | 8 | 4 | 8 | 8 | 8 |
|  | T-70 | 8 | 7 | 5 | 5 | 5 | 5 |
| Total: | T-34 | 40 | 29 | 17 | 16 | 16 | 16 |
|  | T-70 | 16 | 16 | 12 | 12 | 12 | 12 |
| **7th Guards Mechanized Corps** |  |  |  |  |  |  |  |
| 33rd Tank Brigade | T-34 | 34 | 11 | 8 | 6 | 6 | 7 |
|  | T-70 | 24 | 22 | 8 | 6 | 6 | 6 |
| 18th Mechanized Brigade | T-34 | 27 | 12 | 9 | 6 | 7 | 8 |
|  | T-70 | 7 | 7 | 7 | 6 | 6 | 6 |
| 34th Mechanized Brigade | T-34 | 29 | 9 | 10 | 6 | 7 | 8 |
|  | T-70 | 7 | 7 | 8 | 5 | 5 | 5 |
| 43rd Mechanized Brigade | T-34 | 25 | 15 | 12 | 6 | 7 | 8 |
|  | T-70 | 7 | 6 | 5 | 4 | 6 | 7 |
| 772nd Signals Battalion | T-34 | 2 | 2 | 2 | 2 | 2 | 2 |
| 33rd Coastal Artillery Battalion | T-70 | 6 | 6 | 4 | 4 | 4 | 4 |
| Total: | T-34 | 117 | 49 | 41 | 26 | 29 | 33 |
|  | T-70 | 51 | 48 | 32 | 25 | 27 | 28 |
| 9th Signals Regiment | T-34 | 5 | 5 | 5 | 5 | 5 | 5 |
| Total for the army: | T-34 | 162 | 83 | 63 | 47 | 50 | 54 |
|  | T-70 | 67 | 64 | 44 | 37 | 39 | 40 |
| Total: |  | 229 | 147 | 107 | 84 | 89 | 94 |

As a result of the combat operations over the period from 27 August to 1 September 1943, the 2nd Tank Army had the following combat losses in tanks: 200 T-34 and 47 T-70, for a total of 247 tanks. These losses were distributed across the following causes: From artillery, anti-tank and tank fire: 113 T-34 and 25 T-70, for a total of 138. A total of 84 tanks were burned-out, including 68 T-34 and 16 T-70. From air strikes: 1 T-70. Due to mechanical breakdowns: 19 T-34 and 5 T-70, for a total of 24 cases. Of the total number of combat losses in tanks, the table below shows the number that had to be written-off as irrecoverable, distributed by type, cause and unit.

**Table 4.13: Irrecoverable tank losses of the 2nd Tank Army**

| Formation | | Type | Irrecoverable tank losses of the 2nd Tank Army | | | |
|---|---|---|---|---|---|---|
| | | | Burned out | Destroyed by artillery fire | Destroyed by aviation | Total losses |
| 3rd Tank Corps | 50th Tank Brigade | T-34 | 10 | 1 | – | 11 |
| | | T-70 | – | – | – | – |
| | 103rd Tank Brigade | T-34 | 12 | 1 | – | 13 |
| | | T-70 | 4 | 1 | – | 5 |
| | Total for the corps | T-34 | 22 | 2 | – | 24 |
| | | T-70 | 4 | 1 | – | 5 |
| 7th Guards Mechanized Corps | 33rd Tank Brigade | T-34 | 9 | – | – | 9 |
| | | T-70 | 10 | 2 | – | 12 |
| | 18th Mech. Brigade | T-34 | 10 | – | – | 10 |
| | | T-70 | – | – | – | – |
| | 34th Mech. Brigade | T-34 | 8 | – | – | 8 |
| | | T-70 | – | – | – | – |
| | 43rd Mech. Brigade | T-34 | 4 | – | – | 4 |
| | | T-70 | 1 | – | – | 1 |
| | 772nd Signals Battalion | T-34 | – | – | – | – |
| | 33rd Coastal Artillery Battery | T-70 | – | 1 | 1 | 2 |
| | Total for the corps | T-34 | 31 | – | – | 31 |
| | | T-70 | 11 | 3 | 1 | 15 |
| 9th Separate Signals Regiment | | T-34 | – | – | – | – |
| Total for the 2nd Tank Army | | T-34 | 53 | 2 | – | 55 |
| | | T-70 | 15 | 4 | 1 | 20 |
| | Altogether: | | 68 | 6 | 1 | 75 |

The army's tank evacuation service worked smoothly and promptly, as the recovery vehicles were located directly among the combat units. Over the period between 27.8 and 1.9.43, 34 T-34 tanks were evacuated to brigade and corps collection stations for disabled vehicles. In addition, over the indicated period, 55 T-34 and 23 T-70, as well as 12 SU-122 (for a total of 90 machines) were recovered and delivered to Collection Station for Disabled Vehicles No.80, before being sent on for major overhauls in industrial factories or to the People's Commissariat of Defense's repair base. Over the period of combat operations between 27.8 and 1.9.1943, 66 tanks (52 T-34 and 14 T-70) were repaired and restored to service. At the moment of departing for refitting, that is, on 2.9.1943, the 2nd Tank Army had 206 tanks. Of them, a total of 82 tanks (46 T-34 and 36 T-70) were operational; 8 tanks (7 T-34 and 1 T-70) were undergoing minor repairs; 58 tanks (49 T-34 and 9 T-70) were undergoing light overhaul; and 58 tanks (49 T-34 and 9 T-70) were undergoing major overhaul.

In comparison with the Orel-Kursk operation, the effectiveness of the German anti-tank artillery fire grew. For example, 72 percent of the tanks that received penetrating hits were left burned out. In the 1943 Sevsk operation, the enemy made almost no use of anti-tank artillery with calibers between 37mm and 50mm; 74 percent of the penetrating hits came from 75mm anti-tank guns, and 26 percent were caused by high explosive anti-tank shells or armor-piercing discarding sabot shells. The number of blown-up tanks now comprises 26 percent of the amount of irrecoverable tank losses.

[Signed] Engineer-Lieutenant Colonel Tanenbaum, Deputy Commander for Combat Vehicles Maintenance and Technical Support, and Major Zemlianukhin, Section Head for Tank Maintenance

On 25 September 1943, Lieutenant General of Tank Forces Bogdanov reported to the Red Army's Main Command of Armored and Tank Forces and gave his opinion regarding the T-70 tank and its suitability in combat:

> The T-70 tank in view of its high mobility best corresponds to the task of pursuing a retreating enemy. In distinction from the T-34 and KV, the tank of the indicated type possesses a relatively quiet engine (the sound of the tank is no greater than that of a car), even when moving at high RPMs, which together with the small dimensions of the tank itself allows the T-70 platoons to approach practically right up to the enemy, without provoking his alarm too soon. If the German artillery gunners can fire at a T-34 tank from a range of 800-1,200 meters, then the small dimensions of the T-70 in the field reduces this range to 500-600 meters. The light weight of the tank facilitates its transportation, both to the front and during the evacuation of knocked-out tanks to the rear. The T-70 tank is simpler to master and handle by poorly-trained drivers, and is amenable to repair in field conditions. All of the available cases of large losses in the T-70 platoons are explained more by the unwise use of them, and not by design flaws in the tank itself. I consider the decision to stop producing the T-70 tank premature. Production of the tank should be maintained, having increased its firepower by switching its main armament to the 45mm Model 1942 gun or the [76mm] Model 1943 Regimental Gun.

### Soldiers of the 2nd Tank Army who distinguished themselves in the 1943 Sevsk operation

Lieutenant Vasilii **Konin**, a T-34 tank company commander with the 103rd Tank Brigade's 420th Tank Battalion. In combat on 27.08.1943 in the vicinity of Moritskii, he personally destroyed 2 anti-tank guns and 2 mortars together with their crews. When the battalion commander was killed, he assumed command of the battalion and continued to carry out the combat mission. In combat he demonstrated skill, courage and resolve. Awarded Order of the Patriotic War 1st Degree.

Guards Senior Lieutenant Petr **Morozov**, commander of a T-34 tank platoon of the 103rd Tank Brigade's 119th Tank Battalion. He displayed courage and daring and was the first to break into the populated settlements of Moritskii and Bukovina. In combat on 27.08.1943, with fire from his gun and machine guns, he destroyed 3 guns, 4 machine guns, 1 self-propelled gun and up to 20 enemy soldiers and officers. Awarded the Order of the Patriotic War 1st Category.

Junior Lieutenant Mikhail **Oleinik**, commander of a T-34 tank platoon of the 103rd Tank Brigade's 119th Tank Battalion. In the battles in the area west of Sevsk, he demonstrated courage and pluck. In combat on 27.08.1943 he destroyed 3 anti-tank guns, 6 machine guns, 1 mortar and up to 30 enemy soldiers and officers. Awarded the Order of the Patriotic War 1st Category.

Senior Sergeant Ivan **Poleshchuk**, commander of a T-34 tank in the 103rd Tank Brigade's 119th Tank Battalion. In the fighting between 27.08 and 29.09.1943, he showed himself to be a courageous and decisive tanker. He personally destroyed 4 anti-tank guns, 3 machine-gun nests, 1 vehicle with its load, and more than 50 enemy soldiers and officers. On 29 August 1943, he fell bravely in battle. Posthumously awarded the Order of the Patriotic War 1st Category.

Guards Lieutenant Colonel Fedor **Artamonov**, commander of the 7th Guards Mechanized Corps' 25th Guards Mechanized Brigade. In the Sevsk operation, the brigade demonstrated model examples of carrying out combat orders. Despite strong resistance, the brigade advanced, liberating populated places and inflicting damage to the enemy: 12 tanks, 21 guns, 7 mortars and up to 3,000 enemy soldiers and officers were destroyed. Fourteen prisoners, 3 vehicles, ammunition dumps and 2 fuel dumps were captured. With its bold actions, the brigade gave great help to the units in seizing the city of Sevsk. Recommended for the Order of the Red Banner.

Lieutenant O. **Tsukanov**, a tank platoon commander with the 50th Tank Brigade. His tank platoon was among the first to burst into Sevsk and destroyed several anti-tank guns and an assault gun.

Captain **Sviatodukh**, commander of a sapper platoon in the 50th Tank Brigade. During the liberation of Sevsk, the soldiers of his platoon laid down an assault bridge across the Sev River, which had a width of more than 12 meters, and secured a crossing of the brigade's motorized rifle-machine gun battalion.

**In the Sevsk operation, the following troops of the 7th Guards Mechanized Corps also showed well:** Guards Junior Sergeant Shul'ba, tank commander Junior Lieutenant P. Opanasenko, artillery battalion commander Captain A. Gudkov, tank battalion commander Captain P. Karpov, mortar battalion commander Captain Riazantsev, chief of staff of a mortar battalion Senior Lieutenant T. Larikov, tank battalion commander Rudnik, scout Sergeant Ovchinnikov, tank company commander Lieutenant Riabtsev, and Junior Sergeant Gribanov.

# 5

# Vinnitsa and Korsun'-Shevchenkovskii, 1944

**The Command Staff of the 2nd Tank Army**
Commander – Lieutenant General Semen Bogdanov
Chief of Staff – Guards Major General Andrei Pavlov
Military Council Member – Major General Petr Latyshev
Deputy Commander for Vehicle Maintenance and Technical Support – Colonel Samuil Krupenin
Deputy Commander for Rear Services – Colonel Petr Antonov
Commander of Artillery – Colonel Grigorii Plaskov
Chief of Operations Department – Colonel Vladimir Chizh
Chief of Intelligence Department – Colonel Ashraf Galimov

**3rd Tank Corps** – Major General Aleksandr Shashin
50th Tank Brigade – Colonel Roman Liberman
51st Tank Brigade – Colonel Semen Mirvoda
103rd Tank Brigade – Lieutenant Colonel Aleksandr Khalaev
57th Motorized Rifle Brigade – Colonel Pavel Shamardin
1540th Heavy Self-Propelled Artillery Regiment (SU-152) – Major N. Shishov; 121st Anti-aircraft Artillery Regiment – Lieutenant Colonel Aleksandr Peshakov; 234th Mortar Regiment – Lieutenant Colonel K. Kovalev; 126th Guards Mortar Battalion (M-13 rocket launchers); 728th Separate Destroyer Anti-tank Artillery Battalion; 74th Motorcycle Battalion; 1818th Self-propelled Artillery Regiment (SU-85); 411th Separate Signals Battalion

**16th Tank Corps** – Major General Ivan Dubovoi
107th Tank Brigade – Colonel Tikhon Abramov
109th Tank Brigade – Colonel Petr Babkovsky
164th Tank Brigade – Colonel Nikolai Kopylov
15th Motorized Rifle Brigade – Colonel Petr Akimochkin
1542nd Heavy Self-Propelled Artillery Regiment (SU-152) – Lieutenant Colonel Dmitrii Gurenko; 1441st Self-propelled Artillery Regiment (SU-85); 51st Motorcycle Battalion; 298th Guards Destroyer Anti-tank Artillery Regiment; 729th Separate Destroyer Anti-tank Artillery Battalion; 1721st Anti-aircraft Artillery Regiment; 89th Guards Mortar Battalion (M-13 rocket launchers), 689th Separate Signals Battalion; 226th Army Mortar Regiment
Units Directly Subordinate to Army Headquarters
11th Guards Tank Brigade – Guards Colonel Nikolai Koshaev
9th Separate Signals Regiment – Lieutenant Colonel Ivan Belenko
87th Motorcycle Battalion; 86th Guards Mortar Regiment (M-13 rocket launchers), 357th Separate Engineer Brigade; 298th Self-propelled Artillery Regiment (SU-76), 1548th Self-propelled

Artillery Regiment (SU-76), 999th Self-propelled Artillery Regiment (SU-76), 754th Self-propelled Artillery Regiment (SU-85), 1219th Self-propelled Artillery Regiment (SU-85)

## Command Staff of the 2nd Tank Army

Semen Bogdanov.

Petr Latyshev.

Aleksandr Shamshin.

Ivan Dubovoi.

Nikolai Koshaev.

Semen Mirvoda.

Petr Akimochkin.

Nikolai Kopylov.

Tikhon Abramov.

Commander of the 50th Tank Brigade R.A. Liberman (left) and the brigade's chief of staff A.M. Kovalevsky. A 1944 photo.

The commander of the 2nd Tank Army S. Bogdanov (right) with the commander of the 11th Guards Tank Brigade Hero of the Soviet Union N. Koshaev.

## In the *Stavka* Reserve

At the beginning of September 1943, the 2nd Tank Army was in the *Stavka* Reserve. Guards Major General Anatolii Shvebig recalls:

> Our 16th Tank Corps was encamped around Makarovka, about 50 kilometers west of Kursk. For the first time, after many days of peregrination among frontline dugouts, the Headquarters and the corps' Department of Technical Support were located in village huts. None of us was counting on a long break, but it was pleasant all the same to have the opportunity to rest and feel like a human' again after the hard combats. The men were undergoing training in this area, while the equipment and repair and recovery means were being prepared. Main attention was focused upon the personnel's training with the equipment, while the command and technical support staff prepared to receive new tanks and worked to process the large number of vehicles in the repair pool. For this purpose, all the repairmen, all the drivers of the wheeled vehicles, and some of the driver-mechanics of the combat vehicles were used.
>
> In October 1943, the corps commander and I were summoned to a meeting of the 2nd Tank Army's Military Council. The new commander, Lieutenant General Semen Il'ich Bogdanov attentively listened to our reports on the condition of the corps' combat equipment without interrupting us, occasionally jotting down notes on the notepad in front of him. From his entire conduct, it was perceptible that he was absorbing every word of our reports. It must be said that tankers loved Bogdanov for his personal bravery, fatherly treatment of his subordinates, rightful exactingness and outstanding organizational skills. Member of the Military Council Petr Latyshev also enjoyed the high respect of the commanders and Red Army men. He remained in this post from the very beginning of the army's formation to the final battles in Berlin.
>
> The tasks given by the Military Council to the 16th Tank Corps were not easy. Approximately 700 of the vehicles that we had in our possession had exceeded their scheduled time for repairs, while the need for more spare parts was obvious. We were receiving them from the army's depots in small quantities. Such a situation was very troubling to the corps commander. At his order, I urgently sent several trucks to Moscow, where we were hoping to acquire very hard to find parts for repairing the vehicles. But our main hope rested upon our repairmen. More than once they had managed to find a way out of similar situations. For example, a team of repairmen under the command of Sergeant G. Masharin of the 145th Mobile Repair Base began to craft individual spare parts through their own efforts. They were restoring gears and created devices for casting and boring connecting rod bearings. Masharin's men over a short period of time repaired 80 batteries and 20 central drive shafts, made repairs to 200 vehicles, and put 35 disabled vehicles back into operation. Other repairmen of Sergeant Volkov's and Sergeant Belotserkovsky's teams matched Masharin. Disregarding time and difficulties, they repaired not only domestically-produced machines, but also machines of foreign brands.
>
> In the middle of November 1943, having secured the support of the new corps commander Major General K. Skorniakov, we held a conference with the corps' engineer and technical staff, during which I summed up the results of the technical support for the units during the Kursk battle. We discussed questions of preparing equipment for use in winter conditions. In the presentations of the deputy commanders of the tank brigades for vehicle maintenance and technical support Karakozov, Maksimov and Iumatov, as well as those of other engineers and technicians, many innovations, which needed to be passed down to all the corps' units, were discussed. The conference held with the engineer and technical staff proved to be very timely. Soon, hard freezes occurred, and at the end of December 1943, the corps as part of the 2nd Tank Army was assembled on the left [eastern] bank of the Dnepr River in the area of

Darnitsy, in a small village that had been destroyed by countless bombing attacks. Then the units of the 16th Tank Corps crossed the Dnepr River over a shaky pontoon bridge, and took up positions west of Kiev at Sviatoshino-Boiarka Station.

From 5 September 1943 the 2nd Tank Army was in the *Stavka* Reserve and was positioned in the L'gov area. At a directive from the *Stavka,* by 5 January 1944 the 2nd Tank Army had reassembled with its main forces in the Sviatoshino (Kiev) area. The army's rear and reserve units were still en route to the new assembly area.

Over this period, the forces of the 1st Ukrainian Front, with successful offensive operations, had seized Zhitomir and Berdichev, and were fighting stubbornly for Vinnitsa. With the aim of exploiting the success on the Vinnitsa axis, by an order from the *Stavka*, the 2nd Tank Army was moved to the Zhitomir area, where it had assembled by the end of 11 January 1944. By this time, the enemy had concentrated major forces in front of the 1st Ukrainian Front, and throughout the second half of January, the Germans were attacking in the general direction of Belaia Tserkov' [Bila Tserkva]. By the end of 26 January, the German main forces had reached the line Rososhna – Iablonovka – Frankovka, and separate panzer groups were continuing to push to the east and north. Back on 16 January 1944, the *Stavka* had directed the 2nd Tank Army to move to the Belaia Tserkov' area, where it was given the task, in case of an enemy breakthrough on the Belaia Tserkov' axis, to prevent a German advance to the north and northeast. As it was preparing a defensive line southwest, south and southeast of Belaia Tserkov', the 2nd Tank Army was simultaneously replenished with materiél (with tanks and self-propelled guns) and received combat supplies. On 20 January 1944, the 2nd Tank Army became part of the 1st Ukrainian Front.

The day before, on 19 January, the commander of the 2nd Tank Army Lieutenant General Bogdanov and Military Council member Major General Latyshev laid out the current situation and upcoming tasks of the army at a conference with the corps commanders, brigade commanders, and chiefs of the army's departments:

> **Bogdanov:** The situation on the front (1st Ukrainian Front) is significantly better than it was three days ago. Today the 40th Army went on the offensive and is having significant success.
>
> 1)  Regarding the <u>organization of the march:</u> Our infantrymen are good; the men are willing, but the march went badly. The 3rd Tank Corps stands out favorably. There is a large percentage of foot sores, especially in the 16th Tank Corps. In the 16th Tank Corps, there is an irritating tardiness in work. The headquarters of the 16th Tank Corps had no plan for the march, as a consequence of which, the corps didn't know where any units were moving. The cause of the poor work is the fact that we are still not in any way switching to a combat footing. There is poor discipline and organization in the units. The commanders of the corps and brigades, and the chiefs of the army's departments, are to pay serious attention to liquidating these shortcomings. Combat morale and discipline must be raised. In places of our disposition, there is no order. The machines are parked with little or no camouflage. In the course of the day tomorrow (20.1.1944), fundamentally switch everything to a new footing, and raise discipline to that level that it was back in L'gov.
>
> This time the 3rd Tank Corps conducted the march four times better than its initial march. The 16th Tank Corps conducted the march significantly better than the first one, but still quite poorly. Immediately rehabilitate the men. For this purpose, the sanitary units must expend every effort. In the shortest possible time, allow all the personnel to bathe. The deputy commanders of the corps and brigades are to be personally engaged with the question of rebuilding the men's health. Elevate the vigor of the officers and

the discipline of all the men. Conduct troop inspections. I am mandating a signal for an alarm drill. The drill will begin at 1.40. Scouts must turn out within 30 minutes. Security must turn out within 30 minutes.

The situation stands badly in the headquarters regarding the processing of documents and the organization of work. Pay serious attention to the conducting and discipline of the march. Throughout the sectors, post trained traffic officers and responsible commanders in a timely manner. Load all the machines with infantry. Seat the infantry in vehicles and on the towed items. The commanders of the corps and the brigades are to have a reserve of fuel and spare vehicles. The accommodation of the headquarters' staffs on the march is poor, a "gypsy caravan". Security is poor. The 16th Tank Corps didn't arrange security for the corps headquarters. The headquarters of the brigades and corps have no rights to lodging or to quarter their subordinates among the local population. From 20 January 1944 we will pass to the control of the 1st Ukrainian Front.

2) Organization of the defense: The 3rd Tank Corps timely organized the local population and properly allocated the forces. The 16th Tank Corps poorly organized the work of the local population. AS QUICKLY AS POSSIBLE ORGANIZE A STIFF DEFENSE. Timetable of work: Complete the primary work today (19.1.1944) by 24.00. Tomorrow (20.1.1944) – complete the secondary work by 24.00. THE MILITARY COUNCIL BELIEVES that work on the defenses is going slowly and that the commanders of the corps and brigades are not overseeing it. The headquarters of the corps and brigades are handling tasks badly. It is necessary to be more engaged with operational-tactical exercises on the implementation of a defense (give thought to firepower, the directions of counterattacks, etc.). The corps and brigade headquarters are to complete the working up of documents regarding the defense by 18.00 on 20.1.1944.

3) ON CONSERVING FUEL: Organize so as to reduce the excess expenditure of fuel. Keep reliable track of fuel, its delivery and receipt. Fix yourselves up with containers. Fabricate oak sleighs that can be hitched to tanks for transporting loads and infantry. We will receive all of our matériel by 25.1.44. Eliminate any and all cases of accidents. Correctly distribute personnel among the units and elements when issuing the equipment.

**Latyshev**: Support for the march was poorly organized. The rendezvousing with the trains was poorly organized. Representatives of the units were not sent forward in order to meet the trains. To this point, there is no practice of towing during movement without loads. The camouflaging of the defensive works, especially in the 103rd "Sevsk" Tank Brigade, is poor. In the same brigade, meals for the men are poorly organized: On 18.1.44, the soldiers each received 400 grams of bread. On 19.1.44 – they received bread only at 18.00. Sanitary conditions are bad. Up to 20 to 30 percent of the men are infested with lice. In the course of the next two to three days, give all the men a thorough scrubbing, replace the underclothing, and conduct a sanitary inspection. Military secrecy is poorly kept. There is a lot of loose talk about the identification of their formations. The local population knows where the 103rd Tank Brigade is located and what it is doing.

Have 2 combat loads of ammunition for weapons of all types. Have 5 refills of fuel for the tanks; 3 refills of fuel for trucks and cars. Throughout the 2nd Tank Army there have been 20 vehicular crashes and more than 25 vehicle breakdowns. Set all the repairmen to work on the vehicles and repair them all within the next three days. Fix all the footgear and uniforms. The main task is to receive the tanks and assemble the crews. Check everywhere whether or not technical commissions exist. Conduct explanatory work among the personnel to reduce accidents, breakdowns and leaks of military secrets. Sum up the results of the march and work on defenses, and eliminate all shortcomings.

On the morning of 24 January 1944, after a powerful artillery preparation and airstrikes, an enemy grouping went on the attack east of Vinnitsa. The 38th Army and the 1st Guards Tank Army with the attached 31st Tank Corps received the enemy attack. Having met the stubborn resistance of the 31st Tank Corps, the Nazi main grouping consisting of the SS Panzer Division *Leibstandarte Adolf Hitler* on 27 January launched an attack to the south, seized Rososha, and began to emerge in the rear of the 8th Guards Mechanized Corps and the rifle divisions of the 38th Army, which were defending on the line Zozov [Zoziv] – Lipovets [Lypovets']. Simultaneously, the 25th Panzer Division and two infantry divisions went on the attack from the front. A unsatisfactory situation developed as well in the Monastyrishche area, where German troops launched an attack to the west, broke through the defenses of the rifle divisions of the 40th Army, and began to develop the offensive toward a link-up with the German grouping that was attacking out of the Vinnitsa area. In order to destroy the penetrating enemy forces, the commander of the 1st Ukrainian Front committed General Bogdanov's 2nd Tank Army, which had arrived out of the *Stavka* Reserve and was located in the Belaia Tserkov' area.

From the combat journal of the 3rd Tank Corps:

> On 11 January 1944, the 3rd Tank Corps was shifted to the Zhitomir area, brought up to table strength in personnel, combat equipment and weapons, and together with other formations of the 2nd Tank Army, it became part of the 1st Ukrainian Front for exploiting an offensive on the Vinnitsa axis. However, before attacking, it had to repel the attacks of major enemy forces. The Hitlerite command had decided at whatever the cost to liquidate the bridgehead in the Kiev area, to retake the capital of the Ukraine, to re-establish a defense along the Dnepr River, and to eliminate the threat to the southern wing of Army Group South. Having assembled significant forces, including up to 500 tanks, the enemy launched a counteroffensive out of the areas of Vinnitsa and Uman', and on 26 January reached the area northeast of Vinnitsa with the forces of two panzer and five infantry divisions, thereby creating a threat of encirclement of our forces. The 3rd Tank Corps, having been replenished with men, combat equipment and weapons by this time, was raised in response to an alarm, and received the task in cooperation with units of the 38th Army (to which the tank corps had been temporarily subordinated) and the 11th Guards Tank Brigade, it was to launch an attack in the direction of Napadovka and Zozov on 27 January 1944.

Having completed its march from the Belaia Tserkov' area, the 2nd Tank Army re-assembled in the Pogrebishche – Ocheretnia – Lipovets Station area. The army had the task on the morning of 27 January 1944 to launch an attack in the general direction of Zozov, to cut off the enemy grouping that had broken through, and to secure the withdrawal of units of the 17th Guards Rifle Corps from the forming pocket.

## The Operational-Tactical Situation by the end of 26 January 1944

The forces of the 1st Ukrainian Front had been conducting a successful offensive on the Vinnitsa axis with the aim of taking Vinnitsa and Zhmerinka. The situation emerged where our forces were threatening the railroad communications of the enemy's entire southern group of forces. With the aim of liquidating the growing threat to his southern grouping, the enemy on 16 January 1944 launched a counterattack out of the area east of Vinnitsa in a southerly direction toward Voronovitsa and Nemirov, and halted the further advance of our units toward Zhmerinka. Simultaneous, with active operations, the enemy was eliminating our Uman' salient in the Tsybuliv, Monastyrishche, Man'kovka, Buki area, and having conducted a regrouping, had formed two strong panzer groupings by 24 January 1944. The first, in the Konstantinovka, Vakhnovka area (northeast of Vinnitsa), consisted of the 1st SS Panzer Division *Leibstandarte Adolf Hitler*, the 25th Panzer Division, an unidentified panzer formation (Heavy Panzer Regiment *Bäke*), the 1st and 254th Infantry Divisions, the 4th *Gebirgs* Division, the 101st *Jäger* Division, and the 18th Artillery Division. The second, in the area northwest of Monastyrishche consisted of the 6th, 16th and 17th Panzer Divisions. Their common aim was to continue the offensive with both groupings in the general direction of Oratov, with the task of destroying our units located to the east of Il'intsy and Lipovets. The total number of tanks and self-propelled guns of both panzer groupings amounted to 450-500, a large portion of which were Panthers and Tigers.

On 24 January 1944, the enemy, consisting of the aforementioned first grouping, went on the offensive from the line Konstantinovka, Vakhnovka toward Rotmistrovka, and by the end of 26 January, had reached the line Ksaverovka State Farm – west of Ocheretnia – Napadovka – Rososha – east of Ul'ianovka – Zozovo – Vakhnovka – Iasenki – Shirokaia Ruda.

The grouping of German forces in the Vinnitsa area, which was opposing the forces of the 2nd Tank Army, had on its roster on 26 January 1944 more than 200 tanks and assault guns. The breakdown of the enemy groupings on that date was as follows:

First grouping: 1st SS Panzer Division – 122 tanks (33 Pz IV, 4 Pz III, 36 Pz V, 9 Pz VI, 34 StuG, 6 Marder), of which 83 were serviceable as of 21 January 1944; Heavy Panzer Regiment *Bäke*, consisting of the headquarters of the 6th Panzer Division's 11th Panzer Regiment, a Panther battalion of the 23rd Panzer Division, the 503rd Heavy Panzer Battalion of Tigers, and a battalion of 88mm anti-aircraft guns plus a brigade of heavy Nebelswerfer rocket launchers of the 18th Artillery Division) – 69 Tigers and 72 Panthers (of which 34 Tigers and 44 Panthers were serviceable on 20 January 1944; the 25th Panzer Division; and the attached 506th Heavy Panzer Battalion (10 Tigers, plus 12 Tigers that arrived on 29-30 January 1944).

Second grouping: The 16th Panzer Division – 116 tanks and assault guns (68 Pz IV, 14 Pz III, 34 StuG) [Author's note: Zetterling gives the figure of 136 tanks and assault guns on 23 January 1944]; 6th Panzer Division – 41 tanks (37 Pz IV, 4 Pz III); and the 17th Panzer Division – 47 tanks (35 Pz IV, 5 Pz III, 7 Pz V).

## The terrain, and the presence and condition of roads

The terrain in the area of the 2nd Tank Army's combat operations was a difficult one for tank operations, with a large number of ravines and water courses: the Ross' River with its Protoka, Kamenka, Rostovshchitsa, Skvira, Beriazanka and Orekhovo tributaries. The presence of water obstacles and deep ravines and the absence of paved roads with bridges capable of bearing the weight of tanks created difficult conditions for the maneuvering of tank formations. There was only one road in the sector of the army's movement and in the area of its combat operations, which by the strength of its bridges and the condition of its road surface was sufficient for the movement of tanks: the Belaia Tserkov' – Skvira – Pogrebishche road.

By the start of the army's combat operations, a sudden thaw had arrived, and the roads from the very first day became difficult to traverse because of the resulting mud. The field and village roads were completely impassable for both tanks and trucks, not only because of the seasonal mud, but also because the existing bridges on these roads had insufficient weight-bearing capacity. In order to secure the army's unobstructed advance, traffic support detachments were assigned from each corps' engineer battalion, which scouted the roads ahead and did work to repair and reinforce bridges. Separate companies of the engineer battalions, because of the lack of motorized transport, moved on foot and comprised rear traffic support detachments. The lack of time to prepare for the march prevented the possibility of making parallel routes ready for the army's movement, so the

2nd Tank Army moved along a single road. The roads, ruined by the early thaw, and the accessibility of the jumping-off positions for the tanks placed the main tasks in front of the combat engineer units: putting the roads and bridges into trafficable condition and covering the forward edge with mine fields.

At the start of the operation, the 2nd Tank Army consisted of a total of 357 armored vehicles (288 T-34, 6 Valentine IX tanks, and 31 SU-85, 19 SU-76, and 13 SU-152 self-propelled guns). Major General Shamshin reported to the commander of the 2nd Tank Army that on 25 January 1944, at the moment of completing the approach march, the 3rd Tank Corps had 197 T-34, 10 Valentine IX, 21 SU-76, 17 SU-85 and 13 SU-152, for a total of 285 armored vehicles. By Order No.09/OP from the 2nd Tank Army on 25 January, the corps was ordered to conduct a 105-kilometer march and arrive in the assembly area Pogrebishche – Pavlovka by 8.00 on 26 January. The corps conducted the march in a single column with a strong advance guard. By 12.00 on 26 January, the corps had assembled in Pogrebishche, with individual lagging combat machines still on the way, along with the 57th Motorized Rifle Brigade, which was making the march on foot. At 19.00 on 26 January 1944, the 3rd Tank Corps, with the exception of its lagging combat vehicles, had 181 T-34, 9 Valentine IX, 19 SU-76, 15 SU-85 and 10 SU-152, for a total of 231 armored vehicles. Thus having completed a march of 150 kilometers, the corps' units were ordered to take up a jumping-off position for an offensive in the Bogdanovka, Napadovka, Rososha direction.

Meanwhile, Major General Dubovoi reported to the 2nd Tank Army commander Guards Lieutenant General Bogdanov that the 16th Tank Corps had begun to receive its combat machines from Belaia Tserkov' Station on 24 January, but they were in need of oil and lubricant changes in order to prepare them for combat. The 16th Tank Corps moved to the area of combat operations in piecemeal fashion, as one or another tank brigade was re-equipped, which complicated the organization of maintenance and repair services. The corps began the march on 25 January out of the Belaia Tserkov' area to the area of Lipovets Station, Sinarna State Farm and Oratov Station with 176 T-34, 10 Valentine IX, 10 SU-85, and 10 ISU-152, for a total of 206 armored vehicles. The road conditions were satisfactory. Each tank brigade had its own repair platoon, radio means, battery charger truck and welding equipment to service its vehicles. On the spot road service from a Type-A quick repair truck was organized in each battalion. The 168th Mobile Repair Base set off along the route after the departure of the 164th and 109th Tank Brigades. The 145th Mobile Repair Base ensured the repair of broken down vehicles along the route of the 107th Tank Brigade.

The 164th Tank Brigade arrived in the area of combat operations at 19.00 on 25 January with 54 tanks. Units of the 89th Separate Guards Mortar Battalion, the 1542nd Heavy Self-propelled Regiment, the 15th Motorized Rifle Brigade and the 51st Separate Motorcycle Battalion arrived together with the brigade. The 109th Tank Brigade was in Belaia Tserkov', receiving and inspecting replacement tanks, a process that didn't end until 15.00 on 27 January. However, because of the pressing situation, the decision was made for the 109th Tank Brigade to set off at 14.00, and the remaining tanks would catch up later. By 14.00 on the next day, it had re-assembled in the Staro-Zhivotiv area with 54 tanks, together with its motorized battalion of submachine gunners and its destroyer anti-tank battalion. The 107th Tank Brigade on 31 January was replenished with tanks up to its table strength (65 T-34 tanks), and having received an additional 4 tanks for the 109th and 164th Tank Brigades, it set off for the area of the corps' defensive operations. By 10.00 on 31 January, the brigade was located on the approaches to Chalnovitsy, where it received an order from the commander of the 1st Ukrainian Front regarding its temporary resubordination to the command of the 6th Tank Army, with the task to assemble in Vinograd by 1 February 1944. Over the course of the 16th Tank Corps' approach march, it lost a total of 7 T-34 tanks that broke down along the way, but within three days these tanks were repaired and put back into service.

On 25 January 1944 at 15.00, the 11th Guards Tank Brigade was activated in response to the alarm, and by midnight that night, having conducted a 170-kilometer march, it was assembling in the Pogrebishche area with 63 tanks, where it became operationally subordinate to the 38th Army. By 7.00 on 26 January, it had arrived in the Ocheretnia area, ready for combat operations.

At 00.30 on 26 January, the 3rd Tank Corps was put on the alert, and by 8.00 26 January, having conducted a 105-kilometer march, it was assembling in the Pogrebishche – Pedosy – Pavlovka area. Later on 26 January, at 19.00, the 16th Tank Corps's 164th Tank Brigade was put on the alert, and having completed a 110-kilometer march, by 6.00 on 27 January it was assembling in the area of Lipovets Station, where it became operationally subordinate to the 3rd Tank Corps, while the remaining units of the 16th Tank Corps were continuing to receive matériel in the Belaia Tserkov' area.

On 26 January 1944, the enemy in the sector of the 38th Army broke through the defenses in the Shenderovka – Britskoe – Rotmistrovka area in separate groups, and forward units advanced in the direction of Dovzhek and Chapaevo (20 kilometers southwest of Pogrebishche). Simultaneously, the enemy's first panzer grouping, having seized Rososha, was striving to link up with the panzer grouping attacking out of the Monastyrishche area. By this time, the latter panzer grouping had seized Oratov and Kazemirovka.

Meanwhile, the forces of the 2nd Tank Army consisting of the 3rd Tank Corps, the 11th Guards Tank Brigade and the 164th Tank Brigade had finished assembling in their jumping-off areas by midnight on 26 January 1944. The 3rd Tank Corps occupied a line stretching from Ochitkov to Lipovets Station; the 164th Tank Brigade was in Lipovets Station, and the 11th Guards Tank Brigade was positioned on the western and southwestern outskirts of Ocheretnia. All were in readiness for combat operations.

## The combat operations of the 2nd Tank Army between 27 January and 4 February 1944

As a result of the counteroffensive, the enemy, having broken through the defenses of the 38th Army, had semi-encircled the 17th Guards Rifle Corps in the area of Lipovets and had begun to advance in the direction of Oratov. Simultaneously, attacking out of the Popivka – Varyianka area, the Germans had seized Gordeevka, Troshcha and Liadskaia Sloboda, and up to a battalion of infantry and 30 tanks had broken through to the Romanov State Farm.

At 17.40 on 28 January, the chief of staff of the 2nd Tank Army Guards Major General Pavlov dashed off a message to General Bogdanov:

> Maksimov (apparently the code name for the commander of the 1st Ukrainian Front) has passed down the order of Iur'ev (Stalin's code name, which was used in coded messages) to hold Khorosha and Romanov Khutor. The 50th Tank Brigade is to attack toward Strizhevka, Babin – to destroy small enemy groups and to hold Tiagun, Babin and Oratov Station. [Signed] Pavlov

There is a penciled note by General Bogdanov on this message that he received it at 02.00 on 29 January.

General Bogdanov also received an update on the 16th Tank Corps early that morning from Colonel Bazanov, which stated:

> I am reporting that the 109th Tank Brigade has been fully refitted and at 13.30 on 28.1.44, the head of its marching column had passed through the western outskirts of Tetiev. The 164th Tank Brigade at 12.30 on 28.1.44 had assembled north of Oratov. The 15th Motorized Rifle Brigade at 13.00 on 28.1.44 – [its] 1st and 2nd Motorized Rifle Battalion in Volodarka; the 3rd Motorized Rifle Battalion and mortar battalion in Rogozno. The 226th Mortar Regiment is moving to the area of Skala. The 1542nd Self-propelled Artillery Regiment is moving to the

area of the southern outskirts of Novyi Zhivotiv. The 51st Separate Motorcycle Battalion is on the march to assemble in the area of Zakrenich'e. The anti-aircraft artillery regiment and the 107th Tank Brigade are in the former area.

On the morning of 27 January, the 2nd Tank Army went on the attack in the general direction of Zozov with the task to cut off and destroy the enemy grouping that had broken through, and to secure the withdrawal of the 17th Guards Rifle Corps out of semi-encirclement. The 11th Guards Tank Brigade had been ordered by the commander of the 38th Army to attack at 13.30 on 26 January in the direction of Point 307.8, Ganovka and Zozov with the task to cut off the enemy grouping that had broken through in the southeastern direction, but the enemy pre-empted the tank brigade's attack with an attack of their own out of the Ksaverovka State Farm – Aleksandrovka – Zozov area toward Ocheretnia with up to 120 tanks and self-propelled guns, supported by groups of 30-40 aircraft. The 11th Guards Tank Brigade, heroically fighting against superior enemy forces, repulsed repeated enemy attacks and stubbornly clung to its occupied line. At 16.30 on 26 January, the enemy against attacked Ocheretnia with up to 40 tanks with air support (28-40 Ju-87 dive bombers). This attack also failed. At 23.00 on 26 January, the tank brigade received an order from the commander of the 38th Army: " … with a single tank battalion and a group of tank riders, go on the attack with the task to strike at the enemy's rear areas with a night attack in the direction of Ganovka and Napadovka."

At 1.00 on 27 January, in conditions of dense fog and a dark night, Guards Senior Lieutenant Khmelinin's 3rd Tank Battalion set off to carry out the army commander's order. At 10.00 on 27 January 1944, the brigade received the order of the 38th Army's commander to go on the attack with the rest of its forces in the direction of Hill 307.8, Ganovka and Slavna, with the objective in cooperation with the 7th Guards Mechanized Corps and the 3rd Tank Corps to cut off and destroy the enemy units that had broken through. By 13.00, the 11th Guards Tank Brigade reached the Hill 299.3 – northeastern outskirts of Ganovka line, while Khmelinin's 3rd Tank Battalion had reached the northern outskirts of Ul'ianovka.

At this point, the enemy launched counterattacks with 15 Tiger tanks out of the area of Hill 296.1 into the rear of the 1st and 2nd Tank Battalion, and with 8 tanks out of the area of Hill 303.2. Simultaneously the 3rd Tank Battalion was counterattacked by 4 Tiger tanks out of the area of Vygoda and 4 assault guns advancing out of Ul'ianovka. The 11th Guards Tank Brigade was forced to accept a difficult combat. Repelling the counterattacks of German tanks, the commander of the 3rd Tank Battalion Guards Senior Lieutenant Khmelinin was able with some of his tanks to break through to the encircled rifle units, and together with them, to fight his way back out of the closing pocket. In the process, Khmelinin's tank was brewed up, while he, now on foot and risking his life, led his battalion out of the battle, thereby having carried out his assigned orders. Conducting a 4-hour battle, suffering heavy losses from enemy fire, the 11th Guards Tank Brigade was compelled to make a fighting withdrawal out of the closing German panzer jaws to the southwestern outskirts of Ocheretnia, where it continued to throw back enemy counterattacks.

The 3rd Tank Corps at 10.30 on 27 January went on the attack with the forces of the 51st and 103rd Tank Brigades from the line Otchetka – Lipovets Station. The 103rd Tank Brigade together with an SU-76 regiment attacked in the direction of Napadovka and Ganovka; together with the 1818th Self-propelled Artillery Regiment, the 51st Tank Brigade attacked toward Rososha and Vitsentovka. The 50th Tank Brigade, supported by the 234th Army Mortar Regiment, took up a defensive position along the southwestern and western outskirts of Spichentsy, while the 164th Tank Brigade, the 3rd Tank Corps commander's reserve, was in the vicinity of Lipovets Station.

The rest of the 16th Tank Corps, back in the Belaia Tserkov' area, was receiving matériel and preparing to move out. Its 109th Tank Brigade, however, received an order to make a night march and to assemble in the area of Staro and Novo Zhitiv by 5.00 on 28 January 1944.

## The 2nd Tank Army, January 1944

Tanks of the 3rd Tank Corps before an attack in the area of Lipovets Station, January 1944 – the Russian caption read, "In ambush – the 3rd Tank Corps."

Motorized infantry of the 16th Tank Corps moving into positions, January 1944.

A T-34 tank crew, January 1944 (a photo of an exposition by the Museum of the Korsun'-Shevchenkovskii Battle).

Tanks of the 2nd Tank Army on the march, January 1944 (a photo from an exposition
by the Museum of the Korsun'-Shevchenkovskii Battle).

### The combat of the 51st and 103rd Tank Brigades for Sinarna State Farm

At 11.00 on 27 January, the 103rd Tank Brigade launched its attack toward Napadovka. At 13.00,
one tank company of the 103rd Tank Brigade reached a ravine south of Vygoda, where it fell into
a devastating crossfire of approximately 90 enemy tanks and self-propelled guns in Vygoda and on
the northwestern outskirts of Napadovka and was completely destroyed. Thirty minutes later, the
420th Tank Battalion and the 2nd Tank Company of the 219th Tank Battalion attacked toward
Vygoda together with a motorized rifle brigade, but once again they came under the deadly crossfire from the very same directions. Having lost 24 tanks, by 14.30 the 103rd Tank Brigade fell back
to a line 1.5 kilometers west of Bogdanovka.

The 51st Tank Brigade took up its jumping-off positions 1 kilometer north of Lipovets Station
at 10.30. At 11.00, it went on the attack in the direction of the northern outskirts of Rososha, with
the further task to take Vitsentovka. The 51st Tank Brigade's 94th Tank Battalion – the brigade
commander's reserve – remained in the woods east of Lipovets Station. The brigade, having
reached a nameless stream flowing from Rososha to the north, blundered into a swamp because
of the failure to reconnoiter the terrain, where 13 tanks got stuck. The brigade commander sent
out his reserve to go around the stream from the north, and eventually it fought its way to a line
1 kilometer north of Rososha. Having lost 42 tanks as a result of the fighting (29 brewed up, 3
knocked out and 13 stuck in the swamp), the brigade at the order of the corps commander fell
back to its jumping-off position with just 15 tanks, and temporarily assumed a defensive posture.

At 2.00 on 28 January 1944 the 103rd Tank Brigade moved out of its defensive positions west
of Bogdanovka, and having conducted a 20-kilometer march, it moved into jumping-off positions at Hill 281.6 for a fresh attack by 7.00. The brigade had 16 T-34 tanks in formation and the
motorized rifle battalion (minus one company). At 9.00 the brigade went on the attack toward

Khorosha and Skripka, and broke into Khorosha with 9 tanks. However, the enemy hurled 25 tanks out of Rososha into a counterattack and forced the 103rd Tank Brigade to fall back to the line Sinarna State Farm – railroad hut 3 kilometers east of Sinarna State Farm. By 22.00 on 28 January, having lost 12 tanks, the 103rd Tank Brigade was in defensive positions together with the 51st Tank Brigade.

The latter brigade had assembled on the Bol'shevik State Farm at 7.00 on 28 January, with the task to seize Khorosha. Having no time to work out cooperation with the infantry, the brigade was attacked at 8.00 by a force of up to 80 tanks with infantry from three directions: up to 50 tanks and two infantry battalions from Skitki; 15 tanks and a company of infantry from Romanov Khutor; and 20 tanks and an infantry battalion from Boliukivka, and it was driven back to the northeastern outskirts of Tiagun. Fighting off powerful attacks by enemy tanks and infantry, the 51st Tank Brigade fell back from line to line, and by 14.30 it was occupying a defense along the northeastern slopes of Hill 252.4. Here, the brigade together with its command wound up encircled. Having organized a breakout attempt, the brigade fought its way out of the encirclement, and by 19.00 on 28 January 1944, it had reached the area of Sinarna State Farm, where it linked up with the 103rd Tank Brigade and together with it took up a defense.

On 29 January, having assembled up to 50 tanks and an infantry regiment in the Sinarskii area, the enemy launched an attack at 12.30 toward the Sinarna State Farm against the right flank of the 103rd Tank Brigade. This attack was repelled, and the Germans left behind 3 tanks knocked-out on the battlefield. At 13.10 the Germans attacked again with up to 28 tanks, but again the attack failed. The enemy repeated fruitless attacks at 13.40 with 22 tanks and at 15.00 with 10 tanks. Only at 15.30, after the fifth enemy attack, was the 103rd Tank Brigade forced to fall back to the southern outskirts of Chagov, having suffered losses.

The day's fighting didn't end with this. Having received 5 tanks from the 50th Tank Brigade, at 19.00 the 103rd Tank Brigade counterattacked, regained the lost ground, and resumed its defense on the line between the Sinarna State Farm and the railroad hut 3 kilometers east of the farm.

From the morning of 30 January 1944, the 51st Tank Brigade numbering 14 tanks (4 tanks of the 103rd Tank Brigade, 5 tanks of the 50th Tank Brigade and 5 of its own tanks) and the 234th Army Mortar Battalion repelled repeated any attempts to seize the Sinarna State Farm. At 9.30 on 31 January, the enemy in strength of 32 tanks attacked out of the area of Oratov Station. Twelve enemy panzers, approaching the crossroads southwest of Hill 279.1, deployed into a combat formation and attacked in the direction of the State Farm. Our tanks with organized fire from fixed positions drove back three enemy attacks with heavy losses to the enemy. Finally, at 13.10 on 31 January, three Tiger tanks carrying submachine gunners and with air support broke into the Sinarna State Farm, forcing the brigade to retreat to the line: Hill 265.5 – Hill 274.0. In the early morning hours of 1 February, the 51st Tank Brigade twice counterattacked Sinarna State Farm, but the attacks were repelled by the enemy and the brigade fell back to the southern slopes of Hill 274.0, where it dug in.

The 3rd Tank Corps had blunted the enemy advance, but under the pressure of superior enemy forces, it was compelled to go over to a defense. Because of the broad front the corps was holding, the brigades were deployed in a single line. Major Shishov's 1540th Heavy Self-propelled Artillery Regiment was in reserve. The tank and motorized rifle brigades deployed their forces into two echelons. Having organized a system of fire, the tankers turned to fortifying the area of defense. The ground was frozen and yielded stubbornly to the shovel, pick axe and crowbar. By morning, the tanks and self-propelled guns were positioned in open revetments. The submachine gunners dug foxholes and trenches.

Fierce fighting for these positions developed. In the course of the next three days, the brigades, reinforced with self-propelled and anti-tank artillery, repelled German attacks by tanks and infantry, supported by strong artillery fire. The combat became particularly difficult for Colonel

Roman Liberman's 50th Tank Brigade in the Bogdanovka – Kozhanka sector, where the enemy launched his main attack. The Germans were attempting to outflank the 3rd Tank Corps. However, on 28 January 1944 the 109th and 164th Tank Brigades of the arriving 16th Tank Corps swung into action and attacked the German grouping in the Oratov area, drove the Nazis out of this village, and adopted a defensive posture on the Salogubovka – Kalenovka line, covering the left flank of the 3rd Tank Corps from attacks. The Soviet troops held their occupied lines and inflicted a heavy check to the foe by preventing a breakthrough to Belaia Tserkov' and Kiev.

General Bogdanov wrote:

> The 3rd Tank Corps played an important role in stopping the enemy counteroffensive. The troops fulfilled their order. They stood fast. They inflicted heavy losses on the enemy. Between 27 January and 3 February 1944 alone, they destroyed 73 hostile tanks and self-propelled assault guns, 27 field guns, and up to 2,000 enemy soldiers and officers. The corps secured the withdrawal of the 17th Guards Rifle Corps out of encirclement, and in cooperation with other formations, stopped the further enemy advance and gave the 38th Army the opportunity to organize a firm defense.

Major General Shamshin, the commander of the 3rd Tank Corps, when summing up the results of the fighting, reiterated that the 3rd Tank Corps had inflicted large losses on the enemy. By doing so, it stripped the enemy of the possibility of a further advance in this sector. The corps not only secured the withdrawal of the 17th Guards Rifle Corps out of semi-encirclement, but also drew significant enemy forces upon itself, which allowed the units of our forces on other sectors of the front to employ active operations. He added, "The main shortcomings, which led to large losses of matériel and personnel of the corps' units are: the hastiness in organizing the 27-28 January attack – the units entered the battle from the march; the lack of reconnoitering the terrain, especially by staff officers; the organization of combat reconnaissance was poor, especially on the flanks; the presence in the area of the corps' operations of a significant number of Tiger tanks, which placed direct fire from a range of 2,000 meters; the absence of artillery or air support; and the lack of infantry – the 57th Motorized Rifle Brigade was on the march, without motorized transport."

## The combat of the 109th and 164th Tank Brigades for Oratov and Oratov Station

As noted in the previous section, the 16th Tank Corps' 109th and 164th Tank Brigades made a timely arrival on the battlefield and with a counterattack, secured the threatened flank of the 3rd Tank Corps. At 19.30 on 27 January, the 164th Tank Brigade had received a new order, and having conducted a 50-kilometer march, by 4.30 on 28 January, it had assembled in the Kalenovka area, where it came under the operational control of the 11th Tank Corps commander. By this time the enemy, exploiting the offensive, had breached the front of our units south of Oratov and was striving to seize the road in the Zhivotivka area. By 11.30, as the brigade approached Zhivotivka, scouts reported that there were no bridges in Oratov, and that up to 50 enemy tanks were present in that area. As the brigade emerged on the southern outskirts of Zhivotivka, it was greeted by the organized fire of enemy tanks and anti-tank artillery and went over to a defense and passed back to the control of the 16th Tank Corps. In the course of the night of 28/29 January, through actions of the brigade's forward detachment, the enemy was driven out of Oratov, and by 8.00 on 29 January, the brigade reached the southern outskirts of Oratov, where it went over to a stiff defense. In the course of 29 January, the enemy in groups of 20-30 tanks with motorized infantry attacked the brigade three times, but incurring heavy losses, fell back to the jumping-off position.

A T-34 rolls across a short bridge. "January 1944: The march in the Vinnitsa area."

On 30 January, the enemy in strength of up to 50 tanks with motorized infantry went on the attack, striving to seize Oratov. With the fire of artillery and tanks from fixed positions, the attacks were repulsed.

The 109th Tank Brigade arrived in the area of Silogubevka by 8.00 on 29 January with the task to set up a defense on the line: Chagov – Hill 291.1 – Lopatinka. On the approach to Hill 274.6, the brigade's motorized rifle battalion was met by enemy tank fire and small arms fire. The brigade was compelled to join battle against the enemy tanks and infantry, and having repelled enemy attacks, the motorized rifle battalion advanced to the Tarasovka area, while the tank battalions reached the western fringe of a patch of woods lying 1 kilometer east of Hill 291.1, where it took up a defense.

Having received an assignment at 13.00 on 29 January to seize Oratov Station and to secure the withdrawal of encircled units of the 135th Rifle Regiment, the brigade went on the attack at 18.45, without arranging cooperation with the infantry, which was supposed to support the attack from the rear and from the direction of Chagov. Initially, with the brigade's unexpected attack, the enemy began to fall back to the south, and the brigade by 21.00 broke into Oratov Station, where it became tied up in bitter fighting. The enemy, with the help of illumination from burning buildings, began to shoot up the brigade's tanks at point-blank range with fire from anti-tank guns, tanks and self-propelled artillery. As a result of heavy losses (25 tanks), the 109th Tank Brigade was withdrawn from combat back to its jumping-off position, where it went over to a defense.

As we've already seen, on 28 January 1944 the 3rd Tank Corps, with the aim of securing the withdrawal of the 17th Guards Rifle Corps from semi-encirclement, had launched an attack in the direction of Skitki and Khorosha. In the course of the day, with savage fighting against superior and counterattacking enemy forces, the corps gave the 17th Guards Rifle Corps the possibility of pulling out of semi-encirclement. By the end of the day, the enemy, committing 45 tanks and up to an infantry battalion into the fighting, achieved a partial success, having seized Lipovets Station and the Kommunar State Farm. By the end of 28 January, with actions out of Frontovka, the enemy had seized Oratov. The units of the 2nd Tank Army in the course of 29 January, with heavy fighting and active operations regained possession of Oratov and Lipovets Station.

In the course of 29 to 31 January 1944, the 2nd Tank Army was defending the line Ocheretnia – Lipovets Station – Sinarna State Farm – Mervin – Lopatinka – Oratov, and was repelling repeated enemy attacks with major forces of tanks and infantry. The Germans in the sector of Sinarna State Farm, undertaking numerous attacks with tanks and infantry and with air support of 20-30 aircraft, shoved back our units at the cost of heavy losses, and seized possession of the Sinarna State Farm on 31 January. In the course of the night between 31 January and 1 February, the enemy went over to a defense on the line: south of Ocheretnia – Hill 291.3 – Rososha – Tel'man State Farm – Sinarna State Farm – Oratov Station – Kazemirovka.

By the end of 30 January 1944, the 2nd Tank Army had 241 operational tanks and self-propelled guns: 197 T-34, 26 Valentine Mark IX, 8 SU-76, 1 SU-85, and 9 SU-152. Table 5.1 shows the number of tanks in the 2nd Tank Army's formations and their status as of 24.00 30 January 1944:

Table 5.1: Data on the availability of tanks in the 2nd Tank Army's formations as of 24.00 on 30 January 1944

| | Type | On the list | Operational | Under repair | | | Losses |
|---|---|---|---|---|---|---|---|
| | | | | Minor repair | Light overhaul | Major overhaul | |
| **3rd Tank Corps** | | | | | | | |
| 50th Tank Brigade | T-34 | 65 | 48 | – | 11 | 3 | 3 |
| 51st Tank Brigade | T-34 | 65 | 4 | 3 | 16 | 2 | 40 |
| 103rd Tank Brigade | T-34 | 65 | 4 | 6 | 4 | 3 | 48 |
| 74th Motorcycle Battalion | MK-9 | 10 | 6 | 2 | 2 | – | – |
| 411th Separate Signals Battalion | T-34 | 2 | – | – | 1 | 1 | – |
| 1540th Heavy Self-propelled Regiment | KV | 1 | – | – | 1 | – | – |
| | SU-152 | 12 | 5 | 3 | 2 | – | – |
| 76mm self-propelled regiment | SU-76 | 21 | 13 | 3 | 3 | – | 9 |
| 1818th Self-propelled Regiment | SU-85 | 16 | 1 | 3 | 3 | – | 9 |
| Altogether for the 3rd Tank Corps | T-34 | 197 | 56 | 9 | 32 | 9 | 91 |
| **16th Tank Corps** | | | | | | | |
| 107th Tank Brigade | T-34 | 65 | 65 | – | – | – | – |
| 109th Tank Brigade | T-34 | 64 | 39 | 4 | 5 | – | 16 |
| 164th Tank Brigade | T-34 | 65 | 37 | 3 | 4 | – | 11 |
| 51st Motorcycle Battalion | MK-9 | 10 | 10 | – | – | – | – |
| **Altogether for the 16th Tank Corps** | T-34 | 194 | 141 | 7 | 9 | – | 27 |
| Total for the 2nd Tank Army: | T-34 | 391 | 197 | 16 | 41 | 9 | 118 |
| | MK-9 | 30 | 26 | 2 | 2 | – | – |
| Total number of tanks: | | 421 | 223 | 18 | 43 | 9 | 118 |

Note: A handwritten not ebelow the table stated: 36 T-34 tanks have been added to the 16th Tank Corps (16 tanks – 107th Tank Brigade, 10 tanks – 109th Tank Brigade and 10 tanks – 164th Tank Brigades, and have already been included in the table) and will arrive by the end of 31.1.44 according to a report over the telephone from Colonel Katerin. [Signed] Deputy chief of staff of the Army – Colonel V. Chizh

At 8.00 on 1 February 1944, Colonel Chizh issued an updated report that provided more detail on the quantity and status of tanks and self-propelled guns in the 2nd Tank Army:

**Table 5.2: Data on the quantity and status of tanks in the 2nd Tank Army's formations as of 08.00 on 1 February 1944**

| | Type | On the list | Operational | Under Repair | | | Losses | | | |
|---|---|---|---|---|---|---|---|---|---|---|
| | | | | Minor | Light overhaul | Major overhaul | Knocked out | Burned out | Abandoned in mud | En route |
| **3rd Tank Corps** | | | | | | | | | | |
| 50th Tank Brigade | T-34 | 65 | 47 | 5 | 4 | 2 | – | 7 | – | – |
| 51st Tank Brigade | T-34 | 65 | 13 | 8 | 3 | 1 | 2 | 38 | – | – |
| 103rd Tank Brigade | T-34 | 65 | 1 | 1 | 3 | 5 | 9 | 46 | – | – |
| 74th Motorcycle Battalion | MK-9 | 10 | 6 | 2 | 2 | – | – | – | – | – |
| 411th Separate Signals Battalion | T-34 | 2 | 1 | – | 1 | – | – | – | – | – |
| 1540th Heavy Self-propelled Regiment | KV | 1 | – | – | 1 | – | – | 1 | – | – |
| | SU-152 | 12 | 4 | 4 | 3 | – | – | – | – | – |
| 76mm self-propelled regiment | SU-76 | 21 | 8 | 7 | – | 3 | 3 | – | – | – |
| 1818th Self-propelled Regiment | SU-85 | 16 | 5 | 1 | – | – | – | 10 | – | – |
| **Altogether for the 3rd Tank Corps** | T-34 | 197 | 62 | 14 | 11 | 8 | 11 | 91 | – | – |
| **16th Tank Corps** | | | | | | | | | | |
| 107th Tank Brigade | T-34 | 49 | Subordinate to the 40th Army | | | | | | | |
| 109th Tank Brigade | T-34 | 54 | 29 | – | 3 | 2 | – | 15 | 3 | 2 |
| 164th Tank Brigade | T-34 | 55 | 27 | 7 | 10 | – | – | 5 | 3 | 3 |
| 51st Motorcycle Battalion | MK-9 | 10 | 9 | – | 1 | – | – | – | – | – |
| 1542nd Heavy Self-propelled Regiment | SU-152 | 10 | 2 | 2 | 1 | 5 | – | – | – | – |
| **Altogether for the 16th Tank Corps** | T-34 | 158 | 56 | 7 | 13 | 2 | – | 20 | 6 | 5 |
| Total for the 2nd Tank Army: | T-34 | 355 | 118 | 21 | 24 | 10 | 11 | 111 | 6 | 5 |
| **Total amount of armor:** | T-34 | **435** | **153** | **37** | **33** | **18** | **14** | **122** | **6** | **5** |

Supplies: 3rd Tank Corps – ammunition – 1 combat load, fuel and lubricants – 1 refill, rations – 3 days; 16th Tank Corps – ammunition – 1.6 combat loads, fuel and lubricants – 1.2 refills of diesel, 0.2 refill of benzene, rations – 3 days

Signed: Deputy chief of staff of the 2nd Tank Army – Colonel V. Chizh

Between 1 February and 3 February 1944, the enemy conducted a regrouping and removed the 1st SS Panzer Division *Leibstandarte Adolf Hitler* and the 16th Panzer Division from the sector of defense. The 2nd Tank Army over this time continued to defend its occupied lines and conducted reconnaissance probes. On 2 February 1944, the assistant commander of the 2nd Tank Army for vehicle maintenance and technical support Guards Engineer-Colonel Krupenin issued another update on the quantity and status of the armored fighting vehicles in the 2nd Tank Army as of 12.00 (see Table 5.3):

**Table 5.3: The quantity and status of the tanks and self-propelled guns in the 2nd Tank Army as of 12.00 on 2 February 1944**

| | Type | On the list | Operational | Under repair: | | | Irrecoverable losses | |
| --- | --- | --- | --- | --- | --- | --- | --- | --- |
| | | | | Minor | Light overhaul | Major overhaul | Written off | Not yet written off |
| **3rd Tank Corps** | | | | | | | | |
| 50th Tank Brigade | T-34 | 65 | 49 | 3 | 6 | – | – | 7 |
| 51st Tank Brigade | T-34 | 65 | 16 | 2 | 3 | – | – | 44 |
| 103rd Tank Brigade | T-34 | 74 | 12 | – | 4 | 3 | – | 55 |
| 744th Motorcycle Battalion | MK-9 | 10 | 6 | 2 | 2 | – | – | – |
| 411th Signals Battalion | T-34 | 2 | 1 | – | 1 | – | – | – |
| Altogether for 3rd Tank Corps | T-34 | 206 | 78 | 5 | 14 | 3 | – | 106 |
| | MK-9 | 10 | 6 | 2 | 2 | – | – | – |
| **16th Tank Corps** | | | | | | | | |
| 109th Tank Brigade | T-34 | 54 | 30 | 3 | 2 | – | – | 19 |
| 164th Tank Brigade | T-34 | 55 | 37 | 3 | 9 | 3 | – | 3 |
| 689th Signals Battalion | T-34 | 2 | 2 | – | – | – | – | – |
| 51st Motorized Battalion | MK-9 | 10 | 9 | 1 | – | – | – | – |
| Altogether for 16th Tank Corps | T-34 | 111 | 69 | 6 | 11 | 3 | – | 22 |
| | MK-9 | 10 | 9 | 1 | – | – | – | – |
| **11th Guards Tank Brigade*** | T-34 | 63 | 36 | – | – | – | 16 | 11 |
| 87th Motorcycle Battalion | MK-9 | 10 | 10 | – | – | – | – | – |
| Total for the Army: | T-34 | 380 | 183 | 11 | 25 | 6 | 16 | 139 |
| | MK-9 | 30 | 25 | 3 | 2 | – | – | – |
| Total tanks: | | 410 | 208 | 14 | 27 | 6 | 16 | 139 |

* In the 38th Army

Comment below table: The 107th Tank Brigade of the 16th Tank Corps with 65 T-34 tanks was operationally transferred to the 6th Tank Army. 30 T-34 tanks have been given to the 40th Army. By 3 February 1944 (end of day), the repair work on 28 T-34 tanks and 2 MK-9 tanks now undergoing minor repairs or light overhauls will be completed. Thus, by the end of 3.2.1944, 238 tanks will be serviceable.

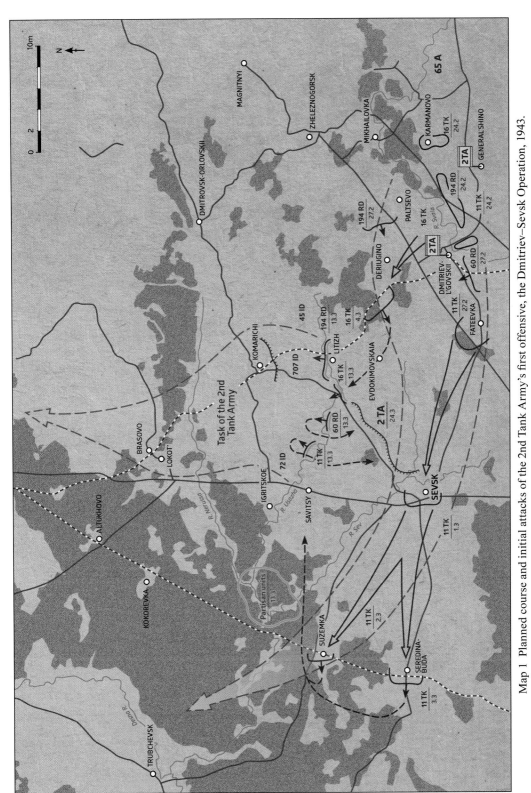

Map 1  Planned course and initial attacks of the 2nd Tank Army's first offensive, the Dmitriev–Sevsk Operation, 1943.

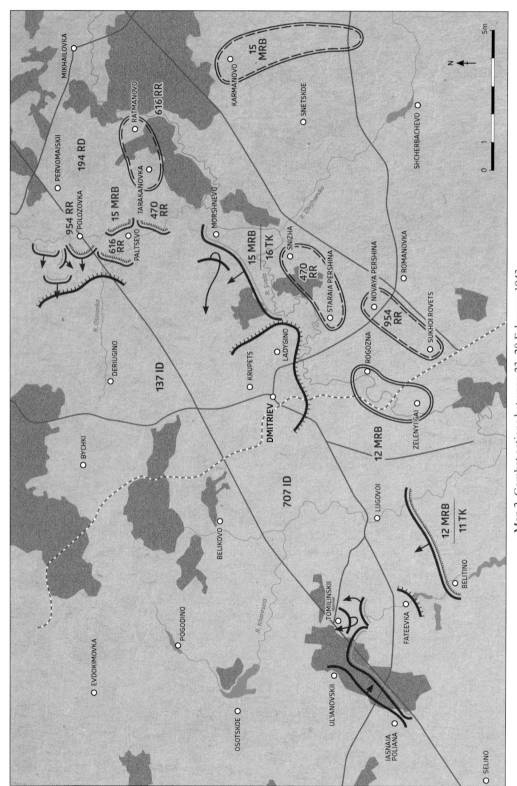

Map 2  Combat actions between 23–28 February 1943.

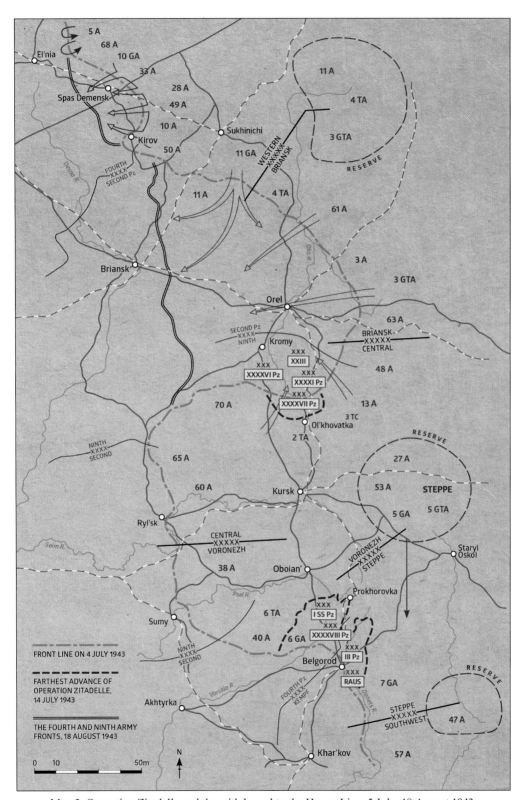

Map 3  Operation Zitadelle and the withdrawal to the Hagen Line, 5 July–18 August 1943.

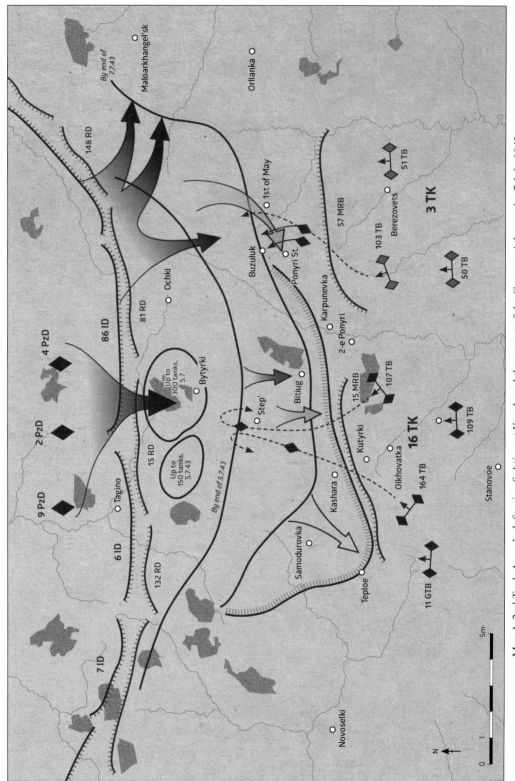

Map 4 2nd Tank Army's defensive fighting at Kursk and the extent of the German Advance by 7 July 1943.

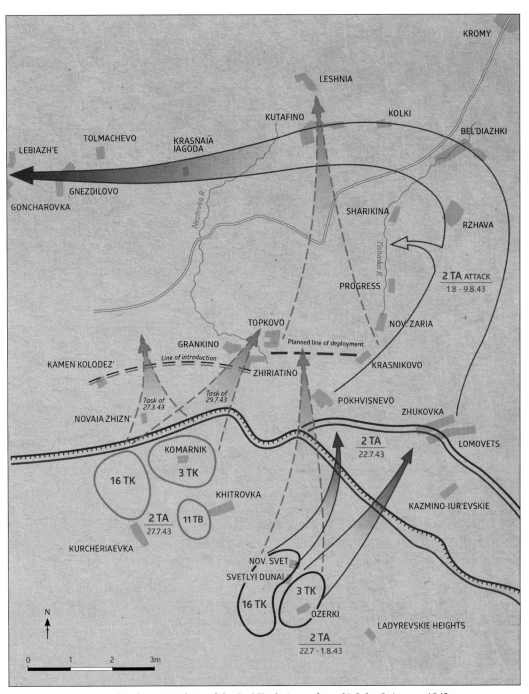

KROMY

LESHNIA

KUTAFINO

KOLKI

BEL'DIAZHKI

TOLMACHEVO

KRASNAIA
IAGODA

LEBIAZH'E

GNEZDILOVO

GONCHAROVKA

SHARIKINA

RZHAVA

*Nezhivka R.*

*Tishinka R.*

PROGRESS

2 TA ATTACK
1.8 - 9.8.43

TOPKOVO

NOV. ZARIA

GRANKINO

Planned line of deployment

KAMEN KOLODEZ'

Line of introduction

KRASNIKOVO

ZHIRIATINO

*Task of
27.3.43*

*Task of
29.7.43*

POKHVISNEVO

ZHUKOVKA

NOVAIA ZHIZN'

LOMOVETS

KOMARNIK

2 TA
22.7.43

16 TK

3 TK

KHITROVKA

KAZMINO-IUR'EVSKIE

2 TA
27.7.43

11 TB

KURCHERIAEVKA

NOV. SVET

SVETLYI DUNAI

3 TK

16 TK

OZERKI

LADYREVSKIE HEIGHTS

2 TA
22.7 - 1.8.43

N

0    1    2    3m

Map 5  Combat operations of the 2nd Tank Army from 21 July–9 August 1943.

Map 6 Map of the combat formations of the 2nd Tank Army's artillery from 17–26 August 1943.

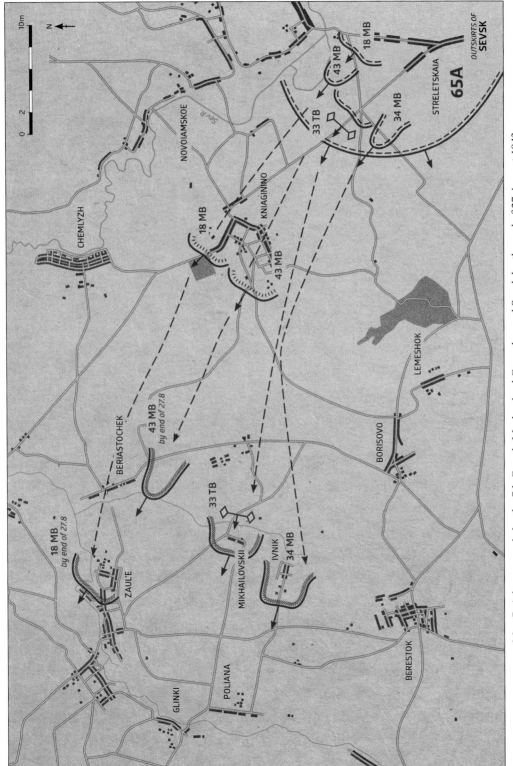

Map 7  Advance made by the 7th Guards Mechanized Corps beyond Sevsk by the end of 27 August 1943.

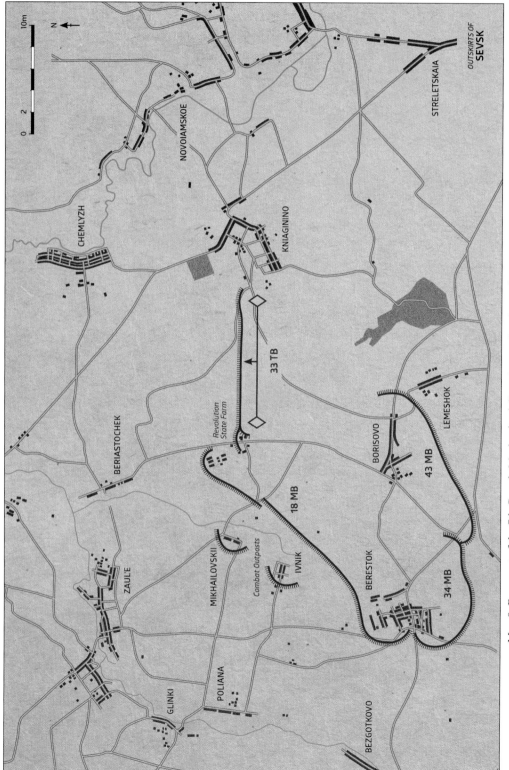

Map 8  Fragment of the 7th Guards Mechanized Corps' operational map for 28 August–30 August 1943.

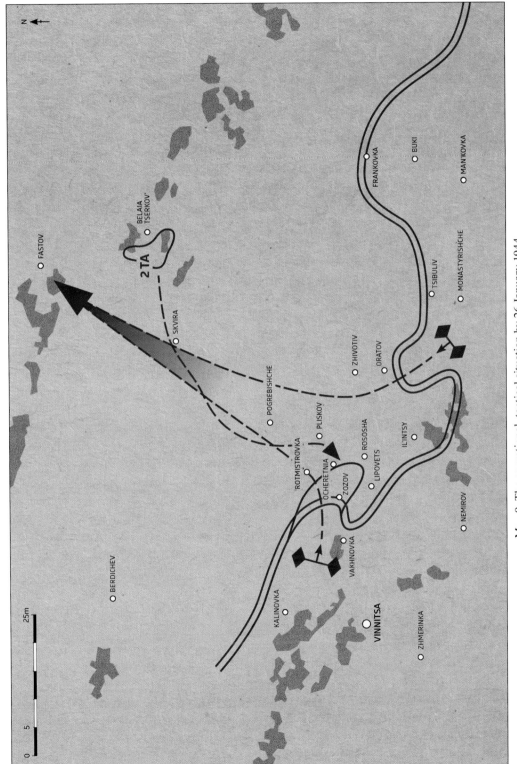

Map 9  The operational–tactical situation by 26 January 1944.

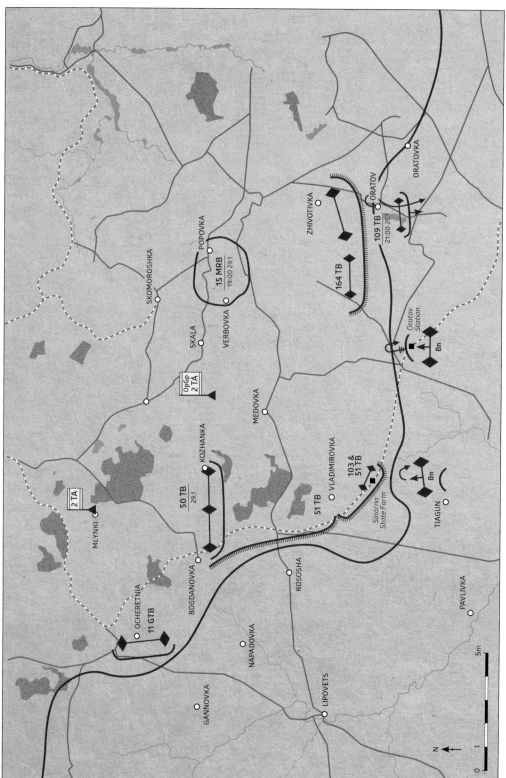

Map 10  The 2nd Tank Army's situation, 29 January 1944.

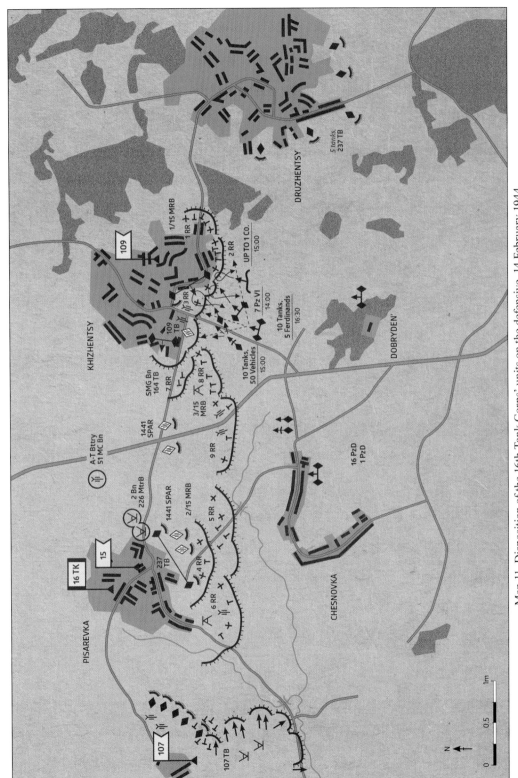

Map 11  Disposition of the 16th Tank Corps' units on the defensive, 14 February 1944.

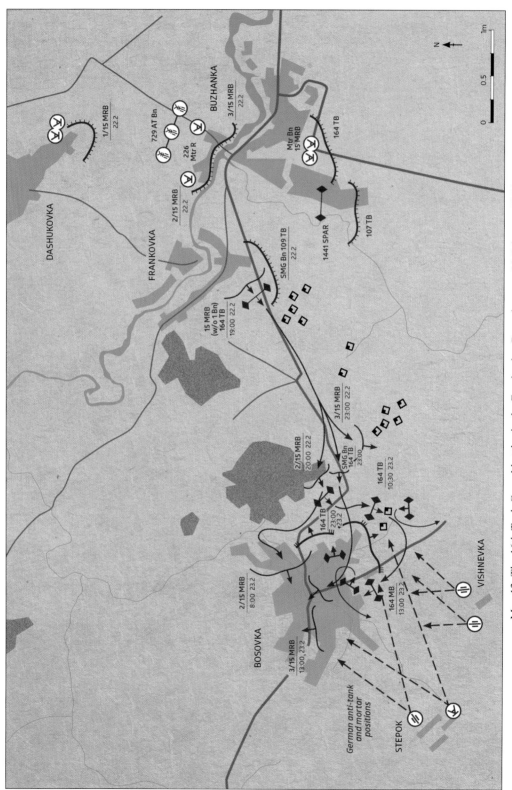

Map 12 The 16th Tank Corps' battles in the Frankovka, Bosovka area, 22 February 1944.

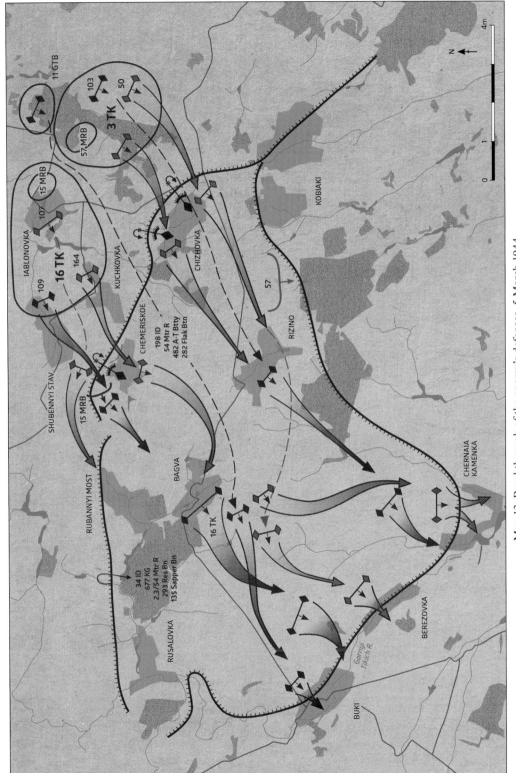

Map 13  Breakthrough of the enemy's defenses, 5 March 1944.

11 GTB

103
50
3 TK
57 MRB

15 MRB
107
IABLONOVKA
16 TK
164
109

KUCHKOVKA
CHEMERISKOE
199 ID
54 Mtr R
482 A-T Btty
282 Flak Btn

CHIZHOVKA

KOBIAKI

57

RIZINO

SHUBENNYI STAV

15 MRB

BAGVA

16 TK

RUBANNYI MOST

CHERNAJA
KAMENKA

34 ID
677 KG
2,3/54 Mtr R
293 Res Bn
135 Sapper Bn

RUSALOVKA

BEREZOVKA

Gornyi
Tikich R.

BUKI

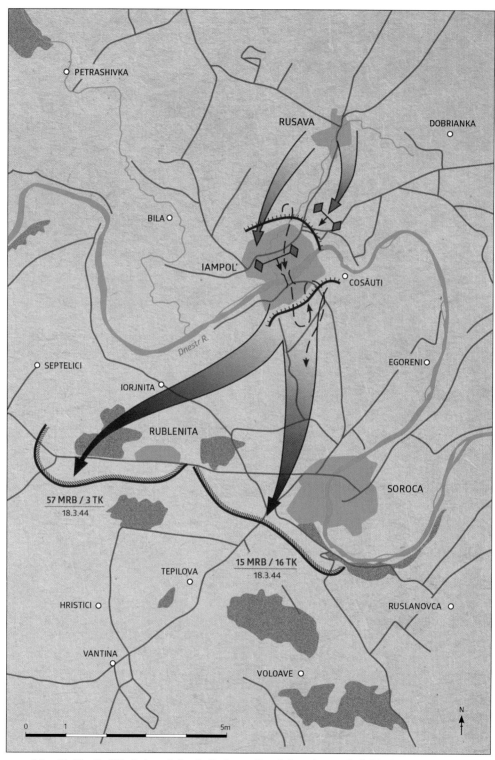

PETRASHIVKA

RUSAVA

DOBRIANKA

BILA

IAMPOL'

COSĂUTI

*Dnestr R.*

SEPTELICI

IORJNITA

EGORENI

RUBLENITA

SOROCA

**57 MRB / 3 TK**
18.3.44

**15 MRB / 16 TK**
18.3.44

TEPILOVA

HRISTICI

RUSLANOVCA

VANTINA

VOLOAVE

N

0    1                    5m

Map 14  The 2nd Tank Army's battle for Iampol' and the seizure of a bridgehead across the
Dnestr River, 17–18 March 1944.

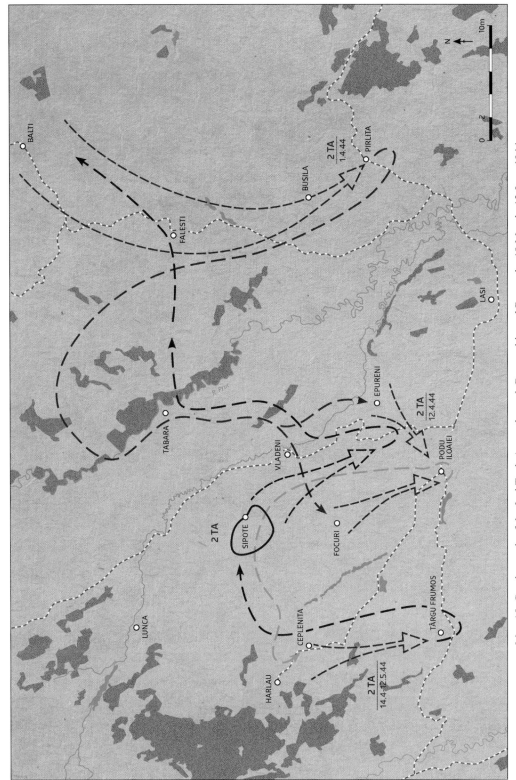

Map 15  Combat path of the 2nd Tank Army through Bessarabia and Romania, 18 March–12 June 1944.

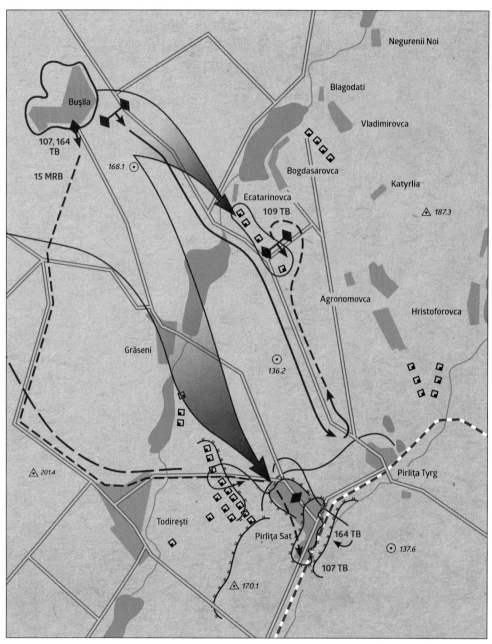

Map 16  The 16th Tank Corps' battle for Pirliţa Tyrg, 29 March–2 April 1944.

The 16th Tank Corps' 107th Tank Brigade, having finally been replenished with tanks up to table strength, set out from Belaia Tserkov' toward the 16th Tank Corps' area of combat operations. Approaching the village of Chelnovitsy while on the march, it received an order to pass to the operational control of the commander of the 6th Tank Army, with the task to assemble in the Vinograd area by the end of 1 February. The 16th Tank Corps, consisting of the 109th Tank Brigade, the 51st Separate Motorcycle Regiment and the corps headquarters on 2 February also transferred to the operational control of the 6th Tank Army, with the task to assemble in the Smil'chentsy area.

As we've seen, the 16th Tank Corps by the end of 28 January 1944 had moved out with its 109th and 164th Tank Brigades against the spearhead of the German panzer grouping that was advancing toward Oratov. The corps commander and the brigade commanders knew that the opponent on this axis had a clear superiority in forces. However, they had decided to attack it. The brigades had deployed and entered the battle from the march. As a result of the surprise attack, the Nazis were driven out of Oratov and thrown back to the south. Subsequently, in view of the enemy's plain superiority in strength, both tank brigades had been compelled to go over to a defense on a line running from Oratov to a point northwest of Kazemirovka.

According to Soviet data, over the period of combat operations running from 27 January to 3 February 1944, the 2nd Tank Army inflicted the following damage to the enemy:

**Table 5.4: The 2nd Tank Army's estimates of the German losses in men and matériel in the fighting between 27 January and 3 February 1944**

| 11th Guards Tank Brigade | | 16th Tank Corps | | 3rd Tank Corps | |
|---|---|---|---|---|---|
| Destroyed: tanks | 33 | Destroyed: tanks | 18 | Destroyed: tanks | 49 |
| Self-propelled guns | 1 | Self-propelled guns | 2 | Self-propelled guns | 34 |
| Vehicles | 21 | Guns of various calibers | 4 | Guns of various calibers | 27 |
| Anti-tank guns | 7 | Vehicles | 19 | Vehicles | 41 |
| Machine guns | 3 | Machine guns | 8 | Machine guns | 29 |
| Wagons | 4 | Wagons with loads | 11 | Wagons with loads | 208 |
| Soldiers and officers | 1,028 | Soldiers and officers | 1,841 | Soldiers and officers | 2,166 |

Over this same period, the 2nd Tank Army lost a total of 193 tanks. The 11th Guards Tank Brigade lost 43 tanks, the 3rd Tank Corps lost 116 tanks, and the 16th Tank Corps lost 34 tanks. Table 5.5 over shows the quantity of tanks in the 2nd Tank Army and their status as of 8.00 on 3 February 1944.

Thus the enemy at the cost of heavy losses succeeded in stopping the offensive by the 1st Ukrainian Front on this axis for a certain time. In the heavy fighting that continued non-stop for five days, the 2nd Tank Army because of its incomplete refitting, as well as its insufficiently rapid maneuvering, was unable to achieve decisive results. In the situation that developed, it was forced to scatter its efforts across a broad front and to enter the battle piecemeal as units and formations arrived. Repelling enemy counterstrokes, the army on all the directions continued to hold and fortify its occupied lines. Simultaneously, its units and formations prepared for a new offensive. The army received a wave of replacements. After short treatment in the medical sanitation battalions, many soldiers returned to active service. In addition, combat equipment was arriving in the army in ever greater numbers.

The document "The Combat Path of the 3rd Tank Corps" states:

An enemy grouping in the Korsun'-Shevchenkovskii area was holding up the further advance of our forces. At the decision of the *Stavka* of the Supreme High Command, forces of the

**Table 5.5: The quantity of tanks and self-propelled guns in the 2nd Tank Army's formations and their status as of 8.00 on 3 February 1944**

| | Type | On the list | Operational | Under repair: Minor repair | Light overhaul | Major overhaul | Irrecoverable losses Written off | Not yet written off | Transferred to other armies |
|---|---|---|---|---|---|---|---|---|---|
| **3rd Tank Corps** | | | | | | | | | |
| 50th Tank Brigade | T-34 | 65 | 49 | 3 | 6 | – | 7 | – | 65 tanks to 6th Tank Army |
| 51st Tank Brigade | T-34 | 65 | 16 | 2 | 3 | – | 44 | – | 33 tanks to 6th Tank Army |
| 103rd Tank Brigade | T-34 | 74 | 11 | – | 2 | 6 | 55 | – | |
| 744th Motorcycle Battalion | MK-9 | 10 | 6 | 2 | 2 | – | – | – | |
| 411th Signals Battalion | T-34 | 2 | 1 | – | 1 | – | – | – | |
| 1540th Heavy Self-propelled Regiment | KV | 1 | – | 1 | – | – | – | – | |
| | SU-152 | 12 | 7 | – | 4 | 1 | 1 | – | |
| 76mm self-propelled regiment | SU-76 | 21 | 10 | 4 | 1 | 1 | 5 | – | |
| 1818th Self-propelled Regiment | SU-85 | 16 | 5 | 1 | – | – | 10 | – | |
| Altogether for 3rd Tank Corps: | T-34 | 206 | 77 | 5 | 12 | 6 | 106 | – | |
| | MK-9 | 10 | 6 | 2 | 2 | – | – | – | |
| **16th Tank Corps:** 30 tanks transferred to 40th Army | | | | | | | | | |
| 107th Tank Brigade | T-34 | 65 | – | – | – | – | – | – | 65 tanks to 6th Tank Army |
| 109th Tank Brigade | T-34 | 54 | – | – | – | 2 | 19 | – | 33 tanks to 6th Tank Army |
| 164th Tank Brigade | T-34 | 55 | 41 | 3 | 5 | 3 | 3 | – | |
| 689th Signals Battalion | T-34 | 2 | – | – | – | – | – | – | 2 tanks to 6th Tank Army |
| 51st Motorcycle Battalion | MK-9 | 10 | – | – | – | – | – | – | 10 tanks to 6th Tank Army |
| 1542nd Heavy Self-propelled Regiment | SU-152 | 10 | 6 | 1 | 2 | 1 | – | – | |
| 1441st Self-propelled Regiment | SU-85 | 16 | – | – | – | – | – | – | 16 SU to 38th Army |
| 298th Guards Self-propelled Regiment | SU-76 | 21 | – | – | – | – | – | – | 21 SU to 27th Army |
| Altogether for 16th Tank Corps | T-34 | 206 | 41 | 3 | 5 | 5 | 22 | – | 130 |
| | MK-9 | 10 | – | – | – | – | – | – | 10 |
| 11th Guards Tank Brigade | T-34 | 63 | – | – | – | – | 11 | 16 | 36 tanks to 38th Army |
| 9th Signals Regiment | T-34 | 2 | 2 | – | – | – | – | – | |
| 87th Motorcycle Battalion | MK-9 | 10 | 10 | – | – | – | – | – | |
| Total for the Army | T-34 | 477 | 120 | 8 | 17 | 11 | 139 | 16 | 186 |
| | MK-9 | 30 | 16 | 2 | 2 | – | 16 | – | 10 |

Supplies: 3rd Tank Corps combat loads for tanks – 1.5; refills: diesel fuel – 2.1, B-70 – 1.1; Type 2 benzene – 0.6; rations – 3 days

16th Tank Corps combat loads for tanks – 1.5; benzene – 0.5; rations – 4 days.

1st and 2nd Ukrainian Fronts on 28 January 1944 launched a simultaneous concentric attack against the base of the Korsun'-Shevchenkovskii salient and linked up in the area of Zvenigorodka. The headquarters of the German XI and XXXXII Corps, seven infantry and one panzer division, and a motorized brigade, as well as other units and assets wound up in encirclement. This forced the German command to halt the counterattacks east of Vinnitsa and north of Uman', and to commit all of the panzer divisions to the rescue of the encircled forces.

The following assessments can be made regarding the operations of the 2nd Tank Army east of Vinnitsa:

1.  The units of the 2nd Tank Army moved out for the area of combat operations in response to an alert. The march was conducted at night, with no preliminary reconnoitering of the routes and the absence of traffic control measures. Because of the deep snow, movement was restricted to roads alone. The arriving thaw worsened the condition of the roads. Traffic jams collected at the bottom of climbs and the top of descents, which delayed the tempo of movement. Because of the absence of fuel and lubricants at the army supply dumps and the poor condition of the roads, wheeled transport carrying combat equipment and the rear services of the army's units failed to arrive in time in the area of combat operations, and the units were not timely replenished with ammunition, fuel and rations. The army's rear services also couldn't fully support the army's combat operations with materiél because of the lack of motorized transport (the army had only one motorized transport battalion, 35 to 40 percent of the vehicles of which needed repair).
2.  The 2nd Tank Army, engaged in offensive and defensive fighting, drew upon itself a significant portion of the enemy's tanks and infantry, thereby freeing up our units on other sectors of the front to operate actively.
3.  The units of the 2nd Tank Army, located in the Belaia Tserkov' area, were caught in the process of refitting, and the units only moved out for the area of combat operations as soon as they received new materiél. For example, on 25 January 1944, the 3rd Tank Corps in its entirety moved out, conducting its march along a single road, with 197 tanks. Of these, only 181 tanks arrived in the area of combat operations. On this same day, the 164th Tank Brigade of the 16th Tank Corps set off with 54 tanks and 10 SU-152 of the 1542nd Heavy Self-propelled Artillery Regiment. The 11th Guards Tank Brigade departed on the next day with 63 tanks. The 16th Tank Corps' 109th Tank Brigade moved out on 27 January 1944 with 54 tanks, and its 107th Tank Brigade followed on 31 January 1944 with 65 tanks, as well as the 24 tanks designated to reinforce the 109th and 164th Tank Brigades. The army was not fully equipped with motorized transport, so the motorized rifle brigades and the motorized rifle battalions of the tank brigades conducted the march on foot. Despite the fact that the because of the uncoordinated introduction of the army's units into the fighting the 2nd Tank Army couldn't operate as a single fist, the units of the army with their impetuous attack halted the enemy's further advance, forced him to go over to a defense, and gave the 38th Army the opportunity to put itself back into order and to set up a new defense.
4.  In all the combat actions, the enemy employed groups of 15 to 40 tanks, primarily Tigers and Panthers, on a narrow front, and on each occasion before an attack, the Germans would target our tanks with direct fire from a range of 2,000 to 2,500 kilometers before moving out on the attack.
5.  The fighting of the 164th Tank Brigade is characterized by the fact that the brigade was passed from the control of one formation to another three times and conducted maneuvers in front of the enemy in difficult nighttime conditions. Because of this frequent change in command, the brigade headquarters didn't have complete information on the enemy, as a result of which the brigade operated sluggishly, while still suffering large losses.

6.   The 2nd Tank Army's combat operations weren't supported by artillery, since the majority of the artillery pieces were still en route due to the arriving muddy season.

7.   The 2nd Tank Army's units were thrown into the fighting from the march, with no time to arrange cooperation with the infantry or to conduct reconnaissance. As a result of this, on 27 January 1944, the 3rd Tank Corps was late by one hour in going on the attack, and the enemy was able to repel the army's attacks in piecemeal fashion: enemy panzers initially counterattacked the units of the 11th Guards Tank Brigade, and then leaving behind a covering screen in the Ocheretnia sector, these same panzers counterattacked the units of the 3rd Tank Corps.

8.   The enemy, unable to achieve success on the front of the 38th Army, on 4 February 1944 conducted a force regrouping and created a new shock panzer grouping in the Konstantinovka – Rubannyi Most area.

## The operational-tactical situation at the end of 4 February 1944

At the end of January 1944, the forces of the 2nd Ukrainian Front, attacking from Kirovograd toward Zvenigorodka, and the forces of the 1st Ukrainian Front, attacking from Tarashch toward Zvenigorodka, had linked up, thereby encircling a major German grouping in the Korsun'-Shevchenkovskii area consisting (in the 2nd Tank Army's assessment) of ten infantry divisions and one panzer division. With the aim of freeing their encircled forces, the Germans created a shock panzer grouping consisting of the 1st SS Panzer Division *Leibstandarte Adolf Hitler*, the 16th and 17th Panzer Divisions, the 34th Infantry Division and the *Kampgruppe 677*, which consisted of the remnants of the 255th Infantry Division. On 4 February 1944, having created a spearhead of six panzer formations (17th Panzer Division – 15 Pz. IV; Heavy Panzer Regiment *Bäke* – 8 Panthers and 8 Tigers; 16th Panzer Division – 40 Panthers, 26 Pz. IV and 18 StuG; sPzAbt. 506 – 8 Tigers; StuG Abt. 249 – 3 StuG; altogether 126 service tanks and assault guns, with more than 150 tanks of the 1st Panzer and 1st SS Panzer Divisions en route) the Germans launched a counteroffensive from the line Konstantinovka – Rubannyi Most, and having broken through the fronts of the 40th Army and 6th Tank Army, began to exploit the success in the direction of Vinograd, Votylevka and Kosiakovka. By the end of 5 February, they had reached the line: Veselyi Kut – Kosiakovka – Kuchkovka.

In response, the 2nd Tank Army consisting of the 3rd Tank Corps, the 164th Tank Brigade, the 11th Guards Tank Brigade and the 86th Guards Motorized Regiment made a forced march out of the area of Lipovets Station and Oratov, and by 5 February reached the Stanislavchik – Fediukovka – Zatonskoe line with the task to block a further advance by the enemy to the northeast, and subsequently to launch a counterstroke in the direction of Vinograd; by the end of 12 February 1944, the main forces of the 2nd Tank Army were to reach a line extending from the southeastern outskirts of Tynovka, through Pavlovka, to Vinograd, where they were to dig in.

On the night of 4/5 February in the conditions of the fully-arrived muddy season, the 3rd Tank Corps conducted a forced march with only tracked vehicles toward the Zhazhkov area along the route Medovka – Tetiev – Piatigory, but as the main forces reached Piatigory, the corps received a new task: to assemble in the Stanislavchik – Fediukovka area with the 50th, 51st and 103rd Tank Brigades and the attached 164th Tank Brigade by 6 February 1944. The 11th Guards Tank Brigade at 4.00 on 7 February set off along the route Andriushevka – Tetiev – Piatigory, and by 24.00 on 7 February, it had assembled in the Stavishche area.

The 16th Tank Corps was still operationally subordinate to the commander of the 6th Tank Army. Its 107th and 109th Tank Brigades were occupying a defense on the line Hill 217.6 – Hill 241.1 – Repki.

## Details regarding the 2nd Tank Army's March to the Stanislavchik area

Essentially in the course of 24 hours (4 February to 5 February) the 2nd Tank Army made a lateral movement along the front; its tanks covered 120 kilometers in the exceptionally difficult conditions of the spring muddy season. The majority of the infantry, left without motorized transport, conducted the march on foot. Ammunition and fuel supplies were carried on the tanks, since the motorized transport couldn't move even along the main thoroughfares. The army's movement to the new assembly area was conducted along the road that connected Zhivotiv Station with Stanislavchik, passing through Iakimovka, Tetiev, Piatigory, and Stavishche. The road over which the army moved passed through terrain that was cut by numerous brooks and streams. Because of the warm weather that had settled over the area, the surface of the road was thawing and dissolving into mud and the passage of vehicles was creating ruts up to 50 centimeters in depth. Tracked vehicles moved along the road only with great difficulty, especially on climbs. Wheeled vehicles were getting stuck in the mud along the entire route, and could move only in the overnight hours, when the temperatures dropped below freezing. In connection with the dissolution of the roads on the entire extent of the army's march, there was no possibility to put them into trafficable condition. The engineer units were moving on foot, and on the march worked to free bogged down machines and to repair bridges. The 2nd Tank Army (without the 16th Tank Corps) after completing the forced march had a total of 94 serviceable armored vehicles, including 87 T-34, 4 SU-85 and 3 SU-152.

General Radzievsky recalls:

> The situation was demanding the immediate introduction of fresh forces. On 5 February, the 2nd Tank Army, which still hadn't completed refitting, was shifted to the point of the enemy breakthrough. Its formations numbered a little more than 160 operable tanks (excluding the 16th Tank Corps, just 94 tanks and SU self-propelled guns), and the personnel strength of the corps were only 40 to 50 percent of authorized strength. In the conditions of the spring muddy season, it conducted a 120-kilometer forced march and successfully carried out its assigned task. The experience of its employment is a quite instructive example of the rapid maneuver of a tank army with the aim of committing it into battle on a threatened axis. The serious situation at the front demanded the introduction of the army's units and formations into the fighting as each arrived in the new area. In order to give them greater self-sufficiency and to simplify command arrangements, at the decision of the army commander General S.I. Bogdanov, composite detachments were created. The 1st Detachment included command organs and tank platoons of the 11th Guards Tank Brigade (without its rear elements), a self-propelled artillery regiment, and a portion of the artillery of the 3rd Tank Corps (altogether this detachment numbered 19 tanks, 12 self-propelled guns, and 6 guns). The 2nd Detachment consisted of elements of two tank brigades and an artillery regiment that had been directly subordinate to the 2nd Tank Army headquarters (46 tanks and 11 guns).
>
> On 3 February, a detachment consisting of platoons of the motorized rifle brigade and of a tank brigade, along with rear elements of the army, was formed and sent to the 6th Tank Army in order to reinforce it. It received the designation of Colonel Maksimov's combat sector (he was the deputy commander of the 16th Tank Corps). From the cited examples it is clear that the formation of composite detachments was a forced measure and was conducted in the difficult conditions of the operational situation given the presence of limited strength and means in the units and formations due to the losses in the preceding fighting. The aim of creating such detachments was to restore the combat capabilities of the formations, units and elements as self-sufficient tactical units and to improve command and control by means of eliminating intermediate command levels and the formation of new organs of command,

or by resurrecting old organs of command on the basis of those command levels that were capable of resolving their inherent tasks.

The creation of composite detachments in the 2nd Tank Army took place by means of re-subordinating the battalions that had been reconstituted from the brigades to the headquarters of one of the corps' tank brigades. For example, a self-propelled artillery regiment and a number of other elements, which had previously been directly subordinate to the army, were reassigned to the command of the 11th Guards Tank Brigade. It is understandable that this was the simplest and most rapid means of creating headquarters for the combined detachments; however, it wasn't always applicable. On the whole, though, the concrete choice of the method of revitalizing the combat capabilities or of creating new organs of leadership over the composite detachments was determined by the available time, the presence of command units, and the degree of staffing of the headquarters with personnel. In the 2nd Tank Army, the army commander directly controlled all of the composite detachments that had been created in the army without any intervening command links. Firstly, the army commander controlled one composite detachment through an operational command group, which focused on bringing the units that had been pulled out of combat back to order. Secondly, the command and control over the three tank corps was ensured by the rapid and organized transfer of them to subordination to all-arms army commands.

## The combat operations of the 16th Tank Corps over the period from 4 February to 5 February 1944

By mid-day on 4 February 1944, the enemy was occupying Pavlovka and Tynovka, and by the end of the day the main body of the German relief forces had reached Votylevka, while simultaneously up to 60 panzers with tank riders penetrated to the Kuchkovka – Kosiakovka – Veselyi Kut area. In response, the 16th Tank Corps, consisting of the 107th and 109th Tank Brigades was urgently shifted to the area of the enemy breakthrough, with the task to prevent a further German advance to the northeast. By the end of 4 February, the 109th Tank Brigade was occupying a line of defense that stretched from Hill 217.6 to the southwestern outskirts of Petrovskoe, with the exception of one tank battalion on the northern outskirts of Tat'ianovka, which had the task to cut off the enemy tanks that had broken through to the Veselyi Kut – Kuchkovka area. The 107th Tank Brigade by 20.00 on 4 February was occupying a defense along the western and northwestern outskirts of Tat'ianovka.

## The combat of the 107th Tank Brigade for Votylevka

At 2.00 on 5 February, the 107th Tank Brigade went on the attack toward Votylevka with the task to seize that place, and with one tank battalion to seize and hold a defense in the Fediukovka area.

At 4.00 the brigade with two tank battalions broke into Votylevka and seized the northern half of it. At 10.00, the Germans brought up tanks and infantry and launched a counterattack, which pushed back the 107th Tank Brigade to the northwestern outskirts of Tat'ianovka, where the tank brigade's resistance stiffened. In the course of the rest of the day, the 107th Tank Brigade launched repeated fruitless attacks toward Votylevka, and having suffered heavy losses in tanks and personnel, it fell back to its jumping off position. Over the day of fighting, the 107th Tank Brigade lost 26 tanks (12 burned-out, 12 knocked-out, and 2 tanks that threw tracks in Votylevka), and had 75 men killed or wounded. In return, it reported knocking out 8 German tanks, including a Tiger, 3 self-propelled guns, and 5 anti-tank guns of various calibers. In view of the extremely muddy conditions and fog, after throwing the 107th Tank Brigade out of Votylevka, the enemy undertook no further active operations.

## The combat operations of the 3rd Tank Corps on 6 February 1944

On 6 February 1944, the enemy continued its counteroffensive with units of the 1st SS Panzer Division and the 16th Panzer Division with the objective of reaching the Medvin, Shenderovka area. The Germans repeatedly attacked with the forces of 20-25 tanks and up to a battalion of infantry with air support. All of the attacks were beaten back.

The 2nd Tank Army, with its main forces, was assembled in the Stanislavchik – Fediukovka area on 6 February, and entered the battle from the march. The 3rd Tank Corps with the 50th Tank Brigade had the task to attack in the direction of Antonovka and Kosiakovka. At 18.45, after brief German resistance, it seized Veselyi Kut in cooperation with the 164th Tank Brigade and the 10th Guards Rifle Regiment, and with a further advance, it had taken Antonovka by the end of the day. The 51st Tank Brigade in cooperation with the 103rd Tank Brigade and the 263rd Guards Rifle Division went on the attack with 10 tanks at 11.00 toward Tynovka, but having taken that place, the infantry didn't have enough time to finish mopping up the remaining Germans in the village and to dig in, before it was counterattacked by 30 enemy panzers with infantry and air support. The infantry fell back to the jumping-off position, and the 51st Tank Brigade made a fighting withdrawal together with it. At 18.00, the 51st Tank Brigade, now consisting of just 3 tanks, was withdrawn to the Stanislavchik area into the reserve of the 3rd Tank Corps commander, where it remained until 10 February 1944, at which point the tank brigade took up a defense along the southern outskirts of Veselyi Kut. The 103rd Tank Brigade, after its attack toward Tynovka, pulled back to the Stanislavchik area with its 6 serviceable tanks at 19.00 on 6 February, and it remained in the reserve of the corps commander until 9 February 1944.

The document "The Combat Path of the 3rd Tank Corps" offers more details on the fighting to contain the German relief grouping:

> The commander of the 2nd Tank Army made the decision to move out the 3rd Tank Corps together with the 164th Tank Brigade and the 11th Guards Tank Brigade to this area, in order to launch an attack against the enemy salient. Because of the poor condition of the road network, the corps moved out along a single road, with the 50th Tank Brigade in the vanguard. Its forward detachment – 14 tanks of Captain V. Esipenko's battalion with Captain V. Svetlov's motorized battalion of submachine gunners encountered up to two enemy panzer battalions near Antonovka. The detachment got the jump on them in deploying for combat, and opened fire at 40 hostile tanks. From the accurate fire of the tankers and the crews of the anti-tank rifles of Lieutenant M. Lazutkin's platoon, 6 enemy tanks burst into flames. This immediately chilled the attacking ardor of the Nazis. The commander of the 50th Tank Brigade R. Liberman deployed his main forces from the march. The brigade attacked the enemy Panthers at the tip of their penetration, with Major M. Khorol'kov's tank battalion on the right and Major M. Slastennikov's battalion on the left. The energetic actions of staff officers Major P. Glebov and Captain N. Demchenko, who led the battalions to their start lines for the attack along routes they had previously scouted, facilitated the rapid deployment and entry into the fighting of the units.
>
> General A.A. Shashin committed the 51st and 103rd Tank Brigades into the battle in the wake of the vanguard, in order to launch attacks against the flank of the advancing enemy in the general direction of Tynovka. The German panzers and panzer grenadiers began to retreat, leaving behind 9 burned-out combat vehicles, 6 smashed mortars and 4 anti-tank guns on the battlefield. The tankers seized Antonovka. The corps' troops increased the pressure. The commanders of the 51st and 103rd Tank Brigades introduced their second echelons into the fighting. By 4.00 on 8 February 1944, they took possession of Veselyi Kut and Tynovka. On 9 February they occupied Kosiakovka. Captain V. Esipenko's tankers destroyed 16 enemy

tanks, two artillery batteries and one mortar battery, and smashed a battalion of infantry. On this same day, units of the 50th Tank Brigade in cooperation with the 107th Tank Brigade defeated the enemy as well in the Kuchkovka area, destroying 6 tanks, 2 artillery batteries, and several mortars and machine guns; they also captured 11 enemy tanks and self-propelled guns, 8 armored halftracks, 10 trucks and 2 motorcycles, all in good working order.

The enemy tanks, numbering up to 60, which had broken through to the Kuchkovka area, wound up encircled by our units. On 7 February, the enemy began to pull back from the Kuchkovka area to the Votylevka area in order to link back up with the main forces.

At 16.00 on 7 February, up to 13 German panzers, unnoticed by the 107th Tank Brigade, crept up under the cover of fog to the outskirts of Tat'ianovka, and opened concentrated fire from a range of just 100-200 meters at the tanks of the 107th and 109th Tank Brigades; a tank clash erupted. As a result of the action and the lack of adequate leadership on the part of the commander of the 107th Tank Brigade, all of the tanks of the brigades, located in the Tat'ianovka area, were knocked out, while the motorized rifle battalions of the tank brigades retreated to the Petrovkskaia area, where they rallied and took up a defense. In this action, the 107th Tank Brigade lost 4 tanks burned-out or knocked-out, and another 4 tanks that didn't return from an attack, but reported destroying 9 enemy tanks. The 109th Tank Brigade, which was defending Tat'ianovka with 10 tanks, lost 3 tanks burned-out, but reported brewing up 2 enemy tanks and knocking out 2 more. In this combat, the commander of the 109th Tank Brigade's 310th Tank Battalion Major Anatolii Khombakh was killed. The enemy took full possession of Tat'ianovka by midnight on 7 February.

The 3rd Tank Corps, having taken Veselyi Kut and Antonovka, went on the attack toward Kosiakovka at 15.30 on 7 February with the forces of the 50th Tank Brigade and the 3rd Battalion of the 10th Guards Rifle Regiment. Fifteen minutes later, having forced a crossing of the Gniloi Tikich River, the motorized rifle battalion broke into the southwestern outskirts of Kosiakovka, and by dawn on 8 February, the 50th Tank Brigade and motorized riflemen had taken full possession of that place. In the course of 8 February, the 50th Tank Brigade, repelling repeated enemy counterattacks in groups of 12-15 panzers, continued the offensive and by the end of the day it had taken full possession of Kuchkovka. On the morning of 9 February 1944, the 50th Tank Brigade dug in on the southern outskirts of Kuchkovka and began to fortify its positions.

Having taken complete possession of Tat'ianovka, the enemy on the morning of 8 February 1944 began stubbornly and persistently to attack the combat formations of our units, striving to seize Petrovskoe and to emerge in the direction of Medvin.

The 109th Tank Brigade and the remnants of the 107th Tank Brigade were stubbornly continuing to cling to Petrovskoe. Experienced in defensive fighting, the tanks were dug into the ground up to their turrets, and with fire from fixed positions at a range of 500-600 meters, they were shooting up enemy tanks and infantry. In the course of the day, 9 furious enemy counterattacks were repelled. In the course of the fighting, the enemy suffered the following losses: 15 tanks, 5 trucks and 2 armored halftracks destroyed, 4 tanks knocked-out, and up to 200 soldiers and officers killed. Soviet losses were 12 tanks burned-out and 5 tanks knocked-out.

The 164th Tank Brigade, with 27 serviceable tanks, went on the attack on the morning of 8 February toward Votylevskie and Tat'ianovka, and created a semi-ring around the enemy in Votylevka. By 10.00 the brigade was occupying Votylevskie, while attacking with its right flank toward the western outskirts of Tat'ianovka. At 15.00 on 8 February, it was engaged in intense combat on the line: Hill 201.7 – western outskirts of Tat'ianovka. The Germans had created a strongpoint in the Tat'ianovka area, with up to 30-40 tanks and up to a battalion of infantry.

At 15.00 on 9 February, the 164th Tank Brigade with the support of one SU-152 and fire support from the tanks of the 107th and 109th Tank Brigades, launched an attack out of the Petrovskoe area toward Tat'ianovka in cooperation with the 10th Guards Rifle Regiment. The

Germans allowed the tanks to approach within close range, and then brought heavy fire from all types of weapons to bear on the tanks and separated them from the infantry. The Soviet infantry, deprived of tank support, dug in on a line 500 meters northeast of Tat'ianovka. The tanks, now lacking infantry support, were compelled to fall back behind the infantry's combat positions, before being withdrawn to the northern outskirts of Fediukovka after leaving behind an ambush in the area of Hill 243.6. As a result of the vicious combat for Tat'ianovka, the 164th Tank Brigade claimed the following damage to the enemy: 46 tanks, 58 trucks, 3 self-propelled guns and 7 anti-tank guns destroyed or knocked-out of action. The losses of the 164th Tank Brigade were 25 tanks destroyed or knocked-out.

The 11th Guards Tank Brigade arrived in the Tat'ianovka area on 10 February 1944, and having replaced the 10th Guards Rifle Regiment, it took up a defense 1.5 kilometers north of Tat'ianovka with one tank battalion and its motorized rifle battalion. The 1st Tank Battalion moved into defensive positions on the southeastern outskirts of Kuchkovka. The next day, the 11th Guards Tank Brigade launched a fresh attack toward Tat'ianovka, and after overcoming strong enemy fire resistance, it took Tat'ianovka at 15.00 before going over to a defense.

Thus, the 2nd Tank Army, having repulsed numerous enemy attempts to expand the break-through, went on the attack and as a result of heavy fighting, forced the enemy to fall back to the line: Hill 227.0 – Krasnyi – Hill 243.3 – west of Tynovka – Votylevka – Vinograd.

Over the period between 6 February and 10 February 1944, the forces of the 2nd Tank Army inflicted the following damage to the enemy: 103 tanks, of which 16 were Tigers, 6 self-propelled guns and 27 guns of various calibers that were destroyed or knocked-out. Over this same period, the 2nd Tank Army lost 46 tanks burned-out and 36 tanks knocked-out, for a total of 82 tanks. Table 5.6 shows the number of tanks remaining in the formations of the 2nd Tank Army as of 12.00 on 10.2.1944.

With the counterattacks in the period between 7 and 10 February 1944, the forces of the 2nd Tank Army drove the enemy out of Kosiakovka and Kuchkovka, before going over to a stiff defense on the line: Tynovka, Votylevskie, Tat'ianovka, Repki. In doing so, the army had carried out its assignment, which was to prevent the enemy tanks from breaking through to the Petrovskoe area and to make a further advance to the northeast, while inflicting heavy losses in combat equipment and personnel on the Germans. The enemy, employing ground assault aircraft and bombers in

Tanks of the 2nd Tank Army, February 1944 (from the archive of Guards Colonel Vitruk).

groups of 30-40 aircraft systematically pounded the army's combat formations, and with ceaseless attacks by tanks and panzer grenadiers, strove at any cost to break the resistance of the army's units on the Fediukovka – Kuchkovka line. All of the enemy's attempts were fruitless and were broken up by the proper use of tanks and artillery, and the iron resolve, tenaciousness and high discipline of the 2nd Tank Army's soldiers and officers. With the combat operations of the army's forces, the enemy was forced to seek opportunities to attack elsewhere along the line.

Officers of the 2nd Tank Army, with tanks of the 3rd Tank Corps in the background, winter 1944.

Moments later, these same officers have stopped to confer.

**Table 5.6: Data on the availability of tanks in the 2nd Tank Army's formations as of 12.00 on 10 February 1944**

| Formation | Type | Serviceable | Note |
|---|---|---|---|
| **3rd Tank Corps** | | | |
| 50th Tank Brigade | T-34 | 5 | Losses of the 3rd Tank Corps for 8.2.44 – |
| 51st Tank Brigade | T-34 | 7 | T-34: burned out – 10 tanks; knocked out |
| 103rd Tank Brigade | T-34 | 5 | – 10 tanks |
| 164th Tank Brigade | T-34 | 7 | |
| 74th Separate Motorcycle Battalion | MK-9 | 1 | |
| **11th Guards Tank Brigade** | T-34 | 39 | Of which 15 tanks are en route |
| 9th Separate Signals Regiment | T-34 | – | |
| 87th Separate Motorcycle Battalion | MK-9 | 10 | 9 tanks in Piatigory, 1 tank in the reconnaissance squad at Army headquarters |
| Altogether for the 2nd Tank Army | T-34 | 63 | |
| | MK-9 | 11 | |
| **16th Tank Corps** | | Data for 8.2.44 | |
| 107th Tank Brigade | T-34 | 4 | Combat losses – 49 tanks; 6 tanks on the |
| 109th Tank Brigade | T-34 | 10 | march; 5 tanks unserviceable, 1 tank at the disposal of the Deputy Army Commander |

Supplies: 3rd Tank Corps: Ammunition – 0.8 combat loads; fuel and lubricants – 0.7 of a refill; 11th Guards Tank Brigade: ammunition – 1.5 combat loads; diesel fuel – 1.2 refills. No grease or daily rations

[Signed] Chief of the 2nd Tank Army's operations department – Colonel V. Chizh

The 2nd Tank Army based its defenses around tank ambushes, the use of forward detachments, as well as the proper allocation of anti-tank means to cover the likely directions of enemy tank advance. The 2nd Tank Army conducted a march along the front over miserable roads, in rain and a sea of mud. Because of the muck, wheeled transport bogged down en route, creating obstacles that held up the following rear services and towed artillery. Thinned out by the difficult march, the army's forces arrived in the area of the enemy's breakthrough with only its tracked armor and a limited amount of fuel, and without waiting for the rest of the combat vehicles to come up, launched a counteroffensive from the march. Once again, the situation compelled the command to feed each unit into the battle as it arrived.

## The operational-tactical situation by the end of 11 February 1944

The Germans, having been rebuffed with serious losses on the Kuchkovka and Kosiakovka directions in the vain attempt to encircle the Soviet forces surrounding the Korsun' pocket, began to withdraw the tanks of the 16th Panzer Division and the 1st SS Panzer Division to the south to the Vinograd – Tarasovka area on the night of 9/10 February. By the end of 10 February, having regrouped the units of its shock grouping [General Hermann Breith's III Panzer Corps] consisting of the 1st SS Panzer Division *Leibstandarte Adolf Hitler* and the 16th and 17th Panzer Divisions, and having reinforced it with the 1st Panzer Division, the 198th Infantry Division and an artillery regiment from the *Führer* Reserve, the Germans on the morning of 11 February resumed their offensive in the direction of Lisianka with the aim of linking-up with the encircled XI and XXXXII Corps in the Shenderovka area. The III Panzer Corps' attack broke through the front of the 6th Tank Army and by the end of 11 February, the Germans had reached the line: Kammenyi Brod – Buzhanka – southern outskirts of Lisianka – western outskirts of Ganzhalovka. Altogether,

155 combat-ready tanks and assault guns of four panzer and one infantry divisions took part in the offensive (Heavy Panzer Regiment *Bäke* – 10 serviceable Tigers and 16 Panthers, plus another 14 tanks that were undergoing minor repairs and were to be ready for the attack on 11 February; 17th Panzer Division – 1 Pz. III, 4 Pz. IV; 16th Panzer Division – 16 Panthers, 16 Pz. IV, 10 StuG, with 10 attached Pz. IV from the 1st SS Panzer Division; 506th Heavy Panzer Battalion – 2 Tigers; 249th StuG Battalion – 4 StuG; 1st Panzer Division – 18 Pz. IV and 48 Panthers; 1st SS Panzer Division – 3 Pz. IV, 3 Panthers, 1 Tiger and 6 StuG).

At an order from the commander of the 1st Ukrainian Front, the 2nd Tank Army with its main forces again by a forced march with only its tanks and the motorized rifle brigade made a lateral movement along the front, and conducted a 40-kilometer night march in the abysmal road conditions of the muddy season. The motorized rifle battalions of the tank brigades followed as best they could on foot. By this time (11 February 1944), the 2nd Tank Army had 98 T-34, 9 Valentine Mark IX, 3 SU-152 and 4 SU-85, for a total of 114 operational tanks and assault guns. It had 1 combat load of ammunition and 1 refill of diesel fuel. Table 5.7 below shows the status of the 2nd Tank Army's armor as of 9.00 on 11 February 1944, according to report from the 2nd Tank Army's deputy chief of staff Colonel V. Chizh:

Between 17.30 and 18.00 on 12 February, the commanders of the 3rd Tank Corps and the 11th Guards Tank Brigade reported on the current situation to Colonel Chizh over the radio. The 11th Guards Tank Brigade commander Koshaev stated, "The situation is unchanged; the brigade is occupying Lisianka. The enemy is quiet. There are up to a company of German submachine gunners and three Panthers in the southern portion of Lisianka. I have a total of 12 serviceable tanks."

The 3rd Tank Corps commander Shamshin gave a fuller report:

a)  The 50th Tank Brigade is in Dashukovka. At 13.10, repulsing an attack by 27 enemy tanks from the direction of the western outskirts of Kammenyi Brod, the brigade knocked out or brewed up 15 enemy tanks.

b)  The 164th Tank Brigade is in the western portion of Lisianka.

c)  The 51st and 103rd Tank Brigades are in their former area – Veselyi Kut. Without the approval of the army commander, I will not authorize their movement.

d)  The 57th Motorized Rifle Brigade with two battalions is defending along the line: southwestern outskirts of Chesnovka – southern outskirts of Chesnovka – southern outskirts of Dobryden'.

e)  The 1540th Heavy Self-propelled Artillery Regiment – is in its firing positions at the crossroads south of Dobryden'.

f)  The 1818th Self-propelled Artillery Regiment – is in its firing positions at the crossroads south of Chesnovka.

The command post of the 3rd Tank Corps is in Chesnovka. The enemy is conducting heavy shelling and air strikes in the sector Dashukovka, 2 kilometers southwest of Dashukovka. There is sporadic artillery and mortar fire in the Lisianka area. The 136th Rifle Division is arriving on the line of the Gniloi Tikich River from Buzhanka to Vsemirnye. I will withdraw the 164th Tank Brigade into my reserve at the onset of darkness, to the area of Dobryden'.

I request: 1) Subordinate the 11th Guards Tank Brigade to me; and 2) Establish telephone communications.

At 10.00 on 13 February 1944, the 1st Ukrainian Front commander transmitted the following orders to the headquarters of the 2nd Tank Army by high-frequency radio: "The enemy has broken through from the direction of Steblev and is fighting in Khitrovka. Quickly dispatch the 107th or the 109th Tank Brigade to Pochapintsy, having first replenished them. Tell Bogdanov and Kravchenko to send a destroyer anti-tank artillery regiment and self-propelled artillery regiment quickly to Lisianka."

**Table 5.7: Data on the availability of tanks in the 2nd Tank Army's formations as of 9.00 on 11.2.1944**

| | Type | On the list | Operational | Irreplaceable losses | En route Serviceable | En route Non-serviceable | Notes |
|---|---|---|---|---|---|---|---|
| **3rd Tank Corps** | | | | | | | |
| 50th Tank Brigade | T-34 | 65 | 21 | 22 | 10 | 12 | 1 missing in action |
| 51st Tank Brigade | T-34 | 65 | 7 | 48 | 6 | 4 | |
| 103rd Tank Brigade | T-34 | 74 | 5 | 57 | – | 12 | |
| Command | T-34 | 2 | – | – | – | 2 | |
| 744th Motorcycle Battalion | Mk-9 | 10 | 1 | – | – | 9 | |
| 1540th Heavy Self-propelled Artillery Regiment | SU-152 | 12 | 4 | 1 | 7 | – | |
| 1818th Self-propelled Artillery Regiment | SU-85 | 16 | – | 11 | 5 | – | |
| Self-propelled artillery regiment | SU-76 | 21 | – | 3 | 10 | 8 | |
| Total for the 3rd Tank Corps | T-34 | 206 | 33 | 127 | 16 | 30 | |
| | Mk-9 | 10 | 1 | – | – | 9 | |
| **16th Tank Corps** | | | | | | | |
| 107th Tank Brigade | T-34 | 30 | – | – | – | – | Transferred |
| 109th Tank Brigade | T-34 | 65 | – | – | – | – | Transferred |
| 164th Tank Brigade | T-34 | 54 | – | – | – | – | Transferred |
| 689th Signals Battalion | T-34 | 55 | 7 | – | – | – | |
| 51st Motorcycle Battalion | Mk-9 | 10 | – | – | – | – | |
| 1542nd Heavy Self-propelled Artillery Regiment | SU-152 | 10 | 4 | – | – | 6 | Transferred |
| 1441st Self-propelled Artillery Regiment | SU-85 | 16 | 8 | 7 | – | 1 | Transferred |
| Total for the 16th Tank Corps: | T-34 | 206 | 7 | – | – | – | |
| | Mk-9 | 10 | – | – | – | – | |
| **11th Guards Tank Brigade** | T-34 | 65 | 25 | 26 | 8 | 6 | |
| 9th Signals Regiment | T-34 | 2 | – | – | – | 2 | |
| 87th Motorcycle Battalion | Mk-9 | 10 | 1 | – | 9 | – | |
| Total for the 2nd Tank Army | T-34 | 479 | 65 | | | | |
| | Mk-9 | 30 | 2 | | | | |

Supplies: 3rd TC – 1 combat load for tanks; 1 refill of fuel and lubricants; no daily rations. 11th Guards Tank Brigade – 1.5 combat load for tanks; 1 refill of fuel and lubricants; no daily rations.

The order was carried out: At 10.40 on 13 February, Colonel Chizh passed down the order over the telephone to Koval', the chief of the 16th Tank Corps headquarters' Operations Department:

> Assemble the 109th Tank Brigade in Pochapintsy, and bring up the remaining 107th and 164th Tank Brigades and prepare them for use on this same axis. Conduct reconnaissance in the direction of Komarovka. Deploy the tanks of the 109th Tank Brigade on the eastern outskirts of Pochapintsy, along the brook, having first taken possession of the road hub. The 754th Self-propelled Artillery Regiment, with four SU-85, is now located in Veselyi Kut; it has been ordered to move out along the route Krasnogorodka – Medvin and to re-assemble in Lisianka by 20.00 on 13.2.44, where it will come under the operational control of the 3rd Tank Corps commander. The regiment in Veselyi Kut is currently without fuel. On the basis of Comrade Nikolaev's directions, I have sent an officer and given an order to the commander of the 3rd Tank Corps for the 51st and 103rd Tank Brigades to be quickly removed and led to Chesnovka, where they are to come under his operational control. The 999th Self-propelled Artillery Regiment, consisting of eight SU-76s and presently located in Dolgaia Greblia, was ordered at 12.30 on 13.2.44 to move out along the route Krasnogorodka – Medvin – Chesnovka, where it was to assemble by 14.00. The regiment commander is to report to the commander of the 3rd Tank Corps for further instructions.
>
> [Signed] 2nd Tank Army Chief of Staff – Guards Major General A. Pavlov; 2nd Tank Army Chief of Operations – Colonel V. Chizh

## The combat operations of the 2nd Tank Army in the area of Dashukovka, Chesnovka and Lisianka

The 2nd Tank Army arrived in the area of the new enemy breakthrough, and after taking position in the Dashukovka – Chesnovka area it had the task to prevent a further German advance to the northeast, toward Frankovka and Lisianka. By 15.00 on 12 February, the 3rd Tank Corps was occupying a line of defense running from the southwestern outskirts of Dashukovka to Hill 285.7. By 10.00 on 13 February, the 16th Tank Corps was defending the line: Brodok – Pisarevka – Khizhentsy. The 11th Guards Tank Brigade was continuing to occupy defensive positions in the area of Tat'ianovka.

At 10.30 on 12 February, the enemy in strength of up to an infantry regiment and 45 tanks, primarily Tigers and self-propelled guns, and with powerful air support from 50-70 JU-87 dive bombers, resumed the attacks toward Chesnovka, Dobryden' and Khizhentsy. The units of the 2nd Tank Army, offering stubborn resistance to the attacking Germans, continued to hold the lines they occupied. The enemy introduced fresh panzer reserves into the fighting, and with increased air strikes and an outflanking maneuver, threatened to isolate the 50th Tank Brigade in Dashukovka. The tank brigade, fighting tenaciously and suffering losses, abandoned Dashukovka and fell back in the direction of Pisarevka, where its remnants (1 tank and 6-7 riflemen) became part of the 103rd Tank Brigade.

Having seized Dashukovka, the enemy attacked toward Chesnovka, where the 57th Motorized Rifle Brigade was defending. Once again using an outflanking maneuver, and having seized Hill 241.5, the Germans broke into the southern outskirts of Chesnovka. Enemy tanks and infantry infiltrated into the western outskirts of Chesnovka and to the church, and with their actions pinned down the 57th Motorized Rifle Brigade. At 18.00, the defenders abandoned Chesnovka and also began to retreat to the north toward Pisarevka.

The 164th Tank Brigade, unable to withstand the enemy onslaught in the Lisianka area, retreated toward Khizhentsy, having abandoned Dobryden', although other units of the 2nd Tank Army, including the 11th Guards Tank Brigade, continued to remain in Lisianka itself. Rolling onward, at 20.00 the Germans seized the southern outskirts of Khizhentsy with a force of 12 panzers and a company of submachine gunners. At the same time, the 50th and 103rd Tank Brigades arrived in the Pisarevka area, whereupon the 51st Tank Brigade, having handed over its remaining tanks and motorized infantry to the 103rd Tank Brigade, set off toward Medvin. The 3rd Tank Corps commander now had operational control over the 109th, 110th, 181st and 237th Tank Brigades and the 136th Rifle Division, each numbering 1-5 tanks and up to 250 active bayonets.

According to German sources, on 12 February 1944 units of Heavy Panzer Regiment *Bäke*, consisting of three Tigers and four Panthers, attacked the hill east of Dashukovka in a dense fog. After the German panzers passed over several small mounds, they ran into the heavy fire of Russian tanks and anti-tank guns, which were positioned on the defense. Four Panthers took hits and burst into flames. The Tigers took heavy damage, and close to being written off, they were evacuated to Potash Station.

At midnight on 14 February, the deputy commander of the 2nd Tank Army for vehicle maintenance and technical support sent the following message to the commanders of the 3rd and 16th Tank Corps:

> The command has ordered: The 21 tanks arriving in the army as replenishments are all to be given to the 51st Tank Brigade. The 103rd Tank Brigade is to turn over 5 tanks and its motorized infantry to the 50th Tank Brigade as replenishments. The 9 serviceable tanks, the 5 tanks located under repair and the motorized infantry of the 107th Tank Brigade are to be turned over to the 109th Tank Brigade. The 103rd and 107th Tank Brigades are to be withdrawn to the Luka area for re-forming and re-fitting. The commander of the 16th Tank Corps is to conduct the replacement of the 107th Tank Brigade and the handover of its sector of defense no later than 21.00 on 15.2.1944. Report on the execution.
> Chief of staff of the 2nd Tank Army – General Pavlov

## The withdrawal of the 2nd Tank Army to the line Pisarevka, Khizhentsy, Dzhurzhentsy, Oktiabr'

The day of 15 February 1944 saw intense, see-saw fighting between the 2nd Tank Army and the III Panzer Corps in the Dashukovka – Chesnovka – Dobryden' – Lisianka area. By this time, the enemy had committed the 16th Panzer Division (numbering 80-90 tanks), the 1st Panzer Division, the 1st SS Panzer Division (numbering 60-80 tanks), Heavy Panzer Regiment *Bäke*, the 506th Heavy Panzer Battalion, and an assault gun battalion to the operation to free the encircled XI and XXXXII Corps. Thus, the total number of German tanks and self-propelled guns in this area, in the estimate of the 2nd Tank Army's command, reached 250-300.

On 15 February 1944, the 16th Tank Corps launched a fresh attack toward Chesnovka and Dobryden', and seized Chesnovka at 9.00 after a fierce tank versus tank combat. The Germans quickly organized a counterattack with the forces of a panzer grenadier regiment and 28 tanks with strong air support. Bitter fighting developed once again in this area, and our units repelled repeated enemy attacks, but at 14.30, after committing another 20 tanks and a panzer grenadier battalion into the fighting, Chesnovka changed hands yet again. Simultaneously, the Germans repeatedly attacked Lisianka with up to a panzer grenadier battalion and 45 tanks with air support. By the end of the day, after paying a high cost in men and armor, they took full possession of Lisianka, leaving them within a dozen kilometers of Shenderovka and the encircled *Gruppe Stemmermann*. The enemy also launched repeated attacks, committing up to a panzer grenadier battalion and

30-35 tanks with the support of up to 40 strike aircraft, and took Oktiabr' by the end of the day, though units of the 2nd Tank Army continued to cling to the northern outskirts of it. As a result of the day's fighting, the 2nd Tank Army had abandoned Dashukovka, Chesnovka and Lisianka, and had fallen back to the line Pisarevka – Khizhentsy – Dzhurzhentsy – Oktiabr', but still stood between the relief grouping and the encircled grouping.

There is a document in the archives about the artillery units of the 2nd Tank Army and their condition on 15 February 1944. This document reveals how little artillery support the 2nd Tank Army's units were receiving at the time:

> The **3rd Tank Corps**: 234th Army Mortar Regiment – 31 120mm mortars (25 on the approach, 6 in their firing positions) and 8 SU-76 (all non-serviceable and en route); the 1540th Self-propelled Artillery Regiment: 3 SU-152, of which 2 are en route and one is non-serviceable; the 1818th Self-propelled Artillery Regiment is without any SU-85 assault guns; the 121st Anti-aircraft Artillery Regiment: 16 guns, all en route; the 728th Separate Destroyer Anti-tank Battalion: 11 85mm guns, all en route; the 126th Separate Guards Mortar Battalion: 8 M-13 rocket launchers, all en route without fuel; the artillery battalions of the 15th Motorized Rifle Brigade: 12 76mm guns, all en route. The **16th Tank Corps**: 1542nd Heavy Self-propelled Artillery Regiment: three SU-152, non-serviceable and en route; the 1441st Heavy Self-propelled Artillery Regiment: three SU-85 in their firing positions; the 226th Army Mortar Regiment: 35 120mm mortars, 17 of which are in their firing positions; the 1721st Anti-aircraft Artillery Regiment: 16 37mm guns, all en route; the 1729th Destroyer Anti-tank Artillery Regiment: 11 85mm guns, en route but not operational; the 89th Separate Guards Mortar Battalion: 8 M-13 rocket launchers, en route; the 298th Self-propelled Artillery Regiment: 12 SU-76, all in firing positions; the 1548th Self-propelled Artillery Regiment: 3 SU-76, 2 SU-85, all in firing positions; the 999th Self-propelled Artillery Regiment: 21 SU-76, 7 of which are in their firing positions, the remaining are under repair en route; the 754th Self-propelled Artillery Regiment: 9 SU-85, 3 of which in firing positions, 6 of which are en route; the 86th Guards Mortar Regiment: 19 M-13 rocket launchers, all in their firing positions and 5 under repair; the 1219th Self-propelled Artillery Regiment: 2 SU-85 in firing positions.

In order to reinforce the battered tank formations of the 2nd Tank Army in their critical position standing between the German relief grouping and the encircled forces, on 16 February the 1st Ukrainian Front command assigned the 13th Guards Heavy Tank Regiment, equipped with the new IS-2 heavy tanks, to it.

At 18.20 on 15 February, General Bogdanov sent messages to the commanders of the 3rd and 16th Corps, ordering them to pinch off the salient that the III Panzer Corps had created toward the encircled XI and XXXXII Corps by midnight:

> To the 3rd Tank Corps Commander:
> By the end of 15.2.44, the Corps is to seize Hill 241.4, Hill 239.8 [a commanding height astride the eventual breakout route of *Gruppe Stemmermann*] and Dobryden' ... [illegible] ... Subsequently take Hill 216.7, northwestern outskirts of Lisianka, and by 24.00 is to reach the Gniloi Tikich River with a forward detachment. Cut the road between Buzhanka and Lisianka. The tanks must advance with infantry escort, and have sappers with mine detectors with the tanks. Don't move along the roads, in order not to trigger mines.
> [Signed] Bogdanov, 18.20, 15.2.1944

To the 16th Tank Corps commander:

By the end of 15.2.44, the Corps is to seize Chesnovka, followed by Dashukovka and Hill 235.8, and by 24.00 it is to reach the Gniloi Tikich River with forward detachments. Have strong forward detachments on the Gniloi Tikich River in the Kammenyi Brod area (north-western and southwestern outskirts). Conduct reconnaissance in the directions of Kammenyi Brod, western outskirts of Buzhanka, and Bosovka. The tanks must advance with infantry escort, and have sappers with mine detectors with the tanks. Don't move along the roads, in order not to trigger mines. The 3rd Tank Corps is attacking to the left of Dobryden', Hill 216.7.

[Signed] Bogdanov

To the commander of the 57th Motorized Rifle Brigade:

[Copies to the commanders of the 16th Tank Corps and 3rd Tank Corps]

1.  The commander of the 57th Motorized Rifle Brigade by 12.00 on 16.2.44 is to turn over its combat sector to the 16th Tank Corps, and by 16.00 16.2.44, following the route Khizhentsy – Dzhurzhentsy, it is to assemble in Oktiabr', where it will come under the control of the commander of the 3rd Tank Corps.
2.  The commander of the 16th Tank Corps is to ensure the occupation of the combat sector within the designated time period.

[Signed] Commander of the 2nd Tank Army Guards Lieutenant General of Tank Forces Bogdanov

[Transmitted over the telephone to Comrade Shamardin (the commander of the 57th Motorized Rifle Brigade at 10.00 on 16 February 1944 and to Comrade Dubovoi (the commander of the 16th Tank Corps at 10.15 on 16 February 1944.]

This was followed by a message from the deputy chief of staff of the 2nd Tank Army Colonel Chizh to the commander of the 16th Tank Corps:

On the basis of a Message No.4981 from the chief of staff of the 1st Ukrainian Front, the commander of the 2nd Tank Army is ordered:

1.  To withdraw the 1542nd Heavy Self-propelled Regiment, without its tanks and self-propelled guns, to Nara Station for refitting, but with all of its personnel, motorized transport, weapons and property, subtracting nothing before departure.
2.  All tanks and self-propelled guns are to be turned over to the 1441st Self-propelled Artillery Regiment.
3.  Provide the departing regiment with 1 refill of fuel and 15 days of rations.
4.  Load the regiment and send it out from Belaia Tserkov' Station on 19.2.44.
5.  Report on the execution.

[Signed] Deputy chief of staff of the 2nd Tank Army Colonel Chizh

The next day again saw savage see-saw fighting. The Germans launched numerous bitter attacks with up to a panzer grenadier regiment and 70 tanks, accompanied by systematic strikes from the air, striving to take Dzhurzhentsy and the key Hill 239. By the end of 16 February, the Germans were holding Vinograd and Kammenyi Brod with the 17th Panzer Division; Chesnovka with the 16th Panzer Division and an assault gun battalion; and Dobryden', Lisianka and Budushche with the 1st Panzer Division, 1st SS Panzer Division *Leibstandarte Adolf Hitler*, Heavy Panzer Regiment *Bäke* and the 506th Heavy Panzer Battalion. According to captured prisoners from the German 57th, 72nd, 88th, 112th, 167th, 168th, 332nd and 389th Infantry Divisions; the 213th Security Division; the 5th SS Panzer Division *Wiking* and the SS Brigade *Wallonia*; and the 1st Panzer and

16th Panzer Divisions, it was established that the III Panzer Corps was attacking in the Lisianka – Oktiabr' – Chesnovka area, striving to link up with the encircled *Gruppe Stemmermann* in the Shenderovka area at whatever the cost, and to hold open an exit corridor for them. At this same time, the encircled Germans in the Shenderovka area had created a breakout group consisting of the 5th SS Panzer Division *Wiking*, and the 72nd and 112th Infantry Divisions, with the task to launch a decisive breakout attack on the morning of 17 February from the Khil'ki, Komarovka line in the directions of Dzhurzhentsy, Pochapintsy and Lisianka, with the aim of linking up with the shock panzer grouping in the Oktiabr', Lisianka area.

### The fighting in the Shenderovka area to destroy the remnants of the encircled grouping

At 23.00 on 16 February, *Gruppe Stemmermann* launched its breakout attempt. Initially, taking advantage of stealth and the hours of darkness, the vanguard, consisting of men of the 115th Infantry Regiment, were able to slip through the positions of the 27th Army, which was holding the inner ring of encirclement, and subsequently the positions of the 2nd Tank Army as well. As the Soviets became alert and the sun rose, however, the following waves of the XI and XXXXII Corps had less luck.

At 4.00 on 17 February 1944, the III Panzer Corps resumed its attacks toward Hill 239 and Dzhurzhentsy out of the Lisianka – Oktiabr' area. Attacking in groups of a panzer grenadier regiment and 30-40 tanks each, the relief grouping was desperately striving to clear a path of withdrawal for the encircled grouping. Meanwhile, the breakout group's assault columns had attacked out of the Khil'ki – Komarovka area, and had broken through the defenses of the 27th Army and were advancing to meet the German relief grouping.

The 2nd Tank Army, locked in combat with the 1st, 1st SS and 16th Panzer Divisions and the Heavy Panzer Regiment *Bäke* in the Oktiabr' – Dzhurzhentsy area, left part of its forces in their occupied defensive lines to repel the enemy relief attacks and conducted a regrouping with its main forces. Having done so, at 8.00 on 17 February the army launched an attack toward Pochapintsy and Komarovka to break up the follow-on waves of Germans seeking to escape the pocket that had breached the 27th Army's line. With this accomplished, the 2nd Tank Army together with the 5th Guards Cavalry Corps turned to the task of destroying the enemy's encircled forces, exacting a fearsome toll from those that were attempting to escape.

In the sector of the 16th Tank Corps, the enemy was moving to break out in detachments of 500-600 men with horse-drawn carts and vehicles. The breakout attempt was made with wild firing and shouts of "Urah!" – designed to induce panic in our units. The majority of the encircled men were unarmed.

From organized tank ambush positions, units of the 16th Tank Corps shot up the German column striving to come out of the encirclement. The enemy, having encountered the organized resistance, scattered through the balkas and ravines, and began to flee to the south and southwest in disorder.

Meanwhile, the 3rd Tank Corps, having adopted an all-round defense and set up tank ambushes in the Dzhurzhentsy – Oktiabr' area, was blocking the main breakout attempt made by the *Gruppe Stemmermann*. At 4.20 on 17 February, the enemy penetrated the corps' defenses, but the advance of his columns was stopped with organized fire, and by 10.00 the Germans were thrown back into the open steppe, where the destruction of the enemy's desperate men continued with fire and tracks. Despite their advantage in numbers, the German seeking to escape the pocket had dissolved into a frenzied mob, seeking to avoid death.

The men of the encircled enemy grouping, seeing their hopeless situation and almost certain deaths, at 5.00 surged toward Petrovskoe in a disorganized mob of 10,000 men. Having been repulsed by our units, the enemy returned to Khil'ki, after which at 6.30, again in a disorganized mass, they pushed toward Komarovka. Here, too, they ran into scathing fire, so they fell back again to Khil'ki. At 7.30, screened by tanks and the local population, the encircled Germans began to push to the south and southwest, between Petrovskoe and Komarovka. At 9.00, tanks of a combat group of the 11th Guards Tank Brigade sliced through the enemy column of 10,000 men, shooting them up at pointblank range with guns and machine guns and crushing enemy troops and materiél under their treads. In the hours between 9.00 and 12.00 on 17 February, the tanks of the brigade roamed freely through the enemy mob, inflicting great damage to it. By 12.00, running short of fuel and ammunition, the tanks were compelled to halt 500 meters to the northwest of Komarovka, where with fire from place they continued to kill the enemy with their remaining shells. By 14.00, the entire field in the area of Komarovka, Khil'ki and Petrovskoe was strewn with enemy corpses, smashed transport and abandoned equipment. Surviving groups of Germans scattered through the gullies and ravines and continued to make their way out of encirclement.

At 7.00 the III Panzer Corps launched an attack in regiment strength out of the Chesnovka – Oktiabr' area toward Pochapintsy. With an outflanking maneuver from the north, it strove to break through to the encircled grouping. Tanks of a second combat group of the 11th Guards Tank Brigade, defending on the western outskirts of Pochapintsy, stubbornly held their occupied positions, inflicting great damage to the enemy. Fighting stubbornly, with fuel and ammunition running low, the tanks fell back to the eastern outskirts of Pochapintsy. Upon entering the northern portion of Pochapintsy, the enemy became disorganized. The commander of the 11th Guards Tank Brigade's 2nd Tank Battalion Guards Captain Ushakov, noticing the opportunity, drove the enemy back out of Pochapintsy and took up a defense along its northwestern outskirts, seizing many prisoners in the process. Observing an enemy mob on the southern fringe of a patch of woods lying 2 kilometers north of Pochapintsy, and having gathered fuel and ammunition from all the tanks in order to resupply two tanks, he attacked the enemy with them. The tanks lunged into the disorganized enemy, isolated them, and with fire and tracks destroyed the foe.

On 18 February 1944, a strong snowstorm swept in, which quickly rendered the roads impassable. In the pre-dawn hours, the 2nd Tank Army, now with 81 T-34 and 19 SU-85, sent forward detachments in the direction of Dashukovka and Chesnovka, in the effort to take those places, and made a reconnaissance in force toward Oktiabr' and Lisianka. The III Panzer Corps put up strong resistance against our forward detachments in the Dashukovka – Chesnovka sector. At 3.00, after a sharp clash, the enemy was driven out of the northern portion of Dashukovka, but regained full possession of that place with a counterattack. The enemy also placed heavy fire on our reconnaissance probes in the direction of Oktiabr' and Lisianka.

Meanwhile, German groups in strength of 1-2 infantry battalions continued to seek to break out of the area of a ravine north of Pochapintsy in the direction of Oktiabr'. The main forces of the 2nd Tank Army continued to mop up encircled remnants of *Gruppe Stemmermann*. The slaughter continued throughout 17 and 18 February 1944. As a result, the units of the 3rd Tank Corps smashed the enemy's XI and XXXXII Corps, and in the process claimed the destruction of 12 tanks, 36 guns of various calibers, 107 trucks, 846 supply wagons along with their loads, and 8,110 enemy soldiers and officers. The 16th Tank Corps claimed the destruction of 4 self-propelled guns, 4 tanks, 9 armored halftracks, 15 guns of various calibers, 300 supply wagons along with their loads, 11 machine guns, and 4,150 enemy soldiers and officers.

In the course of the three days of combat, the 2nd Tank Army claimed the following damage to the enemy: 10,650 soldiers and officers killed and 1,518 taken prisoner; 137 tanks, self-propelled guns and halftracks; 78 guns of various calibers; and the destruction of a lot of other arms and materiél. The process of mopping up remnants of the 57th, 72nd, 88th, 112th, 167th, 168th, 332nd and 389th Infantry Divisions and the 213th Security Division was completed, and the SS Panzer Division *Wiking* and the SS Brigade *Wallonia* were smashed.

After the heavy fighting and frequent reshuffling of forces, the chief of staff of the 2nd Tank Army summarized the current dispositions of the tank brigades and the number of operational tanks still present in each:

> Pisarevka area: Hill 223.8 – the 107th Tank Brigade with 9 T-34 tanks; Pisarevka – 237th Tank Brigade with 7 T-34 tanks. Khizhentsy area: 109th Motorized Rifle Battalion and the 164th Tank Brigade with 12 T-34 tanks; the 87th Separate Motorcycle Battalion – 5 Valentine Mark IX tanks; 237th Tank Brigade [a combat group of the tank brigade] – 5 T-34 tanks.
>
> Dzhurzhentsy area: 103rd Tank Brigade with 14 T-34 tanks; the 13th Guards Heavy Tank Regiment with 19 IS tanks. Wooded area east of Oktiabr' and Hill 239: 50th Tank Brigade, 51st Tank Brigade and 109th Tank Brigade with a total of 42 T-34 tanks. Pochapintsy area: [combat group of the] 11th Guards Tank Brigade – 5 T-34 tanks. Komarovka area: 9 T-34 tanks.
> [Signed] Chief of staff of the 2nd Tank Army Major General A. Pavlov

On the same day, the deputy chief of the Operations Department Major Bulanov gave an account of the operational tanks remaining in the 2nd Tank Army as of 7.00: 18 tanks in the 16th Tank Corps; 34 T-34 and 1 Valentine Mark IX in the 3rd Tank Corps; 19 IS tanks in the 13th Guards Heavy Tank Regiment; 14 T-34 tanks in the 11th Guards Tank Brigade; and 5 Valentine Mark IX in the 87th Separate Motorcycle Battalion for a total of 103 operational tanks.

## The 2nd Tank Army's counteroffensive against the German shock panzer grouping and the emergence of the Army's forces on the Bosovka – Iablonovka – Tikhonovka Line

The enemy, having suffered heavy losses in tanks and having done all it could to breakthrough to the encircled grouping, which by this time had been essentially destroyed, withdrew to the Dashukovka – Sergienko area, leaving behind covering tank screens. At 10.00 on 19 February 1944, the forces of the 2nd Tank Army went on the offensive toward Chesnovka, Hill 235.8, Buzhanka, Oktiabr', Lisianka and Zhabinka. The 16th Tank Corps, having broken the enemy's resistance with a concentric attack, took full possession of Chesnovka. Continuing to advance, units of this corps by 18.00 on 20 February seized Dashukovka and Sergienko, before digging in on their southern outskirts. The enemy, trying to regain its advantageous positions in the Dmitrovka area with the aim of withdrawing his units to the southern bank of the Gniloi Tikich River, launched repeated counterattacks in groups of 12-14 tanks, but each time, having suffered large losses, fell back to the jumping-off position.

Having reached a critical situation with the supply of fuel and lubricants after the fruitless counterattacks, the enemy began to fall back to the south and southwest, leaving behind a lot of wrecked and disabled equipment. At 3.00 on 21 February, the 2nd Tank Army sent forward two mobile detachments in order to pursue the enemy and to seize crossings over the Gniloi Tikich River. The Germans were caught by surprise by the night attacks, and by sunrise on 21 February, a forward detachment of the 164th Tank Brigade had taken possession of the northern outskirts of Buzhanka.

The enemy continued to offer tough resistance, clinging to advantageous lines and the water obstacle of the Gniloi Tikich River, and was stubbornly defending the southern portion of Buzhanka and Frankovka. After a fresh attack by units of the 16th Tank Corps, the Germans made a fighting withdrawal, suffering losses, and units of the tank corps seized all of Buzhanka and reached the southwestern outskirts of Frankovka by 10.30 on 21 February. The enemy, continuing to retreat to the southwest, strove to check the Soviet offensive in the Bosovka area and in a ravine south of it, having fortified this line and set up tank ambushes. Simultaneously, the Germans were conducting mortar and artillery fire out of the Vishnevka – Stepok area. Units of the 16th Tank Corps, continuing to advance, on the morning of 23 February broke into Bosovka and became tied up in street fighting. However, with a simultaneous attack from three directions, they cleared Bosovka of Germans and took possession of the place by 13.00 on 23 February 1944.

The 3rd Tank Corps with the units currently operationally subordinate to it – the 109th Tank Brigade, the 13th and 8th Guards Heavy Tank Regiments, the 27th Guards Motorized Rifle Brigade and the 136th Rifle Division – covered by units of the 160th Fortified District also went on the offensive. At the moment of the attack, the motorized rifle brigades were down to only 10-15 percent of their authorized strength, and the tank brigades had just 5-10 operational tanks each. In the course of 19 February, units of the 3rd Tank Corps were engaged in savage fighting with the enemy, but by 17.00 they had taken complete possession of Oktiabr'. Continuing the offensive, after a nighttime attack and bitter street fighting, the corps by 8.00 on 20 February took Lisianka.

The document "The Combat Path of the 2nd Tank Army" records:

> The fighting was bitter. The 3rd Tank Corps in the course of the day [19 February] tried to drive the Germans out of Lisianka three times, but had no success. Then the corps commander accepted the proposal of the commander of the 57th Motorized Rifle Brigade Colonel Shamardin to attack the hostile units in the Lisianka area at night. At one o'clock in the morning, the 57th Motorized Rifle Brigade broke into Lisianka without any artillery preparation, and by dawn it had taken full possession of this settlement. The attack was a surprise to the Germans. They fled from Lisianka in panic, leaving behind several serviceable tanks, trucks, artillery guns and a lot of other combat gear.

The combat journal of the 3rd Tank Corps observes:

> On 19 February 1944 at the order of the commander of the 2nd Tank Army, the corps' troops went on the offensive in a general direction toward Bosovka and Iablonovka. They retook Lisianka again. In this action, the commander of the 57th Motorized Rifle Brigade Lieutenant Colonel Pavel Shamardin demonstrated high command qualities. An opponent of conventional actions, he proposed to take the important node of resistance – Lisianka – with a surprise night attack without any artillery preparation. The corps commander Shamshin approved his proposal. The chief of staff Lieutenant Colonel Aleksandrin organized a reconnaissance of the enemy, arranged recognition signals in nighttime conditions, worked out a schedule of supporting fire, and established combat supply measures. After a detailed reconnaissance of the approaches to Lisianka, Lieutenant Colonel Shamardin gave each element an attack objective, and a sequence and timetable of mutual actions. Routes were determined for the movement of the elements into their jumping-off positions for the attack. Under the cover of darkness, the elements stealthily took up their jumping-off positions. At the established time, they suddenly and decisively attacked the enemy. The Nazis began to retreat. Many of them were killed, and 2,500 soldiers and officers surrendered. Several tanks were captured.
>
> At 9.30 on 21 February 1944, General Bogdanov issued an order to the 11th Guards Tank Brigade:
> 1. The enemy is defending the southern portion of Buzhanka.
> 2. The 11th Guards Tank Brigade from 11.30 21.2.44 is to move along the route Khizhentsy, Chesnovka and is to assemble in Dashukovka, in readiness to repel enemy counterattacks from the south.
>
> [Signed] Commander of the 2nd Tank Army Lieutenant General Bogdanov
> [Transmitted over the radio at 9.45 21.2.44]

An after-action report described the initial performance of the new heavy tank regiments:

> In February 1944, the breakthrough regiments present in the Red Army, which were equipped with KV tanks, were switched to new tables of organization and equipment. Simultaneously new units equipped with IS machines began to form, which began to be called "heavy tank regiments". At the same time, even during their process of forming up, they acquired the "Guards" title. According to their TO&E, the new regiments numbered 375 men and had four IS tank companies (21 tanks), a company of submachine gunners, a vehicle maintenance and technical support company, an anti-aircraft battery, sapper and administrative platoons, and a regimental medical post. The first two Guards heavy tank regiments of the new TO&E, the 8th and 13th, joined the 2nd Tank Army. The 13th Guards Heavy Tank Regiment was one of the first to enter combat. On 15 February 1944 it arrived in the Fastov – Belaia Tserkov' area with 21 IS-85 tanks [IS-1 heavy tanks equipped with the 85mm gun, the production of which had ended in January 1944]. After a march, the regiment received the task to support the attack of the 109th Tank Brigade toward the village of Lisianka, for which purpose a company of five IS tanks was detached by the regiment commander. On 19 February 1944 at 11.00, the tank company of the 13th Guards Heavy Tank Regiment consisting of five IS-85 tanks was moved out to support the 109th Tank Brigade, which was attacking the enemy strongpoint in Lisianka. At the moment of the tanks introduction into combat, T-34 tanks that were taking part in the 109th Tank Brigade's attack had already been knocked out by the fire of Panthers, which were positioned on the northeastern outskirts of Lisianka. This circumstance allowed the Germans to concentrate fire on the IS-85, having allowed them to approach to a range of 600-800 meters. As a result, two IS tanks erupted in flames, and the other three were knocked out. The entire day of 19 February, the enemy fought to hold their forward edge in Lisianka, but retreated that night, having left behind 21 combat vehicles (16 Panthers, 3 Pz IV and 2 StuG III), some of which were blown up, and some of which were totally serviceable, but without fuel.

In the course of 20 February 1944, the enemy offered stubborn resistance with the remnants of the 1st SS Panzer Division *Leibstandarte Adolf Hitler* in the Buzhanka – Zhabinka area. By the end of 21 February, having crossed the Gniloi Tikich River over the rebuilt bridge in Lisianka, the 3rd Tank Corps seized Zhabinka. Having taken Tikhonovka and having mopped up Iablonovka on 22 February, the corps by 24 February was digging into the lines it had achieved. With the emergence of the units of the 2nd Tank Army on the line Bosovka – Iablonovka – Tikhonovka, the position held by the 6th Tank Army prior to the German relief attack had been fully re-established. At the order of the commander of the 1st Ukrainian Front, the army went over to the defense on the line: southwestern and southern outskirts of Bosovka – Hill 244.7 (1 kilometer south of Iablonovka) – southern outskirts of Tikhonovka.

On 24 February 1944, the 11th Guards Tank Brigade went on the attack out of the Vodianiki area at 7.30 in the direction of Ryzhanovka. By 8.30, the brigade reached the eastern bank of a nameless stream in the center of Ryzhanovka. There, as a result of the lagging behind of the infantry of the 2nd Guards Airborne Division, the brigade lost 5 tanks that were knocked out by German troops equipped with Panzerschrecks. During the attack, the 11th Guards Tank Brigade in return destroyed 4 German tanks and 6 guns, and killed 100 enemy soldiers and officers. At 20.00 on 24 February, the 11th Guards Tank Brigade had 31 T-34 tanks on its list, of which 20 were operational, 1 was undergoing minor repairs, 4 were undergoing light overhauls, 1 was undergoing a major overhaul, plus the 5 tanks that were lost that day, but weren't written off as irrecoverable losses (they had been successfully evacuated).

As a result of the fighting between 27 January and 17 February, the 11th Guards Tank Brigade's 1st Tank Battalion lost 4 tanks (the battalion commander's crew was killed at Ocheretnia; tank commander Gorbunov and 3 men of his crew were killed near Komarovka, and three other tank commanders were killed: Motin, Smirnov and Khalilov). In the 1st Tank Battalion, on 24 February 1944, 6 tanks were knocked out. In the 2nd Tank Battalion, 5 tanks were knocked out. The 3rd Tank Battalion took no part in the combat because of the large losses it had suffered in the raid toward Ganovka, Napadovka and Skitki. In total, the brigade lost 11 tanks in the fighting at Ryzhanovka on 24 February.

In the offensive combat for possession of Ryzhanovka on 24 February, a tank commander of the 11th Guards Tank Brigade's 2nd Tank Battalion Guards Junior Lieutenant Aleksei Gladyshev, demonstrating courage, resolve and heroism, broke into the enemy's first line of defenses, and with fire and the tracks of his tank, inflicted the following damage to the enemy: 2 guns, 1 mortar, 2 machine guns, 2 prime movers were destroyed, and he killed 40 enemy soldiers and officers. In this combat on 24 February, Aleksei Gladyshev was wounded – he lost an eye. He was awarded the Order of the Red Banner. Also on 24 February, another tank commander in the 11th Guards Tank Brigade's 2nd Tank Battalion Guards Junior Lieutenant Viktor Smirnov, having broken into the enemy's forward edge of defenses, with the fire and treads of his tank, destroyed 6 trucks, 4 machine guns, 2 cannons, and 100 enemy soldiers and officers. Viktor Smirnov was also wounded in the fight – his leg was broken. He was awarded the Order of the Red Banner. In the combat for Ryzhanovka, Guards Lieutenant Iurii Kolpakov, yet another tank commander in the 11th Guards Tank Brigade's 2nd Tank Battalion, having penetrated into the depth of the enemy's defenses, destroyed the foe with fire and the treads of his tanks. When his tank was immobilized, Kolpakov continued to fight until his last shell and cartridge. After exhausting his ammunition, enemy infantry climbed up on his tank, wanting to take the crew prisoner. Guards Lieutenant Kolpakov was killed together with his crew inside his damaged and subsequently burning tank. He was posthumously awarded the Order of the Patriotic War 1st Degree.

On 29 February, the 2nd Tank Army's chief of operations Colonel Chizh provided an account of the army's tank pool as of 7.00 that morning (see Table 5.8 below).

The units of the 2nd Tank Army, having worn down the adversary in defensive fighting, went on the offensive and with vigorous attacks broke the enemy's resistance. Something new in the enemy's tactics was the fact that the enemy, when breaking through a defense, assigned the primary role to Tiger tanks. Groups of Tigers would approach our front line, provoke fire upon themselves that would reveal our firing positions, and then fall back, whereupon they would shoot up our tanks and especially our anti-tank guns from long range (2 to 2.5 kilometers). In the given operation, most of the fighting went on for populated places. This type of combat requires the rapid approach of tanks and infantry to the objective. The tanks would then isolate the villages, while the motorized infantry would split the enemy into isolated groups and destroy them piecemeal. The heavy losses of our tank units must be considered due to the lack of time to forge teamwork among the tank crews. The tanks moved out and went into combat directly from the railroad platform. The frequent change in assignments and the operational reshuffling of the units allowed no opportunity to study the enemy, nor even the area of combat operations. Long marches in the conditions of the muddy season reduced the combat worthiness of the units. Practice demonstrated that all of the wheeled transport, as a rule, lagged behind en route, and arrived in the area of combat operations with great delay. The transport of fuel and ammunition was made difficult, which prompted the need to use tanks for the movement of all types of rations. The prolonged operation of the radio sets without the necessary energy supply led to the loss of communications, while the walkie-talkies, as a rule, quit working in the damp weather. Despite all of the problems that were present in the period of the defensive and offensive fighting, the 2nd Tank Army accomplished its task and inflicted great damage to the enemy in men and matériel.

Table 5.8: Data on the condition of the 2nd Tank Army's tank pool as of 7.00 on 29.2.1944

| Unit | Type | On the list | Combat ready | Saw recent combat | Under repair | | | Supply status | | |
|---|---|---|---|---|---|---|---|---|---|---|
| | | | | | Minor | Light overhaul | Major overhaul | Ammunition (in combat loads) | Fuel and lubricants (in refills) | Rations (Days' worth) |
| **3rd Tank Corps** | | | | | | | | | | |
| 50 TBr. | T-34 | 41 | 17 | 17 | – | 14 | 9 | 1.5 | 2.0 | 6 |
| 51 TBr. | T-34 | 27 | 11 | 11 | – | 9 | 5 | 2.0 | 2.0 | 7 |
| 103 TBr | T-34 | 21 | 12 | 12 | – | 4 | 2 | 1.0 | 1.3 | 3 |
| 411 Signals Btn. | T-34 | 3 | 2 | 2 | – | – | 1 | | | |
| 74 MC Btn. | Mk-9 | 7 | 2 | 6 | 1 | – | 1 | 1.0 | 0.5 | 1 |
| 881 SPAR | SU-76 | 16 | 8 | 8 | – | 6 | 2 | 1.1 | 0.6 | 3 |
| 1818 SPAR | SU-85 | 1 | – | – | – | – | 1 | | | |
| 1540 Heavy SPAR | SU-152 | 11 | 5 | 5 | – | 4 | 2 | 1.24 | 1.0 | 5 |
| Total in the corps: | T-34 | 92 | 42 | 42 | – | 27 | 17 | 1.0 | 1.5 diesel, 0.4 high-octane gasoline | |
| | Mk 9 | 7 | 2 | 6 | 1 | – | 1 | | | |
| | SU-76 | 16 | 8 | 8 | – | 6 | 2 | | | |
| | SU-152 | 11 | 5 | 5 | – | 4 | 2 | | | |
| | SU-85 | 1 | – | – | – | – | 1 | | | |
| **16th Tank Corps** | | | | | | | | | | |
| 107 TBr. | T-34 | 25 | 12 | 13 | 1 | 1 | 7 | 1.0 | 1.0 | 1 |
| 109 TBr. | T-34 | 18 | 9 | 20 | 2 | 1 | 6 | 1.0 | 1.0 | 2 |
| 164 TBr. | T-34 | 54 | 19 | 9 | 4 | 17 | 14 | 1.0 | 1.0 | 1.5 |
| 689 Signals Bn. | T-34 | 2 | – | -1 | 1 | – | – | | | |
| 51 MC Bn. | Mk 9 | 10 | 7 | 8 | 1 | 2 | – | | | |
| 1441 SPAR | SU-76 | 12 | 10 | 10 | 1 | 1 | – | 2.0 | 1.2 | 7 |
| | SU-85 | 11 | 8 | 8 | – | 3 | – | | 1.4 | |
| 298 GSPAR | SU-76 | 11 | 9 | 8 | – | 2 | – | 1.5 | 1.5 | |
| Total in the corps: | T-34 | 99 | 40 | 43 | 8 | 19 | 27 | 1 combat load | 1.0 diesel, 0.4 high octane gasoline | 2 |
| | Mk 9 | | | | | | | | | |
| | SU-76 | | | | | | | | | |
| | SU-85 | | | | | | | | | |
| 11 GTBr. | T-34 | 31 | 14 | 14 | – | 2 | – | 1.5 | 2.4 diesel, 0.7 high-octane gasoline | 4 |
| 87 MC Bn. | Mk 9 | 10 | 7 | 7 | 3 | 3 | – | 1.5 | 1.2 | 1 |
| 8 HTR | "IS" | 21 | 18 | 18 | – | 3 | – | | | |
| 13 HTR | "IS" | 19 | 14 | 14 | – | 2 | 3 | | | |
| 1219 SPAR | SU-85 | 10 | 7 | 7 | – | 3 | – | | | |
| 999 SPAR | SU-76 | 16 | 11 | 11 | – | 5 | – | – | – | – |
| Total in the army: | T-34 | 222 | 96 | 99 | 8 | 48 | 44 | 2 | 0.5 | 5 |
| | Mk 9 | 27 | 16 | 21 | 5 | 2 | 1 | | | |
| | "IS" | 40 | 32 | 32 | – | 5 | 3 | | | |
| | SU-76 | 55 | 38 | 38 | 1 | 14 | 2 | | | |
| | SU-85 | 22 | 15 | 15 | – | 6 | 1 | | | |
| | SU-152 | 11 | 5 | 5 | – | 4 | 2 | | | |

## The 2nd Tank Army's artillery in the operation

At the start of combat operations, the 2nd Tank Army had 20 SU-76, 32 SU-85 and 22 SU-152 self-propelled guns. The abrupt changes in the weather in the area of the army's combat operations caused the roads to deteriorate quickly, which placed the resupply of the self-propelled guns with fuel and ammunition under threat. The lengthy marches (up to 300 kilometers) in the mud placed great strain on the engines and to frequent breakdowns. After the initial 120-kilometer march, 17 SU-152s failed to arrive in time at the destination. During the second march to the Stanislavchik area, 9 SU-152, 8 SU-85 and 6 SU-76 broke down and arrived in a completely unserviceable condition. The main cause for mechanical breakdowns was the excessive expenditure of operating hours on the engines and the poor training of the drivers.

Over the period of combat operations, the self-propelled artillery primarily took part in repelling the enemy's powerful tank attacks. It operated out of ambush positions. The SU-85 self-propelled artillery regiment supported the defense from 26 January to 27 January 1944, and then attacked together with the motorized rifle and tank brigades. The SU-152 heavy self-propelled artillery regiments were primarily kept in reserve and moved up to the front whenever wherever Tiger tanks appeared. By the end of combat operations, on 24 February 1944, the 2nd Tank Army had 15 SU-76, 4 SU-85 and 3 SU-152 serviceable.

In the fighting on 13 February 1944 in the Chesnovka area, the SU-85 regiment took up ambush firing positions, and having allowed a large number of enemy tanks to approach to within 100-200 meters, it opened intensive fire from the available 5 self-propelled guns. As a result of the skillful use of the terrain, the tenaciousness of the crews, and the massed fire, the regiment succeeded in destroying 2 German self-propelled guns and 2 Tiger tanks, and disabled another 2 self-propelled guns and 2 Tiger tanks, while losing in the process its final 5 self-propelled guns. The main shortcomings in the struggle with enemy tanks were the inability to select an advantageous, concealed position, and the premature opening of fire, which revealed the self-propelled guns' positions at ranges that were advantageous for the enemy.

Anti-tank guns were used when repelling enemy tank attacks, with surprise concentrated fire out of ambush positions. Given the superiority of the Tiger tanks in the accuracy of long-range fire and the invulnerability of their frontal armor, the Soviet anti-tank artillerymen realized the only way to combat the Tigers successfully was to remain concealed as the Tigers approached, and then to open surprise fire at the close range of 150-300 meters. The order to concentrate the artillery in order to destroy the encircled enemy grouping in the Korsun'-Shevchenkovskii area wasn't carried out in time. The main reason for this was the horrendous road conditions and the lack of a sufficient amount of motorized transport. As a consequence of this, only the self-propelled artillery regiments and separate gun batteries had assembled by 10 February. All the remaining materiél was still in route and arrived in the area of operations only as the combat actions were winding down.

The deployment of artillery in the area of Lipovets Station and Oratov amounted to 11 guns per kilometer of front. In the given sector, the artillery carried out a variety of tasks: the accompaniment of the counterattacking tanks and infantry with fire and movement; the repelling of enemy counterattacks; and the suppression and destruction of the enemy's means of fire. Primarily, the artillery fired over open sights. Later, in the second phase of the 2nd Tank Army's combat operations (in the Lisianka – Chesnovka area), the army's field artillery significantly lagged behind the combat units and operated in separate batteries assigned to the most important sectors.

## Engineering support for the operation

The brevity of the time to prepare for the marches didn't allow an opportunity to set up parallel routes for the movement of the army's formations. After the army's assembly in the new area

(Stanislavchik), the engineer units worked to strengthen bridges and to improve the roads, and to block the probable directions of enemy counterattacks with minefields. On the Lisianka – Chesnovka line, the engineer units worked to repair roads and to place minefields. Groups of combat engineers infiltrated into the enemy rear area to set mines on the roads. On the whole, the army's engineer units, carrying out their support tasks, worked under exceptionally difficult conditions created by the thaw, and despite the fact that they were working by hand, did significant work. More precisely, they built 194 linear meters of new heavy-load bridges; strengthened 292 linear meters of heavy-load bridges; laid 2560 anti-tank mines and 800 anti-personnel mines; and maintained 180 kilometers of roads.

## Material support for the operation

From the moment of the start of combat operations, in order to keep the 2nd Tank Army's formation supplied with the main types of material resources and in order to reduce the burden on transport, separate stockpiles of supplies were established right on the ground. The army had available only a single motorized transport battalion, upon which rested the entire burden of transport. In the conditions of the muddy season, it became difficult to keep the army supplied. The failure of the rear services to keep up with the combat units led to the need to move supply stockpiles closer to the frontline troops and to use tanks to deliver fuel and ammunition. Thanks to the rear facilities' expedience of establishing forward supply stockpiles on the ground and the organization of shuttle runs by the trucks of the motorized transport battalion (if anything in that morass of slush and mud could be called a "run"), the 2nd Tank Army's forces were kept sustained even in difficult moments and didn't experience any acute interruptions in supplies.

The availability of supplies in the army's formations is described by the following data: At the start of combat operations on 25 January 1944, the formations had 1.5 – 2.1 combat loads of ammunition, 1.0 – 2.2 refills with fuel and lubricants, and 2.7 – 8.9 days of rations. On 6 February 1944, they were down to 0.6 – 1.5 combat loads of ammunition, 0.7 – 1.5 refills with fuel and lubricants, and 2.7 – 5.3 days of rations. On 11 February 1944, the 2nd Tank Army's formations had just 0.9 – 1.0 combat loads of ammunition, 0.4 – 1.3 refills with fuel and lubricants, and 2.2 – 2.4 days of rations. By 22 February, they had 0.8 – 1.4 combat loads of ammunition, 0.7 – 0.8 refills with fuel and lubricants, and 3.0 – 5.2 days of rations.

The fluctuation in the number of serviceable armored vehicles and combat equipment over the period of combat operations between 25 January and 25 February 1944 is evident in the data for the following dates:

> **On 25.1.44:** Armor – 264 T-34, 31 Valentine Mark IX, 21 SU-76, 1 SU-85, 12 SU-152; Guns – 28 37mm, 36 76mm, 23 85mm; Mortars – 112 82mm, 84 120mm, and 40 M-13 rocket launchers.
>
> **On 30.1.1944:** Armor – 197 T-34, 26 Valentine Mark IX, 8 SU-76, 1 SU-85, 9 SU-152; Guns – 28 37mm, 20 76mm, 19 85mm; Mortars – 24 82mm, 54 120mm, and 15 M-13 rocket launchers.
>
> **On 15.2.1944:** Armor – 58 T-34, 1 SU-85; Guns – 8 85mm; Mortars – 17 120mm.
>
> **On 18.2.1944:** Armor – 81 T-34 tanks (the increase is due to the tanks in the attached tank brigades), 19 IS-85.
>
> **On 21.2.1944:** Armor – 63 T-34, 7 Valentine Mark IX, 27 IS, 10 SU-85, 2 SU-152; Guns – 15 37mm, 12 76mm, 10 85mm; Mortars: 93 82mm, 82 120mm, and 40 M-13 rocket launchers.

In return, over the period of the army's combat operations between 26 January and 26 February 1944, the 2nd Tank Army claimed the destruction of 534 German tanks, 137 self-propelled guns, 348 guns of various calibers, 95 mortars, 431 machine guns, 18 armored cars, 98 armored halftracks, 959 trucks and cars, 2,078 wagons with their loads, and 16 supply dumps of various types. It also reported killing 39,554 German soldiers and officers, and the taking of 2,550 prisoners.

Every operation has its own characteristics. The operation that was conducted by the 2nd Tank Army between 26 January and 26 February 1944 was unlike any other of its previously conducted operations. The time of year didn't promise anything good. Already at the end of January, a thaw set in. Motorized transport had to stick to macadam roads. Movement along the unpaved roads that ran between the villages was a true ordeal. Nevertheless, the heroic efforts of the soldiers and officers contributed to the fact that the operation was successfully conducted even in such abysmal conditions. At the start of the combat operations, as a consequence of the early thaw, the wheeled vehicles and the artillery and mortars began to lag behind. The delay imposed on the Guards mortar units [rocket-launching units] especially told on the strength of the artillery fire. The special feature of the combat operations consisted in the fact that they had to be conducted in the unusual conditions of the almost total absence of roads. There was even a moment when the threat arose that the tanks and self-propelled guns might be left without fuel and ammunition.

The early thaw also created serious problem in questions of organizing cooperation. While everything remained static, matters went normally. However, in the dynamics of combat, everything was disrupted. The movement of the units in response to the alarm, the lack of time to arrange cooperation according to plan, led to isolated and uncoordinated actions among the army's units. The hastiness in organizing attacks, which excluded even the minimal necessary amount of time for surveillance and reconnoitering, was the main shortcoming in the army's combat actions. The disjointed arrival of the army's understrength formations in the area of combat operations prohibited the massed use of the army's entire power. The tank formations in the majority of cases went into battle without artillery fire support, which led to excessive losses. The frequent reshuffling of the army's units and the frequent change in orders led to the fact that the tank formations wound up isolated from each other and were scattered across the front, which complicated overall command of them.

The enemy, with the aim of eliminating the threat of the emergence of our units in the Vinnitsa – Zhmerinka area, launched a counteroffensive toward Kiev, having created a numerical superiority in tanks and self-propelled guns. Introducing them into the battle in major groups, the Germans achieved success on the front of the 38th Army. In exceptionally difficult conditions, the 2nd Tank Army, having completed the sudden advance to the breakthrough area, halted the enemy's further advance with a vigorous attack, and forced the Germans to go over to a defense.

After the encirclement of the enemy grouping in the Korsun'-Shevchenkovskii area, the Germans launched a relief attack aiming to link up with the encircled forces in the sector of the 40th Army. The 2nd Tank Army made a lateral movement across the front in the most difficult conditions of the early thaw and fought to delay the enemy's advance until the rest of the materiél en route arrived. Then, going over to resolute actions, the 2nd Tank Army attacked the German units that had broken through and forced them to abandon further attacks in this sector.

However, the enemy, showing particular stubbornness in the desire to break through to the encircled grouping, resumed the offensive in the sector of the 6th Tank Army, and using a great numerical superiority in tanks and all-terrain prime movers, the German panzer divisions ground their way forward toward a link-up, and reached Chesnovka by 13 February 1944. At that point, the Germans launched simultaneous actions on the part of the encircled grouping and of the III Panzer Corps that was striving to reach it. At the decision of the command of the 1st Ukrainian Front, the 2nd Tank Army was inserted between the two enemy groupings with the task to prevent a link-up between them. Suffering significant losses, the enemy's shock panzer grouping (the III Panzer Corps) reached its furthest point of advance – the Chesnovka – Oktiabr' – Lisianka line; meanwhile, the encircled *Gruppe Stemmermann* had fought its way out to the Khil'ki – Komarovka line. Thus, only 8 kilometers now separated the two enemy groupings. But if you consider that individual enemy groups had infiltrated toward the Komarovka area, then the gap between the two groupings had narrowed to just 2-3 kilometers. Thus the enemy was striving to break through in this sector with particular ferocity. Unable to do so, the Germans counted upon a withdrawal from encirclement in massed columns. For example, on 17 February, the enemy in a column of up to 1,500 men emerged from Khil'ki, and firing on the move, advanced toward Komarovka, unsuspecting that Komorovka was occupied by our units (the 11th Guards Tank Brigade). The entire column was almost completely crushed and destroyed by the treads and fire of the tank brigade. Later that same day, a second enemy column, taking a slightly different route through ravines, reached Komarovka, where it was destroyed by the fire of our artillery and self-propelled guns.

The insignificant distance between the two enemy groupings gave rise to a tense situation. Success depended upon the maneuverability of the units and keeping them supplied. All of the free transport, right up to staff cars, was mobilized to bring up ammunition. Extreme measures were taken to keep the operating units supplied, right up to employing local citizens, who delivered fuel, lubricants and ammunition on their shoulders.

It should be noted that thanks to these energetic measures, the units of the 2nd Tank Army never sensed an acute need for ammunition, except for the 11th Guards Tank Brigade, which was positioned in Komarovka, where it was even cut-off at one time, but even then, ammunition was delivered to it with the cover of tanks. Thanks to the exertions of the personnel of the units, the 2nd Tank Army, having simultaneously destroyed the German breakout group in the Shenderovka area while still locked in stubborn combat with the III Panzer Corps, was able subsequently to go on the offensive and to regain the former positions held by the 6th Tank Army before the German relief attempt was launched.

The command of the 6th Tank Army and of the People's Commissar of Defense Comrade Stalin expressed their gratitude to the 11th Separate Guards Tank Brigade for destroying remnants of the encircled enemy grouping. Units of the 16th Tank Corps received the official thanks of the Front's Military Council. The 2nd Tank Army, through its actions at critical moments on the fronts of the 38th Army, 40th Army and 6th Tank Army in turn, proved to be the deciding force, and played a major role in the destruction of the encircled Germans in the Korsun'-Shevchenkovskii pocket and in the defeat of the enemy's shock panzer grouping.

### After-action accounts and reports

The after-action report submitted by the 2nd Tank Army headquarters had the following to say:

> The combat actions of the 2nd Tank Army were characterized by lengthy marches and frequent lateral shifts. This requires the full motorization of signals units, engineering troops and the artillery. The command and control over the forces was frequently disrupted in connection with the disorganized changes in location of the formations' command posts and observation posts (especially in the 3rd Tank Corps). It is necessary to demand of subordinate headquarters that they follow the manual for the headquarters' field service. When using artillery, it is necessary to avoid movements of the self-propelled artillery regiments over great distances under their own power, since the lengthy marches negatively affect their combat performance and their equipped vehicles break down prematurely. It is necessary to use the SU-85 self-propelled guns as a means of supporting the tanks. The SU-85 in the recent fighting was the main and almost the sole means to combat the enemy's Tiger tanks. The SU-76 self-propelled

gun, having a weak carriage, weak penetrating capability and light armor, is not very effective as a means of struggle against the enemy tanks. In difficult road conditions for the tanks, it is necessary to set aside some time after the march to service them. Under all conditions, it is necessary to designate the locations of the disabled vehicle collection posts and to use evacuation means to the maximum. In no event allow the use of tanks constantly and in motion, because the shock force of the tank formation lessens due to mechanical breakdowns and the lagging behind of individual vehicles. It is necessary to equip the repair services with vehicles having 50-60 percent better off-road capabilities.

New in the enemy's tactics was the fact that he used heavy tanks in the forward combat echelons, followed by medium tanks and infantry in combat formations, all with the accompaniment of anti-tank artillery. Before an attack, the enemy as a rule conducted combat reconnaissance and exposed first and foremost the anti-tank means in our system of defense, after which Tiger tanks and large-caliber self-propelled guns would shoot up our anti-tank guns and tanks with direct fire from fixed positions at a range of 2-2.5 kilometers. In the period of combat operations, there occurred tank battles that didn't yield positive results, because the 76mm cannon of the T-34 tank could damage Tiger and Panther tanks only from close ranges (500-600 meters), whereas our tanks were opposed by large-caliber guns, which could shoot up our tanks with direct fire from a distance of 1.5-2.5 kilometers. Our units could oppose the enemy's large-caliber guns on their tanks and self-propelled guns only with the SU-85 and SU-152, of which there were not enough in the army for conducting intense combats.

Throughout the entire extent of the operation, no consideration was given to the factor of time for keeping the men fed and warm. This led to the fact that once having received an order, the men were physically not in the condition to carry it out.

The experience of the 2nd Tank Army demonstrated that a tank army is capable of making lengthy marches and conducting successful combats, given the excellent preparation of the tanks and personnel.

Terrain plays a very important role in the operations of tank formations. Wherever the terrain is cut by a multitude of rivers and ravines, there it is the tanks' main foe. In these places the tanks are so restricted in their freedom of maneuver that the main percentage of losses is due to forced halts and exposing the side armor to fire.

Over the period of combat operations between 26 January and 26 February 1944, the 2nd Tank Army inflicted serious damage to the foe. Units of the Army captured 55 tanks and self-propelled guns, as well as a lot of other equipment. Over the month of fighting, the tankers of the 2nd Tank Army captured 2,550 German soldiers and officers. The combat operations in January-February 1944 took place in difficult conditions. The muddy season, the absence of roads, the lack of adequate time to arrange cooperation with other formations – all of this complicated the conducting of the fighting and frequently led to uncoordinated actions. The frequent change in orders in connection with the developing situation led to the fact that the tank formations had to operate isolated from one another and in disassembled pieces. Nevertheless, the operation was successfully implemented. The heroic efforts of the personnel and the bold and aggressive actions of the commanders contributed to this.

The experience of the army's combat operations proved that the muddy season, even given the absence of a network of hard-surface and improved roads cannot be a hindrance to the use of major tank formations. Given good training, a tank army is capable of fighting successfully in the conditions of the muddy season and the absence of roads. The army's command and officers' staff acquired great experience in directing the fighting and organizing it in the most difficult conditions of an operational and tactical situation. The personnel proved to be models of resolve and tenacity on the defense, of great endurance on marches, and of courage and fearlessness on the attack.

General Bogdanov himself wrote:

> In January 1944, in the period of the German counteroffensive on the Vinnitsa axis, and in February 1944, in the period of fighting near Korsun'-Shevchenkovskii, the 2nd Tank Army was thrown into combat against the attacking enemy grouping in the sector of the 38th Army, without waiting to be refitted fully. The army was introduced into the fighting not at full-strength, but in pace with the reception of materiél, and was committed into combat by battalion. No time was given to develop teamwork among the elements and units. As a result of the lack of teamwork of the elements and units, the lagging behind of the rear services and of the recovery means, and in view of the early spring thaw, over the 20 days of uninterrupted fighting the army lost up to 70 percent of its equipment.

The chief of staff of the 2nd Tank Army Major General A. Pavlov provided information on the 2nd Tank Army's losses and gave estimates of the damage inflicted to the enemy:

> Enemy tanks knocked-out or destroyed: 37 Tigers; 145 Pz. IV and Pz. III were brewed up, and 197 tanks of various types were knocked-out, for a total of 379 tanks. In addition, 62 self-propelled guns, 75 mortars, 85 guns of various calibers, 27 armored cars, 197 trucks and cars, 130 machine guns, 45 armored halftracks, 300 horse-drawn carts, and 7 supply dumps were knocked-out or destroyed. The 2nd Tank Army killed 12,780 enemy soldiers and officers, and took 160 prisoner. Over this same period the 2nd Tank Army lost: 125 T-34, 3 Valentine Mark IX, 1 SU-152, 10 SU-85 and 5 SU-76. **Total: 144 machines.** Losses in personnel: 807 killed, 1,099 wounded, and 624 missing in action. Total: 2,530 men.

The commander of the 3rd Tank Corps Major General Aleksandr Shamshin offered the following conclusions regarding the recently-completed operation:

> The 3rd Tank Corps in the recent operations carried out the combat tasks given to it in defensive and offensive battles, despite the exceptionally difficult meteorological conditions and the complete absence of roads. The corps prevented the enemy from linking up with the encircled grouping, and destroyed the enemy grouping that was trying to escape the pocket and up to 10,000 Nazis. It secured the withdrawal of the 17th Rifle Corps from encirclement. It drew upon itself large enemy forces, which thereby facilitated the active operation of units on other sectors of the front.
>
> The Main Shortcomings of the Operation: the untimely distribution of fuel and lubricants from the army bases in the needed quantity; the hastiness in the organization of attacks, which excluded the minimal amount of time necessary for surveillance and reconnoitering; the lack of signals equipment in order to organize two positions, both the current and the future; the frequent change in location of the command posts, which given the absence of reliable communications, resulted in disorganization, and at times even the loss of command and control; the lagging behind of the artillery units, which brought about a reduction in the corps' firepower; the absence of bold maneuvering in the course of the fighting to outflank and encircle the enemy; throughout the entire operation, no consideration was given to the factor of time for keeping the men fed and warm, which led to the fact that having received an order, the men were not in a physical condition to carry it out; the inability to select an advantageous, concealed position and to determine the optimal range to ensure damage to the enemy tanks; the lack of reserve positions and alternate cover for switching from one position to another, once the enemy had detected the location of the tanks and self-propelled guns; the premature opening of fire at the enemy tanks, which leads to the revealing of our

positions and the killing of our tanks, before our guns could be used effectively; the poorly-organized service of technical support and evacuation, of the repair of tanks and evacuation, and of the supply with fuel and lubricants.

Tanks of the 2nd Tank Army moving out toward their jumping-off positions.

Abandoned German vehicles and equipment in the Korsun'-Shevchenkovskii area, February 1944.

**Table 5.9: Irrecoverable losses in armor of the 3rd Tank Corps from 25.1 to 23.2.1944**

| | Type | Dates | | | | | | | | | | | | | Total |
|---|---|---|---|---|---|---|---|---|---|---|---|---|---|---|---|
| | | 27.01 | 28.01 | 29.01 | 30.01 | 31.01 | 1.02 | 8.02 | 13.02 | 16.02 | 19.02 | 20.02 | 22.02 | 23.02 | |
| 50 TBr | T-34 | – | – | 1 | 1 | 5 | – | 8 | 16 | 7 | – | – | – | 6 | 44 |
| 51 TBr | T-34 | 23 | 7 | 6 | 2 | 2 | 4 | 3 | – | 5 | – | – | 2 | 3 | 57 |
| 103 TBr | T-34 | 18 | 11 | 13 | 6 | 7 | – | 3 | – | – | 2 | 3 | – | – | 63 |
| 74 MCBn | Mk 9 | – | – | – | – | – | – | – | 3 | – | – | – | – | – | 3 |
| 1540 HSPAR | SU-152 | – | – | – | – | 1 | – | – | 1 | 2 | – | – | – | – | 4 |
| 1818 SPAR | SU-85 | – | 3 | 6 | – | 1 | – | – | – | 5 | – | – | – | – | 15 |
| SPAR | T-34 | – | – | 1 | – | – | – | – | – | – | – | – | – | – | 1 |
| SPAR | SU-76 | – | – | – | – | 5 | – | – | 6 | – | – | – | – | 3 | 14 |
| Total: | T-34 | 41 | 18 | 21 | 9 | 14 | 4 | 14 | 16 | 12 | 2 | 3 | 2 | 9 | 165 |
| | Mk 9 | – | – | – | – | – | – | – | 3 | – | – | – | – | – | 3 |
| | SU-152 | – | – | – | – | 1 | – | – | 1 | 2 | – | – | – | – | 4 |
| | SU-85 | – | 3 | 6 | – | 1 | – | – | – | 5 | – | – | – | – | 15 |
| | SU-76 | – | – | – | – | 5 | – | – | 6 | – | – | – | – | 3 | 14 |
| **Total losses:** | | **41** | **21** | **27** | **9** | **21** | **4** | **14** | **26** | **19** | **2** | **3** | **2** | **12** | **201** |

The commander of the 16th Tank Corps Major General Ivan Dobovoi offered his conclusions regarding the operation:

> The staggered and incomplete refitting of the corps' formations with tanks and artillery, as well as the piecemeal arrival of the entire corps in the area of combat operations, deprived the possibility of the massed use of all of the corps' power. The tank brigades operated separately from the corps, and in the majority of instances, attacked without artillery fire support. As a result of the separation from the corps and the absence of fire support, the brigades suffered excessive losses in combat. The frequent changes in the subordination of the corps' units and the frequent change in orders led to the fact that the corps' units wound up isolated from each other and operated in a scattered fashion, which complicated the command and control over them and providing them with artillery support. Such a situation prevented the possibility of using the corps in mass to destroy the enemy tank grouping.
>
> As a result of the thaw, the wheeled motorized transport in the period of combat operations in the majority of cases got stuck en route and became separated from the combat units. The supply of units with all types of resources was executed only with the help of tanks and the use of tracked transport, and this created great difficulties in keeping the corps supplied with everything necessary.
>
> In the defensive and offensive fighting, the motorized rifle units, despite the young age of the men and the insufficient forging of teamwork, were models of firmness and resolve on the defense, of great endurance during marches, and of courage and fearlessness on the attack. When on the defense, the motorized infantry were repeatedly subjected to enemy tank overruns of their trenches, and each time the infantry, refusing to abandon their trenches, took on the enemy tanks with point-blank fire of anti-tank rifles and the tossing of hand grenades.

**Table 5.10: Data on losses in personnel of the 3rd Tank Corps' units from 25.01 to 25.02.1944**

| | Killed | | | Wounded | | | Hospitalized with illness | | | Missing in action | | | Total losses | | | Grand totals |
|---|---|---|---|---|---|---|---|---|---|---|---|---|---|---|---|---|
| | Officers' staff | Sergeants' staff | Enlisted men | Officers' staff | Sergeants' staff | Enlisted men | Officers' staff | Sergeants' staff | Enlisted men | Officers' staff | Sergeants' staff | Enlisted men | Officers' staff | Sergeants' staff | Enlisted men | |
| 50th Tank Brigade | 24 | 54 | 32 | 28 | 56 | 110 | – | – | 110 | – | – | – | 52 | 110 | 142 | 304 |
| 51st Tank Brigade | 29 | 84 | 70 | 34 | 86 | 99 | 1 | 2 | 99 | 5 | 1 | 4 | 68 | 173 | 173 | 414 |
| 103rd Tank Brigade | 28 | 55 | 31 | 24 | 60 | 57 | 3 | 1 | 57 | 6 | 45 | 51 | 62 | 161 | 133 | 356 |
| 57th Motorized Rifle Brigade | 24 | 153 | 322 | 54 | 300 | 762 | 3 | 12 | 22 | – | – | – | 81 | 465 | 1,106 | 1,652 |
| 126th Guards Mortar Battalion | – | – | 1 | – | 1 | 3 | – | – | 3 | – | – | – | – | 1 | 4 | 5 |
| 728th Anti-tank Artillery Battalion | – | 1 | 4 | 5 | 7 | 17 | – | 1 | 17 | – | – | 4 | 5 | 9 | 25 | 39 |
| 411th Signals Battalion | – | 2 | – | – | – | – | – | – | – | – | – | – | – | 2 | – | 2 |
| 234th Mortar Regiment | – | – | 2 | 2 | 2 | 5 | – | – | 2 | – | – | – | 2 | 2 | 9 | 13 |
| 64th Separate Chemical Defense Company | – | – | – | – | – | 1 | – | – | 1 | – | – | – | – | – | 1 | 1 |
| 90th Separate Sapper Battalion | 2 | 1 | 9 | – | 4 | 21 | – | 1 | 8 | – | – | – | 2 | 6 | 38 | 46 |
| 1540th Heavy Self-propelled Artillery Regiment | 4 | 3 | 4 | 11 | 4 | 3 | – | – | 3 | – | – | – | 15 | 7 | 7 | 29 |
| 74th Separate Motorcycle Battalion | – | – | – | 1 | 4 | 1 | – | – | 1 | 2 | 3 | 6 | 5 | 7 | 7 | 19 |
| SU-76 Regiment | 6 | 10 | 9 | 12 | 9 | 4 | – | – | 4 | – | – | – | 18 | 19 | 13 | 50 |
| 1818th Self-propelled Artillery Regiment | 5 | 15 | – | 4 | 11 | 1 | – | – | 1 | 4 | 10 | – | 13 | 36 | 1 | 50 |
| 121st Anti-aircraft Artillery Regiment | – | 1 | 1 | 1 | – | 2 | – | – | 2 | – | – | – | 1 | 1 | 3 | 5 |
| Corp headquarters | 1 | – | – | – | – | 1 | – | – | 1 | – | – | – | 1 | – | 1 | 2 |
| Total | 193 | 379 | 485 | 179 | 545 | 1,080 | 4 | 17 | 32 | 17 | 59 | 65 | 393 | 1,000 | 1,662 | 3,055 |

Despite a number of shortcomings, which had their place in the defensive and offensive fighting, the corps' units carried out all the tasks assigned to them by the 2nd Tank Army and 6th Tank Army, and inflicted great damage to the enemy in men and equipment. For their defensive fighting in the Petrovskoe area, the units of the corps received the official gratitude of the Front's Military Council.

**Table 5.11: Data on the losses in personnel of the 16th Tank Corps over the period of combat actions between 27.01 and 25.02.1944**

| | From 25.1 to 5.2.44 | | | | | | | | | From 5.2 to 15.2.44 | | | | | | | | |
| | Killed | | | Wounded | | | Missing | | | Killed | | | Wounded | | | Missing | | |
| | Officers | Sergeants | Enlisted men | Officers | Sergeants | Enlisted men | Officers | Sergeants | Enlisted men | Officers | Sergeants | Enlisted men | Officers | Sergeants | Enlisted men | Officers | Sergeants | Enlisted men |
|---|---|---|---|---|---|---|---|---|---|---|---|---|---|---|---|---|---|---|
| 107 Tank Brigade | 9 | 36 | 14 | 14 | 28 | 18 | – | – | – | 1 | 7 | 1 | 1 | 8 | 13 | – | – | – |
| 109 Tank Brigade | 14 | 74 | 23 | 8 | 37 | 33 | – | – | – | 7 | 16 | 12 | 6 | 17 | 12 | – | – | – |
| 164 Tank Brigade | 5 | 9 | 17 | 3 | 20 | 29 | – | – | – | 5 | 7 | 5 | 9 | 22 | 7 | – | – | – |
| 15 Motorized Rifle Brigade | 1 | 5 | 8 | 2 | 6 | 20 | – | – | – | – | 8 | 16 | 2 | 12 | 35 | – | – | – |
| 226 Mortar Regiment | – | 1 | – | – | – | 2 | – | – | – | – | – | 1 | – | 1 | – | – | – | – |
| 729 Anti-tank Artillery Battalion | – | – | – | – | – | – | – | – | – | – | – | – | – | 1 | – | – | – | – |
| 1441 Self-propelled Artillery Regiment | 1 | 2 | – | 2 | 3 | 2 | – | – | – | – | 1 | – | 2 | 1 | – | – | – | – |
| 51 Motorcycle Battalion | – | – | – | – | – | – | – | – | – | – | – | – | – | – | 3 | – | – | – |
| 205 Signals Battalion | – | – | – | – | – | – | – | – | – | – | – | – | – | – | – | – | – | – |
| 7 Aviation Flight | – | – | – | – | 1 | – | – | – | – | – | – | – | – | – | – | – | – | – |

| | From 15.2 to 25.2.44 | | | | | | | | | From 25.1 to 25.2.44 | | | | | | | | |
| | Killed | | | Wounded | | | Missing | | | Killed | | | Wounded | | | Missing | | |
| | Officers | Sergeants | Enlisted men | Officers | Sergeants | Enlisted men | Officers | Sergeants | Enlisted men | Officers | Sergeants | Enlisted men | Officers | Sergeants | Enlisted men | Officers | Sergeants | Enlisted men |
|---|---|---|---|---|---|---|---|---|---|---|---|---|---|---|---|---|---|---|
| 107th Tank Brigade | – | 13 | 11 | 3 | 13 | 31 | – | – | – | 10 | 56 | 26 | 19 | 49 | 62 | – | – | – |
| 109th Tank Brigade | 2 | 8 | 18 | 10 | 17 | 19 | – | – | – | 23 | 98 | 53 | 24 | 71 | 64 | – | – | – |
| 164th Tank Brigade | 2 | 10 | 4 | 7 | 13 | 29 | – | – | – | 12 | 26 | 26 | 19 | 55 | 65 | | | |
| 15th Motorized Rifle Brigade | 9 | 48 | 136 | 22 | 71 | 180 | – | 5 | 25 | 10 | 61 | 160 | 26 | 89 | 235 | – | 5 | 25 |
| 226th Mortar Regiment | – | – | – | – | – | – | – | – | – | – | 1 | 1 | – | 1 | 2 | – | – | – |
| 729th Anti-tank Artillery Battalion | 1 | 1 | 1 | 1 | 3 | 3 | – | – | – | 1 | 1 | 1 | 1 | 4 | 3 | – | – | – |
| 1441st Self-propelled Artillery Regiment | 1 | 1 | – | 1 | 1 | 1 | – | – | – | 2 | 4 | – | 5 | 5 | 3 | – | – | – |
| 51st Motorcycle Battalion | 1 | – | – | – | 2 | 3 | – | – | – | 1 | – | – | – | 2 | 6 | – | – | – |
| 205th Signals Battalion | – | – | – | – | – | 2 | – | – | – | – | – | – | – | – | 2 | – | – | – |
| 7th Aviation Flight | – | – | – | – | – | – | – | – | – | – | – | – | – | 1 | – | – | – | – |

[Signed] Chief of staff of the 16th Tank Corps Guards Colonel N. Kochtrin

Colonel Nikolai Koshaev, the commander of the 11th Guards Tank Brigade, offered his analysis of his brigade's actions during the operation:

> New in the enemy's tactics: a) the action of tanks on the defensive: In the area of Ocheretnia when assuming a defensive posture, the enemy attached heavy tanks and self-propelled artillery in groups of 4-5 to the infantry units, which operated as mobile firing points, and when repelling the attacks of our units, counterattacked our flanks and rear. The main grouping of enemy tanks was positioned 10-12 kilometers to the rear as a tactical reserve for launching counterattacks depending on the situation. b) In the area of Ryzhanovka, the enemy was defending primarily with infantry, having anti-tank artillery on the southeastern outskirts and tanks and self-propelled guns on the northwestern outskirts. When our tanks broke through to Ryzhanovka, the enemy infantry used new anti-tank grenades. When making contact with the armor, the grenades burned through it, and with a subsequent explosion, knocked out the crew or the engine [Ed.note: These "grenades" were most likely the warheads of Panzerfausts or of the rockets fired by Panzerschrecks]. c) Tanks of the Tiger and Panther type, as well as the self-propelled guns, fire at our tanks from fixed positions and from long ranges. d) In offensive action in order to carry out limited operations, the enemy attached up to 20-30 tanks and self-propelled guns to the infantry.
>
> <u>Shortcomings in the actions of our units:</u> The 11th Guards Tank Brigade in the period of combats from 25.1 to 22.2.44 conducted a 730-kilometer march and was constantly engaged in combat, having no time for conducting mechanical inspections, as a result of which by 22.2.44, of the available machines 70 percent required repair or light overhauls. The majority of tanks now require jump-starting. b) During the offensive in the Ocheretnia area, the brigade was hastily thrown into an attack, having almost no time for organizing reconnaissance or cooperation with other units. As a result, on 27.1.44 the 3rd Tank Corps was late by 1 hour in going on the attack and the enemy was able to repulse the attacks of our tanks piecemeal. Initially he counterattacked units of the 11th Guards Tank Brigade, and then having moved out of cover in the Ocheretnia sector, with these same tanks he counterattacked units of the 3rd Tank Corps. c) During actions on the offensive and on defense, the brigade didn't always operate as a single fist, but was broken up into pieces. In the Tat'ianovka area, the brigade's 2nd Tank Battalion and Motorized Rifle Battalion were on the attack, while the 1st Tank Battalion had been sent to the Lisianovka – Zvenigorodka area, after which it no longer had any contact with the 2nd Tank Battalion and Motorized Rifle Battalion for the next four days. The work of the rear was insufficiently businesslike; the entire rear was stretched out en route because of the bad road, and partially because of the negligence and dawdling of the rear personnel, who didn't take advantage of the nighttime frosts in order to move forward and to supply the units with everything necessary for battle.
>
> Command and control in the battles and on the marches was primarily handled over the radio. Radio communications worked without interruption, which allowed the opportunity to maneuver the units and elements quickly in combat. The conducted combat operations once again demonstrated the courage and bravery of the personnel and the ability to combine fire and maneuver; their resolve and tenacity on the defense, and their intrepidity and energy on the attack.

As we have seen, pursuant to the order of the *Stavka* of the Supreme High Command, two of the five recently formed separate Guards heavy tank regiments joined the 2nd Tank Army during the Korsun'-Shevchenkovskii operation. The 8th and 13th Guards Heavy Tank Regiments, having taken upon themselves the entire burden of the enemy's panzer attack, endured their combat baptism with honor. After the liquidation of the encircled enemy grouping, on 18 February 1944 all of the efforts of our troops were shifted to the outer ring of encirclement. On 19 February, the forces, which now included the 8th and 13th Guards Heavy Tank Regiments, having been urgently sent to this area from near Vinnitsa, drove the enemy's panzer divisions out of the Lisianka area and restored the temporarily lost position. In the Korsun'-Shevchenkovskii operation, of the 42 IS-85 tanks that took part in combat actions, only 3 were irrecoverably lost (one in the 8th Guards Heavy Tank Regiment and two in the 13th Guards Heavy Tank Regiment).

From a report of the commander of the 13th Separate Guards Heavy Tank Regiment Guards Colonel Grishin, who describes the loss of its tanks:

> As a result of the combat in Lisianka, four Panther tanks, one self-propelled gun, two medium tanks and one Tiger were destroyed. The regiment's losses were two IS that were burned out and three IS that were knocked out. Tank No. 17 received a direct hit by a shell fired from a Pz V Panther from a range of 700 meters. The frontal sloping plate wasn't penetrated; there only remained a 15mm deep notch cut into the armor. With a second shell from a Pz V tank from approximately the same range, the tank took a shell hole in the right section of the turret mount. From a range of 400 meters, a third shell, after ricocheting off the lower left section of the turret penetrated the top of the hull near the left-hand fill port of the fuel tank, which ignited a fire inside the tank with a subsequent explosion of the on-board ammunition. The tank cannot be repaired. Tank No. 18 received two through-and-through shell holes in the right side of the turret from a Pz V tank at a range of 400 meters, as a result of which the remaining on-board ammunition detonated. The tank cannot be repaired. Tank No. 13 took a shell from a Pz V tank at a range of 700 meters, which penetrated the right forward part of the turret mount and damaged the fuel tank, the gun elevating mechanism, and the turret drive. The driver-mechanic was killed. A second shell, fired from a Panther from the same range, only left a notch in the right side of the turret with a depth of 40mm. In addition, on the left side the forward roller wheels and the rear support roller were damaged by artillery fire. The tank was sent off for a light overhaul. Tank No. 19 took a penetrating hit in the driver-mechanic's hatch from a 75mm shell fired by a Pz V at a range of 700 meters. The driver-mechanic was killed. A second shell, having struck the forward lower left section of the mud flap, sliced off 30 millimeters of armor and destroyed the welding joint between the turret ring and the side vertical armor plate. The crack created in the armor extended for 600 millimeters. With the ricochet of this same shell, the forward and rear carrier roller brackets were blown away. A third shell penetrated 40 millimeters into the armor of the gun mantlet. The tank was sent back for a light overhaul. Tank No. 16 took a penetrating hit in the lower right front of the hull from a 75mm shell fired by a Panther tank at a range of 700 meters. The driver-mechanic was killed, and the tank caught fire. Through the efforts of the tank commander, the fire was quickly smothered. The rim of the left guide wheel was destroyed by the next shell. The enemy intensified its fire at the now motionless tank, which was continuing to fight. The next shell, striking the lower right vertical plate on the side, only left an impression up to 30mm deep and disabled the middle support roller. In the course of this action, two shells struck the right side of the turret, and one shell struck the left side of it. All three shells left impressions in the armor that were 20 to 45 millimeters deep. This tank was sent back for a major overhaul.

Later, the deputy commander of the 2nd Tank Army for vehicle maintenance and technical support Major General of Engineering-Tank Service Iukin clarified the 2nd Tank Army's losses in a report:

Over the period of combat operations between 27 January and 24 February 1944, the 2nd Tank Army had irrecoverable losses of combat equipment numbering 179 combat machines. Of these there were: 152 T-34, 3 Valentine Mark IX, 2 SU-152, 21 SU-85 and 1 SU-76. In addition, as a result of combat damage and mechanical problems, another 480 combat machines were rendered unserviceable. Of these, there were: 348 T-34, 33 IS-85, 17 Valentine Mark IX, 23 SU-152, 34 SU-85 and 25 SU-76.

**Table 5.12: Condition of non-serviceable tanks and assault guns**

|           | Minor repairs | Light overhaul | Major overhaul |
|-----------|---------------|----------------|----------------|
| T-34      | 140           | 163            | 45             |
| IS-85     | 14            | 16             | 3              |
| Mk IX     | 10            | 6              | 1              |
| SU-152    | 9             | 4              | 10             |
| SU-85     | 17            | 17             | 0              |
| SU-76     | 19            | 6              | 0              |
| **Total:**| **209**       | **212**        | **59**         |

Over the accounted period of tank repairs, the following repair work was done by the army's repair services and the repair shops of the army's units and formations:

**Table 5.13: Number of tanks and assault guns repaired by the army-level repair services and the repair shops of the army's units and formations**

|           | Minor repair | Light overhaul | Total   |
|-----------|--------------|----------------|---------|
| T-34      | 132          | 128            | 260     |
| IS-85     | 14           | 11             | 25      |
| Mk IX     | 8            | 3              | 11      |
| SU-152    | 9            | 4              | 13      |
| SU-85     | 17           | 16             | 33      |
| SU-76     | 10           | 4              | 14      |
| **Total:**| **190**      | **166**        | **356** |

Over the indicated period, a total of 98 tanks were evacuated from the field of battle, no-man's land or extracted from swamps and ravines, before being sent on to the corps-level and brigade-level disabled vehicle collection points. An analysis of the machines that were knocked-out as a result of combat damage over the accounting period indicates that losses due to enemy artillery fire and tanks – 560 machines, or approximately 82 percent of all losses during the operation – occupies the dominating place. Losses from enemy mines, primarily in the first days of the operation, amounted to 11 combat machines. The loss of armor due to enemy aviation sharply decreased in comparison with 1943; over the accounting period, just 2 machines were lost due to this reason, which testifies to the increase in practical experience in the units with camouflaging the machines in places of unloading, while conducting marches, and at stops, as well as to the muddy season, which prevented the wide-scale use of aircraft. The total number of machines rendered unserviceable due to mechanical breakdowns amount to 64 combat machines, or 9.7 percent of the total number of unserviceable machines. Of the indicated number, 6 were SU-152 lost due to exceeding their engines' lifetimes.

The spring thaw and the roads that were not adapted to the use of motorized transport in the period of the muddy season told to a significant extent on the work of the repairmen. However, with the aim of repairing machines for the army's attacking units, separate repair brigades with hand tools were sent forward on tanks and on foot to the acting combat units. The conveyance of parts and components in view of the absence of roads was extremely limited, so the repair teams primarily obtained needed parts and components by removing them from tanks that had been written off as irrecoverable losses. These difficult conditions of the army's combat operations in the accounting period demanded a great deal of flexibility and intense work from the repairmen. Acclimating to the work conditions to restore combat equipment back to service, the repairmen resorted to using tanks that needed long-term repair but still remained mobile as recovery vehicles. They learned how to remove the transmission from a tank.

CONCLUSIONS: The army-level evacuation companies as a consequence of the quickly growing pace of the offensive were unable to follow directly behind the acting units, and were sent to places that were difficult for the wheeled transport to negotiate. In the accounting period, the evacuation companies played a significant role in keeping the wheeled transport moving toward the combat units with fuel, lubricants, ammunition and food.

Of the tanks that equipped the 2nd Tank Army, the one that proved most suitable for work in the muddy terrain conditions and the absence of roads was the domestically-produced T-34. The T-34 tank, despite the difficult road conditions, stood out with its excellent mobility. Cases where T-34 tanks became bogged down were almost not observed. Inoperable T-34 tanks due to mechanical breakdowns should not be regarded as an indicator of the poor quality of the machine or of manufacturing flaws, but were due exclusively to the heavy strain placed on the tank caused by the muddy conditions and absence of roads. The T-34 carried submachine gunners, ammunition supplies and drums of fuel and lubricants, often while taking a vehicle in tow. Among the T-34 tank's positive qualities, its ability to operate longer on a given amount of fuel in comparison with other types of tanks is most valuable in the conditions of the muddy season. The main cause for the disabling of T-34 tanks in the period of the muddy season was the wear on the 1st and 2nd gears, since the tanks used primarily these gears on the entire extent of the march.

Despite the proper organization and the adequate availability of recovery and repair means, the latter were unable to keep up with the acting units because of the melting snow and mud and were forced to fall behind, which unquestionably reflected negatively on the amount of time needed to repair and recover combat equipment.

After the completion of the Korsun'-Shevchenkovskii operation, the formations of the 2nd Tank Army took up defensive positions along the Iablonovka – Tikhonovka (8 kilometers north of Ryzhanovka) line. On 22 February 1944, a directive was received from the headquarters of the 1st Ukrainian Front, in which it was stated: "In fulfillment of the order of the *Stavka* of the Supreme Command, I am ordering the 2nd Tank Army to be placed under the command of the 2nd Ukrainian Front as of 20.00 on 21.2.1944. The army is to remain in the area it occupies until receipt of a special order." In connection with the transfer to the 2nd Ukrainian Front for participation in new offensive battles, on 27 February the army turned over its sector of defense to the 78th Rifle Corps and assembled in the Lisianka area.

The losses of the German panzer divisions that opposed the 2nd Tank Army were also significant. For example, the 1st SS Panzer Division *Leibstandarte Adolf Hitler* had 22 Pz. III and Pz. IV, 16 Panthers and 7 Tigers on 31 December 1943. On 1 March 1944, it had 34 Pz. III and Pz. IV tanks, 58 Panthers and 18 Tigers. However, in January-February 1944 the division had received an additional 20 Pz. IV, 47 Panthers and 23 Tigers from factories. Thus, its irrecoverable losses over

January-February 1944 amounted to approximately 25 tanks (8 Pz. III and Pz. IV, 5 Panthers and 12 Tigers). Zetterling estimates the division's irreplaceable losses over the period between 1 and 18 February 1944 at 20 tanks and self-propelled guns (6 Panther, 1 Pz. IV, 10 StuG, 2 Marder and 1 Wespe). However, it is necessary to keep in mind that of the 110 tanks belonging to the 1st SS Panzer Division on 1 March 1944, only 14 (a little more than 10 percent) were combat-ready, while 96 tanks were undergoing repair. Here we are dealing with "concealed losses", because a majority of the 96 tanks "available but under repair" in fact never again returned to service, but were irrecoverably lost a month later during the German evacuation of "Hube's Pocket".

The same applies to the Heavy Panzer Regiment *Bäke* (the 503rd Heavy Panzer Battalion and a battalion of Panthers from the 23rd Panzer Division); of the 69 Tigers that it had available on 26 January 1944, 21 were destroyed in the combats in the Oratov – Cherkassy area. The losses of Panthers were also high. Of the 72 Panthers that were available on 20 January 1944, by 29 February only 3 were still serviceable (5 percent of the initial number), while according to German records, 25 Panthers had been lost irrevocably. During the retreat on 7 March 1944, the regiment irrevocably lost another 23 Panthers, including 18 Panthers that were being repaired in the Potash area. Here we should also add the losses of the 506th Heavy Panzer Battalion, which at a minimum lost 7 Tigers irrevocably and another 19 knocked out or damaged Tigers that were located in repair shops.

Having 20 Pz. IV and 40 Panthers on 1 January 1944, the 1st Panzer Division had 24 Pz. IV and 30 Panthers on 1 March. Since the division received 28 Pz. IV tanks and 40 Panthers from factories in January-February 1944, **its irrecoverable losses over January and February 1944 amounted to 74 tanks** (24 Pz. IV and 50 Panthers). Zetterling places the division's irrecoverable losses over the period from 5 February to 20 February 1944 at 36 tanks (27 Panthers and 9 Pz. IV). Of the 54 tanks in its possession on 1 March 1944, only 15 (28 percent) were operational, while 39 tanks were undergoing repair. The irrecoverable tank losses of the 16th Panzer Division over January-February 1944 amounted to **75 tanks** (9 Pz. III, 32 Pz. IV and 34 Panthers), while the 17th Panzer Division had to write off **54 tanks** (5 Pz. III and 49 Pz. IV). Zetterling estimates that these two divisions irrevocably lost 48 tanks (32 in the 16th Panzer and 16 in the 17th Panzer) over the period between 5 February and 20 February 1944.

Thus, the German panzer grouping of the III Panzer Corps, which had the order to break through to General Stemmermann's encircled forces, were unable to carry out their task and in the process lost approximately 264 tanks irrevocably, not including the losses in self-propelled and assault guns. To these losses, one should add those of the SS Panzer Division *Wiking*, the SS Brigade *Wallonia*, and of the 228th and 239th Assault Gun Battalions, which when coming out of the Cherkassy pocket, irrevocably lost all their tanks (not less than **54 tanks** in the SS Panzer Division *Wiking*) and assault guns (approximately **42 StuG**), not less than a third of their personnel, and absolutely all of their heavy weapons. Thus the attempts by several Western historians and former Nazi generals to diminish the defeat suffered by the *Wehrmacht* at Korsun'-Shevchenkovskii (Cherkassy) appear unconvincing.

The former artillery commander of the 2nd Tank Army, General Plaskov, left behind detailed personal recollections of General Bogdanov and gave insights into the operation of his headquarters:

> In the first days of September 1943, I was summoned to Front headquarters. There I met Semen Il'ich Bogdanov. "You've been assigned to me," he said. The order had already been signed. In fact, at the Front headquarters they handed me a prepared assignment. But Bogdanov gave me a tug: "Let's go, Grisha; quickly, there is no time. You won't regret it!" We took a seat together in the open body of a Dodge and started off.
>
> Having had a rest in Bogdanov's quarters, now alone I headed to army headquarters. It was located in a small settlement. I looked around for tanks – and didn't see a single one. I only

A T-34 with tank riders aboard passes a burning Tiger tank.

A German Panther, knocked out by Lieutenant Kravtsev's SU-85. The photograph was taken from the driver-mechanic's hatch.

made out thoroughly camouflaged anti-aircraft machine guns. Sentries were posted outside the staff buildings, smartly dressed and well-groomed. With my approach, they sharply snapped to attention. I liked the regimen in the headquarters: a clean, quiet and thoroughly businesslike atmosphere. I became acquainted with my new fellow officers. I was immediately included in the work. The army had recently gone through heavy fighting at Kursk. It had suffered losses in both men and equipment. It was now being replenished. There were a lot of inexperienced soldiers. They were undergoing intense training. A lot of new equipment was arriving straight from the factories – tanks, trucks and guns. I visited the artillery units. There was a lot of artillery – hundreds of barrels – and all of it on mechanized tow. The abundance of anti-aircraft guns and "Katiushas" was pleasing.

The organization of a tank army's artillery was in general little different from that which I had dealt with previously. It was not in vain that Bogdanov had been convincing me: "Your work will be just the same. It is only that there you were supporting infantry, but now you'll be supporting tanks. That's the only difference."

I spent time in the artillery headquarters of the corps and in the regiments and brigades, talking with the men. They were good people. On the morning of my fifth day, Bogdanov summoned me to his headquarters – "Well, how are things?" I told him what I had managed to see. He listened attentively, smiling. Then he said, "I see you're getting along like a brushfire. You've plunged into work. But consider that complaints about you are already coming in."

I understood nothing. It seemed that I'd given nobody a reason to be offended at me. So far, no one had kicked up a ruckus.

"The self-propelled gun crews are complaining," Bogdanov said. "You've dropped by everyone else, but you haven't looked in on them."

"At first I want to find out what they are."

"You'll find out when you get there."

"No, I can't do that."

From Bogdanov, I went straight to the army's technical repair shop. There, several self-propelled guns were being repaired. I climbed all over these powerful machines. They had a lot in common with tanks – the same armor, the same tracks, only the guns were more powerful. Their assignment was to accompany the tanks, and to clear a path forward for them with their fire. I studied the manual for using the self-propelled gun, and the instructions for conducting fire from their cannons. I spent several hours each day with this. I wasn't embarrassed to ask questions of the self-propelled gun commanders, the gunners and the drivers, or of the mechanics that repaired the machines. Only then, once I had familiarized myself with the machines, the crewmen and my job, did I risk travelling to the self-propelled gun units, to check how they were training and carrying out their service. I still hadn't seen self-propelled guns in combat, but I fervently came to love them, and quickly grew close to the cheerful members of the crews of these menacing machines.

At the end of the year, we received an order to restage to Sviatoshino, near Kiev. A 130-kilometer march in the shortest possible amount of time confronted us. The army's artillery headquarters in the course of the night prepared a plan for the march. It wasn't a simple job. You had to think about security on the march; the order of movement of the tracked and wheeled vehicles; rendering assistance to bogged down prime movers and trucks; foresee how the columns would deploy and go into combat in case of the appearance of the enemy; work out systems; and much else, without which the orderly and rapid movement of an enormous mass of vehicles and equipment is unthinkable.

On the next day, we decamped. I had never before happened to see anything similar. The columns of tanks, self-propelled guns, armored carriers, and prime movers with attached guns extended for tens of kilometers. Everything was on tracks or wheels – headquarters, repair shops, supplies and field hospitals. There was not a single person on foot. The tidal surge of machinery began to roll along the road, and the earth was shaking from it weight and the howl of engines.

Bogdanov was racing alongside the column in his open Dodge, urging everyone forward – "Faster, faster!" (It is not in vain that the soldiers nicknamed him "General Forward"!) Semen Il'ich didn't tolerate the least delay. As soon as the slightest hitch arose, he was already there. He acted decisively and irresistibly. Should a tank engine die, at the signal of the army commander two prime movers would quickly roll up to the stopped machine. With steel cable as thick as an arm, they would drag the tank off the road. It would happen sometimes that in the process, the unfortunate tank would topple over onto its side. "It's nothing, you'll make your way out later," Bogdanov would soothe the machine's commander. "You'll catch up. But I won't hold up the entire column for your sake." But he'd already be calling up an engineer: "These guys are stuck. Give them a hand!" Then once again he would go speeding alongside the howling and rumbling wave of machines, alternatingly cheerful and wrathful, but entirely focused.

By the next morning, the army had already arrived at its designated place. The machines, encrusted with mud, quickly took cover in woods. The headquarters set up in a village. Once again, there was not a single tank near it. Indeed, you wouldn't think that the headquarters of a tank army was here.

The 2nd Tank Army advanced toward Zhitomir. We were considered as part of the 1st Ukrainian Front's reserve, but we were almost constantly in combat. The foe, having collected forces, launched an attack against the rifle divisions and began to encircle them. Our 3rd Tank Corps, which was to break through to Lipovets Station and Ochitkov, was sent to bail out the infantry. For the first time I observed a major tank battle. Hundreds of armored vehicles from both sides took part in it. For five days – from 24 to 29 January – fierce clashes didn't cease. Our tankers were fighting heroically. The crews of the self-propelled guns didn't yield to them in courage and skill. On our side we often underestimated these machines. The tankers considered them to be bastardized tanks, while the artillerymen thought of them as inferior guns. In fact, this was a powerful weapon. Self-propelled guns were just as maneuverable as tanks, but their large-caliber guns could penetrate any armor. In combats they moved together with the tanks, and at times even led them, laying down fire on the direction ahead.

The enemy was superior in force, and our 3rd Tank Corps was forced to retreat. The self-propelled guns covered the withdrawal. Over a short period of time, Lieutenant Colonel Dmitrii Gurenko's Guardsmen destroyed sixteen fascist tanks, while losing two self-propelled guns in return. Lieutenant Colonel Boris Kochkarenko's self-propelled guns were also stoutly repelling the enemy tank onslaughts. These two self-propelled gun regiments held the line, until our tanks and motorized infantry had gained separation from the enemy and had re-established a firm line of defense. Only then did the self-propelled guns fall back, under the cover of the fire of heavy guns.

Together with the army's deputy commander for vehicle maintenance and technical support Colonel S.M. Krupenin and the chief of artillery supply Colonel S.N. Fadeev, I hurried to talk with these brave men. How had they survived? How had they escaped? For five days, the German "Ferdinands" [Author's note: Here and further on, the talk is about StuG assault guns and Marder tank destroyers. "Ferdinand" was the nickname given to all German self-propelled guns.] had been firing at them from the front and flanks.

I inspected the machines. There were dents in the armor and deep notches from fragments. Some of the self-propelled guns had broken tracks, or jammed guns. Even so, the enemy had been unable to overcome them, and they had carried out their task.

However, if you will, everything was much harder for the artillerymen manning the field guns. Within the self-propelled guns, the crew was protected by the hard armor against shell fragments and bullets. As long as the carriage was undamaged, it could maneuver, and get out of the line of sight of targeted fire. The artillerymen of the field guns were deprived of these advantages. They didn't even have time to dig in; they fired from open positions, in plain sight of the enemy. Their only hope was the accuracy of their fire. Under the hailstorm of bullets and fragments, protected only by their gun shield, they engaged in mortal combat with enemy tanks, halftracks and infantry.

In the first days of February, the German fascist command assembled a large panzer group and two infantry divisions, which were to launch an attack from the west toward Pochapintsy, in order to liberate the encircled forces in the Korsun'-Shevchenkovskii area. After two days of fighting, the Nazis had somewhat shoved back our units in this area. The 2nd Tank Army was urgently ordered to move to the Antonovka, Fediukovka area, 30 kilometers southwest of the city of Korsun'-Shevchenkovskii. The task was to arrest the enemy's attempts to breach the ring of Soviet forces. Our machines moved out on the march in the early thaw, in the mud, along the disintegrating roads. Less than 24 hours later, they reached the designated line. Already within 14 hours after arriving in the new area, our tanks and artillery launched an attack against the SS Panzer Division *Adolf Hitler*. No sooner had we become tied up in combat, when the Nazis hurled two more divisions against us – the 17th Panzer and the 34th Infantry.

Together with Bogdanov, we hurried to the Medvin area, where the fighting had taken on a particularly savage nature. Our tanks and the enemy tanks were maneuvering against each other at a range of 600-800 meters. The cannon fire and the ringing hits of armor-piercing shells merged into a continuous roar, which never subsided for an instant. The combat was flowing in constant motion. Tanks were coming together and moving apart; in such conditions, it was hard to count upon the accuracy of fire. Thus, we were making very slow progress.

Bogdanov silently observed the battle. Next to him were the member of the army's Military Council Petr Latyshev and the army's Chief of Staff Aleksei Radzievsky. Bogdanov was a decisive and authoritative man, who handled the units' actions boldly, without sidelong glances. However, he never rejected good advice, and paid heed to the opinion of his deputies, the corps commanders, and the service chiefs. Indeed, perhaps, his forte as an army commander resided in this.

The fighting was becoming drawn out. Bogdanov began to get nervous.

"I'm heading to the corps commander," he decided. "Together we'll give thought to what to do." Then he addressed me: "Meanwhile, you figure out what you can do to help the tankers here."

The artillery of the 3rd Tank Corps quickly regrouped, and at 15.40 conducted a brief 10-minute, but heavy artillery barrage. The corps went on the attack again, and with the onset of darkness our tanks and infantry broke into Antonovka.

The enemy attack on 11 February was not a surprise to us. The surprise was the quantity of enemy forces – three panzer and two infantry divisions. A terrible battle went on for the entire day. That night, leaving behind the self-propelled guns and several artillery battalions as cover, our tanks conducted a 45-kilometer march and struck the flank of the attacking German panzer divisions. The Soviet tankers fought stubbornly for two days, but with no clear result.

That night, Bogdanov angrily paced off the dimensions of his office. His Deputy for Vehicle Maintenance and Technical Support Samuil Krupenin entered the room and reported how many knocked-out tanks had been recovered from the battlefield and how many of them could be repaired by the army and corps repair shops. The army commander heard him out, and then gloomily looked at us: "A lot of losses, but little sense."

The arrival of the 3rd Tank Corps commander General Aleksandr Shamshin was being expected. He and Bogdanov were long-time friends from their joint service before the war had started. When he arrived, Bogdanov quickly asked him, "How many tanks do you have left in the corps?" Shamshin replied, "More than might be expected. So we'll do some more fighting." We sat for a long while, pondering what to do next.

Unexpectedly for everyone, Shamshin broke the silence: "I think that we must attack quickly. The Nazis believe that they have smashed us, and that it will take some time before we can bring ourselves back to order. But we'll up and give them a hard rap tonight."

"It is risky," Bogdanov thoughtfully pronounced. But we all understood what he was thinking inside. Then suddenly he gave a smile and twirled a finger by his temple: "Why didn't I think of it?! Let's get busy!" He quickly came up with a decision to send the motorized rifle brigade to Lisianka. Suddenly, with no artillery preparation and without the escort of tanks, it would break into the enemy's position at night. "Once there, we will act according to the situation," he finished, slapping his palm on the table.

On 17 February, the Soviet forces completed the liquidation of the enemy's encircled Korsun'-Shevchenkovskii grouping …

Guards Major General Anatolii Shvebig, the deputy commander of the 16th Tank Corps for vehicle maintenance and technical support recalls:

Having conducted a march in the Zhitomir – Belaia Tserkov' direction, the corps became part of the 1st Ukrainian Front, and on 20 January 1944, in the Belaia Tserkov' area, it began to receive trains carrying replacement armored vehicles. The technical department of the 16th Tank Corps in these days, just as in the days of hot combat, was working intensively. We were controlling the arrival of the equipment. Over a short period of time, 197 T-34, 16 SU-85, 10 British Mark IX and just as many SU-152 arrived to equip the units. The presence of such a large quantity of tanks in the tank brigades forced a re-examination of the personnel and organization of the repair elements. Each tank brigade now had three tank battalions with a total of 65 tanks. Correspondingly, the number of personnel in the vehicle maintenance and technical support companies was increased to 123.

The January frosts were hardening. The officers accompanying the trains carrying the tanks had been compelled to transport the batteries in heated railcars and to drain the water from the machines' systems. In such a condition, the tanks were not ready for combat. It became necessary to organize a special technical service point at an intermediary railroad station 50 kilometers from Belaia Tserkov', where the tanks could be filled with hot water, the batteries could be installed, and the engines could be tested. Engineer-Major Karakozov and battalion commander Captain Kul'biakin directed all this work.

On 20 January 1944, major forces of Nazi infantry and tanks broke through our defenses northeast of Vinnitsa and began to develop the offensive toward Pogrebishche. Soon an order arrived for the units of the 16th Tank Corps to move out to the breakthrough area, minus the 107th Tank Brigade, which still hadn't received all its machines. We were to stop the German offensive by the end of 28 January. However, we were confronted with the need to make a forced march in the conditions of an ice storm. We had to unload the tanks and self-propelled guns quickly. We began to prepare for the march.

Despite the insufficient experience with driving tanks of many of the replacement crews, as well as the difficulty of the road conditions, the corps' units advanced approximately 100 kilometers overnight. For the most part, the march was conducted in an organized manner, without any serious losses in equipment. Minor breakdowns were fixed by specialists of the technical support companies, while more complex problems were repaired by the 168th Repair Base.

The corps commander Major General Ivan Dubovoi and the tank brigade commanders knew that the enemy, approaching the town of Oratov, was superior in force. They decided to attack the Nazis at night. The tank brigades deployed and went on the attack from the march. A night-time tank clash erupted. The Germans couldn't withstand the attack and began to retreat, which gave an opportunity for the encircled units of the 135th Rifle Division to link up with the tankers, and through their joint efforts to drive the Nazis out of Oratov and throw them back to the south.

For example, the tankers of the 109th Tank Brigade enabled a battalion of the 497th Rifle Regiment (135th Rifle Division) to come out of encirclement on the night of 29/30 January 1944. The rifle battalion had been in a hopeless situation in the village of Strizhakovo, with no prospects for an organized exit from encirclement. At 19.30, a heavy exchange of tank and anti-tank fire began in the area of Oratov Station, which gradually intensified. At this time, observation outposts and battalion scouts detected 6 enemy tanks that were patrolling from Oratov Station to Sinarna Station that were preventing the possibility for the battalion and other elements to escape the pocket. In connection with the intensifying combat for Oratov Station, resulting from an attack by the 109th Tank Brigade, the Nazis were compelled to return the patrolling tanks to Oratov Station in order to retain possession of it. As a consequence, the battalion with all of its attached elements of the 135th Rifle Division, numbering 182 men, came out of the encirclement, (about which there is a note from the battalion commander Captain Kerzhavin dated 31 January 1944).

The element of surprise and the night action temporarily secured success. After all, the corps' formations were thrown hastily into the fighting, without accompanying artillery support, or reconnaissance of the enemy and the terrain. Not enough time was given to study the orders and the situation, or to reconnoiter and handle questions regarding cooperation with other units. Later, both brigades in view of the enemy's plain superiority were compelled to go over to a defense on the line Chagov. Merni – Laposhinka – Tarasovka.

In these fierce battles, the repair teams wrote another glorious page in the heroic chronicle of the corps' formations. Under enemy fire, they put 53 tanks back into service, 17 of which had been recovered from the battlefield.

In the course of 4-5 February 1944, the Germans went on the offensive toward Vinograd, Vytylevka, Kosiakovka with the aim of freeing a major grouping of their forces encircled in the Korsun'-Shevchenkovskii area. By the end of 5 February, the Germans had reached the line Veselyi Kut – Kosiakovka – Kuchkovka.

On 2 February, units of the 16th Tank Corps began to arrive in the outer ring of encirclement and received the assignment to block a breakthrough by the foe's shock tank groups from the direction of Lisianka to the divisions trapped in the pocket. The regrouping of the corps' units to the outer ring of encirclement took place in exceptionally difficult conditions. An early thaw had set in. Rains were falling. Snow deposited in the ruts and low-lying places had started to turn brown. The roads, over which tank and vehicle columns were moving in a constant flow, turned into a quagmire. Could the corps in such conditions fulfill an order and move 130 kilometers over 24 hours? The command first of all expected an answer from the officers of the engineer and technical services to this question. Realizing that wheeled transport would inevitably get separated from the tanks, we mounted the repair brigades on the armor, and loaded all the necessary tools and spare parts. Each tank also had 5-6 additional boxes of shells and a 15-member tank-riding team aboard it. The tanks, encrusted with the Ukrainian black earth, were moving in first and second gear. They were scraping the earth with their bellies and digging out wide and deep ruts with their tracks, and at times settled on their bellies. Large areas of broken ground appeared in their wake. After a tank column passed along a road, the road practically ceased to exist.

The repairmen had to crawl beneath the belly of the tanks in the mud in order to fix one problem or other. Wheeled vehicles moved at a pace of 10-15 kilometers a day. Broken down machines awaiting repair fell behind. Unexpectedly, the tactical situation also became complicated. Our rear-echelon and repair elements became cut off from the combat units. They had to make a detour and continue to advance along the route Stanovishche, Tarashcha, Medvin. I reported to the corps commander that given the movement of the tanks in such conditions, there was only enough fuel and oil to reach the assembly area. However, it is impossible to take on fuel on the battlefield. Front Headquarters without delay sent out 15 Studebakers with diesel fuel. This was an enormous help for us. Ten tanks dropped out of the column due to the breakdown of the clutch, the gear mechanisms of the first gear, or the final drive bearing. One tank had a jammed rod and piston group due to engine overheating, while another tank got stuck in a swamp, while a third tank fell into a ravine. Having fully exceeded their engine lifetimes, not a single SU-152 reached the objective, which was as we supposed.

Once again, I had to appeal to the assistance of Captain But and his PO-2 aircraft. We would take off with difficulty from a field covered with slushy snow, and I or Engineer-Major Ekeleovsky would fly together with Captain But over the route taken by the columns. The airplane didn't make any landings en route. We were spotting the location of disabled machines.

The motorized supply columns, promised by the Front, hadn't arrived. In order to search for the Front's transport, search groups on tanks, in the fuel tanks of which the last remaining fuel had been poured, were organized. Soon the commander of the Front's armored and tank forces Colonel General Novikov arrived at the headquarters of the 16th Tank Corps.

"Where are the tanks?" was the commander's first question.

"In their firing positions," replied General Dubovoi.

"You're dissembling," Novikov sharply interrupted him. "Half of your tanks are still en route. You don't know anything!"

Then the commander demanded a report on the condition of the tanks and particularly on those lagging behind. I talked in detail about the reasons for the involuntary halts and showed him the location of each tank that had lagged behind. Having heard me out, Colonel General Novikov observed, "This is a completely different matter. You've informed me that your situation is different." Exchanging glances with Dubovoi, we sighed with relief.

"But why haven't you met the supply column with fuel at the designated place?"

Dubovoi replied, "No one showed up at the designated place, while the organized search groups haven't located the truck column."

"Will you be able to find the fuel vehicles by morning?"

"We will don't know where to look for them. The route taken by the supply column is unknown. It isn't anywhere within a 10-kilometer radius," the corps commander answered.

Midnight arrived, and there was still no word about the fuel trucks. General Novikov asked us a few more questions, made sure that everything was clear for us, and then got ready to leave. I was ordered to escort the commander.

We drove for a long time for some reason through the February pre-dawn hours. Here and there, illumination flares began to burst in the sky. The Willys continued to fly along the back roads between the villages, until it finally stopped. General Novikov asked, "Are there any of our units nearby?" I requested permission to climb out of the jeep to get my bearings. Fifty paces from the road, I spotted the Gniloi Tikich stream in front of me. Quickly heading back, I informed the commander that the command post of a rifle regiment was on a nearby hill, and that a bit further away, sappers were building a bridge. It was cold and raw. A dense mist was rising above the stream. It began to disperse only with the first rays of sunlight. Iumatov, who had only just arrived at the crossing, was standing next to me on the riverbank.

"The Studebakers have to head toward this bridge," he said, wrapped in his overcoat against the early dawn chill. "The corps has no other road available to it."

We crossed over the bridge to the other side of the river and headed out along the side of the road, sinking up to our knees in mud. We had advanced approximately 2 kilometers, when two soldiers in black overalls approached us.

"Who are you?" Iumatov asked.

"We're drivers. We're transporting fuel. The entire column is stuck 1 kilometer from here."

"My dear chaps!" Iumatov exclaimed. "We need you right away. Inform your commander: The bridge across the river isn't ready; park the column alongside the river. We'll ferry the drums with fuel and oil across the river and load them on tanks."

I returned to the command post of the rifle regiment and reported to General Novikov that all the tanks would have a half-tank of fuel by midday. Colonel General Novikov brightened up. Thanking me, he dismissed me. I immediately set off toward the crossing. There, feverish work was underway. With no regard for the cold and the icy water, the tankers and drivers were ferrying the drums to the opposite bank. The crisis point had passed. The tanks, having received fuel, were deploying into combat formations.

Guards Lieutenant Iurchenko left behind a description of one of the combats for the village of Chesnovka during the Korsun'-Shevchenkovskii operation:

In February 1944, our battalion was holding a position in the village of Bradok, preparing for an attack toward the village of Chesnovka. February had turned bitterly cold, with snow squalls. The men's hands were cramped by the cold, their uniforms coated with ice. On 13 February, the order to attack arrived. At the signal to attack, the tanks moved forward. The enemy opened strong artillery and mortar fire. Progress was difficult. The deep snow and wind-blown snow hindered maneuvering on the battlefield. At the end of the day, overcoming obstacles and snowdrifts, three tanks under the command of Captain Donkov broke into the village of Chesnovka. Street fighting erupted. The enemy was firing on our tanks from the roofs of buildings, from windows and from cellars. In the combat for Chesnovka, our three tanks destroyed two enemy tanks, 5 halftracks and up to a company of enemy infantry.

From the recollections of Hero of the Soviet Union Sergei Matsapura:

We underwent our combat baptism in the 107th Tank Brigade in the first days of February, when the forces of the 1st and 2nd Ukrainian Fronts encircled the Nazi Korsun'-Shevchenkovskii grouping. We received an alert in the night and from Belaia Tserkov' moved southward toward the place of battle. This march became a serious trial for the young driver-mechanics. The roads had disintegrated into mud, and heavy, wet snow was falling. In several places on the march, the tanks were literally swimming in the mud, polishing it with their bellies. The tank engines rapidly overheated from such strain. The march went successfully; there was not a single accident in the company. Already close to the front, we found out the reason for such a hasty redeployment of the brigade. Fascist panzer divisions, striving to breach the Korsun'-Shevchenkovskii pocket, had launched a strong attack against the outer ring of encirclement. Among a number of other formations and units, the 107th Tank Brigade was also moved out to meet the enemy. At night, in thick fog, we entered the village of Petrovka, and with tank riders aboard our armor, we moved on, toward the village of Votylevka. A meeting engagement began – tanks against tanks. Our battalion had already penetrated to the outskirts of the village, when an order was received to fall back to Petrovka. We withdrew and camouflaged our machines. At dawn, we prepared a fresh attack toward Votylevka. It sprawled on the far side of a broad, open field. A road, planted on either side with old willow trees, ran along the left edge of the field from Petrovka to Votylevka. Our tank platoon was on the left flank of the battalion's combat formation, which is to say, on the road to Votylevka.

We were sitting in the tank, waiting for the signal. I was picking out a route of advance. At first I would lead the machine through the gardens. The isolated huts and bare cherry orchards of Petrovka, which extended along the road, didn't provide much cover, but nevertheless! Further on were the old willows, and from there, we would make a dash into Votylevka. The tank commander Lieutenant Pogorelov gave the order: "Forward!" The engine roared, and we moved out. My friend Golovnia was driving the tank on my right; further on, other machines were charging across the field. We cleared the planted willows, and now close in front of us were the homes and huts of the village. Somewhere off to our right, German tank guns were firing rapidly. Crossing a hill slope, we broke into Votylevka through some alley. Golovnia's tank was somewhat out ahead of us. He halted briefly and fired. Now I spotted his target. It was a German Panther tank. It hadn't had time to pivot its turret in our direction. Fedia directed his "34" to almost within point-blank range. A shot, and then another shot! The Panther's gun barrel dropped helplessly toward the ground. This happens when the gun's counterbalancing gear is damaged. The crew, perhaps, was still alive, but the tank had been knocked out. We went around the Panther and steered our machines down the street. Golovnia was on the right side, and I was on the left.

"Watch out, a Ferdinand!" Lieutenant Pogorelov called out over the intercom. [Author's note: Here and further, this is reference to a German StuG.] About 100 meters in front of us, having laid a smokescreen, the armored monster was backing out of a yard into the street. Both of our tanks fired and struck the assault gun's right flank and engine compartment. The self-propelled gun erupted in flames. So far, combat fortune was on our side. Plainly, the enemy had overlooked the breakthrough of our two tanks into Votylevka from the direction of the road. All of his attention was focused on the combat with the battalion's main forces, which were attacking from the front across the field.

However, soon we were also engaged. My tank shook from two nearby shell explosions. The fascists were firing from somewhere behind us. "Take cover!" Pogorelov commanded. I drove the machine into a yard, behind a hut. The enemy had to see this. I made a quick advance into the gardens. This he could have hardly seen. Golovnia also placed his tank behind cover – behind a shed on the opposite side of the street. There was no other of our tanks anywhere near us. I could see part of the field between Petrovka and Votylevka. Two T-34s were burning there. Had the battalion's attack been repulsed? But now I had no time to think about this. As long as another "Ferdinand" was lurking in our rear, we were pinned down in our actions. "Keep watch!" Pogorelov ordered.

Through my safety glass in the forward hatch, I could see the street and a corner of the field. Vorob'ev was glued to the turret vision slit. Only the commander had a 360° view. His optical sight was mounted on the turret hatch, but even the Lieutenant couldn't spot the hidden "Ferdinand". Meanwhile, enemy self-propelled guns had spotted the place where Fedor Golovnia had parked his tank. They opened fire. A shell from a "Ferdinand's" cannon, evidently, penetrated the shed, and we heard a loud explosion. Black smoke rose from behind the shed. I had to help my comrades quickly! However, at this moment a German medium Pz. III tank appeared at the far end of the street. It was advancing slowly, firing blindly, since everything around us was blanketed by smoke. The Panther and the "Ferdinand" were burning, as were Golovnia's T-34 and the thatch-covered shed. We allowed the hostile tank to approach a little closer, and the Lieutenant knocked it out with his second shot. But now the enemy had detected our ambush position, and opened aimed fire from both the front and flank; shells were landing ever closer, and we had expended almost all of our ammunition. Lieutenant Pogorelov reported the situation over the radio to the battalion headquarters. The battalion commander ordered a withdrawal from Votylevka.

Passing the shed, we could see the blackened T-34 with a shell hole in its flank. Our comrades were lying on the snow. Three of them – the platoon commander Lieutenant Aleksandrov, driver-mechanic Fedor Golovnia, and the radio operator – had been mortally wounded and died without regaining consciousness. The gun loader, the same one about whom Fedia and I had been speaking, received a bad concussion. However, in the difficult moment for the crew, he had managed to forget his ego, and had attempted to save his comrades. He had dragged all three out of the burning tank. We loaded the bodies and the concussed gun loader aboard our armor, and brought them back to Petrovka.

It turned out that the battalion's attack actually had failed. Having lost several tanks, the battalion had been forced to retreat. The enemy had been firing primarily from the right flank, from well-concealed ambush positions. In addition we, who had broken into Votylevka on the left flank, had also been unable to spot the "Ferdinand" that had brewed up Lieutenant Aleksandrov's tank.

We took Votylevka the next day, but now without our participation. My tank ran over a mine at the very outset of the attack. It was a good thing that the mine exploded under the outside edge of the left track, and the bogey wheels took the full impact of the explosion. Two of the wheels were blown off. Technician-Lieutenant Oreshkin himself towed the stricken tank off the battlefield while under fire. But what to do next? Where to find new bogey wheels? The rear-echelon elements were lagging behind on the ruined roads. "Let's get bogey wheels from any of them," Oreshkin said, gesturing at the field, where knocked-out and burned-out T-34s were standing. However, before removing the wheels, we had to find a machine that had undamaged bogey wheels. So together with Oreshkin, we headed toward those disabled tanks. We were lucky; the first one we reached had intact wheels. We removed them, and then started rolling them by hand. It was hard work; each bogey wheel weighed approximately 200 kilograms, and layer after layer of mud kept accumulating on them with each turn of the wheel. Now and then we had to stop and clean them off. We totally exhausted ourselves, while rolling the first of them to our tank, and then the second one. We mounted the wheels on our tanks, tightened up the track, and by lunchtime the tank was again ready for service.

The recent graduate of a military school Technician-Lieutenant Pavel Oreshkin had passed through his combat baptism at Votylevka with honor – as both a specialist and as a simple soldier. This was his first step toward that high level of esteem, which he soon gained among his peers. After all, thanks to the courage and skill of Oreshkin and his mechanics, who frequently repaired damaged combat machines directly under fire, our platoon, even when suffering losses, always maintained a high level of combat readiness. The 107th Tank Brigade fought for several days at Votylevka, at times repelling the attacks of enemy tank units and at other times counterattacking.

Then the brigade was shifted directly to Lisianka. Here, having gathered a powerful tank fist, the Nazi command made another attempt to break through the outer ring of encirclement. Lisianka changed hands several times. On the night of 12/13 February, the fascists drove our brigade out of this village. Up until 18 February, when the pocket that contained ten enemy divisions was finally reduced, the 107th Tank Brigade continued to operate on the outer ring of encirclement. Only later, when the corps was transferred to the 2nd Ukrainian Front through Pochapintsy, did I managed to see the signs of the slaughter that had taken place on the inner ring of encirclement. The roads, fields and ravines around Pochapintsy were piled with thousands of German corpses and wrecked combat equipment. Here, on the night of a snowstorm, the fascist column had tried to break out of the encirclement, and everyone and everything in it had come under fire.

**Officers and men of the 2nd Tank Army who particularly distinguished themselves in the operation**

Guards Colonel Nikolai Koshaev's 11th Guards Tank Brigade particularly stood out in the fighting, for which it received the honorific title "Korsun'" and was awarded the Order of the Red Banner. The commanders of the subordinate tank battalions Kalashnikov, Khmelinin and Ushakov distinguished themselves in the recent fighting.

Prokofii Kalashnikov –
11th Guards Tank Brigade.

Vladimir Nesvetailov –
11th Guards Tank Brigade.

Alexei Pustovalov –
11th Guards Tank Brigade.

Ivan Ostroverkhov –
16th Tank Corps
(battalion commander).

I.I. Gorbunov –
50th Tank Brigade.

Sergei Matsapura –
107th Tank Brigade.

I.O. Pozdeev –
107th Tank Brigade.

V. Voloznev –
107th Tank Brigade.

K.A. Ishchenko –
109th Tank Brigade.

Alexandr Rybin – 15th
Motorized Rifle Brigade.

Nikandr Panfilov –
51st Tank Brigade.

M.F. Vdovchenko –
11th Guards Tank Brigade.

I.A. Kozhevnikov –
11th Guards Tank Brigade.

I.V. Chupakhin –
11th Guards Tank Brigade.

Petr Krupinov –
11th Guards Tank Brigade.

V.M. Ochkin –
11th Guards Tank Brigade.

M.P. Gedzhadze –
11th Guards Tank Brigade.

M.N. Zhuchkov –
11th Guards Tank Brigade.

M.I. Konev –
3rd Tank Corps.

V.P. Oskov –
3rd Tank Corps.

P.A. Annikov –
86th Guards Mortar
Regiment, 16th Tank Corps.

I.B. Ostrous –86th Guards
Mortar Regiment.

O.G. Antiasov –
107th Tank Brigade.

M.O. Elkin –
107th Tank Brigade.

From the write-up recommending Guards Major Kalashnikov for the title "Hero of the Soviet Union"

> On 27 January 1944, the enemy in strength of up to a regiment of infantry with 20 tanks undertook an attack toward Ocheretnia. Our units fell back under the onslaught of superior enemy forces. Guards Major Kalashnikov with his tank battalion (11th Guards Tank Brigade), having conducted a march of 100 kilometers, engaged the enemy from the march. Having skillfully organized the combat and in the process demonstrating resolve and heroism, he repelled all the enemy's attacks and inflicted great damage to him in men and equipment. Kalashnikov brewed up 8 tanks. Despite heavy bombing from the air, with a skillful maneuver Guards Major Kalashnikov managed to keep his battalion intact. In the fighting for the village of Komarovka, Guards Major Kalashnikov, demonstrating heroism, repaired a bridge while under enemy fire, and with his battalion broke into the village of Komarovka, and inflicted large losses to the enemy in the combat: 19 guns, 10 tanks including 3 Panthers, 7 trucks, 27 machine guns, and 11 mortars, and he destroyed a regimental command post and more than 250 soldiers and officers.

Soldiers of the 2nd Tank Army who distinguished themselves in the operation [excerpts from their letters of citation]:

**Junior Lieutenant Mikhail Oleinik**, a T-34 platoon commander of the 103rd Tank Brigade's 119th Tank Battalion. Involved in the fighting in the area of Lipovets Station, he demonstrated bravery and prowess: On 27.1.44, from an ambush position he destroyed one medium tank and one enemy cannon. On 28.1.44, he took part in repulsing 6 tank attacks. In this fighting, he destroyed two heavy Tiger tanks. He himself was wounded. Awarded the Order of the Red Banner.

**Senior Lieutenant Fedor Korchagin**, a T-34 company commander of the 103rd Tank Brigade's 420th Tank Battalion. On 27.1.44 west of the village of Bogdanovka, he skillfully led his company into battle. The six tanks of his company were one of the first to breach the enemy's defenses and to engage in a fierce tank battle. When enemy tanks from the left flank launched a counterattack, he demonstrated exceptional fortitude. Allowing the enemy tanks to approach within 500 meters, he personally destroyed one Tiger and one Pz. III. His company drove back 3 enemy counterattacks. In the fighting between 27.1 and 31.1.1944, his company destroyed 6 tanks and one self-propelled gun, 3 trucks, and 25 enemy soldiers and officers. Awarded the Order of the Red Banner.

**Guards Captain Vasilii Esipenko**, commander of the 50th Tank Brigade's 254th Tank Battalion. In the fighting for Lopatino, Veselyi Kut, Kosiakovka and Kuchkovka, he skillfully directed the combat, as a result of which his battalion destroyed 18 tanks, 5 halftracks, 4 cannons, 3 machine guns and 940 soldiers and officers. While up among the battalion's combat formations, he had constant contact with the brigade commander and his subordinate companies. By his personal example, he led his men on to carry out combat tasks. He was awarded the Order of the Red Banner.

**Senior Lieutenant Vladimir Beseda**, T-34 company commander in the 164th Tank Brigade's 360th Tank Battalion. On 8.2.1944, he led his company into the attack against Votylevka. By his personal example, he skillfully directed it. His company destroyed 6 tanks, 3 halftracks and up to 70 enemy soldiers and officers. He personally destroyed three tanks and killed up to 18 Nazis. On 9.2.1944, he remained with his tank on the occupied line and drove back two enemy counterattacks. He destroyed another 2 tanks and up to 35 Nazis. Awarded the Order of the Red Banner.

**Guards Senior Lieutenant Vasilii Vykhodtsev**, company commander, 254th Tank Battalion, 50th Tank Brigade. In combat for Dashukovka on 13.02.44, despite a difficult situation, he skillfully handled his company, and personal brewed up a Tiger and knocked out another German tank. He was recommended for the Order of the Red Banner.

**Senior Lieutenant Dem'ian Filonenko**, a platoon commander of T-34 tanks, 360th Tank Battalion, 164th Tank Brigade. In the combat for Votylevka on 8.2.44, he destroyed a Tiger tank and two Pz. IV tanks. He broke into a column of enemy trucks, and with fire and his tracks he destroyed 6 trucks together with their men and loads, and up to 120 Nazis. In this action his tank was damaged, and his driver-mechanic was severely wounded. Filonenko didn't abandon his damaged tank, and risking his life, together with his radio operator he brought it back to a disabled vehicle collection point. He was awarded the Order of the Red Banner.

**Senior Sergeant Georgii Shapka**, a T-34 driver-mechanic with the 164th Tank Brigade's 360th Tank Battalion. In an attack on 8.2.1944 in the Votylevka area, his crew destroyed 3 tanks and up to 18 enemy soldiers and officers. On 9.2.1944, remaining with his tank on the occupied line, under heavy enemy fire, risking his life, together with his crew he gathered ammunition from knocked-out tanks to replenish the ammunition of the still remaining tanks, and before the onset of darkness as part of his crew, he drove back two enemy counterattacks, destroying 2 enemy tanks and up to 35 Nazis. He was awarded the Order of the Red Banner.

**Captain Ivan Ovsienko**, [acting] commander of the 50th Tank Brigade's motorized rifle battalion [after Guards Captain Svetlov's death]. In combats in the area of Dashukovka, Kuchkovka, Lisianka, Buzhanka and Tikhonovka, he proved himself to be a capable commander, always located up with his combat formations, and he skillfully handled his subordinate elements. In the fighting his battalion killed up to 1,000 enemy soldiers and officers and seized 41 trucks, 10 cannons and 21 machine guns. It took prisoner 42 enemy soldiers and officers. He was awarded the Order of the Red Banner.

Commander of the 50th Tank Brigade,
Roman Liberman.

Commander of the 11th Guards Tank Brigade Nikolai Koshaev (on left) and the brigade's deputy political commander Karp Zhuravlev.

**Guards Captain Vasilii Svetlov**, commander of the 50th Tank Brigade's motorized rifle battalion. In combat for Kuchkovka and Kosiakovka, he showed himself to be a fearless and courageous commander. He skillfully organized cooperation with the tank elements, revealing the main strongpoints of the Germans' defenses, which ensured the successful forcing of the Gniloi Tikich River. In one combat alone, his battalion killed up to 200 enemy soldiers and officers and destroyed 2 Pz. IV tanks and 13 trucks. Guards Captain Svetlov, always up with his combat formations, demonstrated personal heroism and inspired his soldiers to follow him. He was killed in action and posthumously awarded the Order of the Patriotic War 1st Degree.

**Guards Senior Lieutenant Dmitrii Barabash**, tank company commander in the 11th Guards Tank Brigade's 1st Tank Battalion. In the fighting between 26.1 and 28.1.1944 in the Ocheretnia area, his company received an order to take up a defense and to prevent an enemy breakthrough. He properly deployed his machines and directed the combat, and repelled all the enemy's attacks. On 16.2 and 17.2.1944, his company devastated the enemy's encircled Korsun'-Shevchenkovskii grouping in the Komarovka area. Thanks to his proper conduct of the fighting, his company inflicted great damage to the enemy: 3 tanks brewed-up, 7 tanks knocked out; 17 anti-tank guns, 380 trucks, 35 machine guns, 13 mortars, 43 prime movers destroyed; and 2,516 enemy soldiers and officers killed, plus 675 taken prisoner. Dmitrii Barabash himself from his tank destroyed 3 anti-tank guns, 2 tanks, 30 trucks, 45 wagons, and 280 enemy soldiers and officers. Awarded the Order of Lenin.

**Guards Junior Lieutenant Vladimir Smirnov**, a T-34 tank commander of the 11th Guards Tank Brigade's 1st Tank Battalion. In combat on 17.2.1944 to destroy the encircled enemy grouping in the Komarovka, Shenderovka area, he showed himself to be exceptionally bold and courageous. He went on the attack three times, and led his tank into the very midst of the foe, destroying him with fire and crushing him with the tracks of his tank. He destroyed 3 anti-tank guns, 60 trucks, 20 machine guns and 6 prime movers, and killed more than 450 Nazis. In this action he was severely wounded, and he later died from his wounds. He was posthumously awarded the Order of the Patriotic War 1st Degree.

**Guards Captain Pavel Ushakov**, commander of the 11th Guards Tank Brigade's 2nd Tank Battalion. While located on the defense with his battalion in the Pochapintsy area, after the death of the brigade's deputy commander, he assumed command and managed to organize a defense in the face of the desperate enemy attempt to break out of encirclement and link back up with friendly forces. He held the occupied line and inflicted damage to the enemy, destroying 12 guns of various calibers, 9 prime movers, 2 halftracks, 19 trucks, 9 mortars, 42 wagons with their loads, and 1,630 enemy soldiers and officers. Having expended all the fuel in the combat machines, Ushakov's battalion continued to rake the enemy with fire from place, thereby preventing a link-up of the encircled grouping with the relief grouping. He was awarded the Order of the Patriotic War 1st Degree.

# 6

# The Uman' Operation

**Command Staff of the 2nd Tank Army**
Commander in Chief – Lieutenant Semen Bogdanov
Military Council Member – Guards Colonel Nikolai Matiushin
Chief of Staff – General Aleksei Radzievsky
Chief of Operations Department – Colonel Il'ia Bazanov
Commander of Artillery – General Grigorii Plaskov
Deputy Commander for Rear Services – Colonel Petr Antonov
Chief of Intelligence Department– Colonel Ashraf Galimov

**16th Tank Corps** – Major General Ivan Dubovoi
107th Tank Brigade – Colonel Tikhon Abramov
109th Tank Brigade – Colonel Petr Babkovsky
164th Tank Brigade – Colonel Nikolai Kopylov
15th Motorized Rifle Brigade – Colonel Petr Akimochkin
1441st Self-propelled Artillery Regiment (SU-85) – Major Dmitrii Gorbatenko; 298th Guards
Self-propelled Artillery Regiment (SU-76) – Guards Colonel Novikov; 226th Mortar Regiment,
1721st Anti-aircraft Artillery Regiment, 51st Motorcycle Battalion, 729th Destroyer Anti-tank
Artillery Regiment

**3rd Tank Corps** – Major General Nikolai Teliakov
50th Tank Brigade – Colonel Roman Liberman/Major Isak Fundovnyi
51st Tank Brigade – Colonel Semen Mirvoda
103rd Tank Brigade – Lieutenant Colonel Vasilii Makarov
57th Motorized Rifle Brigade – Colonel Pavel Shamardin
881st Self-propelled Artillery Regiment (SU-76) – Captain Mikhail Borisenko; 1540th Heavy
Self-propelled Artillery Regiment (SU-152) – Major Nikolai Shishov; 1618th Self-propelled
Artillery Regiment, 74th Motorcycle Battalion, 728th Destroyer Anti-tank Artillery Battalion,
234th Mortar Regiment, 126th Guards Mortar Battalion, 121st Anti-aircraft Artillery Regiment

**Units Directly Subordinate to Army Headquarters**
11th Guards Tank Brigade – Colonel Nikolai Koshaev; (from 10.3.44) – Lieutenant Colonel Ivan
Kurilenko
8th Guards Heavy Tank Regiment – Lieutenant Colonel Andrei Zemlianoi
13th Guards Heavy Tank Regiment – Colonel Nikolai Grishin
86th Guards Mortar Regiment – Lieutenant Colonel Pavel Zazirnyi
5th Engineer-Sapper Brigade – Colonel Aleksandr Miasnikov
283rd Artillery Regiment – Lieutenant Colonel Naum Sherman
9th Separate Signals Regiment – Lieutenant Colonel Ivan Belenko
1219th Self-propelled Artillery Regiment (SU-85), 999th Self-propelled Artillery Regiment
(SU-76), 87th Motorcycle Battalion, 357th Separate Engineer Battalion

Marshal Konev wrote about the Uman' Operation: "The history of the war doesn't know any other operation broader in its scale and deeper in its complexity in an operational sense, which might have been implemented in the conditions of a complete absence of roads and the spring-time flooding of rivers. In my mind's eye I see indelible scenes of the overcoming of the heavy, sticky mud by the soldiers, officers and generals. I recall with what unbelievable labor the soldiers extracted automobiles stuck up to their cab, guns that had sunk up to their gun carriage in the muck, and the tanks coated with black earth. At the same time, they had little else other than manpower."

The badly depleted enemy units that had strived to break through to the encircled Korsun'-Shevchenkovskii grouping were thrown back by units of the 1st and 2nd Ukrainian Fronts on 24.2.1944 to the line: Vinograd, Tolstye Rogi, Bosovka, Iablonovka, Ryzhanovka. The foe was dispirited, disorganized and had suffered heavy losses in men and equipment. It was resolved for the 2nd Tank Army and the 27th Army to break through the enemy's defensive belt on the Shubennyi Stav – Chizhovka front, launching the main attack in the Rizino, Berezovka, Buki direction, to take Khristinovka and with forward detachments to seize crossings on the Southern Bug River in the Bershad' – Osievka area.

## The preparatory stage for the operation, 25 February to 4 March 1944

The 2nd Tank Army, now subordinate to the 2nd Ukrainian Front, set to work to prepare for the new operation. All of the preparatory work was done in a rear assembly area in the course of four days, from 28 February to 2 March 1944. Over this period, the army was replenished with matériel. The army's supply base was still at Belaia Tserkov'; lacking a possibility to reposition its supply bases due to the absence of a functioning railroad, the army, overcoming the springtime mud, deployed forward supply stockpiles on the ground. The army headquarters together with the corps headquarters conducted preliminary work to prepare for the operation, reconnoitering the jumping-off areas, the routes to reach them, and the routes leading out of them. The engineering units constructed and reinforced 144 linear meters of bridges, repaired 30 kilometers of roads, prepared 6 kilometers of disassembled rolling bridges, and assembled means for forcing a crossing of the Gornyi Tikich River. All the questions of cooperating with the 27th Army, as well as within the 2nd Tank Army, were worked out, and questions regarding the operational collaboration with the 52nd and 40th Armies were resolved. A communications network was organized in the jumping-off areas, and command posts and observations posts were set up. Reconnaissance detachments and scouting groups were formed up, and communications with the forward detachments and reconnaissance detachments were organized. In the rear assembly area, the 2nd Tank Army issued an order about the army's deployment in the jumping-off area. The 16th Tank Corps was to deploy on a line extending from the northeastern section of Shubennyi Stav through the northeastern section of Kuchkovka to Iablonovka; the 3rd Tank Corps, together with the 8th and 13th Heavy Tank Regiments was to occupy the area Tikhonovka – woods south of Tikhonovka – Pisarevka – woods northeast of Tikhonovka; the 11th Guards Tank Brigade was to move into the woods northeast of Tikhonovka.

Once in the jumping-off area, on 3-4 March 1944, the vanguard of the all-arms armies probed the enemy's defenses to gather information on the enemy's strength, composition and system of fire. On the basis of this intelligence, the 2nd Ukrainian Front command made adjustments to the attack plans. The artillery moved into firing positions and prepared for battle. Questions regarding cooperation with neighbors were checked and finalized. The 2nd Tank Army command determined the combat formations the tank units would use in the attack. Finally, the anti-air defense of the jumping-off areas was organized.

Table 6.1: The condition of the 2nd Tank Army's tank pool on the eve of the Uman' operation at midnight on 3.3.1944

| Unit | Type | On the list | Serviceable | Took part in recent fighting | Under repair | | | Supplies | | | On the jumping-off line |
|---|---|---|---|---|---|---|---|---|---|---|---|
| | | | | | Minor | Light Overhaul | Major overhaul | Ammunition (in combat loads) | Fuel and lubricants (in refills) | Rations (in days' worth) | |
| **3rd Tank Corps** | | | | | | | | | | | |
| 50 TBr. | T-34 | 41 | 20 | 19 | – | 10 | 9 | 1.5 | 2.0 | 6 | 7 |
| 51 TBr. | T-34 | 27 | 14 | 16 | – | 6 | 5 | 1.5 | 1.3 | 3 | 6 |
| 103 TBr. | T-34 | 21 | 12 | 15 | 1 | 3 | 2 | 1.5 | 1.3 | 7 | 5 |
| 411 Signal Btn. | T-34 | 3 | 2 | 2 | – | – | 1 | | | | |
| 74 MC Btn. | Mk 9 | 7 | 4 | 4 | 2 | – | 1 | | | | |
| 881 SPAR | SU-76 | 25 | 17 | 19 | 3 | 3 | 2 | 1.3 | 0.6 | 8 | 19 |
| 1818 SPAR | SU-85 | – | – | | – | – | – | – | 1.0 | 7 | |
| 1540 HSPAR | SU-152 | 11 | 5 | 6 | – | 4 | 2 | 2.0 | 1.5 | 4 | 5 |
| Total in the corps: | T-34 | 92 | 48 | 52 | 1 | 19 | 17 | | | | 18 |
| | Mk 9 | 7 | 4 | 4 | 2 | – | 1 | | | | |
| | SU-76 | 28 | 20 | 22 | 3 | 3 | 2 | | | | |
| | SU-85 | 10 | 7 | 7 | – | 3 | – | | | | |
| | SU-152 | 11 | 5 | 6 | – | 4 | 2 | | | | |
| **16th Tank Corps** | | | | | | | | | | | |
| 107 TBr. | T-34 | 21 | 12 | 10 | 1 | 2 | 7 | 1.0 | 1.5 | 1 | 4 |
| 109 TBr. | T-34 | 29 | 20 | 20 | 2 | 1 | 6 | 1.5 | 1.9 | 5 | 15 |
| 164 TBr. | T-34 | 46 | 23 | 23 | 3 | 6 | 14 | 1.2 | 1.5 | 1 | 18 |
| 698 Signal Btn. | T-34 | 2 | 1 | 1 | – | 1 | – | | | | 1 |
| 51 MC Btn. | Mk 9 | 10 | 8 | 8 | – | 2 | – | | | | 8 |
| 1441 SPAR | SU-76 | – | – | – | – | – | – | 2.0 | 1.0 | 5 | |
| 298 GPAR | SU-85 | 11 | 11 | 11 | – | 3 | – | 2.0 | 1.5 | 5 | |
| | SU-76 | 23 | 23 | 23 | – | – | – | 2.0 | 1.5 | 5 | |

| Unit | Type | On the list | Serviceable | Took part in recent fighting | Under repair | | | Supplies | | | On the jumping-off line |
|---|---|---|---|---|---|---|---|---|---|---|---|
| | | | | | Minor | Light Overhaul | Major overhaul | Ammunition (in combat loads) | Fuel and lubricants (in refills) | Rations (in days' worth) | |
| Total in the corps: | T-34 | 98 | 56 | 54 | 6 | 10 | 27 | | | | |
| | Mk 9 | 10 | 8 | 8 | – | 2 | – | | | | |
| | SU-76 | 23 | 23 | 23 | – | 3 | – | | | | |
| | SU-85 | 11 | 11 | 11 | – | 3 | – | | | | |
| Separate units: | | | | | | | | | | | |
| 11 GTBr. | T-34 | 19 | 18 | 18 | 1 | = | – | 2.0 | 2.2 diesel, 0.3 high octane gasoline | 5 | 18 |
| 87 MC Btn. | Mk 9 | 10 | 8 | 7 | – | 1 | 1 | | | | |
| 8 HTR | "IS" | 21 | 17 | 17 | – | 4 | – | | | | 17 |
| 13 HTR | "IS" | 15 | 14 | – | 1 | 3 | | | | | 14 |
| 1219 SPAR | SU-85 | | | | | | | | | | |
| 999 SPAR | SU-76 | | | | | | | | | | |
| Total in the army: | T-34 | 209 | 122 | 124 | 7 | 29 | 44 | | | | 74 |
| | Mk 9 | 27 | 19 | 19 | 2 | 3 | 3 | | | | 12 |
| | "IS" | 40 | 32 | 32 | – | 5 | 3 | | | | 31 |
| | SU-76 | 51 | 43 | 43 | 3 | 3 | 2 | | | | 22 |
| | SU-85 | 22 | 16 | 16 | – | 6 | – | | | | 18 |
| | SU-152 | 11 | 5 | 6 | – | 3 | 2 | | | | 5 |

Note: There are some inexplicable discrepancies in the data in this table. For example, the only regiment equipped with SU-85 assault guns in the 3rd Tank Corps has no data entered for it. However, when you look at the totals in the corps, there are suddenly 10 SU-85 assault guns, 7 of which are serviceable and 7 of which saw recent combat. There is also a discrepancy in the number of SU-76 vehicles in the 3rd Tank Corps, as the total number of these assault guns in the 3rd Tank Corps is 3 greater than the number of SU-76 assault guns in the 298th Guards Self-propelled Artillery Regiment. Finally, in some units of the 3rd Tank Corps, the number of vehicles under repair, when added to the number of serviceable vehicles, does not equal the number of tanks or self-propelled guns on the unit's roster.

Table 6.2: The operational status of the 2nd Tank Army's tanks as of midnight on 5.3.1944

| | Type | On the list | Of which: | | | | |
|---|---|---|---|---|---|---|---|
| | | | Serviceable | Under-going minor repair | Under-going light overhaul | Under-going major overhaul | Irreplaceably lost, but not yet written off |
| **3rd Tank Corps** | | | | | | | |
| 50 TBr. | T-34 | 40 | 20 | – | 10 | 10 | – |
| 51 TBr. | T-34 | 25 | 13 | – | 6 | 5 | 1 |
| 103 TBr. | T-34 | 21 | 13 | 3 | 1 | 2 | 2 |
| 411 Signals Bn. | T-34 | 3 | 2 | – | – | 1 | – |
| 74 MC Bn. | Mk 9 | 7 | 4 | 2 | – | 1 | – |
| Total for the corps: | T-34 | 89 | 48 | 3 | 17 | 18 | 3 |
| | Mk 9 | 7 | 4 | 2 | – | 1 | – |
| **16th Tank Corps** | | | | | | | |
| 107 TBr. | T-34 | 21 | 8 | 2 | 4 | 7 | – |
| 109 TBr. | T-34 | 29 | 9 | 2 | 7 | 6 | 5 |
| 164 TBr. | T-34 | 47 | 16 | 4 | 11 | 14 | 2 |
| 689 Signals Bn. | T-34 | 2 | 2 | – | – | – | – |
| 51 MC Bn. | Mk 9 | 10 | 8 | – | 2 | – | – |
| Total for the corps: | T-34 | 99 | 35 | 8 | 22 | 27 | 7 |
| | Mk 9 | 10 | 8 | – | 2 | – | – |
| 11 GTBr. | T-34 | 18 | 17 | 1 | – | – | – |
| 13 GHTR | IS | 19 | 15 | – | 1 | 3 | – |
| 8 GHTR | IS | 21 | 17 | – | 4 | – | – |
| 87 MC Bn. | Mk 9 | 9 | 8 | 1 | – | – | – |
| Total for the army: | T-34 | 206 | 100 | 12 | 39 | 45 | 10 |
| | Mk 9 | 26 | 20 | 3 | 2 | 1 | – |
| | IS | 40 | 32 | – | 5 | 3 | – |

## The operational-tactical situation at the start of the operation

### The Enemy Grouping

Having dug in on the line Rusalovka – Chermisskoe – Rubannyi Most – Chizhovka – Ryzhanovka, the enemy began to withdraw the battered panzer divisions from the front lines to the Man'kovka – Potash Station – Pomoinik area, with the aim of refitting them and bringing them back to order. The panzer divisions were replaced in the front line by infantry divisions. By the end of 4 March 1944, the 2nd Tank Army faced the following enemy grouping: the 80th Infantry Regiment of the 34th Infantry Division, the *Kampfgruppe* 667, III/52nd Mortar Regiment, the 198th Infantry Division, the 54th Mortar Regiment, the 482nd Pontoon Battalion, the 286th Reserve Battalion, I/91st *Gebirgsjäger* Regiment, the 4th *Gebirgsjäger* Division, and the 94th Reserve Battalion. Altogether, this grouping amounted to 7,620 combat troops, 518 machine guns, 161 guns, 63 mortars and 10 tanks.

## The 2nd Tank Army's Grouping

Various figures are available for the amount of armor possessed by the 2nd Tank Army on the eve of the operation. According to an account of the operation, signed off by General Radzievsky, at the end of 4 March 1944 the 2nd Tank Army had 122 T-34, 32 IS-85, 20 Valentine Mark IX, 18 SU-85, 43 SU-76 and 5 SU-152. The 2nd Tank Army's journal of combat operation states that the army had 130 T-34, 32 IS-2 and 19 Valentine Mark IX tanks, as well as 16 SU-85, 6 SU-152 and 43 SU-76, for a total of 246 armored vehicles (181 tanks and 65 self-propelled guns).

In his account, Guards Lieutenant Colonel Shvebig, the assistant commander of the 16th Tank Corps for vehicle maintenance and technical support, wrote that before the start of the operation, the 16th Tank Corps had serviceable 56 T-34, 8 Valentine Mark IX, 11 SU-85 and 20 SU-76, for a total of 95 armored vehicles. The commander of the 3rd Tank Corps reported that the corps was deployed into two echelons for the operation. The first echelon consisted of the 50th Tank Brigade, the 51st Tank Brigade and the 1540th Heavy Self-propelled Artillery Regiment. The second echelon consisted of the 8th and 13th Heavy Tank Regiments together with the 57th Motorized Rifle Brigade. The 103rd Tank Brigade was in reserve. By 5.00 on 5.4.1944, the 3rd Tank Corps had occupied its jumping-off position: the 50th Tank Brigade (with 23 operational T-34) was in the village of Tarasovka; the 51st Tank Brigade (with 17 serviceable T-34) was in Pisarev, together with the 1540th Heavy Self-propelled Artillery Regiment (with 4 serviceable SU-152). The 8th Guards Heavy Tank Regiment (18 IS-2) was positioned 0.5 kilometers east of Hill 242.0; the 13th Guards Heavy Tank Regiment (14 IS-2) was in Dubrovka. Units directly subordinate to army headquarters (with 14 T-34 and 8 BM-13 rocket launchers) were in the Tikhonovka – Dubrovka area, and the 1219th Self-propelled Artillery Regiment (8 SU-85) was in Kotliarovsk. The commander of the 11th Guards Tank Brigade reported that at 24.00 on 6.3.1944, he received a verbal combat order from the commander of the 2nd Tank Army to attack along the Krachkovka – Ivan'ki – Potash Station – Pomoinik – Krasnopolka – Voitovka – Uman' axis. The brigade had 18 T-34 tanks on its roster, of which 11 T-34 were operational and 7 were undergoing repair.

According to a report from the deputy commander of the 2nd Tank Army for technical service Major General of Engineering-Tank Service Iukin, at the moment of the start of combat operations on the Uman' axis on 5 March 1944, the 2nd Tank Army had a total of 205 serviceable tanks (see Table 6.3)

**Table 6.3: Status of the 2nd Tank Army's armor pool on 5 March 1944**

|  | On the list | Serviceable | Under repair | | | Irreplaceable losses, not yet written off |
|---|---|---|---|---|---|---|
|  |  |  | Minor | Light overhaul | Major overhaul |  |
| T-34 | 206 | 100 | 12 | 39 | 45 | 10 |
| IS-85 | 40 | 32 | 0 | 5 | 3 | 0 |
| Mark IX | 26 | 20 | 3 | 2 | 1 | 0 |
| SU-152 | 11 | 6 | 0 | 3 | 2 | 0 |
| SU-85 | 11 | 8 | 1 | 2 | 0 | 0 |
| SU-76 | 48 | 39 | 2 | 4 | 2 | 1 |
| **Total:** | **342** | **205** | **18** | **51** | **57** | **11** |

## The area of operations

The terrain in the sector of the 2nd Tank Army's operations offered relatively level ground with a small number of oak groves. The presence of balkas and small streams, which were difficult even for the tanks to overcome in the spring muddy season, cramped the maneuver of the tank units. The roads, which in the majority were dirt, not hard-surfaced, with crumbly soil, were poorly suited for motorized transport, but in view of the spring thaw, they were all in exceptionally poor condition for the entire period of the operation, as a consequence of which motorized transport was extremely limited. The main roads had one passable rut, the depth of which approached half a meter, as a result of which traffic jams were created by two-way traffic. The rest of the roads were totally impassable for motorized transport, and only tracked vehicles could move along them. Of the wheeled machines, only vehicles with enhanced off-road capabilities (of foreign manufacture) could move along the main arteries with great difficulty, although even they required towing by tanks in the less-trafficable places like bottomlands and balkas, and especially in populated places. On the whole, the poor condition of the road network greatly aggravated the movement of the tank army, the success of which to a great degree depends upon the possibility of unhindered maneuvering. Considering all the above, the commander of the 2nd Tank Army demanded thorough preparation from the commanders of the subordinate formations and superb work by the engineering units.

The 2nd Tank Army's combat operations were connected with overcoming the Gornyi Tikich River, as well as the Southern Bug and Dnestr Rivers during the subsequent advance. The Gornyi Tikich River in the 2nd Tank Army's sector was 15-30 meters wide, with a depth up to 2 meters, and a current flow of 1-1.5 meters a second. The river's channel was stony, and in many places cluttered with rocks. The banks were 0.5 to 1.5 meters high and precipitous in places. The river's basin had a width of 100 to 300 meters, bounded on the right and left banks by hills, the steep slopes of which created bluffs in many places along the river. The Southern Bug River in the Dzhulinki area is 90 to 120 meters wide, with a depth of 1-4 meters, and a current flow of 0.8-1 meter a second. The river bottom is sandy and the banks are sloping, with a height of up to 1.5 meters. The Dnester River has a width of 250-300 meters, a depth of up to 4 meters, and a current flow of up to 1 meter a second. Its bottom is a mixture of sand and silt. The river's banks are sandy and dry, with a height of 3-5 meters.

In sum, the presence of balkas and small streams, which in the majority became obstacles for the tanks in the muddy season, constrained the movement of the tanks and often prevented the possibility of an outflanking maneuver to seize enemy strongpoints. In addition, the springtime thaw had turned the roads into quagmires, as a result of which the rear-echelon units of the 2nd Tank Army couldn't keep pace with the forward units, which disrupted the timely replenishment with ammunition, fuel and lubricants.

## Combat operations of the 2nd Tank Army for the city of Uman'

On 2 March 1944, the 2nd Tank Army's commander issued a combat order:

> The enemy with units of the 198th Infantry Division, the 17th Panzer Division, the 64th Mortar Regiment, the 16th Panzer Division, the 54th Mortar Regiment and the 482nd Panzerjäger Battalion has dug-in along the line: Ruslakovka, Rubannyi Most, Chemeriskoe, Chizhovka, Ryzhanovka. He is hastily throwing up defensive works, intensively mining the roads, villages and the approaches to them. The second defensive line runs along western bank of the Gornyi Tikich River. In reserve are the 1st and 16th Infantry Divisions and the 1st SS Panzer Division *Adolf Hitler*, which have been withdrawn for refitting, presumably to the Man'kovka area.

The 2nd Tank Army together with the 27th Army is to destroy the opposing enemy units and to exploit the success, launching the main attack with the left flank in the direction: southern outskirts of Chizhovka, Rizino, Berezovka, Monastyrek. By the end of the first day of the offensive, force a crossing of the Gornyi Tikich River in the Buki, Chernaia Kamenka sector and seize the Antonovka, Krivets, Ivan'ki, Chernaia Kamenka area. In the future it is to attack along the Dzen'galovka, Ivanovka axis and to seize the Khristinovka, Iagubets, Goliakovka area, having in view the seizure of crossings on the Southern Bug River in the Bershad', Osievka area by forward units.

The 16th Tank Corps – jumping-off area: northeastern outskirts of Shubennyi Stav, northeastern portion of Kuchkovka, Iablonovka. Attack in the direction: Mikhailovka, Hill 242.6, southern outskirts of Bagva, Buki, Popovka and in cooperation with units of the 27th Army, destroy the opposing enemy; by the end of the first day, having forced a crossing of the Gornyi Tikich River in the Buki, Berezovka sector, it is to seize the Hill 237.6, Krivets, Zelenyi Gai, Popovka area, and with a strong forward detachment of not less than a tank brigade with attached self-propelled artillery, it is to take Khristinovka.

The 3rd Tank Corps with the 8th and 13th Heavy Tank Regiments – jumping-off area: Tikhonovka, woods south and northeast of Tikhonovka, Pisarev. Attack in the direction: southern outskirts of Chizhovka, Rizino, Berezovka, Monastyrek; destroy the opposing enemy in conjunction with units of the 27th Army and by the end of the first day, force a crossing of the Gornyi Tikich River in the Berezovka, Chernaia Kamenka sector and seize the Monastyrek, Ivan'ki, Berezovka area, and with a strong forward detachment of not less than a tank brigade with attached self-propelled artillery guns, take Voitovka, having cut the Ivanovka – Uman' road in the vicinity of Hill 244.5.

The army's reserve: the 11th Guards Tank Brigade – jumping-off area the woods northeast of Tikhonovka. Move out behind the 3rd Tank Corps in readiness to repel enemy counterattacks from the directions of Sofievka and Romanovka, and secure the army's left flank.

An aerial view of the city of Uman', March 1944, showing a devastated German column of armor and trucks.

On 5 March 1944, the units of the 2nd Tank Army, having completed assembly in the jumping-off areas, went on the offensive together with units of the 27th Army at 7.50 after an artillery preparation from the line: Shubennyi Stav, Mikhailovka, woods northeast of Chizhovka, and overcoming strong enemy resistance, breached the enemy's defenses. After the rupture of their front line, the enemy abandoned Rubannyi Most, Chemerskoe, Barvinok, Chizhovka, Gruzdka, Bagva and Rizino, and began a fighting withdraw to the southwest toward Buki, with the assignment to hold the line of the Gornyi Tikich River. The withdrawal was accompanied by stubborn resistance. At 12.00, the enemy launched a counterattack out of the Barvinok area toward Chizhovka with up to a battalion of infantry and 5 tanks. The counterattack was repelled, and in the complete absence of roads, the tank units of the 2nd Tank Army continued to pursue the retreating enemy to the Gornyi Tikich River.

At 7.00 on 6 March, the 16th Tank Corps together with the forces of the 15th Motorized Rifle Brigade and attached tanks forced a crossing of the Gornyi Tikich in the Buki area. By the end of the day, having crossed all of its forces, the 16th Tank Corps overcame strong enemy resistance and took Popovka, Krivets, Zelenyi Gai and Khar'kovka, and continued to advance in the general direction of Uman'.

The 3rd Tank Corps, having seized Chizhovka by 12.00 on 5 March, continued to advance and on the morning of 6 March reached Berezovka, having seized a second bridgehead across the Gornyi Tikich River. The army's artillery units, as a consequence of the rapid spring thaw, fell behind the combat formations of the army by 10-12 kilometers on the very first day of the offensive.

The enemy, covering his withdrawal with rear guard detachments behind the banks of small rivers and in villages that had been hastily prepared for a defense, fell back in the direction of Uman'. From the morning of 7 March 1944, the 2nd Tank Army continued to develop the offensive successfully, and overcoming tough enemy resistance, seized Gai, Kishentsy, Monastyrek, Timoshevka, Polkovnich'e, Kinashevka and Ivan'ki, as a result of which the German second defensive line along the Gornyi Tikich River was totally breached. The Germans, with the aim of halting the army's further advance, repeatedly launched counterattacks out of Man'kovka toward Monastyrek and Khar'kovka. All of the enemy counterattacks were beaten back with heavy losses for him.

The 16th Tank Corps, having arrived in the Man'kovka – Khar'kovka area, launched an attack toward the northwestern and western outskirts of Man'kovka with the forces of the 107th and 109th Tank Brigades and the 1st and 2nd Motorized Rifle Battalions of the 15th Motorized Rifle Brigade, and toward the southeastern outskirts of Man'kovka with the forces of the 164th Tank Brigade and the 15th Motorized Rifle Brigade's 3rd Battalion. The 3rd Tank Corps together with the 11th Guards Tank Brigade went on the attack out of the Ivan'ki area toward Potash Station, bypassing Man'kovka on its eastern side. As a result of the 16th Tank Corps' concentric attack and the outflanking maneuver by the 3rd Tank Corps, the 2nd Tank Army seized Man'kovka and Potash Station by the end of 7 March 1944.

In the course of the three days of offensive fighting, the German 34th and 198th Infantry Divisions, the 16th and 17th Panzer Divisions and the 1st SS Panzer Division *Leibstandarte Adolf Hitler* were shattered. In the area of Man'kovka and Potash Station alone, the Germans lost up to 200 tanks, self-propelled guns and halftracks, more than 150 trucks, 37 supply dumps with ammunition and rations, and a lot of other military property. Up to 5,000 German soldiers and officers were killed or wounded, and 800 were taken prisoner. Units of the 75th Infantry Division and remnants of the 34th and 98th Infantry Divisions, covered by rear guard detachments, hastily retreated to the Uman' area, having left behind all their artillery on the battlefield.

The commander of the 11th Guards Tank Brigade Guards Colonel Kurilenko left behind the following account of the brigade's operations:

At 24.00 on 6.3.1944, a verbal order was received from the commander of the 2nd Tank Army to attack along the Krachkovka, Ivan'ki, Potash Station, Pomoinik, Krasnopolka, Voitovka, Uman' axis. The brigade had 18 T-34 tanks on its roster (11 operational and 7 under repair). Because of the poor road conditions, 4 76mm guns and the brigade's rear elements fell behind and were on the march to catch up with the forward units. At 2.00 on 7 March 1944, the brigade went on the attack and by 8.00 on 7.3. 44, it had taken Krachkovka. The enemy managed to blow up both bridges in Krachkovka, and the brigade had to cross the river at a ford. Having crossed over, the brigade reached Ivan'ki by 16.00 on 7.3.44, where the main crossing had already been blown up by the enemy. It had to go around Ivan'ki to the left, which held up the brigade's actions. At 17.30 on 7.3.44, the brigade crossed to the right bank of some nameless stream, which runs through Ivan'ki. At 20.30 on 7.3.44, the brigade's units arrived in the area of Potash Station, where they encountered a large aggregation of enemy tanks. Brigade commander Guards Colonel Koshaev ordered 3 T-34 tanks each to outflank the enemy on both sides, with a simultaneous frontal assault under the cover of darkness. At the designated time, fire was opened up from every weapon and the enemy was attacked. At 21.00, Potash Station was taken, and at 23.00 on 7.3.44, the brigade seized Pomoinik. Continuing to carry out its further assignment, by 4.00 on 8.3.44 the brigade reached the northern outskirts of Krasnopolka. The bridge in Krasnopolka had been blown up. I issued an order for the motorized rifle battalion to repair the bridge and simultaneously to scout for a ford. The enemy in the course of five hours incessantly bombed and shelled the bridge site, which greatly hindered work. At 10.00 on 8.3.44, brigade commander Guards Colonel Koshaev was wounded.

At 20.00 on 8.3.44, the tanks crossed at a ford on the southern outskirts of Krasnopolka. At 21.00, at the order of the 2nd Tank Army commander, Guards Major Rodionov assumed command of the brigade. At 24.00 on 8.3.44, the brigade had 18 tanks in its inventory, of which 3 had been destroyed during the offensive, 4 had been disabled and repaired, and 8 had lagged behind due to mechanical problems (broken tracks). The 4 76mm guns, the brigade's rear elements, and the column of the army's first echelon were approaching Rizino.

At 4.00 on 9.3.44, the brigade went on the offensive toward Voitovka and Uman'. Reaching a fork in the roads 3 kilometers south of Krasnopolka, the brigade ran into the resistance of enemy anti-tank artillery and tanks on the northern outskirts of Voitovka (7 panzers and up to 2 batteries of artillery). With a bold outflanking maneuver, the brigade emerged in the rear of the enemy between Voitovka and Dmitrovskoe, and by 7.30 on 9.3.44, it had crossed over a nameless stream in the Uman' – Sofievka suburban area and had seized the northeastern portion of Sofievka. The enemy in the Voitovka area was paralyzed from the rear and was cut up into small groups, after which he was compelled to retreat to the west and southwest. The liberation of Voitovka created the opportunity of a rapid forward advance to the units acting from the front. From the morning until 16.00, the brigade was fighting with enemy tanks and artillery in the Sofievka area, but by the end of the day it had taken Uman'.

In the course of 10.3.44, the brigade reassembled and put its matériel into order. Deputy commander Guards Lieutenant Colonel Kurilenko assumed command of the brigade.

Over the period from 5 to 8 March 1944, the brigade conducted a 150 kilometer combat march. In the difficult conditions of the march, at the order of the commander of the 2nd Tank Army, it caught up with the 3rd Tank Corps on the Rizino line, and attacking at the head of the column of the army's first echelon, with fighting it seized a crossing over the Gornyi Tikich River. Pushing forward with combat, it seized Potash Station, where the enemy had abandoned a large number of vehicles and tanks.

Disabled German armor in the Potash area, March 1944.

Knocked-out and abandoned Tigers of the 503rd Heavy Panzer Battalion, Potash area, March 1944.

In view of the retreat of the enemy's main grouping toward Uman', the 2nd Tank Army received an order from the commander of the 2nd Ukrainian Front to direct its main attack in the direction of Uman' and Dzhulinki. After a partial regrouping of forces and the arrival of a significant amount of the army's artillery in the area of operations, the army resumed its sweeping offensive and by 15.30 on 8.3.44, it had reached the nearest approaches to the city of Uman' on the line: Berestovets, Krasnopolka, Ksendzovka, Starve Babany, while units of the 16th Tank Corps by 20.00 on 8.3.44 reached the northeastern outskirts of Voitovka (5 kilometers northeast of Uman')

In the course of 9 March 1944, the enemy, with the aim of maintaining possession of Uman' and of liquidating the developing threat of the appearance of the 2nd Tank Army in the rear of his grouping southeast of Uman' on the line: Kochiubeevka, Voitovka, Tinskoe, put up stubborn resistance to the 2nd Tank Army on the approaches to the city with units of the 202nd, 249th and 261st Assault Gun Battalions, the 62nd Heavy Artillery Regiment, the 17th Flak Division, together with the withdrawing remnants of the 1st, 16th and 17th Panzer Divisions, the 1st SS Panzer Division, and the 34th, 75th and 198th Infantry Divisions. Throughout the day, the Germans repeatedly launched battalion-sized counterattacks with the support of up to 15 tanks. The *Luftwaffe* in groups of 30-40 aircraft incessantly and without hindrance bombed the army's combat formations in the areas of Pomoinik, Krasnopolka, Ksendzovka and Voitovka. The 2nd Tank Army shrugged off the German counterattacks and with all its forces forced a crossing of the Revukha River, and as a result of stubborn fighting, breached the enemy's defenses on the approaches to Uman', having seized by the end of the day Voitovka, Dmitrovskoe and Pikovets.

Having captured Voitovka, the 16th Tank Corps, employing the 107th and 109th Tank Brigades in an outflanking maneuver, continued to launch attacks against the northwestern outskirts of Uman', but ran into heavy resistance by fire. Meanwhile, its 164th Tank Brigade continued to

Knocked-out and abandoned Panthers and Tigers of Heavy Panzer Regiment *Bäke*, March 1944.

push in the direction of the northeastern outskirts of Uman'. Simultaneously, the 3rd Tank Corps took Dmitrovskoe by the end of 9 March and launched attacks against the eastern and south-eastern outskirts of Uman', while the 11th Guards Tank Brigade attacked the city from the north. After fierce fighting, at 19.30 on 9 March, the Soviet tanks reached the city center, where they exchanged fire with German anti-aircraft artillery. Motorized infantry by this time had reached the eastern outskirts of Uman' and began to push rapidly toward the center of the city while crushing isolated nests of enemy resistance. In the fighting for the city of Uman', the tank companies of Captain Fedor Donkov (107th Tank Brigade, 16th Tank Corps) and Captain Mikhail Sanachev (51st Tank Brigade, 3rd Tank Corps) particularly distinguished themselves, as did Major Ivan Ostroverkhov's motorized rifle battalion (15th Motorized Rifle Brigade, 16th Tank Corps).

As a result of the concentric attack, by 1.30 on 10 March 1944, the forces of the 2nd Tank Army had taken full possession of the city of Uman'. The 16th Tank Corps had reached the southwestern and southern outskirts of the city, while the 3rd Tank Corps was now on the southeastern outskirts of Uman' and the 11th Guards Tank Brigade was on the western outskirts. The Germans, after the collapse of their resistance in the Uman' area, fearing encirclement, began a retreat to the west and southwest, abandoning combat equipment and other military property. In the fighting for the possession of Uman', more than 200 trucks, 40 tanks, more than 30 guns and mortars, airfield equipment, supply stockpiles of aerial bombs, warehouses with food and a lot of other military property was captured. For their combat actions to destroy the enemy's Uman' – Khristinovka grouping, by order of the Supreme Commander-in-Chief and Marshal of the Soviet Union Stalin, the 3rd and 16th Tank Corps were bestowed the honorific title "Uman'", and by a decree of the Presidium of the Supreme Soviet of the USSR, the 3rd and 16th Tank Corps were awarded the Order of Suvorov, 2nd Degree.

### The 2nd Tank Army in the Uman' Operation of 1944

Booty of the 2nd Tank Army: Abandoned German tanks in the area of Man'kovka, March 1944
(from Guards Colonel S.M. Terekhov's personal collection of photographs).

Units of the 16th
Tank Corps crossing
a flooded stream,
March 1944.

A devastated German
motorized column in
the area of Man'kovka,
March 1944.
A handwritten Cyrillic
caption read, "Abandoned
enemy equipment".

Uman' after
the battle. An
abandoned
German
Nebelwerfer is in
the foreground.
Note also the
camouflage pattern
on the abandoned
German car.

Abandoned German trucks and self-propelled guns in Uman', 1944.

Another shot of abandoned German vehicles on an Uman' city street, 1944.

Disabled and abandoned German Pz. IV tanks, March 1944. Both tanks might have been used as salvage by the Germans; note that both are missing their drive wheels, and the tank in the foreground is missing several bogey wheels.

Vehicles of the 2nd Tank Army, passing between knocked-out and captured German armor, March 1944.

A knocked-out German Pz. IV in the area of Uman', March 1944.

An abandoned German StuG in the same area.

German tanks and halftracks destroyed by forces of the 2nd Tank Army in the area of Uman', March 1944. A Cyrillic caption read, "After accurate strikes".

The command staff of the 51st Tank Brigade. In the center is Colonel Mirvoda, and on the right is Lieutenant Colonel Pisunkov (from S.M. Terekhov's personal collection of photographs).

The award ceremony on 1.10.1944 in the village of Tur, Volynsk Oblast, bestowing the Order of the Red Banner for the liberation of Uman'. On the right is General Latyshev, member of the 2nd Tank Army's Military Council.

In sum, Bogdanov's idea for taking the city of Uman' by a concentric attack was fully realized. The tank corps that were enveloping the city from the northeast and northwest had become separated from their infantry, which were following on foot, and the task of seizing the city was resolved with the introduction of tanks into the city. The attempts by the tank brigade commanders, who had surged ahead of the following infantry, to take the city with tanks from the march demonstrated their audacity and pluck, but also certain rashness in their actions when storming a major city. However, the concentric attack against a demoralized foe was crowned with success. The Germans defending the city were crushed, and the forces of the 2nd Tank Army liberated a major Ukrainian center – the city of Uman'.

## The 2nd Tank Army's combat operations for the town and railroad station of Vapniarka

At the completion of the Uman' operation, the 2nd Tank Army was given the assignment to seize crossings on the Southern Bug River, and then to exploit a success by advancing in the direction of Vapniarka. On 10.3.1944 at 16.30, 2nd Tank Army commander General Bogdanov issued a combat order:

> The 3rd Tank Corps with the 8th Heavy Tank Regiment and the 1st and 2nd Companies of the 257th Engineer Battalion, in cooperation with the 35th and 294th Rifle Divisions, is to attack along the Uman' – Liubashovka road, and by 19.00 on 11.3.44 is to seize a crossing over the Sinitsa River. Take the northwestern outskirts of Ternovka with a strong forward detachment and cut the Ternovka – Serebriia road. Subsequently, it is to attack in the direction of Dzhulinki with the view of reaching the Shliakhova area by the end of 12.3.1944.
>
> The 16th Tank Corps with the 13th Guards Heavy Tank Regiment, in cooperation with the 31st and 294th Rifle Divisions, is to advance behind the 3rd Tank Corps along the Uman' – Liubashovka road, in readiness to exploit a success by the 3rd Tank Corps, and by 19.00 on 11.3.44 is to seize Liubashovka and Iurkovka, and crossings on the Sinitsa River. In the future, it is to attack toward Shliakhova. With a strong forward detachment, take the southeastern outskirts of Ternovka, cutting the Ternovka – Shliakova and Ternovka – Temna roads.
>
> The 11th Guards Tank Brigade with the 86th Guards Mortar Regiment are the army's reserve, and has the task to advance behind the 16th Tank Corps in readiness to exploit the success of the 3rd and 16th Tank Corps, and to be prepared to repel enemy counterattacks from the northwest and southeast.

In addition to this, the commander of the 16th Tank Corps was given a separate order to create a forward detachment consisting of one tank brigade with tank riders aboard the tanks and artillery, and at 21.00 on 10 March 44, it was to dispatch it along the route Uman' – Liubashovka – Ternovka – Dzhulinki, with the assignment to destroy retreating enemy units on its route, to seize a crossing on the Southern Bug River in Dzhulinki by 8.00 on 11 March, and to hold it until the arrival of the 2nd Tank Army's main forces.

The Germans, seeking to avoid the encirclement and complete destruction of its grouping southeast of Uman', began hastily pulling back their forces to the Southern Bug River. In connection with the enemy's rapid retreat, on 11 March there followed a new combat instruction: the 16th Tank Corps was to hasten the tempo of its pursuit of the enemy, and by the end of that day it was to reach the Southern Bug with its main forces and to create a bridgehead on its right bank.

From the morning of 11 March 1944, the enemy, with remnants of the 34th, 75th and 198th Infantry Divisions, the 17th Flak Division, the 249th, 202nd and 261st Assault Gun Battalions, and with special detachments of the 1st, 1st SS, 16th and 17th Panzer Divisions numbering a total of 6,000 active combatants and 45 tanks and self-propelled guns, resisted the advance of our forces with rear guard actions. Nevertheless, by the end of 11 March, the forces of the 2nd Tank Army had made an advance of up to 50 kilometers in the wake of the defeated, retreating foe, and by 21.00 were fighting for possession of Dzhulinki on the Southern Bug River.

The forward detachment of the 16th Tank Corps, consisting of 8 T-34 tanks, 2 SU-76 and a motorized rifle battalion had reached the area of Liubashovka on the Sinitsa River by 9.00 on 11 March. The bridge across the river had been blown up by the retreating enemy. The destruction of this bridge checked the pursuit of the foe by our troops and gave the Germans a possibility to separate from the pursuers and to organize a defense in Ternovka. Having repaired the bridge, the forward detachment, continuing its pursuit of the enemy, from the march broke into the northern outskirts of Ternovka and became tied up in street fighting with the enemy. As a result of the forward detachment's bold and swift actions, by 17.00 on 11 March the enemy had been driven out of this populated place, having had no time to blow up the bridge. Still in pursuit of the retreating enemy, by 22.00 the forward detachment had seized the northern outskirts of Dzhulinki and reached the Southern Bug River.

The enemy, seeking to halt the 2nd Tank Army's offensive on the line of the Southern Bug, threw reserve units from the interior into the battle – a school for junior officers with the Eighth Army and units of the 1st Nebelwerfer Regiment, and began moving up Romanian units to the right bank of the Southern Bug River. In the course of 12 March 1944, the enemy with fire and counterattacks sought to block a forcing of the Southern Bug by our forces. The *Luftwaffe* in groups of 7-25 aircraft incessantly bombed the army's combat formations, the approach route to the crossing over the Southern Bug River in Ternovka, and primarily the vicinity of the crossing itself. At 16.30 on 12 March, General Bogdanov ordered:

> The 2nd Tank Army jointly with the infantry of the 52nd Army, by the end of 12.3.44 is to force a crossing of the Southern Bug River at Dzhulinki, and developing the rapid pursuit of the enemy, by the end of 13.3.44 is to seize the Verkhovka, Tsybulevka, Obodovka area. Subsequently, attacking through Zhabokrich toward Vapniarka, in cooperation with the 6th Tank Army it is to seize Vapniarka by the end of 14.3.44.
>
> The 16th Tank Corps with the 13th Guards Heavy Tank Regiment by 20.30 on 12.3.44, jointly and in cooperation with the 294th Rifle Division and motorized infantry is to use improvised means to force a crossing of the Southern Bug River in the sector between Dzhulinki Station and the church in the center of Dzhulinki, seize a bridgehead on the western bank of the river extending from the southern outskirts of Shumilovo to the shrubs 1 kilometer east of Bol'shoe Nesterovo, and secure the construction of a bridge. By 4.00 on 13.3.44, cross the tank brigades and artillery to the western bank of the Southern Bug River. With an impetuous advance in the direction of Bol'shoe Nesterovo, southern outskirts of Krushinovka, Sumovka, Demidovka and southern outskirts of Budy, seize Verkhovka and Malaia Strateevka by the end of 13.3.44 and the bridges within them. With a strong forward detachment, in cooperation with the 3rd Tank Corps' forward detachment, seize Vapniarka Station. Subsequently, attacking through Levkov, Sokolovka, Sharapanovka, and Hill 298.0, seize the northern outskirts of Vapniarka by the end of 14.3.44.
>
> The 3rd Tank Corps with the 8th Guards Heavy Tank Regiment by 20.30 on 12.3.44 jointly and in cooperation with the 294th Rifle Division and motorized infantry is to force a crossing of the Southern Bug River using improvised means on a front running from the church in the center of Dzhulinki to the southern outskirts of Dzhulinki. Seize a bridgehead on the southern bank of the Southern Bug: [encompassing an area] 1 kilometer east of the thicket of pines near Bol'shoe Nesterovo, 0.5 kilometers north of Ust'e and the western outskirts of Berezki and protect the construction of a bridge. At 6.00 on 13.3.44, in the wake of the 16th Tank Corps, having crossed the tank brigades and artillery to the western bank

of the Southern Bug River, with an impetuous attack on the Berezki – Voitovka – Bershad' –
Byrlovka – Balanovka – Obodovka axis, seize bridges in Bershad', Balanovka and Obodovka,
and by the end of 13.3.44 take Tsybulevka and Tatarovka, and with a strong forward detachment in cooperation with the 16th Tank Corps' forward detachment, seize Vapniarka Station.
Subsequently, attack through Zhabokrich, Zabolotnoe, Kryzhopol' with the task to seize the
southwestern outskirts of Vapniarka and Tsapovka by the end of 14.3.44.

The army's reserve: 11th Guards Tank Brigade with the 86th Guards Mortar Regiment –
move out behind the 3rd Tank Corps in readiness to exploit the success of the 3rd Tank Corps
and to repel possible enemy counterattacks from the southwest.

On 13 March 1944, the 2nd Tank Army with the forces of the 15th and 57th Motorized Rifle
Brigades forced a crossing of the Southern Bug River using improvised means, and by 14.00 took
possession of Berezovki, thereby creating a bridgehead for the construction of bridges. The enemy,
introducing fresh reserves, continued to put up stubborn resistance, striving to prevent the expansion of the bridgehead. The *Luftwaffe* worked over the crossing site and the army's combat formations intensively. In the course of the day, more than 300 individual sorties were counted. On the
night of 13/14 March the 2nd Tank Army finished crossing the Southern Bug River and on the
morning of 14 March, launched a decisive attack. By the end of the day, the 16th Tank Corps had
hurled the enemy back by 53 kilometers and had taken Sokolovka. The 3rd Tank Corps, having
seized Verkhovka, spent the course of 14 and 15 March 1944 in this area for bringing up the
lagging materiél, artillery and vehicles that had become mired in the mud. The 11th Guards Tank
Brigade remained in the northern part of Dzhulinki, ready to repel enemy counterattacks from the
north and northeast. The Germans, refusing battle, pulled their shattered units back to the area of
Vapniarka, where they committed fresh reserves into the fighting – the 9th Infantry Regiment of
the Romanian 5th Infantry Division, the 6th Cavalry Regiment, and the Romanian 6th Battalion,
and strove to retain possession of Vapniarka, which was a key road hub for the enemy's units that
were retreating from various directions.

Pursuing the retreating enemy, the 2nd Tank Army's 16th Tank Corps, with an
outflanking maneuver from south to north, had seized the town and major railroad junction of
Vapniarka by 16.00 on 15 March 1944. In the fight for Vapniarka, Lieutenant Vladimir Kosarev
and his tank crew (driver-mechanic Mikhail Baskov) of the 51st Separate Motorcycle Battalion
particularly distinguished themselves. Their tank was the first to break into the railroad station,
where they destroyed 2 mortar batteries and killed 12 enemy soldiers and officers. With his auda-
cious actions, Kosarev's tank blocked the path of the enemy's retreat, as a result of which the enemy
abandoned up to 200 trucks loaded with gear and supplies.

The enemy was demoralized by the swift and bold actions of our forces when taking Vapniarka
and fled in panic to the west, toward Tomashpol' and Iampol', abandoning equipment and supply
trains. At the Vapniarka train station alone, 500 railroad cars were seized, as well as 2 steam
engines, 2 trains with military property, 300 trucks, 40 artillery supply dumps, and a lot of other
military booty.

The enemy had attempted to obstruct the 2nd Tank Army's unfolding offensive with fresh forces
and a significant increase in *Luftwaffe* activity to support Axis forces. The outflanking maneuver
on the approaches to Vapniarka was bold and corresponded to the situation. The 16th Tank Corps
demonstrated the ability to fight with small forces and the ability to maneuver.

## The 2nd Tank Army Reaches the Line of the Dnestr River

The remnants of the enemy units that had been defeated in the preceding battles were hastily
retreating to Tomashpol' and Iampol', without offering strong resistance to the 2nd Tank Army's

Tanks of the 11th Guards Tank Brigade crossing the Southern Bug River, March 1944.

units. The 3rd Tank Corps by 19.00 on 16 March was assembled in Stepanovka (5 kilometers west of Vapniarka), in readiness to resume the offensive. The 11th Guards Tank Brigade was in Vapniarka. Pursuing the enemy, the forward detachment of the 16th Tank Corps was advancing toward Iampol', on the way scattering isolated groups of enemy troops with its fire. With a rapid march, by 19.00 on 16 March it had reached Rusovo (4 kilometers north of Iampol'), where it met resistance from a Romanian battalion. Attacking it from the march, they drove the Romanians out of the village. There, it took up an all-round defense to wait for the arrival of the main forces.

T-34 tanks of the 11th Guards Tank Brigade being ferried across the Southern Bug, March 1944.

Hero of the Soviet Union Vladimir Kosarev and his tank crew of the 16th Tank Corps' 51st
Separate Motorcycle Regiment enjoy a smoke.

At dawn on 17 March, units of the 2nd Tank Army continued to advance directly toward
Iampol', and by 8.00 it had reached the town, where it attacked the enemy from the march. The
enemy began a gradual withdrawal behind the Dnestr River. On the heels of the retreating foe,
tanks entered the town and drove to the bridge, which had been blown up in two places by the
retreating defenders. By 10.00 on 17 March, Iampol' had been fully mopped up of enemy stragglers. In the combat for Iampol', the army's forces completely destroyed the Romanian 9th Infantry
Regiment of the 5th Infantry Division and remnants of the German 75th Infantry Division.

A Cyrillic caption read, "As it happened". Red Army soldiers in this blurry photo are standing next to their truck, which has become stuck in the deep mud on the road.

At 18.00 on 17 March, the 2nd Tank Army's forces were given a task: "From the march, force a crossing of the Dnestr River and firmly dig in on its right bank, on the line: woods east of Sheptelich, Hill 234.7, Hill 276.1, Rubelnita, Soroca." At this time, the army's motorized rifle units had fully assembled in the area of the crossing site and began to prepare to storm the opposite bank of the river. At 9.00 on 18 March, the assault began and the army's motorized infantry began crossing the Dnestr River using boats. Hurling back the resisting defenders, they continued to attack and by the end of the day after stubborn fighting they had seized Soroca and were holding a firm bridgehead on the right bank of the Dnestr River, along the line: 3rd Tank Corps's 57th Motorized Rifle Brigade – Sheptelich, Hill 276.1, Rubelnita; 16th Tank Corps' 15th Motorized Rifle Brigade – Hill 254.9, southern outskirts of Soroca. The army's tank brigades and artillery were in the Iampol' area, still waiting to cross the river. With the fortification of the bridgehead on the southern bank of the Dnestr River, the operation to destroy the enemy's Uman' – Khristinovka grouping and his fresh reserves, which had been brought up from Romania, came to a successful conclusion.

Over the period of the Uman' offensive operation from 5 to 18 March 1944, the 2nd Tank Army headquarters claimed to have killed 7,148 enemy soldiers and officers, and to have destroyed 912 rifles, 213 machine guns, 42 self-propelled guns, 348 guns of various calibers, 315 tanks, 2 prime movers, 260 halftracks, 41 motorcycles, 33 mortars, 9,768 trucks and cars, and 4 aircraft. In addition, it reported the capture of 144 enemy soldiers and officers, and the prevention of the deportation of 25,000 people of the local population to Germany for slave labor.

In view of the spring thaw and the absence of roads, the rear echelons and transport vehicles were stretched out along the entire route. The entire combat operation was conducted exclusively by tanks and infantry, some of which rode on the tanks, and the rest following on foot. The men obtained food and the tanks obtained fuel from captured German stockpiles and despite the difficult conditions, the assignment given to the 2nd Tank Army was carried out with honor. Over the entire period of combat and conducted marches in difficult conditions, the T-34 tanks proved themselves to be durable, capable of overcoming any obstacles and ensuring the completion of tasks. The personnel demonstrated incomparable valor and courage in the struggle against the German aggressors, pursuing the foe tirelessly through day and night. As a result of the combat operations from 5 to 18 March 1944, the 2nd Tank Army had the following losses in tanks: 99 T-34 due to combat damage and 21 T-34 rendered non-operational due to mechanical problems; the dominating place in the overall losses of combat equipment were the losses due to enemy artillery and anti-tank fire, since the 2nd Tank Army participated in daily fighting without a break.

The 2nd Tank Army, as part of the 2nd Ukrainian Front, carried out one of the most important tasks in the Front's operation. The army was not restrained by the special meteorological conditions (the early spring thaw), and with great sense of purpose and aggression, overcame the enemy's resistance on the path to the city of Uman', and on 10 March 1944 took full control of this city while seizing much booty. Exploiting this success, the 2nd Tank Army over eight days reached the Southern Bug River and forced a crossing of it. Then with a rapid attack, on 15 March 1944 it seized the city and major railroad junction of Vapniarka. In its advance to the Dnestr River, the 2nd Tank Army overcame German attempts to organize a defense with heavy air support in the Iampol' area, and by the end of 18 March 1944, it was holding a firm bridgehead on the right bank of the Dnestr River. Over the period of combat operations from 5 to 18 March 1944, the army's forces, despite the muddy conditions of the spring thaw, advanced up to 300 kilometers with fighting. On average each day, the army advanced up to 23-24 kilometers, and on individual days this pace of advance increased to 50-63 kilometers. In the first days of fighting, thanks to the self-sacrificing work of the supply truck drivers, the troops were kept supplied with the necessary amount of ammunition and fuel. Beginning on 10 March 1944, with the capture of Uman', the army primarily exploited captured stockpiles to keep its units supplied with fuel, lubricants and food. Air drops kept the army's forces supplied with ammunition.

Over the 13 days of the offensive, the 2nd Tank Army gave a drubbing to the enemy forces seeking to stop it, which included the 1st, 16th and 17th Panzer Divisions; the 1st SS Panzer Division *Leibstandarte Adolf Hitler*; the 34th, 75th and 198th Infantry Divisions; the *Kampfgruppe* 677 comprised of units of the 255th Infantry Division, the 4th *Gebirgs* Division, the 54th Mortar Regiment, the 482nd Panzerjäger Battalion, the 280th Flak Battalion; the 202nd, 249th and 261st Assault Gun Battalions; the 62nd Heavy Artillery Regiment; the Eighth Army's school for junior officers; and Romanian units, including the 5th Infantry Division, the 6th Cavalry Regiment and the 6th Workers' Battalion. The absence of air cover for the 2nd Tank Army gave the enemy the opportunity to launch unhindered strikes from the air at the combat formations of our troops, and especially at the crossing sites on the Revukha River, the Southern Bug River and the Dnestr River. This somewhat slowed down the army's drive toward the city of Uman' and held up the construction of bridges across the Southern Bug and Dnestr Rivers. Strong air cover over the combat formations of a tank army is necessary to the entire depth of the fighting.

General Bogdanov later recalled:

> In the Uman' operation, the 2nd Tank Army despite all of the previous operations and combat actions and in spite of being understrength in tanks, thanks to decisive actions in close cooperation with units of the field army and the proper understanding of the role and significance of tanks, broke through the enemy's defenses, and developing the attack, overcame enemy attempts to organize resistance and developed the tactical success into an operational one, thereby contributing to the arrival of the Front's forces on the Dnestr River and subsequently on the Prut River. The Uman' operation was based on bold maneuvering in pursuit of the objective to rupture the enemy's defenses, and with a deep penetration to envelop its

flanks and create the threat of encirclement. The task given to the army fully corresponded to the situation. The success of the operation was secured by a powerful attack against a weak sector of defense, which had only been established after the destruction of the Korsun'-Shevchenkovskii grouping, at the height of the spring thaw.

The experience of the 2nd Tank Army in the operation showed that a tank army, given good preparation of the tanks and the drivers, was capable of conducting successful combats in the conditions of the muddy season and the complete absence of roads. For the combined actions of motorized infantry with tanks, it is necessary to have all-terrain vehicles in the motorized rifle units and formations. In order to ensure the timely delivery of fuel, lubricants, ammunition and rations in the conditions of the springtime muddy season, it is necessary for at least 20-30 percent of the vehicles in the tank formations, the fuel supply companies, the motorized transport battalions and in the *front*-level means for the delivery of fuel and lubricants to have treads.

According to Marshal Konev:

There were a lot of episodes interesting in a tactical respect. Especially instructive were those connected with the crossing of tanks. It is a lot more difficult to cross tanks than infantry. In this case, heavy bridges or ferries were required. The tankers of the 2nd Tank Army showed resourcefulness in the Shumilovo area. They found a relatively small place with a depth of up to 2 meters. The location was thoroughly surveyed and equipped with entrances and signs. The tanks' exhaust pipes were extended upward, and all the hatches were tightly closed, caulked with sealant and coated with grease lubricant. In the middle of the day on 12 March, seven tanks crossed the bottom of the river at a depth of 2 meters. They appeared unexpectedly in front of the enemy and threw him into disarray. Having aggressively pushed the enemy back, these tanks secured the expansion of the bridgehead in the Shumilov – Berezki sector. I am not claiming that this was the first example of such a crossing in the war, but it merits attention that already in the conditions of the Patriotic War, in 1944, we moved tanks across a river underwater along the river bottom – a capability that now has become broadly distributed.

The strength of the 2nd Tank Army diminished rapidly in the course of the operation between 5 and 18 March 1944. Once it concluded, the 2nd Tank Army's chief of staff Major General Radzievsky, deputy chief of staff Colonel Bazanov and Military Council member Major General Latyshev issued a report that tracked the steady decline in serviceable armor and active combatants over the course of the operation:

On **5 March 1944**, the 2nd Tank Army had operational 47 T-34, 8 Mark IX, 8 SU-85, 12 SU-76, 6 M-13 rocket launchers and 820 active bayonets in the **16th Tank Corps**; 54 T-34, 32 I.S. Stalin tanks, 4 SU-152, 8 SU-76, 8 M-13s and 760 active bayonets in the **3rd Tank Corps**; and 11 T-34, 4 76mm anti-tank guns and 206 active bayonets in the **11th Guards Tank Brigade**.

Upon seizing Uman' and reaching the Southern Bug, **on 13 March 1944** the 2nd Tank Army had operational 2 T-34, 2 Mark IX, 2 SU-85, 3 SU-76 and 358 active bayonets in the **16th Tank Corps**; 7 T-34, 5 I.S. Stalin tanks, 4 SU-152, 4 SU-76 and 600 active bayonets in the **3rd Tank Corps**, and 4 T-34, 4 76mm guns, and 71 active bayonets in the **11th Guards Tank Brigade**.

With the arrival on the Dnestr River and the consolidation of a bridgehead **on 18 March 1944**, the 2nd Tank Army had operational 1 T-34, 2 Mark IX, 2 SU-85, 2 SU-76 and 210 active bayonets in the **16th Tank Corps**; 2 T-34, 1 I.S. Stalin, 1 SU-152, 1 SU-76 and 403 active bayonets in the **3rd Tank Corps**; and 3 T-34, 4 76mm guns and 71 active bayonets in the **11th Guards Tank Brigade**.

This report concluded with the recommendation:

> "The operation conducted by the 2nd Tank Army to destroy the enemy's Uman'-Khristinovka grouping is a model of the use of armored forces in the period of a muddy season and should be studied in detail. [Signed] 2nd Tank Army Commander of Troops Guards Major General A. Radzievsky; Member of the Military Council Major General of Tank Forces P. Latyshev; and Deputy Chief of Staff Bazanov."

In sum, then, the 2nd Tank Army's 3rd and 16th Tank Corps and the 11th Guards Tank Brigade had a total of 15 serviceable tanks and self-propelled guns after seizing the bridgehead across the Dnestr River – less than the authorized armored strength of a single tank brigade.

In the opinion of Marshal Konev, the commander of the 2nd Ukrainian Front, great credit in resolving the tasks of the 2nd Tank Army belonged to its army commander and the finely-tuned army command apparatus. Leadership over the combat operations of the 2nd Tank Army, considering the difficult terrain conditions and the weather, was personally executed by army commander S.I. Bogdanov, who was always located directly among the frontline troops. He firmly and confidently led the forces subordinate to him, while [his] headquarters, organizing the command and control and receiving information, kept tabs on the carrying out of the army commander's orders. It needed to be said, according to Marshal Konev, that the personal presence of the army commander up among the combat formations in the situation that existed was of great significance and contributed to the rapid pace of the 2nd Tank Army's offensive.

Marshal Konev:

> Lieutenant General S.I. Bogdanov, whom I first met in the Uman' operation, made a great first impression on me with his appearance, and then his business-like qualities. He was a tall, imposing, handsome man. In all his words, deeds and commands, there was a perceptible high exactingness, strong sense of will and orderliness. After reaching decisions and issuing orders, he always drove out to the frontline troops and acted calmly and without fussiness. The headquarters' staff of the 2nd Tank Army, headed by General A.I. Radzievsky, gave the impression of a tightly integrated organism, upon which the army commander could completely rely. Failures and mistakes were not tolerated in the work of the headquarters. The 2nd Tank Army's Military Council, the member of which was General P.M. Latyshev, was also strongly knit and organized. **This was a well-coordinated army, well-prepared and organized in a combat sense; audacity, drive and great energy were evident in its actions.**

The official history of the 2nd Tank Army states:

> The combat operations between the Bug and the Dnestr were conducted in very difficult conditions. Our troops not only had to overcome strong enemy resistance, but also the difficulties of the absence of roads. The impassable muck restricted the actions of the tanks. The prolonged, uninterrupted and intense fighting gave rise to great fatigue of the troops. There were incidents when the driver-mechanics fell asleep behind the levers of the tank. The situation for the tank army was even more complicated by the fact that because of the abysmal road conditions, the rear echelons of the brigades and tank corps lagged behind. Many tank elements, left without fuel and ammunition, were compelled to halt combat operations and wait for the approach of the rear echelons.

The situation was particularly difficult on the axis of the 16th Tank Corps. Here, the enemy still had a lot of tanks, and put up stubborn resistance with strong rear-guard detachments. The insufficient amount of fuel in the combat machines and the inability to maneuver in the sea of mud meant that the tank corps could not bypass enemy nests of resistance. Having given necessary orders to the army's chief of staff Major General Aleksei Radzievsky about hastening the approach of the rear elements and the planning of the operation to force the Dnestr River, S.I. Bogdanov together with an operational group of the headquarters' staff drove out to be with the combat formations of the 16th Tank Corps. At the command post, the corps commander General Dubovoi reported to the army commander that according to intelligence, the enemy was striving to pull his forces back behind the Dnestr River. The units of the corps were in a difficult position due to the lack of ammunition and fuel. In all of the units, no more than 1/3 of a refill of fuel, 10-12 rounds for the main guns, and 2-3 drums of machine-gun ammunition were left in the tanks. The wheeled transport with the fuel and ammunition had not yet come up.

"What do you intend to do in order to beat the enemy to the crossings on the Dnestr River?" the army commander asked.

The corps commander replied, "I have in the corps 12 repaired tanks in the brigades' rear areas. I've sent an officer there aboard a Po-2 airplane with the instructions to load these tanks with fuel and ammunition and to send them urgently to the 15th Motorized Rifle Brigade. We plan to use this brigade as a forward detachment. I will transfer the repaired tanks to the brigade. This will enable the brigade commander to increase the amount of submachine gunners who can ride upon the tanks."

"Fine," said the army commander. "Our army has long had such experience with the use of tanks. But how much time will this take?"

The corps commander General Dubovoi responded, "By morning this brigade will be ready to cross in pursuit of the enemy."

"By morning? By that time we'll be chasing to catch up with the retreating units, and not in direct contact with them. Pursuit means combat, and if we spend the entire night here, we'll have no one to fight."

S.I. Bogdanov proposed to the commander of the 16th Tank Corps to drive together with him to the 15th Motorized Rifle Brigade, which had been designated to operate as a forward detachment, and to familiarize himself with what was happening there. Having arrived in the 15th Motorized Rifle Brigade, the army commander learned from scouts that the enemy, abandoning vehicles and guns on the roads, was retreating toward the bridges over the Dnestr.

The army commander directed that the remaining fuel and ammunition be transferred to the forward detachments, consisting of the 15th and 57th Motorized Rifle Brigades. Even before the onset of darkness, the forward detachments were ready to move out. On the night of 16/17 March 1944, they began to advance in the directions of Iampol' and Soroca. On the morning of 17 March, the 3rd Tank Corps' 57th Motorized Rifle Brigade captured the city of Iampol', while the 16th Tank Corps' 15th Motorized Rifle Brigade reached the left bank of the Dnestr River in the vicinity of Soroca. The fascists' blew up the bridges here. According to their TO&E, the brigades had no bridging equipment of their own. Time was needed to gather and construct improvised means to cross the river. Thus, the crossing of the river was set for the morning of 18 March. Units of the army used the rest of the day and evening prior to 18 March to build rafts of various sizes. All the soldiers of the motorized rifle and artillery elements took part in preparing for the combat crossing of the river. Sappers, as specialists, were supposed to prepare rafts for the crossing of artillery. The work to gather and assemble the improvised means for the assault across the river went quickly. Everyone understood that to delay meant to give the enemy time to dig in on the right bank of the Dnestr.

By dawn on 18 March 1944, a portion of the 2nd Tank Army's artillery had been brought up to the Dnestr River in the sector between the city of Iampol' and the village of Soroca. This artillery had the task to support the river crossing with their fire. At sunrise, the army's artillery opened fire on the enemy that was occupying trenches on the opposite bank, while the infantry and artillerymen of the motorized rifle brigades rushed toward the river with their hastily-constructed rafts and launched their cross-river assault. Fierce fighting erupted. The German-fascist command hurled a significant amount of aviation at the crossing places, which unceasingly struck our crossings. Knowing that the enemy had tanks, the commanders of the motorized rifle brigades strove to cross anti-tank artillery to the opposite bank as quickly as possible.

Because of the lack of time, the points of the river crossings and the crossing means had been prepared and equipped primitively. The sappers' piers were kept in place by cables. Ordinary boats served as tug boats, to which rafts were attached by cables. After loading, other rafts pushed off from the banks and moved further under oars. Enemy aircraft subjected one such crossing site in the sector of the 57th Motorized Rifle Brigade to heavy bombing. Sappers of the 135th Army Engineer Battalion were supporting the crossing. In spite of the fierce bombing, they didn't cease their work. When one of the rafts left the riverbank, bomb fragments severed the cable attaching it to its tug, and the raft started to drift away in the current. In order to save the raft, sapper A. Koshev displayed promptness and heroism. He plunged into the icy waters, and submerged beneath the surface several times, until he had found the end of the cable and re-attached it to the boat. Koshev saved two artillery crews together with their guns. For this exploit, Private Koshev was awarded the highest title "Hero of the Soviet Union".

Tanks of the 2nd Tank Army in the area of Uman, March 1944.

Red Army troops happily inspect a knocked-out German Panther tank.

By the end of 18 March 1944, after stubborn fighting, the 57th and 15th Motorized Rifle Brigades had seized bridgeheads on the left [sic] bank of the Dnestr River. The actions of the 2nd Tank Army in the offensive fighting from Uman' to the Dnestr River was praised by the *Stavka*. By order of the Supreme Commander-in-Chief, the 107th, 109th and 164th Tank Brigades and the 15th Motorized Rifle Brigade were bestowed the honorific title "Vapniarka". The army commander Lieutenant General of Tank Forces S.I. Bogdanov was given the title "Hero of the Soviet Union", as were the commander of the 16th "Uman'" Tank Corps Major General I.V. Dubovoi, the commander of the 11th Separate Guards Tank Brigade Guards Colonel N.M. Koshaev and other soldiers and officers.

### To the Commander of the 2nd Ukrainian Front's Armored and Motorized Forces Lieutenant General Comrade Kurkin

I am reporting: Units of the Romanian 5th Infantry Division are operating in front of the 2nd Tank Army. As of 20.3.1944, the following number of tanks and self-propelled guns were present in the army's formations: 3rd Tank Corps – 11, 16th Tank Corps – 6, 11th Guards Tank Brigade – 3, 87th Separate Motorcycle Battalion – 3, for a total of 23 armored vehicles. The decision regarding the new assignment has been presented to you in Order No.019/02, and consists of the following: a) firmly to defend and fortify the seized bridgehead on the right bank of the Dnestr River; b) to cross tanks and arriving artillery on ferries; c) in the future together with the 52nd Army to expand the bridgehead as far as the Kainar River and to be ready to seize Bălti [Bel'tsy] together with the 6th Tank Army; d) from 17.3.1944, since the taking of Iampol' and the bridgehead on the right bank of the Dnestr River, only artillery and mortar fire has been exchanged with the enemy, and thus I cannot report on enemy losses. The army is daily suffering losses in personnel and materiél from the incessant activity of the enemy's bomber, ground attack and fighter aviation. e) There have been no captured vehicles since 17.3.44. In turn, I cannot accept reserve vehicles, even though there has been an enormous multitude of them, because I'm constantly advancing and don't have any reserve drivers. f) The 29th Tank Corps is located in Malaia Tsekinovka and hasn't crossed over to the right bank of the Dnestr River.

[Signed] Commander of the 2nd Tank Army, Hero of the Soviet Union, Guards Lieutenant General of Tank Forces Bogdanov, 20.3.1944

General Bogdanov also wrote to Konev, the commander in chief of the 2nd Ukrainian Front, to complain about the absence of air cover for his 2nd Tank Army:

### To the Commander of the 2nd Ukrainian Front

1.  I am reporting that from 18 to 21.3.1944, our aviation has been operating exceptionally poorly. For example, on 20.3.1944 in the interval between 17.00 and 18.00, three fighters refused battle with one enemy bomber; today on 21.3.1944, 30 JU-87 at 17.00 bombed the crossing site, and six of our fighters remained off to one side and didn't approach them before they had dropped all their bombs and departed.
2.  From 18 to 21.3.1944, the enemy has made constant bombing runs in the area of Fleminda, Iampol', Soroca and Rusovo. As a result of this, the crossing has been disrupted 3-4 times a day by direct hits, bomb fragments and strafing runs. The city of Iampol' and the village of Rusava are in complete ruins. Because of the lack of activity by our fighters, the enemy's aviation has absolute superiority in the air, because of which the army has suffered losses in tanks, vehicles and men. It hasn't been possible to work at the crossing, and thus three days have been lost for crossing equipment to the opposite bank of the Dnestr.
3.  I ask that you order our fighters to work actively in the Fleminda, Iampol', Rusava, Soroca area.

[Signed] 2nd Tank Army's commander and Hero of the Soviet Union Lieutenant General of Tank Forces S. Bogdanov; Military Council member Guards Colonel Matiushin; 2nd Tank Army's chief of staff Guards Major General Radzievsky

According to a report from the 2nd Tank Army's chief of the Operations Department Colonel Bazanov, as of 16.00 on 19 March 1944, the day after the seizure of the bridgehead on the right bank of the Dnestr River, the effective combat strength and supply of the 2nd Tank Army's formations were as follows:

**3rd Tank Corps:** Tanks and self-propelled guns: 4 T-34, 5 IS -85, 2 Mark IX, 1 SU-76. Guns and mortars: 3 76mm guns, 2 37mm guns, 7 120mm mortars, 2 M-13 rocket launchers. Available supplies: 0.5 combat load for the tanks and 0.75 of a combat load for the artillery; 0.7 of a refill of fuel and lubricants; 1 day of rations.
**16th Tank Corps:** Tanks and self-propelled guns: 2 T-34, 1 IS-85, 3 Mark IX, 1 SU-85. Guns and mortars: 15 76mm guns and 8 120mm mortars. Available supplies: 0.2 of a combat load for the tanks and 0.75 of a combat load for the artillery; no fuel or lubricants; 1 day of rations.
**11th Guards Tank Brigade:** 3 T-34 tanks and 4 76mm guns. **86th Guards Mortar Regiment**: 18 M-13 rocket launchers, 2 salvoes of ammunition, 2 refills of fuel and lubricants;

and 1 day of rations.

Total number of tanks and self-propelled guns for the army: 9 T-34, 6 IS-85, 5 Mark IX, 1 SU-85 and 1 SU-76.

[Signed] Chief of the 2nd Tank Army's Operations Department Colonel Bazanov

A fuller accounting of the 2nd Tank Army's available armor was generated on the following day and reported by Major General Radzievsky, the 2nd Tank Army's chief of staff, and Colonel Bazanov, the 2nd Tank Army's chief of operations, on 20 March 1944:

Table 6.4: Data on the 2nd Tank Army's available tanks and assault guns as of 20 March 1944

|  | Type and mark | 3rd Tank Corps | 16th Tank Corps | 11th Guards Tank Brigade | Total: |
|---|---|---|---|---|---|
| Serviceable: | T-34 | 4 | 2 | 3 | 9 |
|  | Mk IX | 2 | 3 | – | 5 |
|  | SU-152 | 1 | – | – | 1 |
|  | SU-76 | 1 | 2 | – | 3 |
|  | SU-85 | – | 2 | – | 2 |
| En route: | T-34 | 8 | – | – | 8 |
|  | Mk IX | 1 | 4 | – | 5 |
|  | SU-152 | 3 | – | – | 3 |
|  | SU-76 | 14 | – | – | 14 |
|  | Total: | 34 | 13 | 3 | 50 |

Major General Radzievsky also reported on the army's combat losses in tanks, self-propelled guns and rocket launchers over the period from 5 to 19 March 1944:

Table 6.5: Data on the losses suffered by the 2nd Tank Army over the period between 5 March and 19 March 1944

|  | 3rd Tank Corps | 16th Tank Corps | 11th Guards Tank Brigade | Total: |
|---|---|---|---|---|
| T-34 | 15 | 18 | 7 | 40 |
| Mk IX | – | – | – | – |
| SU-76 | 2 | 6 | – | 8 |
| SU-85 | – | 4 | – | 4 |
| M-13 rocket launchers | – | – | – | 3 |

However, in his report General Radzievsky was referring to total losses (burnt-out tanks or tanks requiring major overhauls). Later, Major General of Engineer-Tank Services Iukin, the 2nd Tank Army's deputy commander for vehicle maintenance and technical support, produced a fuller report on the 2nd Tank Army's losses:

As a consequence of combat offensive operations, the 2nd Tank Army in the period from 5 to 18 March 1944 had the following combat losses in equipment:

a)  Due to combat damage – 99 T-34 tanks, 10 KV-85, 10 SU-85, 8 Mark IX, 18 SU-76, for a total of 145 combat machines; b) knocked-out due to mechanical problems – 21 T-34, 5 KV-85, 4 Mark IX, 5 SU-152, 3 SU-85 and 6 SU-76 for a total of 44 combat machines. In addition, 29 T-34, 11 KV-85, 2 Mark IX, 3 SU-85 and 5 SU-76, for a total of 50 combat machines, received combat damage that didn't render them unserviceable.

Of the total quantity of combat-damaged machines, the irreplaceable losses amount to:

Table 1

|  | Total number of losses | Irreplaceable losses | Percentage of total number of losses |
|---|---|---|---|
| T-34 | 149 | 17 | 11.5 |
| KV-85 | 26 | 5 | 19.0 |
| SU-85 | 16 | 1 | 6.0 |
| SU-76 | 29 | 6 | 20.0 |
| Total: | 220 | 29 | 13.2 |

The army's combat operations in the period from 5 to 18 March 1944 were characterized by the fact that the army took part in daily battles without a break, having daily losses in combat equipment as a result of the pursuit of the enemy and counterattacks by the latter. The analysis of knocked-out machines as a result of combat damage shows the dominating place in the total losses of combat equipment consists of losses due to enemy tanks and artillery fire – 132 combat machines, or 60 percent of the total losses over the operation. The losses due to enemy mines, primarily in the first days of the offensive, amount to 8 combat machines, or 3.7 percent of the total number of losses. Losses from enemy air attack – 5 combat machines. The total number of machines knocked-out of action due to mechanical problems amounted to 44 machines, or 20 percent of the total number of losses. The comparatively large number of disabled tanks and self-propelled guns due to non-combat reasons is explained by the excessive strain placed on the machines by the bad grading of the route, the absence of roads, as well as the inadequate training of the drivers.

### The Repair of Combat Equipment from 5.3 to 18.3.1944

Excluding from the total number of tanks that received combat damage those that were written off as beyond repair and the machines that required major overhauls (22 T-34, 1 IS-85), the repair teams had to repair 137 combat machines that were knocked-out of action over the accounting period. Of them: a) 42 T-34, 5 IS-85, 5 SU-85 and 7 SU-76 (59 tanks and self-propelled guns in total) required minor repairs; b) 39 T-34, 7 IS-85, 13 Mark IX, 5 SU-152, 5 SU-85 and 9 SU-76 (a total of 78 tanks and self-propelled guns) needed light overhauls. Over the period from 5 March to 18 March 1944, 115 tank repair jobs were done by the 2nd Tank Army's repair means. Of them: a) 59 were minor repairs done to 42 T-34 tanks, 5 IS-85 tanks, 5 SU-85 self-propelled guns, and 7 SU-76 self-propelled guns; b) 56 were light overhauls done on 35 T-34, 5 IS-85, 2 Mark IX, 5 SU-85 and 9 SU-76.

### The Evacuation of Materiél from 5.3 to 18.3.44

Over the accounting period, 23 T-34 tanks were evacuated from the battlefield and no-man's land. The evacuation of the tanks was done exclusively by tanks used as recovery vehicles. As a consequence of the quickly accelerating pace of the offensive, the army's evacuation companies were unable to follow directly behind the combat units and were sent instead to locations that were difficult for wheeled transport to negotiate. In so far as keeping the wheeled transport carrying fuel, ammunition and rations moving, the evacuation companies in the period of the muddy season played a significant role. Tractors of the 78th Evacuation Company worked to tow away immobilized armored vehicles and equipment from the Tarashcha – Lisianka – Chizhovka area back to the locations of repair stations. At the moment when the army's combat operations concluded on the Uman' axis on 18 March 1944, the remaining service hours of the engines in the tanks and self-propelled guns still in service were as follows (see Table 2):

**Table 2**

|        | "0" hours remaining | Less than 50 hours remaining |
|--------|---------------------|------------------------------|
| T-34   | 0                   | 15                           |
| KV-85  | 0                   | 4                            |
| Mk IX  | 0                   | 10                           |
| SU-152 | 4                   | 0                            |
| SU-85  | 0                   | 5                            |
| SU-76  | 0                   | 10                           |
| Total: | 4                   | 44                           |

[Signed] Assistant Commander of the 2nd Tank Army for Vehicle Maintenance and Technical Support Major General of Engineering Service Iukin; Chief of 2nd Tank Army's Department of the Repair and Evacuation of Tanks Lieutenant Colonel Zemlianukhin

## Photographs of the 2nd Tank Army in the Uman' Operation of 1944

A T-34 waits in ambush – 2nd Tank Army, March 1944. The Cyrillic caption read "In ambush".

Attacking motorized infantry of the 2nd Tank Army dismount from a halted tank, March 1944.

"What sort of 'technological wonder' is this?"

"Where has their arrogance gone?".

German prisoners, taken
in the Uman' area,
March 1944.

A bridge over the Dnestr River, spring 1944.

Units of the 2nd Tank Army crossing the Dnestr River, March 1944. The Cyrillic captions read, "The crossing of the 34th Guards Motorized Rifle Brigade over the Dnestr River. Motorized rifle brigade commander Colonel P.N. Akimochkin directs the crossing."

Hero of the Soviet Union Captain Fedor Donkov and his tank crew inspect a destroyed German Panther, March 1944. Several days later, the tankers of Donkov's tank company (107th Tank Brigade) would conduct their final exploit in the Pirlița Sat area.

Donkov and his crew inspecting the same knocked-out Panther. The Cyrillic text read, "But what is it like close-up?"

**The losses of the German panzer divisions** that were opposing the 2nd Tank Army were significant. For example, the 503rd Heavy Panzer Battalion lost 23 Tigers in the Potash Station area, where troops of the 2nd Tank Army seized German repair shops, in which 21 disabled Tigers were located that the Germans hadn't been able to evacuate. Two Tigers were lost while defending the station. In the same area on 7 March 1944, soldiers of the 2nd Tank Army destroyed 5 Panthers of II/23rd Panzer Division, which had previously joined the Heavy Panzer Regiment *Bäke*, while another 18 Panthers of this same panzer battalion, which were under repair at the station, were blown up by the Germans as they retreated.

The deputy chief of staff of the 2nd Tank Army for intelligence Colonel Galimov reported:

> In the conducted operation, nothing new was noted in the enemy's tactics and use of tanks. On the contrary, the conducted operation demonstrated that the German command didn't employ the possibility of using tanks on the defensive in the conditions of the muddy season. Having superiority in tanks and personnel, the Germans were unable to secure a compact cover of the main routes of our tanks' advance, while during flank attacks by our tanks and our emergence in the rear of their divisions, they fled in panic, burning and blowing up their equipment. It is confirmed that the enemy skillfully used its aviation, with the aim of slowing the offensive of our units. [The enemy] used massed groups of aircraft, primarily against bridges and crossing sites and the combat formations of our units.
>
> **Conclusions:** As a result of the 2nd Tank Army's offensive operation in the period from 5 to 10.3.1944, the enemy's Uman' grouping consisting of three infantry divisions (34th, 76th and 198th Infantry Divisions); four panzer regiments of four panzer divisions and their specialized elements (1st, 16th, 17th and 1st SS Panzer Divisions); two infantry battalions (the 4th Separate Reserve Battalion of the 4th *Gebirgs* Division and 1/91st *Gebirgs* Regiment); the 471st and 482nd Panzerjäger Battalions; the 202nd, 249th and 261st Assault Gun Battalions; the 54th Mortar Regiment; the 62nd Heavy Artillery Regiment; and units of the 17th Flak Division were destroyed. In the conducted operation, the German command didn't organize

A tank of the 2nd Tank Army enters a Moldavian village, April 1944.

stable resistance to the offensive of units of the 2nd Tank Army given the presence of three water barriers: the Gornyi Tikich, Southern Bug and Dnestr Rivers.

[Signed] Deputy chief of staff of the 2nd Tank Army for intelligence Colonel Galimov and chief of the information section Major Kostromin]

### From the "Opyta boev 2-i Tankovoi Armii" [Experience of the 2nd Tank Army's Combats"]: The teamwork of SU-85 self-propelled gun batteries of the 1441st Self-propelled Artillery Regiment when breaking through the enemy's defense in the battle for Cheremisskoe

After the unsuccessful attempt to break through to the encircled grouping in the Korsun'-Shevchenkovskii area, the enemy hastily went over to the defense in order to prevent complete destruction. The enemy's forces had been worn down by the unsuccessful attacks and by our tank counterattacks. In order not to allow the enemy to consolidate, in the course of a week, work was conducted to repair and return self-propelled guns to service, and an inspection of the equipment and weapons was done. At that time, the enemy's defense was still in the construction stage; it wasn't continuous and presented a number of strongpoints created on directions that were important in a tactical respect. There were no continuous lines of trenches. Minefields had been laid on directions that were vulnerable to tanks. The enemy's artillery was deployed in direct firing positions; the positions were organized tactically and well-camouflaged. The [enemy] aviation wasn't showing activity, having large losses in the preceding fighting. The soldiers' morale had been undermined by the unsuccessful attacks.

On 4.3.1944, the regiment was given the assignment to be ready for offensive combats and to support the attack of the tank brigades. The two batteries were transferred by battery to two tank brigades and were supposed to support the tanks' attack. At 5.00 on 5.3.1944, the regiment took up its jumping-off positions under the cover of darkness: the 1st Battery in the village of Shubennyi Stav; the 2nd Battery in the village of Kuchkovka. Questions regarding the cooperation with the tank brigades had been resolved, and a reconnoitering of the enemy's forward edge of defense and the directions of attack had been conducted with the self-propelled gun commanders. The taking up of the jumping-off positions had been concealed, so that the enemy wouldn't notice the preparatory work, and our offensive was a surprise for him. The batteries of self-propelled guns were supposed to attack at a distance of 100-150 meters behind the combat formations of the tanks in the directions: left-hand group – Cheremisskoe, which the Germans had converted into a major strongpoint, and further on toward the southern outskirts of the village of Vagva; the right-hand group – the crossroads northwest of Cheremisskoe and Vagva. Command of the batteries was implemented over the radio. Communication with the batteries was by visual signals. The commanders of the self-propelled guns maintained observation from bulletproof hatches, since when the main gun fired, dust and gases hindered observation of the battlefield through the optical sights.

At 7.00 the artillery preparation began, after which the batteries went on the attack behind the tanks. As the left-hand group approached the village of Cheremisskoe, it was met by and halted by heavy fire from enemy tanks and anti-tank guns. A collapse of the attack was threatened. At this time, the right-hand group, reaching the western outskirts of Shubennyi Stav and seeing the difficult situation of the left-hand group, engaged the enemy tanks that hindering the advance of the left-hand group. The enemy tanks were caught in an unfavorable position, with their flanks exposed to the fire of our self-propelled guns. The SU-85's main gun was lethal to enemy tanks, since it had greater armor-piercing capability than the 76mm tank guns. The enemy tanks then shifted all their fire to the self-propelled guns. The battery commander, having extensive combat experience, quickly moved his battery up into the tanks' combat formations. This maneuver made it difficult for the enemy to distinguish the self-propelled guns from the tanks. As a result of the brief tank clash, the enemy lost four tanks, and the remaining tanks, seeing their certain destruction, began to retreat. The enemy infantry began to run away in panic after the tanks. Thus, the well-organized fire cooperation of the batteries of self-propelled guns decided the outcome of the battle.

Reaching the western outskirts of Cheremisskoe, the batteries noticed a column of German troops that were in retreat along the Rizino – Vagva road. Opening a lethal fire at the column, they created panic in the enemy ranks. This ultimately decided the outcome of the battle. The enemy without any special resistance abandoned the village of Vagva and began to retreat toward Uman'. As a result of this action, the regiment destroyed 2 enemy tanks, 1 self-propelled gun, 1 anti-tank gun, 1 truck loaded with supplies and weapons, 1 halftrack, and up to 70 enemy soldiers and officers.

**Conclusions:** Thus, the well-organized combat teamwork, the mutual fire support and the demonstrated initiative ensured a breakthrough of the enemy's defenses on the given sector.

The Soviet high command naturally took great interest in the combat performance of its new I.S. Stalin heavy tanks and the recently created heavy tank regiments. The commander of the 8th Separate Guards Tank Regiment Lieutenant Colonel Zemlianoi provided this account of its operations for the period 5 to 19 March 1944:

The combat operations took place in the period of the spring thaw. It was impossible for wheeled motorized transport to move along the dirt roads. As a result, a large gap developed [between the forward units] and the rear echelons with their materiél. The regiment lacked the support with all types of supplies by the wheeled transport.

The regiment as part of the 3rd Tank Corps was introduced into a breakthrough in the Chizhovka – Ryzhanovka sector at 9.00 on 5.3.44, out of the Dubrovka area in the direction of the southern outskirts of Chizhovka, Rizino, Chernaia Kamenka. After the liquidation of the Korsun'-Shevchenkovskii grouping, the enemy was making a fighting withdrawal to the line Rusalovka, Hill 232.1, Rubannyi Most, Hill 241.6, Cheremisskoe, Hill 243.3, Chizhovka, Ryzhanovka, with the aim of shortening their lines and digging-in on a more advantageous line of defense. A second line of defense was being prepared along the southwestern bank of the Gornyi Tikich River. In the sector of operations, the enemy was defending with units of the 17th Infantry Division and the 17th Panzer Division, and with their organized system of fire and multiple counterattacks, he was blocking the advance of our forces and was conducting reconnaissance probes with small groups. His tank reserves – the *Adolf Hitler* Panzer Division and the 16th Panzer Division had been withdrawn for refitting presumably to the area of Molodetskoe and Krasnopolka.

The 3rd Tank Corps with its attached assets in cooperation with the 33rd Rifle Corps had the task to break through the enemy's defenses in the Chizhovka – Kobyliaki sector and to cut the Chizhovka – Rizino road; to seize the bridges across the Gornyi Tikich River in Berezovka and Chernaia Kamenka with a subsequent emergence in the Monastyrek, Timoshevka, Polkovnich'e, Ivanovka, Uman' area. Pursuant to Order No.226 at 22.30 on 2.3.44 from the 3rd Tank Corps commander, the regiment was given the task to move out of the Dubrovka area on the Chizhovka, Rizino, Chernaia Kamenko axis and to cover the corps' left flank, securing the arrival of units of the 51st Tank Brigade on the banks of the Gornyi Tikich River. On our right, the 13th Separate Guards Tank Regiment of the Supreme Command Reserve was operating; on our left there were no tank units. The regiment was ordered by the 3rd Tank Corps commander to carry out its task precisely, in order to secure the forward advance of our units, especially in the fight for the Rizino strongpoint. The village of Rizino with its stone buildings and commanding hilltop location was situated on the axis of the corps' advance, and when bypassing it, the enemy was raking the corps' combat formations with flanking fire from it. The regiment commander decided with part of his tanks to suppress the enemy's artillery batteries with fire from fixed positions, while the second group pinned down the enemy's tanks and destroyed them with fire and maneuver.

The regiment performed this task with success and at 16.30 on 5.3.44 took possession of the Rizino strongpoint. In the fighting for Rizino, 3 Panther tanks, 4 artillery batteries, 83 wagons with military loads and up to a battalion of enemy infantry was destroyed by the regiment.

As a result of an impetuous advance in conjunction with the 51st Tank Brigade, at 10.30 on 6.3.44, the settlement of Chernaia Kamenka was taken from the march. The bridge across the Gornyi Tikich in Chernaia Kamenka was blown up by the enemy when retreating. In view of this, the further pursuit of him with tanks was stopped. In this combat, 8 guns, 47 trucks and 350 supply wagons with their loads were destroyed, and more than 250 enemy soldiers and officers were killed. Booty was taken: 3 guns in good working order, 73 wagons with their supply loads, and 2 operational prime movers.

The losses of the regiment in personnel and equipment in the fighting for Rizino and Chernaia Kamenka were 7 killed (including 2 officers) and 14 wounded (including 2 officers); 1 tank was left blazing in a combat with tanks, and 2 more tanks were knocked-out, but turned over for repair. In the fighting for Rizino and Chernaia Kamenka, the following officers particularly distinguished themselves: Guards Senior Lieutenant Viktor Mel'nikov, the commander of a tank company, and tank commander Guards Lieutenant Nikolai Savin.

The regiment at 6.30 on 9.3.44, having crossed the Gornyi Tikich in Berezovka, went on the pursuit of the enemy on the Krachkovka, Ivan'ki, Man'kovka, Pomoinik, Krasnopolka,

Voitovka, city of Uman' axis with IS-85 tanks, and seized the latter by 18.00 on 9.3.44. The regiment with 12 tanks had reached the edge of a forest lying 3 kilometers northwest of Voitovka, where the commander of the 3rd Tank Corps ordered it to make an outflanking maneuver through a forest firebreak and the western outskirts of Dmitrovskoe, before advancing further along the highway, and to break into the center of Uman' under the cover of darkness with a swift attack in order to take the city. It was also to secure the arrival of motorized infantry and the rest of the units into the city, which would thereby paralyze the Voitovka strongpoint. The regiment carried out its assigned task and at 22.30 on 9.3.44, unexpectedly for the enemy broke into the center of it in the vicinity of the post office and movietheater, and with machine-gun fire and fire from their main guns, the tanks forced the enemy to abandon the city and the area of a military encampment and fall back behind the Umanka River. The enemy, fleeing the city in panic, blew up all the bridges across the Umanka River.

The enemy defending Voitovka and the Uman' airfield, hearing the sounds of combat and the howl of tank engines in the city, abandoned Voitovka without resistance, which by itself secured the further advance of our units. At 23.10 on 9.3.44, our main forces entered the city and began to eliminate groups of enemy stragglers, while 2 hours later the infantry marched into the city. The 57th Motorized Rifle Brigade, which was supposed to be supporting the regiment's offensive, in fact didn't arrive until the morning of 10.3.44.

In the fighting for the city of Uman', the regiment inflicted the following damage to the enemy: 7 guns of various calibers, 23 machine-gun nests, 27 trucks with their cargo, and up to a battalion of enemy infantry was scattered and partially destroyed. Booty was captured: 9 tanks of various marks, up to 600 trucks with their loads, 7 cannons of various calibers, 10 stockpiles of ammunition and rations, 50 light machine guns, and various sorts of fuel – up to 1,000 metric tons. The regiment had no losses in personnel, and no irreplaceable losses in equipment: 1 I.S. tank was knocked-out and 1 I.S. tank was set aflame (but the fire was extinguished through the crew's efforts). Both tanks were repaired and are in service. In the fighting for the city of Uman', the tank company commander Guards Senior Lieutenant Viktor Mel'nikov and tank commander Guards Lieutenant Nikolai Savin [again!] particularly distinguished themselves.

Following the order of the 3rd Tank Corps commander, the regiment jointly with the 50th Tank Brigade at 9.00 on 11.3.44 went on the pursuit of the enemy on the Kocherzhintsy, Liubashevka, Ternovka, Berezovka axis and further toward a bridge across the Southern Bug, and even further toward the Dzhulinki area. The enemy with a portion of his forces north and northwest of Ternovka organized an intermediate strongpoint with the aim of protecting the bridge and withdrawing his personnel and equipment from the Ternovka area. The tanks with a headlong attack struck toward Ternovka and seized it. The enemy in this action lost 2 Panther tanks, 6 guns of various calibers, up to 300 trucks, and up to 200 soldiers and officers. Up to 100 soldiers and officers were taken prisoner. Booty: 50 trucks, up to 200 wagons with combat supplies, and more than 300 horses. In the combat with enemy tanks and artillery that were retreating from Ternovka toward Berezovka, one of our tanks was left blazing and one tank was knocked out by the enemy. The losses of the regiment in personnel: 2 officers, 1 sergeant and 1 private were killed, and 4 were wounded (2 officers). In this battle, Guards Senior Lieutenant Mel'nikov was a model of courage and heroism. His tank was damaged, and then brewed up by a German Panther tank. From the southern outskirts of Berezovka, Senior Lieutenant Mel'nikov, though wounded, sacrificed himself by continuing to fire from the burning tank at enemy tanks, and destroyed one with two shell hits. Mel'nikov burned alive in his tank, but his heroic deed secured the forward advance of the rest of the tanks to the Southern Bug River. For his exemplary conduct while carrying out a command and the heroism and courage that he demonstrated in the process, Comrade Mel'nikov was posthumously nominated for the title "Hero of the Soviet Union".

After the destruction of the enemy's Ternovka grouping, the regiment continued to pursue the enemy and at 20.00 on 11.3.44 took with fighting the town of Dzhulinki, in which there were a lot of Germans. The regiment together with units of the 50th Tank Brigade had taken up a defense on the western outskirts of Dzhulinki, but the absence of our infantry didn't give them the possibility of combing through Dzhulinki (which has more than 2,000 buildings), as a consequence of which there remained a lot of German soldiers and officers in the buildings, who together with a retreating enemy grouping of 4 tanks and 400 soldiers and officers that were striving to cross the bridge over the Southern Bug River that morning, initiated street fighting in Dzhulinki. Lieutenant Smirnov's tank platoon, which was covering the bridge across the Southern Bug, met the enemy with fire from fixed positions and destroyed one Panther tanks and two German self-propelled guns. The defeated enemy in Dzhulinki rendered no resistance to the advance of our forces to the Vapniarka railroad station.

As a result of the fighting for Dzhulinki and the bridge across the Southern Bug River, the enemy suffered the following losses: 4 tanks and self-propelled guns, 2 guns of various calibers, 10 machine-gun nests, 5 trucks, up to 40 wagons with their combat supply loads, and up to 150 enemy soldiers and officers were killed. The regiment as a result of the battle for Dzhulinki lost 1 officer wounded, but had no dead. One tank was knocked-out. In the fighting for Dzhulinki and the bridge across the Southern Bug River, tank commander Guards Lieutenant N.S. Savin and tank platoon commander Guards Lieutenant A.V. Smirnov distinguished themselves.

Conducting an outflanking march along the route Berezki, Bershad', Byrlovka, Zabolotnoe, Kryshepel', Vapniarka railroad station and avoiding combat with the enemy, the regiment on 16.3.44 at 22.40 reached Vapniarka Station. On 16.3.44, the commander of the 3rd Tank Corps gave an assignment jointly with the 51st Tank Brigade to move out of the Vapniarka area toward the southern outskirts of Rusovo, and to seize the city of Iampol' and the bridge across the river with an energetic attack. At 10.40 on 17.3.44, the regiment together with the 51st Tank Brigade (which had only one participating tank) went on the attack toward Iampol' along the Rusovo – Iampol' road, and with an impetuous maneuver broke into the city of Iampol'. Having seized a bridge across the Dnestr River with a load-bearing capacity of up to 6 metric tons, the regiment secured a possibility for our units to cross to the opposite bank and there to develop the success in pursuit of the enemy. In the combat for the city of Iampol' and possession of the bridge across the Dnestr River, the regiment inflicted the following damage to the enemy: 5 guns of various calibers, 5 trucks, 76 wagons with their loads, and up to a battalion of infantry were destroyed. Booty: 8 warehouses with food, 25 wagons, and up to 200 horses.

In the fighting for Iampol' and the bridge across the Dnestr River, tank commander Guards Lieutenant Savin distinguished himself with a decisive, bold and fearless act. Despite the heavy enemy artillery fire from the opposite bank, he was the first to reach the bridge over the Dnestr River and held it, preventing attempts to blow it up.

At 12.00 on 18.3.44, the regiment received Combat Order No.019/op from the headquarters of the 3rd Tank Corps to cross the Dnestr River and to assemble in Tselinova-Mika by 18.00 on 18.3.44. Carrying out the order, the regiment together with the 51st Tank Brigade assembled in the village of Fleminda by 13.00 on 18.3.44 in order to cross the Dnestr River. When conducting the march from Iampol' to Fleminda, 100 meters short of the bridge across the Murafa River in a ryefield on the outskirts of the village of Belaia, 20 enemy JU-87 aircraft attacked the tanks, as a result of which two tanks were set on fire; however, thanks to the courageous and prompt actions of the crews, the flames were extinguished and the tanks remained serviceable. During the air attack on the tanks, tank commander Guards Lieutenant Savin was badly wounded while risking his life under enemy fire to smother the flames that were enveloping his tank. For his repeated demonstration of heroism in combats with the German aggressors and for his disregard for his life for the sake of saving a powerful weapon, an I.S. tank, Comrade Savin was nominated for the title "Hero of the Soviet Union".

**Conclusion**: When introducing the regiment into the breakthrough on 5.3.44, the regiment had 17 tanks operational tanks that were combat-capable, while the other 4 tanks were under repair after the combat operations to liquidate the enemy's Korsun'-Shevchenkovskii grouping. On 19.3.44, the regiment had 6 tanks in the area of the city of Iampol'. Two tanks had been burned-out as a result of enemy artillery fire (irrecoverable losses); 9 tanks were under repair and in transit to the regiment; and 4 tanks were in transit to the city of Iampol'. The tanks' engines, having a service life of 150 hours guaranteed by the factory, in fact had each worked for 230-250 hours in combat conditions. A technical inspection of the tanks is necessary, as is a schedule for replacing separate components.

Over the period of combat operations from 5.3 to 19.3.44, the regiment inflicted the following damage to the enemy in personnel and equipment: <u>Destroyed</u> – 10 tanks and self-propelled guns, 40 guns of various calibers, 33 machine-gun nests, 477 trucks with their cargo, 549 wagons with their combat supply loads, and up to a regiment of enemy infantry. <u>Captured</u> – 9 tanks of various marks, 10 guns of various calibers, 50 light machine guns, 650 serviceable trucks and cars, 2 prime movers in operating condition, 18 stockpiles of food and ammunition, up to 1,000 metric tons of fuel of various sorts, 118 horses, and more than 500 enemy soldiers and officers.

Over the period of combat operations from 5.3 to 19.3.1944, the regiment had losses in personnel and equipment: <u>In personnel</u> – 4 officers and 7 sergeants and privates killed, for a total of 11 men, and 6 officers and 12 sergeants and privates wounded for a total of 18 men. <u>In equipment</u> – 2 irrecoverably lost I.S. Stalin tanks (burned out), and 3 tanks knocked-out (needing major overhauls). The personnel in the conducted battles behaved courageously, decisively and with initiative.

**Overall Conclusion**: The regiment carried out the mission given to it precisely and timely. The officers' staff in the conducted operation acted decisively and energetically, and resolved combat tasks with tactical competence. Command and control over the elements in battle was implemented by the personal example of the regiment commander and by radio. The new I.S. Stalin tanks were employed with tactical skill. Radio communicatons operated without disruptions throughout the entire operation.

[Signed] Commander of the 8th Separate Guards Tank Regiment Guards Lieutenant Colonel Zemlianoi; Chief of Staff Guards Major Demin]

The commander of the 51st Tank Brigade, using very similar language, wrote up a recommendation for the 8th Separate Guards Tank Regiment's officers to be awarded government decorations:

**Battlefield Letter of Recommendation for the 8th Separate Guards Tank Regiment of the RGK [Supreme High Command] for the Period of Actions from 5 to 8 March 1944**

The tank regiment was entrusted to me during the introduction into the breakthrough out of the area of Dubrovka in the direction Rizino, Chernaia Kamenka with the task to cover the corps' left flank, securing the emergence of units of the 51st Tank Brigade at the Gornyi Tikich River. The regiment carried out its given assignment to the letter, which ensured the advance of the units, particularly in the fighting for the strongpoint Rizino. This inhabited locality with its stone buildings and commanding hill was located on the axis of the corps' movement, and when bypassing it, the enemy unleashed flanking fire from all types of weapons against the corps' combat formations. The regiment commander, having assessed the situation, with part of his tanks from fixed positions suppressed the enemy's artillery batteries, and with the rest of his tanks with fire and movement fixed the enemy tanks in position, and then destroyed them. In the fighting for the Rizino strongpoint, up to 2 artillery batteries, 3 tanks and up to 200 enemy soldiers and officers were destroyed by the regiment on the approaches to it, and on the outskirts of the strongpoint, up to 2 artillery batteries, approximately 50 loaded wagons, and up to a battalion of enemy infantry. In the fighting for the settlement of Chernaia Kamenka, the regiment destroyed: 30 trucks, 150 wagons, 3 heavy field guns, and more than 250 soldiers and officers. Booty was seized: 2 serviceable guns, 20 wagons and 2 serviceable prime movers.

**Conclusion:** The regiment carried out its assigned task. In the course of the battle, it had three knocked-out tanks. The regiment's officers acted decisively and gallantly, for which they fully deserve government decorations.

[Signed] Commander of the 51st Tank Brigade Colonel Mirvoda; Chief of Staff of the 51st Tank Brigade Lieutenant Colonel Piskunov

## Veterans' recollections of the fighting

### Guards Junior Sergeant Maripov on the actions of a scout group to seize a bridge:

In order to scout the bridge across the Gornyi Tikich River, a group consisting of 12 men under the command of Senior Lieutenant Belan was detached. The retreating enemy was leaving behind small covering forces along the road, which hindered the advance of our group. Despite these defensive screens, we reached the village of Berezovka. Our group climbed a hill and watched the enemy in the vicinity of the bridge. With the surveillance we established that camouflaged enemy equipment and vehicles were around the bridge. Since we were at close range, we opened heavy fire. The Germans, not expecting the approach of our forces, were thrown into panic and began to scatter into the woods and to the opposite bank of the river. At the command of our group's leader, the group swiftly rushed forward, firing while on the move, as a result of which the enemy's abandoned equipment and the bridge were taken by our group. In the course of the brief nighttime fight, 39 hostile soldiers and officers were killed by the scouts, and 13 men were taken prisoner. At the same time, the following trophies were taken: a staff car of a German battalion with documents, print media and rubber stamps; 9 trucks loaded with a variety of goods; and 20 wagons and 22 horses. Our group of scouts held the seized bridge until the main forces of our units came up. Our group received decorations for this battlefield exploit, while Senior Lieutenant Belan was bestowed the title "Hero of the Soviet Union".

### Guards Senior Lieutenant Galikov:

On 5 March 1944, tank company commander Captain Donkov received an order to drive the enemy out of the village of Cheremisskoe. At 5 o'clock in the morning, Donkov's tanks moved out. The enemy put up savage resistance, but unable to withstand the onslaught of the tanks, turned tail and ran. Captain Donkov, leading by his personal example, pursued the fleeing enemy. Under a hurricane of enemy fire, Donkov was the first to break into the village of Vagva, leaving enemy groups behind himself, which the tanks of his company destroyed. Soon the captain had expended all the shells in his tank, and was running low on fuel. But the brave warrior, returning fire with a machine gun and tossing grenades, waited in the center of the village for ammunition to be brought up. The foe sought in every way to set fire to his machine, but the warrior bravely defended it.

At 22.00 two tanks from his company approached. Having loaded and replenished his tank with ammunition and fuel, Donkov and the two tanks charged toward the village of Ul'ianovka. Seeing the tanks, the enemy took flight in panic, casting aside everything on the way. However, the hero's tanks pursued him. Before reaching Buki, Donkov's tanks stopped, waiting for the approach of other forces. On 6 March 1944, Donkov's tanks burst into Buki and took it. Here, 16 firing points were knocked-out, and 17 loaded trucks, 2 stockpiles of food and 2 regimental banners were taken. The retreating enemy blew up the bridge over the Gornyi Tikich River. With the arrival of darkness, the bridge was repaired.

Having refueled, Donkov's tanks again rolled forward. On 10 March 1944 at 2.00, Captain Donkov was the first to break into the city of Uman' under a storm of enemy fire. The fleeing enemy left behind hundreds of cars and trucks on the city streets, disabled tanks in repair shops, cannons and supply stockpiles.

When liberating Pirliţa Sat, Donkov's tanks were encircled. Captain Donkov was posthumously awarded the title "Hero of the Soviet Union".

### From the recollections of Guards Sergeant Matsapura:

We swiftly outflanked the Nazi Uman' grouping from the northwest – as they say, we caught it by the tail. In the course of this swift advance, we were moving along rail tracks, and on the tracks there was a train carrying enemy tanks – Tigers and Panthers. From everything it was obvious that they were preparing to unload them, and our appearance caught the enemy off-guard. From the train station building, Nazis were running toward the train – some with mess kits in their hands, some with a razor, their faces lathered. Their colleagues were pouring out of the train and leaping out of tank hatches to meet them. Meanwhile, we were spraying all of them with machine-gun fire. The panic was complete. Tigers and Panthers, new ones, straight from the factory, fell into our hands in good working order.

Having liberated Uman' on 10 March, we moved on toward Vapniarka at night. I had already accumulated adequate experience driving a tank at night – both along roads and off roads. This isn't a simple matter. Here it is not enough to have good eyesight. Constant training is needed to acclimatize your eyes to see in the darkness. But that isn't all. An experienced driver-mechanic even with his eyes closed can tell you what sort of soil his machine is traveling – sand, peat or loamy clay under the tracks of his tank. Hearing, which keenly catches changes in the engine's revolutions at a certain speed, helps him in this. A sense of smell helps distinguish the smell of the earth being torn up under the tracks, which wafts into the open forward hatch – dry or damp. The combination of sharp eyesight, hearing and sense of smell, multiplied into an instantaneous reaction, helps the driver-mechanic make the necessary maneuvers in a night action and when driving off-road, when it is pitch-dark.

The combat machines of our company happened to take part in such a night combat approximately 5 kilometers east of Vapniarka, not far from a railroad crossing. Three tanks were moving along the highway, the first – Junior Lieutenant Oleg Matveev's machine; the second – ours; and the third – Junior Lieutenant Viktor Shalgin's. We see in front of us the flashes of gun shots, and determine from their sound that they were our 76mm divisional guns. They are firing at somewhere on the other side of the crossing; there, in the tongues of flames, the outline of a German tank is visible. We drive up to the anti-tank guns; there are two of them. The officer-artilleryman quickly briefed Lieutenant Pogorelov on the situation: beyond the crossing there was a village, and a long, deep and wide ravine ran along the left side of the village. Several enemy tanks were in it. They were plainly intending to set up an ambush, but they themselves fell into one. The artillerymen set aflame the first tank when it tried to attack them. The burning machine blocked the nearer exit from the ravine. But if the far exit could also be sealed, then – here the artilleryman gave a clap – then the Fritzes would be trapped!

"Give them some fire, and pour it on!" Pogorelov requested. "Distract them."

The guns began to fire, ringingly and often, while we led the tanks over the railroad crossing. Once across the railroad, we deployed into a fan-shaped formation. Our machine was rolling forward in the center; Shalgin was on the right, and Matveev – advancing alongside the ravine and village. Matveev's gunner was Nikolai Elkin, a fine fellow, and the best gunner in the battalion. We rolled across a meadow toward the jagged edge of a grove. About 15 or 20 minutes later, there, where according to our calculations, was the far exit of the ravine, shots from Matveev's T-34 rang out. Immediately there came the loud blast of an explosion and a flash of flame, which lit up the far huts of the village. Matveev's crew had started the battle, and Elkin was firing at the fascists like a sniper. Further on I was no longer able to follow the actions of this tank. Enemy anti-tank guns opened fire out of the patch of woods, which lay about 300 meters from us. They were firing at Matveev's tank, and we fired at them. A gun duel flared up.

"Step on it!" Lieutenant Pogorelov hoarsely shouted at me. Across the ruts and potholes filled with slushy snow, I accelerated the tank toward the battery. The flame from the nearby gun muzzle when it fired was blinding; shadows of fleeing soldiers darted, and iron began to grate beneath the tracks. I moved the tank along the wooded edge, overrunning guns, and almost collided with Shalgin's tank, which had also burst into the firing positions of the fascist battery.

"To the ravine!" Pogorelov commanded. We hurried in that direction, guided by the flames of the tanks that Elkin had brewed up. We didn't see Junior Lieutenant Matveev's T-34, but as it later became clear, comrades had arrived just in time to assist. Three or four enemy machines were attacking them. We knocked out two of them, and soon silence reigned over the battlefield. Only in the swale and on the edge of the grove, where the overrun fascist battery had been standing, something was burning fiercely and ammunition was exploding.

Soon the machines of Senior Lieutenant Viktor Benke and Lieutenant Ivan Lisiakov approached us. Battalion commander Captain Kul'biakin had sent them to us as reinforcements, and while we had been overrunning the battery and repelling the tank counterattack, Benke and Lisiakov had bypassed the grove, overrun a column of enemy trucks loaded with fuel and ammunition, and scattered infantry.

Having dispersed and taken up a defense, the five T-34s stood here until dawn. Infantrymen came up, and took up to a hundred Nazis prisoner, who had been lurking in the patch of woods and village. When it became light, we could see our nighttime work – the crushed anti-tank battery, the hulks of burned-out vehicles, and the swale, at the exit of which Nikolai Elkin had knocked out six fascist tanks. Altogether in the night action, the enemy lost nine tanks and four guns. On 15 March, units of the 2nd Tank Army liberated the city and major railroad station of Vapniarka. By an order of the Supreme Commander-in-Chief, the 107th Tank Brigade was given the honorific title "Vapniarka".

**Letters of commendation for those awarded the title "Hero of the Soviet Union" in this operation**

**Semen Mirvoda**, Colonel, commander of 3rd Tank Corps' 51st Tank Brigade. In the period of the corps' preparation for the offensive and the breakthrough of the enemy's defenses in the Chizhovka area, Comrade Mirvoda was able over the short period of time to prepare the equipment and personnel for the breakthrough, and on 5 March 1944 the enemy's defense in the Chizhovka area was breached. Pursuing the retreating enemy, Comrade Mirvoda was always located up in the lead tank of the combat formations of his brigade's units and inflicted severe damage to the enemy in the sector of the brigade's operations on the approaches to Uman', as a result of which the enemy left behind 18 tanks, 37 trucks and 17 guns of various calibers. [The brigade] killed 350 soldiers and officers and took 70 prisoners. Colonel Mirvoda was wounded in this period, but remained on active duty. On 18 March 1944, the brigade was ordered to pursue the retreating enemy in the direction of Iampol', to break into the city, and to seize the bridge across the Dnestr River. Colonel Mirvoda with a group of tanks and submachine gunners, riding in the lead tank, was the first to break into the city of Iampol' and seized the bridge across the Dnestr River. For [his] courage, resolve and heroic deed, as a result of which the city of Iampol' was taken and the bridge over the Dnestr River was seized, Comrade Mirvoda is worthy of acquiring the title "Hero of the Soviet Union".

**Fedor Mekhnin**, Sergeant Major, driver-mechanic of a T-34 tank in the command company of the 3rd Tank Corps' 50th Tank Brigade. He showed himself to be a fearless driver-mechanic. He courageously and decisively directed his tank toward the foe in fighting for the villages of Ternovka and Dzhulinki. His tank was the first to break into Ternovka, and with fire and treads he destroyed 2 self-propelled guns, 4 tanks (2 of which were Panthers) and 23 trucks. Up to 120 dead enemy soldiers and officers were left on the battlefield. In the combat for Dzhulinki, his tank was the first to seize the bridge across the Southern Bug River, and despite desperate enemy attempts to take back the bridge, Sergeant Major Mekhnin, showing no regard for his life, held the bridge until the approach of the main forces, thereby forcing the Germans to plunge directly into the river's water, where up to 150 Nazis drowned. When driving his tank across the seized bridge toward the opposite riverbank, the tank triggered a mine and went to the bottom [of the river] together with the hero. For demonstrated heroism and bravery, for the destruction of enemy personnel and equipment, and for reaching the bridge across the Southern Bug, Sergeant Major Mekhnin has been posthumously awarded the title "Hero of the Soviet Union".

**Alexandr Rybin**, Captain, commander of the 1st Motorized Rifle Battalion of the 16th Tank Corps' 15th Motorized Rifle Battalion. In defensive fighting on 14.2.44 in the village of Khizhentsy, Captain Rybin's battalion stubbornly held its occupied line, and didn't allow enemy infantry and tanks, which were striving to break through to the relief of encircled divisions, to pass. When repelling the attack of enemy infantry and tanks, 13 tanks (including 6 heavy) were knocked out and brewed up by his battalion, and more than 100 Nazis were killed. In fighting south of the village of Druzhintsy on 18-19.2.44 to liquidate the encircled divisions, 889 enemy soldiers and officers were annihilated by Captain Rybin's battalion, and 114 were taken prisoner. In offensive fighting on 6.3.44, his battalion from the march was the first to force a crossing of the Gornyi Tikich River, and having seized a lodgment on the right bank, secured the crossing of other units. On 9.3.44, in fighting for the city of Uman', his battalion with an outflanking maneuver from the right was the first to break into the city, and quickly advanced to its southwestern outskirts. As a result of this bold maneuver, large trophies were captured. On 14.3.44, when repelling an attack of enemy tanks and infantry from the rear, his battalion killed 79 enemy soldiers and officers. Upon reaching the Southern Bug River, the battalion quickly crossed to the right bank under enemy fire using improvised means, and successfully developed the offensive. On 17.3.44, in fighting for the town of Iampol' and the bridge across the Dnestr River, 87 Romanians were killed by his battalion, and 30 were taken prisoner. Arriving at the Dnestr River, [his battalion] quickly crossed to the right bank and continued to pursue the Romanians, tying them up in combat, and captured 50 Romanians and a supply train carrying food, ammunition and weapons. In the period of combat operations, for the successful fulfillment of command assignments, 115 men in the battalion were awarded with Orders and medals. For his model fulfillment of command assignments and for the heroism and courage he demonstrated in the process, Captain Rybin has been awarded the title "Hero of the Soviet Union".

**Fedor Donkov**, Captain, commander of a T-34 tank company of the 16th Tank Corps' 307th Tank Battalion. As commander of a T-34 tank company Captain Fedor Donkov showed himself to be an energetic, hard-driving officer. In battles on the 1st Ukrainian and 2nd Ukrainian Fronts Donkov's company, moving in the vanguard of the units of the 16th Tank Corps, demonstrated its endurance, ability and courage. Despite the very difficult roads, in view of the mud created in the fields as a result of the melting snow, his company dashingly and ceaselessly, without losing a single machine due to breakdowns, accidents or getting bogged down in the mud, conducted a combat march both day and night, without rest, hounding the fleeing foe. Approximately 1,500 enemy soldiers and officers were killed by his company, and several enemy combat and transport vehicles were knocked out. As a result of the impetuous offensive with the active role of his company, dozens of inhabited places were liberated, including Buzhanka, Bagva, Buki, Man'kovka, Uman', Tomashpol', Soroca, Bălti and others. His company destroyed 11 Tigers, 8 Panthers, 12 Pz IV, 36 anti-tank guns, 45 halftracks, 120 trucks and cars, and more than 700 enemy soldiers and officers. Booty was seized: 150 trucks, 18 heavy and 23 medium tanks, 4 supply dumps with fuel, ammunition and food.

In the Man'kovka area, Donkov's crew smashed the headquarters of two German units and seized their banners and documents. During the fighting for Bagva the enemy brought up a large quantity of artillery and tanks, and putting up fierce resistance, prepared to counterattack, which threatened our left flank. Bagva had to be taken straight away. The brave men, bounding foward in their machines, ran into heavy fire and stopped. Then Captain Donkov, showing personal initiative and bravery, surged ahead in one machine, and skillfully maneuvering and shooting up the enemy's firing positions, closed upon them at full speed, rolled across a mined bridge, and breaking into the village, became tied up in street fighting and engaged the enemy until our infantry had crossed a ford and come up. That's how Bagva was taken. The foe fled in panic to Uman', which had to be taken by a daring raid into the rear, so that the enemy couldn't consolidate there and create a firm defense. The tanks, coated with sticky mud, were stretched out along the route and slowly moving forward. Having Sergeant Major Boris Makeev, the best driver-mechanic, in his crew, Captain Donkov decided to break through to the city of Uman' in a single tank and to disrupt the enemy's work on its defenses until the rest of the tanks came up. At midnight, Donkov's tank reached the outskirts of Uman'. The enemy, suspecting nothing, allowed his tank to pass through into the depth of the defenses, where Fedor Donkov immediately initiated daring actions that sowed panic in the city.

**Soldiers of the 2nd Tank Army who particularly distinguished themselves in the Operation**

Evgeni Tyshchik –
50th Tank Brigade.

Fedor Mekhnin –
50th Tank Brigade.

Fedor Donkov –
107th Tank Brigade.

Mikhail Sanachev –
51st Tank Brigade.

Alexandr Rybin – 15th
Motorized Rifle Brigade.

Nikolai Savin – 8th Guards
Heavy Tank Regiment.

Boris Makeev –
107th Tank Brigade.

Melnikov – 8th Guards
Heavy Tank Regiment.

Iakov Telechenko – 11th
Guards Tank Brigade.

**Boris Makeev**, sergeant major, driver-mechanic of Captain Donkov's T-34 tank of the 16th Tank Corps' 307th Tank Battalion. Sergeant Major Makeev passed through a hard school of heavy fighting of the first years of the war. He became a master of driving in the combat condition of tank battles, including the Battle of Kursk. From 1943, as part of the 307th Tank Battalion, he was the driver in the tank of Captain Donkov, the company commander, ensuring his successful actions. Detailed descriptions of the battles have been presented in Captain Donkov's letter of commendation (see above). For demonstrated courage and bravery, skill and fearlessness in combat situations, and his skill as a driver, Sergeant Major Makeev has been awarded the title "Hero of the Soviet Union".

**Viktor Mel'nikov**, Guards senior lieutenant, commander of an IS-85 tank company in the 8th Guards Heavy Tank Regiment. In the breakthough of the German defenses on 5.3.44 in the Chizhovka – Ryzhovka sector, Mel'nikov's tank company, with a decisive attack, crushing anti-tank and anti-infantry obstacles and destroying his [German] equipment and personnel, took the southern outskirts of the village of Chizhovka, not allowing the stunned foe to come to his senses and to organize a resistance. Guards Senior Lieutenant Mel'nikov's tank company swiftly pursued the enemy that was fleeing in panic, and on his boot heels broke into the southern outskirts of Rizino, having from the march destroyed the center of resistance that had been organized within it. As a result of the day of fighting, the company had made an advance of more than 7 kilometers into the depth of the German defenses. On the night of 9/10.3.44, Mel'nikov was given an assignment to seize and hold the city of Uman' until the arrival of the main forces. Mel'nikov's company with an aggressive movement and bold maneuver, bypassing a German anti-tank area, burst into the city. Fierce artillery fire didn't stop the brave officer, who reached the center of Uman' together with his company and held it until the approach of the main tank forces, despite the enemy's numerical superiority and savage resistance.

In the fighting on 11.3.44 for possession of the district center of Dzhulinki and the bridge across the Southern Bug River, the company advanced at the forefront of our units, inspiring them with its attacking elan. On the approaches to the village of Berezovka, Mel'nikov's IS tank encountered heavy enemy fire and accepted an unequal fight. The tank was set aflame and Mel'nkov himself was wounded. Continuing to fire from the burning tank, the commander with accurate shots from his cannon knocked out a heavy enemy tank and three field guns, and scattered and destroyed up to a company of infantry. In this savage combat Mel'nikov continued to fight from his burning tank, securing the rapid advance of our units, until he was consumed along with it by the fire. Inspired by the unparalleled courage of their commander, the tankers impetuously advanced and, having crushed a strong German defense, took the bridge across the Southern Bug.

Over the period of operations from 5.3.44 to 11.3.44, Mel'nikov's company destroyed 3 heavy tanks, 2 medium tanks, 9 guns of various calibers, 89 trucks loaded with various military supplies, and more than 300 enemy soldiers and officers. Guards Senior Lieutenant Mel'nikov has been posthumously awarded the title "Hero of the Soviet Union".

**Nikolai Savin**, Guards lieutenant, commander of an IS-85 tank of the 8th Guards Heavy Tank Regiment. Savin in the fighting in the area of the Rizino strongpoint repeatedly moved out with his tank on reconnaissance in order to expose enemy artillery batteries and tanks, and after revealing them, precisely reported on their locations over the radio.

In the fighting for the city of Uman' Savin together with his crew was the first to break into the city, shooting up soldiers on the streets with a machine gun. When his tank was set aflame, he leapt out of the tank and rushed to smother the flames in spite of taking fire from nearby buildings. As a result of his bold and prompt action as part of a group of tanks, he managed to cut off approximately 600 various trucks and cars in the city; of this number, the great majority were

Tankers of the 2nd Tank Army after being decorated.

serviceable. [In addition] several warehouses filled with food, ammunition and equipment were captured, which sealed the fate of the city's capture in nighttime conditions (23.00 – 9.3.44). Taking part in the seizure of the bridge across the Southern Bug River, in combat he destroyed a Panther tank and self-propelled gun right around the bridge. The bridge was taken with insignificant damage to it.

In the fighting for the city of Iampol', he was the first to break into the city, emerging at the bridge leading to the opposite bank of the Dnestr River. He destroyed 2 cannons and approximately 10 loaded wagons.

When carrying out the combat assignment to reinforce the corps' right flank, in a group of tanks he was subjected to bombing and strafing by JU-87 dive bombers, as a result of which the auxiliary fuel drum on his tank burst into flames. The flames began to enter the engine compartment. As soon as the conflagration was detected, Guards Lieutenant Savin lept out of the tank and started to try to smother the flames, in spite of strafing from airplanes. While fighting the flames, Savin was severely wounded, but refused to abandon his tank until [ensuring] that the machine was saved and remained serviceable. Guards Lieutenant Savin died of his severe wound in a hospital. For his unparalleled bravery in numerous battles and for his self-sacrifice for the sake of his IS-85 combat machine, Guards Senior Lieutenant Savin was posthumously awarded the title "Hero of the Soviet Union".

**Ivan Trukhin**, sergeant, T-34 driver-mechanic in the 94th Tank Battalion of the 3rd Tank Corps' 51st Tank Brigade. Trukhin, taking part in the offensive on the Uman' axis from 7.3.44, along the entire combat path was a driver-mechanic who showed exceptional skill in driving a tank and heroism in the fighting. During the breakthrough of the German defenses, moving in the lead tank, with competent maneuvering he ensured accurate targeted fire for the commander, while boldly heading toward the enemy. On the first day of fighting he crushed 2 guns, 12 machine guns and 70 enemy soldiers and officers with his tracks. In subsequent fighting, demonstrating skill and resourcefulness, he drove his tank onward with combat.

In the period of the offensive toward Uman', driving the tank in nighttime conditions, he boldy steered toward enemy firing points and destroyed them with his tracks. Under a strong enemy artillery fire, he drove the lead tank into the city of Uman'. Maneuvering along the city streets, he ensured the destruction of the enemy with fire, and destroyed 18 machine-gun nests and 50 enemy infantrymen with his tracks. Driving onward on the attack, skillfully maneuvering on the battlefield and destroying enemy infantry with his tracks, he broke into the retreating columns in his tank.

Approaching the city of Iampol', he boldly broke into it and steered his tank to the bridge across the Dnestr River, throwing the enemy into great turmoil, and secured the excellent conducting of fire for the commander and kept the tank undamaged. Throughout the entire extent of the offensive, the tank didn't have a single incident of stopping due to mechanical problems. In the fighting Trukhin showed courage and heroism and was worthy of the title "Hero of the Soviet Union".

**Mikhail Sanachev**, senior lieutenant, commander of a T-34 tank company in the 94th Tank Battalion of 3rd Tank Corps' 51st Tank Brigade. Senior Lieutenant Sanachev, taking part in the fighting on the Uman' axis, showed exceptional ability in commanding the company throughout the entire offensive and displayed personal skill, resourcefulness and heroism. Beginning on 5.3.44, he participated in the breakthrough of the enemy's defenses, accompanying the attacking units with competent fire and maneuver and advancing at the forefront of the attacking forces.

On the first day of the offensive, encountering stubborn enemy resistance in his path, superbly commanding the company, Sanachev destroyed 7 guns and up to 15 enemy machine-gun nests with fire from his tank. In the area of Chizhovka, leading the advance and encountering strong blocking detachments, he destroyed artillery and tanks with fire and crushed infantry with his tracks. On the route from Chizhovka to Chernaia Kamenka, the company destroyed 5 tanks, 35 guns, 23 machine guns, 8 mortars, 45 trucks and killed up to 200 Nazis. Sanachev personally destroyed 3 tanks, 16 guns, 3 mortars, 18 machine guns and 50 soldiers and officers.

In subsequent battles, always advancing at the forefront of the units' attack, with fire and treads he destroyed all of the enemy's firing points, securing the forward progress of our forces. In fighting for the city of Uman', Senior Lieutenant Sanachev, during a night attack, displaying heroism, destroyed the enemy, and maneuvering on the battlefield under heavy enemy artillery fire, was among the first to break into the city of Uman', where he engaged in street fighting with the enemy. Over this period Sanachev together with his company destroyed: 26 tanks, 101 guns, 5 prime movers, 17 machine guns, 3 aircraft at an airbase, 7 supply dumps and 400 soldiers and officers.

Continuing a further advance with fighting and approaching the town of Iampol', he was among the first to enter the town and approached the bridge across the Dnestr River. He mowed down enemy troops from his tank. Placing targeted fire on the right bank of the Dnestr River, he forced the enemy to abandon two occupied locations. Over this period Senior Lieutenant Sanachev with his tanks [of the company] destroyed 14 guns, 42 trucks, 15 motorcycles and 210 soldiers and officers. Along the entire extent of the advance, Sanachev superbly led his platoons and personally displayed exceptional ability, boldness, valor and heroism. By his personal example, he inspired the tankers to heroic exploits. He is worthy of the title "Hero of the Soviet Union".

**Vladimir Kosarev**, lieutenant, commander of a "Valentine" tank of the 16th Tank Corps' 51st Separate Motorcycle Battalion. In the battle for Vapniarka Station, Kosarev and his tank were the first to break into the station, and with fire and treads destroyed up to two mortar batteries and up to 200 enemy soldiers and officers. With his daring surprise actions, he sowed panic among the enemy and with a skillful maneuver blocked the enemy's path of retreat, as a result of which the Germans abandoned up to 2,000 trucks and cars and a horse-drawn supply train carrying loads and ammunition, which were seized by our units in spite of heavy enemy artillery fire. He boldly advanced and ensured the seizure of the station. For demonstrated valor in the fighting, he is worthy of the title "Hero of the Soviet Union".

# The Army's Battles in Moldavia and Romania, 1944

**Command Staff of the 2nd Tank Army**
Commander – Lieutenant General Semen Bogdanov
Military Council member – Guards Colonel Nikolai Matiushin
Chief of Staff – Guards Major General Aleksei Radzievsky
Chief of the Operations Department – Colonel Il'ia Bazanov
Artillery Commander – Major General Grigorii Plaskov
Deputy Commander for Rear Services – Colonel Petr Antonov
Chief of the Intelligence Department – Colonel Ashraf Galimov

**16th Tank Corps** – Major General Ivan Dubovoi
107th Tank Brigade – Colonel Tikhon Abramov
109th Tank Brigade – Colonel Petr Babkovsky
164th Tank Brigade – Colonel Nikolai Kopylov
15th Motorized Rifle Brigade – Colonel Petr Akimochkin
1441st Self-propelled Artillery Regiment (SU-85) – Major Dmitrii Gorbatenko
298th Guards Self-propelled Artillery Regiment (SU-76) – Guards Colonel Novikov

**3rd Tank Corps** – Lieutenant General Vasilii Mishulin
50th Tank Brigade – Major Isak Fundovnyi
51st Tank Brigade – Colonel Semen Mirvoda
103rd Tank Brigade – Lieutenant Colonel Aleksandr Khalaev
57th Motorized Rifle Brigade – Colonel Pavel Shamardin
375th Guards Heavy Self-propelled Artillery Regiment – Guards
Lieutenant Colonel Kharitonov

**Units Subordinate to Army headquarters:**
11th Guards Tank Brigade – Guards Colonel Boris Eremeev
6th Guards Heavy Tank Regiment – Guards Lieutenant
Colonel Iosif Cheriapkin
8th Guards Heavy Tank Regiment – Lieutenant Colonel
Andrei Zemlianoi

Semen Bogdanov.

Nikolai Matiushin.

Aleksei Radzievsky.

Il'ia Bazanov.

Grigorii Plaskov.

Vasilii Mishulin.

Ivan Dubovoi.

Boris Eremeev.

Iosif Cheriapkin.

Pavel Shamardin.

With the completion of the Uman' operation, the 2nd Tank Army had seized a lodgement on the right bank of the Dnestr River and reached the line: Hill 224.7, Hill 276.1, Rubelnita, Soroca, thereby creating a staging area for subsequent offensive operations. The rapid advance of the 2nd Tank Army, the absence of a suitable rail network, the poor condition of the unpaved roads, and the low serviceabilty status of the motorized transport were creating difficult conditions for the troops' actions and for keeping them supplied. With the arrival on the Dnestr River, an intelligence mission organized by the 2nd Tank Army's engineer chief came back with the information that a pontoon bridge on the southeastern outskirts of Iampol' Yampil had been blown up by the retreating Germans and had 65 meters of damaged sections. There was enough material on location to repair it. Quickly, the army's arriving engineer units started work to restore the bridge. Simultaneously, they began to assemble a ferry, and at 10.00 on 18 March 1944, artillery and motorized units began to cross the Dnestr. On 20 March, a second ferry began to operate, with a load bearing of up to 30 metric tons and powered by oars.

In view of the low activity of our aviation, the enemy reigned supreme in the skies. It was almost impossible to work at the crossings. After concentrated air strikes, the pontoon bridge was completely destroyed.

The movement of the wheeled and tracked transport and tanks along a single road, the absence of an adequate traffic control service, the lack of mobile repair shops on the route, and the inexperience of the drivers led to the fact that a majority of the machines en route stood idle for entire days. For these reasons, the army's artillery units at the front had only 35.6 percent of their available number of guns. As of 23 March 1944, the 2nd Tank Army had serviceable 13 T-34, 8 IS-122, 5 Valentine Mark IX, 2 SU-85, 5 SU-76 and 1 SU-152, for a total of 34 tanks and self-propelled guns. The majority of the combat equipment still hadn't crossed to the right bank.

By 7.00 on 25 March 1944, work on the construction of a bridge was completed, and the crossing operation began to work more intensively. All the efforts of the army's apparatus and units were directed to carrying out General Bogdanov's order, demanding the acceleration of the transfer of personnel and equipment to the other side of the Dnestr. By the end of 25 March, the given task was for the most part fulfilled. The defending army, having fortified the bridgehead that it had seized on the right bank, and having set up communications and resolved questions of cooperation with its neighbors, was ready for new battles to expand the bridgehead.

## The operational-tactical situation by the end of 25 March 1944

The 2nd Tank Army's rapid advance on the Iampol' axis and the seizure of the bridgehead across the Dnestr River created a threat to the enemy that our forces could drive into the rear of his Kishinev – Odessa grouping. With the aim of liquidating this threat, the enemy had introduced the Romanian 4th Army Corps, consisting of the 7th, 8th and 14th Infantry Divisions, into the fighting. On 28 March remnants of the German 75th Infantry Division, and the Romanian 8th and 14th Infantry Divisions and 5th Cavalry Division, as well as the 580th, 369th and 213th Security Battalions, which had been resisting on the Dominteni, Trifănești, Alekseevka (Alexeevca), Cernița line [northeast of Bălti], began slowly to fall back with fighting to the Bălti area, with the aim of holding this vital road hub.

## The nature of the terrain and the presence and condition of roads

The terrain in the sector of the 2nd Tank Army's forthcoming operations was moderately rugged, with a large number of ravines and four water barriers – the Dnestr, Reut, Jijia [Zhizhiia] and Bahlui Rivers. For the most part, they didn't present difficulties for tank operations. The roads, except for the Botoșany – Târgu Frumos [Tirgu Frumos] highway, were farm roads and cart tracks.

Once across the Dnestr, the roads had dried out, and the tank units advanced quickly. However, once reaching the Pirlița Tyrg and Cornești Tyrg area, the meteorological conditions didn't bless operations: heavy snow fell, and the roads sharply deteriorated. The movement of trucks and cars became hardly possible, and difficult for tanks. Subsequently, with the arrival in the Focuri – Podu Iloaie area in the sector of the 27th Army, there wasn't a single route that could support a load of 30 metric tons. A nameless stream in the Făcuti area had no passage for tanks.

## The rivers:

The Dnestr River has a width of 300-400 meters, a depth of 1.5 to 2 meters, and had steep banks and bluffs with a height of up to 5 meters. The soil of the banks and river bottom are sandy loam, rocky in places, and the river has an average current flow of 0.9 meters/second.

The Reut River is 40-80 meters wide, with a depth of 0.7 meters. The banks are steep in places, the soil of the banks and river bottom is sandy loam, and the river flows at an average rate of 0.6 meters/second. It had two fords in the zone operation. In order to improve them, rocks were laid across the river bottom to provide more support, and the banks were leveled.

The Jijia River is 10-15 meters wide, with a depth of 0.5 meters. In the vicinity of Cârniceni, a 30-ton bridge was being built through the efforts of the 27th Army. The work wasn't completed in time. The chief of engineers of the 27th Army indicated a different bridge for the passage of tanks in the Borșa – Vlădeni area. This bridge collapsed after the passage of nine tanks. It was repaired by the 2nd Tank Army by 12.00 on 12 April 1944.

The Bahlui River has a width of 5-10 meters and its banks have a height of 6 meters. In addition, the column's route of movement was intercepted by a nameless branch that had a width of 2 to 6 meters and banks as high as 5 meters.

Given the presence of broken ground and water obstacles, it is necessary to have reinforced engineer-sapper units in offensive operations. Materials for the contruction of bridges across water obstacles and swampy ground (pre-fabricated bridges, baffles for treadways, logs, planks, bolts and nails) must be moving behind the combat formations of the tank corps. For their movement, the corps and army sapper battalions must have high-speed, tracked tow vehicles with hitches.

## <u>The combat operations of the 2nd Tank Army from 25 March to 5 May 1944</u>

According to the directive from the 2nd Ukrainian Front, the 2nd Tank Army, having crossed the Dnestr River, was to make a forced march to the Bălti area and to reach it by the end of day on 25 March 1944. Subsequently it was to advance along the Fălești, Pirlița, Cornești, Negurenii Vechi axis. The 16th Tank Corps on the morning of 25 March, having crossed the Dnestr River out of its jumping-off area from the eastern outskirts of Iampol' and Porogi, was to make a forced march through Iampol' toward Frumusica and Bălti, and by the end of the day was to reach the north-western and western portions of Bălti. Subsequently, it was to attack in the direction of Fălești and Pirlița, with the task by the end of 26 March to seize the Pirlița, Nicolaevca, Vladimirovca area. From Bălti it was to dispatch a forward detachment consisting of 8-10 tanks with infantry and sappers in the direction of Pirlița and Tuzara. The 3rd Tank Corps' jumping-off area extended from the western portion of Iampol' to Hal'zhibivka. On the morning of 25 March, having crossed the Dnestr River, it was to set out on a forced march in the wake of the 16th Tank Corps and to reach the southern and southeastern part of Bălti by the end of the day. Subsequently it was to attack along the Fălești, Negurenii Vechi, Cornești axis with the mission to seize the Cornești, Romanovka, Bumbăta area. From Bălti, it was also to send out a forward detachment in the direction of Orhei [Orgeev, Orgiejow]. The 11th Guards Tank Brigade was the army's reserve. Having crossed the Dnestr River, it was to set out behind the 3rd Tank Corps on a forced march and was to reach the northern portion of Bălti by the end of 25 March. Subsequently it was to move out behind the 3rd Tank Corps, with the assignment to secure the army's left flank from possible enemy counterattacks out of the Orhei area. By the end of 26 March, it was to be in the area of Negurenii Vechi.

## a) The 2nd Tank Army's battle for Bălti

The forces of the 2nd Tank Army went on the offensive at 17.30 on 25 March 1944. Units of the lead 16th Tank Corps reached the line of Hill 222.5 and a railroad hut 4 kilometers northeast of Bălti, where they ran into fierce enemy resistance. With a resolute attack by tanks and tank riders of the motorized rifle brigade, the 16th Tank Corps penetrated the enemy's combat positions, broke the enemy's resistance, and on the heels of the retreating enemy, burst into Bălti, where it became tied up in street fighting. Arriving units of the 3rd Tank Corps exploited the success of the 16th Tank Corps, while the 11th Guards Tank Brigade halted in a nameless hamlet 2 kilometers southeast of Cubolta, in readiness to act on the 3rd Tank Corps' left flank.

On the morning of 26 March 1944, the enemy in Bălti, while laying down heavy fire, torched the large buildings, destroyed supply stockpiles, and withdrew his main forces to the south, after blowing up the bridges on the Reut River. From there, conducting artillery fire from Hill 156 and Hill 169.1, they put up fierce resistance, which checked the 2nd Tank Army's offensive toward Fălești.

Tanks of the 2nd Tank Army
being greeted by locals, 1944.

On 26 March, the 2nd Tank Army had serviceable 26 T-34, 7 Valentine Mark IX, and 4 SU-85, for a total of 37 tanks and self-propelled guns. According to a document from the chief of the Operations Department Colonel Bazanov on the condition of the 2nd Tank Army's forces at 24.00 on 28.3.1944:

The 3rd Tank Corps: Serviceable armor 1 T-34, 7 SU-76, 1 SU-85 and 1 SU-152; 7 85mm guns, 3 76mm guns, 3 37mm guns, 8 120mm mortars, 4 82mm mortars and 6 M-13 rocket launchers. En route: 14 120mm mortars, 1 85mm gun, 13 37mm guns, 7 SU-76, 5 76mm guns and 4 57mm guns. Supplies: 1 combat load of ammunition for tanks, 0.3 of a combat load for the mortars, 0.5 of a combat load for the 76mm guns, and 2 salvoes for the M-13 rocket launchers. The vehicles had 1 refill of fuel and lubricants.

The 16th Tank Corps: Serviceable armor 4 T-34, 6 SU-76 and 2 SU-85; 11 120mm mortars, 14 76mm guns, 14 anti-tank rifles and 11 82mm mortars. En route: 17 SU-76 and 5 76mm guns. Supplies: 0.8 of a standard combat load of ammunition, and 0.7 of a refill with diesel fuel.

The 11th Guards Tank Brigade: no operational tanks available, and 4 76mm guns.

87th Separate Motorcycle Battalion: 4 Mark IX tanks operational. 86th Guards Mortar Regiment: 10 M-13 rocket launchers serviceable, 4 rocket launchers en route. Ammunition for 10 of the rocket launchers: 3 salvoes.

[Signed] Chief of 2nd Tank Army's Operations Department– Colonel Bazanov

A 2nd Tank Army command staff offered an analysis of the enemy's combat operations in front of the 2nd Tank Army during the period of fighting between 25 and 31 March 1944:

Enemy actions: In the course of 25.3.1944 the enemy, with fire and counterattacks in strength of a company or battalion of infantry with the support of 4-15 tanks and groups of 3-9 bombers conducted stubborn defensive fighting to retain possession of Bălti. On the morning of 26.3.44, he blew up bridges across the Reut River in the Bălti area, set fire to the major buildings, destroyed supply stockpiles, and simultaneously withdrew the main forces south of Bălti. Up to a battalion of artillery and 3-4 mortar batteries were shelling the combat formations of our forces from the western and northwestern outskirts of Bălti. Up to two companies of infantry with heavy mortars and machine guns were covering the crossing over the bridge in the northern section of Bălti. In the afternoon, unable to hold Bălti, he fell back to the southern bank of the Reut River, offering resistance by fire from Hills 156.0 and 169.1. At the end of 26.3.44, offering no organized resistance by units of the Romanian 14th Infantry Division, covered by groups of 3-5 tanks with infantry support and retreating to the south, [the enemy] fought for possession of Fălești.

On 27.3.44, the enemy, committing the 1st, 2nd and 3rd Ersatz Battalions, formed from men returning from leave and convalescent soldiers and officers of various units, into the battle, strove to restrain our units' offensive. Enemy aircraft in groups of 9-15 bombers struck the combat formations of our units and were exercising control over the roads that lead to the south. In the morning, the enemy, putting up resistance by fire out of the areas of Catranic, Fălești and Albinetul, made a fighting withdrawal to the south, primarily sticking to the roads leading to Bușila and Sculeni.

By the end of 27.3.44, the enemy had been driven out of a number of settlements, was conducting holding actions on the line Vrănești, Stolniceni, Zăzuleni, Teșcureni, and was continuing to retreat in the direction of Sculeni, Petreşti and Buşila. On 28.3.44, the enemy with units of the Romanian 14th Infantry Division; the German 1st, 2nd and 3rd Ersatz Battalions composed of men returning from leave and convalescents of the 75th, 198th and 336th Infantry Divisions; the 404th Security Division; and the 4th *Gebirgs* Division, while offering resistance by fire, were continuing to retreat along the roads leading to Iaşi and Kishinev. In the vicinity of Sărata-Nouă and on the southeastern banks of the adjacent lake, the enemy with a counterattack in strength of up to a battalion of infantry with the support of artillery, mortars and up to 18 bombers strove to check our units' advance on this line. With the swift attack of our units, the resistance was broken. As a result of this action, the enemy was thrown back to the Buşila area. That afternoon, the enemy, having brought up fresh units of the 79th Infantry Division, with a counterattack out of the Ecatarinovca area along the road leading from Ungheni to Pirliţa in the strength of up to a regiment with the support of two tanks, artillery fire and up to 12 bombers shoved our units back to the north and northwest and seized Hill 168.1 (in the Buşila area). At the end of 28.3.44, he was conducting holding actions along the line south of Petreşti, Todireşti, east of Grăseni, Hill 168.1, Blagodati, Negureni Nouă, Teşcureni.

In the course of 29.3 – 30.3.44, the enemy was driven out of Todireşti, Bogdasarovca and Negureni Nouă, but was putting up strong resistance by fire out of the areas of Pirliţa Sat and Pirliţa Tyrg. [Our] neighbor on the right, having forced a crossing of the Prut River and the Jijia River, was fighting on the line: Moineşti, Lăzăreni, Zagarancea and further to the north along Vladnic River.

On 31.3.44, the enemy with fire and counterattacks in strength of up to a battalion of infantry with the support of 4 tanks and more than 25 bombers out of the Blagodati area to the north was offering resistance to our units' offensive. At 13.00 the enemy was driven out of Pirliţa Sat; simultaneously, with small groups of submachine gunners he was putting up resistance by fire 2 kilometers southeast of Buşila and in the area of Blagodati. The activity of all the regiments of the 79th Infantry Division and of the 1st, 2nd and 3rd Ersatz Battalions on their previous directions is confirmed by the capture of prisoners in the Blagodati, Ecatarinovca and Pirliţa areas.

## The 2nd Tank Army, April – May 1944

Motorized infantry of the 2nd Tank Army rest before the offensive, April 1944.

Tanks of the 11th Guards
Tank Brigade on the
march, April 1944.

The commander
of the 2nd Tank
Army Lieutenant
General Semen
Bogdanov, on the
right, bestows
an Order to the
11th Guards Tank
Brigade. On his
right is brigade
commander
Guards Colonel
Boris Eremeev.

Major General
Latyshev at the
11th Guards
Tank Brigade's
award ceremony.
On the right
is brigade
commander
Guards Colonel
Boris Eremeev.

Army commander S.I. Bogdanov taking a look at something off-camera.

Lieutenant Spesivyi's tank crew, which distinguished itself in the fighting in Moldavia and Romania, 1944.

Boris Eremeev, commander of the 11th Guards Tank Brigade.

Captain Petr Zlenko, battalion commander with the 11th Guards Tank Brigade.

Soviet tankers examine their "work".

The 2nd Tank Army's intelligence chief Colonel Galimov, second from right, and on his right, his deputy Lieutenant Colonel Kostromin, 1944.

Tankers of the 50th Tank Brigade of the 2nd Tank Army's 3rd Tank Corps examining a German howitzer that they've knocked out.

Army commander General Bogdanov and Military Council member General Latyshev converse with the commander of the 5th Guards Tank Army General Rotmistrov and staff officers.

A Cyrillic caption read, "May 1944. Romania. An elderly Romanian presents his last remaining sheep to the soldier-liberators of the brigade, who were the first to fight their way into the village."

Tankers of the 11th Guards Tank Brigade. On the right is Guards Lieutenant Vladimir Tolstikov.

Tankers of the 11th Guards Tank Brigade, April 1944; on the left is Guards Lieutenant Vladimir Tolstikov.

On 31 March 1944, the 2nd Tank Army commander General Bogdanov ordered the commanders of the 3rd and 16th Tank Corps and the commander of the 11th Guards Tank Brigade (with a copy to the chief of staff and the artillery commander):

Take the following measures:
1. Replenish the Motorized Rifle Brigades and Motorized Rifle Battalions with personnel by 4.4.44.
2. Bring up the motorcycles of the reconnaissance battalions. Bring up the tank brigades and especially the driver-mechanics of the T-34 tanks for the new tanks by 2.4.44.
3. Replenish the Motorized Rifle Brigades and Motorized Rifle Battalions with light and heavy machine guns, mortars and anti-tank rifles. Find out where all the light and heavy machine guns, anti-tank rifles and 82mm mortars have gone.
4. Take account of the availability and condition of: a) radio sets in the Motorized Rifle Battalions and Motorized Rifle Brigades; b) cable line, which must be replenished; c) fully reassemble the signals battalions; d) replenish mobile means through the use of trucks.
5. Always have available signal flare pistols and flares of various colors in the companies, battalions, brigades and corps.
6. Replenish the headquarters of the brigades and corps with staff officers by 3.4.44.
7. Halt the practice of carrying or having spare fuel drums on tanks and motor vehicles, as a consequence of which they ignite first, and from it the vehicle and tank burns.
8. Bring to justice the guilty parties whose vehicle or tank burns out from aerial attack.
9. Collect the sheepskin jackets from the men and replace them with uniform jackets from 5.4.44.
10. Bring up and assemble the combat units and rear echelons more energetically, more quickly and in a more organized manner.

[Signed] Commander of the 2nd Tank Army Hero of the Soviet Union Guards Lieutenant General of Tank Forces S. Bogdanov

As the order above notes, the 2nd Tank Army's formations received replacement T-34s at the end of March. The chief of the 2nd Tank Army's Operations Department Colonel Bazanov reported on the receipt and condition of the new tanks:

**Information on the Location of the Newly Received Tanks**

1. a) At 20.00 on 28 March 1944, 20 T-34 tanks were dispatched from Vapniarka for the 3rd Tank Corps. Seven of these tanks have broken down on the way between Komargorod and Bălti. Thirteen tanks were handed over to the corps on 30 March. At 2.00 on 30 March 1944, 20 T-34 tanks were dispatched from Komargorod for the 11th Guards Tank Brigade. The chief of staff Rodionov reports 19 tanks had passed through the village of Klembovka at 8.00. At 12.00, 16 T-34 tanks passed through Soroca. Ten T-34 tanks were dispatched from Komargorod at 16.30 on 30 March 1944 for the 51st Tank Brigade. The chief of staff Lieutenant Colonel Piskunov reports that 7 tanks passed through Soroca at 23.00. Nineteen tanks were dispatched at 20.00 on 30 March 1944. Engineer-Major D'iakov reports that 19 tanks passed through Tomaşpol' at 21.00. In total, 69 tanks have been dispatched. b) Broken down on the way as far as Vapniarka inclusively: 1) Zvenigorodka – 4 tanks that require repair of the transmission; 2) Sokolovochka – 1 tank that requires repair of the transmission; 3) Boloshka – 1 tank, bogged down in a swamp; 4) Svinarka – 1 tank that requires repair of the fuel pump; 5) Ust'e – 1 tank that requires repair of the fuel pump; 6) Bershad' – 1 tank that requires repair of the throttle and replacement of lock pins; 7) Vapniarka – 2 tanks that require repair of the transmission. A total of 11 tanks have lagged behind.

2. Four T-34 tanks on 30 March 1944 at 16.00 were filled with fuel and sent from Komargorod. Two of the tanks belong to the 11th Guards Tank Brigade, 1 tank to the 3rd Tank Corps, and 1 tank to the 9th Separate Signals Regiment. Two I.S. tanks were refueled and were to leave Vapniarka on 31.3.44; three SU-85 remain without fuel in Vapniarka.

3. Ten I.S. tanks of the 8th Guards Heavy Tank Regiment are located in the Ternovka – Dzhulinki sector without fuel. These tanks are able to move forward.

4. Tanks, located en route to the army and requiring repair: Budy Station – T-34 tank No.312452 of the 103rd Tank Brigade requires the repair of gears and an engine replacement. T-34 tank No.4154 of the 107th Tank Brigade requires the repair of gears. T-34 tank No.312575 of the 11th Guards Tank Brigade requires the repair of the steering clutch. Trostianets – T-34 tank No.4010027 of the 16th Tank Corps – problems with the engine and a leak in the radiator. Vapniarka – a Mark IX tank of the 87th Separate Motorcycle Battalion. Problems: Engine defects and a rupture in the circuitry. The tank has no security. Total requiring repair – 5 tanks.

5. 40 T-34 tanks have been unloaded at Khristinovka Station. Lieutenant Colonel Zemlianukhin received and is leading the column. Engineer-major Kudriavtsev has flown off to there.

[Signed] Chief of the 2nd Tank Army's Operations Department – Colonel Bazanov

## b) The fighting for Pirliţa-Sat and Pirliţa-Tyrg

Carrying out its assigned task, the 2nd Tank Army continued to pursue the enemy: the 3rd Tank Corps – along the Răuţel – Făleşti – Pirliţa axis; the 16th Tank Corps – on the Pirliţa – Vladimirovca axis. The 11th Guards Tank Brigade was in the army's reserve, following behind the 16th Tank Corps in readiness to repel counterattacks from the west or east.

At 14.00 on 27 March 1944, units of the 16th Tank Corps seized Fălești, and by 21.00 reached the village of Șoltoaia. The 15th Motorized Rifle Brigade reached the hilly area north of Bușila. The *Luftwaffe*, covering the retreat of the ground forces, repeatedly bombed the highway leading from Soroca to Bălti and the adjacent areas in the course of the day. With a counterattack in strength of up to an infantry regiment with the support of 8-10 tanks, the enemy drove back our units in the Bușila area, but by dawn on 29 March, the lost ground had been regained.

The 16th Tank Corps received a supplementary order: Covering the sector stretching from the northern slopes of Hill 168.1 to the nameless hills 2 kilometers northeast of Bușila with the motorized rifle battalions of the 107th and 109th Tank Brigades, in order to prevent an enemy penetration into the Bușila area, it was to attack with the forces of the 15th Motorized Rifle Brigade and the 164th Tank Brigade's motorized rifle battalion along the Hill 143, Todirești, southern outskirts of Pirlița Sat direction in conjunction with the 3rd Tank Corps, 5th Mechanized Corps and 31st Rifle Division, and together with the 3rd Tank Corps it was to encircle and destroy the enemy grouping in the Blagodati, Bogdasarovca, Ecatarinovca area. With the seizure of Pirlița Sat, it was then to attack with its main forces toward Rădenii-Vechi and Temeleuti.

Advancing out of the jumping-off positions, the 107th Tank Brigade consisting of 3 tanks (2 T-34 and 1 Mark III), bypassing Pirlița Tyrg on its western side, circumvented enemy units with a swift advance and reached the southern outskirts of Pirlița Sat, where it took up a defense. The 164th Tank Brigade with 2 T-34 and 2 SU-76, following behind the 107th Tank Brigade, at 13.45 took the eastern outskirts of Pirlița Sat. The 109th Tank Brigade, having reached a valley 1 kilometer north of Bogdasarovca, was stopped because of heavy artillery and machine-gun fire from Hill 168.1. By 22.00, it had dug in among the buildings of Ecatarinovca with the forces of its motorized rifle battalion. The 15th Motorized Rifle Brigade, having seized Todirești, at 17.00 broke into the western outskirts of Pirlița Sat, and by 19.00 it had mopped up the village of the enemy. Thus, units of the 2nd Tank Army had cut the Kishinev – Iași railroad, and with the arrival on the Todirești, Ecatarinovca, Bogdasarovca, Teșcureni line, they had created a serious threat of the encirclement to the enemy's Kishinev grouping.

By 12.00 on 1 April 1944, the 107th Tank Brigade had received 12 T-34 replacement tanks and was occupying a defense on the southeastern outskirts of Bușila. At 14.45, carrying out its previously assigned task, the tanks advanced to the northern outskirts of Pirlița Sat, where they ran into heavy anti-tank fire from the railroad station in Pirlița Tyrg. Having lost one burned-out tank in this area, the tanks fell back to the Ecatarinovca area and took up a defense. With its motorized rifle battalion, the 109th Tank Brigade in the course of the day was fighting 1.5 kilometers south of Ecatarinovca. The 164th Tank Brigade, fighting to retain possession of Pirlița Sat, drove back three enemy counterattacks and continued to hold its positions. With the aim of liquidating the looming threat of encirclement and securing the retreat behind the Prut River, the enemy shifted units from the Kishinev area and reinforced the sector opposite the 2nd Tank Army with units of the 79th Infantry Division, the *Grossdeutschland* Panzer Grenadier Division, the 24th Panzer Division and a *kampfgruppe* of the 13th Panzer Division. Enemy resistance stiffened.

According to a report on the amount of combat-ready tanks and artillery in the 2nd Tank Army and the status of supplies at 24.00 on 1.4.1944:

3rd Tank Corps: 26 T-34, 2 KV, 7 SU-76, 7 M-13 rocket launchers, 7 85mm guns, 6 76mm guns, 8 37mm guns, 8 120mm mortars. The tanks, SU-76, and 76mm and 85mm guns – 1 combat load of ammunition; the M-13 rocket launchers – 1 salvo of rockets; the 120mm mortars – 0.4 of a combat load of ammunition. Fuel and lubricants: 1 refill.

16th Tank Corps: 21 T-34, 1 SU-76, 1 SU-85, 11 120mm mortars, 5 85mm guns, 2 M-13 rocket launchers, 10 76mm guns, 11 82mm mortars. Supplies: Ammunition – 1 combat load; fuel and lubricants – diesel fuel, 1 refill and Type 2 high-octane fuel – 0.5 of a refill. 11th Guards Tank Brigade: no combat-ready tanks, 3 76mm guns. 87th Separate Motorcycle Battalion – 4 Mark IX tanks. 86th Guards Mortar Regiment: 10 M-13 rocket launchers and 3 salvoes of rockets

[Signed] Chief of the 2nd Tank Army's Operations Department – Colonel Bazanov

The enemy, having brought up units of the *Grossdeutschland* Panzer Grenadier Division to Pirliţa Sat, went on the counterattack against the 16th Tank Corps at 8.00 on 1 April. The counterattack particularly fell upon the battalions of the 15th Motorized Rifle Brigade. The brigade went over to an all-round defense. At 9.00, 7 enemy Panther tanks were on the approaches to the southwestern outskirts of Pirliţa Sat. Simultaneously, the Germans committed up to a company of infantry mounted in halftracks into the attack, but the attack was driven back. At 10.00, the enemy renewed the assault. For the next two hours, units of the 16th Tank Corps exchanged fire with the enemy, repelling the attacks of infantry and tanks. The Germans continued to augment their forces and at 12.00 launched an attack with up to 15 tanks and up to 25 halftracks loaded with panzer grenadiers toward the southwestern outskirts of Pirliţa Sat. Another grouping of panzer grenadiers attacked in the direction of Hill 170.1 and some isolated huts wet of Pirliţa Sat with the support of 10 tanks, seeking to envelop the village from the west. Simultaneously, with 5 tanks and panzer grenadiers, the enemy attacked the southwestern outskirts of Pirliţa Sat, and attacked the eastern outskirts of the village with a battalion of infantry. At 13.00 on 1 April 1944, 10 enemy tanks, attacking over Hill 170.1, reached the isolated huts west of Pirliţa Sat and broke into the combat positions of the 3rd Motorized Rifle Battalion, which was putting up stubborn resistance to the enemy. Lacking adequate anti-tank weapons, the 3rd Motorized Rifle Battalion suffered heavy losses and was pushed back to the northwest. The enemy, continuing to advance, struck the southwestern outskirts of Pirliţa Sat with panzer grenadiers, thereby threatening the rear of the 15th Motorized Rifle Brigade. At this time the 1st and 2nd Motorized Rifle Battalions were still offering tough resistance to the enemy and were tied up in savage street fighting.

At 13.30 the commander of 2/248th Rifle Regiment received an order over the radio to withdraw the battalion in small groups from its occupied line and to fall back to Todireşti. The 1st Motorized Rifle Battalion, which was almost completely encircled, yet was continuing to struggle in stubborn street fighting without any anti-tank weapons, wound up in a very difficult situation. Suffering large losses, at 15.00 it fell back to the northwestern outskirts of Pirliţa Sat. The 2nd Motorized Rifle Battalion, continuing to struggle with the enemy, held its defensive positions on the northern outskirts of Pirliţa Sat until 19.30. Thus, the 15th Motorized Rifle Brigade was ultimately unable to hold its occupied sector of defense and fell back to Todireşti, where it took up a defense. The armor of the 164th Tank Brigade, consisting of 2 T-34 and 1 SU-76, covered the withdrawal of the 15th Motorized Rifle Brigade, and after the brigade evacuated Pirliţa Sat, they fell back to the eastern outskirts of Todireşti.

Thus, by the end of 1 April 1944, with fire and counterattacks by tanks and infantry with the support of bomber aircraft, the enemy managed to retake Pirliţa Sat, Vladimirovca and Blagodati. On 2 and 3 April 1944, the Germans continued to hold their occupied line, having reinforced it in the Pirliţa Sat area with the commitment of *Grossdeutschland*'s 1st Panzer Grenadier Regiment. In the course of the day 2 April, the enemy dug entrenchments north and northwest of Pirliţa Tyrg and Pirliţa Sat. At 13.00, the enemy assembled up to a battalion of infantry and tanks in the Ecatarinovca area, having as its aim to force back units of the 16th Tank Corps and to attack to the south along the riverbank, with the task to encircle and destroy our units.

"Fuel for tanks".

At 14.30, observers spotted a column of up to 300 men and supply wagons moving along the turnpike out of Pirliţa Tyrg in the area of Hill 135.2. Three tanks mounted with motorized riflemen of the 107th Tank Brigade were sent forward to destroy the enemy column. With a surprise attack against the column of enemy infantry, by fire and with tracks the enemy column was overrun and scattered. In this action, up to 200 enemy soldiers and officers were killed and up to 100 carts loaded with various military supplies were destroyed. The motorized rifle battalion of the 109th Tank Brigade, in defensive positions 1.5 kilometers south of Ecatarinovca, continued to fight off enemy counterattacks. The 164th Tank Brigade was occupying a defense on the nameless hills 1 kilometer northwest of Pirliţa Sat. The 15th Motorized Rifle Brigade, after the battering it had taken the previous day, was bringing itself back into order and improving its defensive positions.

However, a verbal order came from the commander of the 2nd Tank Army for the units of the 16th Tank Corps to launch a new attack toward Pirliţa Sat. The terrain in the area of the combat operations was hilly, and cut with numerous balkas and ravines. By this time, the weather conditions weren't favorable for offensive actions, because of a snowstorm, which dropped viewing ranges to no more than 20-30 meters. At the same time, the deep snowfall, which gathered in the ravines and balkas, made the route difficult for tanks, and in some places it was completely impassable, while the infantry slogged slowly through the deep, powdery snow.

At 17.00, units of the 16th Tank Corps, carrying out Bogdanov's order, became tied up in fighting in the northern outskirts of Pirliţa Sat. The surprise attack in such weather stunned the Germans, and they retreated out of Pirliţa Sat to the south, southeast and northeast. By 19.00, Pirliţa Sat had been fully mopped up of the enemy, whereupon the units of the 16th Tank Corps went over to an all-round defense.

In the course of 4 April 1944, the enemy launched four counterattacks toward Pirliţa Sat; all the counterattacks were beaten back with heavy losses for the Germans. On the morning of 5 April, the enemy conducted a regrouping of his forces east of Pirliţa Sat, assembling his main forces in Pirliţa Tyrg and behind Hill 170.1. At 11.00 the enemy launched a strong counterattack with 6 Tiger tanks and 5 halftracks carrying panzer grenadiers. Up to ten halftracks were supporting the enemy attack with fire from fixed positions on the western outskirts of Pirliţa Tyrg. At the same time, up to a battalion of infantry attacked from the south with the support of 4 Tigers, from the direction of Niculeni Nouă, and a battalion of infantry attacked from the west, from Hill 137.6.

The enemy, having superiority in numbers of men and tanks, by 18.00 had encircled elements of the 16th Tank Corps in Pirliţa Sat. The corps' units, struggling against superior enemy forces, began to fall back to new lines of defense: the 107th Tank Brigade took up a defense in the Todireşti area, 1.5 kilometers northwest of Pirliţa Sat; the 164th Tank Brigade and a portion of the 107th Tank Brigade's tanks, fighting in semi-encirclement against superior forces of the enemy, began to withdraw to the western outskirts of Pirliţa Sat. Nine T-34 tanks and up to 50 motorized riflemen, cut off from the main forces, continued the unequal fight until 20.00 on 5 April 1944. As a result of the see-saw struggle for Pirliţa Sat, the 16th Tank Corps lost 160 men killed and wounded, and 9 T-34 tanks totally destroyed.

The tanks, which had been covering the withdrawal of the infantry, had fought all day against a superior number of heavy enemy tanks, and were all brewed up. The commander of the tank battalion Senior Lieutenant Aleksei Usachev, who personally destroyed two Tiger tanks and fought until his last shell and bullet, particularly distinguished himself. When attempting to come out of encirclement, his tank was set aflame and Senior Lieutenant Usachev was wounded.

In this same unequal combat, Captain Fedor Donkov, the T-34 tank company commander with the 107th Tank Brigade who had performed so heroically in the Uman' operation, was killed in action. On the day before, his tank company, without losing a single machine and without combat, in a fierce snowstorm that reduced visibility to near zero, had taken the railroad station in Pirliţa Sat, and thereby cut the rail line and terminated all communications along it. The enemy, fleeing in panic, left behind two Tiger tanks, two Panther tanks and four Pz. IV tanks at the station. This daring raid, given the extremely poor visibility, shocked the enemy so much that for the next several days, Germans continued to show up at the station, thinking that it was still in their possession.

Possession of Pirliţa Sat was of critical importance. Our reserves still hadn't come up, while the enemy, having brought up major forces, decided to take the railroad station back at whatever the cost. Captain Donkov was ordered to hold out until the end, but was informed he couldn't count upon help. Having encircled the station with a tight ring of forces, the enemy settled into a siege. For 48 hours, in full encirclement, getting no sleep and sparing the ammunition in the tanks, Captain Donkov's tank company continued to hold the station with combat. When the ammunition and fuel in the tanks ran out, the remnants of the company together with Captain Donkov attempted to break-out, and all were killed while resisting to their final cartridge. That's how the brave tankers, covering themselves with undying glory, died as heroes. Their commander, Hero of the Soviet Union Captain Fedor Donkov, heroically fell in battle together with them.

On the German side, units of the 1st and 2nd Panzer Grenadier Battalions of the *Grossdeutschland* Division took part in this combat, together with a battalion of assault guns reinforced with Tigers from this same panzer division. Hans-Joachim Jung, a former panzer commander in *Panzerregiment "Grossdeutschland"*, writes, "On or about 5 April I moved five tanks of the II./*Panzerregiment "Grossdeutschland"* from the composite tank maintenance facility at Kishinev to Parliti-Sat [Pirliţa Sat], in part by rail." The official history of the *Panzerkorps Grossdeutschland*, written by Helmuth Spaeter, provides details of the German counterattack at Pirliţa Sat:

08.30   Weather: overcast, with good visibility. Beginning of the attack on Parliti Sat [Pirliţa Sat]. The 2nd and 3rd Companies of I Battalion and six assault guns are under the command of Battle Group von Heynitz (CO II Btl.). Swinging north, the 2nd and 3rd (APC) Companies with Leutnant Bader's company in the center, attack the town from the northwest. Meanwhile, two Tigers screen to the north and west toward Tochiresti [Todireşti]. At the same time, the Wechmann Company climbs onto two more Tigers and with these prepares to attack Hill 170.2, about 2 km. southwest of Parliti Sat.

However, in the midst of preparations one Tiger, with a squad and the company H.Q. squad, breaks down; the other two squads and the sole remaining Tiger reach, occupy and hold the hill.

Battle Group von Heynitz (II Btl.) is initially pinned down in front of the town of Parliti Sat by heavy enemy fire.

Hauptmann von Heynitz is killed, battalion adjutant Leutnant Geist is wounded.

Fahnenjunker-Oberfeldwebel Kalinowski dies a hero's death leading 3rd (SPC) Company; Unteroffizier Piepenberg (6th Company) and 4 men are also killed. An assault gun – Reserve Leutnant Josef Hensinger – is hit by an anti-tank gun and blows apart.

09.30   The left company succeeds in breaking into Parliti Sat; the Russians retreat to the west. The town is cleared of the enemy; only in the southern part is a group of Soviet soldiers able to hold out.

12.00   Hauptmann Meyer takes command of II. Battalion. The unit occupies positions from the northwest end of Parliti Sat to and including Point 170.2.

16.00   The remaining enemy group in the southern part of Parliti Sat is destroyed; about 200 Soviets flee along the highway to the south and are wiped out by heavy weapons.

…

Oberleutnant Sturm, commander of the Assault Gun Battalion GD's 3rd Battery, also distinguished himself in this attack. His leadership resulted in the destruction of numerous enemy tanks and, what was more important, the entry into the heavily-occupied town of Parliti Sat. He was recommended for the Knight's Cross of the Iron Cross, which he received a short time later.

The following facts testify to the intensity of the fighting for the Germans. Over five days of combat from 1 to 5 April 1944, *Grossdeutschland*'s 2nd Panzer Grenadier Battalion lost two commanders – Major Betke, who was severely wounded and replaced by Hauptmann von Heynitz, who was himself subsequently killed in Pirliţa Sat on 5 April.

To summarize, given the complete absence of roads, units of the 16th Tank Corps arrived in the area of combat operations at the village of Buşila without their artillery, rear echelons or supply trains, which significantly hampered the course of combat actions. The lack of unified leadership over the units of the 31st Rifle Division and the 16th Tank Corps that were operating in the area of Pirliţa Sat made it possible for the enemy to strike our units piece by piece and to drive our forces out of Pirliţa Sat. The absence of cooperation with the formations operating on the right and left in the Pirliţa Sat area led to the fact that 9 tanks and up to 160 men, being cut off from the main forces, were lost in an unequal struggle.

The assistant chief of staff for personnel of the 107th Tank Brigade reported on the losses in the following hand-written note to the chief of the People's Commissariat of Defense's 5th Department of the Main Command of Cadres:

In reference to your request No. USU/514771 from 5.6.44, I'm reporting that the below named officers of the 107th "Vapniarka" Red Banner Tank Brigade, who wound up encircled at Pirliţa Sat Station in Moldavia's Bălti District on 9.4.44 [sic – according to other operational documents of the 2nd Tank Army and reports of the *Grossdeutschland* Panzer Grenadier Division, this action took place on 5.4.44], must be considered missing-in-action, because their materiél (tanks) were left burned out by German projectiles; the fate of the officers listed below remains unknown:

1. Junior Lieutenant Nikita Zuev
2. Junior Lieutenant Ivan Krupenko
3. Junior Lieutenant Andrei Zanin
4. Junior Lieutenant I.S. Pozniakov
5. Junior Lieutenant Vasilii Chapov
6. Junior Lieutenant Grigorii Kastornyi
7. Junior Lieutenant Aleksei Liamin
8. Lieutenant Vitalii Shapiro
9. Captain Fedor Donkov
10. Junior Technician-Lieutenant Sultan Birmonov

We cannot relay Pozniakov's first name and patronymic and Birmonov's patronymic, because the latter had just arrived with a batch of replacements. From the march, they went straight into battle at night time, which the situation demanded.

[signed] Assistant chief of staff for personnel of the 107th "Vapniarka" Red Banner Tank Brigade, Senior Lieutenant Tkachenko

The "Report on combat operations of the enemy in front of the 2nd Tank Army over the period of fighting between 1.4 and 10.4.1944" states:

The enemy, by transferring units from the Kishinev area, reinforced the Ungheni, Tyrg Cornești sector … and thereby created a blocking force that secured the withdrawal of the Kishinev – Odessa grouping out of the looming threat of encirclement. With the seizure of a large number of prisoners and documents on 1.4.44, the following enemy grouping has been identified: in the sector Zagarancea – Niculeni Nouă, a combat group of the 13th Panzer Division (1 battalion); Niculeni Nouă – Tat'ianovca, 21st Panzer Grenadier Regiment of the 24th Panzer Division; Tat'ianovca – Pirlița Tyrg, 226th Infantry Regiment of the 79th Infantry Division and a panzer grenadier regiment of the *Grossdeutschland* Panzer Grenadier Division; Pirlița Tyrg – Agronomovca, 212th Infantry Regiment of the 79th Infantry Division and the 26th Panzer Grenadier Regiment of the 24th Panzer Division; Agronomovca – Hill 168.3, 208th Infantry Regiment of the 79th Infantry Division and the 1st and 3rd Ersatz Battalions; a security battalion and elements of the 6th Cavalry Regiment of the Romanian 5th Cavalry Division are defending in the area of Romanești and Cornești Tyrg. Altogether in the sector Pirlița Sat – Negureni Nouă (a front of 12 kilometers), 10 battalions of infantry, which amounts to up to 3,400 active bayonets (283 men per kilometer of front); 5 battalions of artillery (87 guns of various calibers, 7.2 guns per kilometer of front); and up to 35 tanks and self-propelled guns and operating in the front line.

Enemy actions: On 1.4.44 the enemy, introducing units of the 24th Panzer Division in the first half of the day, put up stubborn resistance with fire to the actions of our forces. In the afternoon, with fire and counterattacks in strength of a company or battalion of infantry with the support of 5-15 tanks and with groups of more than 30 bombers, he shoved back our units and again took Pirlița Sat, Vladimirovca and Blagodati, and by the end of the day was fighting on the line: Mânzătești, Vechi, along the Vladnin stream, Pirlița Sat, Blagodati, Hill 168.3, Romanești, Cornești Tyrg.

In the course of 2.4 and 3.4.44, showing no activity, the enemy reinforced the combat positions of his units in the Pirliţa Sat area with the introduction of a panzer grenadier regiment of the *Grossdeutschland* Panzer Grenadier Division, which had transferred from the Kishinev axis, and continued to hold the occupied line. In the afternoon [of 3.4.44], putting up stubborn resistance, he was again driven out of Pirliţa Sat. On 4.4.44 the enemy was again driven out of Negureni Nouă and forced off of Hill 168.3 (south of Teşcureni) by the actions of our troops. From 4.00 to 14.00 the enemy in strength of up to a battalion of infantry with 2-4 tanks unsuccessfully counterattacked out of Pirliţa Tyrg toward Pirliţa Sat four times.

On 5.4.44, the enemy with fire and multiple counterattacks in strength of a company or battalion of infantry with the support of 5-10 tanks and self-propelled guns offered stubborn resistance to our units' offensive. As a result of the fighting, the enemy was driven out of Blagodati, Agronomovca and Katyrlia. At 11.00 the enemy counterattacked toward Pirliţa Sat with 10 tanks and up to a battalion of infantry out of the area of Pirliţa Tyrg, and with 4 tanks and 15 armored halftracks out of the area of Tat'ianovca. At 14.00, a company of infantry and 10 tanks counterattacked out of the Vladimirovca area toward Agronomovca. Both counterattacks were repulsed; the enemy suffered heavy losses.

Through observation and combat it has been established that the enemy has up to 25 tanks in combat formation on the southwestern outskirts of Pirliţa Tyrg. The movement of up to a regiment of infantry and 6 tanks from the south toward Vladimirovca has been spotted. Up to three companies of infantry were seen moving from the northeast toward Simonovca. A large aggregation of infantry has been spotted at Pereval Station. The enemy is shifting infantry in armored halftracks and trucks from Bumbăta Station in the direction of Simonovca.

On 6.4.44, showing no activity, the enemy increased the transfer of infantry and equipment out of the Corneşti Tyrg area to the Hristoforovca area. Over the entire day, up to two regiments of infantry, 9 tanks, and 19 guns and up to 20 armored halftracks were shifted. On the left flank, the enemy conducted combat by fire to maintain possession of Pirliţa Tyrg. At 10.00, with a counterattack of up to a company of infantry and two tanks, he pushed back our units and took Agronomovca.

From the morning of 7.4.44 the enemy, with units of the *Grossdeutschland* Panzer Grenadier Division, the 79th Infantry Division, the 1st and 3rd Ersatz Battalions and a portion of the 24th Panzer Division put up heavy fire to resist the advance of our units, and repeatedly launched counterattacks in strength of 1-2 battalions with the support of 8-10 tanks. He continued to reinforce his positions in the Pirliţa Sat area and introduced a forward detachment of the 23rd Panzer Division in the sector Niculeni Nouă, Nov, Bereşti, while simultaneously continuing to withdraw the rear echelons of the Kishinev grouping back behind the Prut River. In the course of the night, the enemy was bringing up infantry, artillery and tanks to the Agronomovca, Hhristoforovca area. Altogether, up to two regiments of infantry, 16 tanks, 17 guns of various calibers and up to 20 armored halftracks were redeployed. In the course of the day, through combat and reconnaissance in the Pirliţa Tyrg, Romaneşti sector, the activity of 6 infantry battalions, approximately 40 tanks, 6 self-propelled guns and 32 guns of various calibers has been established. According to information from the neighbor on the right, reconnaissance spotted the movement of up to 1,000 trucks and cars, 15 tanks and a large quantity of supply trains and evacuated population out of Pirtliţa Tyrg and Ungheni Tyrg. Apparently the enemy was shifting his units out of the Kishinev area by railroad to Corneşti Station and Bumbăta, and then withdrawing them on foot back behind the Prut River.

On 8.4.44, the enemy displayed no activity on the entire sector of the front and was holding his occupied line, throwing up defensive fieldworks, and reinforced the combat positions on this sector with a dozen tanks.

Conclusion: After the destruction of the Uman' grouping, the enemy command, having lost control over their troops, was unable to construct a reliable defense against our forces. As a result of the rapid advance of our forces, the enemy's main lines of communication were cut, which deprived him of the possibility of making timely maneuvers with his forces and of bringing up reserves to the front. As a consequence of such disorganization of the enemy's forces, the [German] command was unable to use the Dnestr River as a defensive obstacle. Having no reserves of German units, the enemy threw Romanian divisions and separate security battalions into the fighting, the chaotic retreat of which only increased the disorganization in the enemy's forces. Covering with the introduction of Romanian units into the fighting, the enemy brought his battered units into order, shifted some of his forces from the Kishinev axis to the Ungheni Tyrg, Corneşti Tyrg sector, and thereby created a blocking force in this sector, which secured the withdrawal of the Kishinev – Odessa grouping back behind the Prut River.

Overnight between 6 and 7 April 1944, 19 T-34 tanks arrived in the 2nd Tank Army's area of combat operations as replacements. After this, having assembled in the Negurenii Vechi, Teşcureni, Blagodati area, the units of the 2nd Tank Army, in cooperation with the 256th Rifle Division, on 7 April 1944 launched an attack in the direction of Corneşti Tyrg, and after stubborn fighting reached the line Hristoforovca, Mirceşti.

On 7 April 1944, the 2nd Tank Army had a total of 49 armored vehicles on its active list: 41 T-34, 4 Valentine Mark IX, and 4 SU-76. Over the period of offensive fighting between 1 and 8 April 1944, the 2nd Tank Army had lost 30 tanks destroyed and 21 knocked-out; personnel losses amounted to 651 killed, 1,713 wounded and 102 missing-in-action.

The 2nd Tank Army's chief of staff Guards Major General Radzievsky and the chief of operations Colonel Bazanov signed off on a report on the replacement T-34 tanks for the 2nd Tank Army as of 24.00 on 7 April 1944:

1.   Unloaded at Potash Station – 20 T-34 tanks; unloaded at Zvenigorodka Station – 60 T-34 tanks; unloaded at Khristinovka – 40 T-34 tanks. Total: 120 T-34 tanks.
2.   Of these, 89 T-34 tanks have arrived in the army's units, of which 7 require light overhauls and 4 need minor repairs. A total of 78 serviceable tanks have been received by the army's units.
3.   On the approach to Bălti – 7 T-34 tanks.
4.   A total of 24 T-34 tanks have been broken down along the route and require repair (50 percent have been picked up by repair teams).

[Signed] 2nd Tank Army chief of staff Guards Major General Radzievsky; 2nd Tank Army's chief of the operations department Colonel Bazanov

## c) Fighting in the area of Podu-Iloaie.

The troops of the 2nd Tank Army received a fresh assignment: having turned over their combat sector to formations of the 52nd Army, by 7.00 on 9 April 1944 they were to assemble fully in the Bolotina, Tomeştnov area. On the night between 9 and 10 April, having crossed the Prut River – they were to attack in the general direction of Focuri, Podu-Iloaie, Iaşi with the aim of seizing the latter. On 10.04.44, the 3rd Tank Corps had 11 serviceable T-34 and 8 T-34 still on the march; the 16th Tank Corps had 13 serviceable T-34, and 6 T-34 and 3 SU-76 on the approach.

On 11 April 1944, the commander of the 2nd Tank Army sent orders and questions to the deputy commander for rear services Colonel Antonov, with copies to his chief of staff General Radzievsky and Military Council member Colonel Matiushin, which show his concerns prior to resuming the offensive:

1. 12 metric tons of fuel have arrived on schedule, but no diesel fuel. As you don't understand, the tanks have traveled 120 kilometers, but there is no diesel fuel. It must arrive tomorrow, 12.4.44.
2. Send three good vehicles for the Operational Group, and do it quickly.
3. Give [us] weapons, and as soon as possible. Especially light and heavy machine guns, anti-tank rifles, submachine guns – send all to me.
4. You must move to Bolotina or closer to the bridge. Leave someone on your behalf in Bălti in order to receive fuel and ammunition.
5. Get foodstuffs delivered to Bolotina or to a different place, but closer to me, on a good road; just not to Borşa.
6. Urgently take measures regarding the uniforms, especially for the infantry. They are already drenched in sweat. Side caps. Forage caps. For officers – uniforms and underclothing.
7. Bring up all the fuel and ammunition closer; the expenditure of fuel will be less.
8. Where are the corps' refueling companies? I don't know. Take energetic and urgent measures. I've had enough of the goofing around. Write a strict order for the corps' rear echelons, as soon as possible. Once again I'm not seeing the brigades trucks. The maneuverability of the motorized rifle brigades must be enhanced; give them their vehicles. Take measures to have the trucks brought up to the motorized rifle brigades by 14.4.44.
9. Your battalions also haven't arrived. How can you tolerate this? What is Korostelev doing? Get him moving. The weather is good, the roads are improving. The vehicles are needed, and as many as possible. I'm bringing this to your attention, because soon they'll be prodding us to advance up to 200 kilometers a day.
10. Organize the repair of vehicles as quickly as possible. Establish control (provide me with a repair plan on 13.4.1944). Comrades Radzievsky and Matiushin are to establish daily control over the assemblage and preparation of the vehicles of the motorized rifle brigades and of the tank brigades' motorized rifle battalions. Establish control over the repair of vehicles. Hold a meeting of the assistant commanders of the corps and brigades for technical support regarding the repair of vehicles. Give Korostelev a rigid schedule and a strict order. Precisely establish the location of the vehicles of the motorized rifle brigades and their number in the 15th and 57th Motorized Rifle Brigades.
11. Make ready the repair of mobile means of communication and motorcycles. Where are the motorcycles? When will they arrive? Who is personally responsible for their delivery?
12. Comrade Radzievsky is to organize and check the light and heavy machine guns and anti-tank rifles in the motorized rifle brigades by 14.4.44.
13. Make a full and final accounting of the tanks. Write-off everything and get rid of hundreds of tanks [probably meaning those needing major overhauls, which had become a burden for the advancing units of the 2nd Tank Army].

On 12 April 1944, the 2nd Tank Army's forces arrived in the designated area, with the 3rd Tank Corps in Focuri and the 16th Tank Corps in Epureni, and at 17.00 they went on the offensive in conjunction with the 202nd Rifle Division in the direction of Podu-Iloaie. Tanks of the 16th Tank Corps, having crushed the resistance and scattered the enemy's infantry, by 20.00 reached a line 200 meters north of Podu-Iloaie Station. Individual tanks entered the outskirts of the station, but

At the command post of the 2nd Tank Army. Seated at the table on the right is the army commander, General Bogdanov.

were forced to retreat from it after running into heavy enemy tank and anti-tank artillery fire. The 16th Tank Corps' motorized rifle battalion and units of the 202nd Rifle Division, cut-off from their own tanks by the enemy tank fire and having no possibility to advance went over to the defense on a nameless hill, north of Hill 150. The tanks, exchanging fire with the enemy tanks, suffered large losses, fell back to the line achieved by the infantry and took up a defense on the southern slopes of the nameless hill north of Hill 150. The enemy attempted to counterattack our units with 8 tanks and 4 halftracks loaded with infantry, with the support of artillery, but was repulsed. In this battle, the 16th Tank Corps lost 7 tanks burned-out and 25 men killed or wounded, including the commander of the 109th Tank Brigade's 3rd Tank Battalion, Major Pavel Gaenko, who fell heroically in battle. The loss of tank officers in the 109th Tank Brigade in the spring offensive of 1944 was particularly heavy, as the following list included in a casualty report shows:

The Main Command of Cadres of the People's Commissariat of Defense

Herewith is the list of the irrevocable losses of officers over the period of the combat operations of the 109th "Vapniarka" Red Banner Tank Brigade from the month of March to 5 May 1944. Altogether, 134 men. Appendix: The list. [signed] Major Korsikov, chief of staff of the 109th Tank Brigade.

The List:

1. Morozov, Viktor Ivanovich, JuniorLieutenant, T-34 platoon commander of the 1st Tank Battalion, killed 5.3.44 (village of Shubennyi Stav, Kiev Oblast).
2. Frolov, Aleksandr Mikhailovich, Lieutenant, T-34 platoon commander of the 1st Tank Battalion, killed 5.3.44 (same place as above).

3.  Shevchenko, Dmitrii Emel'ianovich, Junior Lieutenant, tank commander, killed 7.4.44 in the village of Teşcureni (Bessarabia).
4.  Voronin, Leonid Ivanovich, Lieutenant, tank commander, killed 17.4.44 in the village of Boroşoaia.
5.  Gaenko, Pavel Andreevich, Major, commander of the 3rd Tank Battalion, killed on 12.4.44 near the town of Bălti (Moldavia).
6.  Levkin, Andrei Stepanovich, Lieutenant, commander of a machine-gun platoon in the motorized rifle battalion, killed 10.3.44, village of Voitovka (Kiev Oblast).
7.  Khvatkov, Nikolai Dmitrievich, Junior Lieutenant, commander of a machine-gun platoon in the motorized rifle battalion, killed 11.3.44, Ternovka (Kiev Oblast).
8.  Kulakov, Mikhail Iakovlevich, Junior Lieutenant, commander of an anti-tank rifle platoon, killed 6.3.44, village of Buki (Kiev Oblast).
9.  Aseev, Grigorii Alekseevich, Junior Lieutenant, platoon commander in the motorized rifle battalion, killed 7.4.44, Teşcureni (Bessarabia).
10. Golod, Iakov Maksimovich, Captain, deputy commander of the 2nd Tank Battalion, killed 7.4.44, Teşcureni (Bessarabia).
11. Zhukov, Aleksandr Nikolaevich, Lieutenant, tank commander, killed 2.5.44, village of Făcuti (Romania).
12. Chepurnoi, Nikolai Andreevich, Senior Lieutenant, deputy commander of the motorized rifle battalion, killed 2.5.44, village of Facuti (Romania).
13. Ternovoi, Petr Semenovich, Junior Lieutenant, tank commander, killed 7.4.44, Teşcureni (Bessarabia).
14. Syropiatov, Vasilii Aleksandrovich, Senior Lieutenant, company commander, killed 7.4.44, Teşcureni (Bessarabia).
15. Vol'demar, Boris Arnol'dovich, Junior Lieutenant, tank commander, killed 12.4.44, left in a burning tank in enemy territory.
16. Kolosovsky, Dmitrii Pavlovich, Junior Lieutenant, tank commander, killed 12.4.44, left in a burning tank behind enemy lines.
17. Miniiarov, Fuzar Min'iarovich, Junior Lieutenant, tank commander, killed 12.4.44, left in a burning tank behind enemy lines.
18. Lelenko, Iakov Efremovich, Senior Technical Assistant for technical support, lieutenant, commander of the 109th Tank Brigade's maintenance section, killed 13.4.44, city of Uman'.

The Soviet side claimed the destruction of all 8 tanks and the 4 halftracks; 2 mortar batteries with their crews; 5 machine-gun nests; and reported killing up to 250 enemy soldiers and officers. Over the entire day of 12 April 1944, the enemy lost 8 tanks knocked-out, and up to 500 soldiers and officers killed or wounded. The 2nd Tank Army's losses were 6 T-34 tanks burned-out and 6 knocked-out. After this unsuccessful attack, the 16th Tank Corps was withdrawn from combat and reassembled in the area of Băleni.

The lack of knowledge about the enemy strength and the incorrect estimate of it on the part of the headquarters of the 202nd Rifle Division led to the loss of 7 T-34 tanks, personnel, and the commander of one of the 16th Tank Corps' tank battalions. The lack of anti-aircraft artillery gave the enemy *Luftwaffe* the opportunity to act with impunity, right up to low-altitude strafing runs against the tanks and personnel. The absence of the artillery, both in the 202nd Rifle Division and the 16th Tank Corps, also affected the outcome of the battle.

Here it must be said that contemporary military historians often give distorted information about the fighting in Romania in the spring of 1944, knowingly exaggerating the forces and losses on the Soviet side. Their primary sources are the combat journals of the German 24th Panzer Division and the *Grossdeutschland* Panzer Grenadier Division, as well as lectures given to American

Romania, April-May, 1944.

Tanks of the 2nd Tank Army ford the Prut River – April 1944.

officers after the war by the General Manteuffel, the former commander of *Grossdeutschland*. For example, the American historian David Glantz writes:

> Operating jointly, Trofimenko's and Bogdanov's armies launched their first assault against the 24th Panzer Division's defenses north of Podu-Iloaie late on 12 April with a force of roughly 70 tanks from the 109th Tank and 15th Motorized Rifle Brigades of Dubovoi's 16th Tank Corps, supported by Bronsky's 93rd Guards and Mikhailov's 78th Rifle Divisions from

Goriachev's 35th Guards Rifle and Semenov's 33rd Rifle Corps. The attack struck the German defenses at Totoeşti, three miles due north of Podu-Iloaie, which were manned by four battalions from Edelsheim's 24th Panzer Division. Although the initial Soviet assault succeeded in breaking through the German forward defensive positions, by nightfall a *kampgruppe* of 15 tanks and 30 assault guns from the 24th Panzer Division, which had redeployed rapidly from the village of Domian [Damian] (midway between Podu-Iloaie and Lețcani), counterattacked and drove the Soviets back to their jumping-off positions.

In reality, according to the 2nd Tank Army's Combat Dispatches No.0223/OP and No.0224/OP on 11 April 1944, the 16th Tank Corps had serviceable only 13 T-34 tanks. Thus, Glantz's information about 70 tanks of the 16th Tank Corps and 80 tanks of the 3rd Tank Corps (which he mentioned a bit later) do not correspond to reality and exaggerates the number of tanks of the 2nd Tank Army that took part in these battles by a factor of several times. The historical truth is that the German side had a numerical superiority in tanks and aircraft in these battles. In the period between 9 and 13 April 1944, the enemy had regrouped the 24th Panzer Division and *Grossdeutschland* Panzer Grenadier Division from the Pirlița area to the Podu-Iloaie area with the aim of preventing the 2nd Tank Army's forces from outflanking the city of Iaşi from the northwest.

On the night of 9-10 April 1944, the 3rd Tank Corps crossed the Prut River in the Bederei area and emerged near Focuri. Other formations of the 2nd Tank Army crossed into the bridgehead on the western bank, seized from the foe by divisions of the 27th Army; they had the task to develop a swift offensive in the general direction of Iaşi. On 10.04.44, the 3rd Tank Corps' 50th Tank Brigade, having completed a 120-kilometer march and crossed the Prut River, arrived on Romanian territory and reassembled in the area of Cârniceni, with a subsequent advance to the area of Bârleşti. There the tank brigade became tied up in fighting with the enemy, which had counterattacked with a battalion of infantry and 7 tanks. The brigade, having lost two tanks, abandoned Bârleşti and took up a defense 1 kilometer north of Hill 180.0.

On 12 April 1944, the 51st Tank Brigade in conjunction with units of the 73rd Rifle Division went on the attack in the Bârleşti direction with the order by the end of the day to seize Podu-Iloaie Station, but without adequate support from artillery, and repelling counterattack after counterattack, the brigade was only able to reach Hill 180.0, which it fought to hold. At day's end, at an order from the 3rd Tank Corps' commander, the 51st Tank Brigade turned over all its remaining matériel to the 50th Tank Brigade and withdrew to the Focuri area, where on 13.4.44 6 operational tanks arrived from the rear straight out of repair shops.

On 13 April 1944, the 50th Tank and 51st Tank Brigades renewed the attack toward Bârleşti together with infantry of the 57th Motorized Rifle Brigade and 73rd Rifle Division and took the village, but the attackers were thrown back to their jumping-off positions by a powerful enemy counterattack at 11.00 in strength of up to 19 tanks and up to a regiment of infantry; the 50th Tank Brigade lost 4 tanks and 10 men killed or wounded in the process. In return, the 51st Tank Brigade as the result of the fighting on 13 April claimed the destruction of 5 enemy tanks and 4 machine guns, and the killing of up to 150 German soldiers and officers. In return, the 51st Tank Brigade's losses amounted to 5 tanks burned-out, 12 killed and 3 wounded. Over the day of 13 April, the enemy with fire and counterattacks checked the offensive of our forces. Reluctantly, the 2nd Tank Army's forces fell back to the line of Hill 164 and the southern slopes of the Coarba Burial Mound, where for the rest of the day and throughout 14 April 1944, they conducted stubborn defensive fighting.

Describing the fighting on 13 April, Glantz writes:

Undeterred by this setback, Bogdanov resumed his assaults early on 13 April, this time with about 80 tanks from the 50th and 51st Tank Brigades of Mishulin's 3rd Tank Corps, supported by infantry from the same tank corps' 57th Motorized Rifle Brigade and riflemen from Bronsky's 93rd Guards Rifle Division. This assault struck the Germans' defenses along the northwestern flank of the Totoesti salient. Once again, after the Russians recorded modest initial success, the 24th Panzer Division counterattacked with two *kampfgruppen*, the first equipped with 15 tanks and 30 assault guns and the second with ten tanks and a battalion of assault guns. The combined assaults against the 3rd Tank Corps' flanks quickly brought Bogdanov's assault to a halt and temporarily ended Konev's attempt to resume his offensive in this sector.

In fact, according to the 2nd Tank Army's Combat Dispatches No.0223/OP and 0224/OP from 12 April 1944, the 3rd Tank Corps had 15 serviceable T-34 tanks. On the morning of 13 April, according to its journal of combat operations, the 3rd Tank Corps went on the attack with just 11 operational T-34 tanks.

The 2nd Tank Army's "Report on the Enemy's Combat Actions in front of the 2nd Tank Army over the period of fighting from 13.4 to 17.4.1944" has this to say:

Overall Situation in the Polieni – Domian Sector (a front of 25 kilometers) on 13.4.1944: The enemy, falling back on the road hubs of Târgu Frumos, Podu-Iloaie and Iaşi, with a stubborn defense and repeated counterattacks in strength of up to an infantry regiment with the support of 10-15 tanks, was keeping the offensive of our units in check on the line: along the southwestern banks of the Bahlui River, Erbiceni, Totoeşti, Hills 150, 177, 168, 173, Vulturul, south of Rediu-Aldei, having the strongest grouping in the Podu-Iloaie area. In the period from 9.4 to 13.4.44, he regrouped the 24th Panzer Division and *Grossdeutschland* Panzer Division from the Pirliţa area to the Podu-Iloaie area with the aim of preventing the 2nd Tank Army's forces from outflanking Iaşi from the northwest. With a reconnaissance-in-force and the seizure of prisoners, the following enemy grouping was identified by the end of 12.4.44: the Romanian 8th Infantry Division's 90th Infantry Regiment and the 23rd Panzer Division – in the Belceşti, Erbiceni sector (confirmed by prisoners taken on 10.4.44; the *Grossdeutschland* Panzer Division and the Romanian 8th Infantry Division's 29th Infantry Regiment – in the Erbiceni, stream east of Hill 181 sector (confirmed by prisoners taken on 12.4.44); the 24th Panzer Division, the Romanian 7th Infantry Division's 37th Infantry Regiment, and the Romanian 12th Cavalry Regiment – in the sector Hill 150 – Hill 183. The total number of enemy tanks: in the Târgu Frumos area, 30-40; Podu-Iloaie, 10; Domian, up to 30 tanks and self-propelled guns. There are up to 12 artillery batteries in the entire sector, primarily positioned in the Totoeşti, Hill 150, Hoişeşti and Domian areas. The total number of active bayonets – 8400, guns of various calibers – 74, heavy machine guns – 96, light machine guns – 260, mortars – 56.

Enemy actions: In the course of 13.4.44, the enemy with fire and counterattacks checked the advance of our units. At 11.00 12 tanks with infantry counterattacked our units from the south out of the area of the railroad station south of Totoeşti. At 11.30, 9 self-propelled guns and 8 halftracks with a battalion of infantry counterattacked to the north out of the vicinity of Hill 150. An hour later, the enemy repeated the counterattack in this region in strength of 3 self-propelled guns, 4 halftracks and up to 500 infantrymen. Having no success in this sector, in the course of 14.4.44 the 2nd Tank Army laterally shifted its forces to the Hărmăneşti – Hârlău sector. On 15.4.44, the enemy with units of the Romanian 6th Infantry Division's 27th and 15th Infantry Regiments, the Romanian 8th Infantry Division's 29th and 7th Infantry Regiments, the 23rd Panzer Division and a portion of the *Grossdeutschland* Panzer Division offered resistance to our units' offensive with fire and counterattacks in strength of up to an infantry division with 30 tanks. As a result of the fighting, [the enemy] was driven out of Miruga and Belceşti, and at 20.00 was fighting on the line: Stolniceni, Ruginoasa, Dumbrăviţa, south of Vaşcani, center of Cucuteni, south of Lake Hirbu, Hill 193 and further on along his previous line. In the course of 16.4 and 17.4.44, the enemy with its former grouping put up resistance to our units actions with fire and counterattacks on the line: Ruginoasa, Costeşti, Probota, south of Lake Hirbu, Ulmi Noi.

In the period from 19.4 to 24.4.44, the enemy unsuccessfully conducted active operations in strength of a company, battalion or regiment of infantry, with the support of tanks, and repeatedly attempted to undertake a reconnaissance-in-force, while simultaneously digging in and throwing up fortifications along the entire sector of defense. On 25.44, the enemy in strength of up to 60 tanks and halftracks with infantry, after an artillery preparation, went on the offensive with the support of up to 60 bombers in the direction of Hill 326 and Hărmăneşti, and by 19.00 reached the line of Hill 358, southern outskirts of Hărmăneşti, Hill 372, Vaşcani, Hill 344, where they were stopped by our units.

In the period from 26.4 to 30.4.44, the enemy undertook no active operations. From their occupied positions, the enemy shelled the combat dispositions of our troops with artillery and mortar fire. The enemy unsuccessfully attempted to probe in the Cucuteni area and south of Lake Hirbu in strength of a platoon or company of infantry, with the support of artillery fire and 5 tanks.

Conclusion: Falling back on the road junctions of Târgu Frumos and Iaşi, the enemy has the aim of stopping the advance of our units to the south and keeping possession of the road hubs Târgu Frumos and Iaşi, and the Iaşi – Târgu Frumos highway, which connects him with the Kishinev grouping and is a convenient line of communications for maneuvering and supplying his forces. In the period from 10.4 to 17.4.44, the enemy increased his activity with limited attacks of infantry and tanks out of the Târgu Frumos, Podu Iloaie and Iaşi areas, threw back our units to the north by 5-10 kilometers, and swept clear the Târgu Frumos – Iaşi highway, thereby liquidating the growing threat of our units' appearance on the flank and rear of his entire southern Carpathian grouping. With the commitment of units of the 23rd Panzer Division and *Grossdeutschland* Panzer Grenadier Division north of Târgu Frumos, he reinforced the Romanian units operating in the Ruginoasa – Ulmi Noi sector, placing a strong barrier on the roads leading from the northwest to Târgu Frumos. The enemy, utilizing the Târgu Frumos – Roman and Târgu Frumos – Iaşi lateral roads had the possibility to transfer his tank divisions to the main axis and to create a numerical superiority in tanks in separate sectors.

A batch of documents shows the condition of the 2nd Tank Army in this period of time. A report on the 2nd Tank Army's composition of forces and their supply levels at 6.00 on 13 April 1944 reveals:

Of the 120 T-34 tanks, unloaded for the 2nd Tank Army at the Potash, Zvenigorodka and Khristinovka railroad stations, 110 have been received by the army. Of this number, 103 have arrived in the units. Of the remaining tanks, 5 are stuck in ravines and swamps, and two tanks are continuing to be repaired. Ten tanks of the Front's Armored and Motorized Forces, which lagged behind on the road from Khristinovka to Uman' have been accepted. The 2nd Tank Army, engaged in offensive combat from 1.4 to 7.4.1944 in the Pirliţa Sat, Corneşti Tyrg area, lost 51 tanks, 31 of which were destroyed and 20 of which were knocked-out. In the attack on 12 April 1944, the army lost 6 tanks burned-out and 6 tanks knocked-out. Altogether, 63 T-34 tanks are disabled. Twenty-one tanks have been left behind in the area of the previous location due to mechanical problems, and on the march – 21 tanks. Still operational are 16 T-34 tanks and 3 command tanks.

**Combat roster of the army's formations and supply level**: **3rd Tank Corps:** 12 serviceable tanks; 2 85mm guns and 5 76mm guns; 2 37mm guns. Active bayonets – 340. Ammunition for the 85mm guns – 0.5 of a combat load; for the 76mm and 37mm guns – 1 combat load; rifle cartridges – 0.8 of a combat load; diesel fuel – 0.5 of a refill, Type 2 benzene – none. **16th Tank Corps:** 4 serviceable T-34 tanks; 3 M-13 rocket launchers; 5 76mm guns; 13 130mm mortars. Supplies: shells – 0.3 of a combat load; 76mm rounds – 0.9 of a combat load; rifle cartridges – 0.7 of a combat load; diesel fuel – 0.8 of a refill; Type 2 benzene – none.

[Signed] Chief of the 2nd Tank Army's Operations Department – Colonel Bazanov

Colonel Bazanov's report was accompanied by one from Guards Major General Radzievsky, the 2nd Tank Army's chief of staff:

**Information on the 120 tanks, received by the 2nd Tank Army and their status as of 8.00 on 13.4.1944**
I am reporting that as of 8 April 1944, of the newly arrived T-34 tanks, 45 T-34 tanks have been handed over to the 3rd Tank Corps, and 44 have been sent to the 16th Tank Corps. Total: 89 tanks. On 8.4.44, 5 more T-34 tanks arrived and were handed over to the 3rd Tank Corps. On 9.4.44, 2 T-34 tanks arrived and were given to the 16th Tank Corps. On 10.4.44, 4 T-34 tanks arrived and were handed over to the 16th Tank Corps. On 12.4.44, 3 T-34 tanks arrived and were given to the 3rd Tank Corps. **Total additional tanks:** 14. Out of the total of 120 tanks, which were unloaded at the Khristinovka, Zvenigorodka and Potash railroad stations, 103 T-34 tanks arrived in the army's units on 12.2.44. Seventeen T-34 tanks lagged behind, of which 10 T-34 tanks en route from Zvenigorodka to Iurkovka have been taken under repair by the Front's 92nd Separate Repair Battalion, and are not yet assigned to the army. Seven tanks en route from Kapustiani to Fălești have dropped behind, 5 of which have become stuck in ravines or bogs, and 2 of which are being repaired. As of 13 April 1944, of the new 103 tanks, 63 T-34 are not serviceable, and 36 of these are beyond repair. The 3rd Tank Corps has 14 operational T-34; the 16th Tank Corps has 5 serviceable T-34, for a total of 19 tanks. The other 48 T-34 tanks require light or major overhaul.

[Signed] Army chief of staff Guards Major General A. Radzievsky

Just two days later, on 15 April 1944, the 2nd Tank Army had active 13 T-34 tanks and 3 Mark IX tanks, for a total of 16 tanks. A briefing paper on this date gave updated figures for the status of 2nd Tank Army's formations:

## Information on the Status of the 2nd Tank Army's Forces at 12.00 on 15 April 1944

**3rd Tank Corps:** arrived in the Ceplenița area: 3 T-34 tanks; 3 76mm guns, 4 120mm mortars, 5 82mm mortars; on the march to the Ceplenița area: 4 T-34 tanks; 6 85mm guns; 3 76mm guns; 9 37mm guns; 5 M-13 rocket launchers; 14 120mm mortars. The corps' supply with ammunition for the tanks – 0.8 of a combat load; artillery rounds – 0.4 of a combat load; fuel and lubricants – 0.5 of a refill, Type 2 benzene – 0.5 of a refill.

**16th Tank Corps:** arrived in the Bădeni area: 2 T-34 tanks; 6 76mm guns; 3 M-13 rocket launchers; 11 82mm mortars; 100 submachine gunners; 190 riflemen. On the march to the Bădeni area: 6 T-34 tanks; 9 76mm guns; 2 M-13 rocket launchers; 34 120mm mortars; 2 82mm mortars; 7 85mm guns; 14 37mm guns.

**86th Guards Mortar Regiment**: in the Hârlău area. 12 operational M-13 rocket launchers. Ammunition – 2 salvoes; fuel – 1 refill. Three M-13 rocket launching trucks are still en route, but without fuel.

Total for the army: in the assembly area: 5 T-34 tanks, 4 120mm mortars, 16 82mm mortars, 15 M-13 rocket launchers; 9 76mm guns. On the march: 10 T-34 tanks, 12 85mm guns, 12 76mm guns, 23 37mm cannons; 10 M-13 rocket launchers; 48 120mm mortars, 2 82mm mortars.

[Signed] 2nd Tank Army's chief of operations – Colonel Bazanov

## d) Fighting on the Târgu Frumos axis:

Implementing an order from the commander of the 2nd Ukrainian Front, the 2nd Tank Army spent the day of 14 April 1944 regrouping to a new area: Bădeni, Ceplenița, with the assignment to attack jointly with the 35th Rifle Corps on the morning of 15 April 1944, to seize Târgu Frumos, and subsequently to pivot to the east and advance along the highway leading to Iași.

The 3rd Tank Corps, having assembled in its jumping-off area on the southern outskirts of Cotnari Station was to attack together with units of the 206th Rifle Division on the Lake Hirbu – Hill 184 axis, with the Popa-Mort Burial Mound as its immediate objective, and the eastern outskirts of Târgu Frumos as its following objective. The 50th Tank Brigade was assembled in the Ceplenița area, having been replenished with 5 T-34 tanks and 2 Valentine tanks.

The 16th Tank Corps, having assembled in its jumping-off area on the southeastern outskirts of Cotnari, was to exploit the attack of the units of the 35th Rifle Corps and 3rd Tank Corps in the direction of Hills 222, 197 and 189, with the assignment to to seize Târgu Frumos with an attack from the northwest. The 11th Guards Tank Brigade's motorized rifle battalion was assembled in Fălești. The enemy, with units of the Romanian 23rd and 18th Infantry Divisions, was continuing to defend along the line: Hărmănești, Dumbrăvița, Costești, Pulina Burial Mound and further along the banks of the Bahlui River, fiercely resisting attempts by the 2nd Tank Army to advance.

By 8.00 on 15 April 1944, the 57th Motorized Rifle Brigade had moved into its jumping-off positions for the offensive on the southern outskirts of Cotnari Station, and at 11.30, over-coming enemy resistance, it had taken Balusesti and Stroesti, several kilometers to the southwest of Cotnari Station.

At 5.00 on 16 April 1944, the enemy launched a sudden attack with the support of heavy artil-lery fire and 10 tanks and seized Balș (4 kilometers southeast of Cotnari). However, at 8.00 on 16 April a sharp counterattack by units of the 16th Tank Corps and the 206th Rifle Division seized a nameless hamlet and restored the positions at Balș by 14.00. The enemy, having deployed heavy tanks in the area, began to target our tanks in the nameless hamlet with fire from fixed positions, and forced the latter to fall back out of their zone of fire. Having regrouped his forces, at 18.30 on 16 April, the enemy again attacked our units in strength of up to two battalions of infantry and 14 tanks, and drove the 50th Tank Brigade back to a line 1.5 kilometers south of Cotnari Station. The tank brigade's losses amounted to 5 tanks (2 of which were Valentine Mark IX tanks). Units of the 3rd Tank Corps together with the 57th Motorized Rifle Brigade and the 50th Tank Brigade counterattacked, and by 20.00 reached the southern slopes of a hill lying 500 meters north of Lake Hirbu.

While engaged in see saw defensive fighting on 16 and 17 April 1944, units of the 2nd Tank Army simultaneously worked to repair and bring up more tanks and to resupply them with ammu-nition and fuel. On 18 April 1944, the units of the 2nd Tank Army conducted a regrouping: the 3rd and 16th Tank Corps, having turned over their remaining tanks and defensive sectors to the 11th Guards Tank Brigade, reassembled in the Plugari – Coarnele Caprei area to rest, refit, resupply and to prepare for new battles. The 3rd Tank Corps' 50th Tank Brigade, having turned over its 3 T-34 tanks and sector of defense to the 11th Guards Tank Brigade, moved to the Coarnele Caprei sector. On the same day, its 51st Tank Brigade, having conducted a 20-kilometer march from the Ceplenița area, joined the 50th Tank Brigade in Coarnele Caprei before sunset. Its 103rd Tank Brigade took no part in the fighting between 5 and 18 April 1944 and spent the period putting tanks back in order.

Of the four newly arrived march companies, numbering a total of 40 tanks, 18 had assembled in the Plugari area for the 16th Tank Corps, and 19 had arrived in the Coarnele Caprei area for the 3rd Tank Corps. The 375th Heavy Self-propelled Artillery Regiment was on the march from Bălti to Sculeni with 18 SU-152, where it would come under the command of the 3rd Tank Corps. The 6th Guards Heavy Tank Regiment, assembled in Miclăușeni with 20 JS-122 tanks, was placed under the command of the 16th Tank Corps. The 8th Guards Heavy Tank Regiment was concentrated in Focuri with 5 JS-85 tanks. The 11th Guards Tank Brigade, as noted, was in defensive positions along the southern slopes of Hill 222 and the southern slopes of the hill northeast of Lake Hirbu.

Several reports generated on 18 April, 23 April and 28 April 1944 show the results of the rest and replenishment as the 2nd Tank Army prepared for new fighting:

**Table 7.1: Data on the materiél of the 2nd Tank Army at 6.00 on 18.4.1944**

| | Heavy tank regiments | | | 375th Heavy Self-propelled Artillery Regiment | 11th Guards Tank Brigade | 3rd Tank Corps | 16th Tank Corps | Altogether in the army |
|---|---|---|---|---|---|---|---|---|
| | 8th | 13th | 6th | | | | | |
| Serviceable T-34s | – | – | – | – | – | 4 | 2 | 6 |
| Serviceable Mk IX | – | – | – | – | – | 1 | 1 | 2 |
| Repaired T-34 en route | – | – | – | – | – | – | 2 | 2 |
| Serviceable KV-85 | 3 | – | – | – | – | – | – | 3 |
| Serviceable KV-122 | – | – | 18 | – | – | – | – | 18 |
| Serviceable SU-152 | – | – | – | 19 | – | – | – | 19 |
| Approaching T-34 replenishments | – | – | – | – | – | | | 35 |
| According to plan, T-34s that will be repaired by 23.4.4 | | | | | | 12 | 14 | 26 |
| Total tracked machines | 3 | – | 18 | 19 | – | 17 | 19 | 111 |
| 76mm guns | – | – | – | – | – | 1 | 9 | 10 |
| 85mm guns | – | – | – | – | – | 5 | 6 | 11 |
| 37mm guns | – | – | – | – | – | 6 | 13 | 19 |
| 120mm mortars | – | – | – | – | – | 6 | 13 | 19 |
| 82mm mortars | – | – | – | – | – | 3 | 8 | 11 |
| M-13 rocket launchers | – | – | – | – | – | 4 | 3 | 7 |
| Army-level M-13s | – | – | – | – | – | – | – | 12 |
| Total emplaced barrels | – | – | – | – | – | 25 | 52 | 89 |
| Artillery en route | – | – | – | – | 4 | 23 | 33 | 63 |

Note: The 6th Heavy Tank Regiment consisting of 8 tanks, the technical support company and a company of submachine gunners at 15.30 on 17.4.44 was assembled in Bel'tsy (Bălti). 10 tanks are expected in Bel'tsy by 24.00 on 17.4.1944. The 375th Heavy Self-propelled Artillery Regiment at 19.00 on 17.4.44 consisting of 19 machines was located 19 kilometers away from Bel'tsy. 35 T-34 tanks at 9.00 on 17.4.44 left Bel'tsy for Sculeni. The 8th Guards Heavy Tank Regiment at 18.00 on 16.4.44 was waiting to cross the Prut River. Chief of the 2nd Tank Army's Operations Department – Colonel Bazanov.

Five days later, Colonel Bazanov gave an update on the materiél and supply status of the 2nd Tank Army as of 6.00 on 23 April 1944:

**Table 7.2: Data on the materiél of the 2nd Tank Army at 6.00 on 23.4.44**

| | 11th Guards Tank Brigade | 3rd Tank Corps | 16th Tank Corps | Total for the army |
|---|---|---|---|---|
| Serviceable T-34s | 10 | 21 | 22 | 55 |
| Serviceable KV-122s | – | – | 18 | 18 |
| Serviceable Mk IXs | 1 | – | 1 | 2 |
| Approaching KV-85 on the march | – | – | 9 | 9 |
| Serviceable SU-85 | – | – | 4 | 4 |
| Serviceable SU-76 | – | – | 2 | 2 |
| Serviceable SU-152 | – | 17 | – | 17 |
| Total serviceable tanks and self-propelled guns | 11 | 38 | 56 | 107 |
| Tanks en route with mechanical problems: | | | | |
| KV-122 | – | – | 3 | 3 |
| SU-152 | – | 4 | – | 4 |
| Total en route | – | 4 | 3 | 7 |
| Army's artillery in firing positions: | | | | |
| 85mm guns | – | 5 | 8 | 13 |
| 76mm guns | 4 | 4 | 19 | 27 |
| 37mm guns | – | 12 | 13 | 25 |
| 45mm guns | – | 1 | 2 | 3 |
| 57mm guns | – | 4 | – | 4 |
| 120mm mortars | – | 21 | 27 | 48 |
| 82mm mortars | – | 3 | 18 | 21 |
| M-13 rocket launchers | – | 8 | 3 | 11 |
| Army-level M-13 rocket launchers | – | – | – | 15 |
| Total emplaced barrels: | 4 | 58 | 90 | 167 |
| Artillery tubes en route | – | 23 | 30 | |
| Ammunition supply (in combat loads | | | | |
| For T-34 tanks | 1 | 1.5 | 1.5 | – |
| For KV-122 | – | – | 2.5 | – |
| For SU-152 | – | 1.5 | – | – |
| 85mm rounds | – | 1 | 1 | – |
| 76mm rounds | 1 | 1 | 1 | – |
| 37mm rounds | – | 2.5 | 2.5 | – |
| M-13 rockets | – | 1.2 | 2 | – |
| Rockets for the army-level M-13s | | | | 3 salvoes |
| Fuel and lubricants (in refills): | 1 | 1.5 | 2 | |

Chief of the 2nd Tank Army's Operations Department – Colonel Bazanov

This was followed by another report on the materiél of the 2nd Tank Army, broken down by units, at 15.00 on 28 April 1944:

**Table 7.3: Data on the material and supply levels of the forces of the 2nd Tank Army at 15.00 on 28 April 1944**

| | Serviceable tanks | | | | Total tanks | Supplies | | | Rations |
|---|---|---|---|---|---|---|---|---|---|
| | T-34 | IS-122 | IS-85 | Mk IX | | Ammunition | Diesel fuel | High-octane gasoline | |
| **3rd Tank Corps** | | | | | | | | | |
| 50 TBr | 10 | – | – | – | 10 | 1.5 | 1.5 | 0.3 | 1 |
| 51 TBr | 1 | – | – | – | 1 | 1.5 | 1.5 | 0.3 | 1 |
| 103 TBr | 4 | – | – | – | 4 | 1.5 | 1.5 | 0.3 | 1 |
| 8 GTR | – | – | 5 | – | 5 | 1 | 1 | – | 2 |
| Total: | 29 | – | 5 | – | 34 | 1.5 | 1.5 | 0.3 | 1 |
| **16th Tank Corps** | | | | | | | | | |
| 107 TBr | 10 | – | – | – | 10 | 1.5 | 1.6 | 0.2 | 3 |
| 109 TBr | 9 | – | – | – | 9 | 1.5 | 1.6 | 0.2 | 3 |
| 164 TBr | 11 | – | – | – | 11 | 1.5 | 1.6 | 0.2 | 3 |
| 6 GTR | – | 20 | – | – | 20 | 1.5 | 1.6 | – | 3 |
| Total: | 33 [sic] | 20 | – | 2 | 55 | 1.5 | 1.6 | 0.2 | 3 |
| 11th GTBr | 16 | – | – | 1 | 17 | 1.2 | 0.6 | 0.3 | 3 |
| Amy commanders' tanks | 2 | – | – | – | 2 | 1 | 1 | – | – |
| Total for the army | 80 | 20 | 5 | 3 | 108 | – | – | – | – |
| **Serviceable self-propelled guns:** | | | | | | | | | |
| 3rd TC: 37th HSPAR SU-152 | – | – | – | – | 18 | 1.5 | 2 | – | – |
| 16th TC: 298th GSPAR SU-76 | – | – | – | – | 2 | 1 | 1 | – | 3 |
| 1441st SPAR SU-85 | – | – | – | – | 4 | 1.8 | 1 | – | 3 |
| Total SPGs: | – | – | – | – | 24 | – | – | – | – |
| Total tanks and self-propelled guns for the army | 80 | 20 | 5 | 3 | 132 | – | – | – | – |

| | 3rd Tank Corps | | | 16th Tank Corps | | | 11th Guards Tank Brigade | | |
|---|---|---|---|---|---|---|---|---|---|
| | Tubes | Ammo | Fuel and lubricants | Tubes | Ammo | Fuel and lubricants | Tubes | Ammo | Fuel and lubricants |
| 120mm mortars | 22 | 0.4 | 0.2 | 28 | 0.4 | 0.2 | – | – | – |
| 85mm guns | 6 | 1 | 0.6 | 9 | 1 | 1 | – | – | – |
| M-13s | 8 | 3.5 | 0.3 | 3 | 0.5 | 0.5 | – | – | – |
| 37mm guns | 14 | 2.4 | 0.5 | 15 | 2 | 0.8 | – | – | – |
| 76mm guns | 4 | 1 | 0.1 | 18 | 1.4 | 0 | 4 | 1 | 0.3 |
| 57mm guns | 4 | – | – | 2 | – | – | – | – | – |
| 45mm guns | 3 | 0.2 | – | 7 | – | – | – | – | – |
| 82mm mortars | 5 | – | – | 15 | 1 | – | – | – | – |
| Total | 66 | | | 103 | – | – | 4 | | |

The 2nd Tank Army's chief of operations Colonel Bazanov reported on the status of the tanks and self-propelled guns that arrived in the jumping-off area at 12.00 on 29 April 1944:

> 3rd Tank Corps: 23 T-34 tanks, 4 IS-85 tanks, 16 ISU-152, for a total of 43 tanks and self-propelled guns. Broken down on the way: 6 T-34, 1 IS-85, and 2 ISU-152. 16th Tank Corps: 30 T-34, 19 IS-122, 3 SU-85, and 2 Mark IX, for a total of 51 tanks and self-propelled guns. Broken down on the way: 3 T-34, 2 IS-122, 1 SU-85, and 2 SU-76. Of the IS-122 tanks that have arrived in the jumping-off area, 3 require repair and the replacement of parts. 11th Guards Tank Brigade: 16 serviceable T-34 tanks; 87th Separate Motorcycle Battalion has 1 Mark IX tank.
>
> The 2nd Tank Army has in the jumping-off area a total of 114 tanks and self-propelled guns: 69 T-34, 4 IS-85, 19 IS-122, 3 Mark IX, 16 ISU-152 and 3 SU-85.

[Signed] 2nd Tank Army chief of operations Colonel Bazanov

## e) The Second Stage of Fighting on the Târgu Frumos Axis between 2 and 5 May 1944

The enemy was continuing to hold the Hill 158 – Vaşcani – Cucuteni – Balş – northern slopes of Hill 192 – Ulmi Vechi – Polieni line. A second defensive line had been constructed closer to Târgu Frumos and extended further along the Bahlui River. While the 2nd Tank Army had been rebuilding its strength in the period between 18 April and 28 April, it had simultaneously been reconnoitering routes into the jumping-off positions, repairing roads and bridges along the routes, settling questions of cooperation with the infantry of the 35th Rifle Corps and within the units and formations. Commanders scouted the areas of forthcoming fighting and set up command and observation posts.

On the night of 28-29 April 1944, the 3rd Tank Corps consisting of the 50th, 51st and 103rd Tank Brigades, the 57th Motorized Rifle Brigade, the 8th Guards Heavy Tank Regiment, the 74th Separate Motorcycle Battalion and the 90th Separate Pioneer Battalion, conducted a 30-kilometer march to the area of Cotnari Station, and by 8.00 on 29 April, it had reassembled and taken up its jumping off positions: 50th Tank Brigade – southern outskirts of Balusesti and Stroesti with 10 T-34 tanks and 78 active bayonets of its motorized rifle battalion with 2 82mm mortars and 4 anti-tank rifles; 103rd Tank Brigade – 200 meters north of Băiceni with 9 T-34 tanks and 60 active bayonets of its motorized rifle battalion with 3 radio sets, 1 heavy machine gun, and 3 anti-tank rifles; 51st Tank Brigade – southeastern outskirts of Cotnari Station with 7 T-34 and 69 active bayonets of its motorized rifle battalion with 4 radio sets and 2 82mm mortars; 57th Motorized Rifle Brigade – Băiceni, with 800 active bayonets, 5 heavy and 20 light machine guns, 4 120mm mortars and 5 82mm mortars; 8th Guards Heavy Tank Regiment – 1.5 kilometers south of Cotnari Station, with 5 IS-85 tanks; 375th Heavy Self-propelled Regiment – Moara-Prefectului, with 17 ISU-152. The 3rd Tank Corps headquarters and the units directly subordinate to it were assembled in Cotnari.

The units and formations of the 3rd Tank Corps spent the day of 29 April 1944 putting its matériel back into order after the march into the jumping-off area and camouflaging its jumping-off positions. Between 30 April and 1 May 1944, questions regarding cooperation with the 3rd Guards Airborne Division and the 93rd Guards "Khar'kov" Rifle Division were resolved and put down on paper for each stage of the battle, and commanders reconnoitered the forward edge of the enemy's defenses.

At the combat order of the commander of the 2nd Tank Army No.014/OP, the 3rd Tank Corps received the task to attack in the direction of Hill 256 (the Kalmü), Hill 189 and Hill 184, with the immediate objective of destroying the enemy forces in the Kalmü, Popa Mort Burial Mound area in concert with the 3rd Guards Airborne and 93rd Guards Rifle Divisions. It was then to seize Târgu Frumos with an attack from the northeast in cooperation with the 16th Tank Corps. The commander of the 3rd Tank Corps decided to place the 103rd and 50th Tank Brigades in the first echelon, and covered by the 8th Guards Heavy Tank Regiment on the right flank and the 728th Separate Destroyer Anti-tank Artillery Battalion on the left flank. He intended to launch the main attack with the corps' left flank in close cooperation with the 35th Rifle Corps' 3rd Guards Airborne Division and 93rd Guards Rifle Division, to break through the enemy's defenses, and to seize Târgu Frumos by the end of the day. The 57th Motorized Rifle Brigade would follow closely behind the combat formations of the 50th and 103rd Tank Brigades, and be trailed by the 375th Heavy Self-propelled Artillery Regiment, which was to be ready to repel enemy tank counterattacks. The corps commander's reserve – the 51st Tank Brigade and the 90th Separate Pioneer Battalion – would move up behind the corps' first echelon, in readiness to exploit any success and to repel possible enemy counterattacks.

Units of the 16th Tank Corps, after lengthy offensive and stubborn, maneuvering defensive fighting, had been withdrawn on 18 April 1944 to the Plugari, Boroșoaia, Miletin, Onești area at the order of the 2nd Tank Army Commander to rest and refit. At the start of the operation, the 16th Tank Corps' formations had the following number of tanks, self-propelled guns, anti-tank guns and mortars: 107th Tank Brigade – 10 T-34 tanks; 109th Tank Brigade – 10 T-34 tanks; 164th Tank Brigade – 13 T-34 tanks; 1441st Self-propelled Artillery Regiment – 5 SU-85; 729th Separate Destroyer Anti-tank Artillery Regiment – 8 85mm anti-tank guns; 226th Army Mortar Regiment – 26 120mm mortars; 1721st Artillery Regiment – 15/12 37mm anti-aircraft guns; and the 89th Separate Guards Mortar Battalion – 3 M-13 rocket launchers. Table 7.4 below shows the amount of the 2nd Tank Army's artillery in their firing positions on 29 April 1944.

The 6th Guards Heavy Tank Regiment with 20 IS-122 had assembled in the Onești area by the end of the day on 20 April 1944; two of its IS-122 tanks had broken down on the way and were undergoing repairs. With the arrival of the tanks in the designated assembly area, all of the machines underwent meticulous technical inspection, after which the uncovered defects were eliminated through the efforts of the crews and the regiment's maintenance and repair service. As the tanks were being repaired, they were also serviced and adapted for summertime operation.

Once the process of refitting was complete, the 16th Tank Corps moved out and at 20.00 on 28 April it arrived in its jumping-off area, where its units thereupon took up the following positions by 7.00 on 29 April: the 107th Tank Brigade – southeastern slopes of Hill 192; the 109th Tank Brigade – northern slopes of Hill 193; the 164th Tank Brigade – northern slopes of Hill 193; and the 15th Motorized Rifle Brigade – northern slopes of Hill 192, balka 1 kilometer west of Ulmi Noi.

The 2nd Tank Army's assignment in the looming offensive was to breach the enemy's defenses in the Tetarului, Hodora Burial Mound sector together with the 35th Guards Rifle Corps and in cooperation with the 7th Guards Army and 5th Guards Tank Army, and subsequently to exploit the success in the direction of Târgu Frumos with the aim of seizing the latter. It was then to be ready for operations: a) in the direction of Iași with the task of destroying this enemy grouping; or b) in the direction of Slobozia, with the aim of seizing a pass in the mountains and emerging in the valley of the Barladul [Birlad] River.

By 7.00 on 29 April 1944, the 2nd Tank Army's formations were in their jumping-off positions, in readiness to launch the offensive: 16th Tank Corps – southeastern slopes of Hill 192, northern slopes of Hill 193, balka west of Ulmi Noi; the 3rd Tank Corps – southern outskirts of Balusesti and Stroesti, southeastern outskirts of Cotnari Station, Băiceni, which placed it staggered to the right and behind the line of deployment of the 16th Tank Corps. The 11th Guards Tank Brigade was still holding its occupied sector. By 30 April 1944, the rebuilt 2nd Tank Army had

Table 7.4: The amount of artillery in the 2nd Tank Army in firing positions on 28.4.44

| | SU-152 | SU-85 | Guns | | | | | | Mortars | | | M-13 | Total tubes |
|---|---|---|---|---|---|---|---|---|---|---|---|---|---|
| | | | 85mm | 76mm | 57mm | 45mm | 37mm | | 120mm | 82mm | | |
| **3rd Tank Corps** | | | | | | | | | | | | | |
| 234 Army Mortar Regiment. | – | – | – | – | – | – | – | | 18 | – | – | 18 |
| 728 Anti-tank Battalion | – | – | 6 | – | – | – | – | | – | – | – | 6 |
| 126 Guards Mortar Battalion | – | – | – | – | – | – | – | | – | – | 8 | 8 |
| 121 Anti-aircraft Regiment | – | – | – | – | – | – | 14 | | – | – | – | 14 |
| Art. Battalion of 57 MRBr | – | – | – | 4 | 4 | 3 | – | | 4 | 7 | – | 22 |
| 375 Heavy SPA Regiment | 18 | – | – | – | – | – | – | | – | – | – | 18 |
| **Total:** | 18 | – | 6 | 4 | 4 | 3 | 14 | | 22 | 7 | 8 | 86 |
| **16th Tank Corps** | | | | | | | | | | | | | |
| 226 Army Mortar Regiment | – | – | – | – | – | – | – | | 24 | – | – | 24 |
| 729 Anti-tank Battalion | – | – | 9 | – | – | – | – | | – | – | – | 9 |
| 89 Guards Mortar Battalion | – | – | – | – | – | – | – | | – | – | 3 | 3 |
| 1721 Anti-aircraft Regiment | – | – | – | – | – | – | 15 | | – | – | – | 15 |
| Art. Battalion of 15 MRBr | – | – | – | 10 | – | 7 | – | | 4 | 13 | – | 34 |
| Art. Batteries of tank brigades | – | – | – | 7 | – | – | – | | – | – | – | 7 |
| 51 Motorcycle Battalion | – | – | – | 1 | 2 | – | – | | – | – | – | 3 |
| 1441 SPA Regiment | – | 3 | – | – | – | – | – | | – | – | – | 3 |
| **Total:** | – | 3 | 9 | 18 | 2 | 7 | 15 | | 28 | 13 | 3 | 98 |
| **11 Guards Tank Brigade** | – | – | –4 | 4 | – | – | – | | – | – | – | 4 |
| 86 Guards Mortar Regiment | – | – | – | – | – | – | – | | – | – | 15 | 15 |
| **Total for the army:** | 18 | 3 | 15 | 26 | 6 | 10 | 29 | | 50 | 20 | 26 | 203 |

114 serviceable tanks and self-propelled guns, including 69 T-34, 4 IS-85, 19 IS-122, 3 Valentine Mark IX, 16 SU-152 and 3 SU-85. The dates of 30 and 31 April and 1 May 1944 were devoted to resolving questions of cooperation between neighboring formations and among the rifle units, tank units and artillery.

On 30 April 1944, the command of the 2nd Tank Army issued Order No.217 to its troops on preparing the army's units for the coming offensive:

On preparing the army's units for combat operations: With the aims of the timely and complete preparation of the army's units and formations for forthcoming active combat operations, and the proper and effective conducting of combat, I hereby order commanders of all levels: Familiarize yourselves with the People's Commissariat of Defense's Order No.057 from 22.1.1942 and Order No.325 from 16.10.1942, and Order No.44 of the 2nd Ukrainian Front's Military Council, and organize constant control over the complete and competent execution of these orders. Remember that reconnaissance is the primary means to safeguard the troops. Conduct reconnaissance without interruption with every means, and simultaneously make use of the intelligence of the combined-arms army, as well of the artillery and engineers. Organize and introduce officers' reconnaissance into the system from army headquarters down to the battalion level, and organize surveillance of the battlefield, especially in the depth of the enemy's defenses. The army's chief of intelligence is to organize courses for specialist observers (80-100 men) in the 246th Reserve Battalion.

Pay particular attention to organizing the battle. Ensure the rapid and decisive advance of the infantry with tanks, and maintain a high tempo of attack. The second combat echelons of the corps are to move toward the objective and prod the first echelons forward. On the offensive, ensure the infantry's advance by any and all means, having given strict orders for conducting the battle. "The infantry advances behind the tanks, while the tanks lead the infantry forward." The commanders are to act decisively, boldly and with initiative. Each soldier must know and understand his maneuver. Each crew must have its own attack objective, know its direction of advance and have reference points in the terrain. Each platoon commander must know when, from whom, from where and with what means he will be supported. Battalion commanders and higher must anticipate in the plan of battle the likely directions of enemy counterattack, and secure his flanks and unit boundaries. Surprise – is the main factor of success in combat. All preliminary work must be kept concealed, with the observation of all camouflage measures. Precise teamwork among the tanks, infantry, combat engineers and artillery decides success in battle. Work out questions of cooperation among the tanks, infantry, combat engineers and artillery on the ground down to the tank crew inclusively. Reconnoiter, down to the driver-mechanic inclusively, the routes of approach to the enemy's forward edge of defense.

Up until 16.00 on 1.5.44, organize and conduct exercises to work out cooperation, especially in the depth of the enemy's defenses, at the level of the crew – platoon – company – battalion. Check the infantry's taking up of jumping-off positions in direct proximity to the forward edge (200 meters – "Nestle up to the artillery fire"). Pay serious attention to the cooperation with tanks and artillery. Ensure the constancy and power of the artillery preparation and supporting fire; do not permit any pause between them. The supporting fire must not weaken in the course of the entire battle. Plan the use of rocket launchers both singly and by battery, ensuring the constancy of their action. For immediate support, each motorized rifle battalion should have one artillery battery assigned to it for placing direct fire. Each corps and brigade commander should have "helper" artillery batteries for destroying enemy firing points that are hindering the advance of the tanks during the battle into the depth, or which "come alive" in the process of the battle.

Engineering support to a great degree decides success in battle. Conduct reconnaissance with engineers constantly, especially in the depth. The combat engineer units are to ensure the passage of tanks over water obstacles and through minefields. Prepare the necessary improvised material ahead of time.

The tank commander must see the battlefield; only then can he genuinely direct his powerful weapon. The corps and brigade commanders each must have their own mobile and fixed observation posts. I FORBID commanding from huts, with no view of the battlefield.

Pay special attention to the uninterrupted work of communications. During battle in the depth, communications must not be disrupted. Keep constant contact with your elements and with your superior commander, whom you must keep constantly and accurately informed of the situation. Commanders must demand of their staffs to have constant knowledge of the situation and to analyze it. All tanks and vehicles must have large recognition symbols. Number all the tanks. Make everyone aware of the [identification] numbers on the tanks, operating with the infantry, down to the rank and file.

By the end of 1.5.44, bring up the level of supply of the army's forces: a) For ammunition – up to 2 combat loads (for the ISU-152 – 4 combat loads; for the M-13 rocket launchers – 5 salvoes); b) For diesel fuel – up to 2.5 refills; for Type 2 benzene – up to 2 refills. Fully equip the personnel with the appropriate weapon. Fully supply the motorized rifle brigades with motorized transport by 2.5.44.

Establish iron military discipline and order in the army's units. The privates, sergeants and officers are to have a military appearance. Liquidate amoral manifestations that have a disastrous influence on combat preparation.

Organize courses for light and heavy machine gunners (100 men) in the 227th Reserve Army Regiment. Pay special attention to Party-education work among the new replacements. Make him aware of the army's glorious combat traditions; tell him about its top privates, sergeants and officers; about the army's combat path; and about the tasks that stand in front of him. On the day of 1.5.44, devote all your attention and time preparing for combat operations. Report on the execution of this order by 20.00 on 1.5.44.

[Signed] Bogdanov, Latyshev, Radzievsky

On the eve of the offensive, the 2nd Ukrainian Front's intelligence department provided an estimate of the correlation of forces in tanks, placing it at 4:1 (491 versus 115), although in reality the correlation between the two sides in tanks was closer to 2:1, considering the tanks of the 3rd SS Panzer Division *Totenkopf* and the Romanian 1st Guards Armored Division. The Soviet troops, which were to take part in the fighting at Târgu Frumos, were worn out by the constant fighting since January 1944, and their lines of communications, which kept them supplied with fuel, ammunition and food, now stretched for many hundreds of kilometers. The Front's aviation was experiencing fuel shortages and difficulties with the field airstrips.

General Manteuffel, the former commander of *Grossdeutschland*, after the war gave a lecture to American officers at the General Staff College in Fort Leavenworth, Kansas, in which he gave the following information on the condition of *Grossdeutschland* on 1 May 1944, on the eve of the next stage of fighting for Târgu Frumos [Editor's note: I have borrowed the format and wording from Table 5.3 in David Glantz's *Red Storm over the Balkans*]:

The **Panzer Regiment** comprising:
1.  One battalion of MK IV tanks with four companies and a total of 40 tanks
2.  Two battalions of MK V [Panther] tanks, each battalion with four companies and 40 tanks, for a total of 80 tanks

3.   One battalion of MK VI [Tiger] tanks with four companies and a total of 40 total tanks
4.   For a grand total of 160 tanks

Two infantry regiments [Grenadier and Fusilier], each with three battalions with four companies of 100 men each and heavy weapons companies:

1.   The **Panzer Grenadier Regiment** with one battalion in halftracks and two in lorries
2.   The **Panzer Fusilier Regiment** with one battalion in halftracks and two in scout cars

Two views of an SU-85 seized by the enemy in the Pîrlița Sat area, Romania, April 1944.

A **Reconnaissance Battalion** at two-thirds strength

An **Anti-aircraft Battalion** with three batteries of 88mm guns and one battery of 37mm guns

An **Armored Artillery Regiment** with four battalions, each battalion with three batteries, one tracked and three lorry-drawn

An **Assault Gun Battalion** with about 40 guns

An **Engineer [Pioneer] Battalion**

**Summary**: *Grossdeutschland* Division had 160 tanks, 24 infantry companies with a total bayonet [combat] strength of 2,400 men, 12 artillery batteries, 40 assault guns, and a comprehensive air defense, part of which could be employed in an antitank role

In the future, the data given by Manteuffel in his lecture on the composition of the *Grossdeutschland* Panzer Grenadier Division were repeated in many serious studies of the fighting at Târgu Frumos. For example, Manteuffel's numbers were cited by Helmuth Spaeter and David Glantz in their respective works. However, some scholars question Manteuffel's figures. For example, Hans-Joachim Jung, in his history of *Grossdeutschland*'s panzer regiment, reports that in reality, the panzer regiment never had more than 25 Pz. IV, 12 Pz. V, 10 Pz. VI and 25 StuG combat-fit. This gives a total of approximately 72 tanks and self-propelled guns. This differs from Manteuffel's higher figures by 88 armored vehicles. Thus did Manteuffel double his armor strength? And what was the sense of doing this in his lecture to the American officers? If he stopped the Soviet offensive at Târgu Frumos with only 72 tanks and self-propelled guns, instead of the 160 given by him in the lecture, this would have only have been a major plus for him, for achieving a victory with much less strength.

When preparing his lecture, Manteuffel apparently didn't have any actual reports on the amount of tanks in the division on 1 May 1944, so he gave figures according to the table strength of tanks in the battalions, not their real numbers. In fact, only one Panther battalion of *Grossdeutschland* actually took part in the fighting at Târgu Frumos, namely, I./Pz.Rgt. 26, since the division's own Panther battalion, I./Pz.Rgt. GD, although carried on the unit roster of *Grossdeutschland*, was actually located in France, and arrived on the Eastern Front only in July 1944, whereupon it operated separately from its parent division. There weren't 80 Pz. Vs in his division, as he indicated to his American audiences, but only approximately 40. Thus Manteuffel actually did exaggerate the number of Panthers in his division. According to archival documents, on 1 May 1944 the Panther battalion had 19 combat-ready Panthers, plus 8 Panthers undergoing short-term repairs. More Panthers were undergoing major overhauls.

In addition, there is information that the following replacements had been shipped from the factory for I./Pz.Rgt. 26 alone: 8 Panthers on 22 April 1944 and 16 Panthers on 23 April, which arrived on 1-2 May, but it is unknown whether they were included in a report on the battalion's strength produced on 1 May 1944. Reinforcements were arriving in the battalion throughout the fighting in Romania. For example, another 16 Panthers were sent on 6-7 May. Eight more Panthers arrived for the battalion on 9 May, followed by another 8 Panthers on 28 May. [Source: http://www.panther1944.de/en/sdkfz-171-pzkpfwg-panther/truppenteile/panther-zuweisungslisten/panther-zuweisungsliste-1944.html].

One very important detail: Manteuffel, and many other western scholars of these battles together with him, forgot to mention the assets attached to *Grossdeutschland* in the fighting at Târgu Frumos, but they were significant. For example, Kamen Nevenkin in his book *Fire Brigades*, citing German archival sources, revealed that *Grossdeutschland* in this fighting was reinforced with a Pz. IV battalion and a company of Tigers from the *Totenkopf* Panzer Division, a battery of StuG assault guns from the 325th Assault Gun Brigade, and with at least one battery of the 228th Assault Gun Brigade. Thus, in the fighting near Târgu Frumos between 1 and 10 May

1944, the *Grossdeutschland* Panzer Grenadier Division had one battalion of Panthers (I/Pz.Rgt. 26), two battalions of Pz. IV (its own and the battalion from *Totenkopf*), a battalion of Tigers and a company of Tigers from *Totenkopf*, a battalion of StuG assault guns (its own) and another 2-3 batteries of assault guns. All this adds up to approximately 200 tanks and assault guns alone. A genuine assessment of the *Grossdeutschland* Division at the start of the fighting near Târgu Frumos (on 2 May 1944) would estimate that it had approximately 40 Panthers, 30 Tigers, 80 Pz. IV, and 50 StuG. Thus did Manteuffel really exaggerate the number of tanks and self-propelled guns that he had under his command on 2 May 1944?

As the reader can see, Manteuffel not only didn't exaggerate his strength, but substantially understated the amount of armor in the *Grossdeutschland* Panzer Grenadier Division, and forgot to include its attached assets. In addition to the reinforcements in tanks, *Grossdeutschland* also had reinforcements in the form of infantry and artillery units, about which Manteuffel also modestly kept silent. Thus, on the axis of the main attack launched by the weakened 2nd Tank Army, a very strong German grouping was occupying the defense and preparing for counterattacks. In addition, the 24th Panzer Division was located here, which had redeployed on 30 April 1944 from the Iași area to the area of Podul Iloaie and the Iași – Târgu Frumos highway, where it was given the task to be ready to counterattack the enemy on the right flank of the *Grossdeutschland* Division. According to archival records and the division's combat journal, on 1 May 1944 the 24th Panzer Division had one Bef.Pz.III. 14 StuG III and 33 Pz. IV in the Pz.Rgt.Stb. 24 and III./Pz.Rgt. 24, plus 2 Pz.Beob.III and 4 StuH 42 in I./Pz.Art.Rgt. 24 for a total of 36 tanks and 18 assault guns. It also had two batteries of Hummel and Brumbar self-propelled artillery. Here, the dominance of the *Luftwaffe* in the air should also be noted, which also served to frustrate the Soviet forces' offensive.

## The course of the operation from 2 May to 5 May 1944

On 2 May 1944, after a 65-minute artillery preparation, units of the 2nd Tank Army went on the offensive. The narrative will first discuss the 16th Tank Corps' offensive, before turning to the attack of the 3rd Tank Corps.

The 16th Tank Corps's 107th Tank Brigade advanced together with the 737th Rifle Regiment in the direction of the isolated huts of Bosia, with the assignment to take the northwestern portion of Târgu Frumos with an attack from the northeast; its 109th Tank Brigade attacked in the direction of Făcuti together with the 748th Rifle Regiment; and the 164th Tank Brigade attacked along the axis of Hill 198, Hill 192, Făcuti in cooperation with the 722nd Rifle Regiment. The 15th Motorized Rifle Brigade, advancing behind the combat formations of the 107th and 109th Tank Brigades had the assignment to consolidate the lines seized by the tanks and to push through Târgu Frumos to its southern outskirts.

Our air force was covering the combat formations of the forces with air strikes, targeting the enemy's system of defense and aggregations of tanks and infantry. As the result of an energetic advance, by 11.00 on 2 May, the 107th Tank Brigade reached the Târgu Frumos – Iași highway, 2 kilometers east of Târgu Frumos. The 109th Tank Brigade took possession of Făcuti and continued to pursue the enemy in the direction of Târgu Frumos. The following 164th Tank Brigade reached the line of Hill 192, after which it attacked toward Făcuti to assist the 109th Tank Brigade.

By this time, the left flank had become exposed and was threatening the corps' units from the east. At an order from the commander of the 16th Tank Corps, the 164th Tank Brigade and the 15th Motorized Rifle Brigade pivoted sharply to the east and covered the flank. By 12.00, the Soviet troops had fought their way into the northwestern outskirts of Ulmi Vechi.

The 6th Guards Heavy Tank Regiment moved out on the attack from its jumping-off positions on the northwestern outskirts of Hodora at 5:30 on 2 May and reached the line of deployment at 6.05. At 6.20 the heavy tanks went on the attack, with the 2nd Tank Company following the 107th Tank Brigade, the 1st Tank Company supporting the 109th Tank Brigade, and the left-flank 3rd Tank Company following the 164th Tank Brigade. Its 4th Tank Company trailed the left-flank 3rd Tank Company at a distance of 500-600 meters. At 7.45, the IS Stalin tanks reached the southern slopes of Hill 192. At this time, the enemy launched an infantry counterattack from the direction of the southeastern slopes of Hill 192. The infantry counterattack was repulsed by the rifle units, after which the enemy withdrew the 5-6 tanks on this axis, which hadn't become involved in the fighting. At 9.40 the tanks of the 6th Guards Heavy Tank Regiment approached Făcuti, in the area of which they began to search for a way to cross an obstructing stream, the final obstacle between it and Târgu Frumos. While searching for a ford or bridge, the regiment's tanks moved off to the left (which is to say, to the east).

At 10.30 the enemy in strength of up to 8-10 tanks launched a counterattack from the direction of the southern slopes of Hill 256. At the order of the 16th Tank Corps commander, the 4th Tank Company of the 6th Guards Heavy Tank Regiment was switched to the right flank in order to repel the counterattack. Two enemy tanks were knocked out, and the enemy counterattack was stopped. At 11.30, the enemy undertook an attack from along the Târgu Frumos highway to the north with up to 16 tanks and a battalion of infantry, threatening to envelop the 107th Tank Brigade. At 14.00, this tank brigade fell back to the southern slopes of Hill 184, where the motorized infantry and the 737th Rifle Regiment took up a defense.

Earlier that morning at 9.00, an assault group of the 107th Tank Brigade consisting of three T-34 tanks operating together with infantry had broken into the northern outskirts of Balş, where they were ambushed by 9 enemy tanks. As a result, our tanks had all been brewed up or knocked out.

At 12.30, the 109th Tank Brigade attacking on the Hill 192 – Polieni axis had run into the enemy in strength of up to a battalion of infantry, supported by 12 Tigers and 4 self-propelled guns. Units of the 206th Rifle Division were unable to withstand the enemy's onslaught and began to fall back to Hill 192. The tanks covered the infantry's withdrawal with fire from fixed positions. Having pulled back to the line of Hill 192, the infantry dug in and brought the enemy's advance to a halt.

The 164th Tank Brigade at 12.30 ran into the enemy in strength of up to two infantry companies, supported by 6 Pz. VI tanks, which were counterattacking out of the area of the southern slopes of Hill 180 in the direction of Polieni and Ulmi Vechi. Rebuffing the enemy's attack and suffering losses, the tank brigade was compelled to fall back to a hill west of Ulmi Vechi, where it took up advantageous positions and went over to a firm defense.

In the sector of the 15th Motorized Rifle Brigade, the enemy launched a counterattack at 13.00, aiming the main blow at the brigade's left flank. Simultaneously, up to 30 tanks moved out along the road leading from Ulmi Vechi to Făcuti, which opened fire at the infantry's combat positions. At 15.00 the brigade fell back by 2 kilometers and dug in on the line of the southeastern and northern slopes of Hill 192. In this action, the artillerymen and commander of the rifle brigade's artillery battalion Major Ivanov were high models of resolve. Covering the infantry's retreat, the artillery battalion fired at the enemy's infantry and tanks, and destroyed 4 of the latter.

Early the next morning at 5.00 on 3 May 1944, tanks of the 107th Tank Brigade made an isolated penetration to the outskirts of Târgu Frumos, far in advance of the flanking units. There, they ran into the strong resistance of enemy tanks and engaged them in battle. Lieutenant Grechko fought heroically in this combat action. Using folds in the terrain, he took cover behind a haystack, approached to within 600-800 meters of a Tiger, set it afire with an armor-piercing discarding sabot shell, and then with machine-gun fire shot down the crew as they fled from the burning tank. With an accurately placed high-explosive shell, he destroyed a supply truck loaded with ammunition that was moving along the highway out of Târgu Frumos. After the commander

Grechko was wounded, the turret machine gunner Sergeant Serikaev assumed command of the tank, and with accurate fire, destroyed a hostile tank. The enemy continued to counterattack, and the tanks of the 107th Tank Brigade fell back to the southeastern slopes of Hill 256.

Regarding the 3rd Tank Corps' attack, launched between 5.00 and 6.10 on 2 May 1944, the artillery of the 35th Rifle Corps, the 3rd Tank Corps and of other artillery units conducted an artillery preparation, concentrating on the forward edge and tactical depth of the enemy's defenses. The preparatory barrage was ineffective, because the enemy, aware of the offensive preparations, had pulled back personnel and equipment from the forward edge before it began. Once the artillery barrage ended, the men and equipment moved back into their forward positions. At 6.15 on 2 May, the formations and units of the 3rd Tank Corps went on the attack out of their jumping-off positions in the general direction of Târgu Frumos.

The 103rd Tank Brigade, consisting of 10 T-34 tanks, in cooperation with infantry of the 3rd Guards Airborne Division, broke the resistance of enemy tanks, self-propelled guns and anti-tank guns on the northern outskirts of Cucuteni after savage fighting and reached the northern slopes of Hill 256 by 9.00 on 2 May. In the course of this action, the tank brigade had lost 4 tanks. At 9.00, the enemy counterattacked the 103rd Tank Brigade from the southwestern slopes of Hill 256 with 10 Tiger tanks and a battalion of infantry with air support. The 103rd Tank Brigade repulsed the enemy counterattack, while knocking out or destroying 7 enemy tanks, and dug in on the line it had achieved on the northern slopes of Hill 256, in expectation of the approach of infantry of the 3rd Guards Airborne Division, which had been cut off from the tanks on the southern outskirts of Cucuteni by strong enemy artillery fire and machine-gun fire from Hill 256. Up until 15.00, the enemy launched four counterattacks against the 103rd Tank Brigade in strength of 7-10 Tiger tanks, with the support of two battalions of infantry, artillery fire, and bombers. Repelling the enemy's furious counterattacks, the tank brigade jointly with the 8th Guards Heavy Tank Regiment over the course of 6 hours was engaged in savage combat, which resulted in the loss of 3 T-34 tanks burned-out and 4 T-34 tanks knocked-out; of their crews, 5 men were killed and 10 were wounded.

The remaining three tanks and the motorized rifle battalion of the 103rd Tank Brigade were pulled out of combat back into the reserve at 15.00 on 2 May at the order of the 3rd Tank Corps commander, and took up a defense on the southern outskirts of Balusesti and Stroesti. The 8th Guards Heavy Tank Regiment, having lost two of its heavy tanks, by 15.00 2 May had withdrawn together with units of the 3rd Guards Airborne Division to the northern outskirts of Cucuteni, where it took up a defense behind the combat positions of the 3rd Guards Airborne Division with the assignment to prevent an enemy breakthrough to the north.

The 50th Tank Brigade, consisting of 10 tanks, together with the 57th Motorized Rifle Brigade and acting in concert with units of the 93rd Guards Rifle Division, by 7.30 on 2 May had broken the enemy resistance, seized Hill 197, and was continuing to fight for possession of Hill 184. By 11.30, having overcome bitter resistance of the enemy defending the hill with a force of up to a battalion of infantry, supported by 3 tanks, anti-tank guns and airstrikes, the tank brigade took Hill 184.

At 12.00, the enemy counterattacked the 50th Tank Brigade from the direction of a ravine lying 4 kilometers northeast of Târgu Frumos with a group of 10 Tiger tanks and a battalion of infantry, supported by artillery and bombers. Resisting the enemy counterattack, the 50th Tank Brigade lost 3 tanks and with a bounding retrograde movement fell back to the northern slopes of Hill 197.

The 57th Motorized Rifle Brigade, consisting of three rifle battalions was advancing directly behind the 50th Tank Brigade together with the 375th Heavy Self-propelled Artillery Regiment, and by 11.40 on 2 May, it had come up in support of the tanks of the 50th Tank Brigade on the southern slopes of Hill 197, where together with the tanks of the 50th Tank Brigade they fought to repel the enemy counterattack by tanks and infantry.

At 16.00 on 2 May 1944, the 51st Tank Brigade with 9 tanks and a company of submachine gunners was introduced into the fighting by the commander of the 3rd Tank Corps, and launched an attack along the axis of a nameless hamlet lying 1.5 kilometers northeast of Hill 255, Hill 255, Hill 184, Târgu Frumos from its jumping-off line on the southern outskirts of Balusesti and Stroesti. The 51st Tank Brigade had the order to break through to the eastern outskirts of Târgu Frumos, where it was to cut the highway and railroad and to hold them until the main forces of the 3rd Tank Corps came up.

Together with four tanks of the 50th Tank Brigade and in cooperation with the 57th Motorized Rifle Brigade and the 93rd Guards Rifle Division, the 51st Tank Brigade, struggling against heavy enemy fire and tank counterattacks, by the end of the day had taken the hamlet lying 1.5 kilometers northeast of Hill 255 and had reached the southern slopes of a hill northwest of Hill 184. Not stopping, the 51st Tank Brigade in the course of the night bypassed Hill 184 along a passage it had found through swampy terrain southeast of two nameless lakes, outflanked the enemy defenders, and by 6.00 on 3 May had reached a line just 2 kilometers northeast of Târgu Frumos, where it exchanged fire with enemy tanks and infantry that were defending along the northeastern outskirts of the town. By this time, the infantry of the 57th Motorized Rifle Brigade and the 93rd Guards Rifle Division, with the support of the 50th Tank Brigade's tanks, had taken Hill 184 after some bitter fighting and repeated enemy counterattacks. Further advance by the infantry was stopped by strong artillery and mortar fire and enemy machine-gun fire from Hill 189, another hill lying southeast of Hill 184, and the hamlet of Bosna.

According to the 2nd Tank Army's journal of combat operations, by the end of 2 May 1944, the army had a total of 84 operational tanks and self-propelled guns, including 51 T-34, 9 IS-122, 19 SU-152 and 5 SU-85. Over the day of combat on 2 May, the 2nd Tank Army lost 19 T-34 and 2 IS-122 destroyed, and another 11 T-34 and 9 IS-122 knocked-out, for a total of 41 tanks. In return, it claimed the destruction of 11 enemy tanks and self-propelled guns, 10 halftracks and 4 trucks, and the killing of 400 enemy soldiers and officers. Four prisoners were taken, all from the *Grossdeutschland* Panzer Grenadier Division. General Manteuffel, the former commander of *Grossdeutschland*, estimated that the Soviet forces irrevocably lost 350 tanks on the first day of the offensive, while placing *Grossdeutschland*'s losses at 6 tanks destroyed, and another 8 tanks disabled and evacuated.

A document on the status and supplies of the 2nd Tank Army's forces at 6.00 on 3.5.44 states:

3rd Tank Corps: has combat-fit 19 T-34, 3 IS-85 and 19 ISU-152, for a total of 41 machines. Supply of ammunition for the tanks – 1.5 combat loads, 120mm shells – 0.2 of a combat load; 82mm shells – 0.3 of a combat load. 85mm artillery rounds – 1 combat load, 76mm – 1 combat load, 37mm – 2 combat loads, 45mm – 0.2 of a combat load. Diesel fuel – 1 refill, gasoline – 0.2 of a refill.

16th Tank Corps: has combat-fit 15 T-34, 5 SU-85, 2 Mark IX, 9 IS-122, for a total of 31 machines. Supply of ammunition for the tanks – 1 combat load, 120mm shells – 0.2 of a combat load. Artillery rounds 85mm – 1 combat load, 76mm – 0.4 of a combat load, 37mm – 1.2 combat loads. Diesel fuel – 0.8 of a refill, gasoline – 0.2 of a refill.

11th Guards Tank Brigade: has serviceable 17 T-34 tanks, ammunition – 1.4 combat loads, diesel fuel – 1.4 refills, gasoline – 0.1 of a refill.

In total, the army has 53 T-34, 9 IS-122, 3 Mark IX, 19 ISU-152, 3 IS-85, 5 SU-85, for a total of 92 serviceable tanks and self-propelled guns.

[Signed] Chief of the Operations Department Colonel Bazanov

Although he still lacked the support of infantry, which had lagged behind, the commander of the 51st Tank Brigade continued to follow his orders. Overcoming enemy resistance, the 51st Tank Brigade by 10.00 3 May covered the last 2 kilometers separating it from the town and reached the northern outskirts of Târgu Frumos with three tanks, and the railroad east of Târgu Frumos with six tanks. The brigade then consolidated on the line it had reached in order to wait for the approach of the infantry and artillery, and exchanged fire with the enemy defenders in Târgu Frumos. The tanks of the 50th Tank Brigade were attacking jointly with the infantry, and by 10.00 were exchanging fire with the enemy on the western slopes of Hill 184. The 375th Heavy Self-propelled Artillery Regiment rolled forward in the wake of the advancing infantry, and by 10.00 it was adding to the fire on the enemy atop Hill 184.

At 11.00, the enemy struck the 51st Tank Brigade in the flank with 30 tanks that had approached along the highway from Iaşi, with the support of strong artillery fire and heavy air strikes. Simultaneously, the enemy counterattacked the 93rd Guards Rifle Division, the 57th Motorized Rifle Brigade and the 50th Tank Brigade on the slopes of Hill 184 with up to a battalion of infantry and five tanks. The counterattack was preceded by a strike of 40 enemy bombers against our units, as a result of which two of the 50th Tank Brigade's remaining T-34s were destroyed by direct hits. This enemy counterattack was repulsed with the help of the 375th Heavy Self-propelled Artillery Regiment. Meanwhile, the 51st Tank Brigade was engaged in a fierce 3-hour-long battle with the enemy tanks. The Soviet crews, maneuvering in unfavorable terrain conditions in a cramped sector, fought heroically. As a result of the heavy fighting, the 51st Tank Brigade lost 7 tanks burned-out and an additional tank knocked-out. Among the crews, 11 men were killed and 15 wounded. Eventually, the brigade had to withdraw to the western slopes of a hill lying northwest of Hill 184.

At 17.00 on 3 May, after five air raids by enemy bombers against the positions of the 375th Guards Heavy Self-propelled Regiment, the 57th Motorized Rifle Brigade and the 93rd Guards Rifle Division on Hill 184, the enemy again counterattacked them with 13 tanks from the western slopes of the Bosia hill, and with 7 tanks from Hill 189, supported by the fire of heavy artillery. The enemy attack struck the defenses of the 3rd Tank Corps on Hill 184 with a concentric attack, outflanking it on both the left and the right. The *Luftwaffe* incessantly bombed the combat positions of the corps' defending units with groups of 35-40 aircraft. The 375th Guards Heavy Self-propelled Artillery, maneuvering on the battlefield, fought to repel the enemy's flanking tank attacks. As a result of bitter fighting that lasted for three hours, the 375th Heavy Self-propelled Artillery Regiment repulsed three enemy tank attacks and claimed the destruction of 2 German tanks and to have knocked out 6 more tanks and 3 self-propelled guns. The losses of the 375th Self-propelled Artillery Regiment as a result of the fighting and the enemy airstrikes were 9 ISU-152 destroyed, and three more of the heavy self-propelled guns disabled. Altogether in the course of 3 May, six enemy counterattacks against Hill 184, each with the participation of up to a battalion of infantry and 8-20 tanks, were foiled by the units of the 3rd Tank Corps.

At 9.00 on 3 May, the enemy in strength of up to an infantry regiment with the support of four tanks, two self-propelled guns, artillery and aviation had counterattacked the 3rd Guards Airborne Division and the 8th Guards Heavy Tank Regiment that were defending the northern outskirts of Cucuteni. Having lost both self-propelled guns and up to 200 killed and wounded from the fire from the tanks of the 8th Guards Heavy Tank Regiment, the enemy fell back to the jumping-off position.

By the end of 3 May 1944, units of the 3rd Tank Corps together with units of the 93rd Guards Rifle Division and the 3rd Guards Airborne Division were defending a line running from the southern outskirts of Cucuteni to Hill 184. In the course of the fighting on that day, units of the 3rd Tank Corps knocked out or destroyed 27 enemy tanks and self-propelled guns. In return, the corps lost 9 T-34 destroyed and burned-out, 1 T-34 knocked-out and 9 ISU-152 burned out, with

3 more ISU-152 knocked out, for a total of 22 tanks and self-propelled guns. Having lost up to 60 percent of its tanks and self-propelled guns and a significant number of men in the course of the fighting on 2 and 3 May, on the basis of Combat Order No.077/OP from the commander of the 2nd Tank Army, the units of the 3rd Tank Corps went over to a defense of its achieved lines, with the 57th Motorized Rifle Brigade defending the western slopes of Hill 184; the 51st Tank Brigade (with one T-34 tank and its motorized rifle battalion) – 1 kilometer north of Hill 184; the 50th Tank Brigade (with two T-34 tanks and its motorized rifle battalion – a nameless hill 2 kilometers northwest of Hill 184; the 375th Guards Heavy Self-propelled Artillery Regiment (with four SU-152 self-propelled guns) – the southern outskirts of a nameless hamlet; the 8th Guards Heavy Tank Regiment – the southeastern outskirts of Băiceni; and the 103rd Tank Brigade in the corps commander's reserve on the southern outskirts of Balusesti and Stroesti. By the end of 3 May 1944, the 3rd Tank Corps had only 10 T-34, 8 ISU-152, and 3 IS tanks.

Returning to the 16th Tank Corps' actions, at 5.00 on 3 May 1944 the 107th Tank Brigade with a swift attack had broken into the northern outskirts of Târgu Frumos, but lacking the support of accompanying infantry, it fell back to the southeastern slopes of Hill 256 after heavy fighting. The 109th Tank Brigade, having been switched to the 16th Tank Corps' right flank by the dawn of 3 May, took up jumping-off positions for an attack on a line 2 kilometers east of Hill 184. After a short artillery preparation, the brigade went on the attack toward Hill 184 and the northern outskirts of Târgu Frumos. The enemy was shelling the brigade's combat formations with strong artillery and mortar fire, and in the course of the day launched 4 counterattacks. All of the counterattacks were driven back. Only toward the end of the day, when the enemy began outflanking it on the left and right, did the 109th Tank Brigade fall back to the southern slopes of Hill 192. The 164th Tank Brigade remained in its occupied positions and stubbornly held them, securing the combat operations of the 16th Tank Corps from possible counterattacks by enemy infantry and tanks from the left. The 15th Motorized Rifle Brigade remained in its defensive positions. By the end of the day, units of the corps had firmly dug in on the line: nameless lake northeast of Hill 174 – southeastern slopes of Hill 192 – northern outskirts of Ulmi Vechi. Having deployed the tanks behind the infantry's combat positions, the troops were prepared to repel enemy counterattacks.

In David Glantz's opinion, the 16th Tank Corps' 107th and 109th Tank Brigades had attempted to drive a breach in the German defenses in the sector of Dădești and Hill 189, 3 kilometers northwest of Târgu Frumos, and to exploit in the direction of the city. However, they only managed to make a 2- to 3-kilometer advance, since the main forces of the *Grossdeutschland* Panzer Grenadier Division and of the 24th Panzer Division were blocking their path of advance. By the end of the day, the units of the 16th Tank Corps had returned to their jumping-off areas.

The 6th Guards Heavy Tank Regiment had received a verbal order from the commander of the 16th Tank Corps to advance behind the combat formations of the 107th Tank Brigade in the direction of Târgu Frumos. At 6.00 on 3 May, after the tanks of the 107th Tank Brigade had crossed a stream lying 2 kilometers northwest of Hill 184, the 6th Guards Heavy Tank Regiment moved out, following behind the 107th Tank Brigade at a distance of 500-600 meters. Once the tanks had reached the line of the southern slopes of Hill 184 and the highway leading to Târgu Frumos, the enemy had opened flanking fire from heavy tanks that were deployed in ambush positions on Hill 189 and another hill lying 1.5 kilometers west of Bosia. After a brief exchange of fire, the T-34 tanks had been forced to retreat, which left the heavy IS tanks to contend with the enemy's heavy tanks. The enemy's advantageous position, firing from concealed positions, had its effect. After a two-hour combat, the enemy had managed to disable four IS tanks.

Having brought up infantry, and with the support of concentrated air attacks and artillery, the enemy went on the counterattack along the roads leading to the north. The disabled Soviet tanks, which were immobilized but had continued to fire, were destroyed by the fire of German heavy tanks and by enemy tank-busting aircraft. Over the course of 3 May 1944, the 6th Guards

Joseph Stalin tanks of the 6th Guards Heavy Tank Regiment knocked-out in the area of Târgu Frumos, May 1944.

Heavy Tank Regiment lost a total of six IS tanks burned-out and three IS tanks disabled. Losses in personnel amounted to 76 men. In return, the 6th Guards Heavy Tank Regiment claimed the destruction of 10 German tanks, 20 guns, 18 wheeled vehicles, 8 mortars and up to 80 enemy infantry. On the night of 3-4 May, at an order from the commander of the 16th Tank Corps, the 6th Guards Heavy Tank Regiment was pulled out of combat and re-assembled in the Hodora area for repairs and refitting.

On 2 May 1944, the 11th Guards Tank Brigade had received the assignment to advance in the wake of the 3rd Tank Corps, in readiness to repel enemy counterattacks from the direction of Roman and Iași. At 8.30 on 3 May, the brigade had reached the southern outskirts of a nameless hamlet south of Lake Hirbu with 19 T-34 tanks. At this point, an order had arrived from the commander of the 2nd Tank Army to attack Cucuteni from the southeast and to take that village. The 93rd Guards Rifle Division reported that Cucuteni was occupied, and the 11th Guards Tank Brigade sent four tanks to scout in that direction. At 9.00 on 2 May, the enemy attacked units of the 16th Tank Corps in strength of up to 18 tanks out of the Valea Oilor area to the northwest, and from the outskirts of Polieni with 6 tanks to the west. At the verbal order of the 2nd Tank Army commander, units of the 11th Guards Tank Brigade at 14.00 reached the area south of Polieni-Nouă with the task to counterattack the enemy.

At 16.20 on 2 May 1944, the brigade went on the attack in a general direction to the south toward a point on the highway 1.5 kilometers east of Târgu Frumos; by 21.00, it had reached the southeastern slopes of Hill 192. At 5.30 on 3 May, the 11th Guards Tank Brigade resumed its attack, and by 7.00 the brigade's units had reached the highway 1.5 kilometers east of Târgu Frumos. The attack was energetic; the enemy in panic abandoned up to 30 guns and fled to the south. By 9.00 on 3 May, the 11th Guards Tank Brigade had reached the eastern bank of a nameless stream, which flows beside a tiny settlement 1 kilometer northeast of Târgu Frumos. The commander of the 1st Tank Battalion Guards Major Kalashnikov searched for a crossing with three T-34 tanks, while the other tanks of the brigade supported them with fire from place. At this time, the enemy brought up seven tanks, a mixture of Tigers and Panthers. Lacking support of infantry and artillery, the three T-34 tanks were brewed up in combat. With this, the enemy managed to stabilize his line and to restore order to his units. The tanks of the 11th Guards Tank Brigade, with no artillery support and only a small number of tank riders, continued to struggle against the enemy's tanks and artillery up until 19.40 3 May. As a result, the tank brigade's subsequent attacks had no success and the brigade suffered significant losses.

At 19.30 on 3 May 1944, the enemy attacked out of an area northwest of Târgu Frumos in strength of seven Tiger tanks and out of areas northeast of Târgu Frumos with five tanks with the support of up to a battalion of infantry, threatening to envelop the units of the 11th Guards Tank Brigade. Once the 11th Guards Tank Brigade's strength had dropped to just one tank still capable of offering battle, at an order from the headquarters of the 2nd Tank Army, those tanks still mobile were withdrawn to the area northeast of Hill 184 and took up a defense. In the course of the night between 3 and 4 May 1944, and over the day of 4 May, the 11th Guards Tank Brigade remained on the defense and worked to bring materiél back to working order. On 5 May 1944, the brigade had 7 T-34 tanks combat-ready, with three more T-34 under repair. Nine of its T-34 tanks had been lost irrevocably, having brewed up in the fighting.

### Excerpts from the Letters of Commendation for those soldiers and officers of the 11th Guards Tank Brigade who distinguished themselves in the fighting near Târgu Frumos

**Aleksei Syrov**, Guards Junior Lieutenant, tank commander. On 3.05.44, while scouting with combat and in an attack toward Târgu Frumos, he destroyed 2 enemy cannons and a heavy machine gun, and killed more than 30 soldiers and officers. He gave valuable information about the location of the enemy's infantry and artillery, thanks to which the element carried out its combat task. Worthy of decorating with the Order of the Red Star.

**Grigorii Krivenko**, Guards Junior Lieutenant, tank commander in the 2nd Tank Battalion. In the final action in the area of the city of Târgu Frumos alone, Comrade Krivenko was among the first to break into a village, destroyed 4 enemy guns with fire from his cannon, and slaughtered 30 enemy infantrymen. Worthy of decorating with the Order of the Red Star.

**Aleksei Petrukhin**, Guards Senior Lieutenant, commander of a tank platoon in the 1st Tank Battalion. Participating in the fighting for Târgu Frumos and skillfully handling the platoon, he inflicted great damage to the enemy. During an aerial bombing attack, his tank was set aflame by an enemy bomb. Not losing his cool, he hastily smothered the flames. Having put out the fire, he evacuated the tank to the brigade's collection point for damaged machines. In this fighting he destroyed 2 German tanks, 6 mortars, 4 cannons, 8 machine guns and 256 enemy soldiers and officers. Worthy of decorating with the Order of the Red Star.

**Dmitrii Barabash**, Guards Senior Lieutenant, company commander in the 1st Tank Battalion. In fighting in the Târgu Frumos area, he proved himself to be a bold and decisive company commander. Commanding his company, he fought off several enemy tank attacks. Despite the enemy's aerial bombing and artillery barrage on Hill 192, Barabash personally positioned the tanks and directed the combat. From his tank he personally destroyed (brewed up) two enemy tanks, 5 mortars, 3 cannons, 4 machine guns and up to 100 soldiers and officers. In combat training, Comrade Barabash's company occupies the top place in the battalion. Worthy of decorating with the Order of the Red Star.

**Efim Garkavenko**, Guards Junior Lieutenant, tank platoon commander in the 1st Tank Battalion. In the fighting between 2 and 6 May 1944, he commanded a platoon of T-34 tanks. He skillfully repulsed several hostile enemy tank attacks, in the process demonstrating courage and valor. When his machine was disabled and no longer able to move, he refused to abandon it on the battlefield; having waited for darkness, he repaired it and resumed the attack. Over the period of combat, he inflicted the following damage to the enemy: he destroyed 2 mortars and 3 machine guns, and killed 40 soldiers and officers. Until his final minute, Garkavenko remained on the battlefield and refused to retreat without orders. In combat on 6.05.44, he died the death of the brave. Worthy of decorating with the Order of the Patriotic War, 1st Degree.

According to the 2nd Tank Army's journal of combat operations, by the end of 3 May 1944, the army had a total of just 42 serviceable tanks and self-propelled guns: 26 T-34, 2 IS-85, 4 IS-122, 5 SU-152 and 5 SU-85. The army's losses over the day of combat on 3 May were 16 T-34 tanks and 4 SU-152 self-propelled guns destroyed, plus 3 T-34 tanks knocked-out. Damage inflicted to the enemy: 6 tanks destroyed (including three Tigers), 3 aircraft shot down, 30 guns of various calibers destroyed, as well as 7 anti-tank rifles, 13 machine guns and 2 halftracks.

On the evening of 3 May, the 16th Tank Corps' chief of staff issued a report on the 16th Tank Corps' current combat strength, the losses it had suffered over the day, and the damage it claimed that it inflicted on the enemy:

> 107th Tank Brigade – 3 serviceable tanks, 1 76mm gun, 3 82mm mortars, 6 DShK heavy machine guns. Active combat strength of 48 men. Losses for 3.5.44: 6 tanks knocked-out, 2 tanks destroyed; 36 men killed and 12 men wounded. Enemy losses: 7 tanks, 3 guns of various calibers, 7 machine guns, 2 vehicles and 3 halftracks destroyed; up to 150 soldiers and officers killed.

Commander of a tank battalion
in the 11th Guards Tank Brigade,
Guards Major Prokofii Kalashnikov.

109th Tank Brigade – 4 serviceable tanks, 3 76mm guns, 9 DShK heavy machine guns; active combat strength of 120 men. Losses for 3.5.44: 2 tanks destroyed, 1 tank knocked-out; 7 men killed and 21 men wounded. Enemy losses: 3 machine guns and 30 rifles destroyed, up to 65 soldiers and officers killed.

164th Tank Brigade – 2 serviceable tanks, 2 76mm guns, 2 120mm mortars, 3 RPD light machine guns, 154 riflemen and submachine gunners. Losses for 3.5.44: 4 men wounded. Enemy losses: the fire of 2 mortars suppressed and 8 soldiers killed.

15th Motorized Rifle Brigade – 528 riflemen, 96 submachine gunners; 660 rifles, 443 PPSh submachine guns, 22 82mm mortars, 4 120mm mortars, 7 45mm guns, 7 76mm guns. Losses for 3.5.44: 2 men killed, 7 men wounded. Enemy losses: up to 30 soldiers and officers killed.

6th Guards Tank Regiment – 4 serviceable tanks; losses are being ascertained.

Corps artillery: 226th Army Mortar Regiment – 26 120mm mortars; 729th Destroyer Anti-tank Artillery Regiment – 4 85mm guns; 1441st Self-propelled Artillery Regiment – 4 SU-85; 1721st Anti-aircraft Artillery Regiment – 8 37mm anti-aircraft guns. Losses for 3.5.44: 1 85mm gun destroyed, 1 knocked-out; 1 76mm gun knocked-out; 1 man killed, 2 men wounded.

On the following morning at 6.00, the 2nd Tank Army's chief of operations Colonel Bazanov issued a report on the strength and supplies of the 2nd Tank Army's forces:

> 3rd Tank Corps: has serviceable 11 T-34, 2 IS-85, and 15 ISU-152 for a total of 28 tanks and self-propelled guns. Ammunition for tanks – 2.3 combat loads, for the ISU-152 – 1 combat load, for the rest of the artillery – 1 combat load. Diesel fuel – 1.5 refills; gasoline – 0.2 of a refill. 16th Tank Corps: has serviceable 10 T-34, 5 SU-85, and 4 IS-122 for a total of 19 tanks and self-propelled guns. Ammunition for tanks – 1 combat load; diesel fuel – 1 refill, gasoline – 0.2 of a refill. 11th Guards Tank Brigade: has 5 T-34 tanks serviceable, 1 combat load of ammunition, 1 refill of diesel fuel, and no gasoline. In total, the 2nd Tank Army has 52 serviceable tanks and self-propelled guns: 26 T-34, 4 IS-122, 15 ISU-152, 2 IS-85 and 5 SU-85.
>
> [Signed Chief of 2nd Tank Army's Operations Department – Colonel Bazanov

At 7.00 on 4 May 1944, after a powerful barrage against the defenses of the units of the 3rd Tank Corps, the enemy from the direction of Hill 189 counterattacked the positions of the corps' units on Hill 184 with up to a company of infantry and 15 tanks. The counterattack was driven back by the fire of tanks, SU-152 and the corps' artillery. In the course of 4 May, the enemy counterattacked the positions of the 3rd Tank Corps three times from the direction of Hill 189 in strength of up to 15 tanks and a battalion of infantry, with the support of 40-70 bombers. The corps stubbornly held its occupied line. In the course of repelling the enemy counterattacks on 4 May 1944, the Germans lost 6 tanks knocked-out or destroyed, 6 guns, and up to 500 soldiers and officers. According to the 2nd Tank Army's combat journal, by the end of 4 May, the army had a total of 42 serviceable tanks and self-propelled guns, including 30 T-34, 5 IS-122, 3 SU-152 and 4 SU-85.

On the morning of 5 May 1944 at 6.00, Colonel Bazanov issued another document on the strength and supply levels of the 2nd Tank Army's forces:

> 3rd Tank Corps: has serviceable 11 T-34, 3 IS-85, 5 SU-152 for a total of 19 tanks and self-propelled guns. Ammunition supply for tanks and self-propelled guns – 2 combat loads; 120mm shells – 0.7 of a combat load; 82mm mortar shells – 1.7 combat loads; M-13 rocket – 2 salvoes; 85mm artillery shells – 1.2 combat loads, 76mm – 1.7 combat loads; 57mm – 1 combat load; 45mm – 0.7 of a combat load, 37mm – 1 combat load. Diesel fuel – 2 refills, gasoline – 1 refill. Rations – 2 days. 16th Tank Corps: has serviceable 10 T-34, 3 SU-85, 5 IS-122, for a total of 18 tanks and self-propelled guns. Ammunition supply for tanks – 1 combat load, 120mm shells – 0.4 of a combat load. Artillery shells – 1 combat load. Diesel fuel – 1 refill, gasoline – 0.2 of a refill. Rations: 1 day. 11th Guards Tank Brigade – has serviceable 9 T-34 tanks, 1 combat load of ammunition, 1.6 refills. Tanks of the army's command: 3 T-34, 2 Mark IX. In total, the army has 33 T-34, 5 IS-122, 2 Mark IX, 5 ISU-152, 3 IS-85, 3 SU-85, for a total of 51 tanks and self-propelled guns.
>
> [Signed] Chief of the 2nd Tank Army's Operations Department – Colonel Bazanov

At midnight, the 2nd Tank Army received an order from the command of the 2nd Ukrainian Front:

> Together with the infantry of the 35th Rifle Corps, resume the offensive on the morning of 5.5, resolutely breaking the enemy's resistance, and carry out the previously assigned mission

– the seizure of Târgu Frumos. By 4.00 on 5.5.44, merge all the tanks, motorized infantry battalions and anti-tank batteries of the 3rd Tank Corps' and 16th Tank Corps' tank brigades into a single composite tank brigade in each corps; withdraw all the remaining commands of the tank brigades to the rear, where they are immediately to take up combat training exercises.

On the night of 4-5 March 1944, the materiél and personnel of the 50th and 51st Tank Brigades were transferred to the 103rd Tank Brigade – a total of 13 tanks, plus 3 tanks that had just come up from repair shops, and the 103rd Tank Brigade on the morning of 5 May 1944 went on the attack in cooperation with the 57th Motorized Rifle Brigade. By 13.30, the 103rd Tank Brigade reached the southern slopes of a hill 1 kilometer east of Hill 256, where it took up a defense. In the course of repelling enemy counterattacks, the 103rd Tank Brigade knocked out 4 enemy tanks. The brigade's losses amounted to one T-34 burned-out, and two T-34 tanks knocked-out. At 22.30 on 5 May, on the basis of Combat Order No.079/OP from the 2nd Tank Army's headquarters, the units of the 3rd Tank Corps, with the exception of the 103rd Tank Brigade and the artillery units, having turned over their combat sectors to the 35th Guards Rifle Corps, by 6.00 had assembled in the Pârcovaci – Deleni area. The losses of the 2nd Tank Army in the fighting on 5 May 1944 amounted to 1 T-34 burned-out, 2 T-34 knocked-out, and 1 SU-152 knocked-out.

By the end of the day on 5 May, the 2nd Tank Army had operational 32 T-34, 5 IS-122, 2 IS-85, 2 M4A2, 3 SU-152 and 3 SU-85, for a total of 47 armored vehicles. On 6 May 1944, it was assembled in the Pârcovaci – Maxut – Deleni area, with the exception of the 103rd Tank Brigade, which had taken over the tanks and defensive sector of the 11th Guards Tank Brigade on the slopes of Hill 184; with 15 T-34 tanks, it passed to the operational control of the 35th Guards Rifle Corps. By this same time, the 16th Tank Corps had turned over its combat sectors to the 206th Rifle Division and was assembled in the Ceplenița – Bădeni area.

The 2nd Tank Army's report on the enemy's combat operations over the period of fighting from 2 May to 5 May 1944, written by the army's chief of intelligence Colonel Galimov and the 2nd Tank Army headquarters' chief of the Records Department Major Martynov, had the following to say:

> As a result of the conducted work in the division's new sector of operations, the following enemy grouping has been identified: the Romanian 1st Guards Infantry Division (1st, 2nd and 9th Infantry Regiments and the 3rd and 6th Artillery Regiments), the *Grossdeutschland* Panzer Division, the 99th and 651st Combat Engineer Battalions, the 23rd Panzer Division (201st Panzer Regiment and the 126th and 128th Panzer Grenadier Regiments), and the 24th Panzer Division (24th Panzer Regiment and the 21st and 26th Panzer Grenadier Regiments). Enemy actions: On 2.5.44 after stubborn fighting, the enemy was driven off of Hill 256 and out of Ulmi Noi and Ulmi Vechi. Having regrouped and reinforced the Târgu Frumos grouping with tank units – altogether up to 60 tanks and self-propelled guns with the support of bombers – the enemy at 12.00 launched a counterattack from the line of Hill 184 (5 kilo-meters north of Târgu Frumos) and Hill 148 (3 kilometers southeast of Polieni), regaining his former positions. Between 3.5 and 5.5.44, the enemy in his previous grouping with fire and numerous counterattacks in strength of a company or battalion of infantry with the support of 10-15 tanks and 30-40 bombers was offering resistance to the actions of our forces. By the end of 5.5.44, showing no activity, the enemy was holding and fortifying the line: Heleşteni, De Sus grove, Costeşti, Probota, Hill 256, Hill 184, Ulmi Vechi. From 5.5.44, the units of the 2nd Tank Army were pulled back into the second echelon.

[Signed] Chief of intelligence of the 2nd Tank Army Colonel Galimov; chief of the 2nd Tank Army headquarters' Records Department Major Martynov

On 6 May 1944, the 2nd Tank Army had a total of 49 serviceable tanks and self-propelled guns, including 41 T-34, 4 Mark IX, and 4 SU-76.

On 7 May 1944, the enemy suddenly launched an attack in the direction of Hills 184 and 192. The units of the 206th Rifle Division, unable to withstand the onslaught, began to retreat toward Hill 193. The 16th Tank Corps, having received an urgent coded telegram from the headquarters of the 2nd Tank Army, made a forced march to the area of Hill 193 and together with the units of the 206th Rifle Division restored the situation. Afterwards, at 20.00 on 9 May 1944, it again yielded its sectors to the 27th Army and moved to the Plugari, Oneşti, Boroşoaia area for refitting and combat training.

As a result of the fighting in the Târgu Frumos area, the 16th Tank Corps lost 17 T-34 destroyed or burned-out and 1 T-34 knocked-out; personnel losses numbered 90 men killed and 320 wounded. In addition, it had 1 76mm gun destroyed and 1 damaged, as well as 1 45mm anti-tank gun damaged. Over this same period, it claimed the to have knocked out 16 enemy tanks, 16 guns and 19 machine guns, while killing 1,050 enemy soldiers and officers. The 3rd Tank Corps in the fighting between 2 and 5 May 1944 claimed 26 enemy tanks destroyed and 15 tanks disabled, plus the destruction of 23 guns, 46 machine guns and 8 motor vehicles. Over this same period, the 3rd Tank Corps losses amounted to 10 T-34 tanks burned-out and 6 T-34 knocked-out; 4 ISU-152 knocked-out and 11 ISU-152 burned-out; and 2 IS-85 tanks knocked-out. Personnel losses were 81 men killed and 321 wounded. In the course of 7 May 1944, the 3rd Tank Corps brought its materiél and personnel back to order, and from 8 May 1944 set to combat training while awaiting the arrival of replacement tanks. At 20.30 on 11 May, the 3rd Tank Corps relocated to the Coarnele-Caprei area, where it re-assembled on 12 May. On 16 May, an order of the 2nd Tank Army's Military Council was received about sending 85 crews of the 3rd Tank Corps to Fălești Station in order to receive the arriving new tanks.

After the war, General Manteuffel, the former commander of the *Grossdeutschland* Panzer Grenadier Division gave an interview to the British military historian Liddel Hart, in which he stated: "Approximately 500 tanks from both sides took part in the tank battle at Tirgu [Târgu] Frumos. The Russians' offensive was stopped with large losses for them. Only 60 Russian tanks managed to remain intact among the large number of damaged tanks. I lost only 11 tanks." (Author: according to a report from the command of the 2nd Ukrainian Front's armored forces, on 6 May 1944 both tank armies had a combined total of 264 operational tanks and self-propelled guns, which means the loss of 215 tanks and self-propelled guns between 1 and 6 May 1944. The difference with the data provided by Manteuffel is 204 tanks.)

In its after-action report on the operation, the 2nd Tank Army command observed,

> The enemy used groups of 4-12 tanks to support counterattacking infantry with the simultaneous concerted action of assault artillery, artillery from firing positions and the attack of aircraft in groups of 20-40 bombers. The enemy's heavy tanks, as a rule, were used in front of the combat formations of medium tanks. Assault guns covered the flanks of the tanks. More rarely the enemy used 2-3 heavy tanks as mobile firing points out of ambush positions to combat our tanks. Aircraft in groups of 9-50 bombers with the cover of 4-12 fighters in concerted action with the infantry and tanks attacked the combat positions and rear areas of our forces, primarily working over roads leading to the front. The enemy, redeploying his mobile units (*Grossdeutschland* Panzer Division, 23rd and 24th Panzer Divisions, SS Panzer Division *Totenkopf*) from one sector of the front to another, depending upon the activity of our forces, strove to hold the foreground in front of their main line of resistance, which consisted of permanent fortifications on the line: Heleşteni, Probota, Polieni, Vulturul (north of Iaşi), while simultaneously improving a second defensive line with permanent fortifications along the edge of a forest in the sector: south of Târgu Frumos, south of Iaşi. The enemy

created a grouping in the Stolniceni, Ulmi Noi sector consisting of two battalions of the Romanian 4th Infantry Division, the *Grossdeutschland* Panzer Division and the 46th Infantry Division in the front line, with the rest of the Romanian 4th Infantry, 1st Guards Infantry and 2nd Infantry Divisions, the SS Panzer Division *Totenkopf* and the 24th Panzer Division in the second line and in reserve with the aim of preventing a breakthrough of the fortified line south of Târgu Frumos and the emergence of our forces in the rear of the entire Iaşi grouping, which is holding a passage open in Romania's interior between the Prut and Seret Rivers.

The after-action report concluded:

The 2nd Tank Army over the period of offensive operations between 25 March and 5 May 1944, while inflicting significant damage to the enemy in personnel and equipment, liberated a large part of Moldavia with the cities Bălti, Soroca and Fălești, and pursuant to an order of the Supreme Commander, crossed the Romanian border. With combat operations on the latter's territory, it created a threat of the encirclement and destruction of the Iaşi grouping, forcing the enemy to redeploy more divisions with the aim of preventing a breakthrough of the fortified Târgu Frumos line and the emergence of the army's forces in the rear of the Iaşi grouping

The absence of adequate air cover for the army's actions allowed the enemy in a number of instances to strike our combat formations from the air, and especially bridges, which led to a reduction in the pace of the advance and excessive losses in personnel and equipment. IT IS NECESSARY not only to plan, but also to ensure air cover for the tank formations to the entire depth of the battle in practice. Experience proves that for engineer support of the tank army's offensive operations in difficult terrain with the overcoming of water obstacles, IT IS NECESSARY to have attached engineer-sapper brigades in addition to the army's and corps' engineer battalions. Simultaneously, move up the corresponding materials for the construction of bridges at crossing sites in the wake of the combat formations of the tank corps, and for this purpose, furnish the army's and corps' battalions with speedy tow vehicles with hitches.

Experience demonstrated that of the army's self-propelled regiments, in the conditions of the recent fighting, the most durable were the SU-85. Less suitable because of their weak transmissions and frequent breakdowns were the SU-76. The practice of employing the IS heavy tanks allows one to draw the following conclusions: a) Heavy tanks themselves are obliged to conduct reconnaissance probes with the aim of revealing the enemy's heavy tanks, which do not disclose their positions with the appearance of our medium tanks; b) Escorting units must have more tanks than the heavy tanks present in the regiment, otherwise scouting of the enemy and the terrain, as well as the flanks of the enemy's heavy tanks, isn't secured. In the accompaniment of medium tanks, the heavy tanks (IS-2) must make bounding advances from one hill to the next, occupying commanding heights with the broadest field of fire and view; c) Commanders of the machines must survey the battlefield both from the open hatch of the tank and, given suitable opportunity, from outside the tank as well, advancing to hilltops, from which the ground lying in front is clearly visible; d) It is necessary to cover the flanks of the heavy tank elements with medium or light tanks when conducting reconnaissance probes in order to avoid unexpected flank counterattacks. The successful repulse of enemy tank counterattacks by the heavy tanks can be achieved given the close cooperation of the medium and light tanks with the heavy tanks. Medium tanks also must scout to reveal the ambushes of enemy heavy tanks and should lure the enemy's heavy tanks into the ambushes of our tanks; e) The lack of evacuation means (prime movers authorized by the table of organization and equipment) told on the recovery of disabled tanks. Operational tanks had to be used, as a consequence of which for a certain amount of time they couldn't take direct part in combat. The fighting showed that the enemy on the defensive in hilly terrain is employing new methods of using tanks, attaching them to the infantry in small groups, moving them out to the slopes of hills and keeping low ground under flanking fire.

When the chief of the 2nd Tank Army's Operations Department Colonel Bazanov was preparing another report, he evidently lacked information on the SU-152 self-propelled guns of the 375th Heavy Self-propelled Artillery Regiment, and turned to a staff officer Major Tsumanenko to find out what he could about them. The archive files contain Major Tsumanenko's report to Colonel Bazanov:

**To the chief of the Operations Department Colonel Bazanov – a briefing-report:** At your direction, the location of the SU-152s of the 375th Heavy Self-propelled Artillery Regiment was checked by me on 4 May 1944. As a result of the check, I've established: two SU-152 self-propelled guns of the 375th Heavy Self-propelled Artillery Regiment are located in firing positions in the combat positions of the 57th Motorized Rifle Brigade on the southern slopes of a nameless hill 2 kilometers southeast of Hill 197. Two more of the heavy self-propelled guns are in the reserve of the corps commander in Balș. When returning from the assignment along the route I'd taken, I encountered one SU-152 en route to the area of Cotnari Station from a repair shop. As a result of checking the availability of combat-ready self-propelled guns, from a report of the commander of the 375th Heavy Self-propelled Artillery Regiment to the corps commander and a report from the artillery chief of staff Major Bershadsky to me – it has been established that the 375th Heavy Self-propelled Artillery Regiment entered combat having 19 SU-152 assault guns. At 19.00 on 4 May 1944, the regiment has three SU-152 assault guns operational, two SU-152s undergoing light overhaul, and three SU-152s undergoing major overhauls. Two of assault guns are on the approach. Eleven of the SU-152s have been destroyed. Total: 21 self-propelled guns.

[Signed] Senior Signals Officer of the Operations Department Major Tsumanenko

A document on the loss of materiél of the 2nd Tank Army over the period of combat from 2 to 4 May 1944 reveals:

**2.5.1944 3rd Tank Corps**: 4 T-34 burned-out, 1 T-34 demolished, 5 T-34 knocked-out, for a total of 10 tanks; **16th Tank Corps**: 11 T-34 and 1 IS-122 burned-out; 6 T-34 and 8 IS-122 knocked-out; 1 T-34 demolished; 3 IS-122 were left in enemy hands. Total: 30 tanks. **11th Guards Tank Brigade**: 1 T-34 demolished. Total for 2.5.1944: 16 tanks burned-out, 20 tanks knocked-out, 3 tanks left in enemy hands, and 2 tanks demolished. Total losses: 41 tanks.

**3.5.1944 3rd Tank Corps**: 7 T-34 burned-out, 2 T-34 knocked-out; 3 IS-85 knocked-out; 11 ISU-152 burned-out and 5 ISU-152 knocked-out. Total: 28 tanks and self-propelled guns. **16th Tank Corps**: 4 T-34 and 5 IS-122 burned-out; 7 T-34 and 4 IS-122 knocked-out, for a total of 20 tanks. **11th Guards Tank Brigade**: 10 T-34 burned-out and 3 T-34 knocked-out, for a total of 13 tanks. Altogether over 3.5.1944: 37 tanks and self-propelled guns burned-out and 24 tanks knocked-out. Total losses: 61 armored vehicles.

**4.5.1944 3rd Tank Corps**: 1 T-34 and 1 ISU-152 burned-out, for a total of 2 tanks. No losses in the 16th Tank Corps and 11th Guards Tank Brigade on 4.5.1944.

**TOTAL losses over the period from 2.5 to 4.5.1944 – 104 tanks and self-propelled guns**, including **63 T-34** (37 burned-out, 24 knocked-out, 2 demolished); **21 IS-122** (6 burned-out, 12 knocked-out, 3 left in the enemy's possession); **3 IS-85** (3 knocked-out); **17 ISU-152** (12 burned-out, 5 knocked-out).

[Signed] Chief of the 2nd Tank Army's Operations Department – Colonel Bazanov

Later, Major General A.I. Radzievsky, the 2nd Tank Army's chief of staff reported on the 2nd Tank Army's irrecoverable losses from 1 to 8 May 1944:

3rd Tank Corps: 21 tanks; 16th Tank Corps: 23 tanks; 6th Guards Heavy Tank Regiment: 10 tanks; 11th Guards Tank Brigade: 9 tanks; 375th Self-propelled Artillery Regiment: 11 self-propelled guns. The total irrecoverable losses amounted to 74 tanks and self-propelled guns.

[Signed] Major General A.I. Radzievsky, Chief of Staff of the 2nd Tank Army

Following the unsuccessful offensive and the heavy losses in equipment (65 percent of the tanks and self-propelled guns with which the 2nd Tank Army had started the offensive) in trying to take Târgu Frumos, the subordinate commanders of the 2nd Tank Army came in for sharp criticism. Even before the offensive was sputtering to a halt, General Bogdanov was already harshly criticizing his subordinate officers and announcing formal rebukes, as often happened after a failure:

**Order to the troops of the 2nd Tank Army No. 0229 from 6.5.1944**
The fighting for Târgu Frumos has once again demonstrated that the tank crews, platoons and companies lack direction. They do not know how to fire at enemy tanks, don't survey the battlefield, don't conduct reconnaissance of the objectives, don't maneuver on the battlefield, and don't study the terrain. The brigade commanders are not carrying out the the the People's Commissar of Defense Order No.057-42 and Order No.325, or the order of the 2nd Ukrainian Front and my own orders No. 062, 0103 and 0149. The result was that the tank corps suffered large and unnecessary losses over 2.5 and 3.5.1944. As a consequence of a lack of discipline; the extremely incompetent gunnery and the personnel's poor training; the loss of command and control in the platoons, companies and regiment; and poor observation, reconnaissance and maneuvering the 6th Guards Heavy Tank Regiment over 8 hours lost 100 percent of its powerful and valuable IS-122 tanks, which are able to penetrate the fascist Tigers from a range of 2 to 2.5 kilometers. The 375th Guards Heavy Self-propelled Artillery Regiment (16 tanks), 103rd Tank Brigade (8 tanks) and the 164th Tank Brigade (8 tanks) suffered large losses. As a result of poor command and organization of the battle, and the lack of exactingness and aggression, the 16th Tank Corps suffered totally unjustified losses. Just what are the reasons for the enormous shortcomings in conducting a battle and the loss of tanks? The causes are as follows: a) Corps commanders Major General Dubovoi and Lieutenant General Mishulin, and the commander of the 11th Guards Tank Brigade Guards Colonel Eremeev have not absorbed the experience of previous battles, and have not trained the personnel to win with little blood on the basis of this experience; failed to organize cooperation within the corps among the artillery, tanks and infantry or with the rifle divisions; and have not learned to command on the battlefield with fire and maneuver. b) The corps and brigade commanders and their staffs are not organizing reconnaissance of the terrain and path of advance. Reconnoitering is absent in the brigade, regiment, battalion and company. Tasks are not given on the spot. c) Reconnaissance of the battlefield is not being conducted; target marking and the concentration of fire from tanks, which is to say to focus

the main guns of several tanks on a single target, has not entered the practice of the tankers. d) The commanders of regiments and companies of the 6th Guards Heavy Tank Regiment and the 375th Guards Heavy Self-propelled Artillery Regiment, and the commanders of the 164th and 103rd Tank Brigades do not command with fire and maneuver, do not scout the objectives, have stood idle for hours in a single position without moving, thereby exposing the flanks of the tanks to enemy fire. The tanks are not protected by infantry or by artillery firing over open sights. e) The commanders of the tank platoons and the tanks in the presence of enemy tanks and artillery do not move their tanks from cover to cover, take no account of the terrain, do not reconnoiter the battlefield, and do not observe their targets from their hatches. Fire is slow and not concentrated. The brigade commander – as the main organizer of the battle, is not organizing the combat or coordinating actions. During a battle he doesn't lead, or keep watch on the rear, flanks and boundaries. He isn't using the maneuverability of the tanks in order to fall upon the enemy's flanks or rear, and isn't directing the fire or issuing updated, supplementary orders. The artillery of the tank brigades, as a rule, is lagging behind. All this is taking place because the brigade commanders aren't up in the combat formations. They don't see the battlefield or the battle, or the movement of the tanks, but sit out the fight in a safe location. f) The corps commanders are not demanding actual direction of the combat at the company or battalion level – with flares, tracer bullets, by signal flags or by radio. The platoon and armored vehicle commanders are not reconnoitering their routes. They are not maneuvering on the battlefield; they stand motionlessly with closed hatches. There is no mutual assistance on the battlefield with fire and maneuver. g) During movement, an attack or an exchange of fire, command at the level of the brigade, battalion, company or individual tank, as a rule, is disrupted; the radio doesn't work, while there are no other signals or commands. Instructions are carried out slowly or not at all. The commanders and staffs of the brigades, and the battalion commanders are not taking the necessary and rapid steps to restore communications and control.

The needless losses of tanks and personnel are explained by these flagrant disgraces alone. The tanks are not in battle array. It is time to understand that organization, leadership, constant control over fire and movement, reconnaissance and the concerted action of all types of forces are necessary for victory over the foe.

I am ordering:

1. Precisely carry out the orders of the People's Commissar of Defense No.057 and 325-42, of the Front commander No.103 and 0149-44, and my own instructions and orders. Bring the violators of them to strict accountability. The corps commanders are to forge command and control, reconnaissance, and cooperation among the forces. Demand that the brigade commanders be up in the combat formations, to see the battle and to influence its course. Properly employ the self-propelled gun regiments in battle in full accordance with the instructions of Marshal of Armored Forces Fedorenko.

2. The brigade commanders are to train their battalions and companies to reconnoiter the paths of advance and the battlefield, to fight with fire, to maneuver on the battlefield, to seek out the enemy's flanks and rear, and to act with accurate, deadly fire out of ambushes. Insist upon the deployment of the company or battalion in a combat formation on the battlefield.

3. Once again demand of the brigade commanders to command and to be up with their units, and not to sit out the fight 2-3 kilometers in the rear. [Demand that they] see the entire battlefield and influence the course of the combat with fire and maneuver.

4. I am DECLARING A REPRIMAND to the commander of the 16th Tank Corps Hero of the Soviet Union Major General Dubovoi for the absence of proper command of the corps and for the needless losses of tanks, as well as for the absence of coordination and

reconnaissance, and I demand that he change fundamentally the handling of and exactingness toward his subordinate brigades.

5. Turn the commander of the 6th Guards Heavy Tank Regiment Lieutenant Colonel Cheriapkin over to the Military Tribunal for [his] loss of command and control, the lack of necessary discipline in combat, and for the excessive loss of tanks, which brought great harm to the government.

6. I am DECLARING A REPRIMAND to the commander of the 375th Guards Heavy Self-propelled Artillery Regiment Lieutenant Colonel Kharitonov for the absence of maneuvering on the battlefield; for standing idle in one place; for lagging behind the tanks; for the absence of reconnaissance on the battlefield and for the slow rate of fire at enemy tanks; for the loss of control over the companies on the battlefield; and I'm giving final notice that if in the future he commands the self-propelled guns in this fashion, he will be removed from command.

7. I am DECLARING A REPRIMAND to the commander of the 164th Tank Brigade Colonel Kopylov for sitting out the fighting 2-3 kilometers in the rear; for the lack of proper command and control at the company and battalion level; for the complete absence of direction of the gunnery; for the annihilation of his tanks; and for keeping the tanks standing idle in one place; I'm giving final notice that I forbid directing the combat [from a position] 2-3 kilometers in the rear.

8. I am DECLARING A STRICT REPRMIMAND to the commander of the 103rd Tank Brigade Lieutenant Colonel Makarov for losing control in the brigade and company; for the absence of maneuvering on the battlefield, reconnaissance of the terrain, coordination on the battlefield and the concentration of massed fire, as a consequence of which the brigade suffered needless losses.

9. I am ADMONISHING the commander of the 11th Guards Tank Brigade Guards Colonel Eremeev for the absence of control over the brigade's combat on 3.5.1944, as a result of which the brigade attacked not as a fist, but as scattered groups of tanks; for the incompetent target marking and maneuvering with fire and movement; for the absence of a combat formation on the battlefield. I demand to command the tanks with fire and maneuver, not to stand in place, but to make maneuvers without exposing his tanks to enemy fire.

10. The commanders of the 3rd and 16th Tank Corps are to establish control and monitoring over the course of combat of the brigades, and to use [their] staffs in full measure to direct the fighting. Organize command of the fighting and reconnoiter the terrain and battlefield. I categorically forbid keeping the tanks standing motionless for hours. Set up communications in the battalion and company by radio and by other means, knowing that this is the greatest weakness. Don't disperse the forces, but introduce the brigades into the fighting en mass; properly use the self-propelled gun regiments.

11. Work out the order down to the tank commander by 8.5.44. Report on the implementation by 9.5.44.

[Signed] Bogdanov, Matiushin, Radzievsky

It must be said, however, that the commanders who received rebukes and admonishments drew the proper lessons and already showed better in the June 1944 fighting to repel a German counteroffensive in Romania. For example, the commander of the 375th Self-propelled Artillery Regiment Kharitonov was awarded the Order of the Red Banner for his performance in the June battles. The 6th Guards Heavy Tank Regiment's commander Iosif Cheriapkin and the 11th Guards Tank Brigade's commander Guards Colonel Boris Eremeev stood out for their performance in the June battles. Subsequently, both Cheriapkin and Eremeev would become Heroes of the Soviet Union.

The above order was accompanied by Order No.0230 to the troops of the 2nd Tank Army about eliminating shortcomings in command and control:

The recent fighting clearly exposed the large shortcomings in the command and control of the forces in the process of the fighting. Once again it was shown that the commanders of corps and brigades are not taking up their observation posts, not preparing them in advance, and not organizing supplementary observation. As a rule, lovely homes are being chosen as command posts, with no regard for their suitability for command and camouflaging. The order and discipline at the observation and command posts are low, and no one is overseeing this; vehicles are not being camouflaged, the massed movement of vehicles and men take place, and so forth. The chiefs of staffs of all categories are having nothing to do with the setting up of the command and observation posts. Headquarters commandants are idle. During a battle, all the headquarters and staff officers are sitting in huts, soliciting and squeezing information from subordinates about the situation at the front; spending hours talking over the telephone or radio; writing needless papers; are busy with bureaucratism, avoiding active work regarding the organization of a battle and intelligence work; studying the opponent on paper, and not on the battlefield during a battle. Such work of the headquarters and their leadership over the fighting is no longer tolerable. There are officers who over the entire time of the war have yet to see a battle, but have seen only paper and the telephone receiver.

I am ordering: Cease the direction of fighting on paper and over the telephone in all headquarters. I demand the corps and brigade commanders use staff officers as organizers of the fighting on the battlefield, for studying the enemy on the battlefield, for ensuring victory over the foe in the course of the fighting, and not in a hut over a sheet of paper. Use staff officers: a) to analyze the ground where a battle is anticipated both day and night; on reconnaissance; each staff officers must superbly know the battlefield in reality, and not on paper; b) to study the enemy, his grouping, his weapons, his possible intentions, and his system of defense on the battlefield and during a battle itself. Each staff officers must: a) know the combat assignment of his units, brigades and corps on the ground; organize the combat during a battle, exert leadership over the fighting, and not simple be a fact checker, but must regain control that has been lost during combat; c) must personally conduct constant reconnaissance of the battlefield both day and night, and organize uninterrupted patrols to obtain fresh, supplementary intelligence on the enemy; d) organize communications at any time, especially in the tank battalions and self-propelled artillery regiments; use runners, signal flares, lamps, and flags; wire communications; over the radio and by airplane; d) realign a combat formation of tanks, infantry and artillery that has been disrupted during combat; e) have personal contact with officers who are directing the combat and be up in the frontline units. The atmosphere at the observation posts of the corps and brigades must be businesslike.

Once again, I'm calling the attention of the commanders of the corps, brigades and self-propelled artillery regiments to the fact that: a) the corps commander must observe the battle, direct the fighting, exert control and influence over the course of the fighting with the use of the terrain, fire, combat formation, maneuver, the commitment of his reserve into the fighting or with help from his neighbor; the corps commander absolutely must watch the battle unfold on the axis of the main attack while located in an observation post; b) the commanders of the tank brigades and self-propelled artillery regiments must be located up with the combat units of the brigades and regiments, witness the fighting, and must directly and quickly influence the course of the battle: with the proper use of the terrain; with the adoption of a combat formation in accordance with the terrain and the enemy position; with fire; with maneuver (a strike at the enemy's flank, or envelopment and emerging in his rear); with his reserve and the reserve of a superior commander. I categorically demand direction of the fighting, and not to allow uncontrolled combat and not to entrust direction of the fighting to the company commander or platoon commander. The army's chief of staff must fundamentally rearrange the entire operation of his staff and that of subordinate headquarters. In the future, assess a staff officer not by the amount of time he spends sitting in a hut over a sheet of paper, but by how much the officer personally contributed to a victory over the foe on the battlefield, or to organizing the battle.

Transmit the given order down to the battalion commander. Report on the steps taken to fulfill the order by 12.5.1944.

[Signed] Bogdanov, Matiushin, Radzievsky

The 2nd Tank Army commander also didn't spare the reconnaissance elements and intelligence officers of criticism. On 19 May 1944, Bogdanov issued Order No.0277 to the troops of the 2nd Tank Army regarding the results of the work of the army's intelligence and reconnaissance elements over the period of the latest operation:

The operations conducted in April and May 1944 on the Târgu Frumos axis demonstrated that the army's intelligence and reconnaissance sub-units failed to handle their tasks. The intelligence and reconnaissance elements of the 16th Tank Corps worked exceptionally poorly. The corps, engaged in stubborn fighting between 2.5 and 5.5.1944, didn't know which enemy units were operating in front of it. The commander of the 16th Tank Corps Major General Dubovoi paid no attention to intelligence. As a result of the fighting, the following shortcomings were revealed in the organization of gathering information on the enemy by the army's intelligence and reconnaissance elements: During the preceding operation, the chiefs of staffs of the corps and brigades gave no orders regarding reconnaissance, especially in the 16th Tank Corps. Discipline in the reconnaissance units is low. As a result of this, the reconnaissance units performed poorly. Reconnaissance units are not supplied with communication means. As a result, important information on the enemy is slow in arriving and loses its value. Scout teams are inadequately prepared to snatch prisoners in the conditions of rugged terrain. Little time is spent preparing for a scouting mission. Reconnaissance elements are understaffed, but replacements for them come not from experienced fighters who have distinguished themselves in fighting, but from among fresh replacements, who have no combat experience or training.

I AM ORDERING: By 25.5.44, bring the reconnaissance elements up to strength with personnel from among experienced soldiers, who have distinguished themselves in fighting. In the period from 20.5 to 24.5, conduct five days of meetings with the commanders of platoons and companies, and five days of meetings with the sergeants and men (25.5 to 29.5). The army's chief of signals is to provide one radio set each to the intelligence departments of the army, the corps and the brigades. Create a separate radio network among the army's intelligence organs and staff them with an adequate number of radio operators. The army's chief of intelligence Colonel Galimov is to assess the intelligence officers at the level of the company and platoon. Those unfit for duty are to be replaced by better officers.

[Signed] Bogdanov, Matiushin, Radzievsky

Finally, the command of the 2nd Tank Army turned its attention to the work of the army's artillery in the struggle with enemy tanks, in Order No.0280 to the troops of the 2nd Tank Army issued on 21 May 1944:

The experience of the army's recently conducted combat operations during our forces' successful offensive fighting revealed one characteristic method of struggle in the adversary's tactics with the aim of countering our attacks when breaking through the enemy's defenses and especially when fighting in the depth of those defenses. The enemy began to make widespread use of separate groups of tanks and self-propelled guns, operating very cautiously out of ambushes or patrolling on the battlefield, opening fire at our combat formations at a range of 2 or more kilometers, after which these same groups withdrew behind cover, leaving 1-2 tanks in the previous position for maneuvering, while the remaining tanks redeploy to a different sector and repeat the same tactic. Our troops are still not prepared to struggle with the mobile groups of enemy tanks, and all too often such enemy actions are halting the advance of our forces. Our close-support artillery, having spotted such groups of enemy tanks (self-propelled guns) beyond the range of direct fire, remain silent, and are not adapted for manhandling guns up into positions. Special observers are not posted to keep watch on the enemy tanks, and special signals on the detection of the tanks are not being established. Plainly, many still don't understand that the essence of the artillery's offensive consists in unceasing artillery fire, and that this essential task must manifest itself most clearly when fighting in the depth. With the aims of increasing the effectiveness of the struggle against enemy tanks when fighting in the depth and the tight coordination of the artillery with our tanks, **I AM ORDERING:**

1. During on offensive, have artillery batteries of close-range effect from the destroyer anti-tank artillery battalion in the combat formations of the forward units. Prepare the 85mm anti-aircraft guns for actions out of ambush with the task of destroying the enemy's tanks and self-propelled guns. In battle, set up batteries in ambush and thoroughly camouflage them. Open surprise fire. When carrying out an assignment, gun crews are to change positions quickly, manhandling the gun to an alternate position. All of the battery's officers are to be with it.

2. The commanders of the corps' artillery are to have direct contact by radio or wire with the close-support batteries and heavy guns.

3. By 22.5.1944, at the expense of the artillery's rear echelons, detach and train 3 men for each gun as supplementary manpower for the indicated batteries and close-support artillery batteries. Have cables and slings with all the guns, as well as an entrenching tool.

4. In order to reduce the effectiveness of enemy tank fire, blanket them with smoke. For target direction and the correcting of fire, have artillery observers in the tanks, for which purpose train 1-2 officers in each battalion as special artillery spotters. Have a specially assigned tank for artillery spotting, adjusting fire, and communications in each brigade in combat; keep this tank directly with the artillery chief.

5. Cease commanding the artillery out of dugouts. Each commander, up to the army's artillery commander, is to have personal observation of the battlefield and a nearby telephone. All of the artillery chiefs are to have their own forward observation post. Transmit orders to control the artillery only over the artillery network.

6. All of the commanders of artillery units, from the battalion commander up to the army's artillery commander, are to have a battery on hand in immediate proximity, the fire of which is to be used for pointing out appearing enemy tanks. The explosions of smoke shells (or of spotting tracer rounds) from this battery should serve as the primary signal for the appearance of tanks.

7. The malingering of forward observers is to be viewed as cowardice and as a malicious omission on the part of their superior officers. Have armor-piercing rifle rounds in the battalions for firing at vision slits.

8.  Study the given order and instructions for combatting enemy tanks and self-propelled guns with the entire command staff down to the battalion and company commander inclusively.

[Signed] Bogdanov, Matiushin, Radzievsky

Given the harsh criticism leveled at the commander of the 6th Separate Guards Heavy Tank Regiment in General Bogdanov's order from 4 May 1944 and the dramatic action taken against him, it is perhaps interesting to read the official account of the combat operations of the 6th Separate Guards Heavy Tank Regiment over the period between 9 February and 12 May 1944:

Build-up and Combat Training: The regiment arrived at the Tula Tank Military Encampment (TTME) for its build-up to table strength on 9 February 1944. The regiment was housed in the Tesnitsky camp and after the two days spent bringing itself to order, it set to combat training according to the program released by the Headquarters of the TTME. Upon its arrival at the TTME, the regiment consisted of 22 tank officers and 39 sergeants and men of the tank companies. In addition, of the regiment's elements the following had been fully preserved: a headquarters, a command platoon, a platoon of submachine gunners, a vehicle maintenance and technical support company, and a medical-sanitation unit. In total, the regiment numbered 193 men. The wheeled park numbered 33 vehicles. The regiment had no combat materiél. On the basis of an order of the Chief of the Main Directorate of Combat Training of the Red Army's Armored and Mechanized Forces from 14.2.1944, the regiment's commander and company commanders were sent to Cheliabinsk along with their assistants for vehicle maintenance and technical support to study the "IS-122" tanks. In order to study the IS tank, on 13 February 1944 an "IS-85" tank was received from the 27th Separate Guards Heavy Tank Regiment, which served as a subject for training on the equipment. The exercises were arranged in such a way that the tank was fully used for training purposes. Gunnery training was conducted with the officers of the regiment's command and headquarters every day, and personnel trainings every other day, while twice every 10 days, a 10-hour training period on tactics, topography, the equipment and the Regulations were conducted. On the basis of an order of the Chief of the Main Directorate of Combat Training from 22.2.1944, the personnel of the tank companies were sent to Cheliabinsk for re-training. Thus, only the service elements and headquarters remained in the regiment, which continued exercises according to the program.

On 13 March 1944, the combat materiél in the quantity of 20 "IS-122" tanks arrived in the regiment aboard Train No.10171. Routine spare parts for the tanks and three combat loads of shells arrived with this same train. The machines had been received at the Kirov Factory in Cheliabinsk. The tank crews came primarily from the 7th Replacement Training Tank Regiment's 1st Tank Battalion, and replacements came from this same regiment's 5th Tank Battalion. The regiment's personnel that had been sent to Cheliabinsk for re-training were not returned to the regiment, with the exception of 4 company commanders, their assistants for vehicle maintenance and technical support, and 4 officers. Not a single one of the gun commanders and gun loaders were returned to the regiment. Upon arrival at the Tesnitsky camp, the tanks were put into working order in the course of two days, after which the regiment turned to collective training according to the program released by the Headquarters of the TTME. On 29 March, a regimental training session with the equipment was conducted on the theme, "The regiment's attack as part of a tank corps against a strongly fortified enemy." The training that was conducted received an overall "Good" assessment. In addition to the tactical breaking-in, the personnel of the tank companies were busy with familiarizing themselves with the tank and its weapons.

On the basis of an order from the commander of the TTME, the regiment began to load aboard trains and on 3 April 1944 departed at the order of the commander of the 2nd Ukrainian Front. The regiment traveled by railroad in two trains, as a consequence of which the trains arrived at the destination station with an interval of four days. The first train arrived on 13 April 1944; the second train – on 18 April 1944. The station of unloading was Vapniarka.

On the basis of Combat Order No.091/OP from the headquarters of the 2nd Tank Army dated 18 April 1944, the regiment passed to the control of the 16th Tank Corps and was directed to assemble in Oneşti by 20.00 on 20.4.1944. The personnel and equipment faced a 270-kilometer march over difficult terrain, along dirt and improved roads. The route of movement was: Vapniarka – Iampol' – Soroca – Bălti – Sculeni – Oneşti. The machines traveled a significant portion of the way (25 percent) over waterlogged roads. In addition, along the way, four times the machines had to overcome water obstacles by fording at places where the water was up to a meter deep. There were three instances where machines became stuck; because of the lack of any prime movers, combat machines had to be used to tow them out. On the entire extent of the march, the tanks were loaded with 1 combat load of ammunition, one refill of fuel, and each tank carried five submachine gunners. When conducting the march, halts were made every 80-110 kilometers in order to inspect the tanks, make repairs and service the machines: cleaning the air filters and oil filters and greasing the running gear. On the march, the machines had breakdowns and developed problems, which were fixed quickly by the crews and the regiment's repair services, which were moving at the end of the column as a trailing support element. By the end of the day on 20 April 1944, the regiment had fully assembled in Oneşti with the exception of two tanks. These two tanks, because of mechanical problems and repair work that was underway, were still en route. Upon arrival in the assembly area, all of the machines were subjected to thorough mechanical inspections, after which any revealed problems were fixed through the efforts of the crews and regiment's repair service. Simultaneously, while repair work was being done, the tanks received routine maintenance work and were prepared for summertime operations.

Preparation for Combat: On 23 April 1944, the approach routes leading to the area of the jumping-off positions and the directions of the forthcoming combat actions were reconnoitered by the commanders of the companies, platoons, tanks and the driver-mechanics. The terrain in the area of upcoming combat operations was analyzed with all the personnel of the tank companies. Practical exercises on driving the tanks in the conditions of rugged terrain with the overcoming of steep rises, declines and water barriers were conducted with the driver-mechanics.

On the basis of Combat Order No.1 from the headquarters of the 16th Tank Corps on 28.4.1944, the regiment in full order conducted a march from its assembly area to the area of jumping-off positions along the route: Oneşti – Boroşoaia – Hârlău – Hodora, and by 6.00 on 30 April, it had assembled on the northwestern outskirts of Hodora. Because the launching of the offensive had been postponed until the receipt of a special order, the regiment had the opportunity to inspect its combat equipment once again, to conduct a repeat reconnoitering down to the driver-mechanics inclusively, and to make a detailed reconnaissance of the terrain and passages on the directions of the tank companies'attack. Despite the fact that the tanks in their jumping-off positions had been carefully camouflaged and dug in, on 1.5.1944 the enemy subjected the village of Hodora to an air raid. The regiment suffered personnel losses: one man was killed and another was badly wounded. In the course of 1 May, a final inspection of the readiness of the tanks and personnel for battle was conducted. A verbal combat order was given, which was passed down to each tank crew member. After receiving the combat order, the company commanders headed to the tank brigades of the corps, which each had been instructed to support, and worked out the questions related to coordinating their actions during the battle (target marking and signals)

The regiment received information on the enemy from the headquarters of the 16th Tank Corps. In addition to this, evidence from the rifle units that were positioned on defense was used, as well as information from the regiment's intelligence officer, who was posted with the observers at the regiment's observation post.

The Regiment's Task and Combat Actions: In Combat Order No.33 from the commander of the 16th Tank Corps, the regiment was given the following assignment: "The 6th Separate Guards Heavy Tank Regiment is to advance behind the combat formations of the tank brigades in readiness to repel enemy tank counterattacks and to support the attack of the corps' tanks. Pay special attention to the left flank." Stemming from the assignment laid out in the above order, the directions of attack for the tank companies ran along the axes of the tank brigades' actions. The reserve company was positioned on the left flank.

On 2 May 1944 at 5.30, the tanks moved out of their jumping-off positions on the north-western outskirts of Hodora. They arrived at the line of deployment at 6.05. The regiment's deployment took 10 minutes. At 6.20, the tanks went on the attack in the following forma-tion: on the right – the 2nd Tank Company behind the 107th Tank Brigade; the 1st Tank Company behind the 109th Tank Brigade; and the 3rd Tank Company behind the 164th Tank Brigade. The 4th Tank Company followed behind the 3rd Tank Company on the left flank at a distance of 500-600 meters.

At 7.45 the tanks reached the southern slopes of the Pulina Burial Mound (Hill 192). At this same time, the enemy launched an infantry counterattack from the direction of the southeastern slopes of the Hill 192. The enemy's infantry counterattack was repulsed by the rifle units, after which the enemy withdrew the 5-6 tanks that were in this direction, which had taken no part in the combat.

At 9.40 the regiment's tanks approached Facuti, in the area of which they began to search for crossings over a stream. While searching for a crossing site, the regiment's tanks pivoted to the left, that is, toward the east. At 10.30 the enemy in strength of up to 8-10 tanks went on the counterattack from the direction of the southern slopes of Hill 256. At an order from the commander of the 16th Tank Corps, the 4th Tank Company was shifted to the right flank in order to repel the counterattack. The counterattack was driven back. While repelling the counterattack, two German "Tiger" tanks were knocked out. The 1st, 2nd and 3rd Tank Companies meanwhile continued to search for a way around or over the nameless stream, but had no success.

At 12.00 the enemy counterattacked from the direction of the southern slopes of Hill 148 in strength of up to 15 tanks. Since the reserve 4th Tank Company had been shifted to the right flank, the 1st Tank Company was redeployed to the left in order to repulse the enemy's counterattack. The enemy tanks had been spotted in time. But the 1st Tank Company was unable to shift quickly to the left, because in order to redeploy to the left it had to get around streams and boggy places in a ravine. The counterattacking enemy tanks struck the 1st Tank Company in the flank, and the company suffered losses: 3 tanks were knocked out and 2 tanks were left burning. The 2nd Tank Company also suffered losses: 2 tanks were brewed up. The enemy tank counterattack was repulsed. The following damage was inflicted upon the enemy: 4 tanks were knocked out and one tank was destroyed.

On the basis of a verbal command from the commander of the 16th Tank Corps on 3 May 1944, the regiment received the task to operate behind the combat formations of the 107th Tank Brigade on the Târgu Frumos axis. At 6.00 on 3.5.1944, after the tanks of the 107th

Tank Brigade crossed a nameless stream 2 kilometers northwest of Hill 184, the regiment moved out at a distance of 500-600 meters behind the formations of the 107th Tank Brigade. Upon reaching the line: southern slopes of Hill 184 –highway leading to Târgu Frumos, the enemy opened up with flanking fire from heavy tanks that had been previously deployed in ambush positions. The enemy was firing from the directions of Hill 189 and from a nameless hill lying 1.5 kilometers west of a hill of the Bosia range. The T-34 tanks after a short exchange of fire were compelled to retreat, in which fashion our heavy tanks found themselves in front, and they entered into a solitary struggle with the enemy's heavy tanks. The advantageous enemy position (ambushes) was effective. After a 2-hour battle, the enemy managed to disable 4 of the heavy tanks, and having assembled infantry with the massed support of aircraft and artillery, the enemy launched a counterattack from the above-indicated directions along roads leading to the north. Our damaged tanks, which were continuing to return fire, but unable to move, were brewed up by the fire of heavy enemy tanks and air attacks by bombers. Over 3 May 1944, the regiment suffered losses: 6 tanks destroyed and 3 tanks knocked out. Over two days of fighting, the regiment lost 10 tanks burned out. Personnel losses are given in the table below:

**Losses of personnel of the 6th Separate Guards Tank Regiment over the period from 9 February to 12 May 1944.**

|                   | Officers | Sergeants | Privates |
|-------------------|----------|-----------|----------|
| Killed            | 1        | 6         | 5        |
| Wounded           | 6        | 5         | 12       |
| Missing in action | 9        | 15        | 17       |
| TOTAL:            | 16       | 26        | 34       |

TOTAL: 76 men. Over this same period the following damage was inflicted upon the enemy: 10 tanks, 20 guns of various calibers, 18 wheeled vehicles, 2 mortars, and up to 280 infantrymen.

On the night of 3/4 May 1944, the regiment was pulled out of the fighting at an order of the commander of the 16th Tank Corps and assembled in the Hodora area in order to repair and replace combat equipment. With the arrival in the Hodora area, all the means in the regiment were mobilized and devoted to repair work. Over 3 and 4 May 1944, 6 combat machines were repaired, with which the regiment on 5.5.1944 in response to an alarm moved out into a valley, 500 meters northwest of Hill 192 in readiness to repel enemy counterattacks. The tanks were deployed into defensive positions in the aforementioned valley, while two tanks were sent to an area of vineyards on the northeastern fringes of Ulmi Noi. At the end of the day, an order was received from the headquarters of the 16th Tank Corps for the regiment to assemble in a wooded grove on the southern outskirts of Ceplenița. By 4.00 on 6.5.1944, the regiment had fully assembled in the indicated area; the combat machines and wheeled vehicles were dug in, and the regiment set to work to put them all back into operating condition. In the course of the day, preparation for upcoming combat training exercises was made.

On 7.5.1944, according to a verbal order of the commander of the 16th Tank Corps, the regiment was raised in response to a combat alarm, and at 7.30 it moved out from its deployment area to an area of isolated huts about 1.5 kilometers southeast of Lake Hirbu. The tanks were positioned on the defensive in order to cover a valley that had a road leading out of Târgu Frumos, Hill 192, and the low ground southwest of it. Each tank was given its own sector of fire, and the tank crews filled out inspection records for the tanks. The tanks were dug in and thoroughly camouflaged. A company of submachine gunners had been deployed on the defensive in front of the tanks and as a guard detail.

Between 7 and 12 May 1944, the regiment remained on the defensive in the indicated area in readiness to repel enemy attacks from the south. On the night of 12/13 May 1944, the regiment was ordered to conduct a march to the Oneşti area. By 5.00 on 13.5.1944, the regiment had fully assembled in the indicated area.

Command and Control over the Fighting, and Communications: Radio communications, which worked without a lapse over the entire period of combat, served as the primary means of controlling the regiment in the battle. In order to implement radio communications, there were two radio nets in the regiment: one regimental combat network, which included 21 radios in the tanks, one RBM radio which was located in the corps commander's observation post, and a radio located in the regiment's second echelon. The second network connected the corps' headquarters with the army commander, as well as with the tank brigades operating jointly to carry out the given assignment. Thanks to the good work of the commanders of the radio-equipped vehicles, the regiment commander had a connection with all the tanks for the entire extent of the fighting.

For technical support of the combat, main observation and signal posts, as well as a forward and a main collection station for disabled vehicles were organized. The main observation and signals posts consisted of a tank company's assistant commander for vehicle maintenance and technical support, two mechanics and a radio master. Such main observation and signal posts were present in each tank company; it followed behind the tank company's combat formation of tanks along its axis of movement, monitored the tanks' actions, and rendered immediate assistance to fix minor mechanical problems. From the initiation of combat operations, the forward collection station for disabled vehicles was located in the area of Hill 193. In pace with the tanks' forward advance, on 3 May 1944 it was located in the area of a ravine north of Hill 192. The forward collection station for disabled vehicles had the repair equipment of the regiment's recovery and repair platoon, which worked under the direction of the regiment's chief engineer. The main collection station for disabled vehicles, which was located in the vicinity of Hodora, had attached repair means of the 16th Tank Corps and 2nd Tank Army, a technical service and support company, two combat loads of ammunition and two refills of fuel. The Assistant Chief of Vehicle Maintenance and Technical Support was located here. Disabled tanks were allocated between the forward and main collection station depending on the amount of required repair work. Tanks requiring light or major overhauls were sent to the main collection station for disabled vehicles, while those needing minor repairs were sent to the forward collection station. In some cases, a repair team was sent directly to the area of the tanks' operations. Over the period of fighting, the regiment's repair services performed 8 light overhauls and 3 repair jobs.

[Signed] Commander of the 6th Separate Guards Heavy Tank Regiment Guards Lieutenant Colonel Cheriapkin and chief of staff of the 6th Separate Guards Heavy Tank Regiment Guards Major Golant

The 2nd Tank Army's artillery commander General Plaskov left behind recollections of the tank army's initial operations beyond the Soviet border:

The mood in the army was festive. We were at the border! So therefore we took the Front's new combat order happily: to force the Prut River, and then to seize Iaşi. Everyone rejoiced, except for those who knew the situation at the front well. The army command studied the incoming intelligence with alarm. The German Sixth Army and Romanian Fourth Army

Tanks of the 6th Guards Heavy Tank Regiment.

were defending Iaşi and Kishinev. The enemy was bringing up fresh divisions. At the Military Council, the Chief of Staff A. Radzievsky cited convincing numbers. The enemy had a large superiority in men and equipment. In contrast, we had suffered significant losses over the preceding month. Very few tanks and self-propelled guns remained serviceable, and even they were in need of maintenance and repairs. The men were worn out. The rear services were lagging behind. I also gave a report, and said that the army's artillery was in need of replenishments with both men and equipment, and the situation with ammunition had become very difficult. Bogdanov gloomily heard us out. He said that the Front command knew of our army's condition, but the situation made delay impossible. The exit of Romania from the war was depending a lot on our actions, and this was a matter that didn't allow procrastination. The Front's main forces had joined up with us. Once again, we were to enter a breach in the enemy lines created in the 27th Army's sector.

Several days later, the offensive began. The month of April 1944 was the most difficult, most unproductive month for the 2nd Tank Army. We were expending enormous efforts, but we were grinding in place, unable to break through the enemy's defenses. I have no grievances with a single artilleryman, beginning with the soldier and ending with the corps' artillery commander; they were doing everything that depended on them, in order to assist the infantry and tanks, but there was no success at all. Torshilov and I, and an officer of our staff Knutov, together with the commander of the neighboring 17th Rifle Division's artillery Lieutenant Colonel Stepin and his chief of staff Captain Plavinsky attempted to organize a strike in the flank of the enemy's defenses, and deployed close-support guns. We fired over open sights and indirectly, horribly expending a lot of shells, but the results were pathetic. The Hitlerites were not only refusing to reel back, they were counterattacking. Bogdanov was nervous; his deputy General Goncharov was always up with the forward brigades. Two or three times each, Semen Il'ich asked what I was doing, what the corps commanders were doing, and he himself was driving up to the front. Neither he nor we were accustomed to such a situation. He was rebuking us, dressing us down. "You're making slow progress, spinning your wheels in place," he kept harping to me; "You're cannons are worthless, weak, and firing badly." I wasn't offended by his words. I knew that it was hard for the army commander.

Only two men were calmly going about their work. They were [chief of staff] A.I. Radzievsky and the newly arrived army deputy commander for vehicle maintenance and technical support, Major General N.P. Iukin. Nikolai Pavlovich and his subordinates – engineers, technicians, and mechanics – were driving around the battlefield, towing back disabled vehicles. They were repairing them in the field repair shops and returning them to service. The tankers and self-propelled gunners gazed at Iukin with admiring eyes.

On 11 April, the army commander asked me and the chief of the army's Political Department Colonel M.M. Litviak to drive over to the 49th Brigade to see T.P. Abramov. The brigade was to launch a flank attack against the German defenses, and it was necessary to reinforce it with artillery. I had great respect for Colonel Tikhon Abramov, a valiant and experienced commander. I happily drove to meet him, and brought along the 187th Artillery Regiment together with me.

The brigade moved out in fine fashion, took the first and second line of trenches, but could make no further advance. Dejectedly, Litviak and I started to head back to headquarters. We came under mortar fire on the way. Our Willys jeep was smashed. A fragment sliced open my leg. The driver Filipp Minaev washed the wound with vodka, and then bandaged it with a dish cloth. We made our way back to headquarters aboard a passing vehicle. Litviak and I went in to see Bogdanov. He interrupted my report: "Abramov didn't make any headway? That means your trip was in vain. But now, march off to get bandaged. Your leg is injured, but there is no time to lie around. We're planning a grand offensive. It is set to begin on 2 May."

On 1 May, Bogdanov invited General N.P. Iukin and me to dinner. Although the meal was convivial and the radio kept announcing victories achieved by Soviet forces, this time there was little joy around our table. Bogdanov abruptly rose from his chair several times, and frowning, paced around the room with his long, strong legs. Now and then he went to the telephone and agitatedly spoke with the corps commanders.

The commander of the Front's Armored and Mechanized Forces Colonel General A.V. Kurkin and the commander of the 27th Army S.G. Trofimenko, my old classmate at the academy, came by to see us. At Kurkin's prompting, the Military Council was immediately convened. At it, once again all the questions of the next day's offensive were discussed in detail. It was decided that the 27th Army's 35th Guards Rifle Corps together with our 3rd and 16th Tank Corps would launch a joint attack toward Cepleniţa after a powerful artillery preparation, after which, exploiting a success, we would seize Târgu Frumos from the march.

I had seen General Kurkin for the first time near Uman'. A Willys had come driving up to the forward detachment headed by brigade commander P.N. Akimochkin. Out of it stepped a tall, broad-shouldered general. The army's chief of intelligence was with him. The general questioned Akimochkin about what was holding up the brigade's advance. "Let's give a thought together what to do," he said. So they bent down over a map together. Combat was going on quite nearby. Sometimes shells were landing in the vicinity. But the general didn't pay them any attention. His counsel proved to be very valuable. Akimochkin on the move regrouped his forces, and the advance accelerated.

Such was the man Aleksei Vasil'evich Kurkin. He was often seen up with the combat units, on the march and in combat. It must be stated directly that each of us learned a lot from him. It happened, I'd be standing with him and observing as the artillerymen and tankers fought to drive back the Germans. I wouldn't like the actions of one or another commander, and I'd want to drive over to him, but Aleksei Vasil'evich would clap me on the shoulder: "There's no need. You are more needed here, at the command post; the battery commanders will manage even without you." There was also an occasion once when Bogdanov erupted and began to dress someone down. Kurkin walked up to him, took him by the arm, lead him off to one side, and slowly, drawing out his words, brought him to reason: "Semen, calm down. Remember, at one time you were in just the same position. The mistakes of youth! He'll set things right in the next battle." Bogdanov smiled and gave a wave of his hand: "All right".

I never appealed to Kurkin for anything, but often before leaving he would ask, "Grigorii Davidovich, I'm a Front representative, who can help your artillerymen; do you need anything?" More than once, Kurkin with his advice helped us to conduct our combat operations better. His comments were taken by everyone as right; Aleksei Vasil'evich's authority was unshakeable. In the tank corps they were happy whenever he arrived; they knew him well there and weren't embarrassed to appeal for help.

Just as now, before the offensive, he stayed with us. Together with Bogdanov, Trofimenko and Nikolai Ivanovich Matiushin, who was temporarily carrying out the duty as a member of the army's Military Council after Latyshev's wounding, he drove off to visit the troops.

On 2 May between 6.08 and 6.30, the artillery of both armies and the Front's aviation worked over the designated breakthrough sector to a depth of 7 kilometers. After this, the 35th Guards Rifle Corps and the 3rd and 16th Tank Corps went on the attack. In places, they made a 3- to 4-kilometer advance. Isolated elements reached the western outskirts of Târgu Frumos. But what happened next was unexpected. At the very height of our attack, the foe launched a powerful counterattack. Out of the area of Târgu Frumos to the north and out of the area of Podu Iloaie to the northwest, hundreds of heavy enemy tanks were advancing toward us. Behind them, infantry moved forward on foot and in halftracks. Artillery and mortar fire was mowing down our ranks. The forward units of both sides collided. Everything became jumbled. The commander of the 1643rd Artillery Regiment Lieutenant Colonel A.I. Biriukov, which was supporting the 33rd Motorized Rifle Brigade, opened fire at the enemy infantry. The self-propelled gun regiments – Hero of the Soviet Union Lieutenant Colonel D.G. Gurenko's 369th and Major N.M. Davydov's 368th – were shooting up German tanks at point-blank range. I.M. Glazunov's and A.N. Petrov's batteries, which were advancing along with the tank brigades, were doing the same. The corps artillery shifted fire to the flanks, isolating the approaching hostile units. For approximately an hour, in a sector of the front 5 kilometers wide and 2 kilometers in depth, a bloodbath ensued. From the command post, it was hard to make out what was happening there. Dense, thick smoke, intermingled with the flashes of fire, rose above the battlefield.

The deputy commander of the 16th Tank Corps Colonel G.M. Maksimov and the corps' artillery commander Hero of the Soviet Union Colonel I.I. Taranov set off toward the fighting units in a halftrack [likely an M3 halftrack obtained through Lend-Lease]. Georgii Maksimovich Maksimov had been serving in the tank corps from its day of forming-up (previously he had commanded a brigade). He was a courageous man and an experienced tanker. Just his appearance in the combat formations alone raised the spirits of his subordinates.

S.P. Knutov and I also traveled to the units that were fighting. Men weren't sparing themselves, and were fighting with all their strength. No instructions were required, and it would have been difficult to give them: it was impossible to converse – everything was drowned out by the thunder of explosions and the squeaking of tracks. It was hot from the burning tanks – both the enemy's, and our own. Despite the courage and self-sacrifice of our soldiers, the Hitlerites were pushing us back.

A.I. Radzievsky came rushing up from army headquarters. With an iron hand, he worked to stabilize the situation. At his order, the forces quickly adopted a defensive posture, and our fire became more organized and dense. The foe was forced to halt. For a certain time longer, guns continued to fire, and then became quiet. Silence settled over the battlefield. It was oppressive, ominous.

In a buttoned-up overcoat (in such heat!), S.I. Bogdanov was walking in solitude. I caught up with him. He dragged me over to a truck – "Let's go!" We took a seat in the Dodge; with his powerful physique, it was cramped in a Willys jeep. The commander stopped the truck at the firing position of one of the batteries. He watched a long time as a soldier wiped the blood from the face of a killed comrade with a damp towel. Semen Il'ich touched him on the shoulder. The soldier leaped to his feet and recognized the commanding general: "They've just killed my buddy. I dragged him back to our lines. I must give him a proper burial." Bogdanov praised him, "Fine man, you're acting properly" and nodded to me: "Write down the name: Private Ogloblin." I wrote it down. Before leaving, Bogdanov embraced the soldier. Several days later, I found the name of Petr Gavrilovich Ogloblin on the list of decorated soldiers.

Having searched out the headquarters of one of the units, the army commander stopped the truck and quickly approached the commander. This unit hadn't shown the necessary tenacity during a withdrawal. I was waiting for Bogdanov, as the tankers said, "to give some spirit" to the guilty party. However, to my surprise, the army commander was calm: "I didn't expect this. I thought you were a real commander." He turned around and headed back to the truck. I knew Bogdanov well. If he "didn't give spirit" for a blunder, that meant that he considered the matter unjustifiable, which meant a black mark for the commander. In fact, on the very next day this officer was discharged from the army.

We headed to the 16th Tank Corps, where we met Kurkin and Matiushin. The corps commander I.V. Dubovoi was braced for a hard talk. However, Bogdanov said to him, "I have no grievances with you. Everyone was watching. What happened isn't your fault. You were acting properly."

Semen Il'ich had a talk with all the units and brigades. Some he praised; others, he pointed out their mistakes – always calmly and in a level voice. It turned out that he had tolerance! But we had grown accustomed to consider him too hot-headed ….

About 15.00 the army commander invited Trofimenko, Radzievsky, Matiushin, Goncharov, Levin, the corps commanders and me to a meeting. "We must attack right away", he declared; "before the foe has had time to dig in." Radzievsky and Matiushin attempted to convince him that this was impossible. "All the same, we must," said the army commander; "The people won't forgive us for delaying." Then he grumpily glanced in my direction: "And what are you thinking, Comrade Plaskov?" I replied, "I will follow an order."

After an attack by fire, the tanks rushed into the attack. How few of them we had left! With agitation I watched as the battle unfolded. The foe met our tanks with a hurricane of fire. The first tank burst into flames; then the second … I felt a heavy hand on my shoulder. "If you will, I was hasty" – I heard the choked voice of Bogdanov say. "Grisha, go to Dubovoi. Help him out. Shift as much artillery as you can over there, and help him with your advice." I glanced at the army commander. He was pale. I didn't want to leave him alone in this minute. But he prodded me: "Don't waste time!" Having issued the necessary orders, I hurried off to the attacking tank corps with staff officer G.T. Gorchenkov. It seemed like a miracle that they were still able to move.

I didn't manage to find Dubovoi. I was suddenly blinded. Then black and red spots began to cover the light. Something struck me in the left arm. I felt a warm stream gushing from it. There was a terrible pain. It penetrated my entire body, and it was squeezing my heart. I fell between two tanks – ours and a German tank. They were standing side by side, and both were burning. I regained consciousness already in the medical-sanitation battalion.

A table generated by the 2nd Tank Army's chief of operations Colonel Bazanov shows the status of the army's armor complement on 14 May 1944, the number of tanks and self-propelled guns returning to service from repair shops by 25 May, and the amount of serviceable armored combat vehicles available to the army on 25 May:

**Table 7.5: Data on the status of the tanks and self-propelled guns of the 2nd Tank Army on 14 May 1944**

| Army's composition on 14.5.44 | Leaving repair by 25.5.44 | Army's composition on 25.4.44 |
| --- | --- | --- |
| **3rd Tank Corps:** 18 T-34, 6 ISU-152, Total: 24 | **3rd Tank Corps:** 8 T-34, 1 ISU-152 | **3rd Tank Corps:** 26 T-34, 7 ISU-152, Total: 33 |
| **16th Tank Corps:** 11 T-34, 8 IS-22, 7 SU-85, 2 Mk IX, Total: 29 | **16th Tank Corps:** 16 T-34, 1 IS-122, 2 SU-85 | **16th Tank Corps:** 27 T-34, 9 IS-122, 9 SU-85, 2 Mk IX, Total: 48 |
| **11th Gds Tank Brigade:** 3 T-34 | – | **11th Gds Tank Brigade:** 3 T-34 |
| Tanks of the Army command: 3 T-34, 2 M4A2 | – | Tanks of the Army command: 3 T-34, 2 M4A2 |
| **Altogether: 61 tanks and self-propelled guns** | Altogether: 28 tanks and self-propelled guns | **Total: 89 tanks and self-propelled guns** |
| Chief of the 2nd Tank Army's Operations Department Colonel Bazanov | | |

## Combat operations of the 2nd Tank Army as part of the 2nd Ukrainian Front over the period from 2 to 15 June 1944

After the completion of the Târgu Frumos operation in Romania, the 2nd Tank Army on 13 May 1944 was pulled out of combat from the sector north of Târgu Frumos, and regrouped in the Plugari – Fântânele – Chişcăreni area. From the moment of its re-assembly in the indicated area, the army's units immediately turned to combat training and replenishment with materiél and arms.

### The operational-tactical situation at the end of 1 June 1944

The German Army Group South Ukraine, consisting of the German Sixth and Eighth Armies and Romania's Third and Fourth Armies under the command of Colonel General Schörner, which was defending the strategic axis in Romania, created a panzer grouping on a narrow sector of the front in the Iaşi area. This grouping consisted of the Panzer Grenadier Division *Grossdeutschland*, the 14th, 23rd and 24th Panzer Divisions and the 79th Infantry Division, and the Romanian 3rd and 11th Infantry Divisions. The German command was planning to conduct two pre-emptive counterstrokes with limited objectives, labeled Operations *Sonja* and *Katja*. In order to implement this plan, the German grouping was split into two combat groups, Group Manteuffel and Group Mieth. Group Mieth had General Edelshiem's 24th Panzer Division (Pz.Rgt.Sb. 24, III./Pz.Rgt. 24, and Pz.Art.Rgt. 24), which itself was split into two *kampfgruppen*, "W" under the command of Colonel von Waldenburg (numbering approximately 30 tanks) and "E" under the command of Lieutenant Colonel von Einem (numbering approximately 20 assault guns); Major General Kräber's 23rd Panzer Division, which on 1 June 1944 had serviceable 10 Pz. IV tanks, 17 StuG assault guns and one Bef.Pz.III; and Lieutenant General Unrein's 14th Panzer Division, which was operating in several *kampfgruppen* organized around the 103rd and 108th Panzer Grenadier Regiments and the 36th Panzer Regiment and on 1 June 1944 had serviceable 4 Pz. III, 1 Pz. IV, 3 StuG assault guns and 5 Wespe self-propelled light artillery vehicles mounting the 105mm field howitzer. In order to reinforce the understrength 14th Panzer Division, the 259th and 286th Assault Gun Battalions, which had 15 and 19 StuG assault guns respectively, were attached to it for the operation. Group Manteuffel consisted of the Panzer Grenadier Division *Grossdeutschland*, which had serviceable approximately 100 tanks and self-propelled guns. Altogether, the enemy had not less than 200 tanks and self-propelled guns.

On 2 June 1944, this grouping went on the offensive out of the Iaşi area to the north, with the objective to reach the southern bank of the Jijia River, and subsequently to attack toward the Prut River. As a result of savage attacks, by the end of the day the enemy managed to break through the front of the 27th Army at the cost of heavy losses in men and equipment, and had reached the line: Totoeşti – Coarba hills – Hill 178 – Horleşti – Vulturul – Hill 197 – Bahna – Poleşti.

### The nature of the terrain and the presence and condition of roads

The terrain in the sector of the enemy's operations was open, representing a rolling elevation divided by ravines and balkas. The significant number of the latter made observation of the enemy difficult, and the conditions for camouflage were unsatisfactory. Camouflaging was possible only along the balkas. The sector had no good roads. The available roads were largely dirt tracks that ran between the villages; in dry weather they offered good traction, but movement along them kicked up a lot of dust, which revealed the movement of columns. After rains, these tracks became impassable; the muck made the movement of motorized transport difficult. The basin of the Jijia River is swampy.

Table 7.6 (below) the number of serviceable tanks and self-propelled guns of the 2nd Tank Army at the start of combat operations at 6.00 on 2 June 1944, as well as the available supply of fuel and ammunition.

## The 2nd Tank Army receives an order

The enemy, with units of *Grossdeutschland* and the 14th Panzer Division, and a combat group of the Romanian 3rd Infantry Division and 18th Guards Mountain Infantry Division, breached the defenses of the 27th Army in the Totoeşti – Hill 150 sector and exploited the breakthrough in the direction of Movileni Station [Orsoaei]. On 2 June 1944 at 12.00 by an order of the commander of the 2nd Ukrainian Front, the 2nd Tank Army was given a task: by 16.00 to occupy a defensive line: 3.5 kilometers south of Focuri, the Bolohani Burial Mound, Hill 195, Hill 159, Movileni Station, Epureni, and to prevent the enemy from expanding to the north. In accordance with the received assignment, the commander of the 2nd Tank Army issued an order: "The 16th Tank Corps and 375th Self-propelled Artillery Regiment – are to take up a defense of Hill 195, Hill 159, Movileni Station, Hill 162 and Epureni, with the task to prevent the enemy from expanding in the direction of Larga Jijia, Potângeni and Chişcăreni; the 3rd Tank Corps and the 6th Guards Heavy Tank Regiment – are to take up a defense 3.5 kilometers south of Focuri, the Bolohani Burial Mound and Hill 176, with the task to block the enemy from expanding in the direction of Focuri and Fântânele."

**Table 7.6: Composition of the serviceable armor in the 2nd Tank Army at 6.00 on 2 June 1944**

| | T-34 | IS-122 | M4A2 | ISU-152 | SU-85 | Total for the army | Supplies | |
|---|---|---|---|---|---|---|---|---|
| | | | | | | | Fuel | Ammo |
| **3rd Tank Corps** | | | | | | | | |
| 50 Tank Brigade | 2 | – | – | – | – | 2 | 2.5 | 1.5 |
| 51 Tank Brigade | 3 | – | – | – | – | 3 | 2.5 | 1.5 |
| 103 Tank Brigade | 19 | – | – | – | – | 19 | 2.5 | 1.5 |
| 375 Heavy SPA Rgt. | – | – | – | 7 | – | 7 | 3.0 | 2.7 |
| Total: | 24 | – | – | 7 | – | 31 | – | – |
| **16th Tank Corps** | | | | | | | | |
| 107 Tank Brigade | 8 | – | – | – | – | 8 | 2.2 | 1.9 |
| 109 Tank Brigade | 5 | – | – | – | – | 5 | 2.2 | 1.9 |
| 164 Tank Brigade | 7 | – | – | – | – | 7 | 2.2 | 1.9 |
| 689 Signals Bn. | 1 | – | – | – | – | 1 | – | – |
| 6 Gds Heavy Tank Rgt. | – | 9 | – | – | – | 9 | 2.2 | 3.0 |
| 1481 SPA Regiment | – | – | – | – | 8 | 8 | 2.2 | 1.5 |
| Total: | 21 | 9 | – | – | 8 | 38 | | |
| **11 Gds Tank Brigade** | 14 | – | – | – | – | 14 | 0.9 | 1.5 |
| **9 Signals Regiment** | 3 | – | 2 | – | – | 5 | – | – |
| **246 Training Tank Bn.** | 3 | – | – | – | – | 3 | – | – |
| 86 Guards Mortar Regiment: 18 M-13 | | | | | | | | |
| **Total for the 2nd Army** | 63 | 9 | 2 | 7 | 8 | 91 | – | – |

Chief of the 2nd Tank Army's Operations Department Colonel Bazanov

## Combat actions of the 2nd Tank Army

On the afternoon of 2 June 1944, the forces of the 2nd Tank Army arrived in their indicated defensive areas. The operational subordination of the 103rd Tank Brigade to the commander of the 35th Guards Rifle Corps in the Târgu Frumos area was cancelled, and this tank brigade conducted a rapid march to the area of the 16th Tank Corps' operations. The 11th Guards Tank Brigade and the 86th Guards Mortar Regiment were assembled in the area 1.5 kilometers north of Hill 158 as the 2nd Tank Army's reserve. At 19.00 on 2 June, another order from the commander of the 2nd Ukrainian Front arrived at the headquarters of the 2nd Tank Army: "The 2nd Tank Army at 24.00 on 2.6.44 with the bulk of its forces, together with the 27th Army, is to launch a counterattack with the objective – by the morning of 3.6.44 to destroy the enemy in the area of Movileni Station and to restore the previous position of the 27th Army." In accordance with the received task, the commander of the 2nd Tank Army issued an order:

> The 3rd Tank Corps is to hold the line 3.5 kilometers south of Focuri, Bolohani Burial Mound, Hill 176 with the task to repel enemy attacks. Transfer the 103rd Tank Brigade to the 16th Tank Corps. The 16th Tank Corps and the 103rd Tank Brigade with the 375th Self-propelled Artillery Regiment, in coordination with the 27th Army, are to attack on the Movileni Station – Hill 162 front, and are to regain the former position of the 33rd Rifle Corps by the morning of 3.6.44; the reserve – the 11th Guards Tank Brigade in the Melnela – Sângeri area, the 86th Guards Mortar Regiment in Sângeri – are to be ready to act in concert with the 16th Tank Corps.

In the course of that night, 2nd Tank Army conducted a regrouping with the bulk of its forces for the counteroffensive.

At 6.00 on 3 June 1944, in concert with the 33rd Rifle Corps, the 16th Tank Corps together with the 103rd Tank Brigade and the 375th Self-propelled Artillery Regiment went on the attack toward Hill 178. The attacking tanks were met by the fire of 20 enemy tanks from the northern slopes of Hill 178. The enemy with multiple counterattacks in strength of a battalion or regiment of infantry with the support of 20-30 tanks offered fierce resistance to the army's attack from the north. Having bumped into strong enemy resistance, the 2nd Tank Army's forces, suffering losses and having become separated from the infantry, fell back to their jumping-off position. There, for the rest of the day they fought to repel enemy counterattacks. For example, at 9.00, up to a battalion of infantry and 15 tanks attacked out of Horleşti in the direction of Hill 142. At 13.00, following an artillery barrage on Movileni Station, the enemy attacked out of the area of the northeastern slopes of the Coarba Burial Mound in the direction of the station with up to 1,000 infantry and 30 tanks. At 17.00, an infantry battalion attacked out of Horleşti toward Hill 142. At 17.00 on 3 June, the army's forces again attacked toward Horleşti with part of its strength, and by 20.00 they were fighting on the line: 16th Tank Corps – 1.5 kilometers southwest of Hill 152, south of Epureni, nameless hill 1.5 kilometers east of Movileni Station, Hill 162; the 3rd Tank Corps – the road junction 3.5 kilometers south of Focuri, Bolohani Burial Mound, Hill 176.

By the end of 3 June, the 2nd Tank Army had lost 8 T-34 tanks destroyed. Its combat strength was now 51 T-34, 10 IS-122, 7 ISU-152, and 2 M4A2, for a total of 75 armored vehicles.

Just as after the unsuccessful May offensive near Târgu Frumos, the heavy losses suffered in tanks and materiél again provoked the dissatisfaction of the command and a new draconian order. However, once again the harsh measures proved beneficial with the passage of time. Colonel Vasilii Makarov, who was dismissed from command of the 103rd Tank Brigade, later took command of the 12th Guards Tank Corps' 48th Guards Tank Brigade and led it brilliantly, becoming a Hero of the Soviet Union and a major general before falling in action near Berlin. Colonel Tikhon Abramov, who received a formal rebuke, would later superbly command his 107th Tank Brigade, which would become part of the 16th Tank Corps' forward detachment and stand out for its performance in the Vistula-Oder and Berlin operations. He would become a major general, Hero of the Soviet Union, and would lead the army's composite regiment in the Victory Parade in Berlin.

These punitive measures came down in the 2nd Tank Army command's Order No.0315 from 5 June 1944, which complained about the lack of timely information from lower headquarters and the poorly organized tracking of combat losses:

> Despite my repeated instructions about timely reports on the actions of your units during a battle, thus far the headquarters of the corps and brigades are leaving higher headquarters in the dark about the situation for 5-6 hours at a time. In the fighting on 2.6.1944, the commander of the 107th Tank Brigade Colonel Abramov and the commander of the 103rd Tank Brigade Colonel Makarov and their subordinate staffs didn't fully report to the corps headquarters about their actions and the actions of the enemy. There was no reconnaissance of the enemy. They went on the attack with no knowledge of the arrangement of the enemy's firing positions. On the attack, the crews didn't fire and as a result suffered losses. The crews are still making no effort to tow away a knocked-out or brewed-up tank from the battlefield. For example, the commander of tank No.42356 of the 107th Tank Brigade Junior Lieutenant Iakovlev abandoned his knocked-out tank when it still had a serviceable main gun, without firing a single round at the enemy. The commander of the 16th Tank Corps Major General Dubovoi and his chief of staff Colonel Bibergan displayed feebleness. They failed to take proper measures regarding the organization of communications and command and control over the units. They didn't make inexorable demands with respect to undisciplined officers, such as the commander of the 107th Tank

Brigade Colonel Abramov and the commander of the 103rd Tank Brigade Colonel Makarov revealed themselves to be in the fighting on 3.6.44. As a result of the poorly organized reporting in the units and formations, the commanders and their headquarters often don't know where their units are located and in what combat strength. The tracking of losses of materiél and personnel in the fighting and in the course of 3.6.44 wasn't organized in the 107th and 103rd Tank Brigades. The assistant commander of the 107th Tank Brigade for vehicle maintenance and technical support Engineer-Lieutenant Colonel Karakozov and the assistant commander of the 103rd Tank Brigade for vehicle maintenance and technical support Major Nesterenko failed to keep track of the combat losses, the nature of the losses, and of the evacuation of disabled tanks from the battlefield. There is no scale of the materiél losses. A report on the course of repair work over the day, and on the possibility of returning knocked-out combat machines to service are lacking.

I AM ORDERING:
1. Turn in combat reports and operational summaries within the deadlines that I have strictly established. Report on the course of the fighting every 2 hours and immediately if there is an abrupt change in the situation.
2. Organize constant surveillance of the battlefield by technical officers. Compile an account of the combat losses and the recovery of knocked-out tanks from the battlefield.
3. The corps are poorly organizing record-keeping on the losses of combat materiél and the evacuation of knocked-out and burned-out tanks from the battlefield. I AM DECLARING A REPRIMAND for the assistant commanders of the 107th Tank Brigade and the 103rd Tank Brigade for vehicle maintenance and technical support Engineer-Lieutenant Colonel Karakozov and Major Nesterenko.
4. I AM DECLARING A REPRIMAND for the commander of the 107th Tank Brigade Colonel Abramov for the unjustified loss of tanks, the untimely reporting in combat, and for the poor reconnaissance of the enemy.
5. Remove the commander of the 103rd Tank Brigade Lieutenant Colonel Makarov from his post for his inability to handle his duties as a brigade commander, for the unjustified loss of tanks, the lack of communications or reports in the course of 12 hours, and for the poor reconnaissance of the enemy. I am warning that if in the future Lieutenant Colonel Makarov relates to service duties and the organization of battle in such fashion, then harsher measures will be taken. I AM DECLARING A REPRIMAND for the chief of staff of the 103rd Tank Brigade Lieutenant Colonel Klemenko.
6. I am directing the attention of the commander of the 16th Tank Corps Major General Dubovoi and chief of staff Colonel Bibergan to their feebleness and the absence of a demanding attitude with respect to the undisciplined officers under their command.
7. My assistant for vehicle maintenance and technical support Major General Engineer of Tank Service Iukin is to pay serious attention to the poorly organized record-keeping of losses of combat materiél in the units, and the lack of reports regarding the possibility of restoring knocked-out combat machines to service.
8. The army's procurator is to bring the crews of combat machines who displayed cowardice on the battlefield to justice. Turn over the 107th Tank Brigade's tank commander Junior Lieutenant Iakovlev and his entire crew to trial in front of the Military Tribunal. The procurator is to investigate the case within a two-day period.

[Signed] Bogdanov, Matiushin, Radzievsky

The above order was accompanied by Order No.0316 to the troops of the 2nd Tank Army by the army's command, which pointed to continued problems with reconnaissance, organization of the combat, and command and control in the subordinate formations and units:

> The orders and instructions of the Front commander, and my own instructions on knowing how to conduct observation and reconnaissance, to organize concerted action and to manage a battle, and to suffer as few tank losses as possible, have been taken formally by the commanders of the corps and brigades, without due organization. The headquarters of the corps and the brigades (once again) are not directing the battle, but are sitting out the battle in a safe place far to the rear. The brigade commanders are not leading, but commanding from a distance. As a result of this, there was no real combat, but the 103rd Tank Brigade lost 7 tanks (2 irrevocably), the 107th Tank Brigade lost 11 tanks (5 irrevocably), and 5 crewmembers went missing in action, which is to say, became prisoners. A portion of the crews of the 107th Tank Brigade (tanks No.42845 and No.4365) conducted themselves criminally in the battle, yet no one knows about this and no one wants to know. The commander of the 107th Tank Brigade Colonel Abramov is not commanding the brigade, and is running out of tanks. The commander of the 103rd Tank Brigade Colonel Makarov had no contact with the corps commander or with his battalions for 12 hours, but the 16th Tank Corps headquarters, aware of this, took no action whatsoever. The assistant commanders of the corps and brigades for vehicle maintenance and technical support are working negligently, don't know about the tank losses, and have set up the service of technical observation and recovery unsatisfactorily. The corps artillery commanders have broken up their artillery and don't know where the guns are located or what they are doing, are not directing the fire, have failed to organize observation posts, and the firing positions are located far to the rear. The corps chiefs of staff are not using the reconnaissance battalions for reconnaissance and observation. The army's chief of intelligence Colonel Galimov is directing intelligence operations badly.

> I AM ORDERING:
> 1. Disseminate the order of the Front commander No.00174 and my own instructions down to each soldier and crewmember. Know how to strike the enemy and to inflict large losses upon him.
> 2. The corps commanders are to demand of the brigade and battalion commanders to command the combat formations, to direct the fire and movement of their infantry and tanks. Demand of the corps and brigade chiefs of staff to be true organizers of the fighting, and to busy themselves first and foremost with: a) setting up command and control communications of all types; b) the organization of around-the-clock reconnaissance and observation; c) coordination of the artillery, tanks and infantry (primarily within the corps), and fire, movement and command; d) the organization of the fighting with few losses on our own side and large damage to the enemy.
> 3. Categorically demand of the artillery commanders of the corps and the commanders of the [artillery] regiments, battalions and batteries to carry out the order of the Front commander and my own instructions fully: a) have direct-firing guns in the combat formations of the motorized infantry and tanks; b) make field visits to the open firing positions for confronting enemy tanks; c) conducted targeted, observed fire, and not at areas; d) the observation posts and firing positions absolutely must be checked and their plotting should be precisely determined by an order and over the signature of the battery commanders. The artillery commanders of the corps and the commanders of the [artillery] regiments, battalions and batteries are obliged to see their own targets.

4.  <u>The Military Council for the final time is warning the army's chief of intelligence Colonel Galimov</u> that it is criminal to lead intelligence gathering in such fashion. Three battalions of scouts for the duration of two days of combat failed to seize a single prisoner. Observation has been set up in an off-hand way. Night patrols haven't been organized. Conduct reconnaissance and observation around the clock and organize the reconnaissance and intelligence business so that there will always be a "tongue" [a prisoner willing to talk] on the needed direction or in the relevant area. Demand that the chiefs of intelligence of the corps and brigades be genuine reconnaissance leaders. Place reconnaissance specialists in the tanks on the main axis of advance.

5.  Demand of the assistant commanders for maintenant and technical support of the corps, brigades and battalions to take up seriously the matter of directing the service of technical observation and the evacuation of tanks from the battlefield at any hour of the day or night. Know where a knocked-out tank is located and what needs to be done with it, etc. Thoroughly assess the damage done to knocked-out tanks. Demand that they don't sit in the rear under the guise of repairing tanks. Fully carry out the Front's Order No.00174.

6.  The Military Council catergorically demands of the commanders of the corps and brigades to organize the battle, to direct the combat, and to handle and command the fighting flexibly.

[Signed] Bogdanov, Matiushin, Radzievsky

The enemy offensive, which had placed our defending forces under pressure on the first days of it, had significantly weakened by 4 June 1944. Having suffered losses on the chosen Movileni Station axis, the enemy conducted a partial regrouping and made an attempt to cut off our units from the western bank of the Jijia River by attacking in the direction of Rediu Mitropoliei and Tipileşti. The enemy attack toward Rediu Mitropoliei prompted the necessity of reinforcing this sector and to conduct a partial regrouping of the 2nd Tank Army's forces. In the course of 4 June, the enemy continued to launch furious attacks to the north. The *Luftwaffe* was bombing the army's combat positions in groups of 10-15 aircraft each. Through combat and observation, it was established that the enemy was bringing up and assembling tanks and infantry in the Coarba Burial Mound, Hill 178, and Hill 181 area.

In the course of the day 4 June 1944, the forces of the 2nd Tank Army were throwing back enemy attacks and clinging to the lines: 3rd Tank Corps: 57th Motorized Rifle Brigade – the Bolohani Burial Mound, Vulturul Burial Mound; 51st Tank Brigade – area 1 kilometer south of Gropniţa; 16th Tank Corps: 107th Tank Brigade – southern end of Movileni Station, southern slopes of Hill 162; 15th Motorized Rifle Brigade – Hill 162; 109th Tank Brigade – southern fringes of the patch of woods west of Tipileşti, southern outskirts of Tipileşti; 164th Tank Brigade – southern slopes of a nameless hill 1.5 kilometers south of Potângeni; 103rd Tank Brigade – southern outskirts of Epureni; 375th Heavy Self-propelled Artillery Regiment – 1 kilometers northeast of Movileni Station; 11th Guards Tank Brigade – southern outskirts of Potângeni. As a result of the heavy attacks, the enemy by the end of the day on 4 June 1944 had seized Hill 178 (southwest of Epureni), Hill 181 and Moineşti.

At 18.30 on 4.6.44, the 2nd Tank Army commander issued an order: "The army is to defend Hill 181, Tipileşti, Cazacu, Cailor and Zbantu with the task in cooperation with the 27th Army to prevent the enemy from reaching the southern bank of the Jijia River. Have the defense ready by 3.00 on 5.6.44." The forces of the army on the night of 4/5.6.44 conducted a regrouping with its main forces, and by 3.00 was occupying the defensive line: 16th Tank Corps – Epureni, Coarba Burial Mound; 3rd Tank Corps – Hill 159 – 1 kilometer south of Movileni Station – Hill 162.

Throughout the day of 5 June 1944 the enemy launched repeated attacks with units of the *Grossdeutschland* Panzer Grenadier Division, the 24th Panzer Division and the Romanian 18th Mountain Infantry Division. Especially furious attacks were undertaken in the direction of Coarba. Simultaneously, the enemy was digging in and throwing up fieldworks in the sector Hill 167 – Hill 170. The *Luftwaffe* in the course of the day struck the army's combat positions in groups of 10-15 aircraft, especially in the area of Coarba, Tipileşti and Hill 162. At 5.00 after an hour-long artillery preparation, the enemy in strength of up to an infantry regiment with the support of 10-15 tanks attacked toward Coarba. Between 16.30 and 19.30 up to a company of tanks attacked in the direction of Epureni and Hill 162. Particularly bitter fighting went on in the vicinity of Coarba. According to information from the German side, the 23rd Panzer Division's *kampfgruppe* was attacking Hill 162 together with units of the 14th Panzer Division and the 243rd Assault Gun Brigade with the aim of driving the Soviet defenders off of it. In this fighting, the 243rd Assault Gun Brigade suffered particularly heavy losses. Its commander, as well as several officers together with their crews were killed or burned alive in their assault guns. *Kampfgruppen* of the 24th Panzer Division and the *Grossdeutschland* Panzer Grenadier Division unsuccessfully attacked Hill 183. At 6.30, the enemy in strength of up to two infantry battalions with the support of 10-15 tanks went on the attack out of the area north of Moinesti in the direction of the woods south of Rediu Mitropoliei.

As a result of savage attacks, the enemy managed to reach the southern outskirts of Coarba. With active operations of our forces out of the Tipileşti area, and with the fire of artillery and tanks from fixed positions, the enemy was forced back to the area 600 meters south of Tipileşti. In the Coarba Burial Mound – Hill 167 sector, three enemy attacks were repulsed. Seven enemy attacks were driven back in the Zahorna – Moinesti sector. Especially frequent and stubborn enemy attacks were thrown back in the Rediu Mitropoliei area. At 23.00 on 5 June 1944, the 2nd Tank Army was defending the line: 3rd Tank Corps: 57th Motorized Rifle Brigade – Hill 159, southern slopes of Hill 166, but at 18.00 with part of its strength it attacked in the direction of the railroad and reached a line 1 kilometer northwest of the Coarba Burial Mound; 50th Tank Brigade – 1 kilometer west of Hill 162, Hill 162, Hill 174; 16th Tank Corps: 103rd Tank Brigade with the 164th Tank Brigade's motorized rifle battalion – Hill 162, southern outskirts of Epureni; 15th Motorized Rifle Brigade – southern outskirts of Epureni, woods west of Tipileşti, but at 17.00 attacked jointly with the 206th Rifle Division and reached the northern slopes of Hill 142; 107th Tank Brigade – Coarba Burial Mound, Rediu Mitropoliei; 6th Guards Heavy Tank Regiment – northern outskirts of Epureni; 11th Guards Tank Brigade – in the area of Potângeni. By the end of the day on 5 June 1944, the 2nd Tank Army had serviceable 37 T-34, 9 IS-122, 7 SU-85, and 7 ISU-152, for a total of 60 tanks and self-propelled guns.

The German Eighth Army's Operations *Sonja* and *Katja* failed to achieve substantial successes. Having suffered heavy losses, the enemy had to abandon their plans to reach the Jijia River and to advance to the Prut River. By the end of 5 June 1944, the enemy largely went over to the defense. In the course of 6 June, the enemy launched limited attacks in strength of a company or battalion of infantry with the support of 10 tanks in the direction of the Coarba Burial Mound and Rediu Mitropoliei. In the remaining sectors, the enemy worked to improve their defenses with fieldworks. The *Luftwaffe* bombed the areas of Epureni, Tipileşti and Rediu Mitropoliei with groups of 15-25 aircraft each. The 2nd Tank Army's forces, repelling the enemy's tanks and infantry, kept improving their artillery and tank positions.

At 8.00 on 7 June 1944, units of the army, after a 5-minute artillery preparation, went on the attack together with units of the 33rd Rifle Corps in the direction of Balca, Hill 156, Hill 178, Hill 142 and the crest of Hill 181. In the afternoon, the enemy with repeated counterattacks in strength of a battalion or regiment of infantry with 10-15 tanks and the support of strike aircraft unsuccessfully strove to regain their lines. In the course of the day the 2nd Tank Army, overcoming heavy enemy fire and repulsing numerous enemy counterattacks out of the directions: Hill

178 – an infantry battalion with 5 tanks; Zahorna – an infantry company; Hill 181 – an infantry company; and the ravine southeast of Hill 181 – an infantry battalion with 8 self-propelled guns; made difficult progress and by 21.00 on 7 June 1944, it had reached the line: 3rd Tank Corps: 57th Motorized Rifle Brigade with the 234th Mortar Regiment and 5 tanks of the 11th Guards Tank Brigade – Balca, northern slopes of Hill 156, 1 kilometer south of Hill 167; 51st Tank Brigade and the 50th Tank Brigade's motorized rifle battalion – Hill 178; 16th Tank Corps: 15th Motorized Rifle Brigade together with 3 tanks of the 103rd Tank Brigade – southern slopes of Hill 142; 109th Tank Brigade with the 6th Guards Heavy Tank Regiment and the 1441st Self-propelled Artillery Regiment – 1 kilometer south of the Coarba Burial Mound; 103rd Tank Brigade with the 164th Tank Brigade's motorized rifle battalion – Hill 162, orchard south of Epureni.

The day of hard fighting was reflected in the 2nd Tank Army's armor losses. By the end of 7.6.44, the 2nd Tank Army had operational 13 T-34, 8 IS-122, 5 SU-85 and 6 ISU-152, for a total of just 32 tanks and self-propelled guns.

Throughout the day of 8 June 1944, the enemy in the Mijloc, Moineşti sector continued to offer stiff resistance to the offensive of the 2nd Tank Army's units with numerous counterattacks in strength of a battalion or regiment of infantry with the support of 10-15 tanks and strike aircraft. At 2.00, a company of enemy infantry went on the counterattack together with 5 tanks in the direction of Hill 142. At 4.00, a battalion of enemy infantry after a 10-minute artillery barrage launched another counterattack in the same direction. Both counterattacks were repulsed. At 6.30 a company of infantry and 5 tanks counterattacked out of the Mijloc, Hill 178 area. This was followed at 9.00 by a counterattack out of the Moineşti area with two infantry companies and 12 tanks toward Hill 181. All of the enemy counterattacks were repulsed. At 13.00-14.00, the enemy in strength of up to two infantry battalions and 10 tanks twice counterattacked, but had no success. The Germans were attacking here with a *kampfgruppe* from *Grossdeutschland*'s assault gun battalion under the command of *Oberleutnant* Diddens and *Kampfgruppe* Schroedter from the same division's armored reconnaissance battalion. As the history of the *Grossdeutschland* Division relates, both of the leaders of the *kampfgruppen* went down with serious wounds. The German attack was called off and the Germans began digging in on the line they had attained.

The 2nd Tank Army, having repelled the enemy's counterattacks, at 6.30 on 8 June 1944 resumed its offensive in the direction of Hills 143 and 167 in concert with the 35th Rifle Corps, and by the end of the day had reached the line: Hill 165, grove 1 kilometer southeast of Hill 156. In the course of 9 and 10 June, the enemy was largely quiet; defending its occupied line, the Germans attempted to launch only reconnaissance probes out of the Mijloc and Zahorna areas. For example, at 21.30 on 8 June, an infantry battalion with the support of 3 tanks attacked out of the Mijloc area in the direction of Hill 178. At 9.00 on 9 June, a company of enemy infantry unsuccessfully attacked the 2nd Tank Army's positions from the direction of Zahorna. Throughout the night of 9/10 June 1944, the Germans fought to improve their positions in the Coarba area with up to an infantry battalion and 12 tanks, and in the Zahorna area with up to 200 infantrymen. The 2nd Tank Army, repulsing enemy counterattacks, continued to defend its occupied lines. Due to the return of damaged tanks from the repair shops and replenishments, the 2nd Tank Army's armor complement increased: by the end of 10 June 1944, the 2nd Tank Army had a total of 66 operational tanks and self-propelled guns, including 29 T-34, 7 IS-122, 4 SU-152, 6 SU-85, 8 SU-57 tank destroyers, 10 Mark IX, and 2 M4A2.

At 22.45 on 10 June 1944, a directive from the Red Army's General Staff arrived about dispatching the 2nd Tank Army to a new sector of the Eastern Front. The army's forces were continuing to hold their occupied defensive lines. The 5th Separate Motorcycle Regiment arrived to join the 2nd Tank Army, consisting of a motorcycle battalion, a destroyer anti-tank artillery battalion, a tank company and a machine-gun company.

At 16.00 on 11 June 1944, General Bogdanov issued an order: "The tanks and crews of the 16th Tank Corps and the 11th Guards Tank Brigade are to be turned over to the 25th Tank Regiment, and the tanks of the 3rd Tank Corps – to the 18th Tank Corps. Transfer all self-propelled guns and IS-122 tanks to the 375th Self-propelled Artillery Regiment, which is to be made subordinate to the 27th Army." On 12 June, the army yielded its combat sectors to the 27th Army, and at 22.00 set off on a march to holding areas, where the troops were to board railroad trains.

An after-action report written by the 2nd Tank Army's deputy chief of staff for intelligence Lieutenant Colonel Kostromin discusses enemy actions and losses on the Iași direction over the period of the 2nd Tank Army's combat operations from 1 June to 15 June 1944:

Having assembled the *Grossdeutschland* Panzer Grenadier Division, and the 14th, 23rd and 24th Panzer Divisions in the Totoești – Golaești sector on the night of 1/2 June 1944, on the morning of 2.6.44 the enemy went on the offensive to the north after a two-hour artillery preparation. As a result of furious attacks, by the end of 2.6.44 the enemy at the cost of heavy losses in men and equipment managed to reach the Totoești – Coarba Burial Mound – Hill 178 – Horlești – Vulturul – south of Stânca – Hill 197 – Bahna – Golaești line. On 3.6.44, the 2nd Tank Army was committed into the fighting in the Totoești – Tautești sector. The enemy, with repeated counterattacks by units of the *Grossdeutschland*, 23rd and 24th Panzer Divisions, the Romanian 18th Mountain Infantry Division, 3rd Infantry Division, 7th Cavalry Regiment of the 5th Cavalry Division, in battalion or regiment strength of infantry with the support of 20-30 tanks was offering stubborn resistance to the attack of our units to the south. Enemy aviation in groups of 30-40 aircraft operated ceaselessly against the combat formations of our forces. Altogether over the day, up to 600-700 enemy aircraft sorties were noted. At 5.00 after a 10-minute artillery barrage, up to a battalion of infantry and 10 tanks attacked our units from Hill 178 in a northward direction. At 9.00 up to a battalion of infantry and 15 tanks attacked out of Horlești in the direction of Hill 142. At 13.00, after an artillery barrage on Movileni Station, the enemy in strength of to 1,000 infantry and 30 tanks attacked out of the area northeast of Scati, Coarba Hill in the direction of Movileni Station. At 17.30 an infantry battalion again attacked out of Horlești toward Hill 142. All the enemy attacks were driven back with heavy losses for him.

In the course of 4.6.44 the enemy continued fierce attacks to the north and by the end of the day seized Hill 178 (southwest of Epureni), Hill 181 and Moinești. At 5.40 – 7.00, the enemy in strength of 30 tanks and an infantry battalion twice attacked from Hill 181 toward Moinești. Observers spotted 30 tanks (and self-propelled guns) in the vicinity of Totoești; 19 tanks south of Butulucu; 15 tanks in the Coarba Hill area; 20 tanks on Hill 170 (south of Epureni); 20 tanks on Hill 181; and 40 tanks near Zahorna and Horlești; altogether, 156 tanks and self-propelled guns.

On 5.6.44 the enemy in strength of a battalion to a regiment of infantry with the support of 20-30 tanks and air strikes repeatedly attacked to the north, while simultaneously throwing up earthworks in the sector of Hill 167 – Hill 170. At 5.00 after an hour-long artillery preparation the enemy in strength of up to a regiment of infantry with the support of 10-15 tanks attacked out of the area of Hill 181 in the direction of Coarba. At 6.30 up to two battalions of infantry and 20 tanks attacked out of Moinești in the direction of the woods south of Rediu Mitropoliei. At 16.30 – 19.30, up to a company of infantry and 8 tanks attacked from Hill 170 toward Epureni, and from Hill 167 toward Hill 162. All of the enemy attacks were repulsed.

Over the period of offensive operations from 1.6 to 5.6.44, having achieved no substantial successes and having suffered heavy losses in men and equipment, the enemy had to abandon plans to reach the Jijia River and the development of a subsequent offensive to the Prut River, and by the end of 6.6.44, the enemy had gone over to the defense. Throughout the day of 6.6.44, the enemy defended its achieved line. Enemy aviation in groups of 15-25 bombers bombed Epureni, Tipilești and Rediu Mitropoliei.

On 7.6.44, the enemy was driven out of Balca and forced to yield Hills 156, 178 and 142, and the crest of Hill 181. That afternoon, with multiple counterattacks in strength of a battalion or a regiment of infantry with 10-15 tanks and the support of ground attack aircraft, the enemy unsuccessfully attempted to regain his former positions.

In the course of 8.6.44 in the Mijloc – Moineşti sector, the enemy with units of the Romanian 5th Infantry Division, 18th Mounted Infantry Division and 3rd Infantry Division and the German 24th Panzer Division and *Grossdeutschland* Panzer Grenadier Division put up tenacious resistance with multiple counterattacks in strength of a battalion or regiment of infantry, with the support of 10-15 tanks and strike aircraft. Simultaneously, he conducted a force regrouping and brought up reserves to the front. Between 2.00 and 4.00 the enemy in strength of a company or battalion of infantry with 12 tanks twice counterattacked our units unsuccessfully out of Zahorna in the direction of Hill 142. Between 9.00 and 11.00, up to two companies of infantry and 12 tanks twice unsuccessfully counterattacked out of Moineşti toward Hill 181. In the period between 13.00 and 15.00, up to a battalion of infantry and 6-8 tanks twice counterattacked in the direction of Hill 155 from Hill 150. In the course of the day, observers spotted: 10 tanks on Hill 143; 16 tanks in Mijloc; 25 tanks in the Zahorna, Horleşti area; and 12 tanks in Moineşti.

From 9.6 to 11.6 (up to the point when the 2nd Tank Army was pulled out of combat), the enemy undertook no active operations, and limited himself to reconnaissance probes and fortifying his occupied line. The enemy grouping at the end of 9.6.44 had in the first echelon the Romanian 5th Infantry Division's 8th Infantry Regiment occupying the sector between Hill 155 and the western slopes of Hill 156; the Romanian 18th Mountain Infantry Regiment between Hill 156 and Mijloc; the Romanian 90th and 92nd Mountain Infantry Regiments in the sector between Mijloc and Zahorna; the *Grossdeutschland* Panzer Grenadier Division between Zahorna and Moineşti; and the Romanian 3rd Infantry Division's 1st Infantry Regiment in the sector between Moineşti and the Vulturul Burial Mound. Both the 24th Panzer Division and the *Grossdeutschland* Panzer Grenadier Division were operating in the Mijloc – Moineşti sector, with a total number of 80-100 tanks, which were grouped in the following areas: 8 tanks in the Ochiul Boului sector; 16 tanks in Mijloc; 30 tanks in Zahorna; and 15 tanks in Moineşti. In the second echelon, the activity of up to a battalion of infantry and a battalion of tanks of the SS Panzer Division *Totenkopf* was noted in the Domian – Bogonos sector. The 23rd Panzer Division has been identified in the sector between Rediul-lui-Tataru and Cârligul. The enemy has the Romanian 2nd and 5th Infantry Divisions in reserve. Along the entire front of the 2nd Tank Army in the sector between Hill 155 and Moineşti, up to 20-30 artillery batteries, 8 rocket launchers and up to 10 mortar batteries have been detected. The [enemy's] anti-tank artillery is grouped in the following areas: 2 57mm gun batteries in Ochiul Boului; 3 batteries of 57mm guns in Mijloc; 4 batteries and 2 self-propelled guns in Zahorna; and 2 batteries and 3 self-propelled guns in Moineşti. In each anti-tank area, 3-5 tanks have been detected, which are firing out of ambush positions.

**Enemy losses and booty captured by our forces between 3.6 and 9.6.44**
According to information from prisoners and captured documents, the enemy has lost: 18th Mountain Infantry Division (R) – 2,745 men; 3rd Infantry Division (R) – 975 men; 24th Panzer Division – 1,680 men; *Grossdeutschland* Panzer Division – 1,980 men; 5th Infantry Division's 8th Infantry Regiment (R) – 456 men; altogether, 7,836 men. Losses in equipment: knocked-out and destroyed: 67 tanks, 20 self-propelled guns, 72 guns of various calibers, 190 machine guns, 8 mortar batteries, 15 halftracks, 22 anti-tank rifles, 54 trucks and cars, and 10 aircraft. Captured by our forces: 180 rifles, 13 machine guns, 2 radio sets, 2 mortars, 1 tank and 10,000 small arms cartridges.

### Conclusion

The enemy grouping created in the Iaşi area, consisting of IV Army Corps, XXXX Panzer Corps and I Army Corps (R) with the aim of driving our units out of the Iaşi fortified area with a subsequent development of the offensive to the Prut River had no substantial success. In the course of offensive fighting between 1.6 and 6.6.1944, the enemy, suffering heavy losses in men and equipment, was compelled to go over to a defense without completing his offensive operation, before reaching its objectives.

[Signed] Deputy chief of staff for intelligence of the 2nd Tank Army Lieutenant Colonel Kostromin

At the conclusion of the operation, the 2nd Tank Army's chief of staff compiled the army's losses and tabulated the claims of the damage inflicted upon the enemy over the period from 3 June to 7 June 1944:

1.  Our own losses: Killed in action – 190; wounded – 1,004; missing in action – 60; total – 1,254 men. Tanks: 13 T-34 knocked-out and 18 destroyed, plus 3 left behind on enemy-occupied territory; total – 34 tanks. Self-propelled guns: 3 SU-85 knocked-out and 2 burned-out; total – 5. IS-122 – 1 knocked-out. Total of knocked-out or destroyed tanks and self-propelled guns – 44. KNOCKED-OUT: 1 57mm gun, 4 45mm guns, 1 anti-tank rifle, 1 120mm mortar, 2 motorcycles, 6 trucks. DAMAGED: 2 motorcycles, 1 85mm gun, 2 37mm guns.
2.  Damage inflicted to the enemy: 2,750 soldiers and officers killed. Knocked-out guns of various calibers – 37. Knocked-out or brewed up tanks – 49. DESTROYED: 9 armored cars, 103 machine guns, 1 anti-aircraft battery, 27 trucks, 3 mortar batteries, 2 log bunkers, 4 firing positions, 10 mortars, 4 aircraft shot down, and 1 ammunition dump blown up. BOOTY: 12 machine guns, 2 radio sets, 122 rifles, 10,000 cartridges, and 105 prisoners captured.

[Signed] 2nd Tank Army chief of staff Major General A. Radzievsky

A further report summed up the 2nd Tank Army's losses in tanks and self-propelled guns over the period from 3 to 10 June 1944. According to it, the army lost a total of 38 tanks and self-propelled guns between these two dates, including 31 T-34, 2 IS-122, 3 SU-152 and 2 SU-85.

The chief of the 2nd Tank Army's Department of Staffing Lieutenant Colonel Chuguev provided data on the combat strength of the 2nd Tank Army's formations and units as of 15 June 1944 (see Table 7.7 below).

## Conclusions of the 2nd Tank Army command on the results of the operation

The grouping that the enemy had created in the Iaşi area, which was given the task to clear the south bank of the Jijia River of Soviet units, before pivoting and reaching the Prut River, was unable to drive the Soviet units beyond the Jijia River, while suffering heavy losses in men and equipment. The enemy offensive, met by the organized resistance of the forces of the 2nd Tank Army, was clearly running out of steam by 4.6.1944. Instances where the enemy went over to a defense were noted more frequently. By the end of the operation, the enemy's offensive had been reduced to limited operations to improve their positions.

Having failed to achieve success on the chosen main axis of attack (Movileni Station), the enemy made an attempt to cut off our forces from the western bank of the Jijia River, but here

**Table 7.7: Data on the personnel and matériel of the units and formations of the 2nd Tank Army as of 30 May 1944**

| Formations and units | Personnel | | | | Rifles | Submachine guns | Machine guns | | | Mortars | | Guns | | | | | Anti-tank rifles | Vehicles, all types | Tanks, all types | Rocket launchers | AA-guns | Armored cars |
|---|---|---|---|---|---|---|---|---|---|---|---|---|---|---|---|---|---|---|---|---|---|---|
| | Officers | Sergeants | Enlisted men | Total | | | Light | Heavy | Anti-aircraft | 120mm | 50mm | 122-203mm | 85mm AT | 76mm | 57mm | 45mm | | | | | | |
| 3 TC | 1,400 | 2,576 | 4,429 | 8,345 | 3,380 | 1,757 | 132 | 31 | 39 | 24 | 4 | – | 35 | 12 | 11 | 7 | 111 | 601 | | 8 | 0/15 | 11 |
| 16 TC | 1,458 | 2,816 | 4,759 | 9,033 | 3,317 | 1,958 | 151 | 29 | 49 | 30 | 8 | – | 30 | 11/1 | 12 | 7/1 | 102 | 590 | | 5 | 0/12 | 6 |
| 11 GTBr | 221 | 485 | 494 | 1,200 | 271 | 351 | 19 | 4 | 9 | – | – | – | 6 | 4 | – | – | 14 | 119 | | | | |
| 87 MC Bn. | 36 | 134 | 230 | 400 | 68 | 106 | 13 | – | – | – | – | – | – | – | – | – | – | 18 | | | | |
| 5 MC Rgt. | 110 | 448 | 617 | 1,175 | 55 | 517 | 36 | 12 | 18 | – | – | – | 12 | 4 | – | – | 18 | 62 | | | | |
| **Total** | **3,225** | **6,399** | **10,529** | **20,153** | **7,091** | **4,689** | **351** | **76** | **115** | **54** | **12** | **-** | **83** | **31/1** | **23** | **14/1** | **245** | **1,490** | | **13** | **0/27** | **17** |

Chief of the 2nd Tank Army's Department of Staffing Lieutenant Colonel Chuguev

Notes: Empty columns have been removed from this table to save space, with the exception of "Tanks, all types". This was left in to make clear that the "Vehicles of all types" category did not include tanks and self-propelled guns. The "AA guns" category shows the number of 20-37mm anti-aircraft guns on the right side of the slash, while the left side of the slash reveals the formations had no large-caliber anti-aircraft guns. For the 76mm gun category, the number to the right of the slash gives the number of unserviceable guns.

as well all of his efforts were frustrated by the tenacity of the troops of the 2nd Tank Army and ended in complete failure.

The enemy's attempts to break through in any sector of the Rediu Mitropoliei – Tipileşti direction created the need for frequent regroupings of the army's forces. In essence, every day the area of operations of some element or even formation of the army changed. The shifts as a rule were conducted at night, but there were instances of daytime regroupings, even given the *Luftwaffe*'s high level of activity over the battlefield. The army's tank units frequently had to repel enemy night attacks.

The enemy, before launching the offensive, had diligently prepared for it and had assembled major forces, which promised a successful operation, but thanks to the firmness of the army's personnel, thorough and constant reconnaissance, and good cooperation both within the army and with neighboring formations, all of the enemy's attempts to achieve a decisive success ended in failure. With aggressive counterattacks by the 2nd Tank Army's forces, the enemy in separate sectors was thrown back to the start line. The tank units, having obtained combat experience when operating in the foothills of the Carpathian Mountains, organized a tough defense. In cases where enemy tanks broke through in separate sectors, the self-propelled artillery units were used to thwart them from reaching objectives, which decided the outcome of the operation in our favor. The task given to the 2nd Tank Army, to halt the enemy's drive to the north, was carried out by the army.

### From the account of the deputy commander of the 2nd Tank Army for vehicle maintenance and technical support Major General of Engineering Services Iukin on the Period from 30.5 to 16.6.44

In the period of accounting, the 2nd Tank Army joined the 2nd Ukrainian Front. On 1 June 1944, the presence and condition of the combat matériel in the army was as follows:

**Summary of the combat strength of the units and formations of the 2nd Tank Army as of 15 June 1944**

| | On the list | Serviceable | Undergoing minor repairs | Undergoing light overhauls | Undergoing major overhauls | Irrecoverable losses, not yet written off |
|---|---|---|---|---|---|---|
| **T-34** | | | | | | |
| 3 Tank Corps | 33 | 26 | – | – | 5 | 2 |
| 16 Tank Corps | 34 | 21 | – | – | 13 | – |
| 11 Gds Tank Br. | 6 | 6 | – | – | – | – |
| 9 Signals Bn. | 3 | 3 | – | – | – | – |
| 245 Training Bn. | 3 | 3 | – | – | – | – |
| **SU-152** | | | | | | |
| 375 SPA Rgt. | 10 | 7 | – | 3 | – | – |
| **KV-122** | | | | | | |
| 6 Gds Tank Rgt. | 10 | 7 | 2 | – | 1 | – |
| **KV-85** | | | | | | |
| 6 Gds Tank Rgt. | 1 | 1 | – | – | – | – |
| **SU-85** | | | | | | |
| 1441 SPA Rgt. | 9 | 8 | – | 1 | – | – |
| **Mk IX** | | | | | | |
| 3 Tank Corps | 1 | – | – | – | 1 | – |
| 16 Tank Corps | 2 | – | – | – | 2 | – |
| **M4A2** | | | | | | |
| 9 Signals Bn. | 2 | 2 | – | – | – | – |
| **Total for the army** | 114 | 84 | 2 | 4 | 22 | 2 |

Over the accounting period, the following number of tanks and self-propelled guns of the 2nd Tank Army were rendered unserviceable as a result of combat actions:

**Number of tanks and self-propelled guns rendered unserviceable as a result of combat actions**

| Type | Participated in combat | Knocked-out |
|------|------------------------|-------------|
| T-34 | 126 | 61 |
| KV-122 | 24 | 7 |
| SU-85 | 40 | 12 |
| **Total:** | **190** | **80** |

Combat losses were distributed as follows: 40 – from enemy artillery and tank fire; 23 – due to enemy air strikes; 17 – due to mechanical problems. Over the given period, 182 combat machines were repaired and returned to service by the army's, corps' and combat units' repair mean, including the repair pool of the preceding period. Of these, 156 required minor repairs; 25 required light overhauls; and 1 needed a major overhaul. In the month of June the army took part in combat operations up until 12 June 1944, after which the available combat machines were turned over at an order of the Front to other units, and the army set out to a new assembly area, where it became subordinate to the 1st Belorussian Front.

The German panzer divisions suffered major losses in the fighting in Moldavia and Romania. For example, the German 23rd Panzer Division lost 8 Panthers and 1 Pz. IV in April 1944, in addition to the 16 Panthers lost in the Stanislav area and another 20 Panthers that had been knocked out and evacuated for major overhauls. The German 24th Panzer Division over the month of April 1944 lost 7 tanks (1 Pz. III, 4 Pz. IV and 2 Panthers) and 14 StuG assault guns. Precise figures for the losses of the *Grossdeutschland* Panzer Grenadier Division for the period April-June 1944 are not available, but it is known that they were significant. For example, on 25 April in action against Soviet forces, the assault gun commanded by *Oberleutnant* Raisenhoffer, one of the best officers in *Grossdeutschland*'s assault gun brigade, was destroyed. Raisenoffer was killed together with his crew. The German 14th Panzer Division over this same period irrecoverably lost at least 5 tanks and assault guns. For example, the 243rd Assault Gun Brigade, which was operationally subordinate to the 14th Panzer Division, suffered painful losses in combats with Soviet forces on 1 June 1944: its commander and several other officers together with their crews were killed or burned alive in their assault guns. Of the 10 Panthers available to the SS Panzer Division *Totenkopf* on 20 April 1944, and of the 27 Pz. IV tanks available to it on 1 May 1944, by 1 July 1944 not a single one was still operational. Since this panzer division had received additionally 5 Panthers and 24 Pz. IV tanks in May-June 1944, this means that over two months of fighting, the division irrecoverably lost 38 tanks (23 Pz. IV and 15 Panthers). The precise tank losses for the 23rd and 24th Panzer Division over May-June 1944 are not known, but it is known that the 23rd Panzer Division over the two months of fighting lost 3,141 soldiers and officers either killed or wounded (out of 18,686), while the 24th Panzer Division over this same period lost 1,908 soldiers and officers either killed or wounded (out of the 14,278 reporting for duty on 1 May 1944). In his book on the combat history of the 23rd Panzer Division, Ernst Rebentisch, a former operations officer and regiment commander with the division, gives some information on the panzer division's losses over the period from 30 May to 8 June 1944. On the first day of the offensive – 30 May 1944 – the 23rd Panzer Division lost two Pz. IV tanks irrecoverably, which were destroyed by anti-tank guns. Some of its tanks and halftracks were immobilized by minefields, or became the victims of friendly fire of German artillery and aircraft. As a result, on the second day of the operation, the 23rd Panzer Division's *kampfgruppe* had serviceable only 12 tanks. On 1 June 1944, *Kampfgruppe* Rebentisch of the 23rd Panzer Division), which had set off in the wake of the 24th Panzer Division's panzer group and was advancing in the direction of the Neagra valley, came under heavy fire from 122mm guns in the vicinity of Hill 148. As a result, at a minimum one Pz. IV tank was recorded as destroyed. On this same day in a different combat action, the commander of II/PzGr. 128 *Hauptmann* Schunk was killed. In just one panzer company of the 23rd Panzer Division alone, which had 10 serviceable Pz. IV tanks, there were 13 recorded cases over 9 days of fighting where tanks became immobilized by mines. Over this same period after 30 May 1944, the 23rd Panzer Division had 1,030 wounded.

Here it must be said that the attempts by the former *Wehrmacht* general Manteuffel, as well as by other historians, to depict the battles in Romania in April-May 1944 as a grandiose defeat to the Red Army, which supposedly lost 550 tanks in the fighting for Târgu Frumos alone (Manteuffel wrote that his forces destroyed 350 tanks and knocked out of action another 200 tanks, and then another 70 tanks in the June fighting) appear to be at the very least not objective. The historical truth is that on 1 May 1944, the Soviet 2nd and 5th Guards Tank Armies had a total of 479 operational tanks and self-propelled guns (121 in the 2nd Tank Army and 358 in the 5th Guards Tank Army), so there is no way they could have lost 550 tanks. According to a report of the command of the 2nd Ukrainian Front's armored forces, on 6 May 1944 both tank armies had a combined total of 264 serviceable tanks and self-propelled guns, which means the loss of 215 tanks and self-propelled guns between 1 and 6 May 1944. Though heavy, this figure is two times smaller than the one given by some Western historians. The irrecoverable losses of the German panzer grouping in Romania over May-June 1944 amounted to no less than 130 tanks and self-propelled guns. This figure doesn't include the losses of the Romanian forces.

When speaking about the successful operations of the *Grossdeutschland* Division at Târgu Frumos in May 1944, Western historians forget to mention that this same division at the beginning of June 1944 failed in its attempt to drive the forces of the 2nd Tank Army and of other formations from their bridgeheads across the Jijia River north of Iaşi. In the process, it suffered heavy losses.

In the fighting near Târgu Frumos in May 1944, the commander of *Grossdeutschland*'s Tiger battalion (III/Panzer Regiment GD) Major Herbert Homille was severely wounded. His Tiger was knocked out, and after he changed to a different Tiger, it too was knocked out, and Homille himself was put out of action for a long time. One can read about this in the book by Egon Kleine and Volkmar Kuehne, *Tiger: The History of the Legendary Weapon, 1942-1945* (J.J. Fedorowicz, 2004). Spaeter's *The History of the Panzerkorps Grossdeutschland* (J.J. Fedorowicz, 2000) is silent about this, since this plainly doesn't fit into the version of the fighting near Târgu Frumos created by German authors.

A knocked-out Tiger of the *Grossdeutschland* Panzer Grenadier Division, Romania 1944.

In his after-action report, General Bogdanov later wrote:

> The breakthrough of an enemy's defense together with a field army (the 2nd Tank Army operated together with the 27th and 52nd Armies near Iași and Târgu Frumos) is an undesirable manifestation in combat usage. Such use of the Tank Army should be avoided, since in this case the main advantage of the tank army, as a major operational mobile formation – its shock power, maneuverability and depth of operations – are reduced to resolving tactical tasks and the effect of its combat use is lowered. The structure and organization of the Tank Army doesn't allow it to be scattered and split into pieces in order to carry out tasks of supporting infantry attacks when breaking through an enemy defense, and rearranging it for carrying out such goals is inexpedient. Thus the Tank Army can be used only when the enemy has a weak defense or has taken up a defense hastily, when there are possibilities to break through it from the march and to exploit a success.

## Excerpt from the letters of citation for soldiers of the 2nd Tank Army who particularly distinguished themselves in the operation

Guards Lieutenant Colonel **Stepan Kharitonov**, commander of the 375th Guards Heavy Self-propelled Artillery Regiment of the 3rd Tank Corps. In the period of the corps' combat operations, thanks to maneuver and skillful leadership, the regiment destroyed 10 tanks and self-propelled guns of various marks, 2 mortar batteries, a German observation post, and up to 375 enemy soldiers and officers in the Iași sector. Kharitonov himself was located directly in the midst of the regiment's combat formations and among the crews of the batteries, directing the fighting. On 3.6.1944, the enemy undertook a tank offensive with air support. Despite having a small number of self-propelled guns operationa, the regiment repulsed 7 counterattacks of enemy tanks and infantry. For the exceptional tenacity when repelling all of the enemy's attacks and counterattacks, Kharitonov has been awarded the Order of the Red Banner.

Lieutenant **Nikolai Meleshkov**, a T-34 tank platoon leader in the 51st Tank Brigade's 94th Tank Battalion. On 7.06.44 during an attack against Hill 178 (4 kilometers south of Larga), skillfully maneuvering his tank, he was the first to break into the enemy's positions. With fire from his tank, he destroyed up to a platoon of infantry and 4 enemy machine guns. On 8.06.44 during an attack against Hill 167 in the same area, he was the first to break into the enemy's line of defense and threw up to a company of Romanian soldiers into flight. He killed up to 20 enemy soldiers and officers and destroyed 2 heavy machine guns. He was killed in action. [Posthumously awarded the Order of the Patriotic War 1st Degree.]

Senior Sergeant **Aleksei Shesterskov**, commander of a machine-gun team in the 57th Motorized Rifle Brigade's 3rd Motorized Rifle Battalion. In fighting from 5.6 to 11.6.1944 in the area of Movileni Station, he destroyed two enemy firing positions with his machine gun and wiped out up to 80 Hitlerites. Skillfully maneuvering and firing without pause from his machine gun, he helped a rifle company to seize enemy trenches and to drive back 4 counterattacks by German and Romanian infantry. Being twice-wounded, he refused to leave the battlefield, and continued to direct the actions of his team firmly. Awarded the Order of the Patriotic War 1st Degree.

Lieutenant **Vladimir Burov**, T-34 tank platoon commander in the 51st Tank Brigade's 94th Tank Battalion. On 7.06.1944 during the attack against Hill 178, skillfully maneuvering his tank, he boldly led his tank toward the foe. He killed up to 20 enemy soldiers and officers and destroyed one mortar crew. On 8.06.1944, while repelling an enemy counterattack, he showed resolve and courage. With the fire from his tank he killed up to 23 Hitlerites, which contributed to the collapse of the enemy counterattack. Awarded the Order of the Patriotic War 2nd Degree.

Lieutenant **Nikolai Zinchenko**, T-34 tank platoon commander in the 103rd Tank Brigade's 119th Tank Battalion. In the vicinity of a nameless village on 2.05.44, he demonstrated courage and valor. His platoon was the first to break into the settlement and destroyed one tank, three anti-tank guns and killed up to 50 enemy soldiers and officers. He fought off 2 German counterattacks. Awarded the Order of the Patriotic War 1st Degree.

Lieutenant **Fedor Kirichenko**, commander of a platoon of 85mm guns in the 3rd Tank Corps' 728th Destroyer Anti-tank Artillery Regiment. On 2.06.1944, the enemy in strength of 11 tanks and a company of submachine gunners with air support went on the counterattack in the area of Movileni Station. Lieutenant Kirichenko allowed the enemy tanks to approach to with direct firing range, and opened fire at them. As a result of the combat, one Panther tank was destroyed and one medium tank was knocked-out. On 4.6 and 8.6 1944 in the Epureni area, he repulsed an enemy tank counterattack and brewed up 3 tanks. Awarded the Order of the Patriotic War 2nd Degree.

On 10 June 1944 at 16.00, the Supreme Commander-in-Chief issued an order to the commanders of the 2nd Ukrainian Front and the 2nd Tank Army about relocating the tank army by rail to a new assembly area. The 2nd Tank Army's deputy commander for rear services directed:

The army is to load aboard trains starting at 8.00 on 14 June in the Bălti, Fălești area. The movement request is to be presented to the General Staff on 12 June. The army is to move with the 3rd and 16th Tank Corps, together with all of their attachments and units of combat support, service facilities and the army's rear echelon. All of the units and formations are to move out with all their available personnel, weapons, property and motorized transport, but without the tanks and self-propelled guns; no detractions are to be tolerated. On the route of movement, the army is to be supplied with: 1 combat load of ammunition, 2 refills and 20 days of rations. In order to organize the unloading of the units in the new location and their accommodations and daily rations, the commander of the 2nd Tank Army is to send an operational group headed by his deputy with communications equipment and necessary support staff. Conduct all correspondence and talks regarding the questions connected with the army's departure only with the General Staff. Correspondence and talks regarding these matters with the central command of the People's Commissariat of Defense is forbidden. Make clear to all the personnel and categorically forbid them to reveal to anyone the train's point of departure. Don't give any information to the line organs of the Service of Military Announcements or to the workers of the People's Commissariat of Broadcasting, except for the train's number. At stops of the train, immediately send out strong patrols. Conduct the release of men from the rail wagons in an organized fashion – with commands. Organize meals by wagon. Do not allow lines to form around the kitchens. Camouflage all of the equipment, transport and matériel on the platform cars. After unloading from the trains, direct all the troops to areas of concealment. Confirm the receipt of the directives. Report daily on the process of loading and departure.

[Signed] Antonov – Deputy Commander of the 2nd Tank Army for Rear Services

## Concluding comments

### The conclusions of the commander of the 3rd Tank Corps Lieutenant General Vasilii Mishulin regarding the operation

Throughout the entire extent of the operation, as a result of the great stretching of the lines of communication, the rear services didn't ensure the normal combat work of the units. Broad maneuvering of the tank formation in the conditions of at least a short stabilization of the front was absent. Flexible control by the unit commanders over their subordinate elements was inadequate, especially at the company and battalion level. The organization of the reconnaissance of the enemy was incompetent. Too frequently there was no success in seizing a "tongue". Scouting of the movement routes by engineers was absent. A sense of responsibility for carrying out a given task, primarily among the officers' staff, was absent. As a general rule, the tanks were committed without any thorough reconnaissance of the terrain and forward edge. The day's tasks weren't disseminated down to the tank crews. Changes of decisions were frequent, the setting of tasks unrealistic, with no regard for the presence or absence of means of struggle. The weak air cover allowed the enemy airforce to operate with impunity against the combat formations, which doubtlessly restricted the actions of the forces. In all cases, field artillery was carrying out the work of the tanks' close-support artillery. Other than this, the corps' artillery almost played no part in the fighting throughout the operation.

[Signed] Commander of the 3rd Tank Corps Hero of the Soviet Union Lieutenant Colonel Mishulin; Chief of Staff of the 3rd Tank Corps Colonel Shevtsov

### The conclusions of the commander of the 16th Tank Corps Major General Dubovoi regarding the operation:

From the experience of the Corps' combat actions in the Carpathian foothills it is evident that the main stubborn fighting arises for possession of roads, road hubs and commanding heights. The use of tank units is possible not along the entire extent of the front, but only on directions accessible for tanks. During the movement of the tanks into an attack – the infantry is obliged to conduct reconnaissance of the terrain for the tanks, to guide them through difficult pieces of terrain, as well as to point out enemy tanks. The 10 days of preparation of the operation on the Târgu Frumos axis allowed the possibility for all of the brigade's personnel to prepare well – to work out coordination and to reconnoiter the directions of the brigades' probable actions in the Corps as a whole down to the tank commander and driver-mechanic.

[Signed] Commander of the 16th Uman' Order of Suvorov Tank Corps Major General of Tank Forces Dubovoi; Chief of Staff of the 16th Tank Corps Colonel Bibergan]

### Conclusions of the commander of the 11th Guards Tank Brigade Guards Lieutenant Colonel Kurilenko regarding the operation:

The enemy on the defense in hilly terrain is adopting new methods for using tanks, attaching them to the infantry in small groups, moving them out on the slopes of hills and keeping the valleys under flanking fire. The tank commanders, especially the tank battalion commanders, forgot about covering their flanks and didn't deploy tanks to cover the flanks. The tankers because of little combat experience in hilly terrain are not conducting sufficient reconnaissance of the battlefield and losing sight of the enemy. All this gives the enemy the opportunity to fall upon the flanks with 2-3 tanks and to knock our tanks out of action. The commanders of the platoons and tanks, because of the lack of topographical maps, were unable to study the routes of advance throughout the extent of the combat operations. In future battles, it is necessary to provide all of the tank crews with topographical maps, to give the crews ahead of time the chance to analyze the terrain along the routes of advance in the entire depth of the combat task. It is necessary to allot a sufficient amount of time before the start of an operation for the reconnoitering of the terrain and to work out the coordination of actions with other arms, in order to allow the possibility of thorough reconnoitering, down to the driver-mechanics.

[Signed] Commander of the 11th Guards Korsun' Order of Suvorov Tank Brigade Lieutenant Colonel Kurilenko; chief of staff of the 11th Guards Korsun' Order of Suvorov Tank Brigade Lieutenant Colonel Rodionov [Unclear]

## Conclusions of the commander of the 57th Motorized Rifle Brigade Lieutenant Colonel Shamardin regarding the operation

In the course of three months of combat, the brigade, lacking the authorized amount of motorized transport, conducted its movements on foot, as a result of which the brigade's rear elements stretched for hundreds of kilometers. In spite of the lack of motorized transport and fuel for the available vehicles, the brigade was always receiving and carrying out assignments as a motorized rifle unit. As a result of this, the combat capability of the personnel was reduced significantly, since the marches were always forced, and the men frequently entered combat from the march. For this same reason, the artillery systematically lagged behind the brigade, lowering its combat strength. However, in spite of all the difficulties of the actions given the poor equipping with transport, which meant as well the poor support of the units with everything necessary for battle, the brigade carried out the combat tasks that it faced with honor.

[Signed] Commander of the 57th Motorized Rifle Brigade Lieutenant Colonel Shamardin

## The recollections of participants in the fighting

Guards Sergeant Major Bondar', a gun commander of an IS-2 tank in the 6th Separate Guards Heavy Tank Regiment recalls:

In the month of May 1944, our units neared the town of Iaşi and took up a defense. The Germans in this sector went on the offensive with major forces of tanks, aviation and infantry, but all of the attacks were successfully driven back by our troops. After the battle near the city of Târgu Frumos, which is northwest of Iaşi, the 6th Separate Guards Tank Regiment was regrouped to the area north of Iaşi, where by this time a tense situation had developed. Our units took up a defense on high ground that extended along the bank of the small Jijia River. Level ground stretched behind us. We arrived near Iaşi on the evening of 2 June 1944 and moved into position. The tanks were dug into the earth and camouflaged from the enemy's ground observation and aerial surveillance. Several days passed. The enemy didn't undertake any attacks, apparently sensing that the menacing IS-2 tanks were in front of them. On the night of 7/8 June 1944, two of the IS-2 tanks were moved up in front of the remaining platoons and companies and were deployed as a vanguard 500-600 meters behind our infantry. I was the gun commander in one of these tanks. Guards Lieutenant Aleksandrov commanded the tank crew.

At 6.30 on 8.6.44, we were given a brief order over the radio: "Seven Tigers and Panthers are moving toward our forward edge; move out and destroy them." We were given precise coordinates of the location of the enemy's tanks and their direction of movement. The tank commander Guards Lieutenant Aleksandrov directed to start up the motor and to move out in front of our infantry's positions. When we reached the forward edge of our infantry, we pivoted 90 degrees to the left and climbed a hill, from which point the enemy's tanks that were advancing toward three of our T-34 tanks that had been immobilized by mines, were clearly visible. I quickly calculated the range to the enemy tanks once they reached our frontline infantry and we had the possibility of firing at their flanks. At the order of the tank commander, I opened fire at the enemy tanks. The Germans immediately spotted our tank and opened up heavy, disorganized fire. However, only the turret of our tank was visible to the Germans. The combat lasted for just 5-10 minutes. I fired 8 shells and knocked out or brewed up three tanks, while the other four tanks, firing wildly, retreated.

At 12.00 the commander of the 16th Tank Corps Major General Ivan Dubovoi congratulated us over the radio and awarded us with Orders. At 23.00 on 8.6.44, the tank commander Guards Lieutenant Aleksandrov was awarded the Order of the Red Star. The rest of the crew received the Order of the Patriotic War 2nd Degree. Over the day of combat on 8.6.44, three Tiger tanks, 3 machine guns and up to 50 enemy soldiers and officers were destroyed by our crew.

Guards Senior Sergeant Chizov remembered:

In the battle on the approaches to the city of Iaşi our platoon received an order to take Hill 178. Submachine-gun platoon commander Lieutenant Kriukov gave our squad an order to move up 50-75 meters toward the enemy's trenches, and after they were worked over by rocket artillery and artillery, we were to break into the trenches, disrupt communications, sow panic in the enemy's combat positions, and destroy two machine-gun nests in the depth of the defense. The task was not easy: The approaches to the hill were exposed and a ravine was blocking the route of approach. From the ravine, we would have to make a 100-meter-high climb up the hill to reach the enemy. The ravine was exposed to the enemy's view and was being swept by flanking machine-gun fire.

Having prepared the squad for battle, I gave the order to advance and all 6 soldiers started to move to the ravine, crawling through tall grass. We reached the ravine. The enemy on the opposite side might hear our movement. It was necessary to speak and give orders at a whisper. With a quick dash we crossed to the opposite side of the ravine and were now just 50 meters from the enemy. Still unnoticed, we hugged the earth and dug in. Two minutes later the artillery preparation began. Now deeply huddled in their trenches, the enemy no longer had the possibility to observe our movement from the forward trenches. Having waited for the artillery to shift its fire to the depth of the defenses, with a rapid advance we overcame the first trenchline and moved out along the communication trenchs to a point in the rear of the machine-gun nests. With shouts of "Ura!", tossing grenades into the German trenches and opening up blistering fire from our submachine guns, our squad spread panic among the German machine-gunners. In fact, stunned by our sudden and unexpected appearance in their rear, they fled, abandoning their machine guns. However, even then we didn't lose our composure, and having taken up advantageous positions in the trenches, we fired at the backs of the fleeing Germans. At this time, our forward elements, having received the possibility to move more freely because the German macine guns were no longer firing, burst into the enemy's defenses and seized the hill. The platoon commander thanked all of us for this and recommended us for government decorations.

Guards Senior Sergeant Matsapura in his memoirs wrote:

The entire month of March went by with constant marches and fighting on Moldavian soil. At the beginning of April, the 2nd Tank Army forced a crossing of the Prut River and arrived on Romanian territory on the Iaşi axis. Here the enemy managed to stop our offensive. Both sides assumed a defensive posture, and the units of the 2nd Tank Army were withdrawn to the rear. The 107th "Vapniarka" Tank Brigade was positioned near the Romanian town of Ceplenița. We were putting our equipment back into order, when the army commander General Bogdanov arrived. As usual, he went around each platoon, chatted with the soldiers, and then gathered all of the brigade's personnel. He spoke briefly and succinctly: "From where are we closer to Berlin?" he asked us all. "From Belorussia!" all the men replied in chorus. "Right!" he said. Then another question:

"Are we all soldiers?"

"Yes, soldiers!"

"Is there a blabbermouth among you that will betray us?"

"Never!"

"Then listen! They're shifting the army to the north – to a point closer to Berlin."

The army commander added that the brigade had to surrender its tanks. In the new deployment site we would receive new machines.

In the first days of June, when the 3rd Tank Battalion was readying its combat equipment for the turnover, an order arrived to head out quickly toward the front lines. Our assembly was so hasty that we already on the march were refastening the rear hull plates that had been removed from the machines. Four machines of our battalion set off on the march, and as I recall, 12-14 in total for the brigade. On the march we were given the order to repulse an enemy tank counterattack, which was pushed our infantry back to the Jijia River. We moved through the night. By dawn we arrived in the designated area, not far from the river. The sun was not yet up, but the infantrymen were already exchanging fire with the enemy. A 57mm battery – three guns – were standing about 100 meters in front of the extended line of skirmishers, covering the withdrawal. They were waiting for us. Two officers quickly briefed the brigade commander Colonel Tikhon Abramov on the situation.

The tanks of the 3rd Battalion were deployed in ambush behind a deep ravine. We camouflaged the machines and waited. At dawn, the fascists intensified their artillery and mortar fire. Then enemy tanks and self-propelled guns – more than 20 of them – moved out from behind distant green hills, advancing directly through vineyards and apple orchards. They were heavy [sic] Pz. V and medium Pz. III tanks. We sat quietly as they approached. At a range of approximately 600 meters, we began to sweep them with fire. The infantry's anti-tank battery was working well, too. About 20-25 minutes later, no less than ten Nazi machines were burning in the vineyards. The remaining tanks had turned back. We waited for a second attack, but it never came. Apparently, the enemy didn't have enough balls for it.

This was our last battle in Romania. That evening, we surrendered our machines, and by dawn we had moved to a railroad, to the loading area.

Guards Junior Sergeant Grishudenko, who served in the 6th Guards Heavy Tank Regiment as a truck driver, recalled:

> I took part in the fighting as a member of the 6th Guards Heavy Tank Regiment from 1944, when the regiment, after forming-up in Tula, joined the 2nd Tank Army near the city of Târgu Frumos. I was a driver who delivered ammunition to the regiment's combat units. In offensive fighting on 2 and 3 May 1944, the enemy tried several times to counterattack and set a lot of tanks in motion that were covered by aviation. My service comrades and I had to bring up ammunition in these difficult circumstances. Once I had an experience that I've not been able to forget. An artillery shell, which exploded during an enemy artillery barrage, damaged the tires and cab of my truck. I understood the situation and knew that this meant I would be late in delivering ammunition to the tankers; exerting all my strength, I worked to put the truck back in working order again, despite the threat of death. When I arrived at the tankers, they thanked me for the fact that we were so selflessly keeping them supplied with ammunition under enemy fire.

### From the memoirs of Guards Major General Anatolii Shvebig:

> We arrived in Moldavia in felt boots, sheepskin jackets and winter fur caps with earflaps, but the temperature there was 25° C. [77° F.]. Lice were eating us up alive. I took off my sheepskin jacket and laid it down, but it budged – so many were the lice. It was impossible to sleep. We took rags, wrapped them around our necks, and immediately a host of lice would rush upon them; we'd take it off, toss it aside and wrap another one around our necks. What else could we do? We were marching without rest, day after day. Later, whcn we managed to get a bit of rest in Romania, we built fires.

Major General Anatolii Shvebig.

The relationships among the senior officers were good; all orders were carried out – and there were no sort of squabbles. Sometimes, of course, someone would raise his voice, but on the whole everything was correct.

There were few specialized prime movers for towing away tanks. What sort did we have? We would remove the turrets from a damaged tank or a tank without a serviceable turret, and convert them into tow vehicles. We made a lot of these. However, at first our losses were not too large for our tow vehicles to manage, yet there was no neeed for the evacuation of knocked-out tanks, because either we would take the position, or the Germans would. It was necessary to abandon knocked-out tanks – it was impossible to remove them from the line of fire.

We didn't use German equipment ourselves. We would use their trucks and cars, but not their tanks – the Germans left behind only burned-out tanks, and moreover we didn't have spare parts for them.

As a technical specialist, I examined German tanks. Initially, we held training exercises with all the crews on the subject of where they had to fire at Tigers, Panthers and so on. This was my assignment – the task of the vehicle maintenance and technical support unit was to conduct such training sessions. By that time we already had some technical data about these tanks. Mainly it was necessary to fire at their flanks and running gear, because their fronts were not badly armored. You could also fire at their rear hull or rear turret, but it was hard to hit them – you could do so only when the tank pivoted.

Yet then we received armor-piercing discarding sabot shells. They easily penetrated the armor of the Tigers and Panthers. Before this we only had armor-piercing shells and high-explosive shells.

The main gun on the German tanks was, of course, excellent. They had the 88mm cannon. In 1944 we now had the 85mm cannon, but it was a little inferor. But in every other aspect they [the German Tigers and Panthers] weren't so special. Because the Tigers were very slow and heavy, how were they used? Not out in front, like our heavy tanks. On the contrary, they had medium tanks moving in front, while the heavy tanks were the ones supporting them. The arrangement, of course, wasn't bad, but it was losing from the point of view of mobility and maneuverability. The Panthers were more mobile and compact – not like the ponderous Tigers.

My primary task as the deputy commander for vehicle maintenance and technical support was to ensure the tanks were combat-ready. Before battle, the technical staff would check the operability, kit, main gun and so forth. The company's deputy commander for technical support would examine everything, and in addition, ask about the combat-readiness of each crew. If the crews said something wasn't working properly, a technician was supposed to check it out and make a decision as to whether the tank was fit for combat. This was a large responsibility, especially a moral one, which each crew faced. There were incidents where crews would render a tank unserviceable. We had technical-control points, and the deputy commander of the technical support company and a company technician would keep watch. It happened that a crew would clamber out of a tank and abandon it. But the observers could see that the tank wasn't burning, yet the crew left it. Such cases took place with especial frequency in Romania. There, a tank would be moving downhill; the crew would jump out of it, while the tank would keep rolling down and would burst into flames, and all of this was visible from the control posts, although the crew was probably thinking that since the terrain was hilly, not level, no one would notice. Such cases, of course, were turned over to SMERSH [literally, a contraction of "Special Methods for Exposing Spies", but known anecdotally as "Death to Spies", the special counter-intelligence service within the Red Army]. But it was hard to say whether a crew deliberately broke something, weakened an idler wheel, or something similar.

The crew would claim a mechanical breakdown, and the technician was supposed to check it and repair whatever was broken. But on the whole, everyone fought honorably.

We left behind tanks that had broken down. Later they returned to service. This was our assignment – to track whether the tanks were being repaired and whether or not they ever returned. Take, for example, the great distances prior to Uman' and after Uman' – tanks were traveling 50-60 kilometers every day. But say one tank had been left 100 kilometers behind, and it had no fuel. It was necessary to organize fueling way stations, in order to refuel tanks on the road. The work to organize repairs was enormous. Everything had to be documented, and the nature of a major overhaul had to be determined. Did it have to be turned over to the army's resources, so that they could send it back to factories in the rear or some place else? We were supposed to examine each burned-out tank, draw up a statement of fact, indicate the location, and establish the cause of the conflagration. Later, so-called control commissions were introduced. Such commissions included a technician, a SMERSH agent and an officer. These three men would make a final decision. Everything was strictly controlled – both burned-out tanks and the receipt of new replacements.

On 12 April 1944, the formations of the 16th Tank Corps were assembled in the area of the Movileni Station and began offensive battles in the direction of Podu Iloaie Station. Here for the first time we began to operate in hilly terrain. Here the tankers had to drive tanks along narrow roads between craggy defiles, and to overcome steep descents and ascents. Thirteen tanks were serviceable and 9 were coming up. Later we fought in the areas of Plugari and Hodora. The new conditions in which the combat operations were taking place required changes in the organization of technical service. The decision was made to move the repair and evacuation means closer to the combat units. It was decided to conduct presentations to the drivers in all the brigades by experienced master drivers, who once again reminded their fellow servicemen about the particularities of driving tanks in hilly and swampy terrain.

By 20 April 1944, there were 40 serviceable T-34 tanks in our three tank brigades. The corps' own pool of repaired tanks in its repair shops in close proximity to the combat units had sharply shrunk, but a large number of damaged tanks had been assembled by the Front and the army at Bălti Station. According to a directive of the Front's Military Council, the 2nd Tank Army had to send the 168th Repair Base to the station in order to perform light overhauls on 32 tanks. The repair workers fulfilled the assignment ahead of schedule, which significantly increased the combat strength of the tank brigades. The 6th Separate Guards Tank Regiment arrived to reinforce the tank corps. It conducted a march to an assembly area on the northwestern outskirts of Hodora. The regiment, which numbered 21 tanks, was equipped with the most powerful tanks in the Red Army, the IS-2. These were the first heavy tanks that appeared on our sector of the front. Factory representatives arrived with the tanks. Engineer-Colonel Petr Voroshilov, the son of Marshal Voroshilov, headed them.

On 2 May 1944, the 16th Tank Corps went on the attack in the general direction of Târgu Frumos. The IS [tanks] moved out of their jumping-off positions in the wake of the combat formations of medium tanks. At first the attack made good progress. The T-34s were forced to retreat when they neared Târgu Frumos. The heavy tanks wound up in front and engaged in solitary combat with the Tigers. After a 2-hour combat, the enemy had managed to knock 4 of our heavy tanks out of action, and launched a counterattack. The regiment put up resistance and fought off the Nazi's attack, but suffered heavy losses. On the night of 3/4 May at a decision of the corps commander General Dubovoi, the IS regiment was withdrawn from combat to the area of Hodora in order to repair tanks. Repair teams were sent to the same place, which over 48 hours repaired 11 combat machines, with which the regiment on 5 May repulsed a Nazi counterattack on the Kurnava – Pulina axis. Serviceable tanks had to be sent to evacuate knocked-out tanks, as a consequence of which for a certain time they didn't take direct part in combat. What should be done with the tanks that were beyond repair, and which remained on the battlefield? I made a decision – to blow them up that night.

Senior Sergeant D'iakonov recalls a mission to snatch a prisoner for interrogation purposes:

In combat in Romania near the city of Iași, I want to relate how we went after an identification prisoner. In order to get a better estimate of the enemy's strength, the command needed a prisoner to interrogate. A group was organized under the command of Lieutenant Tarasevich. He was ordered to select the best scouts in order to carry out this mission. When determining this group, I was the first to raise my hand. The group's members were chosen. Lieutenant Tarasevich gathered this group together, gave us our objective and task, familiarized us with the area on a map, and we headed out in daylight hours to observe the enemy. Through our observation we established that an enemy observation post was located in front of us. We analyzed the approaches to it and the terrain lying in front of it. With the onset of darkness, we prepared to move out. The group's senior ordered, "Take a prisoner at whatever the cost."

When we neared the location of the observation post, we discovered that it was no longer there. We decided to move on, having first sent two men out in front of us. They spotted the silhouettes of men and reported this to the group leader. With observation we determined that this was a German combat outpost. There were three men in it. It was necessary not to waste time, and the group leader Lieutenant Tarasevich decided to approach at a crawl to within grenade-tossing range. We crawled to with 15-20 meters of the Germans, and tossed two grenades as the Lieutenant had ordered, before rushing the position. While checking it out, we found that one of the three Germans was alive, and having caught sight of us, he raised his hands. We took him and headed back to the intelligence department.

In the area of Târgu Frumos, May 1944: a T-34 with an open commander's hatch pauses near the wreckage of a tank that has had its turret blown off.

# Bibliography

## ARCHIVAL SOURCES

### TsAMO

Accounts and Reports about the Combat Operations of the 2nd Tank Army in the 1943 Sevsk Operation: File 307, op.4148, d.145

Account of the Combat Operations of the 3rd Tank Corps over August-September 1943: File 307, op.4148, d.149

Account of the Combat Operations of the 7th Guards Mechanized Corps over August-September 1943: File 307, op.4148, d.140

Account of the Combat Actions of the 11th Guards Tank Brigade over the period from 1 to 9 August 1943

Account of the Combat Operations of the 16th Tank Corps, 3rd Tank Corps and 11th Guards Tank Brigade over the period from 5.3 to 18.3.1944: File 307, op.4148, d.222

Account of the Combat Operations of the 16th Tank Corps, 3rd Tank Corps and 11th Guards Tank Brigade over the period from 25.3 to 5.5.1944: File 307, op.4148, d.222

Account on the Combat Actions of the 3rd Tank Corps over the period from 5 July to 13 August 1943: File 62, Op.343, D.30

Account on the Combat Operations of the 16th Tank Corps, the 3rd Tank Corps and the 11th Guards Tank Brigade over the period from 25.1 to 22.2.1944: File 307, op.4148, d.222

Account on the Material-Technical Support of the Combat Operations of the 2nd Tank Army from 5 July to 11 August 1943: File 307, op. 4148, d. 177, ll. 2-46 (Available in Russian at time of writing at http://podvignaroda.mil.ru/)

Collected materials on the study of the war's experience, No. 11 (March – April 1944). Tank forces in the defense of the Kursk staging area.

Combat Path of the Army: File 307, Folder 184, op. 4148, ll. 1-7

Combat Path of the Army: articles and descriptions of combat episodes and recollections of participants of the Great Patriotic War: File 307, op. 4148, d. 184, ll. 10-19, 626-628

Dmitriev – Sevsk operation of the 2nd Tank Army: File 307, Folder 302, op. 4148, ll. 1-60

Information on the assembly of forces, on their materiél and the condition of the 2nd Tank Army's tank park, and the losses inflicted by the Army's forces: File 307, op.4148, d.266

Journal of Combat Operations of the 2nd Tank Army: File 1

Journal of Combat Operations of the 2nd Tank Army: File 307, op. 4148, d. 1.

Major General M.K. Nozdrunov's "Report: Defensive Operation of the 2nd Tank Army 5-13 July 1943": File 307, op. 4148, d. 147

Marshal Bogdanov's report "On the Combat Use of the 2nd Tank Army": File 307, op.4148, d.476, ll.47-48

Report of Guards Lieutenant Colonel Terekhov about the Operational Use of a Tank Army [based] on the Experience of the 2nd Tank Army

Report on the Combat Operations of the 2nd Tank Army as part of the 1st Ukrainian Front from 25.1 to 25.2.1944: File 307, op.4148, d.221

Report on the Combat Operations of the 2nd Tank Army as part of the 2nd Ukrainian Front in the destruction of the enemy's Uman' grouping of forces from 5.3 to 18.3.1944: File 307, op.4148, d.224

Report on the Combat Operations of the 2nd Tank Army as part of the 2nd Ukrainian Front over the period from 25.3 to 5.5.1944: File 307, op.4148, d.224.

Report on the Combat Operations of the 2nd Tank Army as part of the 2nd Ukrainian Front over the period from 2.6 to 16.6.1944: File 307, op.4148, d.302

Report on the offensive operation of the 2nd Tank Army from 23 February to 18 March 1943: File 307, Folder 154, op. 4148, ll. 13-266

Reports of the tank formations and units of the 2nd Tank Army on the combat actions in the Orel defensive and offensive operations: File 62, op. 343, d. 30

*Additional files:*

File 266, d. 40, op. 321, ll. 174-176

## Bundesarchiv-Militärarchiv

Files of the Gen.Insp.d.Pz.Tr: RH-10

## National Archives, Washington D.C.

Rolls from the T78 series

## Other

Author's correspondence with Martin Block (Germany)
Author's correspondence with Sergei Sergeev (Kiev), 2012
Author's correspondence with Aleksandr Tomzov
Terekhov, S.M., *Boevoi put' Armii* [*Combat path of the Army*] (1992, unpublished manuscript)

## PRINTED SOURCES

Barinov, P.M, Bobrov, B.M., and Deniskin, B.A., *Gvardeiskii Nezhinskii: Boevoi put' 7-go Gvardeiskogo Mexkorpusa* [*Guards Nezhinskii: Combat path of the 7th Guards Mechanized Corps*] (Kemerovo, 1985)

Biriukov, *Tanki Frontu* [*Tanks to the Front*] (Smolensk: Rusich, 2005)

Glantz, David, *Red Storm over the Balkans: The Failed Soviet Invasion of Romania, Spring 1944* (Lawrence KS: University Press of Kansas, 2007)

Iushchik, *Odinnadtsatyi tankovyi v boiakh za Rodinu* [*The 11th Tank Corps in battles for the Motherland*] (Moscow: Voenizdat, 1962)

Jentz, Thomas, *Panzertruppen: The Complete Guide to the Creation & Combat Employment of Germany's Tank Force, 1943-1945*, Volume 2 (Atglen PA: Schiffer, 1996)

Jung, Hans-Joachim, *The History of Panzerregiment Grossdeutschland* (Winnipeg: J.J. Fedorowicz, 2000)

Kazakov, P.D., *Glubokii Sled* [*Deep Imprint*] (Moscow: Voenizdat, 1982)

Kleine, Egon and Kuehn, Volkmar, *Tiger: the History of the Legendary Weapon, 1942-1945* (Winnipeg: J.J. Fedorowicz, 2004)

Krasnitsky, N.F., *2-ia tankovaia armiia v Orlovskoi nastupatel'noi operatsii Tsentral'nogo fronta* [*2nd Tank Army in the Orel offensive operation of the Central Front*] (Moscow: Voenizdat, 1947)

Lochman, Franz-Wilhelm, *Combat History of schwere Panzer Abteilung 503* (Winnipeg: J.J. Fedorowicz, 2000)

Matsapura, S.S., *Tovarishch serzhant* [*Comrade sergeant*] (Moscow: Voenizdat, 1976)

Michulec, Robert, *4. Panzer-Division on the Eastern Front* (Hong Kong: Concord, 1999)

Nash, Douglas E., *Hell's Gate: The Battle of the Cherkassy Pocket, January-February 1944* (Stamford CT: RZM Publishing, 2002)

Nechaev, V.N., *Boevoi put' 9-go tankovogo korpusa* [*Combat path of the 9th Tank Corps*] (Moscow: Voenizdat, 1989)

Neumann, Joachim, *Die 4. Panzer Division, 1938-1943* (Bonn: Privately published, 1985)

Nevenkin, Kamen, *Fire Brigades, The Panzer Divisions 1943-1945* (Winnipeg: J.J. Fedorowicz, 2008)

Newton, Steven H., *Kursk: The German View. Eyewitness Reports of Operation Citadel by the German Commanders* (New York: Da Capo Press, 2002)

Plaskov, G., *Pod grokhot kanonady* [To the roar of a cannonade] (Moscow: Voenizdat, 1976)

Radzievsky, A.I., *Tankovyi Udar* [*Tank Attack*] (Moscow: Voenizdat, 1978)

von Saucken, Dietrich, *4. Panzer-Division* Volume 2 (Aschheim vor München: Peukert, 1969)

Rebentisch, E., *To the Caucasus and the Austrian Alps: The History of the 23. Panzer Division in WWII* (Winnipeg: J.J. Fedorowicz, 2009)

Schneider, Wolfgang, *Tigers in Combat I* (Winnipeg: J.J. Fedorowicz, 2000)

Shvebig, A.P., *I snova v boi* [*And once more into battle*] (Moscow: Voenizdat, 1979)

Spaeter, Helmuth, *The History of the Panzerkorps Grossdeutschland, Vol. 2* (Winnipeg: J.J. Fedorowicz, 1995)

Vysotsky, F.I., Makukhin, M.E., Sarychev, F.M. and Shaposhnikov, M.K., *Gvardeiskaia Tankovaia* [*Guards Tank Army*], (Moscow: Voenizdat, 1963)

Zetterling, Niklas and Frankson, Anders, *The Korsun' Pocket: The Encirclement and Breakout of a German Army in the East, 1944* (Havertown PA: Casemate, 2008)

## WEBSITES

www.iremember.ru.
http://podvignaroda.mil.ru/
http://www.obd-memorial.ru/

# Index

## INDEX OF PEOPLE

Abramov, Colonel Tikhon P., 206-207, 281, 333, 400, 406-408, 424

Akimochkin, Colonel Petr N., 75, 77, 137, 206-207, 281, 316, 333, 400-401

Aleksandrov, Guards Lieutenant, 273, 423

Antonov, Colonel Petr, 206, 281, 333, 354

Artamonov, Guards Lieutenant Colonel Fedor, 173-174, 205

Arzhba, Lieutenant Colonel Anton, 75, 135, 137, 150, 173

Babkovsky, Lieutenant Colonel Petr, 75, 137, 206, 281, 333

Barabash, Guards Senior Lieutenant Dmitrii, 171, 279, 381

Batov, General, 46, 179

Bazanov, Colonel Il'ia, 215, 281, 305-306, 310-311, 333-334, 338, 345, 347, 353, 361-364, 366, 376, 383, 387-388, 403, 405

Belenko, Lieutenant Colonel Ivan, 206, 281

Belkov, Colonel, 24, 146

Bibergan, Colonel, 406-407, 421

Blinov, Senior Lieutenant Konstantin M., 78-79, 105-106, 114, 121, 129

Bogdanov, General Semen Il'ich, 101, 103, 128-129, 137, 146, 148-153, 155-156, 165, 173-174, 176, 178-180, 184-189, 194, 198, 204, 206-210, 212, 214-215, 220, 229, 236, 240-241, 245, 254, 263, 265-268, 281, 298-299, 304, 306-307, 309-310, 333, 335, 340-341, 343-344, 348, 355, 357-359, 370, 388, 390, 392, 394, 399-402, 407, 409, 411, 419, 424

Boikov, Major General, 47, 50

Borisov, Lieutenant Colonel Pavel, 135, 137, 141, 173, 187

Bormotov, Guards Colonel P.L., 149, 163-165

Bronsky, 357, 359

Bubnov, Guards Colonel Nikolai M., 22, 24-25, 50, 53, 65-66, 73, 75-76, 137, 146, 155, 163-165, 171

Bystritsky, Captain Ilia, 125, 132

Bzyrin, Lieutenant Colonel Vasilii, 137, 173, 281

Chagov, Merni, 219, 221, 269

Cheriapkin, Guards Lieutenant Colonel Iosif, 333-334, 390, 398

Chikomasov, Lieutenant Il'ia, 125, 136

Chizh, Colonel Vladimir, 21, 24, 33, 52, 75, 77, 149, 152, 173, 206, 222-223, 235-236, 238, 241, 247

Chuguev, Lieutenant Colonel, 414-415

Davydenko, Lieutenant Colonel Nikita, 24, 41

Deviatov, Colonel, 141, 146

Donkov, Captain Fedor, 121, 271, 293, 316, 324-325, 328-330, 349, 351

Dubovoi, Major General Ivan V., 206-207, 214, 241, 268, 270, 281, 307, 309, 333-334, 357, 388-389, 392, 402-403, 406-407, 421, 423, 427

Eremeev, Guards Colonel Boris, 333-334, 340-341, 388, 390

Esipenko, Guards Captain Vasilii, 231, 277

Fadeev, Colonel Sergei, N., 122, 266

Filonenko, Senior Lieutenant Dem'ian, 122, 278

Fundovnyi, Major Isak, 281, 333

Gaenko, Major Pavel Andreevich, 355-356

Galimov, Colonel Ashraf, 75, 77, 206, 281, 317-318, 333, 342, 384, 392, 408-409

Golovnia, Fedor, 272-273

Goncharov, Major General Mikhail, 24-25, 75, 77, 400, 402

Gorbatenko, Major Dmitrii, 281, 333

Gorbunov, I.I., 247, 274

Gorodishche, Nizhnee, 47, 93, 96, 98, 151

Grechko, Lieutenant, 374-375

Grigor'ev, Major General Vasilii E., 36, 75-76, 91, 9, 123, 137

Grishin, Guards Colonel Nikolai, 260, 281

Gudkov, Captain A., 187, 205

Gurenko, Lieutenant Colonel Dmitrii. G., 206, 266, 401

Gvozdikov, Captain Ivan, 136, 140

Hitler, Adolf, 155, 212-213, 224, 228, 235, 241, 246, 262, 267, 287, 289, 304, 320

Iakovlev, Junior Lieutenant, Mikhail, 406-407
Iukin, Major General N.P., 260, 286, 311, 313, 400, 407, 416

Jung, Hans-Joachim, 349, 372

Kalashnikov, Guards Major Prokofii, 277, 380, 382
Kalashnikov, Prokofii, 274, 382
Kalinichenko, Colonel Petr, I., 24, 29
Kalustov, Guards Colonel Grigorii Sh., 73, 163, 165, 171
Kaminsky, Commander, 31, 37, 62, 178-179
Karakozov, Major, 123-124, 209, 268, 407
Karpov, Captain P., 192, 205
Kazachenko, Guards Senior Lieutenant Grigorii, 71, 73
Kazakov, Colonel, 53, 65-66, 163, 430
Khalaev, Lieutenant Colonel Aleksandr, 137, 173-174, 206, 333
Kharitonov, Guards Lieutenant Colonel Stepan, 167, 333, 390, 419
Khmelinin, Guards Senior Lieutenant, 216, 274
Khombakh, Major Anatolii, 70, 125, 136, 139, 171, 232
Khomenko, Senior Sergeant, 130-131
Kliaro, Colonel Ignatii, 24, 65
Knutov, S.P., 400, 402
Kocherin, Colonel, 68-69, 93, 123
Kokurin, Lieutenant Colonel Georgii A., 75-76, 105
Konev, Marshall M.I., 276, 282, 305-306, 310, 359
Konovalov, Colonel Fedor, 75-76, 135, 137, 141, 146
Kopylov, Colonel Nikolai, 75, 77, 137, 206-207, 281, 333, 390
Korchagin, Guards Lieutenant General Ivan, 173-174, 181, 188, 193
Korol'kov, Senior Lieutenant Ivan, 67, 71
Kosarev, Lieutenant Vladimir, 300, 302, 332
Koshaev, Guards Colonel Nikolai M., 163, 165, 168, 206-208, 236, 259, 274, 279, 281, 290, 309
Kostromin, Lieutenant Colonel, 318, 342, 412, 414
Kozikov, Lieutenant Colonel Sergei, 24, 41
Kramar, Colonel, 35-36
Kriukov, Major General, 31, 46, 50, 57, 423
Krupenin, Colonel Samuil M., 68, 75, 79, 107, 140, 143, 145, 149, 153, 206, 224, 266-267

Kul'biakin, Captain, 268, 326
Kurilenko, Guards Lieutenant Colonel Ivan, 281, 289-290, 421-422
Kurkin, Lieutenant General A.V., 309, 400-402
Kvasha, Guards Lieutenant Ivan, 114, 121

Larikov, Senior Lieutenant T., 192, 205
Latyshev, Major General Petr M., 24-25, 32, 49, 62, 75-76, 132, 137, 149, 152, 156, 173, 185, 206-207, 209-211, 267, 297, 305-306, 340, 343, 370, 401
Lazarev, Major General Ivan, 22, 24-25, 28, 69
Levin, Colonel Isak, 24, 75, 77, 86, 402
Liberman, Colonel Roman A., 206, 208, 219-220, 231, 278, 281
Lugansky, Guards Senior Lieutenant Aleksandr, 67, 71, 73, 78, 171-172

Makarov Colonel Vasilii, 281, 390, 406-408
Makeev, Sergeant Major Boris, 328-330
Maksimov, Colonel Georgii Maksimovich, 75-76, 101, 105, 172, 187, 209, 215, 229, 401
Malinin, Lieutenant General, 84, 99, 139
Manteuffel, General, 139, 357, 370, 372-373, 376, 385, 403-404, 418
Maripov, Guards Junior Sergeant, 324
Maslov, Major General Aleksei, 22, 24-25, 36
Matiushin, Guards Colonel Nikolai Ivanovich, 281, 310, 333-334, 354, 401
Matsapura, Guards Senior Sergeant, Sergei, 271, 274, 424
Matveev, Junior Lieutenant Oleg, 325-326
Matveevich, Nikolai, 66, 163
Mekhnin, Sergeant Major Fedor, 327, 329
Mel'nikov, Guards Senior Lieutenant Viktor, 320-322, 330
Merkulovka, Iuzhnaia, 32, 41
Mikhailov, M.G., 71, 357
Mirvoda, Colonel Semen, 206-207, 281, 297, 324, 327, 333
Mishulin, Lieutenant General Vasilii , 333-334, 358, 388, 421

Nesvetailov, Vladimir I., 71, 78, 274
Novikov, Colonel General, 270-271, 281, 333

Oleinik, Junior Lieutenant Mikhail, 204, 277
Opiakin, Guards Colonel Pavel, 24, 65
Ostroverkhov, Major Ivan, 274, 293

Pavlov, Guards Major General Andrei, 206, 215, 238-239, 244, 254
Pavlov, Lieutenant Colonel Petr, 75, 137

Petrukhin, Senior Lieutenant Aleksei, 72, 381
Piskunov, Lieutenant Colonel, 297, 324, 345
Plaskov, General Grigorii, 206, 263, 281, 333-334, 398, 402
Pogorelov, Lieutenant, 272, 325-326
Poliana, Shirokaia, 193, 148, 189, 194
Potemkin, Guards Major, 180-181
Preisman, Colonel, Grigorii 75-76, 93, 137, 149, 173
Pupko, Colonel Leonid, 24, 36

Radzievsky, Guards Major General Aleksei I., 79, 154-155, 229, 267, 281, 286, 305-307, 310-311, 333-334, 353-354, 361, 370, 388, 390, 392, 394, 399-400, 402, 407, 409, 414
von Rappard, General, 185-186
Riazantsev, Captain, 193, 205
Rodin, Guards Lieutenant General Aleksei, 23-24, 28, 32, 37, 47, 49, 62, 68, 75-76, 86, 91, 93, 95, 98, 103, 131, 137, 140-141, 143, 146
Rodionov, Guards Lieutenant Colonel, 168, 290, 345, 422
Rokossovsky, Colonel General K.K., 91, 95, 131, 141-142, 151, 176, 178-179
von Roman, Lieutenant General Rudolf Freiherr, 185, 188
Romanenko, Lieutenant General Prokofii, 21-23
Roshcha, Shirokaia, 61, 179
Rybin, Captain Alexandr, 275, 327-329

Safronov, Colonel, 153, 169, 195
Sanachev, Captain Mikhail, 293, 329, 332
Sankovsky, Colonel Aleksei, 24, 65, 120
Savin, Guards Senior Lieutenant Nikolai S., 320-323, 329-331
Schneider, Major General Erich, 50, 52
Semenov, Georgii, 172, 358
Shalgin, Junior Lieutenant Viktor, 325-326
Shamardin, Colonel Pavel, 206, 245, 281, 333-334, 422

Shamshin, Major General Aleksandr, 207, 214, 220, 236, 245, 254, 267-268
Shashin, Major General Aleksandr A., 206, 231
Shilov, Guards Junior Lieutenant Aleksandr, 72-73
Shishov, Major Nikolai, 206, 219
Shvebig, Major General Anatolii, 68, 123, 209, 268, 286, 425
Shvetsov, Colonel, 182, 195
Silov, Lieutenant Colonel Ivan, 173, 188
Sinenko, Major General Maksim S., 75, 93, 98, 135, 137, 141, 147, 150, 153, 168, 173
Slobodka, Verkhniaia, 137, 139-140, 194
Smoly, Lieutenant Colonel Iosif 24, 75, 77
Sosnovikov, Major General Vladimir, 24, 75
Stalin, Joseph, 21-22, 128, 215, 252, 293
Stoliarov, Junior Lieutenant Andrei, 114, 121
Svetlov, Guards Captain Vasilii, 231, 278-279

Teliakov, Major General Nikolai M., 24, 75, 77, 82, 123-124, 137, 281
Terekhov, Guards Colonel S.M., 293, 297
Ternovka, 298-299, 321-322, 327, 345, 356
Tkachenko, Lieutenant, 148, 351
Tolstikov, Guards Lieutenant Vladimir, 343-344
Trofimenko, S.G., 357, 400-402
Trukhin, Ivan, 331-332
Tsikalo, Colonel Mikhail, 24, 75, 77, 173

Ushakov, Guards Captain Pavel, 243, 274, 280

Vinokurov, Lieutenant Colonel Georgii, 24, 32
Vitruk, Guards Colonel A.A., 82, 233

Weiss, General, 185, 188

Zakrevsky, Captain Dmitrii, 123, 125-127
Zemlianoi, Lieutenant Colonel Andrei, 281, 319, 323
Zemlianukhin, Lieutenant Colonel, 204, 313, 345

## INDEX OF PLACES

1st of May State Farm  43, 70, 85, 98, 101, 103-105, 131, 134, 155

Agronomovca,  351-352
Aleksandrovka,  121, 135-136, 216
Alekseevka,  84, 128, 335
Antonovka,  231-232, 267, 288
Arbuzovo,  31, 36

Bădeni,  361-362, 384
Bagva,  288-289, 328
Bahlui River,  336, 359, 362, 366
Bahna,  404, 412
Băiceni,  366-367, 378
Balca,  410-411, 413
Băleni,  356
The Balkans,  370, 430
Balş,  362, 366, 374, 387
Bălţi,  309, 328, 335-338, 345-346, 350, 353-354, 356, 363, 386, 395, 420, 427
Balusesti,  362, 366-367, 375-376, 378
Bel'diazhki,  137, 139, 150, 164-165, 171
Bel'tsy,  see Bălti
Belaia,  210, 212-216, 220, 225, 227, 241, 246, 268, 271, 282, 322
Belaia Tserkov' Station,  214, 241
Belceşti,  359-360
Berestochek,  184, 189
Berestok,  51, 53, 184, 186-189, 193-195
Berezki,  299-300, 305, 322
Berezovets,  61, 84, 93, 95, 98
Berezovka,  282, 288-289, 320-321, 324, 330
Berezovyi Log,  90, 114
Berlin, 209, 406, 424
Bezgodkovo,  189, 193-194
Bezgorodovka,  186-187
Bitiug,  85, 93, 101-102, 114, 131
Blagodati,  339, 346-347, 351-353
Bobrik,  96-97, 101, 134-135
Bogdanovka,  214, 218, 220, 277
Bogdasarovca,  339, 346
Boguslavka,  39-40, 43
Boguslavskii,  43-44
Bolkhov,  78, 106
Bolohani Burial Mound,  404-406, 409
Bolotina,  353-354
Borisovo,  51, 53, 67, 74, 178, 184, 186-189, 195
Boroşoaia,  356, 367, 385, 395
Borşa,  336, 354
Bosia,  373, 377-378, 397
Bosovka,  241, 244-246, 282

Brasovo,  47-48
Brekhovo,  79, 135-136
Briansk,  21-23, 27, 31, 37, 47-48, 62, 64, 80, 88, 90, 106
Buda,  44-47, 50-51, 61, 69-70, 175-176, 178-179, 185-186, 194
Budy,  53, 299, 345
Bug River,  282, 287-288, 298-302, 304-306, 318, 321-322, 327-328, 330-331
Bugry,  32, 35, 44, 175
Buki,  212, 282, 288-289, 325, 328, 356
Bukovishche,  51, 53, 73-74, 184, 186-187, 189
Bumbăta,  336, 352
Buşila,  338-339, 346, 350
Butyrki,  96-97, 99-100, 121, 123
Buzhanka,  235-236, 240-241, 244-246, 278, 328
Buzuluk,  85, 93, 131, 134-135
Byki,  175, 178
Byrlovka,  300, 322

Caprei  363, 385
Cârniceni,  336, 358
Cepleniţa,  361-363, 384, 397, 400, 424
Chemlyzh,  184, 193
Cheremisskoe,  285, 318-320, 324
Cherkassy,  263, 431
Chernaia Griaz',  32, 36, 44
Chernaia Kamenka,  288, 320, 323-324, 332
Chernatskoe,  175-176
Chesnovka,  236, 238-245, 249-252, 271
Chişcăreni,  403-404
Chizhovka,  282, 285, 287-289, 313, 320, 327, 330, 332
Chuvardino,  141, 164
Coarba Burial Mound,  358, 406, 409-412
Coarba,  358, 404, 406, 409-412
Coarnele Caprei,  363, 385
Corneşti Tyrg,  336, 351-353, 360
Costeşti,  360, 362, 384
Cotnari,  362, 366-367, 387
Cucuteni,  360, 366, 375, 377, 380

Dashukovka,  236, 238-241, 243-245, 278
Deriugino,  29, 32, 37, 40, 43-45, 70, 74
Desna River,  31-32, 50-51, 173, 175-176, 178, 195, 198
Dmitriev,  24, 29-33, 35, 37-40, 43-45, 47, 49, 61, 64, 69, 150, 185
Dmitrovskoe,  290-291, 293, 321
Dnepr River,  209-210, 212

Dnestr River, 287, 300, 302-310, 315-316, 322, 327-328, 331-332, 335-336, 353

Dobrovod'e, 37, 41, 44, 178

Dobruchik, 46, 57

Domian (Damian), 358-359, 413

Donkov, 121, 271, 293, 316-317, 324-325, 328-330, 349, 351

Druzhovetskii, 96, 131, 134-136

Dubrovka, 27, 34, 61, 286, 320, 323

Dumbrăviţa, 360, 362

Duplikovka, 175-176

Dzhulinki, 287, 291, 298-300, 321-322, 327, 330, 345

Dzhurzhentsy, 239-242, 244


Ecatarinovca, 339, 346-348

Efremov, 21-22

Elets, 21-22, 27, 36

Epureni, 354, 404, 406, 409-412, 420

Evdokimovo, 29, 44, 46, 74


Făcuti, 336, 356, 373-374, 396

Făleşti 336-338, 345-346, 361-362, 385-386, 420

Fântânele, 403-404

Fatezh, 27, 33, 36, 49, 61, 84, 86, 96, 104, 130

Fedia, 272-273

Fediukovka, 228, 230-231, 233-234, 267

Fedorovka, 84-85

Filippovo, 175, 178

Fleminda, 310, 322

Focuri, 336, 353-354, 358, 363, 404-406

Frankovka, 210, 238, 244


Gai, 34, 288-289

Ganovka, 216, 247

Glinki, 147, 186-187

Glotovka, 34, 39-40

Gnezdilovo, 140-141, 150-151, 164

Gnilets, 96, 102-103

Gniloi Tikich River, 232, 236, 240-241, 244, 246, 279

Golovnia, 272-273

Goncharovka, 151-152, 165

Gora, 43-44

Goreloe, 131, 134

Gorianovo, 93, 96

Gornyi Tikich River, 282, 287-290, 320, 323-325, 327

Grankino, 141-142, 146

Gremiachevo, 89, 131

Gurovka, 153, 166, 173

Hârlău, 359, 362, 395

Hărmăneşti, 359-360, 362

Heleşteni, 384-385

Hill 142, 406, 410-413

Hill 143, 346, 413

Hill 148, 384, 396, 418

Hill 150, 355, 359, 404, 413

Hill 156, 337, 410-411, 413

Hill 158, 366, 405

Hill 159, 404, 409-410

Hill 162, 404-406, 409-412

Hill 167, 410-412, 419

Hill 168, 339, 346, 351-352

Hill 168.1, 339, 346

Hill 168.3, 351-352

Hill 170, 347, 349-350, 410, 412

Hill 170.1, 347, 349

Hill 174, 378, 410

Hill 176, 404-406

Hill 178, 404, 406, 409-412, 419, 423

Hill 181, 359, 409-413

Hill 183, 359, 410

Hill 184, 362, 366, 374-378, 380, 383-384, 397

Hill 189, 366, 376-378, 383, 397

Hill 192, 366-367, 373-374, 378, 380-381, 396-398

Hill 193, 360, 367, 385, 398

Hill 195, 139, 404

Hill 197, 181, 375, 387, 404, 412

Hill 208.3, 164, 171

Hill 209.6, 187, 195

Hill 216.6, 73-74, 195

Hill 216.7, 240-241

Hill 217.0, 186-187, 194

Hill 217.6, 228, 230

Hill 222, 194, 337, 363

Hill 231.1, 85, 97, 140

Hill 235.8, 241, 244

Hill 235.8, 241, 244

Hill 238.1, 103-104

Hill 239, 131, 173, 240-242, 244

Hill 239.8, 131, 240

Hill 243.3, 233, 320

Hill 244.2, 85, 134

Hill 245.2, 147, 164

Hill 256, 85, 142, 146, 366, 374-375, 378, 384, 396

Hill 256.9, 85, 146

Hill 257, 85, 102, 104-105, 136, 153

Hill 257.1, 85, 104

Hill 260.1, 142, 146

Hill 262.7, 146, 155

Hill 264, 139, 171

Hill 269, 146, 155
Hill 274, 98-99, 104, 219, 221
Hill 274.5, 98, 104
Hill 276.1, 303, 335
Hirbu (Lake), 360, 362-363, 380, 397
Hodora, 367, 373, 380, 395-398, 427
Horleşti, 404, 406, 412-413
Hristoforovca, 352-353

Iablonovets, 141-142
Iablonovka, 210, 244-246, 262, 282, 288
Iamskoe, 173, 179, 182-183, 186-189
Iasenok, 85, 95, 135
Iaşi, 339, 346, 353, 358-360, 362, 367, 373, 377,
    380, 385-386, 398-399, 403-404, 412, 414,
    418-419, 422-424, 428
Iloaie, 336, 353-354, 357-360, 373
Iumatov, 209, 270-271
Iupiter, 178-179
Iurkovka, 298, 361
Ivan'ki, 286, 288-290, 320
Ivanovka, 288, 320
Ivnik, 184-185
Izvichni, 58, 61

Jijia River, 335-336, 339, 404, 409-410, 412, 414,
    418, 422, 424

Kalinin, 21-22, 62, 64
Kalustov, 73, 163, 165, 171
Kamenka Tributary, 36, 40, 134, 176, 213, 288,
    320, 323-324, 332
Kammenyi Brod, 235-236, 241
Karachev, 46-47, 50, 89
Karpun'evka, 85, 103
Kashara, 85, 90, 95, 97, 99, 101-104
Kazemirovka, 215, 222, 225
Khar'kov, 78, 366
Khil'ki, 242-243, 252
Khitrovka, 139, 141-142, 236
Khizhentsy, 238-241, 244-245, 327
Khmelevoe, 86-88, 103-104, 135
Khorosha, 215, 219, 221
Khristinovka, 282, 288, 293, 303, 306, 345,
    360-361
Kiev, 210, 212, 220, 251, 265, 355-356, 430
Kil'kino, 34, 40, 46
Kishinev, 335, 339, 346, 349, 351-353, 360, 399
Kniaginino, 51, 173, 175, 178-179, 182, 184-189,
    192
Kochetki, 34-35, 79
Kolki, 150, 164
Komarichi, 43, 46-48, 50, 57-58, 61

Komarovka, 238, 242-244, 247, 252, 277,
    279-280
Konevo, 28, 34-35
Konotop, 31-32
Konstantinovka, 212-213, 228
Korostovka, 51, 53, 175, 178, 184, 186-189,
    193-194
Kosiakovka, 228, 230-233, 235, 269, 277, 279
Krachkovka, 286, 290, 320
Kramar, 35-36, 99
Krasavka, 95, 97, 102
Krasnaia Iagoda, 148, 150
Krasnaia Roshcha, 141, 148, 150-151, 164
Krasnaia Zaria, 27, 139
Krasnikovo, 139-140, 143, 146, 171
Krasnopolka, 286, 290-291, 320
Krasnyi Klin, 29, 37, 44, 175
Krasnyi, 29, 37, 44, 48, 143, 146, 175, 233
Krivets, 288-289
Kromy River, 23, 48, 62, 64, 78, 84, 89-90, 104,
    113, 136-137, 139, 150, 163-165
Ksaverovka State Farm, 213, 216
Kuchkovka, 228, 230, 232-235, 269, 277-279,
    282, 288, 319
Kudiiar, 51, 53, 67, 73
Kursk, 36, 68, 75, 78-81, 84, 88-91, 96, 98, 101,
    113-114, 120, 123-125, 129-131, 135, 203, 209,
    265, 330, 429, 431, 433
Kutyrki, 85, 93, 96, 104-105
Kuznetsovka, 37, 39, 43

L'gov, 64, 129, 199, 210
L'govskii, 31, 33, 35
Ladyrevskii Heights, 137, 141-142
Larga, 404, 419
Lebiazh'e, 152, 165, 167
Lemeshok, 51, 184, 186-187, 189, 195
Leninskii, 85, 103
Lepeshino, 57-58, 61
Liadskaia Sloboda, 215
Lipki, 40-41
Lipovets, 212-218, 221-222, 228, 249, 266, 277
Lisianka, 235-236, 238-246, 249-250, 252, 260,
    262, 268-269, 273, 278, 313
Litizh, 46-47, 70, 74
Liubashovka, 298-299
Liubazh, 88, 135-136
Livny, 23, 36, 38, 78, 84, 128
Livy, 33, 36
Lobanovskii, 44, 46
Lomovets, 135-136, 139, 141, 143
Lopatinka, 221-222
Lugansky, 67, 71, 73, 78, 157, 171-172

Maksim Sinenko, 75-76, 79, 105, 137, 147, 173
Mal'tsevskii, 48, 57
Maloarkhangel'sk, 85, 93, 113, 135
Man'kovka, 212, 285, 287, 289, 293-294, 320, 328
Maslovskii, 141-142
Matiushin, 281, 310, 333-334, 354, 390, 392, 394, 401-402, 407, 409
Medvin, 231-232, 238-239, 267, 270
Mel, 43-44, 320-322, 330
Melovoe, 37, 44
Mijloc, 411, 413
Mikhailovka, 30-31, 40-41, 288-289
Mikhailovskii, 51, 53, 175-176, 184-186
Milenino, 34-35
Moineşti, 339, 409-413
Moldavia, 333, 341, 350, 356, 386, 417, 425
Molotychi, 85, 95, 98-99, 102, 105, 135-136
Monastyrek, 288-289, 320
Monastyrishche, 212-213, 215
Moritskii, 51, 173, 175, 178, 182, 184-185, 195, 204
Morshneva, 31-32, 34, 39-40
Moscow, 22, 68, 78, 165, 209, 430-431
Mostechnia, 46, 48, 57, 69
Movileni Station, 404-406, 409, 412, 414, 419-420, 427

Napadovka, 212-214, 216, 218, 247
Naryshkino, 136, 151
Negureni Nouă, 339, 351+352
Negurenii Vechi, 336-337, 353
Nerussa River, 47, 57
Nikol'skoe, 95, 98, 102-103, 131
Novaia Zaria, 146, 171
Novgorod, 52, 70, 175-176
Novo-Gnezdilovo, 150, 164
Novo-Iamskoe, 173, 179, 182-183, 186-189
Novo-Ryzhkovskii, 137, 139-140
Novoselki, 95, 136

Obodovka, 299-300
Ocheretnia, 212-213, 215-216, 222, 228, 247, 259, 277, 279
Ochitkov, 215, 266
Ochki, 93, 95, 135
Odessa, 335, 351, 353
Okop, 95, 97
Ol'khovatka, 36, 84, 86, 93, 95-97, 99, 122-123, 129-130, 134, 136
Oneşti, 367, 385, 395, 398
Onuprienko, 24, 32, 62
Oratov, 213-215, 219-222, 225, 228, 249, 263, 268-269

Orel, 23, 41, 47-49, 62, 64, 68, 78-79, 84, 89-90, 96, 98, 101, 113, 124, 134, 136-137, 139, 141, 143, 150-151, 154-156, 161-162, 171, 175, 203
Orhei, 336-337
Orliia, 175, 178, 186, 194, 198
Orsoaei, see Movileni Station
Osievka, 282, 288
Osinovyi, 93, 95, 97
Osmanka River, 29, 34, 47
Ozerki, 93, 137

Pal'tsevo, 34, 36, 39-40
Panskaia, 84, 93
Panskoe, 89-90
Parliti Sat, 349-350
Pavlovka, 214-215, 228, 230
Pavlovskii, 61, 152-153
Pervoavgustovskii, 37, 43-44, 175
Petrovka, 271-273
Petrovskoe, 23, 34, 36, 230, 232-233, 242-243, 258
Petrukhin, 72, 146, 381
Piatigory, 228-229, 235
Pigarevka, 175-176
Pirliţa Sat, 316, 325, 339, 345-352, 360, 371
Pirliţa Tyrg, 336, 339, 345-349, 351-352
Pisarev, 286, 288
Pisarevka, 238-240, 244, 282
Plugari, 363, 367, 385, 403, 427
Pochapintsy, 236, 238, 242-244, 267, 273, 280
Pochep, 31-32
Podsoborovka, 85, 97, 102, 104, 120, 135
Podu Iloaie, 336, 353-354, 357-360, 401, 427
Pogrebishche, 212-215, 268
Pokhvisnevo, 139-140
Pokrovskoe, 137, 180
Polieni, 359, 366, 374, 380, 384-385
Polkovnich'e, 289, 320
Polozovka, 34-37, 39, 46
Pomoinik, 285-286, 290-291, 320
Ponyri, 84-85, 90, 93, 95-99, 101, 103-106, 112-116, 122, 124-125, 128-131, 133-136, 167
Popa Mort Burial Mound, 362, 366
Popovka, 288-289
Popovkino, 37, 40, 44
Potângeni, 404, 409-410
Potash, 239, 263, 285-286, 289-291, 317, 353, 360-361
Prilepy, 85, 131, 134
Probota, 360, 384-385
Probuzhdenie, 96, 131
Proletarskii, 136, 153, 173
Protasovo, 90, 93, 114, 131

Prut River, 304, 339, 346, 352-353, 357-358, 363, 398, 404, 410, 412, 414, 424
Pulina, 362, 396, 427
Pulina Burial Mound, 362, 396

Ratmanovo, 30-31, 34, 37
Rediu Mitropoliei, 409-410, 412, 416
Repki, 228, 233
Reut River, 336-338
Revolution State Farm, 184-185, 187-189, 192-193
Revukha River, 291, 304
Rizino, 282, 288-290, 319-320, 323-324, 330
Romaneşti, 351-352
Romania, 303, 333, 341, 343, 356-357, 371-372, 386, 390, 399, 403, 417-418, 424-426, 428
Romanov Khutor, 215, 219
Romanov State Farm, 215
Romanovka, 35, 288, 336
Romashkovo, 70, 175-176, 178
Rososha, 212-216, 218-219, 222
Rotmistrovka, 213, 215
Rozhdestvenskii, 178-179, 183
Rozhkovskii, 147, 164
Rubannyi Most, 228, 285, 287, 289, 320
Rubelnita, 303, 335
Rusalovka, 285, 320
Rusovo, 301, 310, 322
Rybalko, 139, 179
Ryl'sk, 78, 113
Ryzhanovka, 246-247, 259, 262, 282, 285, 287, 320
Rzhava, 146-147, 150, 163-165, 171
Rzhavets, 96, 134-135
Rzhev, 58, 433

Saborovka, 95-97, 101, 103, 131, 135
Samodurovka, 84, 90, 95, 97, 101-104, 114
Sculeni, 338-339, 363, 395
Sen'kovo, 131, 134-135, 139
Seredina, 44-47, 50-51, 61, 69-70, 175-176, 178-179, 185-186, 194
Sergeevka, 84, 95
Sev River, 29, 41, 173, 175-176, 178-180, 183, 186, 205
Severskii, 52, 70, 175-176
Sevsk, 24, 29-31, 37, 41, 44-45, 47, 50-53, 55-56, 59, 61, 65-67, 69, 73, 78, 129, 150, 173, 176, 178-179, 182-183, 185, 187-192, 195, 198-199, 203-205, 211
Sharykino, 146-147
Shchetinin, 74, 128
Shenderovka, 215, 231, 235, 239, 242, 252, 280
Shepelovo, 136, 143

Shevchenkovskii, 206, 217-218, 225, 227-228, 249, 251-252, 254-255, 259-260, 262-263, 267-269, 271, 279, 282, 305, 318, 320, 323
Shirokoe Boloto, 131, 135
Shmarnoe, 34-35
Shubennyi Stav, 282, 288-289, 319, 355
Shumilovo, 299, 305
Sidorovka, 90, 98
Sinarna State Farm, 214, 218-219, 222
Sinenko, 75-76, 79, 93, 98, 105, 135, 137, 141, 147, 150, 153, 168-169, 173
Sinitsa River, 298-299
Skitki, 219, 221, 247
Snova River, 84, 87, 103, 112
Sofievka, 288, 290
Soglasnyi, 96, 131
Sokolovka, 299-300
Sokolovochka, 345
Soleevka, 34-35
Soroca, 303, 307-308, 310, 328, 335, 345-346, 386, 395
Sorokovye Dvory, 34-35
Southern Bug River, 282, 287-288, 298-301, 304, 321-322, 327-328, 330-331
Stalingrad 22-23
Stanislavchik, 228-229, 231, 249-250
Staro, 214, 216
Staryi Gorod, 30-31, 39-40, 43
Stavishche, 228-229
Stolniceni, 338, 360, 386
Streletskaia, 51, 178-179, 182-184
Stroesti, 362, 366-367, 375-376, 378
Sukhoi Rovets, 30-31
Suzemka, 31, 44-45, 47, 61, 69, 186
Svapa River, 29-30, 34-37, 39-40, 44, 47, 61-62, 85, 104
Svetlyi Dunai, 141-142
Svetova, 185, 194-195, 198
Sviatoshino, 210, 265
Svoboda, 27-28

Tarasovka, 221, 235, 269, 286
Târgu Frumos, 335, 359-360, 362, 366-367, 370, 372-381, 384-386, 388, 392, 396-397, 400-401, 403, 405-406, 418-419, 421-422, 425, 427-428
Tat'ianovca, 351-352
Tat'ianovka, 230, 232-233, 238, 259
Teploe, 87, 90, 95, 97, 101-102, 104-105, 113-114, 130-131
Teşcureni, 338-339, 346, 352-353, 356
Tetiev, 215, 228-229
Tiagun, 215, 219

Tikhonovka, 34, 244, 246, 262, 278, 282, 286, 288
Timoshevka, 289, 320
Tipileşti, 409-410, 412, 416
Tirgu Frumos, *see Târgu Frumos*
Tishinka River, 146-147
Todireşti, 339, 346-347, 349-350
Tolmachevo, 150-151, 164
Topkovo, 142, 146
Torlopovo, 175, 178
Totoeşti, 358-359, 404, 412
Trosna, 84, 96, 139
Tsybulevka, 299-300
Tula, 394, 425
Tur, 136, 297
Tynovka, 228, 230-231, 233

Ugrevichi, 46-48, 57
Ul'ianovka River, 32, 186, 213, 216, 325
Ulmi Noi, 360, 384, 386, 397
Ulmi Vechi, 366, 373-374, 378, 384
Uman, 212, 227, 281-283, 286-291, 293-298,
    303-306, 308-309, 313, 315, 317, 319-321, 325,
    327-328, 330-332, 335, 349, 353, 356, 360, 400,
    421, 427
Unecha, 31-32
Ungheni Tyrg, 339, 351-353
Usozha River, 29, 44-50, 57, 60-61, 87
Uspenskii, 153, 178, 180
Ust'e, 299, 345

Vagva, 319, 324
Vakhnovka, 212-213
Vapniarka, 298-301, 304, 309, 322, 325-326, 332,
    345, 350-351, 355, 395, 424
Vaşcani, 360, 366
Vechi, 336-337, 346, 351, 353, 366, 373-374, 378,
    384

Verkh. Tagino, 87, 90, 94
Verkhovka, 299-300
Veselyi Kut, 228, 230-232, 236, 238, 269, 277
Vetrenka, 103, 136
Vinnitsa, 206, 210, 212-213, 221, 227, 251, 254,
    260, 268
Vinograd, 214, 225, 228, 233, 235, 241, 269,
    282
Vitsentovka, 216, 218
Vladimirovca, 336, 345, 347, 351-352
Voitovka, 286, 288, 290-291, 300, 321, 356
Volobuevo, 148, 151
Voronezh, 23, 78, 89
Votylevka, 228, 230, 232-233, 271-273, 277-278
Votylevskie, 232-233
Vulturul, 359, 385, 404, 409, 412-413
Vulturul Burial Mound, 409, 413
Vygoda, 216, 218
Vysokoe, 152, 173
Vysotsky, 67, 157, 431

Zabolotnoe, 300, 322
Zagarancea, 339, 351
Zahorna, 410-413
Zaul'e, 184-185, 187, 189, 193
Zelenyi Gai, 34, 288-289
Zhabinka, 244, 246
Zhabokrich, 299-300
Zhiriatino, 141-142
Zhitomir, 210, 212, 266, 268
Zhivotiv, 214, 216, 229
Zhizhiia River, *see Jijia River*
Zhmerinka, 212, 251
Zhukovka, 139, 143
Zmievka, 89-90
Zolotukhino, 27, 33, 36, 84, 86, 108, 130
Zvenigorodka, 227-228, 259, 345, 353, 360-361

# INDEX OF GERMAN MILITARY UNITS

**Army Groups:**
Army Group Center, 114, 155

**Armies:**
Second Army, 188-189
Second Panzer Army, 49, 92, 155
Sixth Army, 398
Eighth Army, 299, 304, 403, 410
Ninth Army, 114, 155, 189

**Corps:**
I Army Corps, 414
III Panzer Corps, 235, 239-240, 242-243, 251-252, 263
IV Army Corps, 414
XI Corps, 227, 235, 239-240, 242-243
XIII Corps, 185
XX Corps, 185, 188, 195
XXIII Army Corps, 114
XXXX Panzer Corps, 414
XXXXI Panzer Corps, 88, 98, 101
XXXXII Corps, 227, 235, 239-240, 242-243
XXXXVI Panzer Corps, 88, 114
LVII Panzer Corps, 114

**Divisions:**
*Grossdeutschland* Panzer Grenadier Division, 346-347, 349, 351-352, 356, 358-359, 360, 372-373, 376, 378, 384-386, 403-404, 410-413, 417-418
1st SS Panzer Division *Leibstandarte Adolf Hitler*, 212-213, 224, 228, 231, 235-236, 239, 241, 246, 262-263, 287, 289, 291, 304, 320, 433
2nd Panzer Division, 88, 94, 102, 134
3rd SS Panzer Division *Totenkopf*, 370, 372, 385-386, 413, 417
4th *Gebirgs* Division, 213, 285, 304, 317, 339
4th Panzer Division, 48, 50-53, 55-56, 88, 90, 139, 142-143, 186-189, 198
5th Panzer Division, 89
5th SS Panzer Division *Wiking*, 241-243, 263
6th Infantry Division, 105, 134, 179, 188, 195, 359
6th Panzer Division, 213
7th Infantry Division, 139, 142-143, 178, 184-185, 187, 189, 359
8th Panzer Division, 89, 178, 184, 186-189, 198
9th Panzer Division, 88, 90, 101-102, 134
10th Panzer Grenadier Division, 89-90, 134-135, 154
12th Panzer Division, 89-90, 179
13th Panzer Division, 346, 351
14th Panzer Division, 404, 410, 417

16th Infantry Division, 287
16th Panzer Division, 213, 224, 228, 231, 235-236, 239, 241, 263, 287, 320
17th Flak Division, 291, 298, 317
17th Panzer Division, 213, 228, 235-236, 241, 263, 267, 287, 289, 291, 298, 304, 320
18th Artillery Division, 213
18th Panzer Division, 88-90, 93, 101, 105
20th Panzer Division, 88-90, 98, 101, 104, 134
23rd Panzer Division, 213, 263, 317, 352, 359-360, 384, 404, 410, 413, 417-418
24th Panzer Division, 346, 351-352, 356-359, 373, 378, 384, 386, 403, 410, 413, 417
25th Panzer Division, 212-213
31st Infantry Division, 178, 184, 187, 189
34th Infantry Division, 228, 267, 285
36th Infantry Division, 89
45th Infantry Division, 48, 50, 62
46th Infantry Division, 386
57th Infantry Division, 241, 243
72nd Infantry Division, 48, 50, 58, 62
75th Infantry Division, 289, 302, 335
76th Infantry Division, 317
78th Infantry Division, 134
78th *Sturm* Division, 89-90, 93
79th Infantry Division, 339, 346, 351-352, 403
82nd Infantry Division, 179
86th Infantry Division, 179, 185-186
88th Infantry Division, 241, 243
98th Infantry Division, 289
101st *Jäger* Division, 213
102nd Infantry Division, 48, 139
108th Infantry Division, 47
112th Infantry Division, 242
137th Infantry Division, 37, 40, 45, 47, 50
167th Infantry Division, 241, 243
168th Infantry Division, 241, 243
194th Infantry Division, 48
198th Infantry Division, 235, 285, 287
213th Security Division, 241, 243
216th Infantry Division, 89, 93
251st Infantry Division, 178-179, 184-187
252nd Infantry Division, 90
254th Infantry Division, 213
255th Infantry Division, 228, 304
258th Infantry Division, 89-90
292nd Infantry Division, 90, 135, 154
332nd Infantry Division, 241, 243
336th Infantry Division, 339
389th Infantry Division, 241, 243
404th Security Division, 339
451st Infantry Division, 189

604th Artillery Division,  178
707th Infantry Division,  31, 37, 43, 47-48, 62

**Brigades:**
SS Brigade *Wallonia*,  241, 243, 263
228th Assault Gun Brigade,  372
243rd Assault Gun Brigade,  410, 417
325th Assault Gun Brigade,  372

**Groups** (*Kampfgruppen*)**:**
Group Manteuffel,  403-404
Group Mieth,  403
*Gruppe Stemmermann*,  239, 240, 242-243, 252
*Kampfgruppe* von Heynitz,  350
*Kampfgruppe Kall*,  188
*Kampfgruppe Rebentisch*,  417
*Kampfgruppe Schroedter*,  411
*Kampfgruppe 667*,  285

**Regiments:**
Heavy Panzer Regiment *Bäke*,  213, 228, 236, 239,
    241-242, 263, 292, 317
*Panzerregiment "Grossdeutschland"*,  349
1st Nebelwerfer Regiment,  299
1st Panzer Grenadier Regiment,  347
6th Cavalry Regiment,  300, 304, 351
10th Panzer Regiment,  189
11th Panzer Regiment,  213
12th Infantry Regiment,  184, 189
18th Mountain Infantry Regiment,  413
23rd Panzer Grenadier Regiment,  184
26th Panzer Regiment 26,  372
26th Panzer Grenadier Regiment,  351
28th Panzer Grenadier Regiment,  189
35th Panzer Regiment,  52
36th Panzer Regiment,  404
43rd Artillery Regiment,  143
52nd Panzer Grenadier Regiment,  90, 105
53rd Mortar Regiment,  89
54th Mortar Regiment,  285, 287, 304, 317
61st Infantry Regiment,  178, 187, 189
62nd Heavy Artillery Regiment,  291, 304, 317
63rd Artillery Regiment,  143
64th Mortar Regiment,  287
69th Artillery Regiment,  178, 184
80th Infantry Regiment,  285
91st *Gebirgsjäger* Regiment,  285, 317
105th Infantry Regiment,  48
108th Panzer Grenadier Regiment,  404
115th Infantry Regiment,  242
124th Infantry Regiment,  48
126th Panzer Grenadier Regiment,  384
128th Panzer Grenadier Regiment,  384, 418

133rd Infantry Regiment,  48
201st Panzer Regiment,  384
208th Infantry Regiment,  351
212th Infantry Regiment,  351
226th Infantry Regiment,  351
304th Panzer Grenadier Regiment,  134
451st Infantry Regiment,  179, 189
459th Infantry Regiment,  179
491st Infantry Regiment,  179
656th Heavy Panzerjäger Regiment,  89

**Battalions:**
110th Panzer Reconnaissance Battalion,  89
177th Assault Gun Battalion,  89
185th Assault Gun Battalion,  89
189th Assault Gun Battalion,  89
202nd Assault Gun Battalion,  291, 298, 304, 317
213th Security Battalion,  335
216th Assault Gun Battalion,  88-89
216th Sturmpanzer Battalion,  89
228th Assault Gun Battalion,  263
239th Assault Gun Battalion,  263
244th Assault Gun Battalion,  89
245th Assault Gun Battalion,  89
249th Assault Gun Battalion,  291, 298, 304, 317
249th Assault Gun Battalion,  236
259th Assault Gun Battalion,  404
261st Assault Gun Battalion,  291, 298, 304, 317
280th Flak Battalion,  304
286th Assault Gun Battalion,  404
286th Reserve Battalion,  285
313th Security Battalion,  48
369th Security Battalion,  335
471st Panzerjäger Battalion,  317
482nd Panzerjäger Battalion,  287, 304, 317
482nd Pontoon Battalion,  285
503rd Heavy Panzer Battalion,  213, 263, 291, 317
505th Heavy Panzer Battalion,  88-89, 114, 155
506th Heavy Panzer Battalion,  213, 236, 239,
    241, 263
580th Security Battalion,  335
604th Artillery Battalion,  184
620th Artillery Battalion,  143
651st Combat Engineer Battalion,  384
653rd Heavy Panzerjäger Battalion,  89
654th Assault Gun Battalion,  89
654th Heavy Panzerjäger Battalion,  89
656th Assault Gun Battalion,  89
656th Heavy Tank Destroyer Battalion,  114
851st Artillery Battalion,  143,
851st Assault Gun Battalion,  143
904th Assault Gun Battalion,  52, 89
909th Assault Gun Battalion,  89

## INDEX OF HUNGARIAN MILITARY UNITS

Hungarian VIII Army Corps,  32

## INDEX OF ROMANIAN MILITARY UNITS

Romanian Third Army, 403
Romanian Fourth Army,  398, 403
Romanian 4th Army Corps,  335
Romanian 1st Guards Armored Division,  370
Romanian 1st Guards Infantry Division,  384
Romanian 2nd Infantry Division, 386
Romanian 3rd Infantry Division, 403-404,
    412-413
Romanian 4th Infantry Division,  386
Romanian 5th Cavalry Division,  351
Romanian 5th Infantry Division,  300, 302, 304,
    309, 413

Romanian 6th Infantry Division's, 359
Romanian 7th Infantry Division's, 359
Romanian 8th Infantry Division,  359
Romanian 11th Infantry Division, 403
Romanian 14th Infantry Division,  338-339
Romanian 18th Guards Mountain Infantry
    Division,  404, 410, 412-413
Romanian 18th Infantry Division, 362
Romanian 23rd Infantry Division, 362
Romanian 12th Cavalry Regiment,  359
Romanian 90th Mountain Infantry Regiment, 413
Romanian 92nd Mountain Infantry Regiment, 413

## INDEX OF SOVIET MILITARY UNITS

**Fronts:**
Central Front, 23, 30-32, 35-36, 43, 46-48, 50, 57,
    61, 64-65, 67-68, 82, 84-85, 88-89, 95-96, 98,
    103, 106, 112-114, 131, 137, 139, 141, 146, 148,
    151-152, 173, 176, 183-184, 195, 198
1st Ukrainian Front, 210-212, 214-215, 225, 228,
    236, 240-241, 246, 251, 262, 266, 268
2nd Ukrainian Front  228, 262, 273, 282, 291,
    304, 306, 309-310, 336, 362, 369-370, 383,
    385, 388, 395, 403-405, 416, 418, 420

**Armies:**
1st Guards Tank Army, 212
2nd Tank Army, 21-48, 50-53, 57-58, 61-65,
    68-69, 75-76, 79-99, 101-114, 116-118, 122,
    128, 131, 133-155, 158, 160-162, 164-168,
    171, 173, 175-176, 178-189, 193-196, 198-204,
    206-218, 222-231, 233-255, 258-263, 266-267,
    274, 277, 281-283, 285-291, 293, 296-300,
    302-306, 308-314, 316-318, 326, 329, 331, 333,
    335-340, 342, 344-348, 351, 353-369, 373, 376,
    378, 380-381, 383-388, 391-392, 395, 398-399,
    403-406, 408-420, 424-425, 427
3rd Guards Tank Army,  151, 179, 199
3rd Reserve Army,  21-22
5th Guards Tank Army, 343, 367, 418
6th Tank Army,  214, 224-226, 228-229, 235, 246,
    251-252, 258, 299, 309
7th Guards Army,  367

13th Army, 84-86, 88-89, 91-99, 101-103, 105-106,
    110-113, 123, 131, 134-135, 198
16th Air Army,  86, 92, 94, 102, 104-105, 142,
    151, 176, 178
27th Army,  226, 242, 282, 288-289, 336, 358,
    385, 399-400, 404-405, 409, 412
38th Army,  212, 215-216, 220, 224, 226-228,
    251-252, 254
40th Army,  210, 212, 223-224, 226, 228, 251-252
48th Army, 85, 113
52nd Army,  299, 309, 353
60th Army,  186, 195, 198
65th Army,  31, 46, 48, 57, 61, 65, 173, 175-176,
    178-179, 182-184, 187, 189, 194-195
70th Army,  41, 88, 92, 95-96, 103, 105, 135, 137,
    139-143, 146, 148-149, 151-153

**Corps:**
2nd Guards Cavalry Corps,  28, 49-51, 53, 57-58,
    61, 65
3rd Tank Corps, 75-76, 78-80, 83-84, 93, 95-99,
    101, 103, 105-107, 109-112, 114, 126, 128, 131,
    134-142, 145-147, 149-153, 160-162, 164, 166,
    168-169, 173, 175-178, 180-187, 189, 194-195,
    197, 200-203, 206, 210-212, 214-217, 219-229,
    231-232, 234-246, 248, 252, 254, 256-257, 259,
    266-267, 276, 281-286, 288-290, 293, 298-301,
    303, 305-307, 309-311, 320-322, 327, 331-333,
    336-338, 342, 345-346, 353-354, 358-359,

361-368, 373, 375-378, 380, 383-385, 387-388, 403-406, 409-412, 415-416, 419-421
4th Artillery Corps, 97, 142
5th Guards Cavalry Corps, 242
5th Mechanized Corps, 346
7th Guards Mechanized Corps, 173, 175-181, 184-189, 192-195, 198, 200-203, 205, 216
8th Guards Mechanized Corps, 212
9th Tank Corps, 85, 88, 131, 147-148, 187, 198
11th Tank Corps, 21-22, 24-28, 32, 34-37, 39-42, 44-46, 48-49, 57-58, 61-62, 65, 69-70, 79, 220
15th Rifle Corps, 97, 111
16th Tank Corps, 21-28, 32, 34-37, 39-40, 42-46, 48-49, 57-58, 60-61, 67-68, 70, 75-76, 79-80, 82-85, 88, 93-105, 109-110, 112, 114, 121-124, 133-134, 136-142, 145-150, 152-153, 160-162, 173, 175, 180, 200, 206, 209-211, 214-217, 220, 222-230, 235, 237-245, 248, 252, 256, 258, 268-270, 274, 276, 281-283, 285-286, 288-289, 291, 293-294, 298-303, 305-307, 309-311, 327-328, 330, 332-333, 336-338, 344-350, 353-358, 361-368, 373-374, 376, 378, 380-381, 383-385, 387-390, 392, 395-398, 400-411, 415-416, 420-421, 423, 427
17th Guards Rifle Corps, 84, 95-98, 101, 104, 111-113, 212, 215-216, 220-221, 254
18th Guards Rifle Corps, 85, 94, 131
18th Tank Corps, 412
19th Tank Corps, 61, 82, 85-86, 88, 95-98, 101-106, 108, 111-112, 136
29th Rifle Corps, 141-142, 146
31st Tank Corps, 212
33rd Rifle Corps, 320, 358, 405-406, 410
35th Guards Rifle Corps, 358, 362, 366-367, 375, 383-384, 400-401, 405, 411
78th Rifle Corps, 262

**Divisions:**
1st Anti-aircraft Artillery Division, 47, 175
2nd Guards Airborne Division, 246
3rd Guards Airborne Division, 366-367, 375, 377
3rd Guards Cavalry Division, 51
6th Rifle Division, 102
10th Anti-aircraft Division, 36
15th Rifle Division, 94, 97
16th Lithuanian Rifle Division, 22
17th Rifle Division, 400
31st Rifle Division, 346, 350
35th Rifle Division, 298
43rd Guards Latvian Rifle Division, 21
55th Rifle Division, 141
60th Rifle Division, 24, 26-28, 34-37, 39-40, 42, 44-45, 48-49, 57, 61, 65

69th Rifle Division, 185
70th Rifle Division, 98
73rd Rifle Division, 358
74th Rifle Division, 98
75th Guards Rifle Division, 102, 123
78th Rifle Division, 357
81st Rifle Division, 97
93rd Guards Rifle Division, 357, 359, 366-367, 375-377, 380
112th Rifle Division, 24, 37-38, 40, 42-45, 62
132nd Rifle Division, 31, 37, 96
135th Rifle Division, 269
136th Rifle Division, 236, 239, 245
140th Rifle Division, 102, 104
175th Rifle Division, 102
181st Rifle Division, 61
183rd Rifle Division, 21
194th Rifle Division, 21-22, 24, 34-37, 39-40, 42-46, 57, 61, 65
202nd Rifle Division, 354-356
206th Rifle Division, 362, 374, 384-385, 410
256th Rifle Division, 353
263rd Guards Rifle Division, 231
294th Rifle Division, 299
307th Rifle Division, 98, 101, 103, 105-106
374th Rifle Division, 21

**Brigades:**
5th Engineer-Sapper Brigade, 281
8th Motorized Rifle Brigade, 88, 147
11th Guards Tank Brigade, 23, 25-28, 32, 34-37, 39, 42, 44, 46, 48-54, 58, 61-62, 71-76, 78-80, 83, 85, 88, 92-95, 98-99, 103-104, 108-110, 114, 133, 135-138, 141-142, 145-149, 151-153, 155, 160, 162, 164-166, 168, 171-173, 175, 180, 200, 206, 208, 212, 214-216, 224-231, 233, 235-239, 243-248, 252, 259, 274-277, 279-282, 284-286, 288-289, 293, 298, 300-302, 305-306, 309-311, 329, 333, 336-338, 340-341, 343-345, 347, 362-368, 376, 380, 382-384, 387-388, 390, 403, 405, 409-411, 415-416, 421-422
11th Separate Guards Tank Brigade, 21-22, 24, 50, 65, 252, 309
12th Motorized Rifle Brigade, 22, 24, 29, 32, 40, 42
13th Destroyer Anti-tank Brigade, 122, 152
13th Separate Destroyer Anti-tank Brigade, 122
14th Destroyer Brigade, 177
15th Motorized Rifle Brigade, 22, 24, 34, 39-40, 42, 48, 74-75, 77, 83, 93, 99, 104, 122, 130, 133, 137-138, 152-153, 160, 206, 214-215, 240, 258, 275, 281, 289, 293, 303, 307, 309, 329, 333, 346-348, 367, 373-374, 378, 382, 409-411

15th Separate Rifle Brigade, 21

18th Mechanized Brigade, 176, 180-181, 189, 193, 195, 200-203

20th Separate Rifle Brigade, 21

23rd Separate Rifle Brigade, 21

23rd Tank Brigade, 147

24th Guards Mechanized Brigade, 173, 193

25th Guards Mechanized Brigade, 173-174, 205

26th Guards Mechanized Brigade, 173, 180, 185, 187, 192-193

26th Motorized Rifle Brigade, 102

27th Guards Motorized Rifle Brigade, 245

33rd Motorized Rifle Brigade, 401

33rd Separate Rifle Brigade, 21

33rd Tank Brigade, 176, 180-181, 184, 189, 193, 200-203

34th Guards Motorized Rifle Brigade, 316

34th Mechanized Brigade, 176, 180-181, 184, 200-203

34th Tank Brigade, 189, 193

43rd Mechanized Brigade, 176, 180-181, 185, 189, 193, 200-203

43rd Tank Brigade, 187

48th Guards Tank Brigade, 406

49th Brigade, 400

50th Tank Brigade, 75-76, 83, 98, 107, 109, 131, 135, 137-142, 146, 153, 160-162, 173, 176, 182, 184, 189, 194, 200-203, 205-206, 208, 215-216, 219-220, 222-224, 226, 231-232, 235-239, 244, 257, 274, 277-279, 281, 286, 321-322, 327, 329, 333, 342, 358, 362-363, 366, 375-378, 405, 410-411

51st Motorcycle Brigade, 26

51st Tank Brigade, 75-76, 83, 103, 105, 109, 131, 135, 137-139, 141, 150, 160-162, 173, 182, 189, 194, 206, 216, 218-219, 222-224, 226, 231, 235, 237, 239, 244, 257, 275, 281, 286, 293, 297, 320, 322-324, 327, 329, 331-333, 345, 358, 363, 366-367, 375-378, 405, 409, 411, 419

53rd Separate Tank Brigade, 37

53rd Tank Brigade, 24, 34, 39, 42, 44, 49, 57, 61

57th Brigade, 193

57th Guards Tank Brigade, 173

57th Motorized Rifle Brigade, 75, 83, 98, 131, 135, 137-138, 150, 160, 173, 176, 182, 187, 206, 214, 220, 236, 238, 241, 245, 257, 281, 286, 303, 307-308, 321, 333, 358-359, 362, 366-367, 375-378, 384, 387, 409-411, 419, 422

59th Tank Brigade, 24, 34, 39, 41-42, 49, 57, 61

60th Tank Brigade, 42

74th Motorcycle Brigade, 75

79th Tank Brigade, 88, 97, 102

95th Tank Brigade, 147

101st Tank Brigade, 97, 102

103rd Tank Brigade, 75-76, 78-79, 83, 97-99, 101, 103, 105, 109, 114, 121, 128-129, 131, 134-135, 137-140, 146-148, 153, 160-162, 172-174, 176, 182, 185, 187, 189, 194, 200-204, 206, 211, 216, 218-219, 222-224, 226, 231, 235, 237-239, 244, 248, 256-257, 277, 281, 283, 285-286, 333, 345, 363, 365-366, 375, 378, 384, 388, 390, 405-411, 420

107th Tank Brigade, 24, 34, 39, 42, 61, 70, 74-75, 77, 82-83, 93, 97, 99, 101, 104, 109-110, 114, 121, 123, 133, 136-139, 160-162, 206, 214, 216, 222-227, 230, 232, 235, 237, 239, 244, 248, 258, 268, 271, 273-276, 281, 283, 285, 293, 316, 326, 329, 333, 345-346, 348-351, 365, 367, 373-375, 378, 381, 396-397, 405-410, 424

108th Tank Brigade, 88, 147

109th Tank Brigade, 24, 34, 39, 42, 61, 70, 74-75, 83, 93, 99, 102, 104, 109, 133, 136-140, 160-162, 171, 206, 214-216, 221-227, 230, 232, 235-239, 244-246, 248, 258, 269, 275, 281, 283, 285, 333, 346, 348, 355-356, 365, 367, 373-374, 378, 382, 396, 405, 409, 411

110th Tank Brigade, 239

115th Rifle Brigade, 48

115th Separate Rifle Brigade, 23-24, 32, 34, 37-38, 45, 50, 57, 61-62

115th Special Rifle Brigade, 42, 65

129th Tank Brigade, 88

160th Tank Brigade, 24, 34, 39, 41, 49, 57, 61-62, 70

164th Tank Brigade, 24, 34, 39, 42, 61, 70, 75, 77, 83, 93, 97, 99, 101, 109, 133, 136-139, 160-162, 206, 214-216, 220, 222-224, 226-228, 231-233, 235-237, 239, 244, 248, 258, 277-278, 281, 283, 285, 289, 291, 333, 346-349, 365, 367, 373-374, 378, 382, 388, 390, 396, 405, 409-411

181st Tank Brigade, 239

202nd Tank Brigade, 88, 97, 102

234th Mortar Brigade, 137

237th Tank Brigade, 244

357th Separate Engineer Brigade, 206

**Regiments:**

5th Separate Motorcycle Regiment, 411, 415

6th Guards Heavy Tank Regiment, 333, 363, 365, 367, 373-374, 378-380, 388-390, 394, 396-399, 404-405, 410-411, 416, 422, 425, 427

7th Replacement Training Tank Regiment, 394

8th Guards Heavy Tank Regiment, 248, 260, 281, 284-286, 298-299, 319, 323, 329-330, 333, 345, 363, 365-367, 375, 377-378

9th Separate Signals Regiment, 21, 23-24, 75, 137, 142, 145, 162, 173, 202-203, 206, 226, 235, 237, 281, 345, 405

10th Guards Rifle Regiment, 231-233

13th Guards Heavy Tank Regiment, 240, 244, 246, 248, 260, 281-282, 284-286, 288, 298-299, 320

15th Cavalry Regiment, 74

16th Cavalry Regiment, 74

25th Tank Regiment, 411

27th Guards Tank Regiment, 39, 41-42, 61

27th Separate Guards Breakthrough Heavy Tank Regiment, 24

29th Guards Tank Regiment, 23, 34-37, 39-40, 42-44, 46, 61

29th Separate Guards Breakthrough Heavy Tank Regiment, 21-22, 24

37th Guards Mortar Regiment, 23-24, 26, 36, 47, 57

37th Guards Motorcycle Regiment, 22

48th Tank Regiment, 102

51st Separate Motorcycle Regiment, 83, 138, 160, 214, 216, 225, 300, 302, 332

58th Tank Regiment, 102

79th Anti-tank Regiment, 177

79th Destroyer Anti-tank Artillery Regiment, 176

86th Guards Mortar Regiment, 36, 206, 240, 276, 281, 298, 300, 310, 338, 347, 362, 368, 405

86th Guards Motorized Regiment, 228

121st Anti-aircraft Artillery Regiment, 75, 79, 83, 88, 131, 138, 160, 173, 176-177, 182, 206, 240, 257, 281, 368

130th Destroyer Anti-tank Artillery Regiment, 88

135th Rifle Regiment, 221

143rd Mortar Regiment, 24, 36, 62

187th Artillery Regiment, 400

226th Mortar Regiment, 75, 83, 99, 133, 137-138, 160, 206, 215, 240, 258, 281, 367-368, 382

227th Reserve Army Regiment, 370

227th Reserve Rifle Regiment, 142, 145

227th Reserve Training Regiment, 80

234th Mortar Regiment, 75, 83, 105, 131, 138, 160, 173, 177, 182, 206, 216, 240, 257, 281, 411

283rd Artillery Regiment, 281

288th Anti-aircraft Artillery Regiment, 173

291st Destroyer Anti-tank Artillery Regiment, 173

298th Guards Destroyer Anti-tank Artillery Regiment, 206

298th Guards Self-propelled Artillery Regiment, 206, 226, 240, 248, 281, 283-284, 333, 365

375th Heavy Self-propelled Artillery Regiment, 333, 363, 366-368, 375, 377-378, 387-390, 404-406, 409, 412, 416, 419

410th Separate Guards Mortar Regiment, 177

449th Destroyer Anti-tank Artillery Regiment, 131

468th Mortar Regiment, 173, 177

470th Rifle Regiment, 34, 36

497th Rifle Regiment, 269

563rd Anti-tank Regiment, 26, 42

563rd Destroyer Anti-tank Artillery Regiment, 24

567th Anti-tank Regiment, 26

567th Destroyer Anti-tank Artillery Regiment, 24

614th Anti-tank Regiment, 83, 138, 160

614th Destroyer Anti-tank Artillery Regiment, 75, 93, 102, 133, 137

616th Rifle Regiment, 34, 36

722nd Rifle Regiment, 373

728th Destroyer Anti-tank Artillery Regiment, 420

729th Separate Destroyer Anti-tank Artillery Regiment, 367

737th Rifle Regiment, 373-374

748th Rifle Regiment, 373

754th Self-propelled Artillery Regiment, 207, 238, 240

881st Anti-tank Artillery Regiment, 83, 138, 160

881st Destroyer Anti-tank Artillery Regiment, 75, 97-99, 131, 137, 147, 173, 176-177, 182

881st Self-propelled Artillery Regiment, 248, 281, 283

934th Rifle Regiment, 34

954th Rifle Regiment, 36

999th Self-propelled Artillery Regiment, 207, 238, 240, 248, 281, 284

1042nd Anti-Aircraft Regiment, 133

1068th Anti-Aircraft Artillery Regiment, 131

1085th Anti-Aircraft Regiment, 83, 133, 138, 160

1118th Destroyer Anti-tank Artillery Regiment, 24, 62

1180th Destroyer Anti-tank Artillery Regiment, 122, 131

1188th Destroyer Anti-tank Artillery Regiment, 36, 47, 62

1219th Self-propelled Artillery Regiment, 207, 240, 248, 281, 284, 286

1283rd Rifle Regiment, 41, 44

1323rd Destroyer Anti-tank Artillery Regiment, 131

1329th Destroyer Anti-tank Artillery Regiment, 131

1418th Self-propelled Artillery Regiment, 173, 176, 180-181

1441st Self-propelled Artillery Regiment, 131, 137, 145, 173, 206, 226, 237, 240-241, 248, 258, 281, 283, 318, 333, 367-368, 382, 411, 416

1442nd Self-propelled Artillery Regiment, 145, 176-177, 182

1481th Self-propelled Artillery Regiment, 405

1540th Heavy Self-propelled Artillery Regiment 206, 219, 222-223, 226, 236-237, 240, 248, 256-257, 281, 283, 286

1541st Self-propelled Artillery Regiment, 120, 133, 137, 145, 152

1542nd Heavy Self-Propelled Artillery Regiment, 206, 214-215, 223, 226-227, 237, 240-241

1548th Self-propelled Artillery Regiment, 206, 240

1618th Self-propelled Artillery Regiment, 281

1643rd Artillery Regiment, 401

1706th Anti-aircraft Artillery Regiment, 177

1721st Anti-aircraft Artillery Regiment, 206, 240, 281, 367-368, 382

1729th Destroyer Anti-tank Artillery Regiment, 240

1818th Self-propelled Artillery Regiment, 206, 216, 222-223, 226, 236-237, 240, 248, 256-257, 283

**Battalions:**

9th Separate Combat Engineer Battalion, 124

9th Separate Signals Battalion, 200-201, 416

10th Anti-air Battalion, 42

18th Mortar Battalion, 143

24th Reconnaissance Battalion, 126

24th Separate Reconnaissance Battalion, 83, 126, 138, 160

33rd Coastal Artillery Battalion, 200-202

50th Tank Battalion, 146

51st Motorcycle Battalion, 24, 42, 75, 137, 206, 222-223, 226, 237, 248, 258, 281, 283, 285, 368

51st Motorized Battalion, 224

51st Separate Motorcycle Battalion, 83, 138, 160, 214, 216, 300, 332

57th Destroyer Anti-tank Battalion, 173

68th Separate Motorcycle Battalion, 181

74th Motorcycle Battalion, 137, 173, 206, 222-223, 248, 281, 283, 285

74th Separate Motorcycle Battalion, 79, 131, 235, 257, 366

87th Motorcycle Battalion, 206, 224, 226, 237, 248, 281, 284-285, 415

87th Separate Motorcycle Battalion, 206, 224, 226, 235, 237, 244, 248, 281, 284-285, 309, 338, 345, 347, 366, 415

89th Separate Guards Mortar Battalion, 206, 214, 240, 367-368

90th Separate Pioneer Battalion, 366-367

90th Separate Sapper Battalion, 79, 257

92nd Separate Repair Battalion, 361

94th Tank Battalion, 135, 218, 331-332, 419

109th Motorized Rifle Battalion, 244

119th Tank Battalion, 128, 140, 146, 148, 204, 277, 420

126th Guards Mortar Battalion, 206, 257, 281, 368

126th Separate Guards Mortar Battalion, 240

135th Army Engineer Battalion, 308

205th Sapper Battalion, 133

205th Signals Battalion, 258

234th Army Mortar Battalion, 219, 368

245th Training Battalion, 416

246th Training Tank Battalion, 405

254th Tank Battalion, 135, 277-278

255th Tank Battalion, 135

307th Tank Battalion, 136, 140, 328, 330

310th Tank Battalion, 70, 136, 139, 232

352nd Tank Battalion, 69-70

357th Separate Engineer Battalion, 281

360th Tank Battalion, 136, 277-278

411th Separate Signals Battalion, 79, 206, 222-224, 226, 257, 283, 285, 248

420th Tank Battalion, 140, 204, 218, 277

689th Separate Signals Battalion, 206

689th Signals Battalion, 224, 226, 237, 248, 285, 405

698th Signal Battalion, 283

728th Destroyer Anti-tank Artillery Battalion, 75, 79, 83, 98, 105, 131, 137-138, 160, 173, 176-177, 182, 206, 240, 257, 281, 367-368

729th Anti-tank Artillery Battalion, 83, 75, 122, 133, 137-138, 160, 206, 258, 368

734th Separate Destroyer Anti-tank Battalion, 176-177

744th Motorcycle Battalion, 224, 226, 237

772nd Separate Signals Battalion, 173, 180-181, 200-203

816th Separate Motorized Transport Battalion, 27

850th Separate Motorized Transport Battalion, 27

# Related titles published by Helion & Company

*Adventures in my Youth.
A German Soldier on the
Eastern Front 1941-45*
Armin Scheiderbauer
ISBN 978-1-906033-77-4
(paperback
ISBN 978-1-907677-49-6
(eBook)

*The Rzhev Slaughterhouse. The
Red Army's Forgotten 15-Month
Campaign Against Army Group
Center 1942-1943*
Svetlana Gerasimova
Translated and edited by
Stuart Britton
ISBN 978-1-908916-51-8
(hardback)
ISBN 978-1-910294-17-8 (eBook)

*Tomb of the Panzerwaffe: The
Defeat of the Sixth SS Panzer
Army in Hungary 1945*
A. Isaev & M. Kolomiets
Translated and edited by
Stuart Britton
ISBN 978-1-909982-16-1
(hardback)

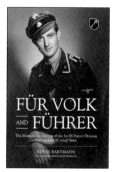

*Für Volk and Führer.
The Memoir of a Veteran of the
1st SS Panzer Division
Leibstandarte Adolf Hitler*
by Erwin Bartmann
ISBN 978-1-909384-53-8
(hardback),
ISBN 978-1-910294-27-7
(eBook)

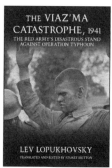

*The Viaz'ma Catastrophe.
The Red Army's Disastrous Stand
Against Operation Typhoon*
Lev Lopukhovsky
Translated and edited
by Stuart Britton
ISBN 978-1-908916-50-1
(hardback)
ISBN 978-1-910294-18-5
(eBook)

*Demolishing the Myth.
The Tank Battle at
Prokhorovka, Kursk, July 1943.
An Operational Narrative*
Valeriy Zamulin
Translated and edited
by Stuart Britton
ISBN 978-1-906033-89-7
(hardback),

**HELION & COMPANY**
26 Willow Road, Solihull, West Midlands B91 1UE, England
Telephone 0121 705 3393 Fax 0121 711 4075
Website: http://www.helion.co.uk